D0005007

BERLIN·NEW YORK

Like and Unlike

BERLIN

Like and Unlike

NEW YORK

**Essays on Architecture and Art
from 1870 to the Present**

**Edited by Josef Paul Kleihues
and Christina Rathgeber**

RIZZOLI
NEW YORK

First published in the United States of America in 1993
by Rizzoli International Publications, Inc.
300 Park Avenue South, New York, NY 10010

Library of Congress Cataloging-in-Publications Data

Berlin/New York : like and unlike : essays on architecture and art
    from 1870 to the present / edited by Josef Paul Kleihues.
        p.   cm.
ISBN 0-8478-1657-5
1. Art, German—Germany—Berlin.   2. Art. Modern—19th
century-Germany—Berlin.   3. Art, Modern—20th century—
Germany—Berlin.   4. Art, American—New York, N.Y.   5. Art,
Modern—19th century—New York, N.Y.   6. Art, Modern—20th
century—New York, N.Y.   7. Art. Comparative. I. Kleihues, Josef
Paul.
N7428.5.B47   1993   92-37372
709'.431'5509034—dc20   CIP

Translations from the German by Susan Cox, John Gabriel, and
Christina Rathgeber

Design by Abigail Sturges

Printed and bound in the United States of America

Contents

9 Acknowledgments
   Josef Paul Kleihues

Part One: 1870–1918

13 The City as Creator and Creation
    Thomas P. Hughes

33 The Development of the Dock, Rail, and Bridge
    System of New York City 1870–1920
    Carl Condit

47 The Metropolis as a Construction:
    Engineering Structures in Berlin 1871–1914
    Hans Kollhoff

59 The Berlin Tiergarten
    Folkwin Wendland

71 Central Park
    Jordan Mejias

81 The Berlin Garden City of Falkenberg:
    A Successful Example of Planning from
    the German Garden City Movement
    Kristiana Hartmann

93 New York and the Garden City Movement
    Between the Wars
    Daniel Schaffer

111 Going in Style: The Architecture of Transportation
     in the Glory Days of Metropolitanism
     Robert A. M. Stern

129 Architecture and Urban Planning 1850–1914
     Hartwig Schmidt

145 The Berlin *Mietskaserne* and Its Reforms
     Dietrich Worbs

159 On the Uses of Air:
     Perfecting the New York Tenement 1850–1901
     Richard A. Plunz

181 The Birth Pangs of Modernism
     Eberhard Roters

195 The Art World in New York 1900–1919
     Patricia Hills

211 The City and Entertainment:
     Coney Island and Haus Vaterland
     Roger Green

224 Observations

Part Two: 1918–1945

231 Searching for the New Dimensions of the City
Nicholas Bullock

249 Modernism and the Metropolis:
Plans for Central Berlin 1910–41
Vittorio M. Lampugnani

265 Neighborhood Block and Garden Court:
New York City Housing Between the World Wars
Richard Pommer

281 Between America and Germany:
Werner Hegemann's Approach to Urban Planning
Werner Oechslin

297 Moses and Ammann: Notes on the Modernization
of the Empire State
Kenneth Frampton

315 Manhattan Transfer: The New York Myth and Berlin
Architecture in the Context of Ludwig Hilberseimer's
High-Rise City
Fritz Neumeyer

331 Art Deco Skyscrapers: Towers of Modern Babel
Rosemary Haag Bletter

341 Post Expressionism: Notes on Dada, Neue Sachlichkeit,
and Bauhaus
Wieland Schmied

357 The New York Art World During the Interwar Years
Garnett McCoy

367 Berlin and New York: A Personal Involvement
Michael Blackwood

374 Observations

Part Three: 1945 to the Present

385 Collage and Chaos
Peter Blake

395 From the Destruction to the Critical Reconstruction
of the City: Urban Design in Berlin after 1945
Josef Paul Kleihues

411 Manhattan Montage: The Art of
Spatial Restructuring 1945–88
M. Christine Boyer

423 In Dialogue with Witnesses to the Past:
The Architecture of West Berlin
Peter Rumpf

435 In Search of Lost Research
Herbert Muschamp

441 Vicissitudes: The Art World in Postwar Berlin
Karl Ruhrberg

459 The New York Art World Since 1945
Dore Ashton

475 Competition of the Fragments:
Challenges for Tomorrow's Berlin
Michael Mönninger

481 Competition of the Centers: A Cultural
and Philosophical Comparison
Mathias Schreiber

494 Observations

505 Index

Acknowledgments

Josef Paul Kleihues

On November 16 and 17, 1987, a conference took place at the Aspen Institute in Berlin under the direction of Professor Shepard Stone. It was one of approximately three hundred conferences that occurred during Shepard Stone's long and wise stewardship. Its topic was "The City of the 21st Century."

Because they can be understood as the metropoles of the modern world, the discussion at the conference revolved around the problems and opportunities facing not only Berlin but also New York. Although many problems had to be overcome, it was this discussion that prompted the idea for the publication of *Berlin · New York: Like and Unlike.* Together with Shepard Stone, the members of the advisory board—John Brademas, Barbara Jakobson, Wilhelm A. Kewenig, Bill Lacy, Thomas M. Messer, Julius Posener, H. Beate Schöpp-Schilling, and Wolf Jobst Siedler—lent their ready support to the idea. The editorial committee, comprised of Kenneth Frampton, Vittorio M. Lampugnani, John Russell, Wieland Schmied, and myself, decided on the book's structure and general topics and made suggestions on possible authors.

The realization of the project only became possible, however, with the aid of the Stiftung Preußischer Seehandel and we owe this institution a special thanks for its generous financial support. We are also greatly indebted to Dr. Peter Raue, who has long been committed to Berlin and a friend of New York, for the active support that he showed us. Finally, the publication of this book—delayed in part because of the technical difficulties involved in coordinating a manuscript of this size—owes much to the unflagging patience and care shown by Dr. Christina Rathgeber. She was also responsible for acquiring the majority of the illustrations and for translating some of the German texts into English. I am deeply grateful for her efforts.

During the course of the conference that took place on the city of the twenty-first century, Shepard Stone mentioned almost in passing that he had lived for twenty years in New York, six years in Paris, two or three in London, and had at that point been living for thirteen years in Berlin. He was convinced that the Wall would not stand for another twenty years and that because of its geographical location alone, Berlin would inevitably once again take on a special role "when East and West became more sensitive to each other." That was in November 1987.

Shepard Stone loved Berlin and gave much to this city that only he was able to give because of his tolerance and wisdom. He saw the Wall come down.

This book is dedicated to Shepard Stone, who knew Berlin and New York, like and unlike, so well.

Part One
1870–1918

1

2

1. *Lower Manhattan Island in 1875 during construction of the Brooklyn Bridge, 1875.* From *Scientific American* 99 (1908).

2. *Lower Manhattan Island in 1908 showing transformation wrought by modern construction methods.* From *Scientific American* 99 (1908).

The City as Creator and Creation

Thomas P. Hughes

Thomas P. Hughes is Mellon Professor for the history of sociology of science at the University of Pennsylvania. He is also visiting research professor at the Wissenschaftszentrum Berlin and Thorsten Althin Professor at the Royal Institute of Technology in Sweden. A member of the Royal Academy of Engineering Sciences in Stockholm and the American Academy of Arts and Sciences in Cambridge, Massachusetts, Hughes is author of American Genesis: A Century of Invention and Technological Enthusiasm *(1989; German edition, 1990), and editor with Agatha C. Hughes of* Lewis Mumford: Public Intellectual *(1990).*

Technology cannot permanently be understood as an end in itself, but gains in value and significance just at that point at which it is recognized as the most defined means of achieving a culture. A mature culture, however, speaks only through the language of art. —Peter Behrens, 1910[1]

During the half century after 1870, Berlin and New York became technological metropolises. Earlier, London, Paris, Vienna, and Rome had become mother cities, although primarily government and commercial activities, not urban technology, stimulated and sustained their growth and prestige. The wealth of Victorian London, concentrated in the City with its banks and investment houses, derived from colonial enterprise and the heavy industrialization of the Midlands and the north of England. The rich agriculture and gradual industrialization of France fed the government and the cultural, as well as commercial, activities of Paris, but modern technology did not sustain it. Vienna was the cultural and governmental center of the multinational Austro-Hungarian empire. Rome flourished as a museum of culture, the site of the Papal See, and later as capital of a newly united Italy. Berlin and New York after 1870 experienced a kind of stimulation and growth different from that of the other cities. Berlin and New York became creatures and creators of a new technology, the technology of a second industrial revolution and urban development. A metropolis, in contrast to a large city, is an urban creation that expresses the history, the multifold social and cultural activities, and the aspirations of the larger national or regional society of which it is a part.[2] Berlin and New York were alike in that both, among other characteristics, expressed the technological, that is a creative, exuberance of their countries during the second industrial revolution that began around 1870 and reached its apogee between the two world wars.

The first great technological and industrial revolution occurred in Britain during the eighteenth and early nineteenth centuries; then it spread to Western Europe and America. It involved the exploitation of coal and iron, the expansion of factory production, the spread of mainline railway networks, and the rapid population and industrial growth in districts rich in raw materials, such as Birmingham in England, the Ruhr in Germany, and Pittsburgh, Pennsylvania, in the United States, and increased factory production in places such as New England and Manchester. Heroic canal builders, railroad-construction engineers, and textile-machinery inventors played significant roles in the British industrial revolution. In contrast, the second industrial revolution that shaped the rapid development of New York and Berlin involved the new power sources of electricity and internal combustion; new materials such as steel, glass, and reinforced concrete; the development of intraurban and highway transportation; and the organization of massive systems of production and communication. The revolution also depended on the inventions (especially in the United States) of independent inventors, the amassing of knowledge in technical colleges, universities, and private and government research institutions especially in Germany, as well as modern management techniques. Smoke, fire, and masses of workers comprise our image of the first industrial revolution; humming dynamos, city streets illuminated by electric arcs and incandescents, intraurban electric transit,

3. (Left to right) Emil Rathenau, founder of Allgemeine Elektrizitats-Gesellschaft, and Thomas Edison in Berlin central station Moabit, 1911. Berliner Kraft und Licht AG.

city planning and urban housing developments of an international style, engineers bent over drawing boards, Edisonian inventiveness, scientific managers, and white-coated scientists working in industrial laboratories and research institutes characterize the second. Berlin and New York, not smoky Pennsylvania or Ruhr Valley towns, were the sites of the managerial, institutional, technical, and scientific developments of the second industrial revolution. Both cities had skilled workers who were experienced and gifted in practicing the high-technology arts of the day, such as fine machine work and complex electrical engineering.[3]

Berlin and New York were creators of modern technology; they were also the creatures of it. The role of technology in the making of modern New York and Berlin has not yet been adequately recognized. The rapid growth of the two cities during the late nineteenth and early twentieth centuries has been conventionally attributed mainly to events such as the unification of Germany and the establishment of Berlin as its capital in 1871 and to the rise of the United States to world-power status and industrial preeminence. Relatively little attention has been given to the technology that has made possible the artifactual wonder—the modern metropolis. Except in specialist studies, for instance, the history of the electrification of transportation and communication in the two cities is rarely explored. Only infrequently has it been stressed that independent inventors, the source of much late nineteenth-century innovation, chose to do their creative work in New York and that the great research institutions of Germany found their home in Berlin. Too often the interweaving of financial potential and technological awareness by the investment banks and houses of New York and Berlin has been overlooked. Only a few historians have seen that power drawn from integrated networks of electrical transmission and distribution lines and applied in myriad ways in office, factory, and home have made possible modern Berlin and New York. Walther Rathenau, social critic, statesman, and head of Allgemeine Elektrizitats-Gesellschaft (AEG), the German electrical manufacturing company founded by his father, Emil, wrote of the electrical and other urban networks:

In their structure and mechanical order all great cities of the white world are identical. Imbedded in a web of rails, they spread their net of highways over the countryside. Visible and invisible networks move streaming traffic underground and through city canyons, pumping masses of people from the suburbs into the heart of the city twice daily. A second, third, and fourth network distribute water, heat, and power; an electrical nerve system pulsates with life of the city. Food and goods glide on rails; water flows through the city; and waste empties through canals.[4]

Historian Carl Condit has written:

If there was a particular time in which the modern city of New York emerged in a discernible outline of what it was to become in its maturity—the electrified, steel-framed, high-rise, bridged and tunneled, architecturally urbane, civically conscious, multi-ethnic city, a world center of the performing, building, literary, and visual arts—it was the decade of the 1880s, for it was then that the necessary technological and architectural as well as the sociopolitical bases were established.[5]

While the two cities were similar in many ways, they also had their differences. During the nineteenth and twentieth centuries, great cosmopolitan cities drew on an international pool in technology. Engineers, scientists, and managers in Berlin knew what their counterparts in New York were doing. Yet despite the common pool available, they did not create identical buildings, machines, processes, or technological systems for transportation, communication, and production. Each city's framework for creativity and invention was unique. Using technology to solve problems has not homogenized the world. Because, for instance, the geography, demography, politics, economics, and history of Berlin differed from those of New York, a Berlin style—and a New York style—of technology emerged. Style permits us to speak of the unlike; the common pool of technology engenders the like.

We shall, then, observe in this essay how these cities nurtured, and imposed distinctive styles on, innovative networks of inventors. In order to savor in several ways the creative vigor of Berlin and New York during the opening decades of the second industrial revolution, we shall also consider their responses with modern technology and architecture to nearly overwhelming problems of transportation and housing. First, however, we shall see how the two cities expressed a leading trend of the era by taking on the character of modern electropolises.

Berlin and New York as Electropolises

Berlin, a center of electrical manufacturing, has aptly been named an "elektropolis."[6] Modern New York, too, was an electropolis, but mainly because electrical technology made the modern New York physically possible, not because New York was a center of electrical manufacturing. In contrast, two of the world's largest electrical manufacturers, Siemens & Halske and AEG, had located in Berlin by 1890. In each city the presence of one of the world's leading suppliers of electrictiy—Berliner Elekricitats-Werke in Berlin and Consolidated Edison in New York—also contributed to the rise of these electropolises. The electrical supply networks of these utilities rapidly developed between 1880 and 1920 and made possible the communication, lighting, and horizontal and vertical transportation that were the identifying characteristics of these modern technological cities.

The history of electrical manufacturing and supply in Berlin had its beginning near and in New York. The independent inventor Thomas A. Edison and his associates, working at Menlo Park, New Jersey—only a short train ride from New York—invented and developed an incandescent lighting system that was installed on Pearl Street in the Wall Street district of New York in 1882. In 1881 Emil Rathenau, who had established himself in Berlin in mechanical engineering, visited the Paris International Electrical Exhibition and was so impressed by the Edison electrical lighting display that he acquired its patent rights in Germany. Financed by German banks, including Jacob Landau of Berlin, Rathenau founded in 1883 the Deutsche Edison Gesellschaft für angewandte Electricität (German Edison Company for Applied Electricity). There fol-

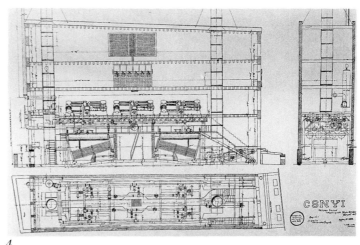

4

5

4. *Engineer's renderings of Edison's first urban electrical central station, Pearl Street, New York, 1882.* From Association of Edison Illuminating Companies, *Edisonia* (New York, 1904).

5. *Interior of the electrical central station, Markgrafenstrasse, Berlin, 1886.* Courtesy of Rudolf von Miller.

*6. Bird's eye view of Manhattan
showing the fourteen subway and
main-line railway tunnels and three
major long-span bridges either
under construction or opened
between 1895 and 1910. From*
Scientific American *99 (1908).*

lowed between the Rathenau interests and the long-established telegraph and electrical manufacturing firm of Siemens & Halske an agreement that, because of its cooperative character, was far more characteristic of Berlin and Germany than of New York and the United States. They concurred that Deutsche Edison would manufacture incandescent lamps and install the Edison system but that the Siemens company would manufacture the large equipment for the electrical systems. Deutsche Edison proceeded to install an Edison system at Friedrichstrasse 85 to supply the renowned Café Bauer in Berlin and then to construct, in 1885, a central lighting station on Markgraffenstrasse and a distribution system much like the one that Edison had installed in New York. Rathenau also established the Berliner Elekricitäts-Werke and transformed Deutsche Edison into Allgemeine Elektrizitats-Gesellschaft, which soon became, with Siemens, the best-known electrical enterprise in Europe. AEG and Siemens—creators of technology; employers of engineers, scientists, and thousands of workers; designers of factory and worker-housing settlements; and powerful economic and political movers—became the core of the Berlin electropolis.[7] By contrast, the great electrical manufacturers in the United States, though deeply dependent on the inventions of Edison and other Americans, several of whom did much of their work in New York or its environs, established themselves in Schenectady, New York (General Electric Company), and Pittsburgh, Pennsylvania (Westinghouse Company).

Berlin and New York not only manufactured or invented electrical devices but by using them defined their own characteristics as cities. Before 1870, applied electricity was associated primarily with the telegraph. The electrical telegraph originated in the first half of the nineteenth century when it conveyed messages from one city center to another. Later, ingenious inventors showed how it could be used within cities form a network of commercial communication, spread stock market reports, and carry fire alarms and police messages. After 1850, bold overland lines and transatlantic cables made cities nodal points of world communications. In 1876, Alexander Graham Bell, probably influenced by the earlier telephone experiments of the German Philipp Reis, introduced the speaking telegraph—or telephone—a communication system that within a decade was spreading a network of personal communication throughout large cities. The telegraph and the telephone changed the tempo of and brought precision to both communication and control activities. Communication at the speed of light transcended space and time. From New York or Berlin such investment bankers as J. P. Morgan in New York and George Siemens in Berlin, a cousin of the inventor Werner, oversaw, helped coordinate, and sometimes controlled far-flung commercial-industrial empires, including those involved in telephone and electrical manufacturing.

Electric lighting came to the cities first as brilliant arc lighting and then as soft incandescent lighting in the 1880s. Because distribution lines for electric current constituted a prime cost for the electrical supply utilities, such lines were established first in the densely populated cities. Berlin and New York quickly forged ahead of Paris and London in adopting the new lighting. Arc lighting in the streets and incandescent lighting in the interior spaces changed the rhythm of city life. Oil and gas lighting had shown the possibilities of nightlife, for pleasure and work, but electricity brought a dazzling illumination that suffused the evening hours with a glow and clarity that rivaled the stimulation of a sunlit day. Urbanites no longer ventured out into the dark; they strode along great white ways. For pleasure and excitement, Times Square at night contended with Central Park by day. Offices, workshops, and factories that needed brilliantly lit workplaces for fine accounting and machine tending turned quickly to incandescent light. Newspaper publishers could readily set type and run presses for their morning editions. The bright new lights, however, were long in coming to dark tenements.

Electric motors came to the cities about a decade after incandescent lighting. Many industrial establishments in Berlin first drove their electric motors with current from their own power plants, but by 1900 the rapidly expanding Berliner Elekrizitäts-Werke could persuade industry that it was economically feasible to close down its isolated generating plants and take power from the urban network or grid of distribution lines that the utility was extending through Berlin. In New York, Consolidated Edison brought industry onto the network even more rapidly. Electric motors in factories made possible the reorganization of the workplace and of work. Previously, the central steam engines, with their geometrically extended labyrinth of transmission belts driving various machines, had severely constrained their placement and prevented subtle variations in factory layout and architecture. Once individual electric motors were attached to the various machines, experts in factory organization and managers of labor opened for themselves a plethora of redesign and reorganization opportunities. It is not coincidental that scientific management, assembly-line production, and industrial electrification rose in tandem during the early decades of the twentieth century.

Unlike steam power, electric light and power spread through cities as a great interconnected network, an urban system. An impressive sequence of inventions and developments made possible by 1900 the supplying of electric power and light to Berlin and New York from several large central stations generating alternating, or polyphase, power. Transformers, motor-generators, synchronous generators, high-voltage transmission lines, and low-voltage distribution lines interconnected arc lights, incandescent lights, home appliances, giant industrial motors, and the motors for streetcars, subways, elevated and later mainline trains. A few persons in several centrally located dispatching, or control, centers matched the generating capacity of the central stations to the consumption of the millions of diverse consumers. Berlin and New York might have seemed chaotic at times, but well-ordered systems of supply such as electricity, gas, and water bound people and things together in a great net of dependency.

Berlin and New York took early leads in developing electric power for transportation. Werner Siemens and his company took a historic step when they built an electric urban railroad in Berlin in 1879 on the occasion of the International Trades Exposition. The Siemens company operated the small electric railway with a locomotive, pulling several cars at four miles per hour around a circle of track. More than eighty-six thousand passengers were excited, even thrilled, by the experience, but the city did not build subways and elevated railroads with electric locomotives until 1896.[8] A year earlier, city-owned electric streetcars began operating in Berlin. In New York by 1902, electric locomotives had replaced the steam locomotives that drew trains along elevated railroads above Second, Third, Sixth, and Ninth avenues. In 1905, the elevated train transported 250 million passengers. Electric streetcars were common in New York in 1899 and by 1910 they were carrying 500 million passengers per year. The New York Rapid Transit Commission opened the first of its electrified subways in 1904, a line extending from City Hall northward to the Bronx. In 1907, another line from the City Hall Park extended under the East River to Brooklyn. This remarkable story of elevated, subway, bridge, and tunnel construction, however, can be seen in the context of British historian Arnold Toynbee's challenge-and-response frame as developed in his multivolumed *A Study of History.*[9] He argued that repeated instances of physical challenges to communities and their responses had occurred throughout history. Inventive and successful responses brought growth and change; inadequate responses led to stagnation and decay. Barriers to communication and transportation created by nature, such as high mountains and deep valleys, deserts, and swamp lands, have threatened to retard social development; the Hudson River and the physical confines of Manhattan posed such a challenge to New York.

Electricity Provides Three Dimensions

On Manhattan Island, New York's use of electricity in conjunction with railroad technology responded to a Toynbeean challenge that threatened to paralyze transportation. By 1900, horses, horse-drawn vehicles, electric streetcars, and pedestrians all filled the streets, competing for space. New York had special problems because the deep and powerful Hudson River and the East River paralleling its north-south flow only a few miles away concentrated and constrained the movement of people and freight. About two million people lived in Manhattan by this time and almost as many commuters entered and left the island each day.

New York had become a great international ocean port with ships sailing or steaming past the Statue of Liberty and docking at the piers along the West Side of Manhattan. But while the Hudson provided access to the ocean, it acted as a barrier against the flow of people and goods from Manhattan westward. Until nearly the end of the nineteenth century, the deep river defied tunnel constructors and, until the twentieth, bridge builders as well. Until then, ferries had transported people and goods from New Jersey across the Hudson, but chaos prevailed at ferry terminals during peak hours, and the lack of adequate rail and street transportation stifled movement into and throughout Manhattan. As early as 1864, an engineer observed that if the trend in traffic continued, surface transportation would be impossible. "The streets would be absolutely blocked and the time occupied by the trip would be a loss from the occupations of the city which would be unen-

durable."[10] Then the population of the Greater New York area was about 1.5 million; by 1900, it was about 3.5 million. By 1885, six mainline railroads operated freight yards, piers, and stations in Manhattan to receive and transfer freight brought by ocean, ferry, and rail. Ultimately the railroads operated forty freight piers along the Hudson River and seven along the East River. Forty-one ferry routes served Manhattan Island, carrying about 625,000 people each weekday.[11] After the turn of the century, New York found a long-term, if not final, solution to the problem and in so doing provided the urban world an example to technological achievement.

Since 1840, the United States had been constructing mainline railroads from the Atlantic ports of New York, Baltimore, Philadelphia, and Boston westward through and over the north-south–ranging Allegheny mountains, into the Great Plains of the Midwest, across the Mississippi River, up into the Rocky Mountains, and down to the cities of the Pacific coast. The first transcontinental railroad was completed in 1869. To achieve this goal, railroad engineers, laborers, managers, and financiers had to organize and operate a gigantic construction system that could pass railroads over and under mountains and across broad rivers. A nearly level route had to be extended across an undulating continent. In the first decades of railroad building, American engineers tended to go around the hills and deep depressions in order to avoid the technical and costly problems of excavating, embanking, bridging, and tunneling. In the second half of the century, drawing on European experience and having gathered their own, Americans surpassed the world in the scale of their railroad activity. More than fifty thousand miles of railway had been opened in the United States. Nowhere else were there as many experienced railroad engineers and laborers as in America, a human task force ready to transform the face—and the ground beneath the face—of the earth. Railway technology was by then taken for granted as the means of leveling natural obstacles for ease and economy of transportation and for establishing routine and regular transportation over great distances.[12]

Unforeseen circumstances brought the railway solution to the New York problem: railroad engineers and laborers transferred their accumulated knowledge and skill from the interurban to the intraurban world. By 1880, the basic railway network was nearly complete and the rate of mainline railway construction in the United States declined. Railway construction became a solution seeking a problem. By chance, as mainline railway construction lost its position as a preeminent stimulator of technological change, the great urban market for technology, including New York City, took over the role.[13] Congested Manhattan traffic presented a likely problem, a pressing need. The population of Greater New York, and especially Manhattan, experienced its greatest growth between 1890 and 1900, and the city's transportation network suffered its greatest congestion, just as the railway engineers and managers began to seek new challenges. The prodigious building of skyscrapers in lower Manhattan after 1900 added to the density of population during the workday and increased commuter travel in early morning and late afternoon.[14] Railroad engineers proposed that railroads be laid in tunnels under rivers and streets and that bridges be erected above. Within the urban context these would be known not as railroads but as "subways" and "elevateds." These experienced railroad engineers, laborers, and managers joined with their counterparts in the electric-power industry to produce three of the greatest achievements of American building art—Pennsylvania Station and Grand Central Terminal with their underground access routes and the largest subway system in the world with it tubes beneath the Hudson and East rivers.[15] In the short span of years from 1895 to 1910, they built no less than fourteen river tunnels, subway and mainline railways, and three of the greatest long-span bridges in the world.[16]

Pennsylvania Station was far more than a terminal building. Certainly the most awe-inspiring technological achievement of the period, it was a system that included a surface terminal in midtown Manhattan, a surface railroad across the New Jersey meadows from the system's western end in Newark to the west face of Bergen Hill that intervenes between the meadows and the Hudson, and tunnels under the hill and the Hudson, from the Hudson under Manhattan to the surface terminal, from the surface terminal under Manhattan and the East River, and from the East River to Sunnyside, Queens. When the system was in operation after 1910, it connected the main lines of the Pennsylvania Railroad with the Long Island Railroad, a majority of whose stock was owned by the Pennsylvania. Electric trains moved throughout the system. Passengers and freight from New England could then pass easily through New York and then down the Atlantic coast.

The Pennsylvania Railroad, with its four thousand miles of track in highly industrialized Pennsylvania and New Jersey, announced its plans in December 1901 for a Pennsylvania terminal system.[17] The opening in 1900 of the electrified Gare d'Orsay in Paris and the successful completion and operation of an electrified mainline railway tunnel into Baltimore in 1895 encouraged the planners of the system. The accumulated wealth of the Pennsylvania Railroad also favored the mammoth project. In 1902, the railroad's total revenues were $112 million and the net income after all fixed charges amounted to $26 million.[18] With substantial resources and the construction of a great cross-country transportation network in place, the Pennsylvania Railroad faced a problem: where to invest its capital. Such circumstances helped focus the momentum of railway, tunneling, and bridge-building technology—the solution looking for a problem—on the New York challenge.

The use of tunneling shields based on the one used by the engineer James H. Greathead in constructing the tunnels of London's subway and improved by his associate Charles M. Jacobs, a tunnel engineer who served on the advisory board of the Pennsylvania terminal system, greatly facilitated tunneling under the Hudson. The architectural office of McKim, Mead & White designed the Manhattan terminal building that "undoubtedly represented the largest, most difficult, and most rewarding commission for any architect of the time, or any other time in American architectural history."[19] The essential problem was to provide a monumental gateway to the city and to move a quarter of a million people per day from four street entrances to the grand concourse and downstairs to trains be-

7. Levels of transportation on Manhattan at 33rd Street, c. 1910. The tunnel of the Pennsylvania Railroad is at the lowest level; above it are electrified subways, street railways, and elevated trains. From Scientific American 99 (1908).

8

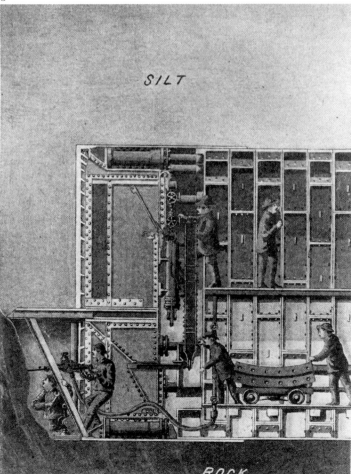

9

low. Neoclassical in style and of a design thought to be of noble simplicity appropriate for a modern world metropolis, the building covered a two-block area. For vertical transportation of passengers, baggage, mail, and other goods, there were fifty-two elevators, some hydraulic, others electric. The controlling brain for the terminal system, which dispatched 525 trains per weekday in 1911–12, was the most complex, interlocking train-control system then existing. Various control centers distanced along the system used signals of German design and were connected first by telegraph and telephone and later by radio. Passengers could move easily from railroad trains to the Manhattan subway system.

Construction of the world's largest subway system called forth the talents of several remarkable engineers, among them William Barclay Parsons. His career provides an excellent example of the transfer of technology from mainline railway construction to urban transit. He served as chief of engineering for the construction of the Fort Worth and Rio Grande Railroad in Texas, and then led a small party of American engineers making a survey for a thousand miles of railway from Hankow to Canton in China that passed through the closed province of Hu-nan. In China, he became known for his diplomacy as well as for his engineering skill and wrote about his experiences in *An American Engineer in China* (1900). Subsequently, he became chief engineer for the first section of the electrified subway system of the New York Transit Commission. This assignment, too, demanded political, as well as engineering, skills. In designing and constructing the subway, he established design standards for subways that were adopted throughout the world. In 1905, he supervised construction of the Steinway tunnel under the East River in New York; later he consulted and advised on urban traffic problems in London, San Francisco, Detroit, Toronto, and Chicago. During World War I, he was an army colonel with the United States Corps of Engineers and wrote of his experiences in *The American Engineers in France* (1920). A cultured man interested in engineering history, he also wrote *Engineers and Engineering in the Renaissance* (1939).

Bridges across the East River helped fill out the transportation network during this remarkable decade and a half of technological achievement. The Brooklyn Bridge, opened in 1883, is perhaps the most widely acclaimed and the most aesthetically impressive, but the Williamsburg Bridge, completed in 1903, the Queensboro (Blackwell's Island), opened in 1909, and the Manhattan Bridge, opened in 1910, each had notable characteristics. The Williamsburg suspension bridge had a longer main span than the Brooklyn and far greater weight and carrying capacity; the Manhattan Bridge on completion had the largest carrying capacity of any suspension bridge, providing for eight railroad tracks and a thirty-five-foot roadway. The Queensboro was a massive cantilever bridge, the design of which caused its builders considerable anxiety after the collapse of a similar structure, the Quebec Bridge in Canada, just as the Queensboro neared completion.

10

11

12

8. Tunnels of the Pennsylvania Railroad beneath the Hudson River with external diameters of twenty-three feet and internal diameters of nineteen feet. Driven with the aid of a shield, the tunnels achieved a maximum rate of advance through mud and silt of thirty-seven and a half feet per day. From *Scientific American* 99 (1908).

9. Shield used in constructing the tunnels of the Hudson companies under the Hudson River. A projecting roof protected workers as they drilled and blasted out reefs of rocks. From *Scientific American* 99 (1908).

10. Williamsburg Bridge. Construction began in 1896; the bridge opened in 1903 with a span of 1,600 feet. It was built to carry two subway tracks, four surface-railway tracks, two roadways, and two footwalks. From *Scientific American* 99 (1908).

11. Manhattan Bridge under construction in 1908; its main span was 1,470 feet. The bridge was designed to carry four subway tracks, four surface-railway tracks, a roadway, and two footwalks. From *Scientific American* 99 (1908).

12. Queensboro (Blackwell's Island) Bridge under construction in 1908. Total length, including approaches, was 8,600 feet. Although the bridge had been planned for four subway tracks, four surface tracks, a roadway, and two footwalks, it was found to be overstressed, and design changes were made during construction. From *Scientific American* 99 (1908).

13

13. *Martin Wagner second from left, and Hans Poelzig second from right, c. 1925.* Sammlung Baukunst, Akademie der Künste, Berlin.

14. *For mass production of housing, Wagner advocated labor-saving machinery, rational materials layout, and orderly work procedures. Photograph shows concrete panel construction originating in the United States and introduced in Germany by a Dutch firm, Occident Gesellschaft, c. 1926.* From Martin Wagner, "Gross-Siedlungen: Der Weg zur Rationalisierung des Wohnungsbaues," *Wohnungswirtschaft 3* (1926). Courtesy of Sammlung Baukunst, Akademie der Künste, Berlin.

15. *Labor-saving crane in use at Hufeisensiedlung Britz, c. 1924.* Sammlung Baukunst, Akademie der Kunste, Berlin.

16. *Earth-moving equipment and rails for efficient flow of work process at Hufeisensiedlung Britz, c. 1924.* Sammlung Baukunst, Akademie der Künste, Berlin.

Challenge and Response: Martin Wagner and the Siedlungen

After World War I, Berliners reacted to the shortage of housing with much of the resourcefulness shown by New Yorkers in responding to transportation-related congestion in Manhattan. Their housing problem was also a Toynbeean challenge. By 1900, Berlin was believed to be the most densely populated city in the world. In the case of New York, the transportation problem was seen as primarily geographical, physical, and economic; in the case of Berlin, the housing problem was viewed as essentially political and social. In both situations, however, the solutions called for technological ingenuity and audacity. These similar and dissimilar challenges and responses suggest the distinctive technological styles of the two metropolises.

Following the war, the housing problem in Berlin became "catastrophic."[20] Shortages of materials had postponed building, and economic depression and deflation had further delayed the construction of housing acutely needed by returning soldiers and their growing families. Even before the war, housing for low-income Berliners was among the worst in Europe. In 1910, government statistics counted seven percent of the Berlin population living in twenty thousand apartments with at least five people per room. By 1925, the situation had worsened: more than seventy thousand Berliners lived in cellars.[21] Countless factory workers, artisans, and lower-middle-class office workers lived in *Mietskasernen,* large, multistory, square tenements with often only a single window on a dark, dank, inner court per apartment. Frequently only one room of a two-room apartment was heated. Many apartments had no running water or toilets, and residents were forced to share facilities. In these buildings there were sometimes four or more people in each room. With such housing conditions in Berlin and elsewhere in Europe after the war, it was not surprising that the French architect Le Corbusier had predicted architecture (housing) or revolution.[22]

In Berlin, architect and city planner Martin Wagner took action. He believed that new technology, especially American production technology, offered the most likely solution to the dire housing problem.[23] Other avant-garde architects in Germany and Berlin shared his approach. Among them were Bruno Taut, also in Berlin, Walter Gropius at the Bauhaus in Dessau, and Ernst May in Frankfurt. In their enthusiasm for modern technology, they were like independent inventors who had flourished several decades earlier in the United States, especially in New York. The architects were among the principal founders of the modern, or international, style of architecture much as the independent inventors were originators of twentieth-century, or modern, technology. Wagner served as architect and *Stadtbaurat* (municipal city planner) in Berlin from 1919 to 1932. The "leading engineer-architect of his era,"[24] he was politically and philosophically deeply committed to the Social Democratic Party and to socialism. He used technology and architecture to solve the pressing social problems of his day. Through housing, Wagner sought to bring "light, air, and sun," dignity, and order to persons of limited income.[25] He is best remembered in Berlin as the architect of several major *Siedlungen* (housing settlements), especially the first stage of the Hufeisensiedlung built at Britz, which he designed in association with Bruno Taut.

Enthusiastic about American production technology, Wagner despised American capitalism. In 1924, after an intensive three-week study tour of the American construction industry, he returned to Germany persuaded that the massive flow of traffic in American cities, the plethora of skyscrapers as tall as the Cologne cathedral, and the bright lights of New York's Broadway could not mask the greedy dehumanizing materialism of a civilization dedicated to the dollar.[26] Yet his animadversion toward capitalism did not keep him from appreciating the American production techniques that he associated with the reforms of Frederick W. Taylor, the father of scientific management. He observed that in Germany there was much talk of Taylorism but little practice. In America, he heard relatively little discussion but witnessed widespread applications of scientific management doctrines. Like so many other Germans at the time, he also wanted to adopt the mass-production techniques associated with Henry Ford. Wagner believed that mass production of housing and consumer goods would ensure the loyalty of the working class to the newly established and fragile Weimar Republic. Leninist reformers in the Soviet Union held similar views at about the same time.

Drawing on American practices, Wagner articulated the ways in which costs could be lowered in the construction industry and a system of mass production introduced. He insisted that only through these economies could the financial means be found to solve the dire housing problem in Berlin. For the government to tax other sectors of a poor economy to subsidize the housing sector was, in his opinion, not in the national interest. He advocated mass production of housing through the specialization of labor and the substitution of machines for labor. He also wanted to standardize building components. He contrasted this method with the almost medieval construction techniques still used in Germany.[27] The program for mass housing that he worked out with Gropius, Taut, and May specified the use of nontraditional and inexpensive building materials, the avoidance of labor-intensive practices such as building interior walls of small, hand-laid bricks, and the reduction of transportation costs by use of local materials and the newest materials-handling techniques. Perceptively observing that mass-production achievements depended on organizational and financial inventions and innovations as well as technical ones, he called for the vertical integration of organizations such as those involved in raw-materials production, building-components manufacture, and housing construction. Wagner realized that the cost of mechanization and administration had to be spread over many units of production (apartments or houses) in order to justify the investment in high-cost machinery and processes. From the managers of large-scale, industrial production enterprises, he also borrowed the cardinal principle of using capital and labor to capacity. He understood that idle labor and capital, especially that caused by poor scheduling and coordination of work, added greatly to unit costs. Work stoppages on the building site because of poor weather were a special problem of the housing industry. To counter it, he wanted more building components to be made in factories rather than on the open site.[28]

14

15

16

Like many other inventive persons, Wagner relied heavily on the use of analogy. Before embarking on mass production, Wagner insisted that architect-engineer entrepreneurs, like the great manufacturers, had to analyze the market carefully, for housing needs were localized and houses were not transportable. Following the most recent trends in industrial practice, he wanted to establish a research laboratory to develop new materials and processes. He also recommended that architect-engineers, like automobile producers engaged in mass production, design and construct experimental models of housing before embarking on mass production. As in manufacturing, housing construction needed, Wagner maintained, large hierarchical organizations presided over by entrepreneurs to coordinate its numerous branches and phases.[29] Henry Ford and his managers coordinating and controlling a massive system of production involving mines, rubber plantations, raw-materials processors, railways and ships, assembly lines, and dealer networks provided an example for those wishing to rationalize housing production.

Estimating that about eighty percent of the costs of an apartment in a housing settlement stemmed from construction and only about twenty percent from land, closing, interest, and administrative costs, Wagner concentrated in his reform of construction practices on replacing labor with machines. He offered as a prime example of wasteful labor the use of standard bricks. Wagner calculated that 24,500 bricks would be needed in each apartment in a housing development he was planning and, therefore, 24.5 million would be required for the thousand apartments to be constructed. He estimated that each brick had to be handled ten times, so workers would have to handle bricks 245 million times during construction. From the United States might come, he predicted, the solution to this labor-intensive process in the form of poured concrete or concrete-panel construction. He had reference, especially, to an American concrete-panel mode of construction that had been introduced in Berlin by the Dutch firm Occident. In 1926, however, he decided that further development of the process had to take place before it could be extensively employed.[30]

Wagner's opportunity to respond on a large scale to the Berlin housing problem had come in 1925, with the commission for the Hufeisensiedlurg. Capital shortage and conservative labor practices kept him from introducing much of the new building technology that he had seen in America and articulated for mass housing in Germany. Nevertheless, the Hufeisensiedlurg is a milestone in the history of modern housing construction and Wagner's ideas served as a model for the rationalization of city planning in Germany.[31] The layout of buildings and streets in the housing settlement facilitated the handling of materials, and a power excavator replaced hand labor. Traveling cranes moved materials to the workers.[32] Apartment buildings were limited to four basic types. Coordination of the project by a centralized administration also provided an example of rationalization. Yet there were disappointing failures in this early rationalized *Siedlung* venture. Wagner complained that a thousand housing units were not enough to take full advantage of the economies of scale. In addition the newly designed mechanical excavator had numerous breakdowns.

Changes in design of the four basic housing types during construction raised costs, which ultimately became higher than projected, so that few low-income workers could afford to live in the apartments.

Despite this, more apartments at the Hufeisensiedlung were added to those designed by Wagner and Taut. Over eight years, 2,317 housing units were constructed; Taut continued as architect for most of the period. These units served as a precedent and model for Onkel Toms Hutte (Waldsiedlung Zehlendorf), Siemensstadt, and Weisse Stadt, three other major housing developments begun in Berlin during the era of the Weimar Republic. Almost 2,000 apartments were constructed between 1926 and 1932 at Onkel Toms Hutte, for which Taut served as one of the architects; 1,370 for Siemensstadt in 1930–31, for which Walter Gropius, Hans Scharoun, and others were the architects; and in 1930–31, 1,286 for Weisse Stadt. Seventeen major *Siedlungen* were constructed in Berlin during the Weimar era.[33] Construction of the Berlin *Siedlungen* was a substantial technological achievement. Not as dramatic as the New York response to the transportation problem, the Berlin solution to the housing problem demonstrated impressively how technology could be organized on a large scale and directed to social, even political, ends.

During the interwar years, the *Siedlungen* architecture of Wagner, Taut, Gropius, Scharoun, Hugo Haring, and other avant-garde architects introduced not only modern production technology, but also a modern, or international, style of design. As Gropius characterized the style, it embraced precisely impressed or cast forms, carefully controlled processes, pronounced contrasts of form and materials, orderly arrangement of building elements, and overall unity of design and color.[34] The concepts were obviously borrowed from mechanical technology. The architects believed that the International Style, with its plain surfaces and rectilinear forms, was particularly well suited, like Henry Ford's Model T automobile, to construction using modern techniques.

Peter Behrens, architect and designer for AEG, also designed Berlin buildings expressing the order, control, and rationality of modern production technology. After 1908, Behrens designed a series of factory buildings for AEG in Berlin-Wedding. Included among them was the turbine construction building on Huttenstrasse now regarded as a major twentieth-century architectural statement. The characteristics of these buildings influenced the designs of other architects, including Gropius, Ludwig Mies van der Rohe, and Le Corbusier, all of whom worked in his atelier around 1910. Behrens insisted that the functionalism of engineering calculation would never fully express a modern style; the artistic sensibility of the architect was needed as well.

His factory buildings embodied new materials such as glass and steel. Offended by the nineteenth-century practice of cladding buildings with ornament to make historical references, he designed factories manifesting the technological processes taking place within them. He created appropriate spaces for the orderly process of manufacture and large expanses of glass and vertical supports of steel that provided

17. Hufeisensiedlung Britz, c. 1926.
Sammlung Baukunst, Akademie
der Künste, Berlin.

18

19

20

21

18. *Bronze bust of Nikola Tesla by Fran Menegelo-Dincic.* Deutsches Museum, Munich.

19. *Tesla experimenting with high-voltage electrical discharges.* Burndy Library, Norwalk, Connecticut

20. *Elmer Sperry, left, independent inventor, experimenting with small model of device that he developed into a gyro ship stabilizer.*

21. *At the Franklin Institute, Philadelphia, April 20, 1928, left to right: Elihu Thomson, inventor of electric welding, co-inventor of arc lighting; F. J. Sprague, inventor of arc lighting on trolley systems and motors; Charles F. Brush, inventor of arc-lighting dynamo and the electric storage battery; Elmer Sperry, inventor of Sperry gyroscope compass, gyroscopic stabilizer, gyroscopic helmsman; E. E. Rice, former president of General Electric Company.*

proper lighting for work. Avoiding flat, banal functionalism by presenting walls of steel, masonry cladding, and glass, he achieved volumetric effects with the play of light and shadow. His use of a rhythmic sequencing of prominent features, such as column supports, suggested the order of serial mass production. Behrens wrote of the "articulation of large areas, a lucid contrast between prominent features and widely stretched flat planes, and a unified repeating sequence of essential features."[35]

New York Inventors

The avant-garde architects of Berlin have a place in history because of the remarkable creativity they expressed over a short period in a concentrated area. In New York, professional inventors flourished, contributing a disproportionate number of breakthroughs during the decades between 1870 and 1910, when America achieved technological preeminence. Berlin did not produce or attract this same kind of inventor. Edison, Elmer Sperry, Nikola Tesla, Lee de Forest, and Frank Julian Sprague rank among the dozen or so leading inventors of American history. All chose to live or work in the New York area at some time during the period from 1870 to 1915, when they and other professional inventors introduced the high technology of the second industrial revolution. All worked independent of institutional constraints, electing to avoid salaried positions with the engineering departments—later the industrial research laboratories—of manufacturing companies, although occasionally they would act as consultants for them. The New York inventors formed their own companies based on their inventions, and unlike their counterparts in Berlin, were not affiliated with engineering schools or universities.

The American independents are remembered mainly for their major inventions. Edison invented and introduced in 1882 a system of incandescent lighting for large cities. Sperry, in many ways a more professional inventor than Edison because of his unwavering dedication to the creative craft, is recalled as the father of cybernetic, or feedback, controls, including those now used on airplanes and ships. Tesla's place in history is assured by his invention of a polyphase system of electrical power distribution that became the American standard. De Forest was responsible for the three-element vacuum tube, the invention that opened the electronic era. Sprague invented and introduced modern electrical traction, vertical and horizontal, into large cities. As is invariably the case, the uniqueness of their contributions has often been overstated, for other inventors in America and abroad were solving the same problems in almost the same ways, but these American independents stand out among their peers because of a slight priority with a breakthrough invention, because they established companies to manufacture them, or because of the large number of inventions they made.

The story of Edison inventing in his laboratory in Menlo Park and later in West Orange, New Jersey, has often been told. He chose to locate both of these laboratories less than an hour by train from Manhattan in order to have access to the resources of the city. Much less well known are the two periods when Edison worked and lived in Manhattan. From 1869 to 1871 he lived there to concentrate on telegraph inventions; between 1881 and 1886 during his supervision of the construction and early operating years of his first major urban central lighting station, he and his family lived in a hotel adjacent to Gramercy Park. He had offices in a brownstone mansion at 65 Fifth Avenue. Not far away on Goerck Street, he established a small laboratory. At 65 Fifth Avenue, the "genius of electricity" received prominent visitors from the worlds of finance and large enterprise, among them the financiers William H. Vanderbilt and J. P. Morgan, the German entrepreneur Henry Villard, and Norvin Green, head of Western Union Telegraph Company.[36] When Edison could escape from the pressing financial and business problems associated with the introduction of his lighting system, he enjoyed calling for a few hours on his associate, the German craftsman and factory owner Sigmund Bergmann, who made models and manufactured some of Edison's inventions. A favorite meeting place was a nearby German restaurant.

Wall Street's venture capital financiers and the city's skilled mechanics, instrument makers, and model builders, many of them immigrants who had learned their craft in Germany, England, or Switzerland, attracted other inventors besides Edison to Manhattan. They flourished in New York because it used their inventions—their incandescent lighting, electrified rapid transit, wireless communications, and marine innovations. The U.S. Navy had a major yard in Brooklyn and shipping lines were headquartered in New York. In addition, the principal engineering societies and engineering publishing houses, all sources for the inventors of vital information about technological problems and solutions, were located in Manhattan.

Sperry came to New York in 1907 and soon began to use the skilled model builders and mechanics there to build the ship gyrostabilizers, gyrocompasses, gunfire control devices, and automatic airplane controls that he invented and manufactured for the United States and British navies. In 1910, he established the Sperry Gyroscope Company in a building on Manhattan Bridge Plaza not far from the U.S. Navy yard. Merchant and naval ships from throughout the world came to the port of New York to be outfitted with Sperry compasses and automatic pilots. His was the high technology of the day.

Tesla, born on the northernmost coast of Dalmatia, found the New York environment exhilarating.[37] His most creative years were spent largely in Manhattan, where he lived in the finest New York hotels, entertained lavishly, and delighted in the company of the city's financial and cultural elite. They visited his laboratories, first in 1887 at 33-35 South Fifth Avenue and later in 1895 at 46 East Houston Street. Tesla's demonstrations of his inventions, especially those involving extremely high voltages, were dramatic, enhanced by his sartorial elegance and handsome presence. He, too, depended on New York financiers, including J. P. Morgan, for funds.[38] De Forest also gravitated to New York because of money and the market for his wireless system. Soliciting funds from New York capitalists, many of whom were his Yale classmates, he caught their attention by dramatic demonstra-

22. *Werner von Siemens, electrical engineer, inventor, and industrialist.* Deutsches Museum, Munich.

23. *August Wilhelm von Hofmann, chemist and professor.* Deutsches Museum, Munich.

24. *Adolf Slaby, inventor and professor of electrical engineering.* Deutsches Museum, Munich.

25. *Friedrich von Hefner-Alteneck, inventor and electrical engineer.* Deutsches Museum, Munich.

23

24

25

tions of radio transmissions of the latest market information, including ones across the New York bay, from off-shore yacht races, and to automobiles parked in front of Wall Street brokerage houses.

For Sprague, New York was a prime market for his inventions. During his lifetime, he became known in the electrical engineering profession as the father of electric traction, for vertical as well as horizontal transportation. His motors and systems of control found application in streetcars, elevators, elevateds, and subways of the great urban centers. Like other American independent inventors, he established a number of small companies to manufacture and market his inventions and then sold these companies to such large manufacturers as General Electric Company. The Sprague Electric Railway and Motor Company in which he was variously electrical engineer, manager, treasurer, and office boy, introduced a constant-speed motor widely adopted after 1887 for electric traction. Nearly three thousand Sprague motors found application in various industries before the Edison General Electric Company absorbed his company in 1889. Two years later, Sprague established the Sprague Electric Elevator Company that built six hundred elevators and also electrical control systems for elevators before he sold it to the Otis Elevator Company. Drawing on his experience with electric controls for elevators, Sprague invented a system of electric train controls that allowed the drive motor to be installed in individual cars rather than on a simple locomotive. Subways and elevateds quickly adopted multiple-unit control, and in 1902, the General Electric Company bought the Sprague Electric Company.[39]

Siemens and Edison: Contrasting Styles

The pronounced differences between the inventive styles of Werner Siemens and Edison suggest the contrast between Berlin and New York as sites of creative, especially technological, activity. Siemens demonstrated in 1866 that an electrical generator did not need permanent magnets but could itself produce the electromagnetic field needed for the generation of electricity. This opened the way for the development of the modern electrical generator. In addition, Siemens invented numerous improvements in land and underwater electrical telegraphs. Both Siemens and Edison were major inventors of electrical devices, but there the likeness ends. Edison flaunted his lack of formal education; Siemens took pride in the scientific grounding he had obtained as a Prussian military cadet in artillery and engineering schools. Edison never tried to hide or alter his plain speech, dress, and manners; he was proud of his rural Canadian and midwestern American roots. In his memoirs, Siemens stated that "although the fact that I owe my position in life to my own efforts I have always gratefully acknowledged that my path was smoothed by my admission into the Russian army [as an officer] and therewith into the State of the great Frederick [of Prussia]. It was very valuable in Prussia to belong as an officer to the court-retinue and to have entree to all social circles."[40] In early life, Edison relished the ribald company of the mechanics and model builders who worked with him in his laboratories; later he treasured rural retreats with Ford, Harvey Firestone, and other captains of industry. Siemens boasted of his close contacts with men of science in Berlin—among them Emil du Bois-Reymond, an eminent physiologist and leader of the scientific community. Edison acquired numerous patents; Siemens's memoirs stress scholarly articles more than patents. He highly valued his membership in the Berlin Academy of Sciences and an honorary degree from the University of Berlin. In interviews with newspaper reporters, Edison was given to irresponsible remarks about his disdain for long-haired academics and their impractical theories. Siemens established his Berlin electrical manufacturing company and played an active role in its management the remainder of his life. Edison, like the other American independent inventors, characteristically cast off organizational shackles whenever he could. Siemens contributed greatly to the establishment of scientific and technological institutions in Berlin, including a chair for electrical engineering at Charlottenburg (Berlin) Technische Hochschule (formerly technical college, now technical university) and, in 1887, the Physikalisch-Technische Reichsanstalt for research and the establishment of national technical and scientific standards.

Berlin Inventors

Other leading inventors in Berlin shared Siemens's characteristics. They welcomed affiliations with academic, industrial, and government institutions. Unlike the American inventors, they were not wary that institutions might constrain their freedom of choice of problems on which they wished to work. Countless inventive persons and numerous important inventions came out of Berlin during the decades between 1870 and 1915, but major inventors in Berlin were mostly associated with the Charlottenburg Technische Hochschule, the University of Berlin, or one of the large, innovative manufacturing companies, such as Siemens & Halske or AEG. Those who were academics, however, often headed their own research institutes. Berlin inventors working for large companies concentrated on problems related to the manufacturing processes and products of those companies. Because so many electrical inventions came from the laboratories or engineering departments of the large manufacturers, the inventions tended to be improvements in existing processes or products rather than breakthrough inventions. Berlin is far better known than New York for its numerous discoveries chemistry. Berliners active in chemistry were often university professors; most of those responsible for major electrical inventions worked for Siemens or AEG.

Among those in Berlin responsible for major inventions between 1870 and 1915 were August Wilhelm von Hofmann, a University of Berlin chemist; Adolf Slaby, a professor of electrical engineering at the Charlottenburg Technische Hochschule; Friedrich Hefner-Alteneck, an electrical engineer with Siemens & Halske; and Michael Dolivo-Dobrowolsky, and electrical engineer at AEG. An exception to the general rule of institutional affiliation, Adolf Frank succeeded impressively as an independent inventor who, like the Americans, established companies to manufacture his inventions. A brief survey of these Berlin inventors suggests the highly institutionalized environment in which they pursued their technical and scientific interests.[41]

Hofmann studied chemistry under Justus Liebig, who blazed a trail in the application of chemistry to practical problems, especially agriculture. The British called Hofmann to London to introduce the Liebig style of laboratory research there, and he became known for his discovery of organic dyes from coal tar, which made possible the rapid growth of the German dyestuff industry in the second half of the nineteenth century. Despite the place he had made for himself in Britain, in 1865, Hofmann accepted a call to the University of Berlin, where he established a large chemical research laboratory for himself and co-workers as well as a private laboratory in his home. A founder and leader of the Deutsche Chemische Gesellschaft that included leading German chemists among its members, he was also an influential member of the Berlin Akademie der Wissenschaften (Academy of Sciences). He published more than 150 papers describing his discoveries in chemistry, many of them of industrial importance. He was the first president of the Gesellschaft deutscher Naturforscher und Arzte.[42] Slaby studied in Berlin and was a private lecturer in mechanical engineering until the major inventions of Siemens stimulated his interest in electrical engineering. In 1883, Slaby was named to the first professorial chair in electrical engineering at the Charlottenburg Technische Hochschule, where he established his own research laboratory with emphasis on industrial applications. After witnessing Guglielmo Marconi's experiments with wireless telegraphy and studying the principles of wireless transmission, Slaby and an assistant, Graf von Arco, along with Ferdinand Braun of Strassburg, invented various components for a wireless system that broke a Marconi monopoly in Germany.

Hefner-Alteneck possessed an imaginative and creative drive similar to that of the New York independent inventors, although he chose to work for Siemens & Halske. His father was an art historian who became head of the Bayerisches National Museum. Probably because of this early exposure to the arts, the son later displayed more interest in visual concepts than in mathematical ones in his technical work. After studying engineering at the technical institutes in Munich and Zurich, he fulfilled his goal of obtaining a position with Siemens & Halske, where his abilities soon persuaded Siemens to place him in charge of the development of apparatus for the Indo-European telegraph line. Soon he headed what today would be called a research and development department for electrical machinery. He invented major improvements (e.g., drum armature, innerpole dynamo) in electrical generators and motors and arc lighting. He also established a unit of measurement that became a standard for electric lighting. Hefner-Alteneck published in scholarly journals and was a member of the Berlin Academy of Sciences.

Dolivo-Dobrowolsky was born in Saint Petersburg, Russia, but studied at the Darmstadt Technische Hochschule in Germany. As an engineer with AEG, he concentrated on the development of an efficient and economical system of polyphase electrical transmission that set standards for the field. The company manufactured equipment of his design, as chief en-

26

27

gineer, that greatly contributed to the displacement of direct by polyphase current as the worldwide standard. Subsequently, however, he anticipated the development of direct-current transmission that would supersede polyphase current at extremely high voltages; but his early death cut short his forward-looking experiments.

Unlike the institution-bound inventor typical of Berlin, Frank thrived when he was inventing and establishing companies in varied fields. After apprenticing as a pharmacist, he decided he needed systematic knowledge and studied chemistry in Berlin and at the University of Gottingen. He concentrated on improvements in beet sugar and in potash fertilizers. Establishing a factory in Stassfurt to use his patented process for making potassium chloride, he was a founder of the potassium industry in Germany. In 1876, he gave up his position as a leading industrialist, moved to Charlottenburg, now a part of greater Berlin, and founded a factory for making glass containers. He invented coloring for brown glass that preserved beer longer than the green glass formerly used and developed a process for making mosaic glass (*fondi d'oro*). In 1883, Frank changed direction once again and pioneered in the use of iron slag in fertilizer. In 1885, he styled himself an independent consulting chemist and engineer and contributed to the invention of a widely adopted industrial process for making cellulose. Turning to one of the most pressing problems of this day—obtaining nitrogen from the atmosphere for fertilizer and other purposes— he invented and patented in 1895–96 with Nikodem Caro the calcium cyanamid process for production of cyanide and ammonia (nitrogen compound). This, too, became widely used in industry. Others of his processes were used for the making of nitric acid, carbide, acetylene, and hydrogen out of water gas, which was needed for the great zeppelins being constructed then. Despite these remarkably varied contributions, Frank did not enjoy the honors and prestige bestowed on inventors and chemists associated with great universities, well-established manufacturing enterprises, or government service.[43]

Conclusion

During the early decades of the second industrial revolution, both Berlin and New York were creators as well as creations of modern technology. In Berlin, however, creative or inventive activity was mediated by influential institutions such as universities and manufacturing firms. In New York, such creative achievement was highly individualistic, as exemplified in the activities of the independent inventors. Berlin was also unlike New York in that *Siedlungen* builders not only utilized the modern technology of mass production, as did builders in New York, but made efforts to find new symbols and forms expressing their commitment to modern values such as rationality and economic democracy. The modern International Style first took root in Berlin, not in New York. By contrast, builders of great bridges, railroad stations, and high-rise buildings in New York cloaked their stark technical achievements in historical forms and symbols until the third or fourth decade of the twentieth century. On the other hand, New York displayed its remarkable technological prowess by creating an urban transportation system of unprecedented size in an unprecedentedly short time. There was little effort to find forms and symbols expressive of a new age; the raw and imposing nature of the technology said enough. New York's dramatic technology directly served the commercial life of the city; Berlin made efforts to integrate technology and culture, to find ways of relating technology to social and aesthetic, not simply economic, goals.

Notes

1. Peter Behrens, "Art and Technology," Tilmann Buddensieg, ed., *Industriekultur: Peter Behrens and the AEG, 1907–1914* (Cambridge: M.I.T. Press, 1984), 215.
2. Karl Schwarz, "Die Metropolen wollen: Berlin als Metropole woolen," in Schwarz, ed., *Die Zukunft der Metropolen: Paris, London New York, and Berlin*, vol. 1 (Berlin: Technische Universitat, 1984), 21.
3. Ingrid Thienel-Saage, "Verkehrstechnologie und raumfunktionale Specialisierung als Gestaltungskrafte der Metropole Berlin im 19: Jahrhundert," in Schwarz, ed., *Die Zukunft*, 316.
4. Walther Rathenau, *Zur Kritik der Zeit* (Berlin: S. Fischer Verlag, 1921), 15.
5. Carl Condit, *The Port of New York: A History of the Rail and Terminal System from the Beginnings to Pennsylvania Station* (Chicago: University of Chicago Press, 1980), 105.
6. Sigfrid von Weiher, *Berlins Weg zur Elektropolis* (Berlin: Stapp Verlag, 1974).
7. Thomas P. Hughes, *Networks of Power: Electrification in Western Society, 1880–1930* (Baltimore: The Johns Hopkins University Press, 1983), 66–78.
8. Von Weiher, *Elektropolis*, 170.
9. Arnold Toynbee, *A Study of History* (London: Oxford University Press, 1961), 12, 254–63.
10. James Blaine Walker, *Fifty Years of Rapid Transit, 1864–1917* (New York: The Law Printing Company, 1918), 18.
11. Condit, *The Port of New York*, 111, 241.
12. Thomas P. Hughes, "A Technological Frontier: The Railway," in Bruce Mazlish, ed., *The Railroad and the Space Program: An Exploration in Historical Analogy* (Cambridge: M.I.T. Press, 1965), 65.
13. Alfred D. Chandler, Jr., "The Beginnings of Big Business' in American Industry," in *Publications in the Humanities* 30 (Cambridge: Department of the Humanities, Massachusetts Institute of Technology [n. d].), 1.
14. The availability of Bessemer steel for the structural skeleton of the buildings, of electric elevators, and the steep increase of real estate prices in lower Manhattan greatly stimulated the building of the skyscrapers. The land was the most expensive in the world and the buildings were the tallest. In 1908, the Metropolitan Life Tower with its fifty stores and 8,100 tons of steel was the "loftiest building in the world." It was not unusual for the site of a building to cost more than the building itself. Land for the Flatiron Building on Broadway and Fifth Avenue cost approximately $250,000. "New York, 1898–1908," *Scientific American* 99 (December 5, 1908): 400–402.
15. Condit, *Port of New York*, 79.
16. "New York, 1898–1908," 391.
17. Condit, *Port of New York*, 266.
18. Ibid., 268.
19. Ibid., 277.
20. Norbert Huse, "Grossiedlungen der 20er Jahre-heute," in *Vier Berliner Siedlungen der Weimarer Republic: Britz; Onkel Toms Hutte; Siemensstadt; Weisse Stadt* (Berlin: Bauhaus-Archiv, 1984), 9.
21. Hans Jorg Duvigneau, "Die Bedeutung der Berliner Grossiedlungen fur die Wohnungsversorgung-damals und heute," in *Vier Berliner*, 13.
22. Le Corbusier, *Vers une architecture* (Paris: Editions Gres, 1923).
23. Ludovica Scarpa, *Martin Wagner und Berlin: Architektur und Stadtebau in der Weimarer Republik* (Braunschweig/Wiesbaden: Friedr. Vieweg & Sohn, 1986), 15.
24. *Munchner Merkur*, May 28, 1957.
25. Sabine Schurer-Wagner, "Architekten-Portrat," *Der Architekt* (December 1985).
26. Martin Wagner, "Das ist Amerika," *Gewerkaschafts-Zeitung* 34 (December 6, 1924): 483.
27. Martin Wagner, "Gross-Siedlungen: Der Weg zur Rationalisierung des Wohnungsbaues," *Wohnungswirtschaft* 3 (June 1, 1926): 83.
28. Martin Wagner, "Ersparnismoglichkeiten in Wohnungsbau," typescript in Bauhaus Archiv, Berlin. File: Wohnmachine; Folder: Korrespondenz, 1924–26.
29. Wagner, "Gross-Siedlungen, " 87–92.
30. Ibid., 108–9.
31. Ludovica Scarpa, "Das Grossiedlungs-Modell: Von Rationalisierung zum Stadtebau," in *Vier Berliner*, 21.
32. Scarpa, *Martin Wagner*, 37.
33. Paper by Gunther Schulz (Bonn) given at conference on Berlin and London in the 1920s organized by Das Deutsche Historische Institut (London) and held in Berlin. Repr. *Der Tagespiegel* ,Sonntag (May 15, 1988): 44.
34. Fritz Neumeyer, "Im Schatten des mechanischen Haines: Versuchsordnungen zur Metropole," in Schwarz, ed., *Die Zukunft* 274.
35. Behrens, "Art and Technology," 218.
36. Matthew Josephson, *Edison: A Biography* (London: Eyre & Spottiswoode, 1961), 273.
37. On Sperry in Brooklyn and New York, see Thomas P. Hughes, *Elmer Sperry: Inventor and Engineer* (Baltimore.: The Johns Hopkins University Press, 1973), 116, 134, and 237.
38. John J. O'Neill, *Prodigal Genius: The Life of Nikola Tesla* (London: Neville Spearman, 1968), 66–67, 123–24, 195–99, 214, and 287.
39. Harriet Sprague, *Frank J. Sprague and the Edison Myth* (New York: The William-Frederick Press, 947), passim.
40. *Personal Recollections of Werner von Siemens*, trans. W. C. Coupland (London: Asher & Co., 1893), 360–61.
41. The five persons chosen to represent invention in Berlin all appear in Conrad Matschoss, *Manner der Technik (*Berlin: VDI-Verlag, 1925). Frank, Hefner-Altenneck, and von Hofmann are also distinguished by three or more entries between 1870 and 1907 in Ludwig Darmstaedters, *Handbuch zur Geschichte der Naturwissenschaften und der Technik* (Berlin: J. Springer, 1908), See also, *Geschichte der Technik.*, hrsg. Michael Matthes (Dusseldorf: ECON, 1983).
42. B. Lepsius, "A. W. von Hofmann," in G. Bugge, ed., *Das Buch der Grossen Chemiker*, vol. 2 (Berlin: Verlag Chemie, 1930), 136–53.
43. H. Grossman, "Adolf Frank," in Bugge, ed., *Das Buch* 310–20.

Acknowledgment

I wish to acknowledge the editorial and research assistance of Agatha C. Hughes.

1

2

1. Municipal ferry pier, 1907–09.
Pen end of ferry house, facing the
water. Terminal at South Ferry for
service to 39th Street, Brooklyn, now
part of the Battery Maritime
Building. New York City
Department of Ports, International
Trade, and Commerce.

2. Bush terminal complex,
39th–51st streets, Brooklyn,
1902–17. Typical warehouse and
industrial buildings. New York City
Department of Ports, International
Trade, and Commerce.

The Development of the Dock, Rail, and Bridge System of New York City 1870–1920

Carl Condit

Carl Condit is professor emeritus of history, art history, and urban affairs at Northwestern University. His many publications deal with the history of urban technology and urban development, with emphasis on building, planning, and transportation. Condit's chief honors include the Leonardo da Vinci Medal of the Society for the History of Technology and the Heritage Award of the American Society of Civil Engineers.

Waterfront Structures: Piers and Ferry Slips

Among the great harbors of the world, New York is unique by virtue of its extensive area of water in embayments of the sea and its physiographic and geological complexity. The city itself now extends over three islands and the southernmost part of the mainland of New York State; the metropolitan area includes northern New Jersey on the west and Connecticut on the east. In considering the future, city planners faced two overriding needs—first, to build up the harbor works necessary to transatlantic shipping, and second, to knit the metropolitan area's geographically distinct segments into a unified circulatory system.

Its ocean site compelled the municipality to build shipping and other harbor facilities from the very beginning of its history. The Dutch began to construct docks of primitive wooden form when they founded the colony of Nieuw Amsterdam in 1624. When the British replaced the Dutch in 1664, they constructed the first stone piers, probably composed chiefly of rock fill in timber cribbing. The systematic emplacement of docks and associated harbor works did not begin in Brooklyn until 1840. By 1870, the Dutch, the British, and the citizens of the new American republic had built 126 piers along the Manhattan shore.

The construction of waterfront shipping and circulatory facilities was an anarchic process in which private, colonial, and later state and municipal interests were frequently in conflict. They clashed over land reclamation, the building of docks, warehouses, and other commercial structures; the extension of streets; and the enlargement of property holdings through landfills undertaken by private citizens. The promise of order and the multiplication of docks, in number and size commensurate with the city's rapidly expanding marine commerce, came with the establishment of the New York City Department of Docks in 1871. George S. Greene, Jr., was appointed chief engineer in 1875 and held the position until 1897. He designed and supervised construction of piers in the Chelsea district of the Hudson River, the first group built in the period 1875–83, and the major part, in both number and structural character, from 1897 to 1910. These came to be known as the Chelsea-Gansevoort piers, extending along the waterfront from Bloomfield street on the south to 23rd Street on the north. The pressure to build ever longer and more substantial piers is indicated by the following table showing the constant increase in the length of steamships between 1870 and 1920:

Vessel	Construction Date	Length (ft.)
Oceanic	1872	425
Arizona	1880	475
Umbria	1884	500
Campania	1893	628
Baltic	1903	724
Olympic	1910	882
Majestic	1920	956

The dock plan of 1871 was revised in 1880. The various piers and ferry slips built between 1880 and 1910 followed variations on a fundamental structural system, the variations mostly dependent on function and on the depth of bedrock, which drops from a minimum of eighteen feet below mean low water to more than fifty feet along the Hudson River in the Chelsea district. All this construction was associated with the rebuilding of the bulkhead wall, along the length of the Hudson River from the Battery to 23rd Street.

Pier A, at the Battery, designed by Greene, was constructed in 1884–86 for the use of the Police Department's Harbor Patrol and is the oldest surviving example of work accomplished by the Docks Department in the 1880–1910 period. Since bedrock at this point lies only eighteen feet below mean low water, the concrete bag and block foundation could be laid directly on the rock surface, cleared of overburden by dredging. The concrete-supported granite blocks were faced with masonry. A series of parallel sub-piers, joined by concrete arches spanning between iron girders, formed the base of the floor of granite blocks covered with a three-inch layer of mortar. The building rose above the flooring, enclosed by a wall of brick and terra cotta at the shore end, a tin roof on iron trusses, and walls of galvanized iron siding on a timber frame. The walls were well insulated: a stud frame supported tongue-and-groove sheathing, two layers of tar paper, and mineral wool between studs. Utilities were advanced: a boiler generated steam for radiators, gas lights provided illumination, and a water supply from the street served plumbing fixtures. The Cunard Steamship Line pier built in 1908–09 at 16th Street was typical of the Chelsea group. Its underfloor construction was carried on pilings driven into the riverbed; the flooring consisted of long narrow stone slabs, and walls and upper floor were carried on a steel frame, with roof supported by steel trusses spanning between wall posts. By this date, the maximum steamship length was approaching nine hundred feet.

The carfloat terminal requires a special kind of waterfront structure designed for freight handling. The railroad carfloat, invented in 1866 by John Starin, was a barge operated by tugs and designed to transfer freight cars between the float terminals, where they could be loaded or dispatched in outbound trains. Since only one rail line provided freight service on Manhattan, the first carfloat terminal served the New York Central and Hudson River Railroad's West Side line at 60th Street. A second terminal was built at Port Morris in the Bronx to serve four New Jersey roads and became part of the city's waterfront system with the expansion of the urban area on January 1, 1898. The largest installation was at Bay Ridge in Brooklyn, another borough added to the city area in the 1898 enlargement.

In this water-laced city, ferry service was an obvious necessity for the movement of passengers and delivery wagons (later trucks). The first steam-driven vessel in the United States was the *Clermont*, built by Robert Fulton and piloted by him on its first successful run from New York to Albany on August 17, 1807. The idea of local ferry service followed in a few years. The first steam-powered vessel, the *Raritan*, was successfully operated between the Battery and Perth Amboy, South Amboy, and Elizabethport, New Jersey, on May 1, 1810. Regular service on a fixed route was inaugurated by Fulton between

Jersey City and the foot of Broadway (later designated South Ferry) on July 17, 1812. The great expansion of ferry service came with the introduction of the railroads in 1832. By 1910, forty-one ferry routes united Manhattan with New Jersey, Staten Island, Long Island, and the smaller islands of the harbor and the East River. A total of thirty-four ferry terminals ringed the island.

An example of the carefully designed ferry terminal was built in 1907–09 for the Manhattan–South Brooklyn service, inaugurated in 1887. The structure later became one of the piers of the Department of Marine and Aviation and later housed the offices of the department on the third floor (fig. 1). Since it is located at South Ferry, with bedrock at a minimum depth, the foundation rests directly on the rock. The enclosure of painted steel sheathing is supported by a steel frame with flat roof trusses. The walls are decorated in the Beaux-Arts style. At the water end are three arched openings for the ferry slips, the arches springing from four huge pilasters with capitals in the form of scroll brackets. A promenade at the upper-deck of the ferry, which is the third floor of the building, is supported by steel arches springing from columns.

The prime example of shipping, warehouse, and industrial facilities on the Brooklyn waterfront is the extensive complex of docks and industrial and shipping facilities of the Bush Terminal Company, which was established in 1902 and which completed its development in 1917 (fig. 2). Its plan was to construct and operate piers, warehouses, rail-freight terminals, workers' housing, and switching trackage over an area of twenty blocks along the waterfront from 39th to 51st streets in Brooklyn. The development included 7 piers, 103 warehouses, 18 industrial buildings, workers' housing, an office building at 100 Broad Street, New York, and an exhibition building and buyers' center on 42nd Street at Sixth Avenue.

Demolition, construction, and reconstruction of waterfront facilities—shipping piers, service docks, ferry, and carfloat terminals—continued over the years to World War II, the grand total of all structures reaching a maximum of 190 on the Manhattan waterfront, one in the Bronx, three in Queens, and 106 in Brooklyn (determined from the most reliable maps available).

Early Years of the New York Metropolitan Rail System

The railroad history of New York City (which was synonymous with Manhattan Island until the expansion in 1898) began with the construction of the New York and Harlem Railroad, initiated on February 25, 1832. The company operated the first horsecar service in New York but by mid-century began to conduct operations by means of steam locomotives. The line was pushed steadily northward, crossing the Harlem River in 1839–40, the Bronx River in 1842, and up to Chatham, New York, in 1852, where a connection with the Western Railroad of Massachusetts gave it entry to the New York state capital at Albany. The railroad company built several stations in New York, the largest of which was completed in 1845 at Madison Square, the intersection of Madison and Fourth (later Park) avenues with 27th Street. The rapidly expanding traffic necessitated two enlargements, completed in 1851 and 1857. The number of trains suddenly increased in 1848, when the newly completed New York and New Haven Railroad began to operate trains by trackage rights over the Harlem from Woodlawn, New York, to the Madison Square terminal. This arrangement lasted through the subsequent history of the New York rail system.

Direct service to Albany came with the construction of the Hudson River Railroad over the years 1846–51. The line lay on the West Side of Manhattan close to the river shore, where it remained throughout the distance northward to Albany. The railroad was built under the direction of John B. Jervis, one of the great creative engineers of his time, who also designed and supervised the construction of New York City's first public water supply system, the Croton Aqueduct and associated dams and reservoirs (1839–42). To put the Hudson River line in operating order required extensive construction on the West Side: a downtown passenger terminal on Chambers Street (1851), freight and passenger depots and repair shops in the blocks bounded by Tenth and Eleventh avenues between 30th and 32nd streets (1850–51), a bridge over Spuyten Duyvil (1853) in the Bronx, and a spacious freight terminal at Saint John's Park (1867–68). The famous railroad tycoon Cornelius Vanderbilt acquired control of the line and merged it with his New York Central Railroad in 1869 to provide a continuous through route from New York to Central via Buffalo and to give the pioneer New York and Harlem line the status of a local railroad that was eventually to become a division of the New York Central Railroad.

To the east of the city, in the future boroughs of Queens and Brooklyn, the Long Island Rail Road (LIRR) began its corporate life with the nucleus of the Brooklyn and Jamaica Railroad, established in 1834. Acquired by and merged with the LIRR in 1836, the extended line reached the east end of the island at Greenport ten years later. For a few years, the combination of rail, ferry, and steamship service provided a through route from New York to Boston. The network of rail lines that constituted the Long Island Rail Road was created over the years by the merger of a number of small companies that extended over the length of the island. The unified system built two major terminals that superseded the earlier local stations. The first was constructed at Hunter's Point in Long Island City in 1861 and remained in service until the LIRR gained entry to Pennsylvania Station in New York in 1910. The second, built to coincide with the electrification of the Atlantic Avenue line between Brooklyn and Jamaica in Queens, was constructed in 1902–04 at the intersection of Atlantic and Flatbush avenues in Brooklyn and is still in use.

The New Jersey rail lines and terminals formed an integral part of the metropolitan system, but their history is unusually tangled in spatial distribution as well as chronology. This complexity is further increased by the fact that the large trunk lines that built the great terminal stations were usually formed by merger or lease of numerous smaller companies. Perhaps the most convenient way to treat the construction of the New Jersey facilities is to take them up in geographical order, from

south to north, which corresponds fairly closely to their chronological order. The first, then, would be the Central Railroad of New Jersey, which in 1864, built its first rail-ferry terminal in Jersey City, directly behind both Ellis Island and the Statue of Liberty. This was replaced with a much larger structure in 1887–89 and enlarged extensively in 1914. Next, again in Jersey City, were the successive terminals of the Erie Railroad and its predecessors. The nucleus of the large rail line, the Paterson and Hudson River Railroad, built its first New Jersey station in 1838. The Erie acquired a great number of small companies in the metropolitan area of northern New Jersey, including the Paterson, and constructed the first unified terminal in 1886–88. The entire station complex was demolished during the decline of rail passenger traffic in the United States following the World War II. The original company of those that formed the Pennsylvania Railroad opened a Jersey City terminal in 1838, which was replaced three times. The last, constructed in 1888–92, attracted international attention for its huge vaulted train shed carried on three-hinged arched trusses. It, too, fell before the wreckers in the melancholy years following World War II.

The first road to reach the Hudson River outside the dense and overloaded web of Jersey City lines was the Morris and Essex Railroad, which built a station in Hoboken in 1859–62. The company, along with a number of small lines, was leased to the Delaware, Lackawanna & Western Railroad, which constructed a unified terminal in the same city in 1905–07. This structure also included in innovative engineering feature: its train shed was a series of low parallel vaults each spanning two tracks and an associated platform. It was called the Bush shed after its inventor, Lincoln Bush, chief engineer of the Lackawanna. The terminal is the only one that survives to this day. The northernmost of the north Jersey phalanx of freight and passenger stations and last to be opened to service was the joint terminal of the New York, West Shore & Buffalo, and the New York, Ontario & Western railroads, built between 1881 and 1885. The facilities were eventually demolished, and the minor, traffic-starved Ontario Railroad abandoned its entire line. The extension of the Baltimore and Ohio Railroad to Staten Island (Richmond Borough of New York City) in 1887–89 very nearly marked the end of construction history for the New Jersey lines, with only completion of the Pennsylvania Railroad's great ferry terminal yet to come.

The pattern of railroad freight stations, transfer lines, spur tracks, and yards in the New York metropolitan area is so vast and intricate that it would be impossible to describe it in general terms (figs. 13, 14). For the city itself, the various roads built a total of nine carfloat terminals and thirteen freight stations, comprising a total of thirty-eight tracks. The essential characteristic of this vast web was that, for all practical purposes, the continental rail system terminated at the New Jersey waterfront, but the freight-handling piers of the transoceanic vessels lined the Manhattan and Brooklyn shores. The result was that New York became the greatest lighterage and carfloat terminal in the world, and perhaps its most extraordinary feature was that the whole tangle of intersecting and overlapping lines of shipping could be made to work at all. The port and various shipping facilities broke down during

3. Grand Central Depot, 1869–71.
View of the head house facade
along 42nd Street.

World War I and had to be rescued, along with all the railroads themselves, by the federal government.

The Manhattan Railroad Stations

The first of the palatial railroad terminals of Manhattan was Grand Central Depot, constructed in 1869–71 at the intersection of 42nd Street and Fourth (later Park) Avenue (figs. 3, 4). The architect of the station building, or head house, was John B. Snook; the engineer in charge of the project was Isaac C. Buckout, chief engineer of the New York and Harlem Railroad; and the architect-engineer of the train shed was Robert G. Hatfield, perhaps the leading constructive architect of New York at the time. Since the whole complex was designed to provide unified terminal facilities for the Harlem, New York and New Haven, and newly formed New York Central and Hudson River railroads, the first step in the implementation of the plan was the construction of the Spuyten Duyvil and Port Morris Railroad, opened shortly before the completion of the station, to connect the Hudson River line on the West Side with the Harlem tracks on Fourth Avenue. Grand Central Depot was divided into the usual head house, which contained all public and service spaces, and track-platform area under its vaulted train shed. The head house was a narrow, elongated **L** in plan, embracing two sides of the track area. The formal treatment of the building was drawn from Renaissance and Second Empire motifs. The main part of the building, comprising the chief public areas such as waiting room and concourse, was divided into three pavilions along 42nd Street, identifying in elevation the three internal divisions serving the three railroad companies. The prominent features of this tripartite scheme were the curving mansard roofs that covered and served to distinguish the separate pavilions. The head house constituted the first of the great railroad palaces, although it included many defects in planning. The most advanced element of the terminal complex was the train shed, a semicircular vault of glass and galvanized, corrugated iron that measured 652 feet in length and 199 feet in span. Carried on thirty-two wrought–iron, arched trusses fixed in cast-iron shoes at the springing points, it was the grandest work of its kind in the United States at the time and a creditable counterpart of the leading train sheds in Europe in the mid-nineteenth century. The approach tracks running down the middle of Fourth Avenue were roofed over in 1872–75 to form the Park Avenue tunnel that helped to compel adoption of electrical operation of the terminal after the turn of the century. Traffic grew at the rate of ten percent per annum to reach fifty thousand passengers and three hundred trains per day in 1900.

The growth of traffic forced the station beyond its limits in less than thirty years. Overloaded track and platform space, overcrowded office space, and chaotic circulation forced the railroad companies to undertake a program of renovation and expansion. The mixture of the old and new terminal, now known as Grand Central Station and designed by the architect Samuel Huckel, Jr., was rebuilt in 1899–1901 (fig. 5). The revised plans included enlarged space for passengers and staff, improved circulation through reduction in conflicting lines of

4. *Grand Central Depot, interior of the train shed, looking toward the head house.*

foot traffic, and direct movement from street of waiting room to trains; but there were no changes in the existing track-platform system. The new formal design of the head house was less ostentatious: severe Renaissance details with modest tourelles at the corners replaced the Second Empire mansards of 1871. The station had scarcely opened, however, when the rising flood of traffic and the overheated, smoke-filled Park Avenue tunnel required far more drastic solutions.

A combination of legislative demands and irresistible operating pressures led to the decision to sweep away everything that had gone before and replace it with a new electrified terminal that was to emerge as the world's foremost work of railroad engineering and architecture. Both American and European precedents were available to provide the necessary models. The first successful application of electric traction to the operation of trains came with the City and South London Railway, constructed as a subway line in London over the years 1887–90. More important for the New York stations was the use of electric power in heavy-duty standard railroad operations. The first of its kind was the electrification of the Baltimore Belt Railroad, a subsidiary of the Baltimore and Ohio, in 1892–95. The decisive event was the construction of the world's first electrified railway terminal, the Gare d'Orsay in Paris, in 1897–1900. A series of proposals between 1899 and 1902 underlay the decision to introduce electrical operation at Grand Central Terminal. The first was offered by the electrical inventor and engineer Frank J. Sprague in 1899; the second came from William J. Wilgus, the author of the original Grand Central plan, in the same year; and the third from the transportation planner Bion J. Arnold, who conducted an exhaustive series of tests in 1901–02 and submitted a report to the directors of the railroad company. On the basis of the Arnold report, the company decided on direct-current electrification, began extensive testing of an experimental locomotive manufactured by the General Electric Company in 1904, and inaugurated regular service between the terminal and High Bridge, New York City, in September 1906. The operation was later extended northward on both the Hudson River and the New York and Harlem lines. The New Haven Railroad, which used the New York and Harlem tracks from Woodlawn, New York, to the terminal, followed in 1906–07 with a considerably more innovative system, the first alternating-current installation for a standard steam-operated railroad.

Meanwhile, the directors of the companies owning Grand Central Terminal made the radical decision to sweep away the overloaded station and replace it with a double-level terminal that remains the largest such structure in the world. The original plan was advanced by W. J. Wilgus in March 1903, but it was soon enlarged from fifty-seven to sixty-seven station tracks, distributed between forty-two tracks on the upper or through train level and twenty-five on the lower or suburban train level. Construction of the terminal complex was initiated in the spring of 1903, with Wilgus acting as chief engineer and director of the vast project; the architects of the head house and appurtenant buildings were originally Reed & Stem of Saint Paul, Minnesota, but they were later joined in a loose association by the New York firm of Warren and Wetmore. The entire episode, involving choice and retention of architects,

forms one of the sorriest chapters in the history of American architecture, since Warren and Wetmore unilaterally and illegally terminated the contract held by the original architects. In a lawsuit that went through the courts until 1922, the New York firm was compelled to make restitution in the sum of five hundred thousand dollars paid to Allen Stem and the Charles Reed estate. The process of design was as chaotic as the relations among the architects, but the giant structure was eventually completed in February 1913.

The head house as designed is a product of the principles taught at the Ecole des Beaux-Arts in Paris, and the chief elevation, facing 42nd Street, was based in part on the Petit Trianon at Versailles (fig. 6). The terminal complex, filling the area between 42nd and 45th streets, its axis centered on the line of Park Avenue, includes mail, express, and baggage-handling facilities as well as the head house. The subsidiary yard, storage, service, and repair trackage ultimately gave the terminal a total of 189 electrified subgrade tracks underlying an area of ten city blocks in midtown Manhattan. It is by far the largest rail terminal ever built and made possible an immense air-rights development that brought the New York Central Railroad and its successors a handsome rental income.

Pennsylvania Station, facing Seventh Avenue between 31st and 33rd streets, opened two-and-a-half years before Grand Central, as the first terminal of the Pennsylvania Railroad on Manhattan Island. The station proper is the nucleus of an immense program of construction and electrification extending from Harrison, New Jersey, on the west to the eastern area of Queens on the east, where the line connects with that of the New York Connecting Railroad and the New York, New Haven, and Hartford Railroad's Harlem River Branch. The main part of the system, lying between its west point and Sunnyside Yard in Queens, is known as the New York Extension of the Pennsylvania Railroad; the remainder, to the New Haven connection, is the New York Connecting Railroad. Planning for this project began more than ten years before the inception of construction, but the exact beginning is difficult to establish. Perhaps the ancestral origin was the ambitious proposal put forth by Austin Corbin, president of the Long Island Rail Road, in 1891, to bring his railroad into New York City and to extend the city's transit system to New Jersey. Both were eventually realized, but only in part through the achievements of the Long Island and the Pennsylvania railroads. The idea of building a New York station had by then taken root in the minds of the Pennsylvania Railroad's officers. In the year following the Corbin plan, Samuel Rea, assistant to the president of the railroad, submitted a report to President George N. Roberts describing five alternate plans for a New York extension, but it was the end of the century before any of them were set into motion. The opening of the Gare d'Orsay profoundly influenced the Pennsylvania Railroad's new president, Alexander Cassatt, and the decision to undertake this extraordinary and costly project soon followed. The entire program, except for the New York Connecting Railroad, was placed under construction in 1903 and opened to the public on November 27, 1910. The architects selected for the station building were McKim, Mead & White, the most prestigious firm in New York, and the chief engineer was George W. Raymond (fig. 7).

5

6

7

5. *Grand Central Station, c. 1900.*
Vanderbilt and Park Avenue
elevations after reconstruction and
expansion.

6. *Reed & Stern and Warren &*
Wetmore. Grand Central Terminal
as it appeared about 1930. The
Commodore Hotel stands on the
right, and the New York Central
office building in the background.

7. *McKim, Mead & White.*
Pennsylvania Station.
Seventh Avenue elevation.

His field commanders were drawn from the leading engineering talent of the nation.

The New York Extension embraced so many different architectural and engineering techniques that it can be described only by following the engineering and physiographic divisions of the construction process. The Meadows Division is a double-track embankment that extends from Manhattan Transfer, one mile east of Newark, New Jersey, to the west face of Bergen Hill, a great basaltic sill that forms the Hudson River Palisades. The North River Division consists of two single-track cylindrical tunnels of cast iron, lined with concrete, which extend through Bergen Hill and under the Hudson River and the West Side of Manhattan to about Tenth Avenue. These tunnels, mined through soft river sediments and dense metamorphic rock, required the most heroic efforts on the part of the construction crews.

The terminal and its head house is twenty-one-track through station, occupying the two blocks bounded by Seventh and Eighth avenues between 31st and 33rd streets. The station filled the east half of this space, but the track area, with supporting yards between the west and east throat extended from Tenth Avenue on the west to Sixth Avenue on the east. The head house was powerful work of Roman Imperial design, drawn chiefly from the Thermae of Caracalla in Rome as a precedent, and the splendid climax of its interior space was the glass and steel vault over the concourse. The magnificent structure was demolished in 1963–66, to mark the worst act of civic and architectural vandalism in the history of American building. The East River Division embraces the most complex series of engineering works. The four single-track tunnels are designated the Crosstown—under the east half of Manhattan Island, the East River, and the Queens—from the borough on the east side of the river. The tunnel exit tracks terminate in the junctions with the Long Island and the New York Connecting railroads and the Sunnyside Yard, the largest railroad coach yard in the world. The entire work—the grandeur of its architecture and its extraordinary engineering feats—constituted the single greatest work of American structural art of the time.

The electrification of Pennsylvania Station and its approach tracks involved considerable experimentation in the design of motive power and fixed equipment, and in a strictly chronological sense the Long Island Rail Road, which was a party to the whole station program, was the pioneer. The initial stage of the Long Island program was the electrification of the Atlantic Avenue line in Brooklyn, from Jamaica station to Flatbush Avenue, carried out in 1903–05. The conversion of the main stem, from Jamaica station to the junction with the Pennsylvania, was a part of the terminal program itself, the installation put in place in 1906–10. The essential characteristics of the Long Island-Pennsylvania program marked a clear step forward: the power generated was three-phase alternating current transmitted at eleven thousand volts; this was converted and stepped down for distribution, by third rail, to 650 volts direct current. The locomotives were unique, and the form was never exactly duplicated in the subsequent evolution of electric motive power. The motor in each locomotive unit was of extraordinary size, rated at two thousand horsepower, and the armature was connected to the driving wheels by means of an inclined, counterweighted jackshaft and a horizontal driving rod. They were rugged in construction, powerful, easily controlled, and so reliable in operation over the years that the steam locomotive seemed merely primitive by comparison. Great expansion of electrified mileage and the progressive evolution of electric locomotives eventually placed the Pennsylvania Railroad in the position of world leadership. Most of the railroad's motive power, however, disappeared with the decline of rail traffic in the eastern United States, a melancholy parallel to the brutal destruction of the company's great New York station. Transportation in mid-century America became a sorry tale of blindly misplaced technologies.

The Bridges of Manhattan

The first of the major bridges to join Manhattan with the Long Island and mainland boroughs quickly became one of the most impressive monuments of modern structural engineering. The Brooklyn Bridge, constructed in 1869–83, became a national symbol and elevated its German-born creator, John Augustus Roebling, to the status of national hero (fig. 8). The East and the Hudson rivers proved formidable barriers to the bridge-builder's art, and it was only when Roebling had carried suspension bridge construction to a mature level that the task could be undertaken. Sadly, Roebling was never to see his supreme achievement realized. While conducting the final survey for the construction project in the summer of 1869, he injured his foot so severely that partial amputation was necessary. He died of the resulting tetanus infection and his son Washington became chief engineer in his place. The actual construction began on January 2, 1870, in which the first task was to erect the masonry towers founded on bedrock by means of pneumatic caissons. The wire-cable bridge, marked by numerous technical innovations, was opened on May 24, 1883 and immediately became a world sensation because of its unprecedented size. The main span extends 1,595 feet 6 inches between cable saddles, and the side or anchor spans extend an additional 930 feet shoreward of each tower. The towers rose to an overall height of 271 feet 6 inches above mean high water and were the highest structures in the skyscraper city of New York until the Pulitzer Building finally topped them in 1890. Traditional and innovative techniques came together in the Brooklyn Bridge, whose towers and anchorages are solid masonry, but the cables, suspenders, and stays are composed of steel wire. These last elements in the suspension system were first used by Roebling: they form a dense network radiating outward and downward from the saddles and serve as stiffeners to increase the rigidity of the flexible suspension structure. Roebling was an authority on the aerodynamic stability of such spans, and the lessons he taught were not finally learned until the collapse of the Tacoma Narrows Bridge over Puget Sound in 1940.

The spans that followed Brooklyn over the East River might have seemed anticlimactic beside their predecessor, but in truth they all embodied noteworthy features of bridge engineering. The next in both spatial and chronological order is the Williamsburg Bridge, constructed between 1897 and 1903 not far to the north of the pioneer work. The chief engineer was Leffert L. Buck; he was an accomplished engineer, but there are controversial features of the span that prevent it from standing in the front rank of suspension bridge design. The entire structure is heavily redundant, the longitudinal stiffening trusses, for example, introduced to render the bridge rigid against wind loads, are forty feet deep, quickly seen to be nearly double the necessary depth. The posts or vertical elements at the sides of the towers lean inward in an awkward form the violates the ruling geometry of the whole complex. The structure embodies technical innovations, however, that give the bridge some distinction. Its main span of sixteen hundred feet exceeded that of the Brooklyn Bridge; its towers are the first all-steel constructions among the New York spans; and the bridge was the first to carry a rapid transit line. It is the appearance of the bridge, more than anything else, that is its only real defect, and it is generally deplored by structural purists.

The third East River crossing marked a considerable improvement, and it was the first for which architects were associated with the engineers in the process of design (fig. 9). The Manhattan Bridge, constructed between 1901 and 1909, was the work of chief engineer Othiel F. Nichols and his staff and the architectural firm of Carrère and Hastings, who were simultaneously working on the design of the New York Public Library, one of the city's architectural masterpieces. A narrowing of the river made it possible to reduce the main span to 1,470 feet, but piers, berthing space, and other waterfront structures required unusually long anchor spans. The span was the first double-deck suspension bridge in New York and the second to carry a transit line. The towers in the form of steel bents or frames were designed to allow deflection in the line of the bridge without excessive bending forces when subject to unequal tension caused by temperature changes. The presence of architectural designers guaranteed that the Manhattan Bridge would possess a unity of structural form and ornamental detail that made the bridge superior to its immediate predecessor.

The bridge immediately north of the Manhattan marked a radical departure from the monopoly of the suspension form. The Queensboro Bridge, along 60th Street in Manhattan, was erected between 1901 and 1908 from the plans of Gustav Lindenthal and his staff (fig. 10). The Queensboro Bridge is a cantilever truss bridge and stood among the largest of its kind at the time of its completion. It crosses the river at Roosevelt (formerly Blackwell's) Island, and the five spans, with a total end-to-end length of a little more than 3700 feet, are nearly symmetrical about the midpoint over the island. The bridge is a succession of cantilever and anchor spans, of which the two long cantilevers over the main channel of the river form a clear span between bearings of 1,182 feet. The unusual feature of this part of the structure is that the two trusses of the channel span are pure cantilevers without a suspended span between them, the presence of which is common practice. The huge bridge, visually impressive for its weight and power and the complicated interplay of web members in the subdivided Pratt trusses, carries a busy double-deck roadway, which for-

8. *John A. Roebling and Washington Roebling. Brooklyn Bridge, 1869–83.*

9. *Carrère & Hastings and Leon Moisieff. Manhattan Bridge, 1901–09.* New York Public Library.

10. *Henry Hornbostel and Gustav Lindenthal. Queensboro Bridge, 1901–08.* New York City Landmarks Preservation Commission.

11. *Henry Hornbostel and Gustav Lindenthal. Hell Gate Bridge as constructed, 1914–16 with a portion of the Triborough Bridge in the foreground.* New York Public Library.

12. *William R. Hutton and Edward H. Kendall. Washington Bridge (Harlem Bridge), 1886–89.*

9

10

11

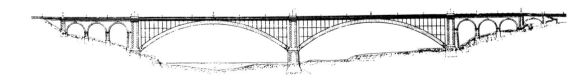

12

merly included trolley lines on the upper deck and transit on the lower.

The only railroad bridge and the only arch bridge over the major bounding waterways of Manhattan is Hell Gate Bridge, which crosses the East River at the turbulent confluence of main river and subsidiary channels from which the bridge takes its name. The great arch is another world-famous New York bridge and forms the centerpiece of a short but exceedingly expensive railroad line. The New York Connecting Railroad was incorporated in 1892 and was constructed in 1912–18 between the New Haven Railroad's Harlem River Branch at 142nd Street in the Bronx and the Long Island Rail Road line at Fresh Pond Junction in Queens. Along the way there is a connection with the Pennsylvania Railroad at Sunnyside, and the Long Island Rail Road beyond Fresh Pond gave access to the Bay Ridge carfloat terminal in Brooklyn. This was the east end of the carfloat route whose west end was the terminal of the Pennsylvania Railroad at Greenville Piers in Jersey City. These tedious details indicate the crucial link that the little Connecting Railroad provided. It was the means for uniting the rail lines of New England and eastern Canada with the numerous connections of the Pennsylvania to the south and west. The record cost of the line arose from the fact that a high proportion of its twelve-mile length lies on bridges and viaducts. The tracks diverge from the New Haven in a flyover junction at 142nd Street, extend on a concrete-walled fill to 138th Street, cross a local shipping channel on a double-leaf bascule bridge, lie on a steel plate-girder viaduct to 132nd Street, on another double-leaf bascule bridge over the Bronx Kills, a second plate-girder viaduct over Randall's Island, a four-span steel bridge on inverted bowstring trusses over Little Hell Gate, the major Hell Gate Bridge, and on a third plate-girder viaduct through Queens. Much of the remainder is on a fill requiring plate-girder and concrete arch bridges at the street intersections.

The masterpiece in this extraordinary exhibition of bridge engineering is the Hell Gate arch, constructed between 1914 and 1916 from the design of chief engineer Lindenthal and his staff, and the architect Henry Hornbostel (fig. 11). The steel structure is a two-hinged arch carrying a four-track rail line and spanning 977 feet 6 inches clear, between centers of the hinges. It remained the largest such bridge in the world until the completion of the Bayonne Bridge over Kill van Kull between Staten Island and New Jersey in 1931. Only the lower rib of the structure provides arch action; the upper rib is the top chord of a stiffening truss designed to resist the bending forces arising from moving traffic loads. The overall form of the Hell Gate Bridge might be regarded as deceptive because the massive masonry towers at the ends and the covered hinges at the springing points of the arch give the appearance of a fixed arch. There were, however, reasons for this formal design. The top chord had to be recurved at the ends to provide sufficient clearance for the distribution and transmission lines of the electrical system. The resulting appearance of the ends would have been misleading and aesthetically unacceptable. The architect felt that the towers were essential to offer a strong visual closure or containment of the arch thrust, even though that thrust is concentrated at the hinges. It is doubtful

whether the controversy will ever be resolved to everyone's satisfaction.

The Harlem River bridges offered no comparable structural sensations to those over the East and Hudson rivers because the tidal waterway has only a modest width compared to the major bounding waters. A total of fourteen bridges crossed the Harlem, the original in 1693 to carry the Albany Post Road over Spuyten Duyvil, and of these, thirteen remain, having been constructed over the years from 1839 to 1963. Two are noteworthy works of the bridge builder's art and a third deserves historical identification. The oldest of the surviving bridges is High (originally Aqueduct) Bridge, constructed between 1839 and 1842 as part of the Croton Dam and Aqueduct, the city's original public water supply system, built under the direction of John B. Jervis. The structure was originally a multispan bridge of full-centered masonry arches, but five of these were replaced by a steel-plate arch over the Harlem Ship Canal and the New York Central Railroad line in 1927. The bridge is a handsome work of masonry arches in the Roman style, but its most unusual characteristic is hidden. Jervis developed an ingenious method for distributing the heavy water load of the aqueduct pipes to the arches; in the hollow space between the spandrel walls, he introduced longitudinal walls that carried the load directly to the extrados of each arch, then added lateral walls to help distribute the load as uniformly as possible. The laterals are braced by diagonal stone struts set between the lateral and longitudinal elements. Equally important as engineering but radically different in form is the Washington Bridge, constructed between 1886 and 1889 from the design of a number of talents (fig. 12). The fundamental design was the work of Charles C. Schneider, a leading bridge engineer, and his assistant Wilhelm Hildebrand; the design of the structure as built was the work of the engineer William R. Hutton and the architect Edward H. Kendall; the contract drawings were prepared by Theodore Cooper, another noted bridge engineer, and William J. McAlpine. The resulting bridge is virtually unique in form and size. The approaches are carried on traditional masonry arches, but the two main spans are composed of two-hinged arches built up of steel plate to an unprecedented size. The clear span of each arch is 508 feet 9 inches center to center of the hinges and the rise is 89 feet 10 inches from the center line of the hinges to the center line of the arches at the crown. No attempt was made to disguise the form of the arches: the hinges are plainly visible, and the steel-plate members contract at the springing points to a depth no greater than the diameter of the hinges. This contraction reflects the fact that there is no bending force at the hinge.

The third of the Harlem River spans that deserves the historian's attention is the University Heights Bridge, originally built between 1893 and 1895 from the plans of the engineers Alfred P. Boller and William H. Burr, both distinguished members of their profession. The structure is a center-pivoted swing bridge, which means that in the open position the two halves of the span are cantilevers, each acting as the anchor span for the other. As a consequence, traffic and dead loads on the bridge result in maximum bending at the center, over the circular pier around which the span rotates. This fact is clearly

13. Map showing the passenger-carrying rail lines and the passenger terminals of the New York metropolitan area, 1925.

14. Map showing the freight-carrying rail lines and the principal freight terminals of the New York metropolitan area, 1925.

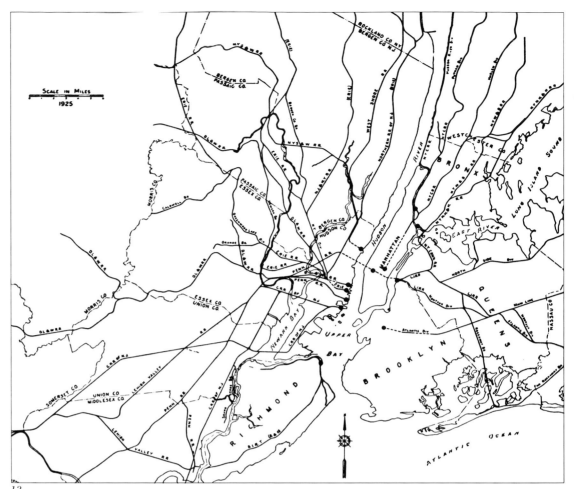

13

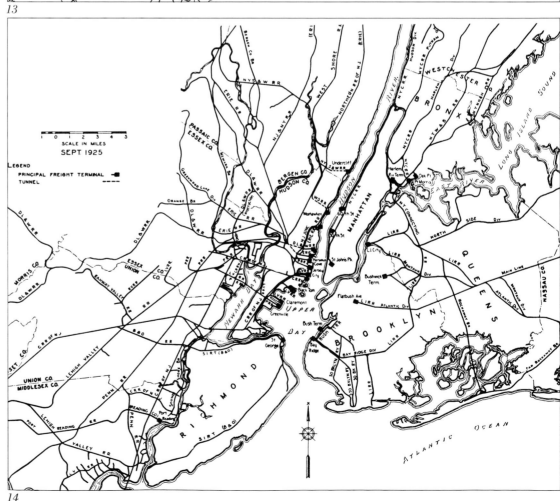

14

reflected in the form of the trusses, the depth of which decreases from a maximum over the pier to a minimum at the free ends.

The great age of bridge building in New York came between the years 1870 and 1910. After a relatively short hiatus, it was renewed with a series of magnificent suspension bridges and one steel arch span that finally eclipsed Hell Gate in length of clear span. The first bridge to cross the Hudson was the George Washington, constructed in 1927–31, its Manhattan end close to the scenic beauties of Fort Tryon Park. The engineer was Othmar H. Ammann, who had been associated with Gustav Lindenthal, and the architect Cass Gilbert, designer of the Woolworth Building. The one exception to the second suspension monopoly is the Bayonne Bridge 1928–31, built to cross Kill Van Kull between Staten Island (Richmond borough) and Bayonne, New Jersey. Ammann and Gilbert were again engineer and architect. A two-hinged arch with a clear span of 1,650 feet between hinges, it held the record for length for over twenty years. The municipal government returned to the suspension form with the Triborough Bridge (1933–36), a three-armed complex of bridges uniting the boroughs of Manhattan, Queens, and Bronx. Two bridges cross the easternmost length of the East River: the Bronx-Whitestone (1937–39) and the Throg's Neck (1959–61) are particularly handsome examples of the suspended form. The Verrazano-Narrows Bridge, construct between 1959 and 1969 for some years held the record length for clear span at 4,260 feet. The majestic span, stunning in its very simplicity, crosses the Narrows between Staten Island and Brooklyn, and the first part of its name comes from that of Giovanni da Verrazano, who on April 17, 1524 became the first European to sail into New York Harbor. By the end of World War I, New York had laid out the most extensive system of urban transportation ever devised, one that covered the surface of the land and water, the air above, and the earth below both land and water. It was a multidimensional hierarchical network that embraced surface car lines, later supplemented by buses, elevated transit, subways, ferries, and standard railroad lines (fig. 13, 14). The vastly ramifying system had no counterpart for sheer magnitude and capacity—the rail system alone was capable of carrying more than one million passengers per day— and it offered the supreme example of urban mobility combined with a new kind of urban order, built up, we sometimes think, to serve precisely the ever-restless and impatient New Yorkers. The automobile as a device for mass transportation seems primitive by comparison.

References

Baedeker, Karl. "New York," in *The United States*. Leipzig: Karl Baedeker, 10–81

Buttenwieser, Ann L. *Manhattan Water-Bound: Planning and Development Manhattan's Waterfront from the Seventeenth Century to the Present*. New York: New York University Press, 1987.

"Carroll Street Bridge, over the Gowanus Canal, Borough of Brooklyn". New York City Landmarks Preservation Commission. Unpublished report, October 1987. Includes bibliography.

Condit, Carl W. *American Building Art: The Nineteenth Century*. New York: Oxford University Press, 1960. Includes short bibliography.

———. *American Building Art: The Twentieth Century*. New York: Oxford University Press Includes extensive bibliography.

———. *The Port of New York: A History of the Rail and Terminal System from the Beginning to Pennsylvania Station*. Chicago: University of Chicago Press, 1980. Includes comprehensive bibliography.

1. Jungfern Bridge, Berlin, 1901.
Landesbildstelle, Berlin.

The Metropolis as a Construction: Engineering Structures in Berlin 1871–1914

Hans Kollhoff

Hans Kollhoff is an architect and a visiting professor at the Eidgenössische Technische Hochschule in Zurich. He was director of the Summer Academy for Architecure in Berlin and has also held teaching positions at Cornell University, Ithaca; Technische Universität Berlin; Hochschule der Künste Berlin; and the University of Dortmund.

To celebrate the 750th year of its existence, in 1988, the city of Berlin gave itself a present: the conversion of the former Hamburg Station into an imposing new exhibition site. This gesture is symptomatic of an era that has begun to make itself comfortable in nineteenth-century structures and, under the pretext of preserving historical monuments, to sun itself in the borrowed light of the Wilhelmine era—in which a newly united Germany grew in economic and military power with Berlin as its capital. Berlin has again and again shown its inability to carry on the tradition of turn-of-the-century urban buildings and public spaces, resigning itself instead to architectural and urban design patterns that were little more than symbols of status and power even when they were new. Something very important has been lost from sight in the process: the impulses that made Berlin, with breathtaking rapidity, into a world center.

Ever since the 1920s, people have been talking about metropolitan architecture, seemingly unaware that such architecture had actually been built before the First World War. This was the period when factories, railway stations, shopping arcades, greenhouses, market halls, hotels, exhibition buildings, and fairgrounds emerged that established a typology of structures for the Industrial Age. Built by private investors and speculators, they provided the backdrop for the legendary 1920s, when the flight from the corrupt city set in and thousands dreamed of a better future out-of-doors, in the green belts and garden cities of cooperative projects.

The vision of a metropolitan architecture that emerged in Germany after World War I like an awakening from a troubled dream attracted enormous journalistic interest. Still, it remained largely retrospective in character and really can only be understood as an unconscious attempt to come to terms with the past. After the AEG buildings (Allgemeine Elektricitäts-Gesellschaft) in 1907, metropolitan architecture in Berlin came to a standstill. The brute force of the declining nineteenth century dwindled to nothingness as architectural volumes began to do without articulation and the lucid outlines of pared-down geometrical solids replaced decorative forms. It remained for the 1920s to speculate and philosophize about the big city and develop utopian ideas that in turn culminated in orderly, basically anti-big-city systems. Unlike art, literature, and film, modern architecture proved unable to accept the chaos of the metropolis of our day.

In the interest of a truly urban architecture, then, it is time to consider the Wilhelmine era as more than the mere soil from which the flowering of the 1920s sprang. Rather, it was the period in which urban architecture in Berlin was born and grew to maturity.

It would be wrong, however, if the only lesson we learned from this era was a fixation on style, as if it were enough to reinstall "Hardenberg" cast-iron street lamps, slap peaked helmets on projecting bays, and refurbish stripped facades with stucco ornament. To do so would be to repeat the mistake of 1870, when Karl Friedrich Schinkel was seen as a stylistic virtuoso rather than a visionary architect and urban designer. The way in which glittering glass pyramids and cupolas are currently

47

being placed in front of depressing hotel boxes in Berlin or in which Wilhelmine square designs are being retraced in banalized form, is an indication of that lack of substance, economic and cultural, from which the city has always suffered. "Everything here is *pauvre*," wrote Theodor Fontane, "and there was not never nothing good come of being *pauvre*."[1]

The period between 1879 and 1914 in Berlin was the period of a newly united Germany and soon thereafter a world center. By the end of this period Berlin had caught up with the enormous, well-nigh frightening technological lead enjoyed by London, Paris, and the great American cities. Berlin became the upstart among world centers, "a colonial city," as Karl Scheffler remarked in 1910, "whose suddenness of development had more in common with American cities than with the old metropolises of Europe, recklessly expanding, violent, and established in a kind of no-man's land, far from the terrain of European culture."[2]

Not surprisingly, the result was a cultural inferiority complex that led to a compulsive effort to create style and thus compensate for the city's respectable but internationally modest achievements in technology and the emergent field of engineering. Conversely, no effort was spared to bolster the self-confidence of the fledgling Reich with the aid of the most advanced technology available.

While swinging between technology and ostentation, Berlin produced nothing in the way of architecture or urban design that could be considered significant enough to include in an architectural history. In Leonardo Benevolo's *History of Nineteenth- and Twentieth-Century Architecture*, for instance, Schinkel's design for the Marschall Bridge (1818), appears in company with English and French bridges (all of which, apart from the Marschall, were designed by engineers). But this is the only mention of a Berlin structure in the entire first half of this voluminous book; in the second half another Berlin example appears—Peter Behrens's AEG turbine factory of 1907. To today's eyes, even a technical curiosity like the Jungfern Bridge of the mid-eighteenth century appears more progressive than any of the bridges of Wilhelmine Berlin (fig. 1).

The national monument to Emperor William I, on the Kupfergraben, embodied the artistic and technological potential of the period with metaphoric concision (fig. 2). It was mounted on a foundation 240 feet long, paralleling the front of the palace and extending far into the Spree River; a separate canal had to be built beneath the monument to deal with overflow. The building compendium, *Berlin und seine Bauten (Berlin and Its Buildings,* 1896) devoted five full pages to describing the elaborate, though quite invisible, technical tricks that were required to erect this monster. It was located on a completely unsuitable site, sandwiched between the palace and the Architectural Academy, which contemporaries would have liked to see torn down.

In the essay "The Most Beautiful City in the World," published in 1899 in Maximilian Harden's journal *Zukunft,* Walther Rathenau took a sarcastic stab at the monument fever and pomposity of Wilhelmine Berlin. Comparing it with the world centers of London, Paris, and New York, Rathenau spared no detail of its overladen and tasteless architecture. "One feels overcome by delirium," wrote Rathenau, "when one is compelled to hurry through the grand avenues of Western Berlin. Here an Assyrian temple, abutted by a patrician house from Nuremberg, then a piece of Versailles, followed by reminiscences of Broadway, of Italy, of Egypt—horrific premature births of polytechnical, beer-induced visions. Thousands of misconceived forms ooze from the walls of these petty bourgeois domiciles. Into noodles and curls, braids and ringlets their borrowed glory of plaster, stucco, artificial mortar and cement swells and congeals."[3]

Karl Scheffler called Berlin the "most faceless and ugly of Germany's larger cities." In his book *Berlin, Ein Stadtschicksal* (1910), he described it as producing a mixture of fascination and nausea, as possessing a "barbarian monumentality," a hypertrophic Americanism and amorphousness that could only be understood as a product of inorganic growth. City planners had been replaced by unscrupulous speculators, who had created the "utilitaristic city on the Spree."[4]

There is a certain tragedy in the fact that this period, which more strongly and lastingly shaped the face of Berlin than any other, should have been artistically and technologically so insignificant, although it had forces at its disposal of which present-day Berlin can only dream. A closer look at the period between 1871 and 1914 becomes interesting, although—or perhaps because—we know our search for cornerstones of architectural history will be in vain. With extreme rapidity, indeed brutality, an urban topography was stamped out during these years that is both frightening and fascinating—residential blocks truncated by railroad tracks, an urban structure dissected by railroad lines, harsh juxtapositions of buildings, bridges, underpasses, embankments, colossal artifacts—gas meters, water towers—floating disembodied in the cityscapes. It was not until the beginning of the twentieth century that a certain beauty was discovered in these things, a beauty that, as August Endell admitted, seemed initially rather strange:

Our big cities are still so young that their beauty is only now being discovered. . . . The period that produced an enormous expansion of cities also gave birth to poets and painters who began to sense their beauty and build their works upon it. . . . It is enough to recall the iron sheds, bridges, elevators, refineries, and especially the machines themselves. They possess a beauty that might at first sight seem to be a pseudo-aesthetic, because these configurations were made to serve a purpose.[5]

Despite its "boring, depressing, uninspired, pompous and pretentious-looking" buildings, Endell believed the city deserved viewing afresh (fig. 3). The example he chose was an iron bridge,

assembled of hundreds of load-bearing members, each stressed according to its strength, slightly stretching and then elastically contracting with every load, the main parts working against one another, the effortless whole with its steel joints and roller platforms that shift under the influence of burdens, the sun, the cold, in a silent, barely detectable oscillation of expansion and contraction. It is strangely pleasurable to enter, in thought, into the private life of these monsters.[6]

Gradually there came to be discovered in the works of engineers, especially in iron and steel construction, an aesthetic of a unique kind. Gottfried Semper's verdict that whoever accepted iron construction would find a meager soil for art made way for the insight that engineering structures were not intrinsically ugly, even when their utilitarian character was fully evident; in other words, there was no longer any reason to hide them behind a mask.

In 1908, the year that Endell's book appeared, Karl Scheffler noted in connection with the building of elevated railways in Berlin:

While they were still in process of building, there were occasional sensations. . . . As long as the constructional intention alone was at work, as long as the skeleton itself, unclad, still revealed the purpose and function of every part and the assemblers were tackling their job, as it were, from the nodal points of the static problem, these rudiments often appeared to contain the promise of art. . . . All in all, the strongest architectural impressions to be had nowadays are received in the presence of half-finished buildings. A rough structure without doors and windows, unplastered, in the delicate, powdery hue of Mark Brandenburg bricks, with its clear vertical striving still uninterrupted by stucco ornament, with the monumental proportions of its large, undetailed masses, affects one for all its primitivity as being beautiful—or at least powerful.[7]

The self-confidence of German engineers, however, was still relatively undeveloped. In the field of architecture they had no achievements to show that could match those of English, French, or American engineers. Neither Berlin nor Germany as a whole could boast a Telford, an Eiffel, a Roebling. Nor, of course, did the challenges exist—the bridging of great rivers, the world's fairs—that would have brought them forth. German engineers were able to unfold their skills only in areas where they were not blocked by architects or reduced to supernumeraries—in the field of machine building itself or in that of the technical facilities of the urban infrastructure.

Nevertheless, it was the accomplishments of engineers that shaped Berlin during the years from 1871 to 1914. By rapidly and directly reacting to the needs of the period they lent a lucid expression to the forces in society that commands our respect and admiration today. Not only the great urban spaces that still survive but also the anonymous components of the city possess a lasting fascination: the many miles of graceful archways supporting the interurban rail lines, the subway viaducts, the interurban embankments, the canals, the countless bridges that conduct these various transportation systems over and under one another, the giant railyards, and not least, the commercial and industrial yards that managed to survive war and renewal.

The low opinion in which such engineering accomplishments were still held in the late nineteenth century becomes evident from an entry in *Berlin und seine Bauten,* the standard work on the city's architecture. As late as 1877, the authors could still write, "The earlier history of Berlin only rarely mentions construction projects to which we would apply the modern term, 'engineering structure.'"[8] Yet in its emergent phase the term engineering structure actually covered a broad range of build-

2

3

2. *Unveiling of the monument to Emperor William I, 1897.* Landesbildstelle, Berlin.

3. *Bridge at the Stettin Train Station, Berlin 1897.* From Janos Frecot and Helmut Geisert, *Berlin in frühen Fotografien, 1857–1913* (Munich, 1984).

4

5

4. New National Gallery, Berlin,
1967. Hydraulic presses raise the
steel-roof construction.
Landesbildstelle, Berlin.

5. Stator of a three-phase current
generator, 1912. From Tilmann
Buddensieg and Henning Rogge,
*Industrie-Kultur, Peter Behrens und
die AEG* (Berlin, 1981).

6. Potsdam Train Station. Site
plans, 1838, 1868. From *Berlin und
seine Bauten*, vol. 1 (Berlin, 1896).

7. Plan of Berlin's railway track
system, 1896. From *Berlin und
seine Bauten*, vol. 1 (Berlin, 1896).

ings whose functions lacked the status or grandeur that would
have made them worthy of an architect's attention. Until the
end of the century these buildings included factories.

Friedrich Gilly already sensed the danger of separating architects from engineers; and Schinkel and the engineer Peter
Beuth, with whom he had traveled to England, managed to reunite the diverging disciplines under the roof of the Academy
of Architecture. It was not until 1879, however, when the fac-
ulties were split at the new Technical College in Charlottenburg, that engineers as specialists in the mathematical sciences could face architects as aesthetic specialists in a
partnership of equals. In the meantime, methods of calculat-
ing highly complex types of steel construction had been found.
In 1863, J. W. Schwedler had succeeded in computing spheroidal roofs for locomotive sheds and natural-gas tanks, and E.
Winkler followed with double- and triple-articulated arches.
Steel construction theory, which until then had limped behind
practice, especially in the experimental field of greenhouse
building, could now find creative application.

The construction of gas container buildings of large diameter gave
Schwedler the opportunity to free the rafter construction previously
used for the roofs of these structures from their internal tie-rods, and
to transfer by an arrangement of rings and groins all of the constructional elements into the spheroidal roof surface, thereby transforming the earlier beams system into a dome system. Since 1863,
Schwedler's domed roof has been employed in every gas container
building erected in Berlin. . . . As regards installation, the central
section of the domes, measuring 23.66 meters in diameter, was fully
assembled and riveted on the floor of the water basin, resting on several trestles. The raising of this approximately 12,000 kilogram section was carried out with the aid of twelve lever jacks which were installed on a projecting, gallery-like scaffolding.[9]

The raising took eight to ten hours, which meant that it could
easily be accomplished in a day. The assembly process is
comparable to that used to erect the roof of Berlin's New National Gallery in 1968 (fig. 4), one of the several reasons why
we must attribute to Mies's building a power that has more in
common with the nineteenth century than with the Neues
Bauen of the early twentieth—particularly in the girder supports, coffered ceilings, and not least the urbanity of its interi-
or, which is the sole postwar example that can rival interiors
produced before World War I.

In the National Gallery the conflict between industrial product and architectural detail was first settled, a conflict that
had made life difficult for turn-of-the-century architects. As
technical possibilities increased, building materials no longer
presented sufficient resistance to the designer, and the result
was an indecision or arbitrariness of expression. The first
building to face this issue, and which came to embody it, was
Peter Behrens's AEG turbine factory (1907). "Behrens produced mass," says Julius Posener, who also said he knows of
only one large building in Germany that employed the new
methods of steel construction as an architectural means, the
Frankfurt Exhibition Hall by Friedrich Thiersch (1908).
Berlin, Posener admits, has nothing to compare.

With the onset of industrialization, Berlin developed into the

50

largest industrial metropolis on the European continent in the space of a few decades, assisted by modern technology industrial capital, and an efficient transportation system. Stimulated by state subsidies, private enterprise was at last able to take up England's lead, even though the Berlin region entirely lacked sources of raw materials.

With the establishment of the Royal Iron Foundry outside the New Gate in 1804, the stage was set for Berlin firms pioneering in machine building to move to Chausseestrasse, which came to be popularly known as Fireland. Instead of the enclosed industrial yards that predominated in the south and east, these factories in the northwestern part of the city, ranged as freestanding, solitary structures along the streets, providing the model for the emergent typology of large industrial spaces that came to maturity in the AEG assembly buildings of Peter Behrens (fig. 5). Yet Chausseestrasse was soon overcrowded, and in 1847 the Borsig Company was obliged to shift its operations to the district of Moabit on the Spree and eventually, in 1898, from there to Tegel. This migration to the periphery, which affected all of the expanding large enterprises, necessitated an expansion of mass transportation and municipal services, which in turned opened up new locations on the city's outskirts. When Berlin became capital of the German Empire in 1871, these developments accelerated dramatically. By 1877, its population numbered one million, and by 1905, it had surpassed the two million mark.

The initial step in the expansion was the construction and improvement of highways and waterways; the first steamship appeared on the Spree River in 1815. By 1825, regular steamer traffic commenced, and the old Schafgraben was excavated, based on Peter Joseph Lenné's plans, to become the Landwehr Canal. In 1853, Schöneberg Harbor went into operation, and followed in 1859 by the Berlin-Spandau shipping canal.

The extension of the rail network began in 1838 with the inauguration of the Berlin-Potsdam Railway, allowing not only an increased flow of goods and raw materials into the city but a growing migration of labor. When Berlin became the capital, the need for transportation grew ever more urgent. In 1868, horse-drawn buses were introduced; building commenced on the belt railway in 1871, on the interurban railway in 1882, and on the subway system in 1902 (figs. 6, 7). The first electric trolley in the world went into operation in 1881 in the Lichterfelde district of Berlin.

Tracks proliferated and extended into every nook and cranny of the city until they could go no further, and came up short at the bumper of a terminal. Station after station was constructed, altering the face of Berlin entirely and driving every well-meaning urban planner to distraction. It may well be that the impossibility of city planning was demonstrated here before it even had the chance to establish itself as a discipline.

Hamburg Station (fig. 8), the last of Berlin's early station buildings after Anhalt (1840) and Stettin stations (1842), was a glazed, triple-vaulted terminal designed by Friedrich Neuhaus, supplied by the Borsig Company, and erected in 1845–47. The three-story, yellow brick building was given a

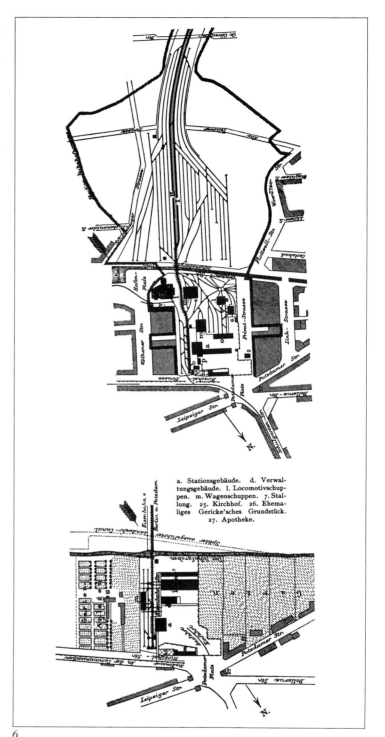

a. Stationsgebäude. d. Verwaltungsgebäude. 1. Locomotivschuppen. m. Wagenschuppen. 7. Stallung. 25. Kirchhof. 26. Ehemaliges Gericke'sches Grundstück. 27. Apotheke.

6

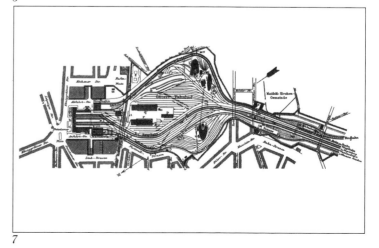

7

striking facade with two flanking towers and two central, round-arched portals for the locomotives, which reversed direction by means of a turntable located in front of the terminal. The turntable was replaced in 1874 by a sliding platform on the south side of the station hall. The passenger station was closed in 1884, when the demand far exceeded its capacity. Still, Hamburg Station with its central hall and two long aisles remained a model for railway terminals in Berlin. And in 1906 it became the site of the Transportation and Building Museum, which was inaugurated by Kaiser Wilhelm II in person.

The interurban Stadtbahn, a four-track system that served as both a belt and a long-distance line, was the first viaduct railway in Europe. In the built-up areas of the city, its route was elevated on arched brick viaducts, with wooden truss bridges at river crossings and simple riveted steel girders at road crossings. Boasting 731 viaduct arches, 597 of which were open to business occupancy, the Stadtbahn represented the largest contiguous urban structure in Berlin, a chain of shops, storerooms, warehouses, workshops, and pubs that with the market halls guaranteed the provisioning of the city. Interurban and belt lines were designed to compensate for the deficits that had resulted from the configuration of competing terminals. Berlin never had a main or central station, only a number of terminal stations, each of which served a single main line coming in from a different direction. By 1875, there existed eight such stations, arranged like the points of a star around the historical town core. Passengers who wanted to transfer from one line to another had to take cabs or walk through the city center to reach their connecting trains.

Alexanderplatz and Friedrichstrasse stations, glazed, triple-jointed arched halls that were huge by Berlin standards dominated the cityscape. Friedrichstrasse in particular (fig. 9), with its glazed walls and looming mass covering an area of 132 by 5,456 feet, became a favorite picture-postcard motif.

Wonderful Friedrichstrasse Station, when one stands on the outside platform over the Spree, where one sees nothing of the "architecture" but only the huge surface of the glass walls; and the contrast to the shabby confusion of the surrounding buildings is especially lovely when twilight shadows cause the rag-tag environs to merge into a single whole and the many tiny windowpanes begin to reflect the setting sun, bringing the whole area to colorful, shimmering life, stretching afar over the dark, low, monstrous cleft out of which the broad-chested locomotives threateningly emerge. And then what an intensification when one enters the darkened hall, which is still suffused with hesitant daylight: the huge, gradually arching form indistinct in a murky haze, a sea of gray hues just tinged with color, from the brightness of rising steam to the heavy darkness of the roof-skin and the absolute black of the bellowing engines arriving from the East; but above them, glowing in the murky surface of the glazing like a sharp, red shimmering pinnacle, appears the gable of a building, set luridly ablaze by the evening sun.[10]

With the invention of the dynamo in 1866 by Werner von Siemens, the generation and use of power now functioned independently of one another. Instead of a locomotive, a small electric motor could be installed in the first carriage of a passenger train, fed by power plants placed anywhere along the line. This development gave rise to the idea of a flexible inner-city transport system that, inspired by New York's example, could be built above the streets—an elevated train. After several plans had been rejected by the authorities, including a line through Friedrichstrasse, in 1891, Siemens received permission to construct a section of the belt line he envisioned between Gitschiner and Skalitzer Strasse, which was to connect the main-line terminals. In the meantime his company, Siemens & Halske, had built the subway system in Budapest and a network of electric streetcars in southern Berlin.

With the directness of engineering plans the tracks pushed themselves forward until they encountered some obstacle, which was duly tunneled through and the opening equipped with a frame—a ruthless procedure that gave rise to one of the most delightful and spectacular, but not untypical, situations along the trunk line of Berlin's elevated railway, the tenement-tunnel on Bülowstrasse.

The junction point known as Gleisdreieck (fig. 10) received its characteristic triangular shape on account of the need to connect the east-west trunk line with Potsdamer Platz without the use of crossings, for on September 26, 1908, two trains had collided, casting one of their motor carriages off the viaduct and killing twenty-one people. To ensure adequate train frequency all three branches were provided with separated tracks so that each line could be operated independently of the others. The substructure, a stone viaduct, had to be replaced by five iron bridges. Differing from one another in length, direction, gradient, and height above the ground, they were combined in an extremely complex and apparently daredevil way into a filigree, three-dimensional grid.

The elevated-train viaducts of riveted rolled steel, designed by the engineer Heinrich Schwieger, soon drew harsh criticism because of their utilitarian plainness (fig. 11).

Popular opinion initially turned against the elevated out of a latent aesthetic aversion to iron as an artistically expressive building material, an aversion that even affects experts and that probably has its source in the fact that people are used to considering iron an aesthetically inferior material that is employed for supports, train rails, and so forth. . . . This obliged the Association for Electric Elevated and Subway trains to earmark a considerable sum for the artistic design of the viaducts and stations, and from that point on, construction took place as if under continual public supervision.[11]

A competition was held; first prize went to Bruno Möhring. Since the constructive elements had to be made of wrought iron, freedom of design was limited to the cast parts at their base and top. The gradual evolution of the elevated viaduct eventually led to organically mature solutions in which the contributions of engineers could no longer be distinguished from those of architects. A merely utilitarian employment of materials made way for sophisticated architectural design.

Ornamentation was replaced by careful structural detailing, precisely placed rivets, and supports whose shape followed the play of forces within the viaduct. Necessity itself became a subject of artistic interpretation, with a view to finding an adequate expression of the building task based on its static

8

8. Hamburg Train Station. Arrival hall, view from the rear, c. 1865. From Holger Steinle, *Ein Bahnhof auf dem Abstellgleis* (Berlin, 1983).

9. Friedrichstrasse Train Station with taxi ramp, 1910. Landesbildstelle, Berlin.

10. Gleisdreieck after redesign, c. 1915. Landesbildstelle, Berlin.

9

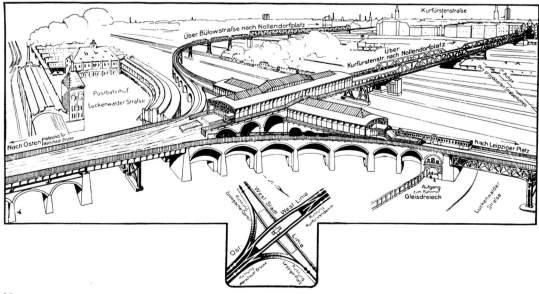

10

11. Bridge for elevated train over the Landwehr Canal, c. 1900. Landesbildstelle, Berlin.

12. The Large Palm House in the Botanical Gardens, Berlin, shortly before its demolition in 1910. From Stefan Koppelkamm, Künstliche Paradiese (Berlin, 1988).

13. Central Hotel, Berlin. View of the conservatory, c. 1880. Engraving. From Georg Kohlmeier and Barna V. Sartory, Das Glashaus (Munich, 1981).

11

12

13

function and the nature of the materials; it was a form of expression that avoided short cuts.

At Nollendorfplatz, the rails had to go underground in order not to disturb the peace of the posh West End. The cumbersome viaducts and noise would have disrupted Tauentzienstrasse. Technically, the U-Bahn posed little problem to Siemens and Halske after their experience in Budapest. The architectural demands were reduced as well, for the stations were invisible and therefore much easier to design than the obtrusive above-ground stations, which tended to dominate the cityscape.

Long ignored by architectural history, greenhouses evolved into vast iron translucent structures in which to cultivate and exhibit subtropical and tropical plants. Under a filigree shell of iron and glass an exotic climate could be produced in the midst of cold northern cities. The conservatories attached to hotels, restaurants, and dance halls became favorite gathering places for society (fig. 13). Unhampered by building codes and relatively free of the aesthetic obsessions of the Wilhelmine period, this building type could develop according to function alone, making it the predecessor of types of construction whose prime aim was to reduce mass to a minimum.

Even less hampered than greenhouses by questions of style were the structural experiments carried out in connection with man's first attempts to fly. The Airship Hall (fig. 14), built in 1911 on Johannistal Airfield, was a miracle of spidery iron construction comparable in every way to the flexible skeleton of Otto Lilienthal's flying machines.

If there was one single type of building, however, that characterized the waning nineteenth century in Berlin, it was the Panorama (fig. 15). No less a man than the young Schinkel introduced the Berliners to paintings arranged in panoramic form. The Sedan Panorama at Alexanderplatz Station, a seventeen-sided structure measuring 128 feet in diameter and 49 feet in height, had a Schwedler domed roof with a glazed rim 23 feet wide. The outside ring of the stepped platform, 36 feet in diameter, was rotatable, each rotation lasting twenty minutes.

Located five-and-one-half meters above the floor of the platform is a walkway covered with vellums, which is suspended from the roof beams and which fulfills the regulations of ventilation and lighting. The thorny problem of illumination by night has been satisfactorily solved here for the first time, by means of seventeen differential lamps, or arc lamps, based on the Siemens and Halske system and installed over the walkway railing, for which electricity is provided by generators located in the basement.[12]

In 1892, when interest in panoramas was already on the wane, Berlin's most impressive example of this genre was built, the Hohenzollern Panorama. It was a massive, sixteen-sided stucco building, 131 feet in diameter, located on the axis of Moltke Bridge between the Packhof (Custom House) and Lehrte Station. Representing a quarter millenium of Brandenburg-Prussian history, the Hohenzollern Panorama apparently bored the Berliners despite—or perhaps because of—all its pomp and circumstance, and so it was replaced before the in-

14

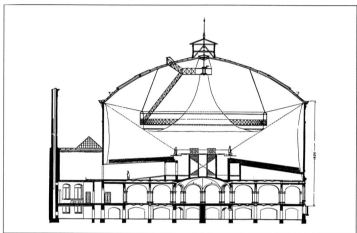

15

14. Airship hangar under construction, c. 1918. Landesbildstelle, Berlin.

15. Sedan Panorama, designed c. 1810. Cross-section. From *Berlin und seine Bauten*, vol II (Berlin, 1896).

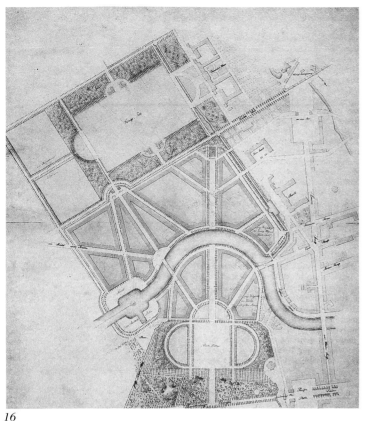

16

17

16. *Peter Joseph Lenné,* Plan for the
Pülvermühlengelände, Berlin,
1839. From Harri Günther, *Peter
Joseph Lenné* (East Berlin, 1985).

17. *Hans Kollhoff, Berlin-Moabit
Design Seminar, ETH Zurich,
1988.*

augural year was out by a depiction of "A Lloyd Steamship
Entering New York Harbor."

We actually feel as if we were on the deck of a great steamer just
pulling into the huge basin of New York Harbor. . . . On our left we
see the gigantic Statue of Liberty. . . . And there, right in front of us,
to the right of the bow, New York's colossal suspension bridge arches at a dizzying height over the East River to the neighboring town.
Like a fantastic, brightly shimmering mirage it soars through the
sunny sky high above the whitish smoke of the steamers covering the
water. At its left end, enormous red and white buildings bristle
above the sea of New York's houses, which rise from the harbor
shore to Broadway, the most magnificent of its streets.[13]

Their own city having nothing comparable, Berliners were reduced to goggling at the technological wonders of skyscrapers
or the Brooklyn Bridge in a panorama or, as the author of the
newspaper article suggested, to rushing down to Karl Stan-
gen's travel agency at 10 Mohrenstrasse and buying a passage
to New York. What they could boast, however, was an urban
drainage system that was the most modern in the world in its
day and one of the finest achievements of Berlin engineering.
Until 1878, the disposal of all the city's sewage, including human wastes, was effected by means of cesspools that were
manually emptied into stinking open carts. "As a big city,"
wrote August Bebel, "Berlin did not really pass from a bar-
baric to a civilized state until after the year 1870." The so-
called reform of latrine facilities occupied engineers and local
authorities for decades on end. The process began in 1859
when James Hobrecht, a thirty-two-year old master of waterway and railway construction, was made head of the Commission for the Preparation of Building Plans for the Environs of
Berlin. Part of his job was to work out a "drainage system for
the projected streets, squares, and surrounding terrain."

After an inspection trip in 1860 to Paris, London, and Hamburg, Hobrecht designed a system of drainage based on "the
principle of dividing the city into various separate districts or
radial systems and disposing of sewage water on surrounding
fields by means of irrigation. Machine power would be employed to pump the water up from the separate radial systems
though pipes arranged in a radial manner to outlying properties which were to be purchased by the city."[13] After the plan
was approved by the magistrate and city council, the first
phase of construction began in August 1872. The principal,
technologically revolutionary feature of Hobrecht's conception of a closed system of water supply, sewers, and biological
clarification of waste water was that instead of being emptied
into the river, sewage was channeled away from it by means of
pump stations and radial piping to fields on the extreme periphery of the city. Human feces were no longer treated as
waste but as a valuable raw material for fertilizer, filtered
through the soil and, thus purified, reintroduced into the
ground water. The project involved dividing the city into
twelve drainage districts each with its own pump station,
which permitted the system to be expanded as the city grew.

It was only logical that Hobrecht devoted himself as well to
the construction plan for Berlin, which came into force in
1862 and remained valid until 1919. Already in its initial
phase, a debate had raged over the extent and stringency of

56

the plan's stipulations, which, it was feared, might prove an obstruction to future developments. Although on the one hand its limitations did prove ineffective and led to the "biggest tenement city in the world," on the other hand, for the enterprising spirit, the plan represented an incentive to develop farther areas beyond its boundaries. The avenues envisaged by the plan, criticized at the time as being excessively wide, have stood the test of increasing traffic to this day. Only at those points where Hobrecht left the firm ground of engineering and adapted grand public-square designs from earlier plans (Generalszug, Pulvermühlengelände) or projected new ones such as Humboldthain was his plan overtaken by subsequent developments. Even during Schinkel's and Lenné's day, the interests of private property owners, above all the railroads, had thwarted all attempts at comprehensive planning. Lenné had still hoped that the leveling tendencies of industrialization could be counteracted by a harmonious urban planning that combined "beauty with utility." But just as Hamburg Station elbowed its way into Lenné's Pulvermühlengelände plan, Potsdam and Anhalt stations dislodged the Generalszug which still ends in a cul-de-sac, although today's Yorckstrasse turns to the south and passes under the railway bridges. The result, as so often happened when Berlin plans failed or were distorted beyond recognition, is one of the most fascinating situations in the cityscape.

Perhaps the clearest idea of the apparently chaotic development of Wilhelmine Berlin is conveyed by the district of Moabit, as represented in 1888 in the Liebenow plan. The plan reveals Berlin as a city of engineers and at the same time a field of battle upon which countless architectural designs met their doom. Gathered in Moabit in a small space is the entire typology of large buildings, infrastructure, public housing, and places of amusement; the most progressive of industrial plants rubs shoulders with the most bizarre of exhibition buildings. Yet detectable in this chaos beyond the control of architects and city planners is an urban-design utopia of a kind that Schinkel had predicted. Schinkel was prepared to bring the confusion under control without resorting to baroque notions of the well-ordered city. As early as 1822, when he not only planned the museum but suggested moving the Packhof to the northern tip of Museum Island, he conceived of an urban space determined by relationships of tension among great, freestanding structures that would replace the former axial relationships and the limited spatial typology of street, square, and courtyard (fig. 16). This was a vision of the city as a landscape, aiming at long, deep perspectives and consciously producing voids that would heighten the effect of mass in a controlled way. As the hesitant design process that was documented in his sketches indicates, Schinkel tried to establish fixed points with extreme precision (fig. 17). The Academy of Architecture in its uncompromising position within the frame of reference established by the palace, museum, armory, and Packhof buildings, embodies the quintessence of this planning approach. The formal Baroque dinner party has ended; the guests are standing and have begun to communicate with each other.

Notes

1. Karl Scheffler, *Berlin. Ein stadtschicksal,* Berlin 1910 (Nachdruck, Berlin 1989).
2. Walter Rathenau, *Die schönste Stadt der Welt* (Leipzig, 1902).
3. Scheffler, *Berlin.*
4. August Endell, *Die Schönheit der grossen Stadt* (Berlin, 1908).
5. Ibid.
6. Karl Scheffler, *Moderne Baukunst* (Leipzig, 1908).
7. *Berlin und seine Bauten* (Berlin, 1877).
8. Ibid.
9. Julius Posener, *Berlin auf dem Wege zur einer neuen Architektur* (München, 1979).
10. Endell, *Die Schonheit de grossen Stadt.*
11. Stephan Oettermann, *Das Panorama* (Frankfurt am Main, 1980).
12. Ibid.
13. Ibid.
14. *Berlin und seine Bauten* (Berlin, 1896).

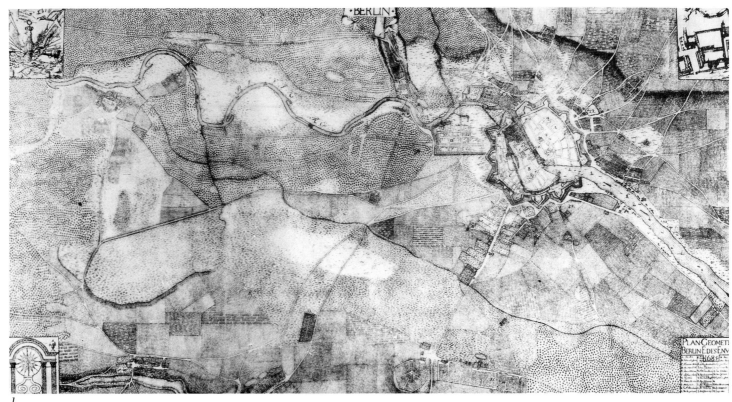

1

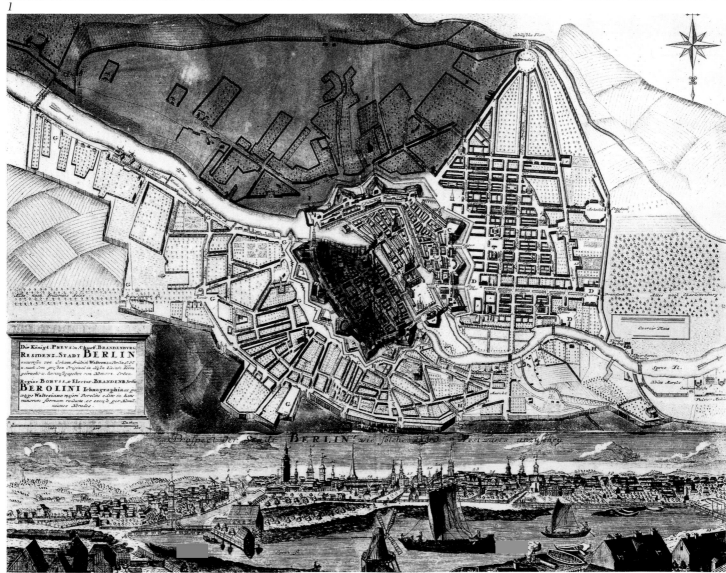

2

The Berlin Tiergarten

Folkwin Wendland

Folkwin Wendland is a member of the Arbeitskreis "Historische Gärten" in der Deutschen Gesellschaft für Gartenkunst und Landschaftspflege and since 1987 has been an honorary member of the Pückler-Gesellschaft in Berlin. Wendland worked as a horticulturist and as a garden architect directly involved in the reconstuction projects for numerous historical gardens and parks, including those in Weimar, Rheinsberg, Mosigkau, and Friedrichsfelde.

Geographically the Tiergarten forms the center of Berlin. It began to be developed in the early sixteenth century. Its origins can be traced to a wooded area that lay in a glacial valley about one mile west of the medieval town. As was the case with many of their princely contemporaries, the electoral princes of Brandenburg not only had a garden on the grounds of their residence but also fenced in an area that lay beside it to indulge their passion for the hunt. Most of this terrain was already in their possession, and because of its diverse vegetation, it was an optimal area for all manner of big and small game as well as game birds. It contained a timber forest with enclosed fields in the east; moors farther to the south; meadows with forests along the Spree River; a former arm of the river with still water; and marsh forests, mires, and ditches. There was further terrain on the other side of the Spree, toward the north, although this was primarily moorland. Grazing areas were created and barns were built to store hay for the winter. The fence made the hunting grounds into a garden for game or animals; the word *Garten* means a fenced in or protected terrain.

For almost two hundred years, the Tiergarten was a hunting ground and game preserve for Brandenburg's electoral princes and Prussia's monarchs. This function was interrupted during the Thirty Years War (1618–48), when the fence could no longer be maintained and the game therefore dispersed or was decimated by marauding soldiers. Moreover, during these years the electoral prince's court was usually not in Berlin but in Königsberg, in East Prussia. Between 1656 and 1657, the Great Elector, Frederick William, substantially enlarged the terrain north of the Spree, fenced it in, and had it stocked with game. Since this date, there have been two sections to the Tiergarten. At the front, there is the large Tiergarten—the area today referred to in an abbreviated form as "the Tiergarten"—and at the back, there is a much smaller section, of which only a small green space—known as "the small Tiergarten"—still remains in the district of Moabit (fig. 1).

In 1695, the first Prussian monarch, Frederick I, had a large avenue built through the Tiergarten's forest. It began immediately behind the gate to the Tiergarten and continued along the route now called Unter den Linden, a street created by his father. This avenue's primary function was to link the royal capital to the newly constructed summer palace of his wife, Sophie Charlotte. The palace was located in Lietzow, or as it is known today, Charlottenburg. In the approximate center of the avenue a so-called hunting star was laid out. Eight radial avenues met here and for this reason it is still known today as the Great Star. Similarly, an area on the bank of the Spree was created in a semicircular form with seven radial avenues. These rays, or avenues, would later acquire names, and they became one of the Tiergarten's distinguishing features.

On the order of Frederick I's successor, Frederick William I, the Tiergarten ceased to be a game preserve, and its fence was torn down. Between 1723 and 1734 this monarch had a strip of forest cleared that was about 1,640 feet wide. Located on the eastern border of the Tiergarten, this area was added to the new districts that were emerging around Unter den Linden and Friedrichstrasse (fig. 2). A sixteen-foot wall was built

1. Plan of Berlin with environs. The Tiergarten is depicted as a forest. Drawing: La Vigne, 1685.

2. Plan of Berlin with the new districts of Friedrichstadt and Dorotheenstadt. The plan is oriented towards the south. Drawing: Johann Friedrich Walter, 1732.

59

3. Large Tiergarten, Berlin. Overall plan with Bellevue and pheasant-run. Drawing: Anonymous, 1765.

4. Large Tiergarten. In "the tents." Drawing: F. Calau, 1793.

5. Large Tiergarten. The "new part" with Rousseau Island. Drawing: J.J. Müller, c. 1800.

6. Large Tiergarten. Overall plan with Bellevue and the pheasant-run. Drawing: Anonymous. Copied from Haas's plan, 1795.

3

4

5

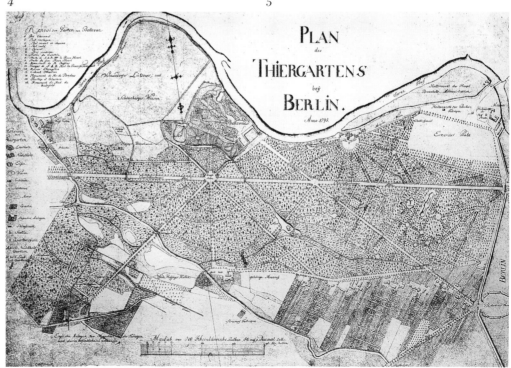

6

around these districts, and the newly constructed gate between Unter den Linden and the Tiergarten was now known as the Brandenburg Gate. It was, however, not yet the monumental construction with which we are familiar today. With the development of the new districts, Dorotheenstadt and Friedrichstadt, the city was now in very close proximity to the Tiergarten. Most of its houses still had gardens, but since many people rented flats within these houses, they began to visit the Tiergarten. Its new function was recognized by Frederick II (the Great), who came to the throne in 1740. He instructed his architect, Georg Wenzeslaus von Knobelsdorff, to redesign the Tiergarten as a park. In accordance with the artistic tastes of his era, Knobelsdorff laid out broad avenues and placed seats (so-called cabinets) at their intersections. The Great Star was bordered with hedges, decorated with statues, and surrounded with labyrinths, whose paths were both straight and curved and went in every possible direction. There were also many open areas where benches, statues, and decorative trees were placed. The existing ditches were cleaned and connected with the Spree so that the extremely low lying terrain could be adequately drained. In the vicinity of the Brandenburg Gate a pond was created, surrounded by hedges and small, pruned trees. A statue of Venus was placed in this pond, referred to as the Venus Basin. (It was later known as the Goldfish Pond.) The star-shaped area beside the Spree, as well as its avenues, were also bordered with hedges (fig. 3). It was named *der Kreis* (the Circle) and the seven avenues that led out from it were known as the seven electoral princes, a reference to the group who elected the Holy Roman Emperor. Because of its beautiful location beside the river, the Circle quickly became a favored spot for visitors to the park. They welcomed the many new possibilities the Tiergarten now provided for walks. Trees were planted on both sides of the broader avenues. The more narrow avenues were essentially paths that had been cut through the forest. The wooded terrain and marshland on the other side of the Landwehrgraben (a former army trench) were made into a pheasant run and were thereby no longer a part of the Tiergarten.

In 1745, after the monarch allowed two Huguenots to sell refreshments to summer visitors in two linen tents on the Circle, this area immediately became an even more popular place to visit. It became known as the Tent Place or simply the Tents. A broad avenue, the Tent Avenue, connected it with the Brandenburg Gate and made it accessible to coaches and horseback riders (fig. 4). The original stipulation that refreshments should only be offered in the summer and inside of the tents was soon forgotten or ignored. Two tents quickly became four. The stern "old Fritz" was succeeded by the good-natured Frederick William II, and the tents were replaced with lightweight wooden constructions surrounded by tables and wooden benches. Visitors to the park could now obtain refreshments not only at the northern end of the Tiergarten, beside the Spree, but also in the southern part of the park. A number of garden cafés were established in this area. Located along the present-day Tiergartenstrasse, they successfully competed with the attractions offered by the Tents. They included Richards Kaffeegarten, later Kempers Hof, which lay approximately on the spot graced today by the Philharmonic Hall; as well as the Michaelis Garten on the Mattheikirchstrasse, the

Odeum, Teichmanns Blumengarten, the Taronescher Kaffeegarten, and the Hofjäger. The latter was the best-known garden café and lay at the southern end of the Hofjägerallee, where today Klingelhöferstrasse leads into Lützowplatz. In 1784, Frederick II's youngest brother, Prince Ferdinand, had bought a piece of land in the northwestern part of the Tiergarten. It had once been a mulberry tree plantation and was then turned into a dairy farm by Knobelsdorff. Under Ferdinand's ownership, it became the site of his classicist palace, Bellevue. His purchase of bordering land, which belonged to the Schöneberg meadows, augmented the palace's scenic park and large kitchen garden (fig. 6).

It was during the reign of Frederick William II, in 1792, that for the first time an area of the park reflected the influence of the new natural style of landscape architecture known as the English style, which had become popular throughout Europe. On the initiative of Forestry Minister Frederick William von Arnim, the royal gardener, Christian Ludwig Samuel Sello, enlarged one of the watercourses leading to a small lake with choppy water at its shore and a small island. A few years later, a monument was placed on the island commemorating the philosopher Jean-Jacques Rousseau. His grave in Ermenonville Park in Paris was also on an island. In this era of heightened and self-conscious sensibility, Rousseau's followers were deeply affected by his ideas of a new understanding and consciousness of nature and wished to re-create a site holy to an entire epoch. The island was mentioned in all of the contemporary descriptions of Berlin (fig. 5).

An important new development of the Tiergarten took place between 1798 and 1799, when the pitted sand path leading to Charlottenburg was transformed into a paved street, the Charlottenburger Chausee. This street was only paved in the middle, however, and on either side the so-called summer paths remained. The construction of such a street had become a pressing necessity, for it had taken the royal coach four hours to travel from the palace in Berlin to Charlottenburg. The Great Star was the resting place on this route. At approximately the same time (1788–91), the new construction of the Brandenburg Gate was undertaken by Carl Gotthard Langhans.

Visitors to the Tiergarten came from all parts of Berlin, but primarily from the neighboring residential districts of Friedrichstadt and Dorotheenstadt and from Friedrich-Wilhelm-Vorstadt, north of the Spree. To this point the city had expanded alongside the major arterial roads. In the first decades of the nineteenth century, however, there was constant construction along Potsdamer Strasse in the Tiergarten district and in the area north of the Spree. It was here that the former colony of smallholders, established during the reign of Frederick William I on the grounds of the small Tiergarten and known as Moabit, gradually became a suburb of country houses. A direct connection to Berlin did not yet exist, for the grounds belonging to the gunpowder factory stretched out so far that they interrupted the construction of residential buildings. Since there was not yet any public transportation, the eastern part of the Tiergarten attracted far more visitors than the western part around the Great Star. For a Berliner who lived at Alexanderplatz and neither owned a carriage nor had the means to rent one, it was a day's journey to get to the Tents or the Hofjäger. This situation led to the creation of a popular idiomatic expression. When somebody had undertaken an activity that had lasted a long time, it was described as *bis in die Puppen dauern* (lasting to the dolls)—the dolls referring to the statues at the Great Star. Change occurred only with the continued construction within the area—including the western side—and with the establishment, at the end of the eighteenth century, of a carriage service that ran between the Brandenburg Gate and Charlottenburg and Spandau.

Before that, however, there was a decisive change in the Tiergarten as a result of the Napoleonic Wars between 1806–07 and 1813–15. The years of crisis between and subsequent to these wars meant that little could be done to maintain the Tiergarten. It became heavily overgrown, and as the irrigation ditches fell into disrepair, parts of the park became marshland.

In 1818 Peter Joseph Lenné, who had been hired as a journeyman gardener for Sanssouci two years earlier, was instructed by the commissioner of forests to draw up a plan, with a cost estimate, for redesigning the area around the Tents. Frederick William II rejected both the plan and the estimate. The highly qualified Lenné recognized, however, that the Tiergarten was desperately in need of a new design. Although he had no direct instructions to do so, he drew up a design for the entire Tiergarten, which he presented to the monarch in February 1819, along with a comprehensive analysis of what had to be done. The plan and the analysis are significant, for they mark the first time that Lenné used the term *Volksgarten* (garden for the people) with respect to the Tiergarten.

It seems to me, however, that it would greatly improve and perfect the *Tiergarten* if it were understood as a *Volksgarten*. As such, it would be able to satisfy the different tastes of those who stroll through it. Beautiful well-kept paths, which have a natural form, could wind their way through thick clusters of groves or through one graceful grove.[1]

Lenné wanted to erect a memorial to the Berliners and heroes who had fallen in the Wars of Liberation.

My humble proposal is that it be a hall of people, constructed in a simple, noble manner. . . . It should immortalize the names of the Berliners who gave their lives in the struggle for freedom, for king and fatherland, in the years between 1813 and 1815. . . . Nowhere is the heart and the imagination so receptive to the impressions which this type of memorial makes upon our feelings as when we are in nature. Were the Tiergarten adorned in this way, it would become a great national monument.[2]

Lenné also envisioned further functions for the Tiergarten.

The tents represent a major public attraction for Berliners. On nice summer days people come here from all directions, by wagon, by horse, and on foot. I think it is necessary, therefore, to retain all of the existing avenues which lead toward the tents and to add natural looking footpaths through the beautiful woods and groves.[3]

Lenné's ideas were indebted to the work of the Kiel professor Christian Cay Lorenz Hirschfeld. In his five-volume work (1779–85) on the theory of landscape architecture, he had argued for the establishment of "national gardens" in large royal capitals. These were to have the character of "places of learning for the nation," in which the "spirit of the people would be uplifted."

He proposed a "patriotic landscape architecture" in the form of a *Volksgarten*, through which the populace would be educated "while it was amusing itself."[4] Instead of the copies of antique sculptures found in the well-ordered gardens of the seventeenth and eighteenth centuries, he wanted to see statues of "heroes, law-givers, saviors, and philosophers . . . as is befitting their services to the nation."[5] He and the Berlin scholar Johann Georg Sulzer were of the opinion that only the scenic garden, with its diversity of natural forms, which constantly provided new surprises and impressions, represented this new type of garden. Both were still thinking of the sentimental, romantic garden that belonged to the first phase of the scenic style. Indicative of the great interest such questions held for the era's leading thinkers, in the late eighteenth and early nineteenth centuries Immanuel Kant, Johann Gottfried Herder, Friedrich Schiller, Johann Wolfgang von Goethe, and Georg Wilhelm Friedrich Hegel all concerned themselves with the issue of landscape architecture as an independent artistic movement, and they exerted a lasting influence on the development of the scenic garden from its sentimental to its classical manifestation.

Lenné's first comprehensive design for the Tiergarten must be seen against this intellectual background. The decisive aspect was the connection between the *Volksgarten* and the idea of a national monument, with retention of the baroque avenues as the park's basic structure. The latter is very surprising at this early stage, for only two years earlier, in his major design for Sanssouci, Lenné had proposed a radical effacement of the avenues. Since Lenné's designs were based on practical as well as formal considerations, however, he was very much in favor of retaining the radial avenues around the Tents and the Circle for the use of the many visitors to these major attractions. At first, Frederick William III rejected both his proposal and the competing plan of the Tiergarten's head forester, Karl Frederick Simon Fintelmann. The latter had drawn up his plan with his brother Ferdinand, who was the royal gardener on the Pfaueninsel (Peacock Island). The proposals for a redesign remained untouched for over a decade until the state councillor, Christoph Wilhelm Hufeland (the former physician to Queen Louise), wrote to the monarch in 1832. He emphasized the medical importance for Berlin's population of a properly maintained green area instead of the overgrown Tiergarten. A similar point had already been raised in 1788 by Karl von Eckartshausen, a member of the Bavarian Academy of Sciences. He had proposed that the marshes be drained and the forests tended in order to improve the air. This made a deep impression on Frederick William III, and he allowed the first measures to be taken. The minister of finance, who had jurisdiction over the Tiergarten's administration, judged this to be an opportune moment to have Lenné draw up another comprehensive plan with a cost estimate for the entire park. Lenné submitted his plan on December 8, 1832. His enclosed estimate came to 62,970.20 thalers. The head of the Planning Department, Eytelwein, requested a further 24,600 thalers for the rebuilding of bridges and other necessary construction work—a laughable sum when one considers the millions spent on such work today. In his enclosed memorandum, Lenné directed particular attention to the conditions Hufeland had criticized, and he emphasized questions of hygiene rather than aesthetic considerations.

In the Tiergarten, there are no sunny paths and few open spaces, although these are really a necessity in the spring and fall. The few broad paths, on which one can still catch a little bit of open air and sunshine are so crowded on nice days that they become unbearable. . . . It is strange, that the Berlin Tiergarten, this large . . . expanse of forest immediately beside the walls of a city, otherwise bereft of almost all of nature's charms, is visited so rarely by a large population which actually has a great need of what this park could offer. . . . It is only on Sundays and holidays that crowds of people surge along the few avenues which lie either on the edge of the park or lead toward its center. They make their way to the restaurants and pleasure spots, while the inner forest, full of magnificent trees, remains unused. It is only now and then that a solitary visitor finds himself lost on the narrow paths. . . . The main elements in the new design are the large waterways. Above all, the park must be healthy and in such a condition that it can be used and enjoyed. . . . Many curving and new paths will be created for those who have the time to take a leisurely stroll. . . . Provisions should be made for enough light and shade on all of the newly designed paths for carriages, horses, and pedestrians. . . . Moreover, the new plan will provide the poorer classes in the royal residence with extra employment during the winter months.[6]

The extremely thrifty, even stingy, monarch rejected both plans. He could see no justification in spending 90,000 thalers on a park. He did not, however, rule out the possibility of individual improvements. Since Lenné now had some experience in how the monarch could be persuaded to support larger building projects, it was probably his idea to carry out the entire project piece by piece. At the beginning of 1833, the minister of finance assigned Lenné the task of undertaking a small improvement in the western part of the Tiergarten, between Charlottenburg Chausee, the Great Star, Fasanerieallee, and Landwehrgraben. At a cost of 8,750 thalers, the area was leveled and drained. A part of it was planted with new greenery, and new paths were created. By fall, the work was completed. In a conversation with Hufeland (which Hufeland then reported to Lenné), the monarch praised Lenné's work and declared that he would be favorably disposed toward further suggestions (fig. 7). Hufeland's emphatic appeals on behalf of public health, which were echoed by Lenné in his memoranda for his rejected comprehensive design of 1832 and his design for a part of the park in 1833, had had an effect on the monarch. By the end of 1838, improvements on the remaining six areas had been completed (fig. 8). During these five years, however, Lenné and his senior colleagues constantly had to struggle against the ministerial bureaucracy and demand additional funds. In general, the bureaucracy had little knowledge of this huge, often marshy area or of the sort of measures required. Despite his notorious thrift, Frederick William III did not object to granting the additional funds, for he was very familiar with the Tiergarten. He often walked or rode through the park, either alone or accompanied only by an

7

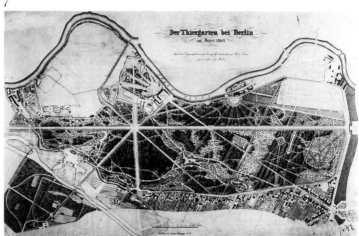

8

7. *Johann Heinrich Stürmer,* In the Tiergarten, *1835.*

8. *Large Tiergarten. Overall plan with Bellevue and the pheasant-run after the redesign by P.J. Lenné. Drawing: G. Koeber, 1840.*

adjutant. Lenné and his team of workers did everything they could to ensure that the construction costs did not exceed the budget. Broken bricks and waste products from the porcelain factory rather than expensive gravel and stone chips were used for the paths. When land was cleared, young plants were saved and then replanted, or they were given to the Tiergarten's new tree nursery. Masonry and carpentry work were done by Lenné's team of workers to avoid employing craftsmen from the city, for then as now, they charged high fees. The minister did his best to placate the bureaucrats, particularly since Lenné, who was in charge of the restoration, had threatened to resign. Lenné was successful in seeing that funds were also provided for the upkeep of the new grounds. When his work on the Tiergarten was finished, he also made sure that his colleagues were employed in succession as the inspectors responsible for the Tiergarten and that they received an appropriate salary.

Lenné drew up as many as six different designs for each of the seven separate areas. Most of them still exist today. The unusually broad variation between the plans is noteworthy. This variation was necessary because the monarch often had his own ideas, and it was difficult to persuade him of the validity of Lenné's far more qualified opinions. Nevertheless, Lenné never lost sight of a larger concept for the park, as is confirmed by the three comprehensive designs of 1834, 1834–35, and 1840. These designs were not requested by any higher authority, nor were they submitted to the monarch or his ministry. One must assume, therefore, that Lenné wanted to record his ideal concept for the Tiergarten and demonstrate that even if he had to accept compromises in the work on the individual areas, he was certainly capable of producing a unified and well-balanced solution to the problems facing the entire park. The first design, in 1834 (fig. 9), reveals a completely new variant, for in it Lenné attempted to place what would later be the Zoological Gardens on a centrally located island. The surrounding watercourses were meant to replace the fence. Had the zoo been located there, however, it would never have been able to expand to its current size and would have remained a small menagerie. In the second design (fig. 10), Lenné no longer included the zoo project, for the monarch had not approved of it. Instead, he created a large lake, with many bays and islands, from a bog located in the southwest, between the Tiergarten and the pheasant run. Ten years later, while the Landwehr Canal was being built, a lake was created here (the Neuer See or the New Lake), but it was much smaller than the one envisioned by Lenné. As with all of the other designs, the third design has not only an extensive, well-balanced network of paths augmenting the existing avenues, but it also has a variety of waterways and the Neuer See, as well as broad meadows that stretch from Luiseninsel (Louise Island) to Rousseau Island in the north. In the opinion of the Prussian architect Johann Arnold Nehring, this was Lenné's most scenic design and was characterized by its well-balanced relationship between groups of trees, water, meadows, and paths. The design was a clear reflection of Lenné's own intentions. "Neither nature nor man-made creations can offer anything more beautiful than the combination of forest and water . . . with the many lakelike ponds, small islands, charming lawns, the diversity of elevations, and the many clusters of trees."[7]

An important feature of all of these designs was that Lenné did not pay any attention to the surrounding buildings. Apart from the Brandenburg Gate and the Bellevue Palace, there was no building in the developed eastern and southern areas (there was nothing at all in the north and west) that would have merited visual inclusion in his designs.

Second, in all of these designs, he retained the baroque avenues, which he considered to be unique, characteristic features of the Tiergarten and very useful for the visitor's orientation. The restoration and reintegration of these avenues between 1985 and 1987 by Berlin's Department for the Preservation of Historical Gardens was of decisive importance in recovering of the Tiergarten's original identity.

While the Tiergarten was being reshaped it became clear that the old army trench would have to be enlarged. A canal was required, for the locks in the inner city could no longer cope with the steadily increasing ship traffic and a drainage system was a pressing necessity for both the southern Friedrichstrasse and the planned expansion of the city onto the so-called Köpenick field. Lenné marked out the route and included a number of small harbors and promenades. The canal was to begin at the Silesian Gate and, embedded in the trench, reach the lower Spree, underneath the Tiergarten mill. In its last section, it was to be redirected. The major problems in the construction of the canal had to do with the gradient and water level. The hydraulic engineers wanted to have a much lower water level than did Lenné. He was afraid that such a low water level would kill the ancient oaks and other trees in the Tiergarten. The long discussion ended with a compromise. Between 1845 and 1850, the canal was built with a water level that lay between the two proposals. In the immediate proximity of the pheasant run, which was turned into a zoo during these years, a lock with a canal was placed into the Landwehr Canal, thereby creating an island (Schleuseninsel).

While the canal was being built, Neuer See was formed (fig. 11); on the southern part of the Schleuseninsel, outside the zoo and extending toward the Charlottenburg Chausee, a hippodrome was created. Lenné once again provided a number of designs for both of these projects; they soon became new attractions for the residents of the neighboring districts, rounding off the Tiergarten in the west in a most effective manner and representing Lenné's last designs for the park.

It was some years after the reshaping of the park that work was begun on converting the military parade ground in the northeast into a green space. This took place more or less at the same time as the work in the west was nearing completion. Almost a decade later, the park was opened toward the north. The construction on the southeastern border of Moabit (fig. 12) —in the areas where the gunpowder factory had once stood— and the erection of the Moltke (1864–65) and Luther (1891– 92) bridges meant that on this side of the Tiergarten, the city was growing ever closer together. The park, which had once been outside the city, was now taking on a central location. Construction in the west was also moving closer to the Tiergarten, for Charlottenburg was beginning to expand up to and even beyond what is today Ernst-Reuter-Platz. At the same

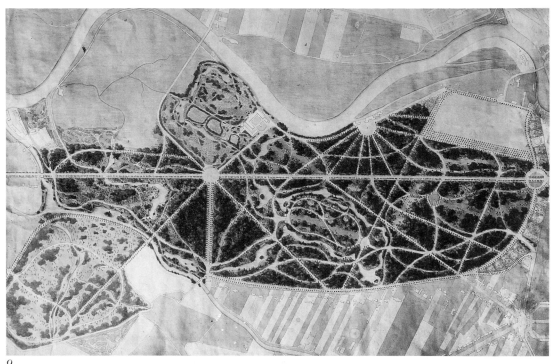

9

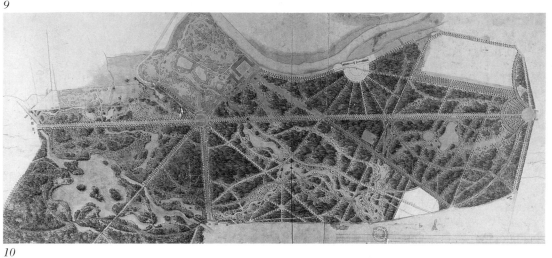

10

11

9. *Large Tiergarten. Overall design by P.J. Lenné with Bellevue and the pheasant-run. Plan for a small zoological garden in the vicinity of Rousseau Island. Drawing: P.J. Lenné and G. Koeber, 1834.*

10. *Large Tiergarten. Overall design by P.J. Lenné with Bellevue and the pheasant-run. Drawing: P.J. Lenné, 1834/35.*

11. *Large Tiergarten. Neuer See, c. 1850. Aquarelle on pencil drawing: F.A. Borchel.*

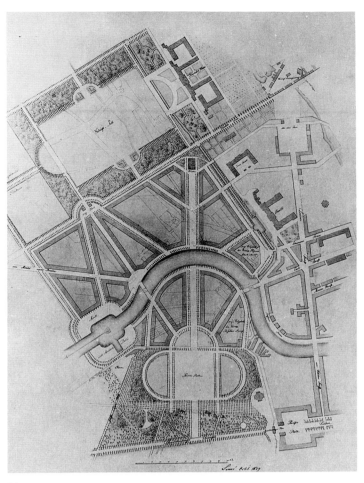

12

12. P.J. Lenné's plan for construction on the gunpowder factory grounds and in the area of the military parade ground, 1839. Drawing: G. Koeber.

13. Large Tiergarten. View of Königsplatz from the west, with Berlin's skyline in background, c. 1850. Drawing: J. Gottheil.

14. Large Tiergarten. A typical scene, 1898.

15. Large Tiergarten. Path along the last remaining part of the former army trench at Neuer See, 1934.

time in the south, along Tiergartenstrasse, the era of the garden cafés had come to an end. The area that extended to the Landwehr Canal was now traversed by new roads built on land where these cafés had once stood. These included Bendlerstrasse, Mattheikirchstrasse, Viktoriastrasse, Margaretenstrasse, Hildebrandstrasse, and Friedrich Wilhelm Strasse. Although it was still primarily individual buildings that were being put up on these streets, a closed street front could already be found on Bellevuestrasse, Schulgartenstrasse (later Königstrasse and then Friedrich Ebert Strasse), and on Potsdamer Strasse. This situation is readily apparent on G. Koeber's well-known plan of the Tiergarten in 1840 (fig. 8), which also provides a clear impression of the unique character of the Tiergarten at this time. A typical feature was the absence of any large expanse of meadow. In the west and north, the plan shows areas of thick forest and undergrowth, which are only alleviated by numerous paths and waterways. Toward the south and east it shows a sparser, primarily grovelike terrain.

Decisive for the Tiergarten's structure were the baroque avenues Lenné had fought to retain, but he was only permitted to clear out their undergrowth. The limitations the monarch placed on Lenné's plans gave the Tiergarten its unique forestlike character. Today, this forest park has disappeared, but the watercourses survived the destruction at the end of World War II and still have the form Lenné once gave them.

The slow encroachment on the Tiergarten in the north was completed with the construction of two large buildings on the borders of the former military parade ground (the Raczynski Palace on the east [fig. 13] and Kroll's Restaurant on the west) and by construction on the former dairy meadows in the curve of the Spree. Although this area had belonged to the Tiergarten, neither Knobelsdorff nor Lenné had made use of it in their plans, and its loss had no real effect upon the park. The construction of the victory column commemorating three Prussian victories within one decade in the middle of the new military parade ground (Königsplatz), marked the beginning of a flood of historical monuments that would dot the Tiergarten in the following decades, not always to its enhancement.

Two new traffic arteries led straight through the Tiergarten once the Siegesallee and the Friedensallee were built. Although they were certainly useful for the new residential area in the curve of the Spree (Alsenviertel), they brought noise and commotion into the eastern part of the park.

The same thing happened in the western part, where in 1872 the renowned garden café Zum Hofjäger disappeared and its land was used for building a connecting street between Lützowplatz and Hofjägerallee. This street was Friedrich Wilhelm Strasse (today Klingelhöferstrasse), which was lined with high and impressive apartment houses. The horse-drawn tram and later the streetcar also used the street and branched out at the Great Star toward the Brandenburg Gate, drove along Spreeweg and over the Luther Bridge to the district of Alt-Moabit and through Altonastrasse into the residential area of Hansaviertel. Similar to the Alsenviertel at Königsplatz, the Hansaviertel had also been built up on land that had once belonged to the Tiergarten. The so-called Schöneberg and Wilmersdorf meadows had been included in the terrain that had been fenced in for the Tiergarten, but they had remained largely in private ownership. When the Hohenzollern monarchs ceased to use the Tiergarten as a hunting ground and game preserve, they also ceased to have any interest in purchasing these meadows. They were not included by Knobelsdorff in his plans for the park, nor were they included in any other plans made before or after him. It was out of the question for Lenné to include them in his designs. He was all too aware that he could not expect his stingy monarch to pay for the changes he had planned for the Tiergarten and to buy these meadows as well. Although Lenné would have welcomed rounding off and bordering the Bellevue Park with land belonging to the Tiergarten and thereby including it visually in the park, he also knew that if he suggested to the monarch that he buy the meadows, he would be jeopardizing the entire project. The result was that the meadows were built up. The owners actually offered to sell their properties to the monarch's agents, who deluded themselves in hoping that villas with large gardens (as on the Tiergartenstrasse) and not tenement houses would be built there. Later some land belonging to Bellevue Park even had to be given up for the city railroad. The inclusion of the Spree in the park was also neglected at this time, and its banks were not planted with greenery, although it would have been possible to do so on the state-owned terrain belonging to the gunpowder factory. Nor were meadows across from Bellevue purchased; they too, had been offered for sale to the monarch's agents. The consequences of this decision were much worse. The Spree would subsequently be bordered by a freight depot, a custom house, and storage sheds and sites. It is only in very recent times and with a great deal of effort that a green area has been created across from Bellevue. The National Garden Show 1995 is planning to transform the area between Luther Bridge and Moltke Bridge into a green oasis; one will then be able to see trees, shrubs, and perhaps even lawns when looking out over the river from the Tiergarten.

Apart from the construction of the Siegesallee, after Lenné, no more fundamental changes were undertaken in the Tiergarten. Subsequent directors of the park restricted their work to the preservation and maintenance of the existing landscape (figs. 14, 15). Naturally, at the turn of the century, an increasing number of playgrounds were added to the park. They were situated at its periphery and comprised little more than the usual sandbox and a bench for mothers. A great deal of money had to be spent on rectifying the consequences (foreseen by Lenné) of the construction of the Landwehr Canal. Because the canal had been built without an adequate outfall, its waters began to stagnate, stink, and become marshy. After a waterworks was built for the Tiergarten, which pumped new water into the canal, an irrigation system was also built, for the paths that were heavily used by both pedestrians and horseback riders had to be watered regularly. Indeed, in the opinion of Heinrich Fintelmann, the superintendent of Potsdam's gardens, even if one allowed for its use as a *Volksgarten*, there were still far too many paths in the Tiergarten. "In particular, there are too many bridle paths. As far as the landscaping is concerned, these paths give the impression that the attempt

13

14

15

16

17

18

16. *Large Tiergarten. Horseback-riding on the Grosser Sternallee.*

17. *Large Tiergarten. Garden Café, Tent 4, 1915.*

18. *Large Tiergarten. Changing the baton on Charlottenburger Chaussee during the Potsdam-Berlin relay race, 1912.*

has been made to emulate the buffalo paths of the North America prairie in Berlin. There are limits to the concessions which should be made to the traffic demands of an emerging metropolis. The best example of what I mean can be found at Floraplatz, with its circular bridle paths. I would suggest that it would be a logical step to place Flora herself on horseback."[8] Roughly fifteen years later, this suggestion would be carried out—albeit unintentionally—when Flora was replaced with Tuaillon's statue of an Amazon on horseback.

The bridle paths were especially popular among the members of the army's general staff (at Königsplatz) and the many diplomats who lived in the Alsenviertel and Tiergartenviertel. They made use of the opportunity to go horseback riding in the city rather than having to take the long trip to the forest (Grünewald) on the city's periphery (fig. 16).

In the same essay on the Tiergarten, Fintelmann continued in a critical vein. "If one looks at the slow but sure way in which the capital's streets and buildings . . . are spreading out toward the west and toward the park's northern and southern sides, then it is obvious that it will not be much longer before one will be speaking of the Tiergarten in Berlin."[9] Until the beginning of the 1890s, the Tiergarten plans still referred to the *Tiergarten near Berlin* (author's italics).

With the construction of P. Wallot's building for the Reichstag (1884–94), Königsplatz became a city square. Formerly a part of the Tiergarten, it was now only its appendage. The steadily increasing flood of visitors from the neighboring residential areas was often drawn to the showy restaurants—the Tents—which were also built at this time. In Tents 1–5 and in Kroll's Restaurant, there was room for thousands of people, either inside or in the beer and coffee gardens. Since 1865, there had been a horse-drawn tram for the routes along Charlottenburg Strasse from the Brandenburg Gate to Charlottenburg and along Hofjägerallee, Fasanerieallee, Altonaer Strasse, Brückenallee, and Spreeweg.

As a result of the constant improvements in the municipal railway network and of the expansion of the streetcar network to the suburbs, it became easier to visit the many forests and lakes that surrounded Berlin. The Tiergarten was no longer the only green area where the urban dweller could go for relaxation. This also meant, however, that the park was now visited by people who lived at some distance from it. They no longer had to cover this distance by foot, as had been the case a hundred years previously.

Until 1881 the Tiergarten belonged to the district of Teltow. After that date, the park, including Bellevue, became a part of Berlin's municipal area. Over the years its administration was under the control of different Prussian ministries, but it always belonged to the royal house. After great hesitation, the city of Berlin began to contribute financially to the park's maintenance in 1879. This sum of ten thousand marks was intended primarily, however, for the upkeep, lighting, and irrigation of the major arterial roads. The sum was then raised to thirty thousand marks per year. After lengthy negotiations between the kaiser's cabinet and the municipal authorities, it was agreed that as of 1909 the city would pay fifty thousand marks per year. It was a real bargain for the city—whose citizens could have full use of the park—when one considers that in 1903 the total budget of the Tiergarten's administration was 270,840 marks. After 1918, the Tiergarten became the property of the Prussian state, and its administration belonged to the domain of the Prussian finance minister. Since 1945—following the dissolution of Prussia—the Tiergarten has belonged to the city of Berlin.

Over centuries, the Tiergarten slowly became Berlin's centerpiece and until its destruction in 1945, it enjoyed the unalloyed affections of Berliners from all social classes. Its trees were not cut down at this time out of blind fury on the part of the populace but rather because of its desperate need for fuel. In any case, it would have been necessary to fell the many trees that had been torn apart by the bombs and grenades of the last, bitter battles of April 1945.

Although all that remained was a virtually treeless wasteland, the idea of building on this terrain was never even considered; the person who dared propose doing so would have had to face an outraged public. When restoration work on the park began and land that Berliners had begun to use was needed, they gave it up without a complaint, so that they could once again have "their Tiergarten." Many thought it would never be possible, but the Tiergarten once again became Berlin's heart and center.

Notes

1. Quoted in Gerhard Hinz, *Peter Joseph Lenné und seine bedeutendsten Schöpfungen in Berlin und Potsdam* (Berlin 1937), 141.
2. Ibid.
3. Ibid.
4. Christian Cay Lorenz Hirschfeld, *Theorie der Gartenkunst*, (1785), 70.
5. Ibid.
6. Quoted in Hinz, *P. J. Lenné*, 145.
7. Quoted in Dorothee Nering, *Stadtparkanlagen in der ersten Halfte des 19. Jahrhunderts* (Berlin, 1979), 145.
8. H. Fintelmann, "Der Tiergarten bei Berlin," *Jahrbuch für Gartenkunst und Botanik* (1888/1889) 6. 328.
9. Ibid. 242.

*1. View of Central Park, looking
north, 1853.* New-York Historical
Society.

Central Park

Jordan Mejias

*Jordan Mejias is a writer and editor who obtained degrees in Romance
languages and music from the University of Frankfurt am Main and a
master of music degree from the Manhattan School of Music. Mejias writes
about the United States for German newspapers, magazines, and radio. He
is a member of the New York editorial staff of the* Frankfurter Allgemeine
Magazin.

"Such a show!" Walt Whitman's amazement in the nineteenth
century is shared by today's visitor to Central Park. No, the
poet did not exaggerate. If anything, the "show" that he observed and described more than a hundred years ago has become even more colorful and fascinating.

On the surface, things have certainly changed. Gone are the
carriages and coaches and the nineteenth-century vision of
the well-to-do on a stroll, with servants and lapdogs in tow. Instead of footmen in impeccable uniforms, there are casually
attired cyclists, roller skaters, skateboard artists, joggers, and
a wide variety of athletes and passersby. T-shirts, sweatpants,
and jeans have replaced top hats and frock coats, and scores
of professional and amateur conga drummers, saxophonists,
and guitarists entertain the crowd instead of officially sanctioned brass bands. But when today's horseback riders trot
through the park on sunny weekends or when families get
away from the stone and pavement and relax on the soft grass,
the mood is almost the same as it was a hundred years ago. In-
veterate city dwellers and visitors test what remains of their
love for nature by making sure that they do not miss out on this
free, open-air presentation of big-city life.

In 1879, when Whitman observed the original show, Central
Park was exactly twenty years old. New Yorkers had become
used to the park and took for granted that it was an inseparable part of their city, but it was still endangered. Complica-
tions that had delayed the park's development were still in evidence after its opening; the majority of public officials had
opposed it from the beginning. In fact, Central Park's very existence—as a successful example of urban design, a social experiment, and a work of art—is owed to the work of two farsighted men. Its creators and guardian angels, the architect
Calvert Vaux and the farmer, failed journalist, and genius of
American landscape architecture Frederick Law Olmsted,
were often scorned. No doubt it was precisely because of such
opposition that the park quickly became a monument of public pride and a municipal and even national symbol.

The idea of laying out a park at this location had actually been
considered for decades. In 1811 a law was passed that regulated future construction on Manhattan within an elongated
grid, with intersections at right angles; shortly thereafter, demands were made for leisure space within the confines of the
grid. Nobody took notice. In close affinity with real estate
magnates and speculators, public officials generally had a
very different idea about the well-being of the rapidly expanding city and its inhabitants. They considered Manhattan's
ground space too valuable to waste on what they considered an
artificial oasis, an oasis, moreover, which would not bring in
revenue from taxes but would require such revenue.

The urban nature lovers were not silenced, however, and as
the city continued to grow, their arguments became ever more
persuasive. They were right when they warned that New York
was in danger of becoming a city of stone. Waves of immigrants were pushing housing complexes to the northern borders of the city, row upon row of houses devouring farmland
and meadows. Advocates of green spaces published warnings
in newspapers, but the city government showed no interest.

2

3

4

2. *Shanties on the Central Park site, 1862.* Museum of the City of New York.

3. *Calvert Vaux.* Society for the Preservation of New England Antiquities.

4. *Frederick Law Olmsted.* National Park Service. Frederick Law Olmsted National Historic Site.

Undaunted by the outcry, politicians directed public attention instead to the numerous rivers and bodies of water located nearby and argued that these made parks of any kind in the city unnecessary. It was not until the mayoral election in 1854, accompanied by promises from demagogic candidates and corrupt party politicians, that change in that position finally became apparent. The city had to break with custom. Its usually unfettered concentration on profit now had to be given up in favor of the long neglected public welfare. Authorized by the state, the city bought just over 840 acres of land for a park, and the early history of Central Park ended with a democratic victory, a triumph of people over government.

The area designated for the park was a desolate piece of land originally planned for garbage dumping to the north and south of the main water reservoir. Located in the center of the island, this elongated rectangle was difficult to get to and certainly far from being a "central park." Poor immigrants found shelter in its caves, ravines, and abandoned quarries, fattening their pigs on the garbage of the more fortunate. Before one could even think of trees, shrubs, paths, lakes, and meadows, this slough had to go. For a while, however, nothing happened. The political establishment had recovered from its bout of concern for the public welfare and used every possible excuse to delay cleanup. Once again, without public pressure, perhaps all would have been lost. This new test of strength persisted until 1857, when workers finally began to appear between Fifth and Eighth avenues and between 59th and 110th streets. Supervising the project was the thirty-five-year-old Olmsted.

But a plan for the future park still did not exist, and a designer had yet to be hired. Andrew Jackson Downing, the nation's most renowned landscape architect had recently died and there was no obvious choice. A competition was arranged by the Central Park committee, and Calvert Vaux, who was brought into the country from England by Downing as a partner and consultant, recognized Olmsted's dormant talent and encouraged him to participate. Together they submitted the winning entry.

Their design was based naturally on the English garden tradition. Olmsted had toured England extensively and had lived in London as well. In any case, the era of formal gardens in the French and Italian styles had long passed. Starkly geometrical and symmetrical gardens, with flowerbeds at regular intervals between pruned, submissive shrubbery, and straight promenades and grand avenues, belonged to a different age. Once nature had been tamed by gardeners and forced to honor a single prince; now it was permitted to be itself. Andre Le Nôtre, landscape architect of Versailles and Vaux-le-Vicomte, was succeeded on the other side of the Channel by William Kent, Capability Brown, and Humphrey Repton. They perceived themselves as nature's partners and tried to develop the park within the landscape, repeatedly declaring that their goal was to improve nature and not to distort it. This was often not enough, however, for the advocates of picturesque landscapes. Richard Payne Knight, Uvedale Price, and William Gilpin would have liked to see parks that resembled the idyllic scenes depicted by Claude Lorrain.

5

6

5. The Conservatory Water.
Museum of the City of New York.

6.The Conservatory Water and
Krebs Memorial Boat House, 1990.
Laurie Watters.

7

7. *A camel from the Menagerie helped mow the grass in 1860.* Central Park Conservancy.

8. *Bethesda Terrace, 1896.* Museum of the City of New York.

9. *The Mall, 1894.* Museum of the City of New York.

Olmsted and Vaux developed their own style out of necessity. Where was "nature" in the Central Park site? The terrain they had to work with after removal of the garbage was noted chiefly for its bleakness. There was not a tree in sight. It seems the ice age left behind enormous boulders, and the soil covering Manhattan's hard substratum could not be used. Depressions for meadows and groves were blown out of the bedrock and filled with thousands of cart-loads of fertile soil from Long Island and New Jersey. Mere trickles of water were transformed into lakes whose water was directed through a sixty-mile complex of pipes into basins whose irregular shapes looked deceptively natural. During the following three years, hundreds of thousands, even millions, of plants, bushes, and trees were planted. No municipal park is comparable to Central Park in this respect. In addition to its astonishing botanical variety, the park is often cited for its sheer volume of natural life and works of art. Statisticians have now counted 25,000 trees with a diameter of more than six inches, 57 sculptures, statues, and fountains, 36 arches and bridges, no less than 269 species of birds, and a medieval castle. To quote Walt Whitman once again, the park is good for a show, even without the public.

Creating miracles is an American specialty. Olmsted did more than this, however; for out of the miracles, he created a work of art. As it turned out, the tabula rasa he had to work with made the job easier. There was almost nothing in the landscape that could either hinder or stimulate his artistic freedom or the transformation of his visions into reality. What appears to be natural in Central Park is almost always a naturalistic setting. The southern section, with its meadows, ponds, rolling hills, and gently curving paths, recalls the landscapes of Kent or Brown. North of the reservoirs, where nature takes on a more picturesque intensity, the park offers wild thickets and thrilling, beautiful gorges.

Olmsted combined both English styles harmoniously, creating landscapes rich in variety yet well-balanced. French formality had no place here. Perhaps one should say almost no place, for in one corner the stiff splendor of the ancient régime is apparent. The handsome mall, shaded by rows of huge elm trees, follows a short but stately and straight path through the park. It comes to an end at Bethesda Fountain. Crinolines and powdered wigs would not be out of place here. Is it an anachronism? No! The average citizen should feel free to strut about as if a king or queen.

Olmsted agreed with Vaux that the continuing industrialization of society must be balanced by nature, man-made or otherwise. Central Park should be all of that, which the modern city of New York was not. The beauty of meadows and fields, of green pastures and still waters was to be rough to the urban dweller. *Rus in urbe:* the country should be experienced in the city. Olmsted wanted this refuge to provide relaxation and peace for himself and his fellow citizens. He had never had any doubt about the edifying and uplifting effects of untramelled nature upon the individual. At the same time, he saw the park as the quintessence of a liberal and democratic ideal of society. From the very beginning, he wanted to satisfy both rich and poor. All should have equal access. The rich

8

9

should be able to stroll down the impressive mall or wave from their carriages and, for a few hours, the poor should have the chance to forget their wretched living conditions. With an elegant trick he managed to minimize the anticipated traffic problems. He laid out separate paths and lanes for pedestrians, horseback riders, and coaches. To avoid congested intersections, Vaux designed slender bridges and underpasses. Traffic across the park was directed along four sunken traverse roads that were hidden from view.

Despite the gloomy prophecies, Olmsted's social experiment was success. As he had always predicted, the soothing nature of the park was triumphant, and opponents of parks in New York had been defeated.

Right up to opening day, they had warned against the robbers' nest and loafer's paradise that was being built with the taxpayers' money and had criticized the extravagance of the whole project. Beginning in June 1859, the park was opened, piece by piece, to the public and, slowly but surely, the detractors were proved wrong. The public immediately took possession of its garden. By 1862, its custodians had already counted two million visitors on foot and seven hundred thousand in coaches. Ten years later, there were ten million visitors to the now largely completed urban arcadia. Moreover, they were not fighting with each other. People from all social classes could be found in the park, but the atmosphere remained completely peaceful. The park, which had been decried as supporting undemocratic and antisocial behavior, had once again revealed itself to be absolutely democratic.

Central Park became the city's pride and its green jewel. Surely only a fool would still attempt to oppose this park, but in 1870, public officials disposed of the controlling authority and began to make decisions themselves. In no time at all their lackeys and cronies had chopped down trees, torn up bushes, and destroyed Olmsted's carefully composed landscapes. Space was needed, after all, for the buildings they were planning to construct. Thankfully, a political scandal prevented the worst from happening.

The clique that succeeded them was not much better. Vaux and Olmsted, who had been abruptly fired, were reinstated in their positions. They could do nothing, however, against the continuing corruption, intrigues, and patronage. Year by year, they lost influence in the development of their park, and in 1878, they were finally stripped of all authority and retired to honorary positions. The embittered Olmsted moved to Massachusetts and buried himself in work and commissions from all over the country. Central Park had made him into America's leading landscape architect.

His New York masterpiece continued to be changed, redesigned, and disfigured. The inventiveness displayed by his successors was truly amazing. Hedges and bushes disappeared because of the disorderly way in which they nestled against bare walls. A row of trees was felled because a park commissioner with a particular sensitivity for technology wished to have an unobstructed view of the elevated train. Why should the city not put a zoo into its park? Why not stage

a world exposition here? Why not build a mile-and-a-half-long racetrack? Five weeks after final permission had been granted by the state authority, the people once again spoke out, and the latter project was over-ruled.

Of course it would be incorrect to present Olmsted as being in constant harmony with popular opinion. It would quickly become apparent that many New Yorkers had no inclination for enjoying the more contemplative pleasures of the countryside. Olmsted's artistry did not lead them to tiptoe around the park and pay their respects to nature's loveliness in hushed tones. They wanted to ice-skate in the winter and boat in the summer. The meadows might have been meant to direct their attention toward artistically planted landscape scenes, but they wanted to run around and play ball or lie down and listen to concerts. They wanted to eat a hot dog or an ice cream, have a coffee, and take their children to a playground. In short they did not just want to admire Central Park; they wanted to use it. Olmsted opposed such defacement of his creation with all of his steadily decreasing authority. With the exception of skating, he did not approve of any sports in the park. For him, the idea of swings and carousels in a pastoral setting was outrageous. His opposition had no effect. The sportsmen staked out their territory. Musicians unpacked their instruments, and ice-cream vendors set up their stands. Sculptures and statues, most of them of questionable quality, sprouted out of the earth more quickly than the surrounding trees. The dream of enjoying the uncorrupted pleasures of the countryside within the city was destroyed by this city. It was too egotistic to adapt itself to the park, and the park was to gentle too restrain it.

Nevertheless, the city's inhabitants managed to maintain a sense of proportion in their demands upon this vulnerable enclave. Without waiting for the experts' opinions, they rejected a hippodrome and an amusement park. Far less concern, even unscrupulousness, was displayed, however, by the park's official guardians. None of them broke as radically with Olmsted's concepts as did Robert Moses. He came to office in 1934, and for the next twenty-five years of his controversial regime he directed his considerable energies toward creating the park anew. It would have been a Herculean task simply to restore the park. Dead trees, brown deserts instead of meadows and paths, and bridges and underpasses that had fallen into disuse gave sad testimony to decades of neglect. Moses was not satisfied, however, with mere repairs. He instigated the further development of the park with projects that included a zoo, numerous sports grounds, twenty playgrounds, a restaurant built on the site of the former sheepfold, a small formal garden, a roller-skating rink, brick buildings, straightened streets for cars and paved paths for pedestrians. The work was carried out by twenty-five hundred workers. Olmsted had not had more.

Moses no longer saw the park as a natural remedy for the problems of urban life. It would have been inconceivable for him to devote his energies to the illusion of unbounded nature. *Rus in urbe?* Far from it. A planner who moved with the times, what he had in mind was not to reproduce the Garden of Eden but rather to create a large leisure-time machine. But trees and grass were certainly welcome. Indeed, Central Park's current

11

10. *View across the Park to the West Side, 1990.* Laurie Watters.

11 & 12. *Roller skating and bicycling, two popular sports today.* Laurie Watters.

13. *Statue of Hans Christian Andersen.* Laurie Watters.

12

13

stock of trees stems almost entirely from Moses's period of office. At the most, there are only fifty still around from Olmsted's days. At least as important as forests and meadows for Moses, however, were streets, bicycle paths, sports grounds, and playgrounds. Under his energetic direction, the city park became more like the city.

Today the pendulum is swinging back. Olmsted's passion for nature is preferred to Moses's love affair with progress. Incredibly, the first indication for this change in attitude was displayed in 1966 by the municipal administration that closed the park to traffic on weekends. In recent decades, the administration has been well disposed toward the park, and politicians and commissioners have treated it with more care than ever before in its history. They even succeeded in having it recognized as a national landmark, a posthumous homage to Vaux and Olmsted. Their original plans, which were altered and thwarted so often in the course of time, are now being used by the park's conservationists. Currently, the park is undergoing a general overhaul. The first results are impressive. When did New Yorkers ever lie on softer meadows or walk on cleaner paths? When were the lakes and ponds ever clearer? Bethesda Terrace sparkles in fresh, carefully restored grandeur and the Shakespeare Garden is utterly charming. Although Olmsted would have considered it scandalous to place a zoo in a naturalistic park, in its new, $35 million form, the zoo is a hit with both children and architecture critics. Grand Army Plaza, the Mall, and Harlem Meer are being cured of the inflictions incurred of old age and neglect.

This all costs money, and the public pocket is chronically empty. Who could help in a situation such as this? Private sponsors—who else? Since its establishment in 1980, the Central Park Conservancy, a nonprofit organization, has collected close to $50 million for the park, an emphatic expression of the affection New Yorkers have for their garden. This sum has been generously augmented by subsidies from the city. Municipal politicians—at least the clever ones—have drawn their conclusions from this and have sided with the garden friends. Both politicians and citizens sense, however, that money alone will never solve the park's basic problems.

These problems always faced the park's commissioners, from Olmsted to Moses, to the commissioner in the 1990s, Henry J. Stern. They stem from the permanent tug-of-war between visitors to the park who want to follow Olmsted's example by being one with nature and those who tend more toward Moses by wanting to jog around the reservoirs, fly kites on the Sheep Meadow, play football on the Great Lawn, dance to music from transistor radios at the Angel of the Waters Fountain, go rowing and skateboarding, ride bicycles, roller-skate and ice-skate, ride horses and train dogs.

The major problems facing the park are the same as those facing the city. The rural refuge Olmsted envisaged was finally only a phantom, and now it is not even that. Far from being an oasis for quiet contemplation, Central Park is often a mirror image of life in New York. Although the unusual contrast of compressed nature against a skyscraper background is justly famed, this is not the whole story. In botanic, architectonic, artistic, and cultural terms, the park obviously deserves to be praised. Yet in the final analysis, it is not so much the flowerbeds and statues that define the park as the quarter million people who visit it on an average summer day. Park and city merge. Olmsted's social utopia had been overtaken by the reality of day-to-day life in the city.

Central Park stretches from white and wealthy mid-Manhattan to black and impoverished Harlem. It is one of the few places were citizens of all classes and skin colors come in contact with each other. But just like the city, the park suffers from a portentous division. In its nicely renovated southern section, whites feel at home, while most of the visitors to its rundown northern part are black. This is not the only similarity it shares with the city. It too has to weigh the rights of the homeless against those of the working population. It too is engaged in a never-ending struggle against vandalism, graffiti, and crime. In 1988, the police investigated two murders and ten rapes that took place here. In comparison, neighboring residential areas were actually more dangerous. Nevertheless, as far as safety is concerned, the park does not have a very good reputation. Somehow, it is as if a crime committed within this refuge is twice as bad as if it were committed elsewhere. And finally, in the same way as the city, the park would like to be all things to all people. For those seeking rest, it is a natural wonder in full bloom. For music lovers, it is a concert hall where the Metropolitan Opera, the New York Philharmonic Orchestra, jazz bands, and rock groups perform. For theater enthusiasts, it is a stage where both Shakespeare and musicals are performed. For athletes, it is a multipurpose stadium.

In contrast, Olmsted and Vaux hoped to create a park that would be able to defy the urban Moloch—a park whose design was stimulated by some of the best European examples and by the instructive and upright ideals of the farmers who founded America. The triumph of benevolent nature would be to the emotional and physical well-being of the urban dweller. It all turned out a bit differently. Central Park is increasingly subject to the city that surrounds it. The city can destroy it or be generous and tolerate it. The park is less powerful. Its harmonious coexistence with and within nature is limited and therefore all the more precious. Its task, to quote Henry James, is certainly unique and wonderful but it can almost be crushed by it. The park is a vital luxury for the city. The park can make the city bearable, but it has to do this from a weak position. It is unfortunately to its own detriment that the city is stronger.

1. Stone houses make stone hearts!
Bruno Taut's graphic depiction of
the concept of the garden city in
Auflösung der Städte, Hagen 1920.

The Berlin Garden City of Falkenberg: A Successful Example of Planning from the German Garden City Movement

Kristiana Hartmann

Kristiana Hartmann is professor of the history of architecture and urban design at the Technische Universität in Braunschweig. Dr. Hartmann's research has concentrated on architectural history since the Enlightenment and the history of housing estates and urban planning. She has also prepared reports and inventories for urban restoration, and monument preservation.

Suppose people lived in little communities among gardens and green fields, so that you could be in the country in five minutes' walk, and had few wants, almost no furniture for instance, and no servants, and studied the (difficult) arts of enjoying life, and finding out what they really wanted: then I think one might hope civilization had really begun.[1]

These words written by William Morris in a letter reflect the ambivalence of reform approaches of the type adopted and developed by the German garden city movement. The German reformers pursued similar, two-pronged aims to those expressed in Morris's utopian novel *News from Nowhere*. Looking backward as a strategy for reaching a future goal was as common a practice in Wilhelmine Germany as it was in Victorian England.

These aims covered a variety of often mutually contradictory hopes. For instance, in the synthesis of city and country as a means of combating the ugly aspects of capitalism. Then there was the notion of an escape from the city, from bourgeois conventions of prosperity and status seeking, accompanied by the demand that people ought to be allowed to shape their own lives instead of submitting to established norms. Indeed, the hopes of the garden city reformers included a liberation of imagination, of sensuous experience, and of sexuality. What goaded them most was middle-class morality and its oscillation between prudishness and prostitution. The projection of a new, garden city world was predicated on an entire spectrum of hopes, from ideologies of purification to dreams of liberation, from escapism to emancipation, from regression to progress.[2]

The German Garden City Movement Emerged in Berlin

The German garden city movement was founded in 1902, indicatively, by a writers' commune dedicated to social reform called *die neue Gemeinschaft* (New Community). The group had moved in 1900 from the Berlin suburb of Friedrichshagen, where members referred to themselves as the Friedrichshagen Friends, to Schlachtensee in the western part of the city. They were not, as might be expected, a group or institution concerned directly with the housing and planning deficits of the day. Formed by the Hart brothers, Heinrich and Julius, Bernhard Kampffmeyer, Gustav Landauer, and other intellectuals, the New Community in 1901 received an offer from a banker by the name of Securius, "a longtime supporter of the nature-cure movement and Stamm's land reforms," to take "a cheap lease on a handsome building with a large garden in Berlin-Schlachtensee."[3]

At the end of the nineteenth century, the outlying, rural suburbs of Berlin offered a welcome refuge for city dwellers overcome by nostalgia for the soil. "They were all passionate believers in social ideas, admirers of nature, and this in the exaggerated form characterized the sentimental epoch of German romanticism at the start of the nineteenth century. I myself saw the way they joined hands and danced around an ancient oak, the way they adorned their hats with oak leaves and sang hymns in honor of humaneness, freedom, and brotherly love—oh, how naive they pretended to be."[4]

2

2. *Members of the New Community at a Spring Feast, 1902. All are expecting a new alternative and autonomous form of life. Dortmund, Stadt- und Landesbibliothek.*

3. *Members of the Berlin-Neukölln Wandervogel (Wandering Birds) Club, 1915. Bildarchiv, Staatsbibliothek Berlin.*

4. *Self-portrait of Hugo Hoeppener, member of the German Garden City Association, 1890.*

5. *Architect Paul Robert Tautz, board member of the German Garden City Association, 1931.*

3

4

5

For the high-minded armchair socialists of the New Community, the English garden city idea held great appeal.[5] But of course it was not so much the down-to-earth, practical reforms of Ebenezer Howard's conception that won these sentimental intellectuals' approval. They took up the idea because of the similarities it seemed to bear to their own enthusiasm for nature and to the communal life they lived in Schlachtensee. To those who envisioned a holistic reform for soul, spirit, and body, Howard's conception came as a godsend. The time was ripe for the English example, and armed with visions of the garden cities of the future, New Community forged ahead to new, unexplored shores. The first, propagandistic pamphlets of the German Garden City Association (*Deutsche Gartenstadtgesellschaft*) were produced from the pen of forty-seven-year-old Heinrich Hart.

Although in the course of its development the German Garden City Association had distanced itself from the rebellious literary naturalists of the New Community and soberly attempted to further reforms in living and housing conditions, it was never quite able to shake off the sins of its youth; socialist idealism set the tone of the activities of the association throughout its early years.

The first board members of the German Garden City Association in its founding year,[6] were Wilhelm Boelsche, author, natural philosopher, and free-thinker; Hugo Hoeppener, known as Fidus, printmaker, painter, and health reformer; and Henriette Lyon, author. With these members, cultural critique and life-reform approaches had a strong representation on the board. More practical and pragmatic points of view were advanced by Professor Paul Förster, educator; Dr. Franz Oppenheimer), economist and sociologist; and Adolf Otto, economist and later secretary general of the Greater Berlin Public Building Cooperative, which was to found the garden city of Falkenberg. The final founding member was the architect Paul Robert Tautz, who like Adolf Otto would later collaborate in the Falkenberg project.

Soon after the association was established, then, the board of directors consisted of a mixture of educated middle-class people with a neoromantic flair who saw their reform efforts aided by national awareness, along much the same lines as the journal *Kunstwart* edited by Ferdinand Avenarius. The *Mitteilungen der Deutschen Gartenstadtgesellschaft (Bulletin of the German Garden City Association)*, published until 1906 in pamphlet form, began to appear in 1907 in the renowned *Hohe Warte*, an "illustrated semimonthly for the artistic, intellectual, and financial interests of urban culture," edited by Joseph August Lux. The association's members were anything but unpatriotic, despite the fact that Bernhard Kampffmeyer, *littérateur*, gardener, and health reformer, displayed a sympathy for the anarchist ideas of Piotr Kropotkin.

The professionalization of the German garden city think tank—board members of the association—increased throughout the first propaganda phase, which lasted until 1907. Still, during the key phase of the movement, up to the First World War, the designers of German garden cities adhered to a comprehensive, almost holistic conception of reformist thought.

Their critique was directed against the entire range of ills that afflicted big cities in the late nineteenth century—hygienic, moral, spiritual. Their agitation, based on motives of more than a philosophic or social nature, was intended to ward off political evils. An important consideration for them was that national honor and the self-image of the German people were endangered by the conditions in German cities.

A cure for these urban abuses threatening the fiber of the nation was seen in Howard's new model city with its democratic decision-making structure, its just distribution and use of land, and its integrated facilities for public education and recreation. To the German planners, the concept "garden city" conveyed a reform idea that extended to all fields of life. If the short-term aim was improved housing, long-term goals included reforms in education, fashion, nutrition, the arts, views of sexuality, and last but not least, the political system of government. The struggle for reform implied a will to emancipation, the projection of a new, liberated style of life.

The republican humaneness envisioned by the reformers could only be realized piecemeal in the face of opposition from the Wilhelmine system of imperial Germany. This obviously required courage and persistence on the part of its advocates, individuals working within their own communities and places of employment, their level of involvement often determined by their own personal capacity for coping with hostility and conflict. But achieving reforms also required solidarity with the social goal of the garden city architects, who, with various degrees of commitment, were all very much players in the progressive architectural and planning discussion. Yet they neither belonged to the phalanx of neobaroque revivalists, such as Wilhelm Kreis or Bruno Schmitz, who were part of the circle around William II, nor did they stand in the vanguard of the young design revolutionaries exemplified by Henry van de Velde and the protagonists of Art Nouveau.

Goals of Garden City Planning: Reform

The planning of garden cities required a willingness to become involved in a process far more complex than the object-related design for which most architects were trained. The various specialized fields—area utilization planning, zoning, transportation planning, infrastructure, landscaping—all had to be integrated in a single planning process with problems solved through teamwork. Also included were the organization of production and recreation and the provision of a maximum of amenities for life and leisure in the new districts.

The Design of Space

Parallel to this general cooperative approach was the understanding from the outset that garden city planning should include the definition, design, and most effective utilization of available space. Although it is surprising in view of Howard's rather vague scheme, the first English garden city architects, Raymond Unwin and Berry Parker, had already developed concrete spatial conceptions as a setting for reform. In contrast to the purely utilitarian architecture of monotonous mass housing, Unwin and Parker planned strikingly designed spaces in the public areas of the garden city centers and visually provocative solutions for the more private dwelling areas in accordance with Camillo Sitte's much-discussed urban planning ideas of 1889 (City-Planning According to Its Artistic Principles).

Hans Kampffmeyer, one of the foremost and probably the most eloquent advocate of the early garden city period in Germany—he was an economist, not an architect—summed up the hope that the design of space could lead to an improved and more humane existence as early as 1911:

If in a garden city the individual houses are concentrated into unified groups and blocks, this is neither accidental nor arbitrary; it is the manifest, logical expression of an existing social community. Just as in a cooperative the individual must to a certain extent subordinate his own, personal wishes to the general will of the community . . . his house will not demand to be separated from its neighbor but will merge with it to produce a unified overall effect.[7]

The new, communitarian social aesthetic was linked to the expectation that the effect of design on sense perception, the psyche, and productivity would be recognized. Even though corresponding expectations may since have proven naive and certainly not entirely practicable, at the time the insight was new and untested and deserves special attention. Around the turn of the century, unprecedented and highly interesting empirical investigations of the human psyche were being made (by Alfred Adler and Sigmund Freud, among others). The fact that the garden city reformers attempted to find practical applications for the insights of psychology perhaps represents one of the most significant achievements of the urban reform conception. Quality of design was not an abstract, theoretical formula, nor was it a key to the exercise of power, intended to give architectural expression to gestures meant to impress or threaten others. Rather, design quality was to serve the purpose of creating a new, liberated, peaceful, emancipated society within a new kind of city.

Land Reform

The basis and condition for planning activity in the new garden cities were property law reforms. To ensure a strict control of property transactions and abolish laissez-faire policy such instruments as community ownership of land, community property, cooperative ownership, and hereditary tenure were foreseen. The reformers were convinced that the economic goal of land reform could be achieved only through organizational reform aiming at the creation of cooperatives or at least of nonprofit, public-service enterprises.

Health and Hygiene

The social problems observed in medium-size and large cities of the nineteenth century, especially the environmentally influenced epidemics to which doctors, hygienists, and statisti-

cians repeatedly drew attention, were the point of departure for the formulation of new planning goals. A few devices for this—zoning codes, housing supervisory agencies—had already been discussed and in part implemented since the 1870s. The promoters of garden cities, in agreement with and to a large extent personally contiguous with the Association for Social Policy (1887), the German Association for Public Health (1873), the Association for the National Housing Bill, and land reformers in general, never tired of pressuring the legislative bodies of the Reichstag to take account of these factors in the drafting of general planning and building laws. The mental and physical health of the populace were to be guaranteed by hygienically improved living conditions. The demands for better hygiene, apart from purely humanitarian considerations, were not seldom based on national interest; after all, the First World War was imminent and fitness for military service was a general concern. The pauperization theory of socialism mobilized many, especially the revisionary wing of the Social Democratic Party, which provided key support for the garden city movement.

Community Ideology

An important component of garden city reform efforts was the demand for self-government, decentralized organization, and anticapitalist, nonprofit forms of financing. Cultural and social policy ran under the slogan "community work creates community spirit." What the sociologist Ferdinand Tönnies had described as the superiority of "community" as something organic (and German) over "society" as something artificially constructed (and French) was adopted by the reformers and associated with the hope that an "island of the blessed," a garden city, would be an antidote to smoldering social conflicts. It was not so much the precise analyses of actual conditions in imperial Germany that provoked a change in course but far more Nietzsche's mythic, elevated utopian dreams of a new, just, healthy, and heroic world.

Planning Deficits in the Imperial Capital of Berlin

Turn-of-the-century Berlin, capital of the empire, was no exception in being beset by housing shortages and social injustice. From 1898 to 1908, the population increased by about ninety thousand annually,[8] but the ownership of the city's buildings remained in the hands of only one percent.

Several attempts to institute overall planning schemes for Berlin were made, but most failed. In 1892, the Association of Berlin Architects sponsored a Competition for the Layout of a World Fair, in which the prize-winning entries bore the highly indicative titles, "Love's Labours Lost," "Vain Desires," "God Bless You, It Was So Lovely," and "Dream."[9]

In 1898, the Royal Academy of Architecture in Berlin (established May 9, 1880) proclaimed that the architectural development of the city should be planned according to both artistic and technical criteria. Their suggestions remained unheeded outside the academic microcosm of the institution.[10] It was not until 1906 that the idea of an overall planning scheme was revived. At a meeting of the Berlin Architects Association held on January 18, a motion advanced by Emanuel Heimann, government building supervisor, Theodor Goecke, and Albert Hofmann was accepted, "to draw up a unified building plan for Greater Berlin which would conform to the requirements of modern city planning and which, in particular, would ensure that relatively large areas would remain exempt from construction."[11]

The imperial capital, its architects agreed, should at long last be made aware of its responsibility and its dignity. For, as Werner Hegemann complained,

The city did not have any true citizens with influence and taste, but suffered from an absenteeism that, in view of its consequences, could only be called criminal. Whoever felt the need for art went to Italy or enthused about Nuremberg, and let the Gendarmenmarkt or Opernplatz go to the dogs in the meantime. Whoever wanted a taste of nature went to Tyrol, and abandoned the Grunewald and Tempelhofer Field to construction.[12]

6

Greater Berlin Settlement Association, 1908

Dissatisfaction was widespread; the time was ripe for action. However, two full years had to pass until the planning suggestions were taken up by socially committed, pragmatic men. One of these was Karl von Mangoldt, who on February 13, 1908, established the Greater Berlin Settlement Association (*Ansiedlungsverein Gross-Berlin*).

In its publications, this group attacked private corporate monopolies on land and challenged the government to establish a "city expansion agency for Greater Berlin." Legal bases for hereditary building rights, pensions in the form of land, and cooperative holdings were to be worked out, and skyrocketing rents halted.[13] The brochures of the Settlement Association were published by the same company as the pamphlets of the German Garden City Association. Both had the support of the anarcho-utopian New Community despite the fact that the garden city movement hoped to further its purposes, at least initially, without becoming involved in state bureaucracy.

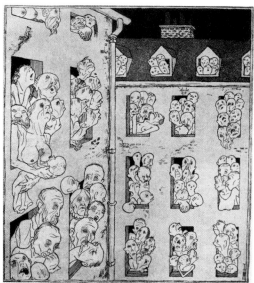

7

6. Typical, densely built block showing the Berlin Mietskaserne.

7. The housing shortage as depicted by Thomas Theodor Heine in Simplizissmus.

In the first issue of the journal *Gartenstadt* in 1908, there promptly appeared a "Call for the Establishment of a Garden City near Berlin," which was sent to numerous newspapers and specialized journals for reprinting and also distributed in industrial circles.[14] In 1909, the Eighth General Meeting of the German Garden City Association passed a resolution:

[We] protest most strongly against any attempt to water down the Greater Berlin building regulations once again, by permitting a greater building density. On the contrary, the association declares, in conformance with the intent of the projected General Building Plan, that a thorough-going reform . . . in terms of a much more extensive provision of open space and an inclusion of the small house, is absolutely necessary and will brook no delay.[15]

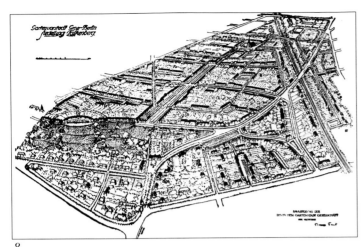

8

9

8. *Bruno Taut's design for Falkenberg, 1913.*

9. *Taut also used the concept of the crescent in "50 Family Community of Farmworkers Instead of the Manor-House" in Auflösung der Städte, Hagen, 1920.*

Greater Berlin Nonprofit Building Cooperative

The year 1910 marked two key events in Berlin: the famous and much-acclaimed City Planning Exhibition and the founding of the building cooperative Gemeinnützige Baugenossenschaft Gross-Berlin e.v.[16] While Karl Scheffler[17] and Theodor Goecke[18] put their authority as experts at the disposal of the idea of building a garden city in Berlin, a certain B. Wehl, writing in the journal *Städtebau*, pointed out the obstacles involved: "There is no profit to be made from a garden city, which explains why private capital . . . has not yet gone into this line of business. . . . The opponents of garden city settlements are the communities which resist them for antisocial or tax reasons, and, innocently, express their resistance by means of arbitrarily high road-construction levies."[19]

At Last: The Garden City of Falkenberg, near Grünau

After the founding of the Greater Berlin Nonprofit Building Cooperative in 1910, three years passed in the search for a suitable site for Berlin's first garden city. The two final alternatives were a piece of land in Eichwalde and the property that was finally secured by purchase option, the 150-acre Falkenberg Estate owned by Second Lieutenant Richter and located near Grünau in the county of Altglienicke. "What difficulties were involved even where land was to be had," wrote Bruno Taut, "was something we sufficiently experienced here in Falkenberg, where no means was left untried to prevent us 'proles, atheists, apple and chicken thieves, and anarchists' from obtaining a modest share of German soil."[20]

The garden city of Falkenberg was ultimately to comprise fifteen hundred houses for approximately seven thousand people. The initial plans were drawn up by Hans Bernoulli, a Swiss architect from Basel who had earlier worked in Berlin, but they did not conform to the wishes of the community and left certain local conditions out of account. In 1913, with Bernoulli's aid, Taut became active for the German Garden City Association, adopting Bernoulli's preliminary project for Falkenberg.

Despite the architect's many and eloquent pleas for the design process as an individual accomplishment, for "architecture as art," Taut considered planning an integral part of a comprehensive effort to bring about a new era. The formal aesthetic aspects of modern housing, Taut believed, should be understood as adjunct to the social aesthetic program of the garden city, and not abstractly, as mere art for art's sake, or in isolation from the social context. The "morphologically new," he stated, was to find its true purpose and confirmation in the "socially new."

A new idea has taken shape, a truly modern idea, an idea that promises to become a philosophy, a generally accepted axiom that will make the great challenges that face us more difficult than ever. This idea is the social idea . . . (building of small apartments, creating colonies, reforming the content of life). It goes . . . without saying that this thought has found its finest expression in our garden city efforts, and that it is here that the contemporary architect's task lies.

This is the field in which we architects can find an expression for our era. Our era has no need of luxuries.[21]

Taut observed with increasing interest the contemporary tendencies in the field of estate and general urban planning and council housing, and published in *Gartenstadt* a detailed description of his Falkenberg project, which reveals borrowings from Unwin and Parker's Letchworth, a much-discussed model of modern urban planning at the time. The Falkenberg plan had a plazalike, low traffic density avenue of 100 to 120 feet in width that sets the topographical theme of the entire layout, serving as a backbone for the adjacent communal infrastructure—churches, schools, teachers' residence, gymnasium, shops. The residential streets issuing into the main avenue, with their generous landscaping, interesting viewpoints, and space-defining perspectives, are other typical features of Berlin garden city planning.

In formal terms, Falkenberg differed hardly at all from traditional developments, apart from the fact that Taut consciously avoided references to romantic, medieval German city design. Although Taut's row and individual houses may have been less strictly functional, less dry and puritanical than, say, those designed by Heinrich Tessenow for the first German garden city, Hellerau near Dresden, Taut nevertheless made every effort to avoid historical citations and the kind of quaintness that appeals to popular taste.

The first construction phase, in 1913, brought the completion of the Akazienhof; many of its features were familiar from the English garden city. The Akazienhof plan is symmetrical: rowhouses line a two-story apartment building situated in the center whose facade is set back considerably from the front of the row. This house serves to emphasize the lateral axis of the small square. Its longitudinal axis would seem to be compositionally marked as well, at least on first sight. However, the square is actually not entered on the axis, and the short, symmetrical final row is shifted out of the axis in the opposite direction.

It would be incorrect to describe these deviations as a diminishment of a baroque square configuration. In place of a composed space in the baroque sense, the observer experiences a juxtaposition of structures arranged around an open space. Taut created no cityscape here, neither a baroque nor a medieval one. What he did was to demonstrate a new kind of coexistence among residential buildings.[22]

Conceived as a cul-de-sac, the plan excludes through traffic. Although it was not an urgent matter at the time of construction, this element has since proven to be a far-seeing and communication-enhancing achievement, since it permits relatively unhindered pedestrian traffic and children's play. In this plan, the street—especially when enlivened by trees and front gardens, as is the Akazienhof—represents not a danger factor but a semipublic extension of the private living space around it.

Of the thirty-four apartments in Akazienhof, twenty-six were planned as detached houses or as rowhouses and eight as upstairs apartments with various types of ground plans. They were to be ready for occupancy in September 1913.

10

11

12

10. Bruno Taut, c. 1913.

11. First three construction phases of Falkenberg, 1913; Akazienhof is at the bottom left (aus "Gartenstadt" 1913).

12. Simple rowhouses with classical symmetry at Falkenberg.

13

14

13. *Falkenberg entranceways, 1969.*

14. *The paintbox estate's festival banner. Kurt Junghanns.*

The early employment of color at Falkenberg as an inexpensive yet enlivening design element deserves particular recognition. Popularly known as the paintbox estate, Falkenberg was soon to play a key role in the cultural policy of Berlin during the Weimar Republic.

Tenant Self-Government in Falkenberg

Not only the planning and projecting of the various house types but also the determination and definition of future tenants' wishes were discussed at meetings on the basis of plans, drawings, and models. As Taut recalled, "the majority of the cooperative members had to give their final Yes."[23] The importance of an active involvement with the desires and needs of the inhabitants was repeatedly stressed by Taut:

But what is the most important condition for any housing development, if the quality of its design and the harmony of life in it are to reach the highest level? It is the interest of the inhabitants in everything concerning the estate. This interest must extend beyond the fence around one's own house (which really no longer has any justification in a public estate) and include the interests of the entire estate. The only way to awaken and maintain this interest is to form a cooperative, to which everyone who lives in the estate should belong. Membership gives everyone the right to participate in decisions relating to their own house or apartment or to the estate as a whole, while at the same time . . . giving them responsibilities, not only to keep their own house and its surroundings in order, show consideration for their neighbors, etc., but to concern themselves with the whole estate. This will give rise to a cooperative spirit.[24]

Community Instead of Society

During the first two construction phases before the outbreak of war (which made them the last), the homogeneity of Falkenberg's inhabitants and their early inclusion in the planning and design process contributed to the emergence of a remarkably active community life that was observed with interest not only by Taut himself but by the planners of public housing during the 1920s in Berlin. The shared bulk purchase of consumer articles and household appliances, the founding of a nursery, kindergarten, school garden, and library, establishment of a dancing and singing club, and the holding of artistic soirees for adults were among the activities by which the Falkenbergers hoped to create community spirit through community work. An elected tenants' committee organized gymnastics and games days for schoolchildren; school graduates gathered in Labor Youth and Tourist Clubs, the latter known as the Friends of Nature (Die Naturfreunde). Music, singing, and chess groups offered the inhabitants an opportunity to get together in their leisure hours. Their health, finally, was in the care of an estate physician with infirmary and an estate-run health insurance plan.

Most famous of all these activities were the Falkenberg Festivals, the first of which took place just before the outbreak of war, in July 1914.[25] The subsequent festivities in 1921, 1924, 1926, and 1927 were not only a gathering place for the inhabitants of Falkenberg but attracted thousands of visitors, mostly working people, from all over Berlin. The broad range of cultural activities at the estate cannot, of course, be attributed to Bruno Taut alone. It was primarily the efforts of those who lived there that kept Falkenberg from becoming just another dormitory suburb. The close relationship between the inhabitants and their architect—as they called him—was to play a role once again in 1924, ten years after the completion of the first section, when in the course of extension plans Taut drew up on an honorary basis a festival hall for Falkenberg. For financial reasons, this project was never realized.

The organization and program of the Falkenberg Festivals enjoyed the support of members of two important Berlin theaters of the day, the Freie Volksbühne and the Reinhardt-Bühne. Georg Büchner's *Danton's Death* was performed there; members of the Friedrichshagen group, Julius Hart, Erich Mühsam, and the Kampffmeyers held lectures in Falkenberg. Erich Weinert recited his stirring poem "Der rote Feuerwehrmann"; Sergei M. Eisenstein's film *Battleship Potemkin* had its premiere screening at the Falkenberg open-air theater; and Gret Palucca instructed a Falkenberg gymnastics group in expressive dance.

Falkenberg Sets the Example for Later Projects

The Falkenberg Festivals inspired many subsequent events held at the estates Taut designed in the 1920s, as well as at Schiller Park and at developments in the Britz and Zehlendorf districts of Berlin. The social aesthetics formulated by the theoreticians of prewar reform—designing living space intended to further communal cohesion—was put into practice in a compelling and generally understandable way in the public estate projects of the postwar decade.

Mindful of prewar insights, Taut remained true to the cultural aims of the reform movement. When the Garden City Association conducted a survey in 1931 on the question "What is a large estate and what meaning does it have for the garden city?" Taut was one of the most prominent and qualified of those who replied. Large developments, he explained, were not large in size for arbitrary reasons but because they ensured an organic articulation of all of the life needs of their inhabitants. Size was not only a requirement of rational construction and administration, but equally and even more importantly a necessity for the ordering of relationships between the community and the individual.

The term order, to us, means a social state in which the needs common to all are fulfilled in common, centrally, collectively . . . such that truly individual needs have even greater scope to develop. The possibility of enjoying one's privacy belongs in the range of needs shared in common. Contained in this definition of the large estate, of course, are not only central laundries, central nurseries for children, kindergartens, etc.; beyond this, the community must arrange for provision of groceries and regulate the distribution of consumer goods. In other words, the lonely existence of wives who feel less and less like sitting at home, will be replaced by opportunities such as community libraries, practice and lecture rooms, community centers and the like, which in turn will probably lead to a redesign of apartment plans. . . . The question we ask ourselves should not be, how

Brieda, laßt det Sorjen, heute woll'n wa lustij sein, hat doch jeda Morjen seine eijne Pein.

15

16

15. Invitation to the party "Uffn Akazienhof," 1914.

16. Collage from the festival magazine, Fest im Fischtal, 1932. (Onkel Tom's Hütte, Berlin-Zehlendorf. The architect was also Bruno Taut.)

17. The concept of the crescent in the Hufeisensiedlung.

18. Falkenberg's symmetry would be systematized and simplified by Berlin's modernist architects.

18

are we going to make apartments smaller? but, how are we going to make the life of the community and the individual richer and more productive?[26]

With this last question, Taut took a definite stand on an issue that had been hotly debated in German planning circles since 1928, that of the minimum-existence flat. Mere economic feasibility could not be the guideline in the designing of public housing, of that Taut was convinced. The main goals, and in his eyes the guarantors of a new era, were social emancipation and individual self-realization.

Conceived by literary eccentrics with a penchant for health food and open collars, the German garden city movement came close to achieving its aim of a comprehensive reform in living conditions and life-style during the Roaring Twenties in Berlin. Although Falkenberg itself remained a fragment the ideas behind it reverberated throughout the city and beyond. Today, this pioneering estate in Grünau is a protected historical site.

Postscript

Since the fall of the Berlin Wall, plans have been made to complete and expand the garden city of Falkenberg. A competition is being prepared. The "paintbox estate" is seen as an aid in solving the growing city's housing problem. It is to be hoped, that the spirit and aims of Berlin's early supporters of the garden city will find adequate contemporary expression.

Notes

1. William Morris, 1874. Quoted in Arthur Leslie Morton, (London, 1952)
2. On this topic, see also Janos Frecot, "Die Lebensreformbewegung," in Klaus Vondung, ed., *Das wilhelminische Bildungsbürgertum. Zur sozialgeschichte seiner Ideen* (Göttingen, 1976), 138ff.
3. Adolf Damaschke, *Aus meinem Leben* (Berlin, 1928), 220.
4. Stanislaw Przybyszewski, *Erinnerung an das literarische Berlin* (Munich, 1965), 111. See also Herbert Scherer, *Bürgerlich-oppositionelle Literaten und sozialdemokratische Arbeiterbewegung nach 1890* (Stuttgart, 1974).
5. See the article by D. N. Schmidt on the Hart Brothers Heinrich und Julius, in *Neue deutsche Biographie*, vol. 7 (Berlin, 1966), 706ff.
6. See Kristiana Hartmann, *Deutsche Gartenstadtbewegung. Kulturpolitik und Gesellschaftsreform* (Munich, 1976).
7. Hans Kampffmeyer, "Die Bedeutung der wirtschaftlichen und sozialen Grundlagen der Gartenstadt für den Städtebau," in Karl Keller, Hermann Wagner, Karl Ernst Osthaus, and Bernhard Kampffmeyer, eds., *Bauordnung und Bebauungsplan, ihre Bedeutung für die Gartenstadtbewegung* (lectures held at the annual meeting of the German Garden City Association, DGG) (Berlin, 1911).
8. First pamphlet of the Ansiedlungsverein Gross-Berlin (1908), authored by Karl von Mangoldt.
9. Werner Hegemann, *Der Städtebau nach den Ergebnissen der allgemeinen Städtebau-Ausstellung*, sec. 1 (Berlin, 1911), 76.
10. Albert Hofmann, "Gross-Berlin, sein Verhältnis zur modernen Grosstadtbewegung," *Deutsche Bauzeitung* 4 (1910): 184.
11. Ibid., 197.
12. Hegemann, *Der Städtebau*, 87.
13. First pamphlet of the Ansiedlungsverein Gross-Berlin.
14. *Gartenstadt* 2; 1–2 (1908; supplement to the journal *Hohe Warte*).
15. *Gartenstadt* 3 (November 1909). The resolution was authored by Karl von Mangoldt.
16. See *Der Falkenberg* 1 (1915) and *Gartenstadt* 8 (July 1914).
17. Karl Scheffler, *Berlin. Ein Stadtschicksal*, 2nd ed. (Berlin, 1910), 258: "land for dwellings, such that around the industrial and working city a wreath of garden cities will develop, with good connections to each other and to the center, each a little organism in itself, where living is good and comfortable and healthy."
18. Theodor Goecke, "Die bauliche Ausgestaltung von Gross-Berlin," *Neudeutsche Bauzeitung* (1913), 58: "As I once said, From greater Berlin to the garden city—what a distance!"
19. B. Wehl, "Warum gibt es noch keine Gartenstadt bei Berlin?" *Der Städtebau* 9; 3 (1912): 33ff.
20. Adolf Otto, "Wie es war und wie es wurde," *Denkschrift Falkenberg* (1913–23): 22.
21. Bruno Taut, *Kleinhausbau und Landaufschliessung*, lecture manuscript, 1913, p. 3.
22. Julius Posener, *Berlin auf dem Wege zu einer neuen Architektur. Das Zeitalter Wilhelm II* (Munich, 1979), 558ff.
23. Bruno Taut, *Siedlungsmemoiren*, manuscript, Shorin-san, Jassau, August 24, 1936, p. 3.
24. Bruno Taut, *Siedlungen für Japan*, manuscript.
25. Otto, "Wie es war und wie es wurde," 24ff.
26. Quoted in *Gartenstadt* 15; cf. *Denkschrift Falkenberg* 1913–1923, pp. 24f.1 (1931): 9ff.

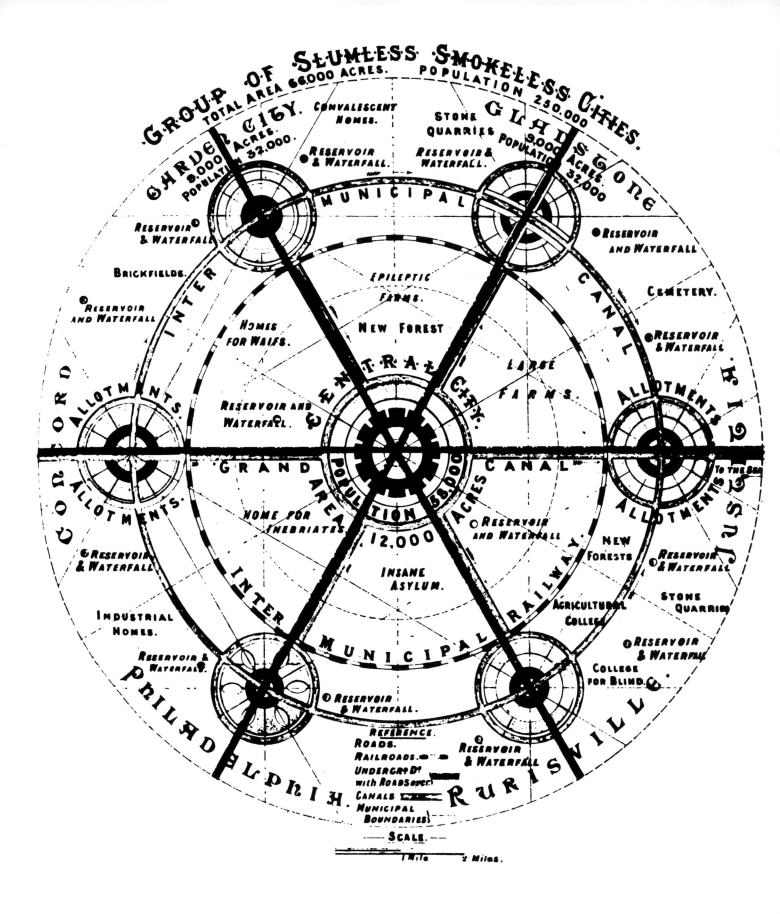

1. Ebenezer Howard's matrix of a garden of cities from Garden City of Tomorrow: A Peaceful Path to Real Reform, *1898.*

New York and the Garden City Movement Between the Wars

Daniel Schaffer

Daniel Schaffer is assistant director at the University of Tennessee's Energy, Environment, and Resource Center and Editor-in-Chief of Forum for Applied Research and Public Policy. *He is the author of* Garden Cities for America: The Radburn Experience *(1982) and editor of* Two Centuries of American Planning *(1988).*

The garden city movement, although never widely discussed in the general population, is considered a key instrument of urban and metropolitan reform among professional urban planners and architects. The movement began with the publication of Ebenezer Howard's *Garden City of Tomorrow: A Peaceful Path to Real Reform.* It has enjoyed periods of international interest and application—for example, at the turn of the century, in the 1930s, in the immediate post-World War II period, and in the 1960s. The movement's design elements are best described by centralized population pockets surrounded by open space. Its visual contents have stood in contrast to urban overpopulation and suburban sprawl.

The garden city movement in the United States, in many respects, reached its zenith in the 1920s. The movement's power and influence was not due to its broad-based support. Most Americans were as familiar with the garden city as they were with the opera. Even among intellectuals the movement's influence was limited. Indeed much of the discussion and experimentation surrounding the American garden city in the 1920s took place within twenty miles of Manhattan. This important chapter of a movement—with worldwide consequences for planners and public officials—was largely confined in concrete terms to the New York metropolitan region.

This essay will trace the garden city movement in America from its beginnings at the turn of the century to its world renowned experiments at Sunnyside Gardens, Queens, and Radburn, New Jersey, in the 1920s. It will explore both the design elements that gave the garden city its unique physical definition and the intellectual and political elements that made the movement more than an important chapter in the history of American urban design—elevating it to a symbol of social reform.

What social and economic conditions did garden city advocates hope to improve through this new urban form? Why did New York prove such fertile ground for their efforts? How successful were they? What can we learn from their experience not only about urban design, but also about the nature of political and social reform in the United States? And, is the American garden city experience in New York during the 1920s unique—that is, although part of an international movement, does it represent a significant variation in both physical form and political content from other plans for metropolitan growth?

A Movement Is Born

In 1906, a small group of New York City intellectuals and reform-minded businessmen created the Garden Cities Association of America. The organization took shape eight years after the publication of Ebenezer Howard's garden city manifesto, *Garden Cities of Tomorrow: A Peaceful Path to Real Reform,* and seven years after a similar association was formed in England to advance a similar goal.[1]

Howard, a nondescript English court stenographer, gained much public notoriety in his native land with the publication of *Garden Cities,* the only monograph he ever wrote. In response to the poverty and overcrowding found in England's industrial cities, Howard called for the creation of a new regional form that would meld the best qualities of town and country. He envisioned a city blessed with modest housing for all residents, an urban design where noxious factories would be segregated from residential areas, a town with broad, picturesque boulevards and ample parklands, and perhaps most importantly a system of regional development in which one city would be separated from another by forests and farmland. Such a regional form, Howard contended, would arrest the sprawling decay of late nineteenth-century English cities and create instead a pleasant pattern of cellular development—a series of "social cities," as he referred to his vision.[2]

Howard gained a strong following in England, particularly among wealthy and influential liberal reformers. An association was formed and enough money collected to launch the world's first "garden city" experiment in 1903 at Letchworth, forty miles north of London.[3]

Howard's American disciples, however, were not as successful as the master. The Garden Cities Association of America and its members are now largely lost to history. Grandiose plans for a series of garden cities in the Northeast, to house 350,000 families, quickly were pared to a single proposed experiment on Long Island, New York. Even that modest initiative faltered, and the entire organization languished and died a slow death. When it officially disbanded in 1921, dated editions of its journal, *The Village,* are all it left behind.[4]

Despite its lack of success, the first American garden city association displayed many elements that were to characterize its successors. First, it is important to note that members of the association belonged to New York's conservative elite, that is, wealthy executives, intellectuals, and political leaders. The garden city may have had its radical elements, but it was in fact an elite movement.

Second, garden city advocates were reacting to the extraordinary social and economic circumstances of the United States at the turn of the century. The Spanish-American War signaled America's emergence as a world power, and the expanding strength of corporate giants such as United States Steel and Standard Oil symbolized its economic prowess. Beneath these triumphs of power and wealth, however, resided an uneasiness and despair that threatened to tear the fabric of American society apart.

The nation at the turn of the century was being jolted by conflicting impulses. Signs of wealth and power abounded, but so did signs of despair and neglect. No other period in United States history, except the 1930s, experienced such a wave of labor unrest and protest. The violent and destructive Pullman strike, the Haymarket riot, and labor unrest at Homestead all have been painfully etched on the portrait of America on the eve of the twentieth century.[5] So too have been depictions of urban poverty and overcrowding, in Chicago's Back of the Yards, Philadelphia's Kesington, Boston's Back Bay, and especially New York's Lower East Side where it was estimated that a portion of one ward housed 936 persons per acre (higher than the "outcast" ward of Koombarwara in Bombay, India, which was thought to be the most densely populated place on earth).[6]

To use a more contemporary vocabulary, turn-of-the-century America displayed characteristics of both First and Third World nations. Contradictions, so vividly conveyed in so many aspects of American life, preoccupied much of American thought. It was reflected in the writings of Edward Bellamy and others who hoped that America's economic and technological prowess could magically transform the nation into a harmonious society of peaceful bliss.[7] It could be found in the Social Gospel of Josiah Strong and Washington Gladden who urged fellow Christians to follow moral precepts and do good work here on earth.[8] And it was shown through the ubiquitous presence of so-called good works organizations such as the Salvation Army, the Boy Scouts, and others, which believed that a helping hand and guiding light could do much to lift the burdens and brighten the dark sides of American life.[9]

The first American garden city movement fit the times. It was another expression of the nation's growing concern for the contradictions in American society. Like other organizations, it acknowledged that serious social and economic problems plagued the United States. Like the others, it also believed that a resolution to these problems did not require violence or profound systemic change. Rather, meaningful social and economic improvement, garden city advocates hoped, could be attained through ingenuity, voluntary commitment, and self-imposed limits on personal greed. It should not be surprising that New York City, plagued by the nation's most troublesome urban problems on the one hand and endowed with the nation's liveliest intellectual community and reformist impulses on the other, should be home to America's first garden city association.[10] After all, it would seem illogical to have such an organization trace its roots to Duluth, Minnesota, or Wichita, Kansas.

Slow Growth

Between the demise of America's first garden city and the beginning of World War I, the American Garden City movement experienced a period of slow growth, both in terms of actual examples in community design and of intellectual discussions and organizational efforts.

Nevertheless, a number of town-planning projects in the United States adopted the basic garden city principle of town and country planning. These communities, despite their innovative design elements, were seen primarily as singularly unique communities, and rarely as important components of a larger whole. Englishmen residing in Howard's first town-planning experiment at Letchworth would proudly accept the town's title as England's first garden city. Conversely, neither the residents of John Nalens's Country Club District in Kansas City, Missouri, nor those of Earl Draper's Kingsport, Tennessee, would comfortably wear such a badge.[11] Without an organization to bind their garden city efforts, America's town planners were essentially on their own. The communities

2

3

*2. Letchworth, the first English
garden city. View of Nevell's Road
in 1905.* British Information
Services, Central Office of
Information, London.

*3. Forest Hills Gardens, general
view of group two.* Department of
Manuscripts and University
Archives, Cornell University
Libraries, Cornell University,
Ithaca, New York.

95

these planners created may have adopted some of Howard's concepts and may have successfully generated some of the spirit of Howard's design, but for the most part these communities were viewed as innovative suburbs or milltowns—an adoption of an evolving theme, not a radically new addition to the nation's design vocabulary. Likewise, the social purpose behind the physical form, which Howard viewed as the essence of his idea, failed to achieve prominence on this side of the Atlantic.

In New York City, the most significant contribution during this early period of garden city development was Forest Hills, built on a 160-acre site in Queens, New York, in the decade before World War I. The fact that Forest Hills is better known as the previous home of the United States Tennis Open than as a unique planned community says something about both its design and its intent—and, more generally, about the inability of American town planning to establish a living tradition beyond the academe and one-time examples of historical interest.[12]

Forest Hills was built as a suburban enclave for wealthy entrepreneurs and professionals who worked in nearby Manhattan. It succeeded admirably along those lines. The staying power of housing prices and the community's persistent upper-middle-class appeal speaks well of the Forest Hills plan. It was built to last and it has, but on its own terms, which emphasized physical design elements at the expense of social concerns. There was no mixing of income groups at Forest Hills and no attempt to solve the enormously difficult problem of low-income housing—just a desire to build a more pleasant community for those who could already afford it.

With the interstate highway system decades away, living in the shadow of the city was unavoidable, and intelligently designed communities such as Forest Hills seemed like a reasonable solution to the upper-middle-class problem of balancing one's work with one's family life. Like Marietta, Ohio, Palos Verdes Estates, California, and other planned suburbs, Forest Hills was not a radical design statement offered in opposition to prevailing trends; rather it was presented as an accommodation to the problems of twentieth-century living confronted by a growing number of upper-middle-class families—how does the head of a household work in the city, move the family to the suburbs, and find the time for all to enjoy the good life?

Not that Forest Hills planners did not think about larger social issues. They simply found such goals to be economically unfeasible. And so Forest Hills and other American garden suburbs of the pre-World War I period illustrated, however, unwittingly, another abiding principle of the garden city movement in America, an iron-clad principle that was to entrap the movement throughout its history. The physical design elements of the garden city proved attractive not only to planners but to house buyers as well. Building those elements, however, was an expensive proposition. America's system of private land development for profit welcomed the garden city's progressive design. But communities built with such design elements were to be opened only to those who could afford the price of entry.

The contribution of Forest Hills to the garden city movement, however, was more than just a vague, unintended reaffirmation of the movement's social and economic limitations. The Forest Hills design introduced a planning concept—the neighborhood unit—that was to become as important as Howard's original garden city ideas.[13]

Simply put, the neighborhood unit was a design principle that sought to cluster the major elements of a neighborhood—house, school, and shopping center—into a safe and convenient environment. For garden city advocates, such clustering that had occurred naturally in the past was now being unraveled by the forces of industrialization. Specialization may have made sense on the factory floors, they contended, but it generated serious problems when applied to living. It increased the distance between home and work, home and school, and home and shopping. For adults, this increased distance also added unnecessary time and effort into an already busy day; for children, it could be isolating and even dangerous particularly if traffic patterns interfered with their daily walks to school and play.

The neighborhood unit attempted to reintegrate these now-separate elements by reintroducing schools and shops into the core of the neighborhood. In a sense, the notion of self-contained cities envisioned by Howard on a regional scale (in his system of social cities) was applied on a micro, or neighborhood, level in the neighborhood unit. Or, as historian Walter Creese has suggested, the "external green" portrayed by Howard was now complemented by an "internal green" of self-contained and self-reliant neighborhoods.[14]

In an American society at the threshold of the age of the automobile, this breakthrough was to have a dramatic impact on reshaping the American garden city movement. Howard had given garden city advocates the broad brushstrokes of a new regional form; the neighborhood unit concept first expressed in Forest Hills provided a level of design detail that would take the movement into the post-World War I period.

After the War

The first decades of the twentieth century in America were a time of great concern and great optimism. The Progressive era, as historians have come to call it, did not deny that difficult problems beset the United States, but there was a sense that the nation enjoyed both the resources and the will to solve them. That optimism accompanied America's entry into World War I in 1917. In the words of President Woodrow Wilson, this was not just a war to destroy oppression, injustice, and imperialism (daunting goals in their own right), it was to be a "war to end all wars."[15]

For many Americans, including much of the nation's intellectual community, the war—despite the triumph of the United States—was a cruel hoax. The war's purpose became increasingly vague as the fighting progressed. Patriotic fervor fueled by the war effort helped to undermine some of the nation's most basic democratic principles, a trend most vividly displayed by government-sanctioned raids against ethnic groups and political radicals accused, without proof, of abetting the enemy. Congressional bills against espionage and treason were passed under the publicly stated purpose of protecting the nation against foreign subversion. But many in Congress supported these bills as a means to quell legitimate protest against the war—a justification for suppression with which many patriotic Americans concurred.[16]

Perhaps, most importantly, the war did not end all wars. In fact, the Axis defeat left a legacy of international suspicion and tension from which few nations, including the United States, could escape. Witness Woodrow Wilson's failure to achieve American approval for the League of Nations—a defeat he suffered at the hands of the United States Senate. Witness too the bitter peace France and England imposed on Germany, and the civil war in the Soviet Union in which the Allied powers (including the United States) felt compelled to lend military support to the non-Soviet White Army.

Compounding all of these political and diplomatic troubles was a postwar economy reeling from inflation and labor unrest. For many American intellectuals, World War I and its aftermath marked the end of an age of innocence and optimism—and they escaped the harsh reality of their native land by migrating to Europe as expatriates of a nation that had promised so much but delivered so little.[17]

There was a diverse group of intellectuals in the United States—educator John Dewey, historian Charles Beard, and economist John Commons, among others—however, who held tight to a vision of a better future. Their optimism was not based on a blind belief in the goodness of America; nor were they oblivious to the price that the United States had paid for victory in World War I—not just in lives and injuries but also in the dilution of cherished American values.

What moved these intellectuals in part was a firm belief in the goodness of the individual, a fundamental American notion that could be traced to Emerson and Thoreau. But this optimism grew from more than just philosophical principles; it evolved as well from a distinct interpretation of recent political and social events which made them believe that the United States was at the threshold of a new era of prosperity. This era of well-being, these intellectuals believed, could be shared democratically, both here and abroad, if the appropriate plans and policies were put in place.

Two forces in particular bolstered their hopes. One was an uncompromising belief that modernization held great promise if the power of the machine could be harnessed to serve man instead of profits. The other was less grandiose but equally important. During World War I, the power of government had been coordinated and expanded as never before—and to great effect. Federal agencies determined the nation's production schedules in defense-related factories, regulated transport on the rail and shipping lanes, and even built houses and communities to assure an adequate workforce was available to labor in the nation's defense plants.[18]

For these intellectuals, individual goals achieved through co-operative effort became a hallmark of the new frontier in America, and the positive role of government in improving the nation's plight emerged as an abiding concept. Such abstract ideas were rooted in reality by the standard American device of remaining nonideological and practical.

These broadly conceived ideas may seem far afield from the houses, roadways, shops, and parks that ultimately gave meaning to the American garden city movement in the 1920s. But the ideas nevertheless proved essential in shaping the American garden city's reformist impulses. Most importantly, they provide the context for understanding how such a potentially radical idea as comprehensive land development could reach such a level of political acceptability (if not acceptance in practice) during one of the most conservative decades in American history.

Toward a Second American Garden City Association

The second American garden city association, which was organized in the summer of 1923, did not evolve from a grand strategic plan. Rather, it developed informally over time from a growing network of friendships among people who shared similar ideas on how to build better cities and a better society. The group's collegiality was a source of both strength and weakness. On the one hand, it provided an informal dynamic environment were ideas could be tested and refined. Perhaps for this reason, the group—despite its small size and minuscule budget—briefly emerged as the most influential planning association of its day.

That same informality, however, also compromised its ability to work effectively in the political arena—to translate its ideas from the parlors of discussion and debate and one-time demonstrations into the mainstream of American political thought and action.

Individually, members of the second garden city association—which came to be called the Regional Planning Association of America (RPAA)—all carved important careers of their own. There was Lewis Mumford, the internationally acclaimed writer;[19] Benton MacKaye, first president of the National Wildlife Federation and the mind behind the Appalachian Trail;[20] Catherine Bauer Wurster, who became one of the nation's most insightful critics on housing and federal housing policy;[21] and Stuart Chase, a respected economist who helped to popularize the ideas of Franklin D. Roosevelt's New Deal.[22] The personal fame of these people exceeded the notoriety they achieved as members of the RPAA. Nevertheless, each was quick to note the fundamental influence that the RPAA was to have on their thoughts and actions.[23]

Mumford gave the group a broad social vision and an imaginative pen that allowed it to break out into the world of opinion and influence. MacKaye's Thoreauvian ideas—his love of the wilderness and his disdain for technocratic solutions—gave the RPAA an unmistakably American stamp, despite its European garden city roots. These two intellectuals—Mumford who was born and bred in New York City and MacKaye who spent much time there as a child accompanying his playwright father to the theater—had instrumental roles in the development of the RPAA.

Two other members, however, translated the abstract ideas of regional design formulated by Mumford and MacKaye into a tangible community form. Clarence Stein, who was born and raised in New York City not far from Mumford, was a man of distinctive organizational skills, trained in the design vocabulary of the Beaux Arts yet an early convert to garden city ideals. Henry Wright was born and bred in the Midwest and moved eastward after World War I to find a more hospitable environment for his innovative town-planning concepts. Collectively, Stein and Wright would reach the height of their creative powers while teamed together as members of the RPAA. Indeed, Stein's position as president of the organization allowed him to exercise his organization talents in ways that would never again be available to him; and Wright's association with a group of individuals of powerful intellect and imagination enabled him to refine his considerable talents in town-planning design.[24]

The formation of the group began modestly and was instigated by an outside source who, although responsible for the initial spark, ultimately played an insignificant role in the RPAA's growth and evolution. Charles Whitaker, the editor of the *Journal of the American Institute of Architects* (*JAIA*) and a staunch advocate of Henry George's single tax theories, was searching for ways to reduce *JAIA*'s preoccupation with physical design elements and raise the publication's concern for social issues. The severe United States housing shortage following the end of World War I gave Whitaker ample opportunity to explore the relationship between town planning and a productive and humane society; future members of the RPAA provided him with provocative copy to explore that theme.[25]

For example, Whitaker commissioned architect and future RPAA member Frederick L. Ackerman to investigate postwar housing plans in England. While there, Ackerman learned of the influence of the garden city on English town-planning policies and spoke favorably of these efforts when he returned.[26] Whitaker also sponsored the early writings of Lewis Mumford. In fact, at the age of twenty-four, Mumford published one of his first articles in *JAIA*: "The Heritage of the Cities in America: An Historical Survey." Although lacking the sophistication of Mumford's later evaluations of urban America, it showed the young critic's allegiance to garden city concepts, particularly as conveyed by the Scottish academician Patrick Geddes, whom Mumford considered his mentor.[27] Finally, Whitaker's *JAIA* opened its pages to Benton MacKaye's inspired vision of an Appalachian Trail. In the *JAIA*'s October 1921 edition, MacKaye outlined his blueprint for a wilderness footpath stretching from Georgia to Maine.[28]

As Whitaker provided a literary forum for the ideas of the garden city, New York governor Alfred E. Smith created a housing committee in 1919 to grapple with the anticipated problems the state would face in meeting the challenges of postwar housing. In so doing, Smith unwittingly created a nascent po-

litical forum for future RPAA members. Heading that committee was Clarence Stein; among its members were Ackerman, Robert D. Kohn, and Alexander Bing—all future participants in the RPAA. The committee's recommendations, which included a call for local housing boards and publicly subsidized housing, were largely ignored by the state legislature—as were similar recommendations by the state's subsequent Commission on Housing and Regional Planning, also led by Stein.[30] But what these state-supported commissions lacked in political punch, they more than made up for in intellectual energy and the cooperative spirit of exchange. Together with Whitaker's *JAIA*, Smith's postwar housing commissions provided the framework around which the RPAA was built.

Limited Dividend Housing

The RPAA was never bankrupt for ideas. Without capital, however, it could not have moved from the abstract world of intellectual exchange to the street-smart environment of real estate development. That capital was provided by Alexander Bing, a benevolent capitalist who believed that profit and decent housing for all people were compatible goals—as long as investors willingly limited the rate of return on their investment.

Like Mumford and Stein, Bing was bred in New York City. Ironically, he and his brother had earned a fortune early in the century through real estate speculation; they bought tracks of land along Fifth Avenue in Manhattan and then benefited from skyrocketing land prices after the elevated railroad tracks were removed and Fifth Avenue became a fashionable place for development. Like other benevolent capitalists of his day, he thought he owed society something in return for his personal wealth. At first, he dabbled in labor issues, but then persuaded by Stein he turned his attention to housing—a burning issue in the post-World War I period as war-delayed construction and postwar inflation generated a shortage of affordable housing, especially in burgeoning cities such as New York.[31]

Bing's limited dividend solution, that is placing a ceiling of, for example, six or seven percent on the rate of return for capital invested in his housing company, was not revolutionary—nor even unique. Reform-minded capitalists in the United States had experimented with limited dividend investment schemes since the mid-nineteenth century.

New York City, because it magnified America's dilemma of wealth and poverty, became home to most of the nation's limited dividend housing projects. Spearheaded by New York reformers Alfred T. White and Elgin R. L. Gould, the New York Association for the Improvement of the Condition of the Poor, the Children's Aid Society, the State Charities Aid Association, and the City and Suburban Homes Company all promoted limited dividend housing.[32] As historian Roy Lubove has written, "Neither White nor his contemporary housing reformers were radical, toying with imaginative reconstructions of the social and economic order. Their aim was more modest—to provide safe, comfortable, and even pleasant housing for low-income groups within the framework of the capitalist-profit system."[33]

Bing drew upon this tradition when he established the City Housing Corporation (CHC) in 1924. Its dividends were to be limited to six percent. Its goal was to provide low-cost housing to moderate- and low-income families. Its vision was to apply as extensively as possible the ideas of Ebenezer Howard's garden city to new development in the New York metropolitan area. And finally, like Howard, Bing hoped that if successful, the CHC could serve as a prototype for real estate and housing development throughout the United States.

Sunnyside Up

Stein, who had led the design effort, and Bing, who had led the effort for capitalization, decided to attack New York City's housing problems as quickly as possible—and they decided to direct their attack not at the core among the tenement blocks of Manhattan but rather at the flank along yet undeveloped land in Queens, a borough that rested within the shadow of Manhattan and was ripe for development.

There was a logic to Bing and Stein's approach that fit both the design elements and the economic viability they hoped to achieve. Because of the high price of urban land on which tenement housing was built, slum clearance and tenement redevelopment would be costly. Capital for good design and quality construction would be consumed by the cost of land. Such an investment pattern may have benefited real estate speculators, Bing and Stein contended, but it returned little to residents who would ultimately live in the houses built there. Undeveloped land was not only cheaper, it also provided a clean slate upon which innovative design concepts could be sketched. Finally, although Bing and Stein would have preferred to construct a complete garden city modeled after Howard's ideal, they realized the complexity of the task and acknowledged their lack of experience in grappling with a project of that magnitude. They chose instead to begin on a small-scale and with a site well-connected to a larger urban entity—Manhattan.

Today Queens is a fully developed borough of New York with densely populated residential neighborhoods, shopping centers, industry, and commerce. More than 1.8 million people live there.[34] In the 1920s, Queens was by no means a rural paradise, but there was plenty of open space waiting to be cleared for housing. In effect, Queens was at the eastern edge of the New York metropolitan region, and there was little doubt the city was about to move forcefully into its sparsely populated neighborhoods. The question was not if Queens would be developed, but rather when and how. Already, strips of densely packed rowhouses lining newly developed Queens streets foretold of an urban pattern not substantially different from lower Manhattan, Brooklyn, or the Bronx—boroughs that already experienced the relentless outward thrust of New York metropolitan population growth.

Bing and Stein hoped to offer an alternative vision of development not only for Queens but for the rest of America. It was a tall order for a nondescript seventy-six-acre site sliced from a swatch of land just fifteen minutes from Grand Central Station

4. Fifth Avenue and 42nd Street, 1923. Department of Manuscripts and University archives, Cornell University Libraries, Cornell University, Ithaca, New York.

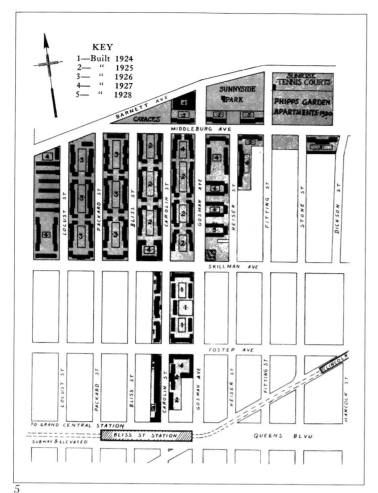

KEY
1—Built 1924
2— " 1925
3— " 1926
4— " 1927
5— " 1928

5. *Clarence S. Stein. Sunnyside Gardens, New York. Street plan.* M.I.T. Press.

6. *Clarence S. Stein. Sunnyside Gardens, New York. Street level.* Department of Manuscripts and University Archives, Cornell University Libraries, Cornell University, Ithaca, New York.

in Manhattan. But members of both the RPAA and the CHC viewed Sunnyside not as a final commercial real estate product but rather as an experimental "urban laboratory," which would lay a foundation for greater success in the future. As Columbia University economics professor Richard T. Ely proclaimed, Sunnyside Gardens hopes to show "that private enterprise can improve standards without sacrificing reasonable profits, without sweeping government aid or subsidy, and without demoralizing the housing market."[35]

Between 1924 and 1928, the CHC built twelve hundred housing units at Sunnyside. Costs were contained not only by limiting dividends but by a systematic construction plan that increased labor productivity by ensuring the availability of work in both winter and summer. Bing and Stein may have been idealists when it came to low-cost housing and community design, but they were unflinching realists when the issue was economics. Carrying costs could kill the project. Therefore, it was essential to keep labor costs to a minimum and to ensure the units were occupied as quickly as possible.[36]

Such concerns did not compromise the use of innovative design concepts. Stein and his design partner, Henry Wright, Sr., were operating under certain constraints at Sunnyside that prevented them from fully exploring radical alternatives to New York City's urban grid. Existing zoning ordinances and city plans for Sunnyside called for the construction of right-angled streets to frame city blocks typical of New York City and almost all of urban America. The CHC and RPAA asked city officials for an exemption to free Sunnyside's planners from the city's "cramped stage" but were denied the request.[37]

Within this grid, Stein and Wright turned the houses ninety degrees. Thus instead of knifing into the block and creating alleys between the buildings, Sunnyside houses faced the street in a broadside fashion that welcomed light and air. In Sunnyside, buildings covered only twenty-eight percent of the total area, compared to seventy percent on typical tenement blocks in Manhattan. Equally important, the alleys were replaced by interior common parkland that gave all residents access to open space and natural settings.[38]

Aesthetically, Sunnyside houses were a success but economically the results were mixed. Houses were priced between $4,300 and $17,800. Although by no means exclusive, the price was beyond the means of most low-income families.[39] Sunnyside cooperatives were more reasonable, but even those units required an annual wage of $2,500 to purchase and maintain—an income earned by only four percent of all urban families at that time.[40] Indeed the median annual income for Sunnyside families in the 1920s was $3,000 (for private homeowners and cooperative dwellers). In the United States, two-thirds of all families earned less than that.

Within this high plateau of earnings, Sunnyside enjoyed a demographic diversity not common to other subdivisions either then or now. This was due partially to Sunnyside's competitive prices, partially to innovative financial schemes offered by Bing's CHC to attract lower income groups, and partially to the town's experimental nature, which enticed a select number of

100

New York City intellectuals and academics. As Lewis Mumford, an eleven-year resident of Sunnyside, wrote: "In the block where I lived there was a grocer's clerk who earned $1,200 to $1,400 a year, and a physician who earned $10,000—then a large salary. So this effort at an acceptable minimum in housing achieved something even more important; a mixed community, not the economically segregated kind that the high costs of a well-planned, middle-class suburb demand."[41]

If the success of Sunnyside's demand-side economics (based on housing prices) remained opened to debate, the success of its supply-side economics (based on its ability to generate investment and profits) seemed irrefutable. Bing's CHC met its overhead costs, the carrying charges on Sunnyside's vacant land and, as promised, accumulated enough capital to reward investors with a six-percent return on their investment. Sales at Sunnyside achieved all these goals and still generated a surplus of three hundred thousand dollars, a nest egg that could be used for larger, more ambitious town-planning projects in the future.[42]

Little wonder that the CHC promotional literature in the late 1920s delighted in the company's accomplishments. Sunnyside, one pamphlet read, "stands as a consciously successful demonstration of how much can be done to better housing conditions, provide garden and play space for children and put these advantages within the financial reach of wage earners and other moderate income families—all by the course of a sound, conservative business operation."[43]

The Road to Radburn

The second project produced by the collaborative efforts of the RPAA and CHC would assure these organizations a significant place in the history of planned communities. Fifteen miles west of the northern tip of Manhattan was the small community of Fair Lawn, New Jersey. Today, Fair Lawn is engulfed by metropolitan sprawl that reaches fifty miles beyond the town's borders. Its checkerboard suburban neighborhoods form part of an endless puzzle of metropolitan growth that now includes twenty million people and covers portions of three states—New York, New Jersey, and Connecticut.

In the 1920s, however, Fair Lawn was much like Queens—an area of open space waiting for the reach of the metropolis to touch its borders. Indeed portions of Fair Lawn remained in a rural state, much as they had since the colonial days of the first Dutch settlers who quickly began to cultivate the area's rich soil. When representatives of the CHC began to knock on Fair Lawn's doors in the late 1920s to acquire the acreage for their next town-planning experiment, they sometimes encountered truck farmers who earned a good living selling spinach and other produce to residents close at hand—much as their ancestors had 150 years before.[44]

At Radburn, the cramped stage gave way to an open theater where innovative town planning concepts could be freely explored. One square mile (or 640 acres of land) was purchased;

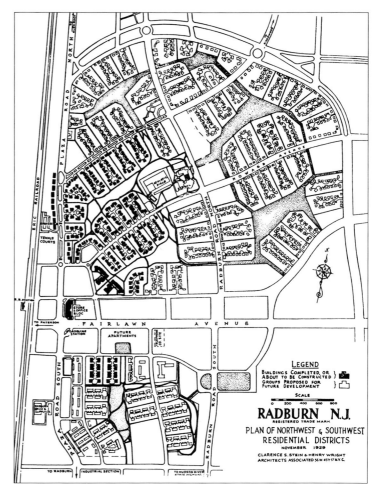

7. Radburn, Fair Lawn, New Jersey. Original plan, c. 1930.

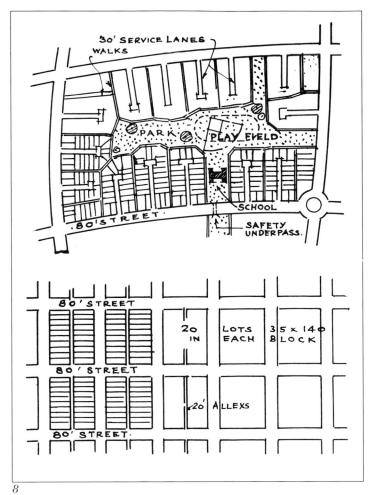

8

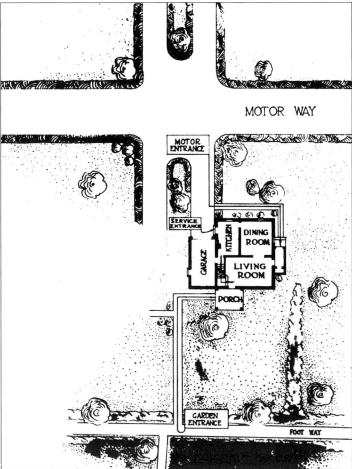

9

a town of thirty thousand people living and working in the same area, if not the same town, was envisioned.[45]

The Superblock and Beyond

The centerpiece of the Radburn idea was the superblock. At a simple level of perception, the superblock was an enlarged version of Sunnyside's town plan—houses were placed along a block's periphery with the interior reserved for common open space. But the differences between the design of Radburn and Sunnyside were qualitative as well as quantitative. Whereas Sunnyside represented a reorientation of the prevailing urban grid (a variation on the American streetscape), Radburn was a radically new concept that promised to provide the physical and intellectual scaffolding for an entirely new city.

The CHC advertised Radburn as "the town for the motor age." Twenty years after its construction, Stein claimed the "Radburn idea" sought to discover "how to live with the automobile"—or perhaps more precisely, "how to live in spite of it."[46] A series of cul-de-sacs or dead-end streets cut into the superblock without transecting it. Houses were lined along the cul-de-sacs on eighth of an acre lots—with the savings in private yard space transferred to common parkland that all could enjoy. Without streets interfering with the setting, the common area was truly a place for residents not automobiles. It called for a permanent community of relaxation and play, not a transitory environment best observed and enjoyed fleetingly while driving an automobile.

To enhance the community's orientation to people (rather than automobiles), a separate system of pedestrian walkways also was created. These walkways led from the house to the parkland and also to the school and shopping center. The intent was to enable residents to get about without ever having to get into their cars. Each neighborhood unit, consisting of two superblocks and approximately ten thousand residents, was to be relatively self-contained. Families could thus satisfy their routine needs in comfort and without confronting the inconveniences and dangers posed by the automobile. Rather than acquiesce to the automobile's demand for space and primary presence, Radburn's designers hoped to put the car in its place.[47]

These physical design concepts were significant. By trying to introduce humane elements into an increasingly technological society, the Radburn plan echoed the concerns of the garden city's earliest advocates. By concentrating on the impact of the automobile, the plan proved to be truly American for its time. No other nation so thoroughly embraced the automobile as the United States and no other nation so unquestionably accepted its presence: for Americans, the automobile promised to close the nation's vast open spaces to bring individual freedom to a society straddled by the limits of public transportation and allowed urban dwellers the opportunity to enjoy the countryside. It is interesting to note that the same year that ground was broken for Radburn, 1928, Henry Ford introduced his Model A automobile. Radburn offered a note of caution about the destructive force of the automobile; Ford's Model A was a

10

11

12

8. Comparison of Radburn
superblock and a conventional grid
pattern.

9. City Housing Corporation.
Radburn turned-around houses,
with living rooms facing the park
and utility rooms facing the street,
1929. Radburn Association
Archives.

10. Radburn, interior parkland, c.
1932. Radburn Association
Archives.

11. Radburn overpass, separating
pedestrian and vehicular traffic.
Department of Manuscripts and
University Archives, Cornell
University Libraries, Cornell
University, Ithaca, New York.

12. Radburn, children at play, c.
1930.

celebration of its mass appeal. History tells us who won the hearts and minds of the American people, but it also shows us at what cost to the nation's social fabric.[48]

Thus Radburn's superblock construction was sparked by a concern for the automobile. Such concern not only brought the garden city into the twentieth century, it helped to transplant the concept onto the American landscape. Before Radburn, the garden city was a European idea that had attracted a few American planners and intellectuals concerned about the course of urban and metropolitan growth. After Radburn, the garden city's superblock became one of the most enduring terms of America's (and the world's) design vocabulary—retaining a prominent place in the lexicon throughout the post-World War II period and finding expression in design among both public housing projects and suburban subdivisions. Again, it should be no surprise that the New York metropolitan region led the charge—from its public-housing projects in Manhattan where multi-storied apartments were set in superblocks to Levittown, Long Island, the postwar suburban paradise accented by cul-de-sacs and neighborhood schools and shopping centers.

Overcoming Economic and Spatial Segregation

Beyond its more visible physical design elements, Radburn also held a broad social vision. That vision was rooted in American values that cherished equalitarianism. The Jeffersonian ideal of a homogeneous society of yeomen farmers, leaving aside the question of whether it ever existed as a prominent force in American history, had long since given way to a society of class and distinction. Social classes were not just reflected in professions and personal wealth but in the unmistakable lines of division that separated neighborhoods. Whereas Americans in the colonial period and early nineteenth century had resided in cities and towns where rich and poor often lived side by side (a function of limited transportation more than personal or social preference), America in the 1920s was marked increasingly by ghetto neighborhoods and exclusive suburbs in which rich and poor rarely interacted beyond working hours.[49] Again, the New York metropolitan area with its Lower East Side ghettos and glistening Westchester and northern New Jersey suburbs seemed to exemplify, if not spearhead, this larger trend.

Radburn designers hoped to arrest this development—or at least demonstrate that there were alternatives to the current forces of economic and spatial segregation. It was not, of course, in their power to make America more equalitarian. They did believe, however, that communities could be planned to accommodate a broad spectrum of social classes. Private privilege would remain unchallenged, a function of inheritance and income, but public amenities could be shared regardless of a resident's personal status or family wealth.

To advance this vision, a variety of housing types were constructed at Radburn: apartment houses for young childless couples with small incomes; garden apartments for families of modest means; rowhouses (now called town houses to disguise

their urban roots); and single-unit dwellings comparable to the houses in any 1920s upper-middle-class subdivision except that the rooms and yard space were made somewhat smaller to provide for the common parkland.

Social and economic segregation was one sin that Radburn's designers hoped to correct; spatial segregation was another. Again, in the colonial period and the early decades of the Republic, home and work remained virtually unseparated—sometimes shops were found on the first floor and living quarters on the second; sometimes they were separated by clusters (a few houses followed by a few commercial or manufacturing establishments). Rarely, however, was there great distance between the two.

By the mid-nineteenth century, this informal mixing of living and working areas began to give way to a more spatially segregated landscape. As manufacturing became a less attractive and more intrusive process, those who could afford to do so began to move away—and they had no intention of having factories follow them to their new residential neighborhoods.[50] Indeed in the early twentieth century, zoning was established largely as an administrative measure to prevent the mixing of unlike functions—and by implication to prevent the mixing of unlike classes. It was the poor who were left behind to share urban space with unappealing factories and large commercial establishments. As transportation improved and incomes for the upper middle class rose, the space between home and work lengthened for those who could afford the expense of commuting.[51]

Radburn hoped to stymie this trend as well. Factories and large commercial establishments would not be placed within the residential settings of the superblock but would be built within the community (in the town's southwestern corner). Radburn's planners realized that not all of the town's working adults would find—or even seek—employment there. The region's complex employment base was too diverse and scattered to expect that to happen. It was hoped, however, that Radburn would provide the opportunity for many who lived in the town to work close by, thus eliminating the drudgery of commuting and simultaneously providing the town with a tax base to finance its community-wide social activities.[52]

A Road Blocked

In its physical design elements (intended to address problems created by the automobile), Radburn succeeded admirably. To this day, it is cited in planning literature as an intelligent solution to the most compelling problem of twentieth-century planning: What do you do with the automobile? How do you acknowledge its importance without allowing it to run roughshod over the environment? On the larger social questions, however, of integrating economic classes and multiple land-use functions into a coherent and livable pattern, Radburn failed.

It failed on the first count because building decent housing in a decent setting cost more than low-income families could afford. The average price of a single-family home in Radburn in the late 1920s ranged between $7,900 and $18,200, more than twice the average price of a house in the United States. Limited dividends might place a ceiling on investor profits, but they did not effect the cost of land, material, and labor. Good housing cost good money, and unless the incomes of workers were raised it was unlikely that any formula for investment—regardless of how humane or well-intended—would be sufficient to meet low-income housing needs.[53]

Radburn failed on the second count—in its inability to attract industry—for several reasons. Stein would later claim that its location was not conducive to industrial development. Although a rail line passed alongside Radburn, it was a secondary route. Moreover, a planned highway to connect the town with the George Washington Bridge (then under construction) and thus Manhattan was only on the drawing board. "We found," Stein lamented, "that industry lives in the present."[54] What Radburn also found was that any town—regardless of its intentions to be self-sufficient—was part of a larger, highly competitive regional network. Radburn's pleasant residential neighborhoods were attractive and could easily compete against other subdivisions. Its industrial lots, however, suffered from significant handicaps which they could not overcome. For most investors seeking a new plant site, Radburn simply did not compare favorably with other locations that offered better access to transportation and the region's centers of population.

In time, Radburn may have surmounted these marketing problems. But if it found itself at a disadvantage in terms of larger regional developments, it would soon find itself overwhelmed by a national economic disaster from which there was no escape—the Great Depression.

13. Clarence S. Stein. The only section of Radburn to have been completed. M.I.T. Press.

The End of the Road

When ground breaking took place at Radburn in 1927, the CHC had all the trappings of a successful corporation. It enjoyed $4 million in assets and an additional $3 million in stocks. John D. Rockefeller was so impressed with the accomplishments of the CHC that he extended the company a $5 million loan, and large financial institutions—such as Equitable Life Assurance and Irving Trust—began to make large amounts of mortgage money available to prospective Sunnyside and Radburn homeowners (once assured that the CHC had guaranteed the first mortgages).[55] Indeed, both communities received national publicity: Sunnyside's success was analyzed at length in well-respected journals across the nation, and the announcement of the construction of Radburn was met with a great deal of interest and anticipation.[56]

When the first residents arrived in January 1929, Radburn was still on track—and so was the CHC. The town plan was praised not only by American public officials and opinion makers, it also proved appealing to the buying public. Not even the initial jolt of the October stock-market crash could set the town off course. Before the end of 1929, 170 single-family homes, 19 two-family homes, and a group of garden apartments with 92 units had all been completed.[57] On the first anniversary of Radburn's opening, the town was home to 202 families and 587 people. This rapid growth prompted the *New York Times* to editorialize that "if Radburn hasn't already received the Census Bureau's prize for the fastest growing community, it ought to be awarded without further delay."[58]

In the dark days of the early Depression, when housing emerged second only to unemployment as a critical national problem, it is not surprising that Radburn's success was greeted with such praise. Its physical design, based on the superblock, was hailed as "automobile proof"; its financial strategy, based on the limited dividend concept, was viewed as "depression-proof."

But the praise was premature. Radburn and the CHC could not weather the Depression's economic storms any more successfully than more conventional developments and developers. Indeed, the CHC may have depended more on continuous economic expansion than other realtors. Its six-percent bonds and stocks were secured largely through the mortgages held by Sunnyside and Radburn home buyers (mortgages often cosigned by the CHC itself). Because these mortgages served as collateral for CHC stocks and bonds, mortgage defaults not only jeopardized the company's primary means of capitalization, it made the company liable for payment as well. For conventional developers, bad times meant bad business and perhaps bankruptcy due to a lack of work. For the CHC, bad times assured bankruptcy because the company was not only a developer but had assumed ultimate responsibility for the payment of many mortgages. At the same time that its revenues were shrinking, the CHC's economic liabilities were rising dramatically. Once the downward spiral of the Depression pulled the CHC into its relentless orbit, it did not take an economic genius to realize that the company had created a formula for disaster.

Indeed the CHC's vulnerable economic state began to appear as early as 1930, when dividends were paid not from earnings but from the company's accumulated surplus. If *Business Week* had known that this state of affairs existed, it might not have been so eager to claim during the same year that the Depression "had practically no effect" upon Radburn's growth.[59] The CHC's depletion of funds accelerated at such a rapid pace that the company experienced its first deficit in 1931—a year in which only sixteen housing units were sold in Radburn. Not even the opening of the much-heralded George Washington Bridge could stem the tide. In 1932, a year after the first vehicles crossed the bridge, only eleven more units were built. In 1933, just ten more houses were added, making for a total of thirty-seven in a three-year span. Clearly, the CHC was on the ropes. In 1934, all construction ceased and the company declared bankruptcy. The road to success had not just reached a roadblock; rather, the entire CHC enterprise had fallen off the precipice into the abyss of the Depression. It was not to survive.[60]

As the CHC's insurmountable problems enveloped the company, words of praise turned to caution and criticism—almost as quickly as the company's fortunes. Just three years before,

the limited dividend concept had been hailed as an effective weapon that could ward off the ills of the Depression. Now it was greeted with skepticism—viewed as a device that may have added to the CHC's economic woes. As one social critic, commenting on the precarious state of the limited dividend concept, said, it "is neither fish, flesh, nor fowl—it's not straight public housing, nor is it cooperative housing nor commercial housing."[61] Or as one irate Sunnyside homeowner, threatened with foreclosure and eviction, proclaimed, "God protect us from the philanthropists—against commercial swindlers we can protect ourselves."[62] In the end, trying to be both capitalistic (profit-making) and socially sensitive (shielding its customers from the vagaries of the marketplace), the CHC could be neither.

A False Pathway to Reform

What does the experience of the CHC tell us about the New York metropolitan region in the 1920s and early 1930s? More importantly, what does it say about the nature of real estate development and social reform in the United States during the twentieth century? What made the garden city such a rising force for such a short time, glistening on the landscape and hailed by diverse groups as a new beginning only to dissipate before it ever had a significant impact?

The New York metropolitan region between the end of World War I and the onset of the Depression represented a unique intellectual and cultural environment in which garden city concepts could be nurtured and developed.[63] National developments, such as the successful efforts to gear the nation's domestic economy to the war effort and postwar emphasis on private initiative and enterprise, helped to shape garden city development in the 1920s. Wartime work on the domestic front gave planning—indeed long-term planning—a legitimacy it could never have achieved on its own, and the conservatism of the postwar period—led by the presidential administrations of Warren Harding, Calvin Coolidge, and Herbert Hoover—assured that if town planning were to take hold, it would have to be within the hands of the private, not public, sector.

Thus a blending of progressive elements (an elevated faith in the value of planning) and conservative elements (a blind commitment to the private sector not unlike what we have witnessed in the 1980s) gave garden city advocates a unique environment in which to flourish. MacKaye, Stein, and other RPAA members may have preferred direct support from the public sector, but they fully realized it was not forthcoming. Bing and the private, limited dividend CHC were the only source of funding available. Without CHC support, RPAA ideas would have remained abstractions. Moreover, because of its semiphilanthropic nature, the company was viewed favorably by conservatives and liberals alike. Here was a group that practiced welfare capitalism—valiantly trying to prove that private investment could turn a profit and meet the nation's social needs as well.

But if such broad-based trends gave the RPAA and CHC a national presence, it was New York City and its metropolitan surroundings that gave them the locale in which to operate. No other city in the United States could have served this purpose as well. First, there was a history of social concern for housing dating back to the mid-nineteenth century. No other American city, except perhaps Philadelphia, displayed the same depth of concern or level of activity. Second, no other city in America matched New York's population, cultural ferment, or intellectual curiosity. As the national center for art and literature, it is not surprising that New York City also proved a conducive environment for garden city ideas—a movement with strong intellectual traditions. Moreover, New York City was the American city with the strongest European ties—which were strengthened on the one hand by the city's literary and artistic interests and, on the other, by its large immigrant population. Whereas other cities might have found the European traditions of the garden city alien to their own sentiments, New York welcomed them as part of its diverse and iconoclastic setting.

If New York had some of the positive attributes that made the garden city an appealing alternative to traditional methods of real estate development, it also had some negative ones that made the concept worthy of consideration. All American cities in the early decades of the twentieth century suffered from poverty and overcrowding, but none to the extent of New York City. Here the numbers alone added to the magnitude of the problem. Just as Howard viewed with disdain the teeming, overpopulated streets of London and Manchester at the turn of the century and envisioned a more humane environment for their citizens, so too did Stein and Mumford in the 1920s look at the streets of Lower Manhattan and conclude that the garden city offered a more attractive alternative for housing the working class.

Indeed, for its advocates, the garden city concept formed a compelling solution to the problems of wealth and poverty that New York City seemed to embody. In the 1920s, the suburbs had not yet overshadowed the center city. The city, in fact, stood supreme as the heart and soul of the metropolis. Aided by a comprehensive plan, such as the garden city, advocates thought that the city, suburb, and hinterland could be melded into an aesthetically pleasing and economic whole. Garden city advocates believed they could step outside the economic system, show a better way, and then draw an increasing number of converts to their cause. For a brief moment, the garden city pilgrimage seemed to be making progress. Ultimately, however, garden city advocates found themselves trapped by the same economic forces that encircled conventional developers, and they emerged from their journey as unwitting victims of dramatic market fluctuations and sweeping economic cycles (although the Depression was more dramatic than most). In the process, they displayed the uniqueness of the New York metropolitan regions but also showed that when it came to forces of economic growth and stagnation, neither they nor New York were that unique at all.

14. *Aerial view of Radburn, c. 1929.*

Notes

1. Ebenezer Howard, *Garden Cities of To-morrow* (Cambridge, Mass.: M.I.T. Press, 1902; reprint, 1965). Members of the Garden Cities Association of America included former Senator Louis Child, who served as president; Episcopal Bishop Henry C. Potter; Ralph Peters, head of the Long Island Rail Road; Christian socialist ministers D. P. Bliss and Josiah Strong; Elgin R. L. Gould, president of the City and Suburban Homes Company; Felix Adler of Columbia University; and New York banker August Belmont. See Daniel Schaffer, *Garden Cities for America: The Radburn Experience* (Philadelphia: Temple University Press, 1982), 32.

2. Howard, *Garden Cities of To-morrow*, 142.

3. For a laudatory description of Letchworth, see C. D. Purdom, *The Letchworth Achievement* (London: J. M. Dent and Sons, 1963). For a balanced scholarly treatment, see Robert Fishman, *Urban Utopias in the Twentieth Century: Ebenezer Howard, Frank Lloyd Wright, and Le Corbusier* (New York: Basic Books, 1977), 64–75.

4. For a brief discussion of the Garden Cities Association of America, see Joseph Arnold, *The New Deal in the Suburbs: A History of the Greenbelt Town Program: 1935–1954* (Columbus: Ohio State University Press, 1971), ch. 1, especially pp. 6–7; Mel Scott, *American City Planning Since 1890* (Berkeley: University of California Press, 1971), 90.

5. For a discussion of the American working-class culture and labor-industrial relations, see Herbert G. Gutman, *Work, Culture, and Society in Industrializing America* (New York: Knopf, 1976). Also see David Brody, *Workers in Industrial America* (New York: Oxford University Press, 1980). For a discussion of the rise of big business, see Alfred D. Chandler, *The Visible Hand: Managerial Revolution in American Business* (Cambridge, Mass.: Belknap, 1977); Glenn Porter, *The Rise of Big Business, 1860–1919* (New York: Crowell, 1973); Samuel P. Hays, *The Response to Industrialism* (Chicago: University of Chicago Press, 1957); and E. C. Kirkland, *Industry Comes of Age: Business, Labor, and Public Policy: 1860–1897* (New York: Rhinehart and Winston, 1961).

6. For a discussion of overcrowding during the turn of the century, see Scott, *American City Planning*, 10. For a general discussion of urban poverty, congestion, and the reform measures proposed to deal with these problems (with special reference to New York), see Roy Lubove, *The Progressive and the Slums: Tenement House Reform in New York City: 1890–1917* (Pittsburgh: University of Pittsburgh Press, 1962).

7. Edward Bellamy, *Looking Backward* (orig. pub. in 1808; Cambridge, Mass.: Belknap Press, 1967).

8. See, for example, Josiah Strong, *Our County* (reprod. of 1891 ed.; Cambridge, Mass.: Belknap Press, 1963). Also see Charles H. Hopkins, *The Rise of the Social Gospel in American Protestantism: 1865–1915* (New Haven: Yale University Press, 1967), and Henry F. May, *Protestant Churches and Industrial America* (orig. pub. 1945; New York: Octagon Books, 1963).

9. See, for example, Robert H. Breamer, *From the Depths: The Discovery of Poverty in the United States* (New York: New York University Press, 1956).

10. For the problems of poverty and housing with particular reference to New York City, see Anthony Jackson, *A Place Called Home* (Cambridge, Mass.: M.I.T. Press, 1976). For a discussion of the New York intellect, see Thomas Bender, *New York Intellect* (New York: Knopf, 1987).

11. For a description and in-depth analysis of the Country Club district in Kansas City, see John Hancock, "John Nolen and the American City Planning Movement: A History of Culture, Change, and Community Response, 1900–1940" (Ph.D. diss., University of Pennsylvania, 1964). For an in-depth look at Kingsport, see Margaret Wolfe, *Kingsport, Tennessee: A Planned American City* (Lexington: University of Kentucky Press, 1987).

12. For a discussion of Forest Hills, see Scott, *American City Planning*, 90–91.

13. Planner and social critic Clarence Perry was responsible for devising the neighborhood unit concept. Its basic elements were embodied in the Forest Hills plan. For a written description of this planning tool, see Perry, "The Neighborhood Unit, a Scheme of Arrangement for the Family-Life Community," in Thomas Adams, ed., *The Regional Survey of New York and Its Environs*, vol. 7 (New York: New York Committee on the Regional Plan of New York and Its Environs, 1924–1931). For a discussion of the context in which Perry's ideas took shape, see Lewis Mumford, *The City in History* (New York: Harcourt, Brace, and World, 1961), 500, and "What Is a City?" *Architectural Record* (November 1937): 59–62.

14. Walter Creese, *The Search for Environment: The Garden City, Before and After* (New Haven: Yale University Press, 1966), 303.

15. For a broad-based discussion of the Progressive Era, see Robert H. Wiebe, *The Search for Order: 1877–1920* (New York: Hill and Wang, 1966). Also see William L. O'Neill, *The Progressive Years: America Comes of Age* (New York: Dodd, Mead, 1975); David M. Kennedy, ed., *Progressivism: The Critical Issues* (Boston: Little, Brown, 1971); Robert M. Crunden, *The Progressives' Achievement in American Civilization: 1889–1920* (New York: Basic Books, 1982).

16. See John Higham, *Strangers in the Land: Patterns of American Nativism, 1860–1925* (New York: Atheneum, 1963). Also see William Preston, *Aliens and Dissenters: Federal Suppression of Radicals* (New York: Harper and Row, 1966; and Robert K. Murray, *The Red Scare: A Study of National Hysteria, 1919–1920* (Minneapolis: University of Minnesota Press, 1955).

17. See Malcolm Cowley, *Exiler's Return* (New York: Norton, 1934); and Alfred Kazin, *On Native Grounds* (New York: Reynal and Hitchcock, 1942).

18. For a discussion of the impact of the role of government during World War I and its continued impact after the war, see William E. Leuchtenburg, *The Perils of Prosperity, 1914–1932*. Also see Ellis W. Hawley, *The Great War and the Search for Modern Order: A History of the American People and Their Institutions* (New York: St. Martin's Press, 1979); and Paul Carter, *Another Part of the Twenties* (New York: Columbia University Press, 1977). For the earliest expression among historians of social and economic continuity between the Progressive Era and the conservative 1920s, see Arthur Link, "What Happened to the Progressive Movement in the 1920s," *American Historical Review* (July 1959): 833–51.

19. Mumford writings are voluminous. Among his more important works on the city and urban planning are *Sticks and Stones* (1924 reprint; New York: Dover, 1955); *The Culture of Cities* (orig. pub. 1938; New York: Harcourt, Brace, and Jovanovich, 1970); *City Development* (New York: Harcourt, Brace, 1945); *The City in History* (New York: Harcourt, Brace, and World, 1961); *The Highway and the City* (New York: Harcourt, Brace, and World, 1963); and *Urban Prospect* (New York: Harcourt, Brace, and World, 1968).

20. MacKaye's writings are limited, but his unique intellectual insight and friendships enabled him to influence planning thoughts and ideas far beyond the reach of his published works. See *The New Exploration: A Philosophy of Regional Planning* (reprint ed., Urbana: University of Illinois Press, 1962); *From Geography to Geotechnics*, ed. Paul T. Bryant (Chicago: University of Illinois Press, 1976).

21. Catherine Bauer Wurster's most noted work in the pre-World War II period was *Modern Housing* (1934 reprint ed.; New York: Arno Press, 1974).

22. Stuart Chase was not as active in the RPAA as some other members. Perhaps his greatest contribution was his ability to popularize the economic and social policies subsequently associated with Franklin D. Roosevelt's New Deal. See *The Tragedy of Waste* (New York: MacMillan, 1925); *Prosperity: Fact or Myth* (New York: Boni, 1930); *Rich Land, Poor Land* (New York: Harper and Brothers, 1935).

23. For an overview of the RPAA, see Carl Sussman, ed., *Planning the Fourth Migration* (Cambridge, Mass.: M.I.T. Press, 1976). Many of these articles originally appeared in a special edition of *Survey Graphic* 54 (May 1, 1925).

24. For a brief, but insightful, discussion of the RPAA's development and its organizational strengths and weaknesses, see Roy Lubove, *Community Planning in the 1920s: The Contribution of the Regional Planning Association of America* (Pittsburgh: University of Pittsburgh Press, 1962).

25. RPAA members Clarence Stein, Henry Wright, Lewis Mumford, Benton MacKaye, and Frederick L. Ackerman all published extensively in the *Journal of the American Institute of Architects*. Their contributions have led one historian to describe the *JAIA* as "one of the liveliest technical publications in the period." See Park Dixon Goist, "The City as Organism: Two Recent American Theories of the City" (Ph.D. diss., University of Rochester, 1967), 324.

26. See Frederick L. Ackerman, "The Significance of England's Program of Building Workmen's Houses," *Journal of the American Institute of Architects* 5 (November 1917): 539.

27. See Lewis Mumford, "The Heritage of the Cities Movement in America: An Historical Survey," *Journal of the American Institute of Architects* 7 (August 1919): 349–54.

28. See Benton MacKaye, "An Appalachian Trail: A Project in Regional Planning," *Journal of the American Institute of Architects* 9 (October 1921): 15.

29. See New York, Reconstruction Commission, Housing Committee, Report on Housing Conditions (Albany, March 26, 1920). Also see Clarence S. Stein, "Amsterdam—Old and New," *Journal of the American Institute of Ar-*

chitects 10 (October 1922): 310–27. For a historical evaluation of the committee's work, see Lubove, *Community Planning*.

30. For a description of the recommendations of the New York Commission on Housing and Regional Planning, see New York, Commission on Housing and Regional Planning, Leg. Doc. 1926, *Permanent Housing Relief*. Also see Clarence Stein, "Housing the People," *The Nation* 122 (March 10, 1926): 246, "Housing New York's Two-Thirds," *The Survey* 51 (February 15, 1924): 509–10, and "The Housing Crisis in New York," *The Survey* 44 (September 1, 1920): 652–62.

31. See Lewis Mumford, "A Modest Man's Enduring Contributions to Urban and Regional Planning," *Journal of the American Institute of Architects* 65 (December 1976): 20.

32. Other prominent reformers in early efforts to improve housing conditions for America's working class were Lawrence Veiller and Robert W. de Forest. For an excellent detailed discussion of housing reform during the late nineteenth and early twentieth centuries (with special attention to the problems of housing reform in New York City, see Roy Lubove, *The Progressives and the Slums* (Pittsburgh: University of Pittsburgh Press, 1962). Also see Scott, *American City Planning*, especially 7–12. For a critical view of planning's avoidance of housing issues, see Peter Marcuse, "Housing in Early City Planning," *Journal of Urban History* 6 (February 1990): 153–76. For critical assessments of why efforts to produce low-cost housing have failed, see Lawrence M. Friedman, *Government and Slum Housing: A Century of Frustration* (Chicago: Rand McNally, 1968); and Jackson, *A Place Called Home*.

33. Lubove, *The Progressives and the Slums*, 37.

34. *1980 Census Bureau of Population, Characteristics of the Population*, vol. 7 (Washington, D.C.: U.S. Department of Commerce, Bureau of the Census, 1980), Table 171, 134–929.

35. Richard T. Ely, "The City Housing Corporation and Sunnyside," *Journal of Land and Public Utility Economics* 2 (April 1926): 184.

36. See Rosiland Tough, "Production Costs of Urban Land in Sunnyside, Long Island," *Journal of Land and Public Utility Economics* 8 (February 1932): 49.

37. Clarence S. Stein, "Radburn and the Radburn Idea," unpub. ms., August 19, 1943, Stein papers, Olin Library, Cornell University, Ithaca, New York.

38. Henry Wright, Sr., *Rehousing America* (New York: Columbia University Press, 1935), 75; Lewis Mumford, "Houses—Sunnyside-Up," *The Nation* 120 (February 4, 1925): 115–16; Clarence S. Stein, "A New Venture in Housing," *American City* 32 (March 1925): 277–81.

39. Alexander Bing, "Sunnyside Gardens: A Successful Experiment in Good Housing at Moderate Prices," *Municipal Review* 15 (June 1926): 335.

40. City Housing Corporation promotional pamphlets, Stein papers, Cornell University: "Your Share in Better Housing" and "Sunnyside and the Housing Problem," April 1924; and "Brick Garden Homes at Madison Court," June 1927.

41. Lewis Mumford to Daniel Schaffer, October 27, 1977.

42. Bing, "Sunnyside Gardens," 2.

43. City Housing Corporation promotional pamphlet, Stein papers, Cornell University, "Expert Opinion," April 15, 1928.

44. The City Housing Corporation hired a real estate firm from nearby Hackensack, New Jersey, to bid secretly on the land. The company feared that if local residents learned of the project's magnitude, they would demand a higher price for their land. See Schaffer, *Garden Cities for America*, 147–48.

45. See Geddes Smith, "A Town for the Motor Age," *Survey* 59 (March 1, 1928): 695.

46. Clarence Stein, *Toward New Towns for America* (Cambridge, Mass.: M.I.T. Press, 1973), 17.

47. For the most comprehensive description of Radburn's physical design elements, see Stein, *Toward New Towns*, especially ch. 2.

48. For a brilliant discussion of Henry Ford and the American Dream, see Warren I. Sussman, *Culture as History: The Transformation of American Society in the Twentieth Century* (New York: Pantheon Books, 1984), 131–41. For a discussion of Ford's impact on American manufacturing and the nation's landscape, see Kenneth T. Jackson, *Crabgrass Frontier: The Suburbanization of the United States* (New York: Oxford University Press, 1985), especially 160–63. Also see David L. Lewis, *The Public Image of Henry Ford: An American Folk Hero and His Company* (Detroit: Wayne State University Press, 1976); Reynold M. Wik, *Henry Ford and Grassroots America* (Ann Arbor: University of Michigan Press, 1972); and the classic account of

Allan Nevins and Frank Ernest Hill, *Ford: Expansion and Challenge* (New York: Arno Press, 1954; repr. 1976).

49. For the best account of spatial arrangements in nineteenth-century urban America, see Sam Bass Warner, Jr., *Streetcar Suburbs: The Process of Growth in Boston, 1870–1900* (New York: Atheneum, 1974), and *The Private City: Philadelphia in Three Periods of Its Growth* (Philadelphia: University of Pennsylvania Press, 1968).

50. For a discussion of the growing spatial segregation of residential and living quarters during the nineteenth century, see Henry Binford, *The First Suburbs: Residential Communities on the Boston Periphery, 1815–1860* (Chicago: University of Chicago Press, 1985).

51. See Jackson, *Crabgrass Frontier*, especially ch. 9–15.

52. For a more detailed discussion of Radburn's unfulfilled desires to attract industry and commerce, see Stein, *Toward New Towns*, ch. 2; and Schaffer, *Garden Cities for America*, 159–61.

53. The lowest-priced house in Radburn was seventy percent more than the cheapest Sunnyside house. Thus in terms of fulfilling the garden city's social mandate for mixed income groups, Radburn represented a step backward not forward. The first survey of Radburn homeowners, conducted in 1933, showed that eighty-seven percent of the men had some college education and that almost all of them held white-collar or professional jobs. For the prices of houses in Radburn, see Louis Brownlow, "New Town Planned for the Motor Age," *International Housing and Town Planning Bulletin* (February 1930): 4–11. For Radburn's demographic composition in the early stages of development, see Robert Bowman Hudson, *Radburn: A Plan for Living* (New York: American Association for Adult Education, 1934).

54. Stein, *Toward New Towns*, 39.

55. *Fourth Annual Report to Stockholders of the City Housing Corporation* (New York: City Housing Corporation, 1927), Radburn Papers, Radburn Library, Fair Lawn, New Jersey. Also interview with Charles Ascher, conducted by author, December 1, 1977, New York City.

56. On Sunnyside, see for example, Ely, "The City Housing Corporation and Sunnyside"; Lewis Mumford, "Houses: Sunnyside Up," *The Nation* 120 (February 4, 1925); Rosiland Tough, "Production Costs"; and Clarence S. Stein, "A New Venture in Housing," *American City* 32 (March 1925). On Radburn, see for example, Henry M. Propper, "Construction Work Now Under Way on the 'Town for the Motor Age,'" *American City* 39 (October 1928); Smith, "A Town for the Motor Age"; *New York Times*, April 27, 1930, section 12 ("Real Estate"), 12; *New York Times*, May 26, 1930, 20.

57. *Eighth Annual Report to Stockholders of the City Housing Corporation* (New York: City Housing Corporation, 1931), Radburn papers; *Ninth Annual Report to Stockholders of the City Housing Corporation* (New York: City Housing Corporation, 1932), Radburn papers; Tenth Annual Report to Stockholders of the City Housing Corporation (New York: City Housing Corporation, 1933), Radburn papers.

58. *New York Times*, April 27, 1930, section 12 ("Real estate"), 12.

59. *Business Week*, July 9, 1930, 2.

60. Eighth, ninth, and tenth *Annual Reports to Stockholders of the City Housing Corporation*, (1931, 1932, and 1933), Radburn papers.

61. Loula D. Lasker, "Sunnyside Up and Down," *Survey Graphic* 25 (July 1936): 441.

62. Benjamin Ginzburg, "Sunnyside Back and Forth," *Survey Graphic* (August 1936): 496.

63. For an insightful treatment of New York's unique intellectual environment, see Bender, *The New York Intellect*.

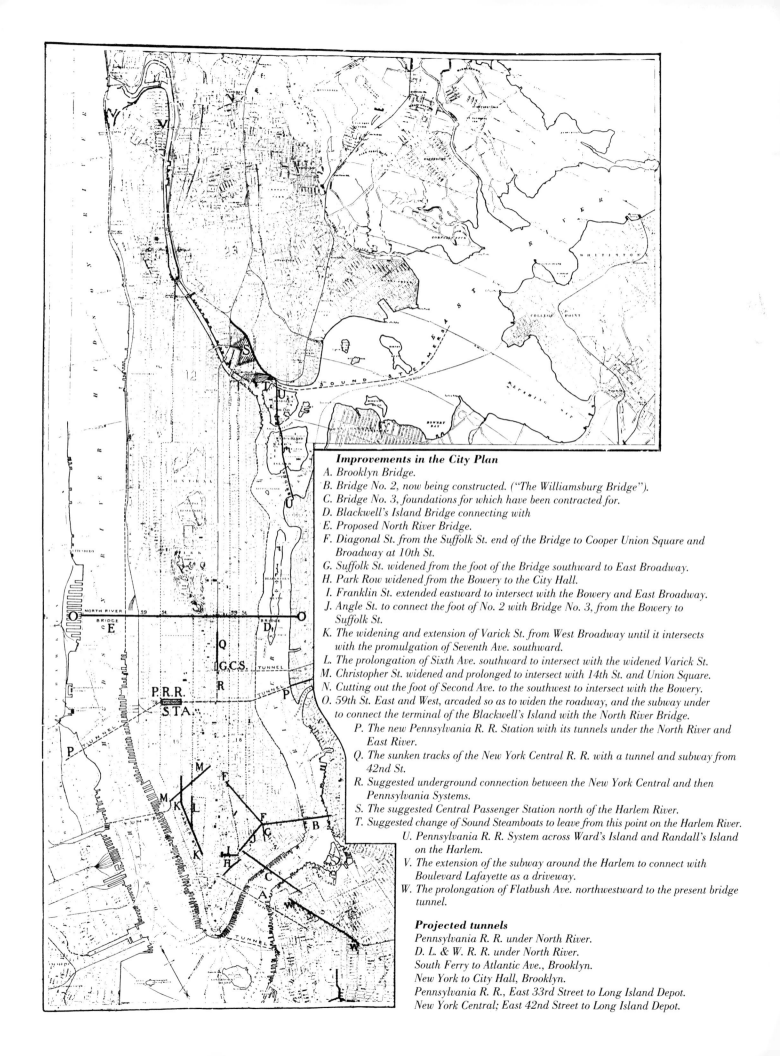

Improvements in the City Plan

A. Brooklyn Bridge.

B. Bridge No. 2, now being constructed. ("The Williamsburg Bridge").

C. Bridge No. 3, foundations for which have been contracted for.

D. Blackwell's Island Bridge connecting with

E. Proposed North River Bridge.

F. Diagonal St. from the Suffolk St. end of the Bridge to Cooper Union Square and Broadway at 10th St.

G. Suffolk St. widened from the foot of the Bridge southward to East Broadway.

H. Park Row widened from the Bowery to the City Hall.

I. Franklin St. extended eastward to intersect with the Bowery and East Broadway.

J. Angle St. to connect the foot of No. 2 with Bridge No. 3, from the Bowery to Suffolk St.

K. The widening and extension of Varick St. from West Broadway until it intersects with the promulgation of Seventh Ave. southward.

L. The prolongation of Sixth Ave. southward to intersect with the widened Varick St.

M. Christopher St. widened and prolonged to intersect with 14th St. and Union Square.

N. Cutting out the foot of Second Ave. to the southwest to intersect with the Bowery.

O. 59th St. East and West, arcaded so as to widen the roadway, and the subway under to connect the terminal of the Blackwell's Island with the North River Bridge.

P. The new Pennsylvania R. R. Station with its tunnels under the North River and East River.

Q. The sunken tracks of the New York Central R. R. with a tunnel and subway from 42nd St.

R. Suggested underground connection between the New York Central and then Pennsylvania Systems.

S. The suggested Central Passenger Station north of the Harlem River.

T. Suggested change of Sound Steamboats to leave from this point on the Harlem River.

U. Pennsylvania R. R. System across Ward's Island and Randall's Island on the Harlem.

V. The extension of the subway around the Harlem to connect with Boulevard Lafayette as a driveway.

W. The prolongation of Flatbush Ave. northwestward to the present bridge tunnel.

Projected tunnels

Pennsylvania R. R. under North River.

D. L. & W. R. R. under North River.

South Ferry to Atlantic Ave., Brooklyn.

New York to City Hall, Brooklyn.

Pennsylvania R. R., East 33rd Street to Long Island Depot.

New York Central; East 42nd Street to Long Island Depot.

Going in Style: The Architecture of Transportation in the Glory Days of Metropolitanism

Robert A. M. Stern

Robert A. M. Stern, a practicing architect, writer, and teacher, is principal in the firm of Robert A. M. Stern Architects. Professor of architecture at Columbia University, he served as the first director of the Temple Hoyne Buell Center for the Study of American Architecture. He is the author of many publications on architectural subjects, including New Directions in American Architecture; George Howe: Toward a Modern American Architecture; New York 1900; New York 1930; *and* Pride of Place, *the companion book to his eight-part documentary television series on American architecture.*

Architects, historians, and the general public share a fascination with the turning point of the nineteenth into the twentieth century. Most widely known by French designations—*fin de siècle* and *La Belle Epoque*—the period is sometimes referred to in America as the Mauve Decades.[1] Much of the allure of that time is surely rooted in nostalgia, an appropriate attitude for the era of Marcel Proust, Henry James, and Edith Wharton. Yet the reasons for our fascination are much more complex than mere sentimentality. The simultaneous presence of cultural unity and heterogeneity ensure the durability of the great metropolises of 1900 as cultural artifacts. In short, we look back to turn-of-the-century London, Paris, Brussels, Barcelona, Vienna, Berlin, and New York in order to better understand their urbanism and to establish a standard against which to measure our own era.[2]

Unlike most great metropolises, which are political capitals, New York City achieved its stature purely on the basis of its geographical advantages, the energy of its citizenry, and the vision of its entrepreneurs and their artists and architects. New York is such a central force in American thought that we tend to think it has always been a major metropolis, but, in fact, its preeminence only dates from the latter half of the nineteenth century, when its great year-round port and splendid water and rail connections to the interior of the continent made it a center of both national and international commerce.

New York began to assume this position around 1876. Enriched by the Civil War and Reconstruction, the city was in the thrall of a period of staggering economic and physical growth. Caught up in the burst of activity that followed America's centennial, New York artists and architects possessed a sense of both a lost past and a bountiful future. They fiercely sought to transform the cultural and commercial programs of the day into glorious monuments commensurate with those of the past.[3]

As the nation fully entered into an imperial age in the final decade of the nineteenth century, marked by territorial expansion abroad—the acquisition of protectorates in the Caribbean and South Pacific—so too did its leading city, annexing whole sections of the mainland, the villages that constituted Queens County on Long Island and Staten Island and joining with its sister city Brooklyn to form Greater New York in 1898. The event "touched public pride," Herbert Croly observed, and resulted in an "awakening of municipal vanity."[4] Faced with the consequences of virtually uncontrolled growth, New Yorkers developed a sensitivity to the environment, fostering the development of a hitherto virtually unrecognized concept of city planning and a demand that each new work of architecture express civic pride and purpose. For a contemporary writer in *Harper's Monthly*, the new awareness demonstrated "the transition from individualism to civicism as the vital force."[5]

The era's heightened sense of civicism was given vivid architectural representation in the design of transportation facilities, which were, perhaps more than any other, a democratic building type that could be used and enjoyed by the broadest cross section of society; the great train stations, subway sys-

1. Map of turn-of-the-century transportation projects. Avery Library, Columbia University.

111

2. Bradford Gilbert. Grand Central Terminal, north side of 42nd Street at Park Avenue, 1898–1900. View from north with exposed train tracks. Museum of the City of New York.

3. Reed & Stem and Warren & Wetmore. Grand Central Terminal, north side of 42nd Street at Park Avenue, 1903–13. View from 42nd Street. Museum of the City of New York.

4. Reed & Stem and Warren & Wetmore. Grand Central Terminal, north side of 42nd Street at Park Avenue, 1903–13. Perspective from north showing property available for air-rights development. Museum of the City of New York.

5. Reed & Stem and Warren & Wetmore. Grand Central Terminal, north side of 42nd Street at Park Avenue, 1903–13. Concourse. Museum of the City of New York.

6. Reed & Stem and Warren & Wetmore. Grand Central Terminal, north side of 42nd Street at Park Avenue, 1903–13. Concourse detail. Museum of the City of New York.

2

3

4

tems, and bridges were designed not simply to allow movement through the city but to celebrate it. Synthesizing the high Roman-inspired classicism of the so-called American Renaissance and the urbanistic ambitions of the City Beautiful movement with the most recent advances in technology, architects in turn-of-the-century New York translated unprecedented problems of engineering into symbolic gateways of the metropolitan city.[6]

Grand Central Terminal (1903–13) and Pennsylvania Station (1906–10) achieved an appropriate sense of public place through a remarkable reconciliation of innovative planning, traditional architectural form, and modern production techniques. The two railroad stations, as the historian Carl Condit has observed, "from their conspicuous architectural features to their hidden elements, possessed a grandeur and a power that placed them in the front rank of modern technical-artistic achievements. They are . . . the greatest architectural-engineering works ever undertaken in the United States. They are the centerpieces of a rail and waterway network of unprecedented magnitude and complexity."[7]

5

6

The present Grand Central Terminal is the second building on the site between Vanderbilt and Lexington avenues, 42nd and 45th streets. The original was erected in 1871, at the time of the consolidation of the New York Central lines. From 1898 to 1900, the station was extensively renovated and enlarged, although its inherent functional and symbolic inadequacies were still apparent. Plans were already under way for its replacement when a serious accident in the steam-filled Park Avenue tunnel leading to the terminal occurred on January 22, 1902, killing seventeen passengers and prompting the state to pass a law requiring the railroad to electrify its track south of the Harlem River. But the decision to build a new station was neither completely altruistic nor functionally determined, since New York Central management realized that the impending tunnel construction under the Hudson River by the rival Philadelphia Railroad would seriously challenge their dominance of the lucrative New York market.[8] The railroad's management also realized that by electrifying their trackage, they could build above the train yards and thus realize a tremendous profit in real estate, creating on their extensive holdings a new urban center that would rival in size and convenience New York's historic downtown financial district.

The genius behind the technological innovations of the New Grand Central was William J. Wilgus, Central Hudson's chief engineer, who formulated the concept that would result in the fullest exploitation of electrified trackage—the use of the land above the right-of-way as an economic resource. Railroad tracks that were usually open or partially covered, allowing the trains' steam to escape, could now be placed within fully closed tunnels. Wilgus also contributed the two-tiered "bunkbed" system of tracks, dividing the terminal into suburban and express levels. By January 15, 1903, sufficient data were prepared under Wilgus's direction for the railroad to solicit design proposals from a number of architects, including McKim, Mead & White of New York, Daniel Burnham of Chicago and Reed & Stem of Saint Paul, Minnesota. McKim, already involved with the Pennsylvania Station design, passed the job of preparing the firm's submission to Stanford White, who proposed a fourteen-story building supporting a sixty-story tower.[9] Crowned by a jet of steam driven three hundred feet in the air and illuminated red at night, the tower would have been the world's tallest and the city's most prominent landmark—if it had been built. White's idea of combining an office building with a railroad station was an innovation. In England, large hotels had frequently been built as part of the terminal head house, but White, recognizing the advantages of electricity over steam, saw the possibilities for a vast, revenue-producing office building placed squarely above the station's tracks.

Reed & Stem were selected as winners of the competition, but after their plan and design were approved by the city in June 1903 they were "persuaded" by William K. Vanderbilt, chairman of the board of the New York Central, to relinquish their role as chief designers to Vanderbilt's cousin, Whitney Warren, and his partner, Charles D. Wetmore. In the final design of Grand Central, Reed & Stem contributed the articulation of Grand Central's elaborate circulation system, but it was unquestionably Whitney Warren who raised the complex to the level of compelling civic art.[10]

The main facade was one of the glories of the modern French classical style in America. The three arched portals flanked by attached columns were clearly a triple repetition of the Arc du Triomphe du Carrousel at the Louvre in Paris and served as a symbolic triumphal arch for the railroad. Although Warren derived the elements of the composition from the Arc du Carrousel, he vastly increased their size while reducing the amount of detail. The seemingly overblown scale of the arches allowed the architecture to hold its own as an urban monument above the encircling traffic. At the same time, the exterior scale prepared the observer for the monumental interior space. For the passengers entering the terminal from the street, the dramatic architectural sequence surpassed that of even the most monumental government buildings. From 42nd Street, the spacious, low entrance portals swept into the bright vertical release of the main waiting room and down to the cavernous Grand Concourse, which could be best appreciated from the head of an intricately planned marble staircase on the Vanderbilt Avenue side that descended from a broad interior terrace to the bustling floor below.

Though a railroad terminal is in fact a point of arrival and departure, the Grand Concourse was conceived as a destination:[11] it is New York's Piazza San Marco. Marrying classical architecture and the American obsession with convenience, the concourse internalizes the outdoor stage of the European public life, protecting hordes of people from the extremes of New York's harsh climate. Though traditional in its language, Grand Central is a quintessentially modern building. The stone-clad steel frames of towering piers screen a Piranesian ramp system that guides the traveler down from street-level entrances to the double level of tracks. The piers rise up powerfully without capitals to support a large but simply articulated entablature crowned by a modern egg-and-dart cornice that skillfully integrates the spotlights needed to illuminate the ceiling. Once planned to be punctuated by skylights, the ceiling is a blue vault painted with the constellations of the zodiac that are drawn as though one were looking down from the heavens rather than up to them.

Reed & Stem's decision to elevate the central pavilion and its surrounding roadway was a stroke of genius. It was, however, initially abandoned by Warren, who called for the terminal and an adjacent office building to be set back behind a plaza facing 42nd Street, with a second major square along its east facade on the future site of the Commodore Hotel. But the need to accommodate the traffic on Park Avenue and not impede its flow toward the developing neighborhood above 42nd Street caused Warren to adopt Reed & Stem's initial plan. The viaduct was completed in 1919,[12] but the system connecting northern and southern Park Avenue was not finished until 1928, when the final link was incorporated into Warren & Wetmore's twenty-eight-story tower for the New York Central Company, with two giant portals accommodating ramps to raise the Park Avenue traffic to the level of the viaduct.[13]

Grand Central is a consummately urban megastructure: the terminal recreates, in miniature, a version of the city as a whole. It presents the traveler with a tempting variety of diversions, including stores, restaurants, and even a bowling alley. Nearly as brilliant as the design of the building and its circulation system was Wilgus's concept for the development of air rights over the covered railroad tracks to the east, west, and north of the terminal. Rather than create isolated properties, Wilgus punctuated a network of buildings with below-grade passageways connecting the buildings with each other and with the station and the newly completed subway system as well. Thus, the buildings constituted a coherent entity called Terminal City. Although never realized in full, by 1931, Terminal City included a post office, two hotels, a YMCA, private clubs, a major exhibition facility (Grand Central Palace), and office buildings. At the core of the development was a bold conception of Park Avenue freed from the deleterious effects of belching steam and transformed into a broad boulevard with a mall through its center wide enough for pedestrians to stroll along a walkway bordered by greenery. The avenue was initially intended to be flanked by continuous blocks of five-story buildings that served as bases for thirteen-story towers to be set back a distance from the street. These height controls were supplanted by those of the zoning ordinance of 1916, which produced a nearly uniform cornice at the thirteenth story along the entire length of the avenue and transformed it into one of the clearest, most consistent reflections of Hausmannesque urbanism in America.[14]

Pennsylvania Station was not blessed with Grand Central's dynamic location. Occupying the blocks bound by Seventh and Eighth avenues, 31st and 33rd streets, it was seen, from the first, as a shot in the arm for a rather dreary neighborhood; together with the General Post Office at its rear, it was expected to foster a new civic center in the west-midtown area.[15] Aside from the hotel that the railroad built and operated on Seventh Avenue, and the department stores and hotels that clustered at nearby Herald Square, the neighborhood languished. But while its location robbed Pennsylvania Station of its higher potential as an urban focus, McKim, Mead & White's extraor-

7

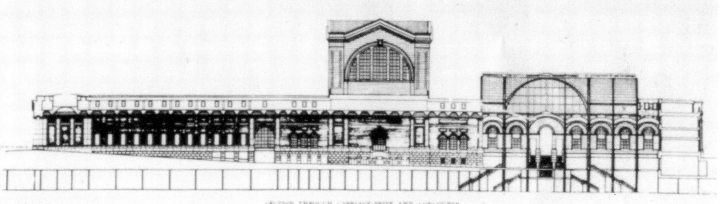

SECTION THROUGH CARRIAGE-DRIVE AND CONCOURSE

8

7. McKim, Mead & White,
Pennsylvania Station. Seventh to
Eighth avenues between 31st and
33rd streets, 1904–10. View from
the northeast. Museum of the City
of New York.

8. McKim, Mead & White,
Pennsylvania Station. Seventh to
Eighth avenues between 31st and
33rd streets, 1904–10. Section
through Carriage Drive and
Concourse. Avery Library,
Columbia University.

9

10

11

dinarily integrative design created a convincing monument for the railroad and the city it served.[16]

Electrification allowed McKim to transform the characteristic symbol of its nineteenth-century predecessors, the vast, glazed shed, into a concourse in which natural light bathed passengers as they descended to the trains a level below. McKim juxtaposed the glazed concourse with a neoclassical waiting room loosely based on the Baths of Caracalla in Rome. Montgomery Schuyler and others criticized the two different styles of the concourse and the waiting room, calling them contradictory,[17] but they could also be seen as an explicit statement of McKim's belief in the continuity of classical form.

McKim wrapped both halls in a low monumental building that formed a perimeter wall around the large block.[18] The waiting room rose above the center of the block, while the concourse sat in a glazed court between the waiting room and the low building on Eighth Avenue. The passage from Seventh Avenue to the waiting room and concourse was a long, carefully modulated system of arcades and corridors that provided a sequence of spaces varying from low to high, narrow to wide, as circulation patterns required swift movement or allowed relaxation. Very clear on paper, and eloquent to those familiar with the station, the sequence was confusing to weary travelers such as Arnold Bennett, the English novelist, who is said to have remarked that "everything could be found there except the trains."[19] But the traveler arriving by taxi found the station uniquely convenient, with covered ramps (one for arriving and one for departing passengers) descending from the two Seventh Avenue corners to the level of the waiting room. The implication that these sunken drives were the canals of the new automobile-oriented city was made explicit by the Venetian-style bridges that carried pedestrians into the building at its midpoint.

To some observers, the station was more than an essential part of a vast transportation system or even a symbolic gateway to the city: it took on the timeless quality of a work of nature. In his novel of 1940, *You Can't Go Home Again*, Thomas Wolfe wrote: "The station . . . was murmurous with the immense and distant sound of time. . . . It had the murmur of a distant sea, the languorous lapse and flow of waters on a beach. It was elemental, detached, indifferent to the lives of men. They contributed to it as drops of rain contribute to a river that draws its flood and movement majestically from great depths, out of purple hills at evening."[20]

The critical presence of the railroad industry in New York resulted in two of its most significant architectural landmarks, but, by and large, the effect of the railroads on the cityscape was devastating, particularly along the west side of Manhattan where freight operations effectively cut off all other activities of the city from the Hudson River waterfront. In 1873, the problem was somewhat ameliorated by Frederick Law Olmsted's plans for Riverside Park, which ensured that the development above 72nd Street would be residential in character. Olmsted's great winding boulevard, Riverside Drive, created a superbly defined edge to the island's Upper West Side; below it, running down to the shorefront railroad tracks, Riverside Park effectively blocked out the sights, if not the sounds, of the belching steam locomotives and rattling freight cars.

In 1885, the city absorbed Twelfth Avenue into Riverside Park and first considered building a waterside roadway on reclaimed land beyond the railroad tracks.[21] As designed by the architect Leopold Eidlitz, the boldly conceived roadway was modeled on London's Rotten Row through Hyde Park's planting; the new roadway was to be built on landfill, the railroad tracks in part roofed over and elsewhere crossed by bridges.[22] The use of landfill to solve problems of development by a process of expansion rather than renewal has been a pattern characteristic of Manhattan since the time of the Dutch, whose influence on the city's urbanism was far greater than the succeeding English colonists.

In 1899 Milton See proposed a more ambitious scheme for what would become known as the West Side Improvement Project. See sought to remedy the inherent limitations of Olmsted's compromises by extending a four-hundred-foot-wide terrace across the tracks from 72nd Street north to Spuyten Duyvil. The new terrace was to be treated not as an extension of Olmsted's naturalistic parkscape but "as a great Italian garden," formally planted and edged with classicizing arcades and balusters.[23] At 116th Street, See suggested an interior lagoon and boat landing for official visitors to the city, with a tree-lined boulevard passing across McKim's new campus for Columbia University and connecting Riverside and Morningside parks. The location of the lagoon foreshadowed the site and program intended for the Robert Fulton Memorial in 1909, another City Beautiful project to conceal the railroad.

In 1913, Arnold W. Brunner and Olmsted submitted a plan for Riverside Drive's extension.[24] As originally laid out, Riverside Drive continued into Boulevard Lafayette, which unlike the Drive was to be flanked on both sides by buildings. Brunner and Olmsted proposed to modify the sharpest curves of Boulevard Lafayette and called for the use of all properties to the west of the roadway, with the exception of the railroad tracks, as parkland. They also urged that the northern tip of Manhattan be acquired as the site of a monumental public building.

Little progress was made on remedying the problem of the railroad for decades. In 1917 the city and the railroad seemed close to an agreement to enhance Riverside Park by covering the railroad's right-of-way in exchange for adding more tracks and to remove the tracks from the city streets below 72nd Street, where the railroad's presence was even more untenable and stymied the entire neighborhood's development; negotiations broke down and no action was taken. By the mid-1920s, when the midtown section of the city had developed into a second business center as complex and congested as Wall Street at the island's tip, Eleventh Avenue, which had a railroad track down much of its length, had come to be known as Death Avenue. So numerous were accidents that a mounted policeman known as the railroad cowboy was employed to herd pedestrian and automobile traffic clear of oncoming trains, which also ran along portions of Tenth and Twelfth avenues,

12

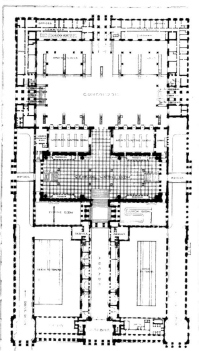

13

9. *McKim, Mead & White. Pennsylvania Station, Seventh to Eighth avenues between 31st and 33rd streets, 1904–10. Waiting room.* New-York Historical Society.

10. *McKim, Mead & White. Pennsylvania Station, Seventh to Eighth avenues between 31st and 33rd streets, 1904–10. Concourse.* New-York Historical Society.

11. *McKim, Mead & White. Pennsylvania Station, Seventh to Eighth avenues between 31st and 33rd streets, 1904–10. Arcade.* Avery Library, Columbia University.

12. *McKim, Mead & White. Pennsylvania Station, Seventh to Eighth avenues between 31st and 33rd streets, 1904–10. Pedestrian bridge over Carriage Drive.* Museum of the City of New York.

13. *McKim, Mead & White. Pennsylvania Station, Seventh to Eighth avenues between 31st and 33rd streets, 1904–10. Plan at street level.* Avery Library, Columbia University.

117

and West, Canal, and Hudson streets. In 1927, construction began on an elevated highway, but the Stock Market Crash of 1929 and the ensuing economic collapse soon halted its progress. It was not until 1932, through the financial and administrative wizardry of Robert Moses, that construction resumed.[25] By 1936, Moses had completed the West Side Improvement, which extended along the entire length of Manhattan. Below 72nd Street, an elevated highway embellished with modern classical decoration brilliantly carried forward turn-of-the-century civic ideals, marrying engineering and architecture. Above 72nd Street, Riverside Park was extended over the railroad, realizing a dream of more than fifty years but ironically throwing up a new barrier to the water in the form of the roadway itself.

At the same time that railroad electrification stimulated significant changes in Manhattan's architecture and urbanism, perhaps its most profound effect was the extension of New York's metropolitanism to previously unimagined limits. The New York, New Haven & Hartford, New York Central, and Long Island railroads electrified their lines to the suburban counties—Westchester, Fairfield, Bergen, and, on Long Island, Nassau—and substantially improved their lines within the as yet largely underdeveloped outer boroughs of the city by eliminating grade crossings and establishing commuter stations in the Bronx and Queens.[26] The improvements brought vast new areas within easy reach of midtown and served to diminish Manhattan's role as a self-sufficient entity.[27]

Impressive though all of the rail termini and their feeder lines were, no rail improvement did as much to transform the city as construction of the subway system, the first segment of which opened in 1904. The scale of the city had begun to change in the early 1870s, when the Ninth Avenue Elevated railway began service, although it was not until 1878 that the Third Avenue Elevated, the first full-fledged, two-track, trunk line, commenced operation between lower Manhattan and Yorkville, then a sleepy country village at 86th Street. While the "Els" relieved congestion, they brought blight with them. The noise and steam from the locomotives, and the darkened streets beneath them, were widely criticized.

The era of elevated railroading reached its peak in 1903, when electrified service was extended along the full length of the east and west sides of Manhattan and into the Bronx and Brooklyn, but the subsequent completion of the first phase of the Interborough Rapid Transit (IRT) subway system soon demonstrated the superiority of underground transportation. The IRT subway had been foreshadowed as early as 1870, when Alfred Ely Beach opened an unusual and short-lived public underground transportation system that was powered by pneumatic air and ran under a section of lower Broadway.[28] But even if the city's political machine had not stopped Beach in order to preserve its own control of the city's existing public transportation, it is doubtful that his pneumatic air system would have proven practical.

In 1899, the Rapid Transit Commission agreed on a subway route proposed by William Barclay Parsons.[29] On February 24, 1900, the city signed a contract with the railway company and ground was broken by Mayor Van Wyck and the socially prominent financier August Belmont, president of the Interborough Rapid Transit Company, in March 1900.[30] The first phase of the subway was completed on October 27, 1904, and ran from City Hall up Fourth Avenue to Grand Central, across to Times Square, then north along Broadway to 145th Street.[31] Later in the year, one section was extended to 157th Street and Broadway and another to 145th Street and Lenox Avenue. By 1906, it would extend its full length along Broadway to Kingsbridge and under the Harlem River as far as 180th Street in the Bronx, and by 1908, to Brooklyn Heights.

While the subway was never conceived of as a major civic ornament, considerable emphasis was placed on the embellishment of the stations, viaducts, and rolling stock. The subway's most outstanding architectural elements were the small street-level kiosks. As designed by the architects Heins & LaFarge, most stations had steel and glass kiosks with a distinctly Parisian character, although they reflected the taste of the Beaux-Arts baroque rather than the art nouveau of Hector Guimard's Metro.[32] Some stations along Broadway—Bowling Green, 72nd, 96th, 103rd, and 116th streets—were built with more substantial control houses of brick and stone that were set like garden pavilions in the avenue's landscaped median strip. These may have been influenced by the elaborate station houses that Otto Wagner designed for the Vienna Stadtbahn between 1894 and 1901.[33]

The design of the stations hardly approached the quality of earlier examples in Paris and Vienna, but most observers did not seem to notice. M. G. Cuniff, writing in *World's Work*, extolled that "For once in a great practical municipal undertaking, beauty had been made an important element in the work . . . the decorations in Rookwood pottery, faience, and marble as well as tiling used in unprecedented quantities, offer a kaleidoscopic variety of color."[34] Yet soon enough, the station's inadequacies were apparent, even to such loyal boosters as the editors of the *Real Estate Record and Guide*: "The experience of a week of subway operations has proved one defect beyond peradventure. The stations and their approaches have not been made as spacious as they should have been . . . the subway should have been designed to handle much larger crowds than the existing stations and their approaches can possibly accommodate."[35]

The handling of the subway stations revealed an intense struggle for architectural expression between the engineers and the architects. The posts along the platform's edge were transformed into columns through a subtle manipulation of the profile at the base and capital, and the ceiling panel of each structural bay was relieved by wide ornamental moldings and rosettes. The walls of each station were carefully articulated in panels of glazed tile and terra cotta, with specially designed decorative panels made for each station depicting a historic building or event that would help the passengers (many of whom did not read English) identify the stations. The plaques at Fulton Street depicted the steamship *Clermont*, Grand Central had a New York Central locomotive, Columbus Circle, the *Santa Maria*, and so on. Unfortunately, as the *American Architect and Building News* quickly pointed out, the plaques as well as the station name panels were "placed where they are of least advantage to those who most need to consult them, the people in the cars."[36] The City Hall station, without doubt the line's grandest architectural statement, was vaulted over in Guastavino tile with the ribs between the vaults sheathed in contrasting glazed tile.

The civic sense evident in the new subway stations also characterized the design of the IRT powerhouse (1900–02). The potent result of a collaboration between Stanford White and the IRT's engineers, the vast facility generated electricity for the network of substations scattered throughout the city. The powerhouse's location at West 59th Street and Eleventh Avenue placed it near the center of the IRT system and allowed direct coal deliveries from ships in the Hudson River, but its presence threatened permanently to hinder the neighborhood's development.[37] At an early stage in the planning process, White volunteered to design the facades. He united the massive block in a continuous colonnade of banded pilasters framing arched windows and covered the facades with delicate, French Renaissance details in a terra cotta that matched the buff-colored Roman brick. The steel trusses above the colonnade supported the facility's coal hoppers and chimneys, which White tapered, suggesting the entasis of a classical column.

In 1911, the city granted the Brooklyn Rapid Transit (BRT) permission to construct a line in Manhattan, inaugurating what came to be called the Dual System of intracity rail transit with two lines, the IRT and the BMT. By 1917, the two linked the east and west sides of Manhattan with the Bronx, Brooklyn, and Queens, but the inefficiencies in the Dual System and the subsequent addition of the city-owned Independent System soon made a mockery of the idea of coordinated subway transportation. Nonetheless, the BMT grandly expanded the city's public transportation and added to the cohesion of the metropolitan city.

The use of representational plaques initiated in the original IRT subway was continued in many of the stations of the expanding network, but the intricacies of paneling, string courses, and articulated column bases and caps were abandoned in favor of more easily maintained smooth surfaces and a more straightforward expression of the engineering. On the whole, the BRT line was more imaginatively designed than the IRT, and its facilities were far more generously proportioned to handle vast crowds. The anonymous BMT designers were influenced by the Paris subways and by Berlin's S-Bahn, as can be seen in the elevated portions of the line, particularly the section that stretched along Queens Boulevard, where the steel structure was dressed, or sheathed, in a sprayed concrete coating that transformed a usually dingy feature into an amenity. The alternation of smooth- and rough-coat surfaces and the extensive use of colorful glazed tiles inset for emphasis helped articulate the basic structural organization.

In the wake of political consolidation, it was the development of a comprehensive subway system that proved itself the critical element in physically unifying the geographically extensive city. But the grandest architectural representations of the city's vast size and complexity were the bridges that linked Manhattan to Brooklyn, Queens, and the Bronx over the East River. Although the bridges were great works of engineering,

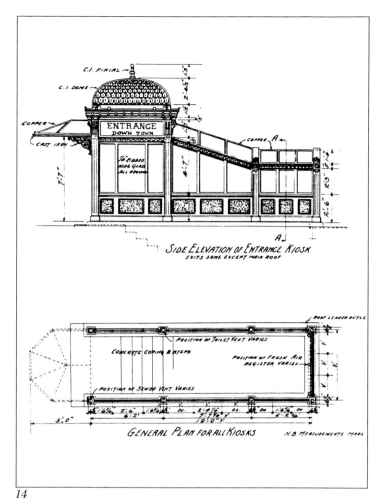

14

15

14. Heins & LaFarge. Standard Kiosk, IRT Subway, 1904. Plan, section and elevations. Museum of the City of New York.

15. Heins & LaFarge. IRT Station, 116th Street and Broadway, 1904. Museum of the City of New York.

16. John A. Roebling and Washington Roebling. Brooklyn Bridge. A 1924 view looking southwest from Brooklyn. Museum of the City of New York.

17. Carrère & Hastings and Leon Moisieff. Manhattan Bridge, 1904–09. Museum of the City of New York.

18. Carrère & Hastings. Manhattan Bridge, 1912. Court of Honor. Museum of the City of New York.

19. Carrère & Hastings and Leon Moisieff. Manhattan Bridge, 1904–09. Detail of tower and pedestrian walkway. Museum of the City of New York.

20. Henry Hornbostel and Gustav Lindenthal. Queensboro Bridge, 1909. Museum of the City of New York.

21. Carrere & Hastings and Leon Moisieff. Manhattan Bridge, 1904–09. Museum of the City of New York.

22. Henry Hornbostel and Gustav Lindenthal. Queensboro Bridge, 1909. Tower finial. Museum of the City of New York.

23. Henry Hornbostel and Gustav Lindenthal. Queensboro Bridge, 1909. Sectional perspective. Museum of the City of New York.

16

17

18

19

there was pressure to make them great works of art: the idea was not to hide the marvels of engineering but to articulate them through architecture.

The first major bridge constructed in New York was the Brooklyn Bridge. Completed in 1883, the Brooklyn Bridge had transformed New Yorkers' sense of their city's geography and proved as significant for the development of New York as the opening of the transcontinental railroad in 1869 had been for the nation as a whole. The Brooklyn Bridge cemented Manhattan's role as the business center of the metropolis and Brooklyn's as a principal dormitory.

By the turn of the century, the Brooklyn Bridge was severely overtaxed and a second crossing, the Williamsburg Bridge, was proposed. Designed in 1896–1903 by the engineer Leffert L. Buck, who had worked with Washington Roebling on the Brooklyn Bridge, the Williamsburg Bridge was planned as a multimodal facility, using steel towers instead of masonry, that would ultimately carry not only pedestrians and horse-drawn vehicles, but also elevated trains and trolleys.[38] In the same year, Buck first submitted plans for the Queensboro Bridge, intended to link midtown with Long Island City in the borough of Queens. The potential visual impact on the riverscape of these two projects triggered a stream of protests, prompting Mayor Seth Low to appoint the distinguished, aesthetically sensitized, and notoriously undiplomatic bridge engineer Gustav Lindenthal as commissioner of the Department of Bridges in 1902 and to refer new bridge designs to the Municipal Art Commission for approval.[39] Distressed by the unconsidered conditions of the approaches to the Williamsburg Bridge and by the squat proportions of its towers, Lindenthal usurped Buck's position and retained the architectural firm of Palmer and Hornbostel as design consultants. Because construction was already well under way, the architects proposed only modest interventions to the bridge itself, reserving their bold moves for its Manhattan approaches, where Hornbostel advocated widening Delancey Street into a landscaped boulevard.[40] The final design still did not meet with critical approval. The notable architectural critic Montgomery Schuyler decried the awkward proportions of the towers, which abruptly changed profile as they rose above the roadway, and deplored their "uncouth and bandy-legged aspect which no cleverness in detail could redeem."[41] The best he could say on behalf of the bridge was "the ugliness of the Williamsburg has been the means of an increased appreciation of the beauty of the East River."[42]

By contrast, Schuyler wrote that the Queensboro and Manhattan bridges, opened within a year of one another in 1901 and 1910 respectively, gave "promise of a final and triumphant refutation of the official European criticism that 'public works in America are executed without reference to art.'"[43] Of the two, the Manhattan Bridge was surely the more grandiloquent monument to the city's recent consolidation. The first plans were drawn by Buck, but in 1903, after Lindenthal became commissioner of bridges, he redesigned the bridge in collaboration with Hornbostel. Lindenthal introduced the use of eyebar cables in place of conventional steel wires, thus making it possible to eliminate the stiffening truss that blocked the view

20

21

22

23

from the roadway.[44] He also proposed towers made up of four columns, which would permit the towers to pivot on their bases and compensate for the expansion and contraction of the cables. But a controversy arose over Lindenthal's technical innovations and Hornbostel's design, which included meeting halls and French-inspired classical touches such as urns and finials on each tower. Lindenthal was dismissed in 1904 by George McClellan, the new mayor, and Leon Moisieff under the direction of George Best, the new bridge commissioner, was brought in. Carrère & Hastings replaced Hornbostel as architectural consultants.[45]

Although the fundamental engineering of the bridge changed, Carrère & Hastings simply improved Hornbostel's design for the towers and the anchorages, which were reshaped and refined so that Schuyler found them "almost more than Roman. They wear, indeed, an aspect of Egyptian immobility."[46] Close attention was paid to articulating the distinction between the cables that held the roadway in tension and the compressive capacities of the steel towers; the contrast between support and supported was made explicit in the manner emphasized by the French theorist of structural expression Viollet-le-Duc. At the Manhattan end of the bridge, an elliptical Court of Honor was distinguished by a triumphal arch based on the Porte Saint Denis in Paris. The court was reserved for vehicular traffic; street cars passed outside the plaza's colonnades, the subway crossed the bridge after it passed under both the plaza and the arch. The Court of Honor was intended as a grand entrance to Manhattan, but from the first it was dwarfed by the scale of the bridge and swamped by the traffic it served.

Though Lindenthal and Hornbostel's Queensboro and Hell Gate bridges may have lacked the grandeur of the Manhattan Bridge, they perhaps represented an even higher level of collaboration between engineer and architect. The Queensboro Bridge, which spans the East River via Blackwell's (later Welfare and now Roosevelt) Island, was the first major bridge in New York to depart from the cable suspension type initiated by Roebling. The first design for the bridge was prepared in 1899 by Buck, who proposed two cantilever spans of unequal length. The use of the cantilever principle made the issue of the anchorages less important than the overall handling of the structural cage that enveloped the roadways and transferred the load from tower to tower. Lindenthal and Hornbostel developed Buck's basic design, manipulating the cross section to add an extra level, which narrowed the overall width of the bridge and transformed its passage into a striking avenue of steel. They based their design on the Pont Mirabeau over the Seine at Neuilly, outside Paris, but they placed their truss above rather than below the roadway. The bridge's entrance was announced by two colossal bronze lanterns and two cast-iron and terra-cotta kiosks leading to an underground terminal for the streetcars that crossed the bridge. The steel superstructure of the bridge began with a low arch across the roadway mounted with bronze commemorative plaques. Four towers crowned by spiky finials rested on masonry pylons of breathtaking slenderness, and Hornbostel's hand could be seen in every detail of bridge design, including the exquisitely worked out patterns of the rivets on the steel work.

The Hell Gate Bridge was the largest steel-arch bridge in the world when it was completed in 1914.[47] The only New York bridge completely engineered and supervised by Lindenthal, it was Lindenthal's and Hornbostel's masterpiece. The gentle reverse curve in the top chord was particularly graceful in its expression of the transfer of forces to the masonry abutments and gave the bridge an uncommonly elegant silhouette. Hornbostel's original proposal for an effusive modern French treatment of the flanking tower buttresses was rejected by the arts commission in 1907 because it was not "strictly utilitarian."[48] In the final design, which was not realized until 1914, the austere towers buttressed and counter pointed Lindenthal's flowing arch with simple masses of stone only slightly out back to reveal emerging pilasters. The viaduct over Ward's and Randall's islands was carried on even simpler, almost slablike piers. Overhead electric wires were strung between tapered pylons with spherical finials that returned architecture to the neoclassicism of the Enlightenment.

The most daring bridge proposal of the era did not link Manhattan with the outer boroughs but rather sought to open the island to its more distant western hinterland across the wide Hudson River. A Hudson River crossing to New Jersey was first proposed in 1884 by Lindenthal, and by 1890, the New York State Legislature passed a bill incorporating the North River Bridge Company for the purpose of building Lindenthal's design. The enormous bridge with its 2,860-foot-long span would have been 1,265 feet longer than that of the Brooklyn Bridge and would have gone further, as the editors of *Architecture and Building* said, "towards making greater New York the foremost city of the world than any other event in the last twenty years."[49] Lindenthal's vision outstripped the imagination of his contemporaries—and possibly their financial resources—and his proposal was never built. The dream of spanning the Hudson was ultimately realized by a former collaborator turned rival, Othmar Hermann Ammann, with the completion of the George Washington Bridge in 1931.[50]

The public transportation projects of the first decades of the twentieth century were monuments to the metropolitan ideal, but they represented an increasingly outmoded technology. The development of the automobile would soon alter the character of urban life, bringing efficient personal transportation to the masses. While the proliferation of highways, which Le Corbusier called "premises of the future city,"[51] would not begin until the 1920s, roadway design began as early as 1870 when horseback and carriage riding became as much a form of urban recreation as transportation. This is easy to understand; by the 1860s, horse-drawn trolleys were in wide use and provided the best means for urbanites to move about. Within ten years, elevated trains would render all means of surface transportation outmoded for any substantial urban journey. So, at least among the upper classes, the fine horses and carriages that had been a practical asset as well as a public symbol of wealth and taste were largely relegated to pleasure journeys. When Olmsted first designed Central Park there were few saddle horses in the city except those kept by riding stables, and his bridle paths and carriage drives were a major factor in stimulating interest in pleasure riding.[52] Olmsted also conceived Riverside Drive as a pleasure drive, and under his di-

123

25. *Ernest Flagg. Automobile Club of America, 253 West 54th and 248 West 55th streets, 1907.* Avery Library, Columbia University.

rection Central Park was linked via Morningside and Saint Nicholas parks to the Harlem River Speedway, which took the fashionable in their carriages to the very tip of Manhattan.

By 1910, the effect of the new automobile era was beginning to be felt all over the city, from the proposed viaduct around Grand Central and the ramps at Pennsylvania Station, to the scale of the individual townhouse at 109 East 40th Street, designed and occupied by the architect Ernest Flagg, which was the first house in New York to incorporate a garage.[53] Designed in 1905, it seemed at first glance to be a conventional red-brick and white-marble townhouse with a *piano nobile* emphasized by a delicate iron balcony stretching across the three front windows. But closer inspection revealed that the arched entryway, with elaborate iron gates, gave access to a *porte-cochère* with an elevator at the rear that could lower the car to a basement garage. Flagg adapted a Parisian model to American conditions, turning to the courtyard of a typical Paris *hôtel* for both the idea of the internalized *porte-cochère* and the general organization of the plan and its complexly shaped spaces.

Public stabling for horses also gave way to garaging for automobiles. Many existing stables were simply converted to garages, but a new building type began to emerge. Many of the early public garages were conceived of as important civic buildings. None was grander than Snelling & Potter's three-story facility of 1906 for Grahm & Goodman on West 93rd Street. Its reinforced concrete structure, sheathed in an elaborate modern French-style brick and limestone facade with a high basement supporting flattened piers, rose to a complex cornice climaxed at its center by a flagpole.[54]

As his house was being completed in 1907, Ernest Flagg was building the Automobile Club of America on West 54th Street.[55] Flagg's design retained an explicit connection to neoclassicism, sheathing the structural frame in a taut, expressive skin of buff brick and subtly polychromed terra-cotta without disguising the presence of the reinforced concrete structure. The decorated skin of the Automobile Club was manipulated to present the building's unusual, hybrid program. Its ground floor was largely devoted to a washroom for cars and the elevators that carried them to garages on the upper floors, articulated with a repetitive pattern of metal-framed, infill windows. The piano nobile, sandwiched between the garage facilities, contained a large assembly room and a grill room for members' use. The terra-cotta balcony and French doors gave the building its public character.

Flagg's design would quickly seem naive. In 1913, Hubert Ladd Towle summarized the developing role of the automobile in an article entitled "The Automobile and Its Mission." Five years earlier it had seemed a "transcendent plaything—thrilling, seductive, desperately expensive," but now it seemed to proffer an entirely new pattern of residential settlement.[56] By then, Henry Ford had begun to mass produce cars on the assembly line, placing a car within reach of virtually every American, and in 1916, the Federal Roads Act initiated a national program of road building. Taken together with new technological advances, including the telephone, radio,

124

movies, and eventually television, the automobile produced an unprecedented freedom of migration for the average citizen and began to transform the scale and character of American geography and urbanism.

In New York, substantial road building began with the fifteen-mile-long Bronx River Parkway, constructed between 1912 and 1925, with Leslie G. Holleran serving as the principal engineer and Hermann W. Merkel acting as consulting landscape architect.[57] The parkway adapted Olmsted's ideas to the requirements of the motor car and was widely admired as an act of land reclamation, innovative road design, and rural beautification, transforming a polluted, muddy stream into a gurgling brook meandering through a linear park. It was, with the exception of a three-mile section of Olmsted's Fenway in Boston and his east-west transverse roads in Central Park, the nation's first highway to eliminate grade crossings, lifting most crossroads above it on a series of bridges.[58] The bridges, constructed of rough-finished field stone and surrounded by lush and naturalistically landscaped rights-of-way, blended into the parklike setting while each adopted a distinctive design by Gilmore D. Clarke, who served as the landscape architect for the Westchester County Park Commission, as well as by the architects Delano & Aldrich, Charles Stoughton, and Bowdin & Webster. Near White Plains, the Westchester County seat, some ten miles from the city line, a more massive and elaborate reinforced-concrete bridge, designed by Palmer and Hornbostel and engineered by Guy Vroman, incorporated a single arch over the parkway and was surmounted by a series of smaller arches supporting the elevated roadway.[59] Above White Plains, another reinforced-concrete bridge, designed by Delano & Aldrich, elevated the parkway itself over a stream and incorporated charming anchorages and supporting columns sheathed in stone.[60]

The Bronx River Parkway set the standard for the plethora of parkways and highways that were soon to be masterminded by Robert Moses and others in the United States. It influenced, no doubt, the design of Germany's Autobahn network.[61] Ironically, the scope and efficiency of New York's transportation system, which at the turn of the century both reflected and stimulated the city's explosive growth and its seemingly boundless self-confidence, would prove the metropolitan city's undoing. At first Moses's highways led urbanites to Long Island's parks and beaches. But soon they triggered uncontrolled suburban land development, subdividing potato fields into quarter-acre parcels of Arcadia, or at least some suburban version of it, and turning New York into merely a node of a new supercity, megalopolis between the two world wars and immediately after.[62]

Today, most of the monumental transportation facilities of New York's great metropolitan era are still intact, daily exerting a powerful presence in the city. True, the Williamsburg Bridge is in a state of near collapse.[63] True, the subway is severely overtaxed, as astute observers predicted it would be over eighty years ago. True, today's straphangers are more likely to be aware of long waits, crime statistics, and graffitti-covered trains than decorative mosaic panels, yet the subway system remains the lifeline of the city.[64] And while the advent of widespread air travel and the concomitant decline of the railroads diminished the luster of opulent train stations, Grand Central survives as the suburban commuter's gateway to the metropolis and as New York's best answer to San Marco.[65] Sadly, McKim, Mead & White's masterful Pennsylvania Station is gone, falling victim to the wrecker's ball in 1963, only to be replaced by Charles Luckman's Madison Square Garden Center of 1968, which buries the railroad facilities within its pathetic banalities. Now it is proposed to relocate the Garden and rebuild the site again, returning to the station some of its dignity.[66] We shall see. . . .

Despite radical changes in New York's architecture and urbanism, the brilliance of the city's bridges and their power as urban icons remain untarnished. These two great urban elements—New York's skyline and its bridges—are like virtuosos singing an antiphony, each enhancing the other's performance. The visual power of lower Manhattan lifts Othmar Hermann Ammann's Verrazano Narrows Bridge of 1964—the city's most recent and the world's longest suspension bridge—which might otherwise be an impressive but somewhat workmanlike example of the engineer's art, far beyond practical consideration to the realm of art.[67] Similarly, the grace and strength of New York's other bridges continue to anchor the sight of the city when seen from afar, helping to maintain it as an indelible image in our minds whatever changes, for better or for worse, the city's skyline undergoes. Perhaps F. Scott Fitzgerald best understood the ideally symbiotic relationship between the city and its bridges that creates the most potent symbol of the city's collective aspiration. In *The Great Gatsby* of 1925, Fitzgerald wrote: "Over the great bridge, with the sunlight through the girders making a constant flicker upon the cars, with the city rising up across the river in white heaps and sugar lumps all built with a wish out of nonolfactory money. The city seen from the Queensboro Bridge is always the city seen for the first time, in its first wild promise of all the mystery and the beauty in the world."[68]

Portions of this essay were adapted from Robert A. M. Stern, Gregory Gilmartin, and John Massengale, *New York 1900: Metropolitan Architecture and Urbanism 1890–1915* (New York: Rizzoli International Publications, 1983), 11–12, 34–59. The term *metropolitanism* describes a complex geographic and social ideal in which the city supplies the same services and benefits as the nation as a whole. The city was perceived not as merely an economic necessity but as the highest representation of cultured life, and its destiny was seen as inextricably linked to that of an optimistic and progressive civilization. "In order to be actually metropolitan," the critic Herbert Croly wrote in 1903, "a city must not only reflect large national tendencies, but it must sum them up and transform them." See Herbert Croly, "New York as the American Metropolis," *Architectural Record* 13 (March 1903): 193–206. A hybrid urban form that reflected its pluralist, democratic society, the metropolis encompassed within its boundaries the most disparate urban forms—from the densely developed business districts to the idyll of the suburbs—linked by the arteries of its mass transportation network. The metropolitan ideal fostered the interaction between the prevailing modes of architectural thought—classical, technological and vernacular—to produce an appropriately complex expression of the modern condition, one born of diversity, special interests, energy, vitality, and a passion for excellence. "The City Spirit and the Metropolitan," *Scribner's* 37 (March 1905), 378.

Notes

1. Thomas Beer, *The Mauve Decade: American Life at the End of the Nineteenth Century* (New York: Knopf, 1926); Roger Shattuck, *The Banquet Years* (Garden City, N.Y.: Doubleday, 1961). Also see Van Wyck Brooks, *The Confident Years 1885–1915* (New York: Dutton, 1952); Ray W. Ginger, *Age of Excess: The United States from 1877 to 1914* (New York: Macmillan, 1965); Howard Mumford Jones, *The Age of Energy: Varieties of American Experience, 1865–1915* (New York: Viking Press, 1971).

2. See Gavin Stamp, ed., "London, 1900," *Architectural Design* 48 (May–June 1978); Alastair Service, *London 1900* (New York: Rizzoli International Publications, 1980); Franco Borsi and Ezio Godoli, *Paris 1900* (Brussels: Vokaer, 1976); Franco Borsi, *Bruxelles 1900* (Brussels: Vokaer, 1979); Alejandro Cirici Pellicer, *1900 in Barcelona: Modern Style, Art Nouveau, Modernismo, Jugendstil* (New York: G. Wittenborn, 1967); Carl Schorske, *Fin-de-Siècle Vienna: Politics and Culture* (New York: Knopf, 1980); Christian M. Nebehay, *Vienna 1900: Architecture and Painting* (Vienna: Verlag Christian Brandstätter, 1984); Robert Waissenberger, ed., *Vienna, 1890–1920* (New York: Rizzoli International Publications, 1984); Franco Borsi and Ezio Godoli, *Vienna 1900: Architecture and Design* (New York: Rizzoli International Publications, 1986); Kirk Varnedoe, *Vienna 1900: Art, Architecture, Design* (New York: Museum of Modern Art, 1986).

3. Richard Guy Wilson, *Charles F. McKim and the Development of the American Renaissance: A Study of Architecture and Culture* (Ph.D. diss., University of Michigan, 1972).

4. Croly, "New York as the American Metropolis," 194.

5. Charles H. Caffin, "Municipal Art," *Harper's Monthly* 100 (April 1900): 655–66.

6. For further discussion of the American renaissance and the City Beautiful movement, see Stern, Gilmartin, and Massengale, *New York 1900*, 18–24.

7. Carl Condit, *The Port of New York: A History of the Rail and Terminal System from the Beginnings to Pennsylvania Station* (Chicago: University of Chicago Press, 1980), 15.

8. Leland Roth, *Urban Architecture of McKim, Mead and White, 1870–1910* (Ph.D. diss., Yale University, 1973), 695–96.

9. Ibid, 693–98.

10. William D. Middleton has ably documented the evolution of the design from Reed & Stem's initial, ingeniously organized proposal to the final, inspired synthesis of planning and aesthetics. Once Warren and Wetmore were involved, many of Charles Reed's strategies for handling pedestrian and vehicular traffic were abandoned as the architects searched for a more monumental expression. See William D. Middleton, *Grand Central: The World's Greatest Railway Terminal* (San Marino, Calif.: Golden West Books, 1977), 63–79; and Deborah Nevins, ed., *Grand Central Terminal: City Within the City* (New York: Municipal Art Society, 1982), 13–16.

11. See Robert A. M. Stern with Thomas Mellins and Raymond Gastil, *Pride of Place: Building the American Dream* (Boston: Houghton Mifflin, 1986), 239–41; and Tony Hiss, "Reflections: Experiencing Places—I," *New Yorker* 63 (June 22, 1987): 45–46ff.

12. "The Park Avenue Viaduct, New York City," *Architecture* 39 (February 1919): 41–44.

13. "New Roadways Around Grand Central Terminal Formally Opened," *Real Estate Record and Guide* 122 (September 15, 1928): 5.

14. See Robert A. M. Stern, Gregory Gilmartin, and Thomas Mellins, *New York 1930: Architecture and Urbanism between the Two World Wars* (New York: Rizzoli International Publications, 1987), 31, 34–45, 395.

15. "A Promising Mercantile Thoroughfare," *Real Estate Record and Guide* 89 (April 13, 1912): 737–38.

16. Lorraine B. Diehl, *The Late, Great Pennsylvania Station* (New York: American Heritage, 1985). See also Condit, *The Port of New York*, 239–311.

17. See Montgomery Schuyler, "The New Pennsylvania Station in New York," *International Studio* 41 (October 1910): 89–94.

18. Alexander Cassatt, president of the Pennsylvania Railroad, wanted a profitable office tower, but McKim prevailed. The decision to build a monumental station rather than an office block sealed the fate of the station. Pennsylvania Station, the culmination of the greatest railroad consolidation in history, only survived fifty years. See Roth, *Urban Architecture*, 700.

19. Quoted in Margaret Clapp, "The Social and Cultural Scene," in Allen Nevins and John Krout, eds., *The Greater City: New York 1898–1948* (New York: Columbia University Press, 1948), 221.

20. Thomas Wolfe, *You Can't Go Home Again* (New York: Charles Scribner's Sons, 1940), 247–48.

21. Arnold W. Brunner and Frederick Law Olmsted, Jr., *Proposed Change of Map for Riverside Drive Extension; Report and Plans* (New York, 1913).

22. "West End Improvement," *Architecture and Building* 13 (November 22, 1890): 294.

23. Milton See, "The Planning of Cities: Paper No. 4," *Public Improvements* 2 (December 1, 1899): 51.

24. Brunner and Olmsted, *Proposed Change of Map*.

25. Incisively recognizing the potential impact of the automobile on patterns of urban development, Robert Moses was responsible, perhaps more than any other individual, for orchestrating the transformation of New York from a distinct metropolis into part of a megalopolis. Moses's brilliance was equalled by a pragmatism which often led to the use of less than democratic methods. The most comprehensive and insightful, though not unbiased, account of Moses is without doubt Robert A. Caro's muckraking biography, *The Power Broker: Robert Moses and the Fall of New York* (New York: Alfred A. Knopf, 1974); for discussion of the West Side Improvement, see 525–66. See also Stern, Gilmartin, and Mellins, *New York 1930*, 713–16.

26. Condit, *Port of New York*, 332–33.

27. See Mel Scott, *American City Planning Since 1890* (Berkeley: University of California Press, 1969), 221–22.

28. S.D.V. Burr, *Rapid Transit in New York City* (New York: Chamber of Commerce of the State of New York, 1905), 10–11.

29. "The Rapid Transit Road," *Public Improvements* 2 (November 1, 1899): 7–8.

30. *Public Improvements* 3 (July 1900): 377.

31. *Interborough Rapid Transit. The New York Subway. Its Construction and Equipment* (New York: IRT Company, 1904).

32. The idea was borrowed from the Budapest subway, where, instead of major aboveground terminals, simple open pavilions (*kushks* in Hungarian) were built to mark the entrances and shelter the steps from rain and snow. See Burr, *Rapid Transit*, 106 and 212.

33. See Nebehay, *Vienna 1900*, 4: 9–11; Borsi and Godoli, *Vienna 1900*, 31–38.

34. M. G. Cuniff, "The New York Subway," *World's Work* 8 (October 1904): 5346–64.

35. *Real Estate Record and Guide* 74 (November 5, 1904): 949.

36. *American Architect and Building News* 86 (December 1904): 73.

37. Roth, *Urban Architecture*, 688–93.

38. F. Nichols, "The New East River Bridge," *Public Improvements* 1 (May 15, 1899): 21–22.

39. George Post, "The Planning of Cities," *Public Improvements* 2 (November 15, 1899): 26–27. For further discussion of Lindenthal and his work, see Sharon Reier, *The Bridges of New York* (New York: Quadrant Press, 1977), 28–65, 90–107. Also see Stern, Gilmartin, and Massengale, *New York 1900*, 50–52, 54–56; Stern, Gilmartin, and Mellins, *New York 1930*, 675–779, 681–82.

40. Montgomery Schuyler, "Our Four Big Bridges," *Architectural Record* 25 (March 1901): 149–60.

41. Ibid., 152.

42. Ibid., 151.

43. Ibid., 160.

44. *American Architect and Building News* 79 (February 14, 1903): 50.

45. *American Architect and Building News* 83 (January 16, 1904): 17.

46. Schuyler, "Our Four Big Bridges," 160.

47. Reier, *The Bridges of New York*, 58–65.

48. *American Architect and Building News* 92 (August 17, 1907): 50.

49. *Architecture and Building* 13 (July 5, 1890): 2.

50. See Stern, Gilmartin, and Mellins, *New York 1930*, 675–79, 681–82.

51. Charles Edoard Jeanneret-Gris (Le Corbusier), *When the Cathedrals Were White*, trans. Francis E. Hyslop, Jr. (New York: Reynal and Hitchcock, 1947; repr., New York: McGraw-Hill, 1964), 196.

52. Marianna Griswold van Rensselaer, "Fifth Avenue," *Century* 47 (November 1893): 5–18.

53. "House of Mr. Ernest Flagg, Architect," *American Architect and Building News* 89 (May 12, 1906): 163–64. In 1904, Andrew Carnegie built a private, separate "automobile house" at 55 East 90th Street; see Christopher Gray, "Not on Our Block: New York's Private Stable Story," *Avenue* 10 (April 1986): 96–103.

54. Development in Garage Construction," *Real Estate Record and Guide* 81 (April 18, 1908): 703.

55. "The Automobile Club of America," *American Architect and Building News* 91 (May 4, 1907): 187.

56. Quoted in David P. Handlin, *The American Home* (Boston: Little, Brown, 1979), 149.

57. The Board of Estimates and Apportionment of the City of New York, The Board of Supervisors of the County of Westchester, *Report of the Bronx Parkway Commission* (New York, 1906, 1912, 1914, 1916, 1917, 1922, 1925).

58. Gilmore D. Clarke, "Collaboration in Bridge Designing. I. The Architect," *Architectural Forum* 48 (May 1928): 729–38.

59. Clarke, "Collaboration," 737.

60. Clarke, "Collaboration," 738.

61. See F. A. Gutheim, "German Highway Design: The Reichsautobahn," *American Magazine of Art* 29 (April 1936): 238–41.

62. See Stern, Gilmartin, and Mellins, *New York 1930*, 41–45, 48.

63. Richard Levine, "A Bridge Dilemma: Patch It or Scrap It," *New York Times* (August 19, 1987): A1ff; "A Bridge to the 21st Century," editorial, *New York Times* (August 23, 1989), 4: 22; Dennis Hevesi, "Taking the Pulse of an Aging Bridge," *New York Times* (November 22, 1987): 50.

64. "Updating 50 Subway Stations: Costly and Late, " *New York Times* (May 11, 1987): A1, ff; "Subway Station Stagnation," editorial, *New York Times* (May 12, 1987): A30; Richard Levine, "On the I.R.T.: New Riders, New Cars, Old Complaints," *New York Times* (July 23, 1987): B1ff.; Richard Levine, "For 463 Subway Stations, A Plan for Top-to-Bottom Sprucing Up," *New York Times* (July 24, 1987): B1–B2; Richard Levine, "42nd Street Shuttle: Cars for Reviled Line," *New York Times* (October 3, 1987): 29; Richard Levine, "Seeking Bearable Subway Discomfort," *New York Times* (October 10, 1987): 33; "Myths About the Metropolis," editorial, *New York Times* (October 11, 1987), 4: 26; Richard Levine, "A Sweepstakes for Brighter, Lighter and Cheaper Subway Cars," *New York Times* (November 11, 1987): B1ff.

65. Carleton Knight, "New York City Landmarks Law Upheld: Grand Central Appeal Wins," *Preservation News* 16 (February 1976): 1ff.; "Grand Central Partisans Fight Against A Tower," *New York Times* (April 22, 1976): 37; "A Grand Building Belongs to All," editorial, *New York Times* (April 27, 1977): 22; Paul Goldberger, "Office Tower Above Grand Central Barred by State Court of Appeals," *New York Times* (June 24, 1977): 1ff; Warren Weaver, Jr., "Tower Over Grand Central Barred as Court Upholds Landmarks Law," *New York Times* (June 27, 1978): A1ff.; Ada Louise Huxtable, "A 'Landmark' Decision on Landmarks," *New York Times* (July 9, 1978), 2: 2ff; "Grand Central Is More Than a Building," editorial, *New York Times* (July 22, 1978): 18; David Dunlap, "Fixing Leaky Roof at Grand Central," *New York Times* (August 24, 1987): B3; Charles Bagli, "Hearing Set on Grand Central Revitalization," *New York Observer* 1 (November 16, 1987): 15; Tim Monahan, "Central Grandeur," *House and Garden* 159 (December 1987): 68A.

66. Frank J. Prial, "Companies Join in Plan for Madison Square Garden," *New York Times* (May 28, 1987): B3; Richard Levine, "Pact Reached on $160 Million Improvement of Penn Station," *New York Times* (June 4, 1987): B1, B28.

67. Triborough Bridge and Tunnel Authority, *Verrazano–Narrows Bridge Cable Spinning: March 7, 1963* (New York: Triborough Bridge and Tunnel Authority, 1963); Gay Talese, *The Bridge* (New York: Harper and Row, 1964); Triborough Bridge and Tunnel Authority, *Spanning the Narrows* (New York: Triborough Bridge and Tunnel Authority, 1964).

68. F. Scott Fitzgerald, *The Great Gatsby* (New York: Charles Scribner's Sons, 1925), 82.

1

2

3

Architecture and Urban Planning 1850–1914

Hartwig Schmidt

Hartwig Schmidt is an architect who has worked for the German Archaeological Institute and the city of Berlin's Department of Architectural Preservation. Since 1985 he has been at the University of Karlruhe, where he is managing a special research project for preservation and restoration of historically significant monuments and sites. His publications include Berlin und die Antike *(1970) (with W. D. Heilmeyer),* Das Tiergatenviertel. Baugeschichte eines Berliner Villenviertels 1790–1870 *(1981), and* Schutzbauten *(1988).*

Unter den Linden

The first stop for anyone visiting Berlin at the turn of the century was Unter den Linden, the city's world-famous boulevard (fig. 1).[1] No traveler's account was complete without words of praise for this avenue at the heart of the city between the Royal Palace and Brandenburg Gate:

Unter den Linden! The mere mention of the name makes every Berliner's heart beat faster. . . . It is the focus of society life in Berlin. Between the magnificent houses, palaces, and hotels that line its sides, a never-ending stream of people flows along the central promenade, the bridle and carriage paths, and the pavements. Not only does all of Berlin's high society gather here, but even busy men of affairs will go out of their way to enjoy the diversity of the display with never-flagging pleasure—the lovely buildings and grand palaces, the superb statues, the officers, horsemen, dandies, and fine ladies, magnificent carriages and glittering uniforms, the grand display windows, the paintings and etchings. . . . Here, free of the atmosphere of workshops and offices, social functions and theater, people meet one another without plan or purpose; everyone is at his leisure, everyone has come to see and be seen. This is the showcase where the fashionable can display their splendor and vanity.[2]

Berlin became capital of the German empire in 1871; the city was the focus of politics, finance, and culture, and an attraction to visitors from around the world. One of its most interesting sights was the Kaisergalerie (figs. 2, 3), opened on March 15, 1873, in the presence of Emperor William I and the cream of the nobility. This elegant shopping arcade was located at 22–23 Unter den Linden and extended to the corner of Behrenstrasse and Friedrichstrasse.[3] With its numerous shops, galleries, banquet halls, restaurants, slide show called the Kaiserpanorama, wax museum, and Castan's Panoptikum the arcade was a landmark of the new, imperial Berlin that completely changed the look of the avenue when baroque townhouses and plain, neoclassical residences were sacrificed for its construction. The building at 27 Unter den Linden had to make way in 1885 for the Kaiserhallen beer emporium, and across the street was Café Bauer, a huge, Viennese-style coffee shop with hundreds of seats and a monumental mural by Anton von Werner entitled *The Roman Art of Enjoying Life*. Number 34, home of Schlesinger's renowned book and music store, whose publications included Weber's opera, *Der Freischütz*, was relinquished to the Prussian Central-Boden-Creditbank. Number 35 was torn down in 1892 to make way for the pompous edifice of the Disconto-Gesellschaft (Ende and Böckmann); Stadt Rom, a modest inn adjacent to the academy was expanded in 1875–76 to become the Grand Hotel de Rome. The buildings at 35 and 36 Unter den Linden were demolished in the 1890s for the erection of Hotel Bristol, Berlin's most luxurious and expensive hotel.

A second arcade was built just down the street from the Kaisergalerie to the west in 1891–92. The Lindengalerie was a huge complex that included a hotel and a theater (the Monopol-Theater of later fame), and the Lindencafé, which was furnished in the typical style of Germany's boom years, the Gründerzeit: "Marbled plaster columns in golden yellow hues, the walls and ceilings adorned with rich rococo ornament in shades of white, cream, and gold, magnificent electric

1. Unter den Linden/Friedrichstrasse, 1898. Landesbildstelle Berlin.

2. Friedrichstrasse/Behrenstrasse, 1900. Landesbildstelle Berlin.

3. Kaisergalerie, 1895. Interior view. Landesbildstelle Berlin.

4

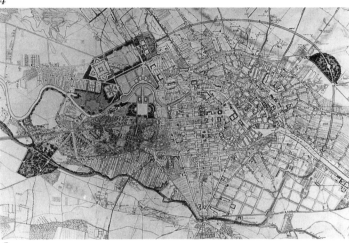

5

4. Eduard Gaertner. Unter den Linden with the Monument to Frederick the Great, *1853.* Neue Nationalgalerie, Berlin.

5. Peter Josef Lenné. Projected Ornamental and Bordering Features of Berlin and Its Close Environs, *1840.* Landesbildstelle Berlin.

chandeliers, and appropriate murals by E. Veith, representing scenes from an Italian *osteria*, an Arabian café, and a Japanese teahouse, quite striking in the pleasing harmony."[4]

Unlike its western end, the eastern end of Unter den Linden, from the academy building to the Royal Palace, remained practically unchanged. In 1851, it had been capped by the monument to Frederick II by Christian Daniel Rauch, an equestrian statue on a tall pedestal that was often copied by the many designers of such monuments in the nineteenth century. The view from the monument to the Royal Palace on a sunny summer day was recorded in 1853 in a large canvas by Eduard Gaertner, the major architectural painter of Berlin during the Biedermeier period (fig. 4).[5] Visible in the far background is the palace, with its high dome rising above the Eosander Portal, then, projecting into the street at the left, is the arsenal, the most significant baroque structure in Berlin apart from the palace. The building in the foreground is the former palace of Prince Henry, the brother of Frederick II, which in 1810 became the seat of Berlin University. Dominating the right side of the avenue is the Royal Opera House with its six-column Corinthian portico designed by Georg Wenzeslaus von Knobelsdorff and built in 1741–43. One of the most modern and admired of its day, the opera house was part of the Forum Fridericianum, a grand square including royal palace that Frederick II conceived and Georg Wenzeslaus von Knobelsdorff designed during their sojourn at Rheinsberg. Instead of the projected palace, Prince Henry's was actually built, and on the west side of the square rose the Royal Library, a replica of the Michaeler Tract of the Vienna Hofburg, begun in 1725 by Fischer von Erlach. Sited at the southern corner of the square was St. Hedwig's Church, the first Catholic church to be erected in Berlin after the Reformation.[6]

Following the Silesian War (1756–63), Frederick II's building activity shifted away from Berlin. While he had initially concentrated on Charlottenburg Palace, whose new, Knobelsdorff-designed wing went up in 1740–48, the monarch resided for the most part in Potsdam after Sanssouci had been completed in 1747. The death of Frederick II in 1786 marked the end of the epoch of royal building projects in Prussia. Under his successor, Frederick William II, architects such as David Gilly, Carl Gotthard Langhans, Friedrich Wilhelm von Erdmannsdorff, and the sculptor Gottfried Schadow were brought to Berlin. Neoclassicism of the typically Prussian variety became the dominating art form of the period. High points of this development were the Brandenburg Gate (1789–91), adapted by Langhans from the Propylaea in Athens, and the Mint, designed by Heinrich Gentz and erected in 1789–1800 on the Werder Market. Gilly's designs for a national theater on the Gendarmenmarkt (1799) and for a monument to Frederick on Leipziger Platz (1797) remained visionary.

When in 1791 an English spinning machine went into operation and two years later the first Berlin steam engine was installed at the Royal Porcelain Factory, a new era had begun. The industrial age transformed Berlin from a provincial Prussian capital into one of the greatest industrial centers in Europe.

Rise of an Industrial Center

If the reign of Frederick William II was marked by the effects of the French Revolution and the ensuing wars with France, the accession of Frederick William III was overshadowed by Prussia's defeat at Jena and Auerstedt in 1806, Napoleon's occupation of Berlin, and the flight of the royal family to Memel in East Prussia. Building activity came to a standstill. It was not until the end of the Napoleonic Wars (1812–14) and the monarch's return to Berlin in October 1815 that a new phase began, a phase that lasted until 1840 and was largely determined by the architectural genius of Karl Friedrich Schinkel and his conception of a romantic neoclassicism.[7]

Schinkel's era coincided with a process of rapid industrialization in Prussia that was fueled by a comprehensive program of state subsidies. The key forms of this support were initiated by Peter Beuth, director of the Technical Deputation for Trade and a good friend of Schinkel's with whom he traveled to Paris and England in 1826. Schinkel's contribution to the development of Prussian enterprise was evident in a voluminous series of designs published from 1821–37 *Vorbilder für Fabrikanten und Handwerker* (Patterns for Manufacturers and Artisans), advocacy of the technique of zinc casting, and improvements in the manufacture of terra cotta for architectural ornament.

Based on the Stein-Hardenberg reforms—emancipation of the peasantry in 1807, municipal incorporation in 1808, freedom of trade in 1810—Beuth's liberal business policies were crowned with success.[8] If in 1820 there were eight steam engines totalling twenty-five horsepower operating in Berlin, by 1830 the number had jumped to twenty-six, and by 1843 to sixty engines producing a total of eight hundred horsepower. This development had begun in 1805 with the inauguration of a model factory, the Royal Iron Foundry on the Panke River. In 1815, the Freund Brothers built the city's first functioning steam engine, followed in 1826 by the manufacturer Franz Anton Egells, who established the first private iron foundry in Berlin, at 3 Chausseestrasse in what was then still a northern suburb. Next door, in 1837, August Borsig set up shop, and by the 1840s, his company had become the largest producer of locomotives in the city.

The industrialization of Berlin was doubtless accelerated by the construction of five railway lines with terminals situated at key points of access around the city's outskirts. In 1838, the first train ran from Berlin to Potsdam, followed in 1841 by the inauguration of the Berlin-Anhalt Railway Company, in 1842 by the Berlin-Stettin line, and in the autumn of that year by the Berlin-Frankfurt line, which established rail connections to Frankfurt on the Oder River to the east. In 1846, when the line to Hamburg was completed, the first phase of railway development came to a close, and Berlin had become a key junction in Germany's rapidly expanding rail network.[9]

Industrialization and a migration of rural workers to the city led to a rapid increase in Berlin's population to 380,000 by 1845. By 1865, the figure had almost doubled and by 1873 had reached 900,000. To regulate construction activity, the building authorities introduced in 1830 a plan covering the entire area within the town walls. Although the king approved the plan, it could not be carried out because the communally administered agricultural lands had yet to be commuted into private property. In 1840, Peter Josef Lenné (1789–1866), royal director of gardens, presented his famous plan *Projektirte Schmuck und Grenzzüge von Berlin mit nächster Umgebung (Projected Ornamental and Bordering Features of Berlin and Its Close Environs)*, a comprehensive design aimed at beautifying the entire region (fig. 5). The plan included all of the projects with which Lenné had been entrusted to that point: the redesign of the Tiergarten, a royal hunting preserve into a landscaped park with a zoo; the creation of a park in the working-class area of northern Berlin (which later became Friedrichshain); a building plan for Luisenstadt including a canal; the planning of the Landwehr Canal, a key inner-city waterway; and a design for the Powder Mill grounds with Mars Field to the north and military drill grounds to the south of the Spree River on the terrain that would later become Königsplatz, site of the Reichstag. The progressive feature of Lenné's plan was a wide, landscaped boulevard that would arc around the northern districts of Berlin and meet the tree-lined promenades lining the Landwehr Canal in the south to form a green belt around the entire city.

Lenné combined the ideas of landscape gardening with the inhabitants' need for new streets, business sites, and general urban expansion. As he explained in his accompanying report, his zoning was intended "to do justice not only to the utilization to be derived for the community from the new arrangements, but also to the recreation of the populace."[10] Although the plan was not put into practice in all respects, it provided the basis for the construction of Luisenstadt, which now forms that part of the Kreuzberg district north of the Landwehr Canal. Construction began in 1842; the canal was built from 1845–50 and the Luisenstädtische Canal from 1848–52 (it was later to be filled in [1926–28]). The latter canal served to link the Spree River with the Landwehr and to provide drainage for the new district; its large basin was simultaneously a harbor and an attractive recreational area. The new suburb was built up within a few decades, in a relatively uniform pattern—four-to five-story apartment houses with side wings, downstairs flats to the front, and stucco facades in the late neoclassical style of the Schinkel school. Small trade premises were located in the courtyard; behind was a garden.[11]

Lenné's grand boulevard around the northern periphery was never built. Berlin's poorest districts were located here—Voigtland, with the earliest housing barracks; the Wülkenitz Family Homes, whose catastrophic living conditions were described in 1843 by Bettina von Arnim in *Dies Buch gehört dem König (This Book Belongs to the King)*; and the working-class districts in the Oranienburg and Rosenthal suburbs, near the iron foundries and machinery factories.[12]

When his patron, Frederick William IV, fell ill in 1858, Lenné lost all influence on Berlin city planning. The initiative shifted to the Royal Police Department, who entrusted James Hobrecht, a surveyor and architect, with the revision of existing

6

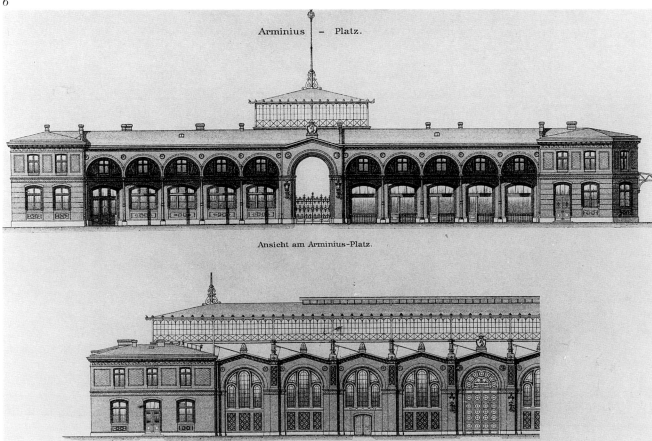

Arminius — Platz.

Ansicht am Arminius-Platz.

7

plans. As it turned out, the continual expansion of the suburbs, the extension of the city limits, and the erection of train stations, which Lenné had not taken into account, necessitated entirely new planning. Still, Lenné's idea of connecting the city's districts by means of wide boulevards was not forgotten. Like the layout of spacious squares, it became a key motif of Hobrecht's *Plan for the Environs of Berlin*, which was published in 1861 (fig. 6).

Actually, the Hobrecht Plan was a pure street plan, merely regulating the width of the thoroughfares and size of the squares. How the intervening spaces were to be used was left up to the building code of 1853, which was aimed primarily at reducing fire hazard. It was this code, together with an extensive utilization of the lots, that gave birth to the Berlin *Mietskaserne*, whose small flats and extremely high density led to the miserable housing conditions for which Berlin—and not only its working-class districts—became notorious.[13]

Rapid population growth and suburban expansion required infrastructural measures on an unprecedented scale—hospitals and schools, market halls and gas works, waterworks and sewers (fig. 7). The building tasks were new, and building types to suit them had yet to be developed.[14] In addition to these noncommercial structures, great numbers of which were built under municipal auspices, churches had to be erected for both Protestant and Catholic congregations, barracks for the large contingents of military in the city, train stations, post offices, and administration buildings. The architecture of the 1860s and 1870s was characterized by brick construction with terra-cotta ornament, and the rounded arches so favored by Berlin architects of the day. Examples are city hall (fig. 8, 1861–69) by F. A. Waesemann, St. Thomas's Church on Mariannenplatz (1864–69) by Friedrich Adler, the General City Hospital in Friedrichshain (1868–74) and the Arts and Crafts Museum (1871–81) by Gropius and Schmieden, Potsdam Station by L. Qassowski, and Friedrich Secondary High School (1871–75) by Hermann Blankenstein, who in 1872 became Berlin's *Stadtbaurat* (director of the City's Department of Urban Planning and Development). Blankenstein also designed the Municipal Market Hall on Arminiusplatz in Moabit. The fourteen market halls built between 1883 and 1892 were all of cast and wrought iron construction with a brick facade. If brick facades were considered durable, the value of their stucco and plaster ornamentation seemed to many merely dubious. Art historian A. Woltmann wrote in 1872 about the prefabricated ornament commonly used on Berlin apartment houses built, he said, out of mere speculation.

Plaster and zinc, stucco and paint produce the glorious facade effects everyone seems to want. They make the most delicate decoration, the richest overabundance of ornament, cheap and easy—all you have to do is order it in cast zinc from Geiss, or in plaster from Dankberg. Not just the ornament itself but the entire facade, which frequently enough tends merely to be pasted onto the architecture, is degraded in many cases to mere frippery in which the materials and workmanship are careless enough. The fate of these buildings is no different from that of ladies' ball gowns, whose appearance at the end of a grand party could not be more disheveled and wilted than that of a modern edifice when rain and snow have defaced the paint or when the playful zephyrs of spring cause the plaster coating on

8

6. *James Hobrecht*. Plans for the Environs of Berlin, *1862.* Landesbildstelle Berlin.

7. *Hermann Blankenstein. Municipal Market Hall No. 10, Arminiusplatz, Moabit, 1883–92.* From A Lindermann, *Die Markethallen Berlins (Berlin, 1899).*

8. *F. A. Waesemann. Berlin City Hall (1861–69), 1902.* Landesbildstelle Berlin.

the brick columns to disintegrate and blow the fragments of the many-figured friezes down the pavement.[16]

It was Schinkel who had introduced zinc castings as an inexpensive means of producing complicated architectural elements, as well as terra cotta to decorate facades. Famous examples are his Feilner House, the Academy of Architecture, and suburban churches.

Prior to the Gründerzeit boom years in Berlin, whose environs yielded only granite or the brittle Rüdersdorf limestone, natural stone was little used as a building material. It was not until the railroads reduced transportation costs and people began to demand more attractive and dignified architecture that the plain walls of yellow or red brick began to disappear and with them the architecture of the Schinkel school.[17]

One of the first buildings with a sandstone facade in the Renaissance style was the new Stock Exchange, designed by Friedrich Hitzig and built from 1859 to 1864 (fig. 9). Its facade based on the colonnades of the Louvre, the structure boasted a trading room with an iron-raftered ceiling that made it the largest interior space in Berlin at the time. Solid stone columns now began to appear on almost every important public building, from the Imperial Bank on Jägerstrasse (F. Hitzig, 1869–76) to the National Gallery (J. H. Strack, 1867–76), from the New Museum to the converted Crown Prince Palace (Strack, 1855–58). Columns also began to grace the suburban houses and villas erected by prosperous Berliners in the Tiergarten district or in Potsdam (fig. 10), whose designs stemmed from a new breed of private master builders: Eduard Knoblauch, Friedrich Hitzig, Eduard Titz, and Carl Schwatlo. The official architects in government service, who to this point had set the style, and the master masons who had been responsible for apartment-house construction, were now joined by freelance architects who built for the well-to-do bourgeoisie and who now began to determine the development of architecture. When in 1857 Martin Gropius and Heino Schmieden joined forces, the era of the great Berlin architectural offices was under way—End and Böckmann (1859–95), Von der Hude and Hennicke (1860–92), Ebe and Benda (1867–91), Kyllmann and Heyden (1868–1902), Kayser and Von Grossheim (1872–1911), and Cremer and Wolffenstein (1882–1919).

To represent their interests, the city's architects had formed the Architects' Association of Berlin in 1824, which from 1875 met in its magnificently furnished clubhouse on Wilhelmstrasse.[18] In 1833, they began publishing a bulletin, *Notizblatt des Architekten-Vereins zu Berlin*, retitled *Zeitschrift für Bauwesen* in 1851,[19] in which interesting new buildings were reviewed and scientific and technical matters discussed. Projects by the members were published in *Das Architektonische Album* (from 1833) and *Das architektonische Skizzenbuch* (1852–86). The official school for architects in the Prussian civil service was the Bauakademie or Academy of Architecture, established in 1799; it was supplemented in 1879 by the Technical College in Charlottenburg. In the 1870s, two new associations were formed: the Architekten- und Ingenieur-Verein zu Berlin (1871), and the Vereinigung Berliner (Privat)

Architekten (1879). The year 1877 marked the publication of a comprehensive review of architectural activities in Berlin, *Berlin und seine Bauten* (*Berlin and Its Buildings*), edited by and with contributions from the association members. The second edition in 1896 had already swelled into a magnificently produced two-volume work.[20]

Two projects were instituted during the reign of Frederick William IV, popularly known as the romantic on the Prussian throne (1841–61), that were to occupy Berlin architects for years to come: the development of the former custom-house yards behind Schinkel's Old Museum into a center of arts and sciences, and the building of a new cathedral with a burial vault for the Hohenzollerns.[21] As a counterpart to the Cologne Cathedral, a Catholic church from the Gothic period on which work was resumed in 1842, the crown prince envisioned a Protestant cathedral for Berlin modeled on the early Christian basilicas of Rome. Plans were drawn up by Friedrich August Stüler; in 1845, the cornerstone was laid, but the revolution of 1848 put an end to construction work.

The development of Museum Island was more propitious. The New Museum, designed by Stüler, was begun in 1843 and its interior finally finished in 1855. With a stairwell conceived as a festival hall and decorated with monumental murals by W. Kaulbach, the New Museum became the most significant work of post-Schinkel neoclassicism. Its interiors, with each room designed in a style suited to the items on display, exerted a considerable influence on museum arrangement. Next to the New Museum, in 1866–76, rose the National Gallery (fig. 11) devoted to contemporary art, a Roman temple on a high socle designed by Stüler with the assistance of Johann Heinrich Strack. There followed in 1898 to 1903 the erection of the Kaiser-Friedrich-Museum (now Bode Museum), based on plans by Royal Building Councillor Ernst Eberhard von Ihne. Situated on the northern tip of Museum Island, bordered by the Spree, the Kupfergraben Canal, and the interurban line, this museum housed the great collection of Renaissance art that had been amassed by Wilhelm von Bode, general director of the Berlin Museums. The final lot on the island, between the interurban line and the New Museum, became the site of the Pergamon Museum, designed by Alfred Messel and built between 1909 and 1930 under the supervision of Ludwig Hoffmann.

Imperial Berlin

On January 18, 1871, the victorious Prussians gathered in the Hall of Mirrors at Versailles to proclaim the German empire. William I, king of Prussia, became German emperor by vote of the assembled princes. It was an elaborate and pompous spectacle in which Bismarck played a leading role, as may be seen from the huge mural by Anton von Werner. The mood of the Berliners on the day war was declared on France was captured by Adolph Menzel in *The King Leaving to Join His Troops on July 31, 1870*, a small, quite unheroic picture that is now in the New National Gallery (fig. 12).

In spite of the Hohenzollerns' respect for Menzel and his rep-

134

9

10

11

9. *Friedrich Hitzig. Berlin Stock Exchange (1859–64), 1890.* Landesbildstelle Berlin.

10. *Friedrich Hitzig. Villas in the Tiergarten district (1861–62), 1899.* Landesbildstelle Berlin.

11. *F. A. Stüler. The National Gallery (1867–76), Museum Island, 1893.* Landesbildstelle Berlin.

utation as the finest painter in Berlin, it was not he but Anton von Werner who was appointed president of the Berlin Academy and who determined the development of art in the city from 1870 to 1900. This decision was very much in keeping with the official policy toward art in Prussia, which in the four decades to the outbreak of World War I was largely determined by the tastes of the court and aristocracy—an anachronism in a period in which Berlin was rapidly developing, in other respects, into a city of international importance.[22]

The upper-middle class, the city, and the state itself all prospered during this period, each willing to spend lavishly. The great stock market crash of 1873 was soon forgotten. Building boomed at the city center as well as between Alexanderplatz and Potsdamer Platz, where office buildings and department stores, municipal services and hotels rose on lots of ever-increasing size. In Friedrichstadt, the face of entire streets, especially the shopping streets, was entirely altered within the course of a few decades.

In 1877 Berlin had a population of one million, by 1890 almost two million, by 1900 2.7 million, and it continued to grow apace. Despite this dire development, urgent municipal projects bogged down in endless discussions on the pros and cons of various systems. It was not until 1873 that the private waterworks came under municipal administration, to be expanded in 1878 by the facility at Tegel. A sewage system was begun in 1872; the first city gasworks went into operation in 1874, followed ten years later by the first city-run electric power plant. The private railroads were gradually transferred to state ownership from 1879 to 1887, after a ring line had been built around the entire circumference of Berlin in 1877. With the opening of this line connecting the various Berlin terminals, industries were in a position to shift their operations from constricted inner-city sites to the periphery, for the most part in the districts of Wedding and Moabit, which rapidly developed into densely populated working-class neighborhoods.

When regular interurban service was established between downtown Berlin and the suburbs, a migration from the teeming inner city to the newly established so-called villa colonies set in. The railway lines that radiated from the center to the environs developed into axes of urban expansion. Despite land speculation and rapidly rising construction prices, the villages on Berlin's margins were soon surrounded by extensive new residential areas.

Fast and comfortable transportation was provided by the new S-Bahn (Stadteisenbahn, or interurban railway), which was inaugurated in 1882 (fig. 13). While this line gave access to the northern part of the city, an electric elevated train, the first section of a projected subway (U-Bahn) opened in 1901, connected Charlottenburg with the downtown business district. Ever since the 1860s, a program of construction and conversion of the stations and rights-of-way of the private railways had been under way, which included such key terminals as Lehrte, Stettin, Potsdam, Frankfurt, and Anhalt stations. By 1882, the number of railway lines connecting Berlin with all points in Germany had risen to twelve.

To expedite goods transport by water, the Havel and Spree rivers were deepened and straightened, the Landwehr and Berlin-Spandau canals were expanded; Teltow Canal was built in 1901–06 to provide a navigable waterway around southern Berlin. New and larger warehouses and storage facilities were erected at Berlin's harbors. The first zeppelin landed at Jungfernheide in 1909, and that same year, Orville Wright pulled his flying machine into the air at Tempelhof Field.

The transformation of Berlin into an imperial capital destroyed the medieval quarter of the inner city, which to that point had survived largely intact. In 1878, historical buildings were razed to connect Kaiser Wilhelm Strasse with Unter den Linden (fig. 14). The gigantic block of police headquarters, designed by City Building Councillor Blankenstein, was built on Alexanderstrasse in 1886–90. In 1897, a row of baroque houses on Schlossfreiheit was demolished to make way for a national monument, and in 1906, the Scheunenviertel was torn down. Older buildings that did not conform to current standards of taste were removed without a second thought.[23] The inner city was transformed from a residential and small-business area into a downtown dominated by office buildings and department stores.

Berlin of the imperial period was a city in which, as contemporary observers continually remarked with astonishment, veritably everything was new—the inhabitants, the buildings, the public facilities, even manners and social intercourse. It was a city of the imperial court and the proletarian masses, of uniforms and parades and workingmen's demonstrations, of new wealth and new poverty. A new pace of life, an acceleration of work, of the exchange of goods and information, even of everyday behavior, characterized Berlin. Tradition counted little; the new was apparently thought preferable to the old in every case.[24]

One definite population trend, evident since the 1880s, was a westward migration of those who could afford it to the western suburbs of Charlottenburg, Schöneberg, and Wilmersdorf, centered around the newly created hub of the Kurfürstendamm and the Memorial Church of Emperor William (fig. 15). The "Ku-Damm," as laconic Berliners soon dubbed it, was a 2.17-mile-long and 115-foot-wide tree-lined avenue with carriageways, bridle paths, and broad sidewalks, created in 1880–86 at the suggestion of Bismarck to connect the central zoo area with the Grunewald forest, the Charlottenburg district with the residential suburb of Grunewald to the west. It began to be built up in 1890, for the most part with five-story, luxury apartment houses whose opulent stucco facades set the example for the side streets as well. The apartments had anywhere from ten to fifteen rooms and were equipped with modern conveniences of every kind; the lobbies were designed to impress, with lavish use of marble, mirrors, and murals.[25]

The architectural tastes of the Wilhelmine period were represented in such landmarks as the new Reichstag Building by Paul Wallot (fig. 16, 1884–91); the new Protestant cathedral on the Spree River (1894–95) by Julius Raschdorff, and the Memorial Church of Emperor William (1891–95) by Franz Schwechten. William II's partiality to a pathos-filled neo-baroque style was best illustrated by the Neptune Fountain in

12

13

14

15

16. *Tauentzienstrasse,*
Charlottenburg, from
Wittenbergplatz, 1904. The tower of
the Emperor William Memorial
Church can also be seen, designed
by F. Schwechten and built in
1890–95. Landesbildstelle Berlin.

17. *In front of the Brandenburg*
Gate, 1899. Landesbildstelle
Berlin.

18. *Ludwig Hoffmann. Town Hall*
(1902–11), 1922. Landesbildstelle
Berlin.

19. *Alfred Messel. Wertheim*
Department Store, Leipziger Platz
(1896–97), 1910. Landesbildstelle
Berlin

16

17

18

19

front of the Berlin Palace (1891), the Bismarck Monument at the Reichstag (1901), and Reinhold Begas's National Monument to Emperor William I (1897). The style and attitude culminated in the Siegesallee, an avenue of victory lined with imposing figures, which was completed in 1901.

However, the Wilhelmine style was short-lived. As early as 1909, the influential art critic Max Osborn noted:

The new political and economic resurgence found no characteristic form in which to express itself, cleaving instead to the academic stereotypes of the Renaissance, which became *de rigueur* for banks and large corporations especially. And the replicas of sixteenth- and seventeenth-century Italian palazzo facades they employed—which at least in keeping with the age's increased need for display were made of authentic materials—now reappeared as well on the apartment buildings of the rapidly developing new streets. External splendor was everywhere. Grandiose portals, magnificent columns and pilasters, pediments stuck over the windows, ornaments from all periods and nations were jumbled together willy-nilly; sometimes even cupolas and towers and roughly fabricated gable statuary, intended to provide a fine residence for the gentleman tailor or glovemaker. A nervous and dissembling brand of architecture, infinitely far removed from true art, elbowed its way into the distinguished intimacy of old Berlin, and at key points in the city it still creates an impression of immaturity and incoherency that renders a feeling of deep pleasure impossible.[26]

In 1896 Ludwig Hoffmann, whose reputation had been established by a new building for the Imperial Court in Leipzig, became Blankenstein's successor as Stadtbaurat.[27] No fashionable eclectic, Hoffmann advocated simplicity and monumentality in architecture; his buildings, which "emerged like islands of good taste from a sea of mundane and pompous banalities,"[28] contributed materially to shaping the face of Berlin prior to 1918. One of his earliest projects was the Märkisches Museum (1901–07). Adapted from the brick Gothic style common to Brandenburg, the historical museum was a picturesquely grouped complex of buildings in which the style of the rooms was in keeping with the items on display. Hoffmann's Rudolf-Virchow-Hospital in Wedding (1898–1906), a city within the city arranged along a broad central avenue, recalled the monasteries of the baroque period in Austria. The Stadthaus (fig. 18; town hall; 1902–11) in a rather heavy, Doric mode, and the Märchenbrunnen (fairy-tale fountain) at Friedrichshain (1913) were among his most popular and well-known projects. After the early death of his boyhood friend, Alfred Messel, Hoffmann assumed responsibility for the erection of the Pergamon Museum (1909–30). Messel himself was a gifted architect, whose major work, and one of Berlin's most highly admired buildings, was the Wertheim Department Store on Leipziger Platz (fig. 19; 1896–97). Its unprecedented combination of thin supports and large areas of glazing provoked paeans of praise, among others from the art critic Alfred Lichtwark, who in the journal *Pan* for 1897 exclaimed: "Liberation! That is the feeling with which a layman is compelled to gape upwards in awe at this magnificent facade, which is more imposing than a hundred government edifices; it radiates a free, creative strength."[29]

Both Hoffmann and Messel were instrumental in overcoming the historical revival styles and rendering Berlin architecture receptive to the innovative approaches of the twentieth century.

Residential Suburbs

In the decades before World War I, as foreseen by the Hobrecht Plan, Berlin expanded beyond its city center and the existing suburbs into the countryside of the Mark Brandenburg. The area encompassed by the ring railway agglomerated into the largest tenement town in the world, the "city of stone" Werner Hegemann so graphically described in his book *Das steinerne Berlin*.[30] Far outside this zone, new suburbs arose—Lichterfelde, Grunewald, Friedenau, residential areas with single- and two-family houses in spacious yards that have remained preferred addresses for Berliners to this day. Their founder was an entrepreneur from Hamburg, J.A.W. Carstenn (later knighted to von Carstenn-Lichterfelde). Already in 1865 he acquired the estates of Lichterfelde and Giesensdorf, extensive sheep-grazing lands between the Potsdam and Anhalt railways, and began to parcel and develop them along English garden-city lines. Stations on the two railways ensured rapid transportation downtown, and reasonable lot prices enabled even people with modest incomes to build their own houses. Increasing numbers of Berliners turned their backs on the *Mietskaserne* and moved out in the country, attracted by the prospect of a home and garden in the suburbs.

In 1869, when William I came to visit him in Lichterfelde, Carstenn replied to the monarch's inquiry as to the further development of Berlin: "Your majesty, after the accomplishments of 1866, Berlin is destined to become the foremost city on the continent, and as regards its territorial expansion, Berlin and Potsdam must become a single city, connected by the Grunewald forest as a park."[31] Carstenn's vision of Berlin as a garden city circumscribed around a densely built-up center became reality—a metropolis with the most extensive residential suburbs in the world, surrounded by and interspersed with woods and lakes.

Industrial Architecture

Mass production, the replacement of steam by electric power, the economic upswing that followed Prussia's defeat of France in 1871, and the advantageous conditions produced by new waterways and railways—these were key factors in the burgeoning of Berlin's industry at the close of the nineteenth century. While in the first half of the century it was English factory construction and manufacturing processes that set the example, in the latter half, it was those of the United States. One of the first built on the American pattern was Ludwig Loewe's sewing machine factory in Moabit. Emil Rathenau, founder of the Allgemeine Elektricitäts-Gesellschaft (AEG), could also rely on personal knowledge of American production methods in designing the plant for his electrical corporation. The transition from the central steam engine with transmission drive to separate electric motors on each machine in a plant influenced the labor process and factory architecture; Peter Behrens's buildings for AEG reflected this change.

20. Peter Behrens. AEG Turbine factory (1908–09), Moabit, 1920. Landesbildstelle Berlin.

Now, sheds of almost unlimited spaciousness could be erected in which the fragile-looking steel supports had merely to extend to the height of the crane track and bear the load of the traveling cranes. The roof above, spanning the entire space, and the thin walls, no more than partitions, had no additional static function. This made it possible to install skylights and windows of any desired size, to admit sufficient daylight to illuminate the premises.[32]

Behrens was named artistic adviser to the corporation in 1906 with responsibility for product design, advertising art, and industrial architecture. His projects in the latter area included a turbine factory in Moabit, erected in 1908–09 (fig. 20), a factory for high-voltage equipment (1910), an assembly shed for large machinery (1911–12), and a small-motor plant in Wedding (1910–13). The turbine factory, a "manifesto of the young art of industrial building,"[33] established Behrens's reputation as an industrial architect. The 361-foot-long hall, in which giant steam turbines were assembled, was a three-joint girder construction with completely glazed curtain walls between the steel uprights. The southern facade, bearing the AEG logo designed by Behrens, was an impressive statement of the company's prestige.

From 1907 to 1911 the staff of Behrens's private office included three young architects who were later to become the most significant in Europe: Walter Gropius, Le Corbusier, and Ludwig Mies van der Rohe. Within the course of only a few years the office produced such major buildings as the exclusive country house of the archaeologist Dr. Wiegand in Berlin-Dahlem (1911–12), the administration offices of the Continental Corporation in Hanover (1911–12), the Mannesmann pipe plant in Düsseldorf (1911–12), and the Imperial German Embassy in Leningrad (1914). In 1910, Gropius left Behrens's firm and formed his own partnership with Adolf Meyer. One of the first projects involved designs for the Benscheidt shoe last factory in Alfeld. Better known as the Fagus Works, this building was probably the major industrial building in pre-1918 Germany apart from Behrens's AEG structures.

The New Style

In 1900, Harry Graf Kessler[34] commissioned a young architect by the name of Henry van de Velde to furnish his apartment at 28 Köthener Strasse in Schöneberg, the so-called privy councillor neighborhood of Berlin between Anhalt and Potsdam stations. The result was a light and airy interior with paneled walls and white lacquered furniture adorned with sparing ornamentation in bronze (figs. 21 and 22). In his autobiography, Van de Velde called the project "an 'elegant' example of my artistic activity."[35] It was as highly admired as Van de Velde's other Berlin projects, which included an outlet of the Havana-Compagnie, at 11–12 Mohrenstrasse (1899), the interior design of the premises of the royal coiffeur, Haby, at 7–8 Mittelstrasse (1901), where the bristling, upturned moustache à la Emperor William was created. For the Paul and Bruno Cassirer Gallery at 35 Victoriastrasse, hub of the Berlin Secession, Van de Velde designed the furnishings and wall coverings of a reading room in which the clientele could peruse international art journals.

Despite the fact that he left Berlin in 1901 to become head of the art school in Weimar, Van de Velde's influence in Berlin proved lasting. Still, rather than developing into a center of Art Nouveau, Berlin tended more to the simplified, even austere forms of neoclassicism. This explains why its architects, in seeking a way to overcome the eclecticism of the historical revival styles, turned to the craft tradition exemplified by the German masters of the late eighteenth and early nineteenth centuries. The resounding success of Paul Mebes's book *Um 1800* (*Around 1800*), is a case in point.[36] Central tenets of the new architecture were simplicity and respect of materials, combined with comfort and utility. The country houses designed in 1905–10 by Hermann Muthesius (1861–1927), located at Rehwiese, in Schlachtensee and Zehlendorf, were indeed delightfully straightforward in design and exceptionally comfortable to live in.[37]

In the years 1869–1903, Muthesius was attached to the German Embassy in London for the purpose of conducting a study of English residential architecture. The result was a three-volume work entitled *Das englische Haus* (1904), whose motto, a quote from Francis Bacon, was "Houses are built to live in, not to look at." The houses Muthesius built were not the stiff and ostentatious villas that dot the Berlin suburbs but true country houses, without basement floors, the garden areas opening out directly from the rooms, each of which was individually designed, very light and airy, and furnished with graceful natural wood furniture. The houses had such typically English detailing as wide windows with white-painted mullions, bow windows, steep roofs with low eaves, and glazed brick facades.

Apartment housing also departed from traditional approaches around 1900.[38] The impetus came not only from public housing associations but from private developers who began conceiving "residential gardens" in which the traditional apartment block was opened up to incorporate large areas of green for common use. An early example of this dispersion of the solid architectural mass was Riehmer's Hofgarten in the Kreuzberg district of Berlin (1855–99), with imposing front buildings on two parallel streets connected by lateral wings flanking a spacious court to which access is provided by a private road. A similar layout was employed for the Versöhnungs-Privatstrasse, an apartment complex in Wedding built by the Vaterländischer Bauverein in 1903–04, whose buildings, in various historical styles, contain nearly three hundred flats ranged around six courtyards. One of the earliest examples of a solid block with an open, landscaped central area was Paul Wolff's design for the Ceciliengärten in Friedenau (1912). In the housing Paul Mebes planned for the Beamten-Wohnungs-Verein zu Berlin (Civil Servants' Housing Association), the interior courtyard was opened out to merge with the public area of the street, as in his projects on Horstweg in Charlottenburg (1907–10), on Fritschweg in Steglitz (1907–08), or in Niederschönhausen (1908–09). The largest single development of this type, however, was the Gartenterrassenstadt built by the Berlinische Boden-Gesellschaft around Rüdesheimer Platz in Schöneberg (1910–14). These apartment buildings, four-story stucco-faced structures in the style of an English country house community, had frontages designed by Paul Jatzow and

21

22

21. Alfred Messel. *Eduard Simon House* (1902–04). Street facade, 1908. From *Blätter für Architektur und Kunsthandwerk* 22 (1908).

22. Alfred Messel. *Eduard Simon House* (1902–04). Garden facade, 1908. From *Blätter für Architektur und Kunsthandwerk* 22 (1908).

23

24

23. & 24. Albert Gessner. Schiller Park and Sophie-Charlotte Park complexes, 1905–07.

were sold under the proviso that the owner agreed not to alter them. The usual front gardens surrounded by high iron fences were replaced by hillocks of lawn, and the space between the buildings extended to 144 feet.

Among the finest inner-city apartment projects of the period were Albert Gessner's buildings in Charlottenburg: the Green House at 2 Niebuhrstrasse (1905–06), the Yellow House at 5 Mommsenstrasse (1906–07), and the Schillerpark and Sophie-Charlottenpark complexes between Bismarck, Schiller, and Grolmannstrasse (figs. 23 and 24; 1905–07). The facades were modeled on country houses, with differently shaped windows on each floor, loggias and corner alcoves, and steep roofs with projecting eaves. To underscore their individuality with respect to the surrounding five-story standard apartment buildings, their roughcast fronts were painted in bright colors—yellow, green, and blue. This tendency to color as a design element was also apparent in the rowhouses by Bruno Taut at the Akazienhof in the garden city of Falkenberg (1913), a means of enlivening the cityscape that Taut continued to employ into the 1920s. "Color is joy in life," wrote Taut in his "Aufruf zum farbigen Bauen" ("An Appeal for Color in Architecture") of 1919: "Dun-colored houses must at long last be replaced by blue, red, yellow, green, black, and white houses, in undiluted brilliant hues."[39]

Paul Mebes's contribution to the garden city was more traditional in nature. His two-story rowhouses in the suburb of Zehlendorf (1912–14) were actually single-family houses combined two by two under a common roof and set parallel to the street. The facades, conceived in a dignified adaptation of the early neoclassical style, had gables over the entrances and a classical order of columns. Paul Schmitthenner's garden town of Staaken, built for the employees of the Spandau munitions factories, was likewise beholden to traditional styles of the kind described by Camillo Sitte in his influential volume *Der Städtebau nach seinen künstlerischen Grundsätzen (1889).* The three hundred single-family houses inside the complex were ensconced within a town wall of two-story row blocks, a feature which, together with the large gardens, produced a sort of regimented intimacy that recalled the small towns of the Frederician era. Hub of the development is the Heidebergplan, a spacious square surrounded by houses whose upswept brick gables call to mind the northern German marketplace of the late Middle Ages. Also located there are two schools, shops for daily needs, and a small church built in 1921 in place of that suggested by Schmitthenner, which would have soared over and dominated the cityscape.

The perimeter city block enclosing spacious green areas in place of the narrow, dark courtyards typical of Berlin's tenement districts, was suggested as early as 1910 by Hermann Jansen, in his first-prize design for the Competition for the Development of a Basic Plan for the Construction of Greater Berlin. The competition stipulated an urban-planning conception for the rapidly expanding metropolis, a complete redesign of the inner city, the regulation of traffic and transport—suggesting central north and south stations to replace the many existing peripheral terminals—designs for projected suburbs, and integration of the forests and green areas encompassing

Berlin. To publicize the plans, an Allgemeine Städtebau-Ausstellung (General City Building Exhibition) was held in Berlin in 1910, and to put them into effect, at least in part, an association called the Zweckverband Gross-Berlin was founded in 1911. Although the divergent interests of the various communities and transport companies prevented the comprehensive building plan from being realized by 1918, the association did succeed, in 1915, in purchasing the Grunewald forest and declaring it a protected area; in 1919, the privately run tramlines came into municipal ownership, the first step toward a united Berlin public transport system.

It was not until after World War I that a certain coherence of planning was ensured by the creation in 1920 of the administrative unit of greater Berlin, incorporating seven towns (Charlottenburg, Wilmersdorf, Schöneberg, Neukölln, Lichtenberg, Köpenick, and Spandau), fifty-nine rural communities, and twenty-seven estates. With a total area of 340 square miles and almost four million inhabitants, Berlin now ranked among the largest metropolitan cities in the world.

Notes

1. Unter den Linden was an avenue divided by four rows of lime trees, conceived in 1647 by Frederick William, the Great Elector, to connect the Lustgarten with the Tiergarten. When Berlin was fortified (1658–83), Unter den Linden lay outside the New Gate. In 1674, Dorotheenstadt was erected on both sides of the avenue, and in 1732, the district was expanded to the west and Unter den Linden capped by a square plaza (Quarré, later Pariser Platz) and the Brandenburg Gate. It soon developed into the most magnificent thoroughfare in the Prussian residence city. See W. Löschburg, *Unter den Linden* ([East] Berlin pub: 1983).

2. Robert Springer, *Berlin, die deutsche Kaiserstadt nebst Potsdam und Charlottenburg mit ihren schönsten Bauwerken und hervorragendsten Monumenten* (Darmstadt, 1878).

3. Jonas F. Geist, *Passagen. Ein Bautyp des 19. Jahrhunderts* (Munich, pub: 1978 (2)), 132–41.

4. Otto Hach, *Kunstgeschichtliche Wanderungen durch Berlin* (Berlin, 1897), 46.

5. Eduard Gaertner, *Strasse Unter den Linden* (Berlin: Neue Nationalgalerie SMPK, 1853).

6. Hans Reuther, *Barock in Berlin* (Berlin, 1969).

7. *Karl Friedrich Schinkel 1781–1841*, exhibition catalogue ([East] Berlin: Staatliche Museen zu Berlin, 1981); also, Hermann G. Pundt, *Schinkel's Berlin* (Cambridge, 1972). A comprehensive review of Schinkel's activity is found in Paul Ortwin Rave and Margarete Kühn, eds., *Schinkelwerk*.

8. Ilja Miek, "Der Staat und die Anfänge des Maschinenbaus in Berlin," in *Berlin: Von der Residenzstadt zur Industriemetropole*, exhibition catalogue (Berlin: Technische Universität Berlin, 1981), 97–109.

9. Wolfgang Klee, *Preussische Eisenbahngeschichte* (Stuttgart, 1982).

10. Harri Günther, *Peter Joseph Lenné* ([East] Berlin, 1985), 175.

11. In connection with the International Building Exhibition in Berlin, a number of excellent studies on the history of Luisenstadt were published: Christiane Bascon-Borgelt et al., *In der Luisenstadt. Studien zur Stadtgeschichte von Berlin-Kreuzberg* (Berlin, 1983); Erika Hausmann and Clarissa Soltendiek, *Von der Wiese zum Baublock. Zur Entwicklungsgeschichte der Kreuzberger Mischung* (Berlin, 1986).

12. Johann Friedrich Geist and Klaus Kürvers, *Das Berliner Mietshaus 1740–1862* (Munich, 1980).

13. Gesine Asmus, ed., *Hinterhof, Keller und Mansarde. Einblicke in Berliner Wohnungselend 1901–1920* (Berlin, 1982).

14. Jochen Boberg et al., eds., *Exerzierfeld der Moderne. Industriekultur in Berlin im 19. Jahrhundert* (Munich, 1984).

15. Manfred Klinkott, "Die Backsteinbaukunst der Berliner Schule. Von K.F. Schinkel bis zum Ausgang des Jahrhunderts," *Die Bauwerke und Kunstdenkmäler von Berlin* 15 (supplement, 1988).

16. A. Woltmann, *Die Baugeschichte Berlins bis auf die Gegenwart* (Berlin, 1872), 252ff.

17. Eva Börsch-Supan, "Berliner Baukunst nach Schinkel 1840-1870," *Studien zur Kunst des neunzehnten Jahrhunderts* 25 (1977).

18. *Berlin und seine Bauten*, vol. 3 (Berlin, 1896), 273ff., figs. 147–716. Conversion by Ende & Böckmann.

19. Edited by Carl Hoffmann and Georg Erbkam, with a large-format plate section based on Ludwig Försters's *Allgemeine Bauzeitung* published in Vienna. Discontinued in 1931.

20. *Berlin und seine Bauten*, compiled and edited by the Architekten-Verein zu Berlin and the Vereinigung Berliner Architekten, Berlin, 1877 (2nd expanded ed., 1896; repr. 1988). Berlin architecture after 1900 is reviewed in subsequent volumes of the series, the first of which was published in 1964 and appears at irregular intervals. *Berlin und seine Bauten* is the most comprehensive work on the city's architectural history.

21. Hans Reuther, *Die Museumsinsel in Berlin* (Berlin, 1978): Renate Petras, *Die Bauten der Berliner Museumsinsel* ([East] Berlin, 1987).

22. Julius Posener, "Berlin auf dem Wege zu einer neuen Architektur," *Studien zur Kunst des 19. Jahrhunderts* 40 (1979).

23. Even such major architectural landmarks as Heinrich Gentz's Mint and Schinkel's Palais Redern were demolished.

24. Reinhard Rurup, "Vergangenheit und Gegenwart der Geschichte. 750 Jahre Berlin," in Ulrich Eckhardt, ed., *Lese- und Programmbuch zum Stadtjubiläum* (Berlin, 1987), 80.

25. Karl-Heinz Metzger and Ulrich Dunker, *Der Kürfürstendamm. Leben und Mythos des Boulevards in 100 Jahren deutscher Geschichte* (Berlin, 1986).

26. Max Osborn, "Berlin," *Berühmte Kunststätten* 43 (1909): 262.

27. Wolfgang Schäche, ed., "Ludwig Hoffmann. Lebenserinnerungen eines Architekten," *Die Bauwerke und Kunstdenkmäler von Berlin* 10 (supplement, 1983).

28. Fritz Stahl, "Ludwig Hoffmann," *Berliner Architekturwelt* 7 (1907): 3.

29. Quoted in Karl-Heinz Hüter, *Architektur in Berlin 1900-1933* (Dresden, 1987), 24.

30. Werner Hegemann, *Das steinerne Berlin* (Lugano, 1930; repr. 1984).

31. Hegemann, *Das steinerne Berlin*, 245.

32. Henning Rogge, "Die Fabrik wird zur Maschine," in Boberg et al., eds., *Exerzierfeld der Moderne*, 330.

33. F. Mannhiemer, "AEG-Bauten," *Jahrbuch des Deutschen Werkbundes* (Jena, 1913), 547; Tilmann Buddensieg and Henning Rogge, *Industriekultur. Peter Behrens und die AEG 1907–1914* (Berlin, 1980).

34. Harry Graf Kessler (1868–1937), art patron and diplomat, co-editor of the journal *Pan*, president of the German Peace Society and advocate of the United Nations. In 1933, Kessler was forced to emigrate, abandoning his priceless art collection and furnishings, to France, where he died in 1937. See Harry Graf Kessler, *Tagebücher 1918-1937* (Frankfurt am Main, 1979).

35. Henry van de Velde, *Geschichte meines Lebens* (rev. ed., Munich, 1986), 161.

36. Paul Mebes, *Um 1800. Architektur und Handwerk im letzten Jahrhundert ihrer traditionellen Entwicklung* (Munich, 1908).

37. H. Muthesius, ed., *Landhäuser von Hermann Muthesius* (Munich, 1912).

38. For an exhaustive description, see *Berlin und seine Bauten*, part 4, in *Wohnungsbau*, vol. B, "Die Wohngebäude—Mehrfamilienhäuser" (Berlin, 1974).

39. Bruno Taut, "Aufruf zum farbigen Bauen," *Die Bauwelt* 10 and 38 (1919).

1. *Meyers Hof, Ackerstrasse*
132–133, Wedding. Aerial view
from south, c. 1930. Landbildstelle
Berlin.

The Berlin *Mietskaserne* and Its Reforms

Dietrich Worbs

Dietrich Worbs is an assistant professor of architectural history at the University of Stuttgart and works for the city of Berlin's Department of Architectural Preservation. Worbs curated the 1983 exhibition "Adolf Loos" at the Akademie der Künste, Berlin, and has worked as an architect and town planner. His publications and lectures deal with the problems of architecture and town planning during the nineteenth and twentieth centuries.

The Berlin Mietskaserne

This essay will not examine the development of Berlin's *Mietskaserne*, or housing barrack, during the eighteenth and nineteenth centuries, as this is already the subject of numerous publications.[1] Instead, I would like to describe the various possibilities for the reform of the *Mietskaserne* after 1900 and the resulting potential for its further development after World War I, suggesting that ossified conditions themselves developed the momentum necessary for reform.

Despite the term's German connotations, the Berlin *Mietskaserne* is neither a uniform nor a standardized construction. The term refers to a wide range of buildings that were built for different social classes and that reflected these differences. It is true, of course, that in almost every case there is a common pattern composed of front house, side wings, and cross houses enclosing inner courtyards, and that the *Mietskaserne* is nearly always five stories high, taking advantage of established height limitations of sixty-five to seventy feet. But, for example, the size of the courtyards depended on the width and depth of the lot and the number and size of the apartments, causing resulting constructions to vary greatly. There are enormous differences between Meyers Hof (fig. 1; 1874) at Ackerstrasse 132–133 in Wedding, with its three hundred apartments, and the houses on Kurfürstendamm (built around 1900) with their ten twelve-room apartments of three thousand square feet or more. It is remarkable that despite the many differences in size, hygiene, and comfort, these apartment houses, whether for the working class, middle class, or even upper class, all share the same basic plan. Moreover, this was a common feature not just for a few years but for the relatively long time span between the unification of Germany in 1871 and the period of highly developed capitalism around 1900. The apartments for the middle and upper classes were incomparably larger and much better equipped—with bathrooms, water closets, heating, and elevator—than those for the working class, but these too were built according to the same principle of maximum utilization of space. Placed more or less closely around inner courtyards and on lots with a high building density, they were not particularly pleasant places in which to live. It is no wonder, therefore, that the first country house colonies in Berlin (for example, Grunewald, Westend, Friedenau, Lichterfelde), which were built in the 1860s and 1870s, were stiff competition for the *Mietskaserne*. This was also at a time in which the latter had reached the final stage in its development toward being a completed system.

The *Mietskaserne* and the urban planning that supported its construction—in particular, the Hobrecht plan (1858–62) for the expansion of the city—were sharply criticized, however, as early as the 1860s and 1870s.[2] In 1877 the city's Architect's Association presented the following defense in *Berlin und seine Bauten (Berlin and Its Buildings)*:

As is true of other areas of life in this peculiar city, Berlin's apartment houses are the brunt of a great deal of biased criticism. The well-meaning desire to rectify their serious shortcomings has often led to a one-sided and exaggerated emphasis upon these shortcomings. Descriptions of the "horror" of "sky-high housing barracks" in

2. Albert Gessner, c. 1920. Gessner
Family Archive.

which "herds" of people have been "packed on top of each other"...
have been used to create the impression that nowhere could there be
more impractical, uncomfortable, unhealthy, and uglier apartment
houses than in Berlin. In response to this, it must be said that, in
general, Berlin's apartment houses are better than their reputation.
It is undeniable that they play a dominating role in the city and that
their capacity for yielding profits is exploited to the utmost. These
unfortunate facts are the results of social conditions, however, and
these cannot be improved easily or through the use of external
means.[3]

An analysis following the association's published comments of
the emergence and development of the *Mietskaserne* layout
and ground plan, making use of statistics from the census of
1871, actually worsened the image of the *Mietskaserne*. While
working-class housing barracks such as Meyers Hof were
strongly criticized, high costs were also bemoaned:

It is obvious that this lay-out creates huge problems. The division of
individual rooms in an apartment by a common corridor makes it impossible to enjoy the comfort of a private home and leads to un-
pleasant encounters amongst the different families. Moreover, these
dark . . . and indirectly ventilated corridors, which are used by a
great number of people, are clearly highly detrimental to the health
of the inhabitants. Nevertheless, to this point it has not been possible to introduce a better system, for this would be substantially more
expensive.[4]

Twenty years later (1896) in the second, expanded edition of
Berlin und seine Bauten, the criticism, defense, and partial
confirmation of the so-called great evils of Berlin's *Mietskaserne* remained basically the same as they had been in
1877.[5]

The most thorough as well as the most devastating criticism
came from Werner Hegemann in 1930. His book *Das steinerne
Berlin (Berlin: City of Stone)*, which he wrote after a long examination of urban planning and construction in Berlin up to
1914, bore the telling subtitle *A History of the World's Largest
City of Housing Barracks*. Hegemann's convincing explanation for the emergence of these barracks in Berlin was that
they had developed from the huge blocks of streets that were
created by the plan for the development of Berlin in 1858–62
and by the city's Building Code of 1853 with its very permis-
sive regulations concerning construction on potential building
sites.

Although the municipal authorities had originally had the laudable
plan of using residential streets to divide the oversize blocks of
buildings, they subsequently decided to let half of Berlin's population live in backyard buildings. Instead of making a decent plan for
the city, they preferred to give this up. They had only one goal. The
compensation that the government would have been obligated to pay
for the land used for streets . . . had to be painlessly diverted to the
landowners. Legally, this was only possible if the landowners could
be persuaded to accept this diversion. . . . The landowners, who controlled the city, were permitted to take part in its planning. The necessary residential streets were left out of the plan. The land needed
for thoroughfares was obtained at no cost. . . for the plan's broad
streets and huge blocks gave landowners the unexpected chance to
exploit to the maximum the dismal Building Code of 1853 in an entirely new way. With the construction of front-facing, side and cross

146

buildings, which measured five to seven storeys in height. . . they were able to enjoy substantial profits.[6]

The Building Code of 1853 remained valid until 1887–97 and, in parts, until 1925. The only restrictions it placed upon the use of a building site was that the height of the eaves could not exceed seventy feet and the courtyard had to be at least seventeen by seventeen feet (the amount of space needed to turn a fire engine). The code did not explicitly forbid window-less rooms; the result of the plan for the development of Berlin, the Hobrecht Plan of 1858–62, and the Building Code of 1853, which Hegemann sarcastically described as "being as perfectly suited to each other as ammunition to a gun or a gun to the appropriate ammunition,"[7] was that by 1900, four million inhabitants of Berlin were quartered in barracks-like housing.

It can come as no surprise that after more than thirty years one had grown weary of the *Mietskaserne*, in all of its different social manifestations, and that one had begun to search for possibilities of its reform. The era of historicism was drawing to a close and the architects who were opposed to its masquerade of style also saw that the quality of life in an apartment house—that is, its floor plan and layout—had to be improved and even reformed. Some of the most instructive books on architecture that appeared shortly after 1900 were devoted to the question of housing reform.[8]

All of the efforts for this were directed toward doing away with the *Mietskaserne* through changing the rigid nature of its ground plan, abandoning the uniform size of the lots, introducing central services (boarding house, one kitchen house), or simply rejecting the apartment house in favor of the town house. It was thought that the town house—which had disappeared long ago from Berlin—could be reintroduced as a multistory terraced house. Workers organized the first building cooperatives and began to construct the first large terraced housing estates.

Examples of Reform: Albert Gessner's Reformed Apartment Houses

Albert Gessner (fig. 2) made a name for himself as both a theoretician and a practicing architect. As was the case with many other Berlin architects, he was not originally from Berlin. Born in Auel/Saxony, he studied in Dresden and Berlin and worked with the firm of Kayser and Von Groszheim and with Alfred Messel before establishing his own company in 1897.

Gessner was one of the first to recognize that the misery of the Berlin *Mietskaserne* represented a failure on the part of architects, and he did everything he could to pay off the debt incurred by members of his profession. He built his first apartment houses, called Yellow Houses, in Charlottenburg at Mommsenstrasse 6 (1903–04), Niebuhrstrasse 78 (1904–05), and Mommsenstrasse 5 (1906–07). His Green House was built at Niebuhrstrasse 2 (1905–06). Together with the two apartment houses built by his brother-in-law Otto Harnisch at Bleib-

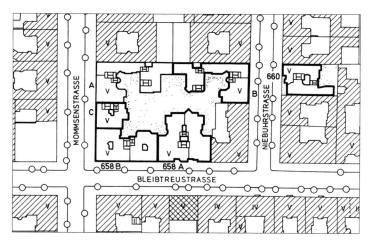

3. Albert Gessner. Yellow Houses I, II, III, and Green House (1903–07), Mommsenstrasse 6, Niebuhrstrasse 78, Mommsenstrasse 5, and Niebuhrstrasse 2, Charlottenberg. Site plan. Also includes houses at Bleibtreustrasse 15–16, 17 designed by Otto Harnisch and others. Architekten-und-Ingenieur Verein zu Berlin.

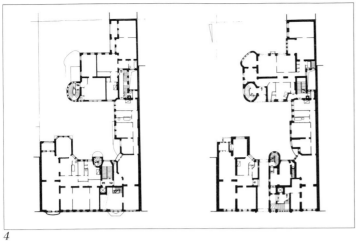

4

5

6

7

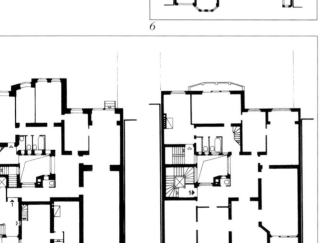

8

9

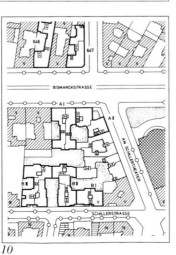

10

11

4. Albert Gessner. Yellow House II (1904–05), Niebuhrstrasse 78. Floor plans of ground and fourth levels. Architekten-und-Ingenieur Verein zu Berlin.

5. Albert Gessner. Yellow House II (1904–05), Niebuhrstrasse 78. From Albert Gessner, *Das deutsche Mietshaus.*

6. Albert Gessner. Green House (1905–06), Niebuhrstrasse 2. Floor plan of second level. Architekten-und-Ingenieur Verein zu Berlin.

7. Albert Gessner. Yellow House III (1906–07), Mommsenstrasse 5. From Albert Gessner, Das deutsche Mietshaus.

8. Albert Gessner. Yellow House III (1906–07), Mommsenstrasse 5. Floor plans of ground and fourth levels. Architekten-und-Ingenieur Verein zu Berlin.

9. Albert Gessner, architect. Green House (1905–06), Niebuhrstrasse 2. From Albert Gessner, Das deutsche Mietshaus.

10. Albert Gessner. Sophie-Charlotte Park and Schiller Park (1905–7), Schillerstrasse 11, 12–16, Grolmanstrasse 1–6, Bismarckstrasse 108–109, Charlottenburg. Site plan. Architekten-und-Ingenieur Verein zu Berlin.

11. Albert Gessner. Sophie-Charlotte Park and Schiller Park (1905–07). Inner courtyard view. From Albert Gessner, Das deutsche Mietshaus.

treustrasse 15/16 and 17 at the corner of Mommsenstrasse (1902–03, 1905), the Yellow Houses formed a complex around a courtyard, which would be of decisive importance in the design of the city's first reformed apartment houses (figs. 3–7).

The ground plans for these buildings reflect their immediate proximity to the garden courtyard. Two buildings (Mommsenstrasse 6 and Niebuhrstrasse 78) form the complex's western end. They each have a front house, a single-loaded side wing, and a shortened cross house. In this way, the courtyard is shielded and structured. The building at Mommsenstrasse 5 only has one front house. Of the two buildings on Bleibtreustrasse, the one at 15/16 has a strong, short middle wing. While the garden courtyard is structured, nowhere is it constrained or split up.

The front houses at Mommsenstrasse 6 and Niebuhrstrasse 78 have two apartments per story. In the cross house and lengthened side wings are either two smaller apartments or one large apartment. These can be reached through a rounded stairwell on the outside of the cross house. The building at Mommsenstrasse 5 has one apartment per story, with an interior light well, which provides light to the main and secondary staircases and, in particular, to the apartment's entrance, hallway, and other rooms.

Apart from the idea of placing single buildings in a block ensemble around the garden courtyard, this light well was Gessner's other invention. He would use it in a number of imaginative variations in his ground plans. The light well allowed not only for the replacement of Berlin's dark apartment corridors with a bright hallway or a small vestibule, it was now also possible to group together functionally related rooms such as the living room and bedrooms, rather than placing them in a row as had traditionally been the case.

The ground plan for the Green House at Niebuhrstrasse 2 is perhaps the best example of how Gessner opened up apartments through a hallway brightened by the light well (figs. 8, 9). Gessner allowed himself a lot of freedom with this building: he created alcoves and terraced loggias, opened up the house front and moved it about, and planted a small garden at the ground story level. The ground plan is practically a jigsaw puzzle in the manner of Muthesius's country houses. Gessner effortlessly achieved the same homey quality and comfort that was displayed by Muthesius in his country houses.

As early as 1905–07, Gessner tested his three inventions—the block ensemble, light wells for the halls, and the clustering together of rooms—on a larger scale. He did this with a group of seven apartment buildings (figs. 10–13; Sophie-Charlotte Park/Schiller Park) that occupied half a residential block between Bismarckstrasse, Grolmanstrasse, and Schillerstrasse. (Bismarckstrasse 108 and 109, Grolmanstrasse 1–6, and Schillerstrasse 11, and 12–16; the complex was partially destroyed during World War II). It was here that Gessner also made use of a further reform element—that of the street courtyard—which, however, had already been developed by others before him. Through the use of such a courtyard, the cross house was opened to the street.

12

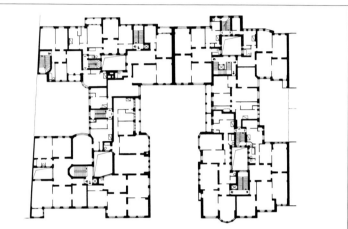

13

12. Albert Gessner. Sophie-Charlotte Park and Schiller Park (1905–07). View of street courtyard from Herderstrasse (south). Landeskonservator Berlin, Fotoarchiv.

13. Albert Gessner. Schiller Park (1905–07), Schillerstrasse 12–15. Floor plan of third level of eastern section. Architekten-und-Ingenieur Verein zu Berlin.

14

14. *Paul Mebes c. 1930.* Mebes Family Archive.

15. *Paul Mebes. Schöneberg (1906–07). Street view from Salzburger Strasse and Warburgstrasse (west).* Beamten-Wohnungs-Verein e.G.

16. *Paul Mebes. Schöneberg (1906–07), Badensche Strasse, Salzburger Strasse, Wartburgstrasse, Martin-Luther-Strasse, Schöneberg. Site plan.* Architekten-und-Ingenieur Verein zu Berlin.

17. *Paul Mebes. Schöneberg (1906–07). Ground plan.* Beamten-Wohnungs-Verein e.G.

The front houses had two apartments per story, and the cross houses had one, two, or three per story. Some of the stairways were in the interior, next to large lightwells, and some overlooked the courtyard. By choosing to design apartments of differing sizes, Gessner was able to include a third apartment on each story of the eastern section, facing the street courtyard. Almost all of the apartments had a foyer that opened into a large hallway that was lit by the lightwell. The study or smoking room could have been entered from the foyer, and directly beside the side entrance and the kitchen was a sizable room for the cook. At this time, such a display of consideration toward household help was not at all the norm.

It was not only Gessner's highly diverse floor plans that were new and unusual. This was also true of his volumetric articulation, his design of the facades, and his use of color. It was important to him that houses had genuinely steeped roofs, usually mansards that sloped down very low and that were given a variegated articulation through crossing gables, oriels, bay windows, loggias, balconies, terraces, and pergolas, as well as through numerous interruptions in the eave alignment. There is nearly a complete absence of historical architectural elements such as pilasters, column arrangements, and ledges, found only in the great variety of openings and in structural articulations such as oriels and gables. Gessner himself wrote, "As far as the work on the exterior of such blocks is concerned, the picturesque principle is a practical one—even if this is not considered to be the highest level of architecture. We Germans have this in our blood."[9] As Julius Posener has already noted, this statement was a swipe at the teachings extolled by Ostendorf.[10] Above all, Gessner's position was one that recognized the real necessities of life, including the need for differentiation, for the picturesque effect of buildings. Perhaps Gessner borrowed these principles from the country house architects of England; not only Muthesius but also Gessner had devoted intensive study to these country houses. In the coloration of his own buildings—yellow, green, violet, ochre—Gessner imparted distinctive features to the cityscape and anticipated trends of the 1920s.

Paul Mebes's Housing Complexes for the Civil Service Housing Association

From the turn of the century until the 1930s, Paul Mebes (fig. 14) played an important role in Berlin's architectonic development, particularly in the sphere of housing (fig. 14). Born in Magdeburg, Mebes studied in Braunschweig and Berlin. Between 1902 and 1905 he worked for the government and from 1906 to 1922, he served as technical director on the executive board of Berlin's Civil Servants' Housing Association (Beamten-Wohnungs-Verein), which had been founded in 1900. In the years between 1906–10, he built five large housing complexes (Schöneberg, Charlottenburg, Steglitz, Niederschönhausen, and Zehlendorf) for the association. Mebes's book *Um 1800* which appeared in 1908, exerted a great deal of influence. It launched a revival of interest in traditional craftsmanship and brought about a more functional approach to design. This was an approach already espoused by the *Deutsche Werkbund*, which Mebes joined in 1912. Between

150

1912–14, he built the Garden City Zehlendorf for the Civil Servants' Housing Association enlarged after the war (1919–21), and in the 1920s, together with Paul Emmerich, Mebes built the large housing estates Friedrich Ebert-Siedlung (1929–31), Haselhorst (1930–32), and the Smokeless City in Steglitz (1930–32).

The five-story housing complex in Schöneberg (figs. 15–17; 1906–07), located between Martin Luther Strasse, Wartburgstrasse, Salzburger Strasse, and Badensche Strasse, contained 217 apartments and eighteen stairwells (figs. 15–17). Ten staircases serviced houses with two apartments per story, and eight staircases serviced houses with three apartments per story. The site itself (which covered an entire residential block) was a trapezoid, an irregular quadrilateral of ninety-two thousand square feet of which sixty-two thousand square feet were covered with buildings. In the middle of the block, there is a quadratic core with an inner courtyard and four staircases; on the core's southern side is an irregular, four-sided structure with five staircases, and on both northeastern and northwestern corners there is a four-sided structure with five and four staircases respectively. The result is an irregular but clear geometric shape with a central inner courtyard that can be entered from the three inner courtyards and from the three street courtyards, resembling a tristar—ample proof of the designer's ability to understand geometrical arrangements. With respect to sunlight, ventilation, and accessibility, the structures on this prescribed, irregularly shaped site were arranged in an optimum manner. At five stories, however, the building density was simply too high. The size of the apartments ranged from two-room apartments at roughly 700 square feet to four-room apartments with one or two storage rooms at 1,340 square feet. Kitchens, bathrooms, and storage rooms were situated next to the inner courtyards, while living and bedrooms were next to the streets or the street courtyards. The stairwells were also located in the inner courtyards so that no living rooms or bedrooms were pushed away from their outside locations. All of the apartments were lit from two sides and had cross or diagonal ventilation; all were equipped with bathrooms and a water closet and with either a balcony or a loggia. In short, insofar as the high building density permitted, the apartments were model examples of hygiene and design.

Because of the three street courtyards, the monotony that often results from long facades is avoided. A diversified vertical articulation of the facades is achieved through the use of flat projections, loggias, that have been either retracted or pushed forward, intersecting gables that divided the mansard roof, ledges, and the alteration of roughcast and clinker brick surfaces. While this moderate animation of the facades did not even approach the differentiated manner of Gessner's animation, Mebes did not aim to design such facades. His friend Walter Curt Behrendt, who showed great support for Mebes's architecture, had the following to say about him.

What we need is an educated and tactful eclecticism which moves along the indicated paths in a dignified manner. This will be beneficial to the development of a civil architecture. It provides the practicing architect with the possibility to concentrate his energies on the necessary task of a new organization of ground plans and gives

15

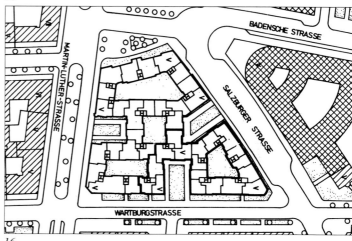

16

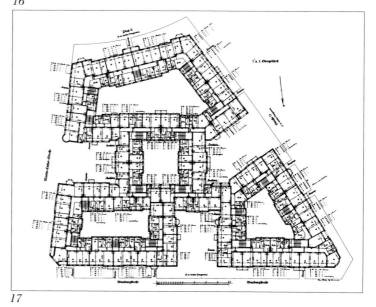

17

18

18. Alfred Messel, c. 1900. From W. C. Behrendt, Alfred Messel.

19. Alfred Messel. Housing complex, Sickingenstrasse 7–8 (1893–94), Tiergarten. Street view from south. Technische Universität Berlin, Plansammlung.

20. Alfred Messel. Housing complex, Sickingenstrasse 7–8, (1893–94), Tiergarten. View of inner courtyard from north. Technische Universität Berlin, Plansammlung.

21. Alfred Messel. Housing complex, Sickingenstrasse 7–8 (1893–94), Tiergarten. Floor plan of upper levels. Berlin auf dem Wege zu einer neuen Architektur.

him the absolutely vital freedom to create an effective and functional architecture. In the final analysis it is this which is important for our uncertain and transitional times.[11]

Alfred Messel's Workers' Apartment Houses for the Berliner Buildings and Savings Association

Alfred Messel (fig. 18) was born in Darmstadt and studied in Berlin (along with his compatriot and friend Ludwig Hoffmann, who would later become Berlin's *Stadtbaurat* (director of the city's department of urban planning and development). From 1878 to 1887, he worked as an architect for the Prussian state government and concentrated on housing, office buildings, and department stores. He achieved worldwide fame with the construction (beginning in 1896) of the department store Wertheim on Leipziger Strasse. In 1892, when the Berliner Building and Savings Association (Berliner Bau- und Sparverien) was founded, Messel became a member of its board and its architect. He built a number of housing complexes for this cooperative, including those on Sickingenstrasse (1893–94), Proskauer Strasse (1897–98), and Stargarder Strasse (1899–1900). He also built a further complex, the Weisbachgruppe (1898–1904), for an association concerned with the improvement of small-sized apartments in Berlin. Messel's earliest housing complex (figs. 19–21), Sickingenstrasse 7/8 in Berlin-Wedding, covered two lots and conformed to the layout of the *Mietskaserne*. Wings bordering the communal courtyard flanked each side of the twin front house; the twin cross house stood on its own, however, separate from the wings. The courtyard, which contained greenery, is unusually large (sixty-six by ninety-eight feet). This complex had approximately ninety apartments. The two-room, one-and-one-half room, and one-room apartments measured respectively roughly 490 square feet, 380 square feet, and 330 square feet, and each had a kitchen and a water closet of its own. The latter is ventilated by a small high window above the pantry. The front houses had three apartments per story, the side wings had two, and the cross house had four. The ground floor plans follow a traditional design.

In the front houses, despite the additional third apartment on each story, the baroque floor plan (as drawn, for example, by Philipp Gerlach in 1735) is clearly recognizable. The living room is on the side facing the street and the bedroom and kitchen are on the side facing the courtyard. In the cross house the ground plan for the apartments which contain a living room, bedroom, and kitchen is in the form of a cross. It has its origins in the ground plan used for the first houses built for day laborers in the eighteenth century. The cross-shaped floor plan is cut in half in the side wings. The two basic and very early types of housing for workers were thus used by Messel—albeit in a revised form—and augmented by a pantry and a water closet.

The complex's low density is surprising. The lot measures 19,355 square feet but there is construction on only 8,600 square feet. Had an additional cross house been constructed, the building density would have risen to such an extent that it would have become unbearable. Messel and the cooperative obviously preferred to avoid this.[1]

152

19

20

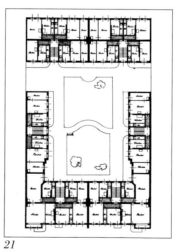

21

22

22. Alfred Messel. *Proskauer Strasse (1897–98), Friedrichshain. Street view from Banschstrasse and Proskauer Strasse.* Technische Universität Berlin, Plansammlung.

23. Alfred Messel. *Proskauer Strasse (1897–98), Proskauer Strasse 14–17, Schreinerstrasse 63–64, Banschstrasse 1, 14, Friedrichshain. Ground plan of Proskauer Strasse and Banschstrasse.* Technische Universität Berlin, Plansammlung.

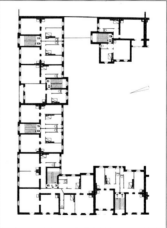

23

A further housing complex designed by Messel demonstrates how determined he was to adhere to his basic principles of creative ground plans, better sanitation facilities, low building density, and large, green courtyards.

Messel's second housing complex (figs. 22, 23; 1897–98) is at Proskauer Strasse, 14-17, Schreinerstrasse, 63, 64, and Bänschstrasse 13, 14 in Berlin-Friedrichshain. Located at the western end of a residential block, the complex was five stories high and U-shaped, with 116 apartments and six additional apartments that were also to be used for commercial purposes. A large courtyard was in the center of the complex. The lot measured 32,580 square feet but construction covered only 1,340 square feet. Messel clearly did not relinquish his intention of maintaining a low building density. He built along the borders of the block, rejecting the construction of side wings and cross houses, although this would have been possible. There was, however, a four-story house—a so-called garden house—with two stairwells servicing sixteen one-room apartments. The large, undivided courtyard was planted with greenery and trees.

The ten stairwells were entered from either the street or the courtyard, servicing two apartments per story. There were two stairwells, however, in the inner corners of the horseshoe that serviced three apartments per story. The size of the apartments ranged from one room (340 or 410 square feet) to the more common one-and-a-half room (490 square feet), and there were also two-room apartments (620 or 720 square feet). The apartments were cross ventilated, with natural light from both sides, and each with a water closet. The ground plan of the predominant one-and-a-half room apartments is the typical living room, kitchen, and bedroom layout, with the living room overlooking the street, and the bedroom and kitchen facing the courtyard. This ground plan, which Messel would continue to use both with and without the additional third apartment per story for his housing projects for workers, had been used in Berlin and Potsdam since the eighteenth century. The shops in the complex's ground story—a bakery, hairdresser's tobacconist, grocery store, and two pubs—met local needs and were, in part, owned by the cooperative. There were also rooms for communal purposes, including a library and a kindergarten, which were also used for a variety of communal functions. The gardenlike courtyard also contained a playground for children.

There is a lively articulation to the U-shaped structure, which is also true of Sickingenstrasse. At Proskauer Strasse, the structure is covered with a steep, saddleback roof which is framed by steep, hipped gables. The latter form the gables of the saddleback roofs over the two side sections of Schreinerstrasse and Bänschstrasse. In the side streets, the roofs are articulated by somewhat historicizing, stepped, or voluted gables. The facades are enlivened through the use of towers for the stairwells and through oriels, balconies, galleries, and loggias. On the courtyard side, however, the forms are simpler.

Apart from individual exceptions, historical stylistic features were used extremely sparingly and in a reduced articulation. Here, as with Gessner's and Mebes's apartment houses, one

can no longer speak of the use of a historical style but rather of a tactful eclecticism on the part of the architect. In so doing, Messel concentrated above all on the solution of fundamental problems to do with the organization of ground plans and the effective arrangement of the housing complex as a whole.[12]

The Ambivalence of the Reform: Stabilization or Radical Change?

Apart from the fundamental endeavor to improve the quality of housing for the upper, middle, and working classes through the development of such housing complexes, there were other, more peripheral attempts to replace the *Mietskaserne*, including the attempt to centralize housekeeping through the one-kitchen apartment house or the boarding house.

There are a number of examples of one-kitchen apartment houses in Berlin; they were built by Gessner on Wilhelmshöher Strasse 17–20 in Friedenau (1909–12) and by Hermann Muthesius on Unter den Eichen/Reichensteiner Weg in Steglitz (1908–09) and on Kuno-Fischer-Strasse[13] in Charlottenburg (1908). Centralized housekeeping in these houses did not last for long, however, for kitchens were soon added to the apartments.

The boarding house was similarly short-lived. The Boarding-Palast, built by Robert Leibnitz (also architect of the Hotel Adlon) in 1911–12 at 193–194 Kurfürstendamm was never very popular and was soon transformed into a Grand Hotel ("Haus Cumberland"). The Boarding-Palast had more than three hundred apartments of varying sizes, ranging from a luxurious three rooms to simply one.

Other attempts to replace the *Mietskaserne* were equally marginal in their success. One of these was the town house. The town houses built in 1904–05 on Sophienstrasse by noted architects such as Bruno Schmitz, Otto March, and Kayser and Von Groszheim were favorably received. Permission was seldom granted, however, to build town houses in areas where there were only apartment houses, to say nothing of areas with detached housing.

In the same way, the *Mietvilla* (rented villa) never really established itself in Berlin. These villas (for example, on Paul-Krause-Strasse in Nikolassee) consisted of two-story units in large buildings. They were of high quality but only a few were built.

Despite the great innovations in architecture and urban planning demonstrated by these housing complexes in their various manifestations, the reform of the *Mietskaserne* remained within the limits defined by the high capitalist era's social, economic, and political system. The crass difference between the misery of the *Mietskaserne* and the examples of reform did not lead to a radical change. Nevertheless, these examples, present in a concrete form, showed what was actually possible.

One building project, the housing estate Freie Scholle (Free Soil; figs. 24–26), in the north of Berlin, which was undertak-

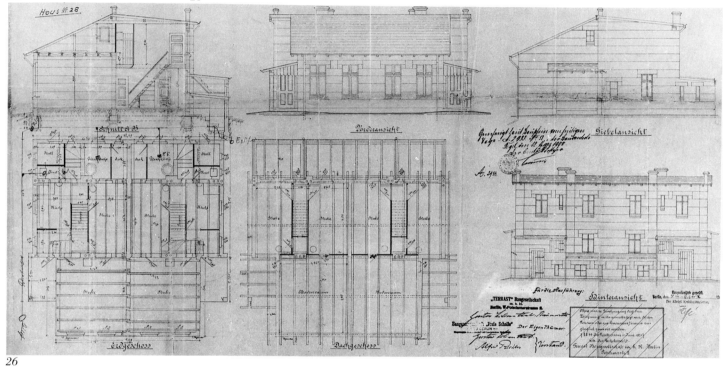

*24. Gustav Lilienthal, c. 1930.
Freie Scholle e.G.*

*25. Gustav Lilienthal. Freie Scholle,
phase one, Egidystrasse,
Reinickendorf (Tegel). South view of
first two duplexes, c. 1910.*

*26. Gustav Lilienthal. Freie Scholle,
phase one, Reinickendorf (Tegel).
Ground plans, section, and
elevation. Freie Scholle e.G.*

*27. Gustav Lilienthal. Freie Scholle,
phase one (1899–1910),
Egidystrasse, Waidmannsluster
Damm, Reinickendorf (Tegel). Site
plan (1899–1937). Freie Scholle
e.G.*

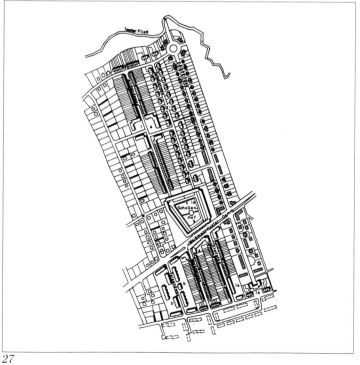

en by the building cooperative of the same name, offered an entirely new perspective on the future. The cooperative was founded by the architect Gustav Lilienthal in 1895, and the first phase of construction of Freie Scholle took place between 1899 and 1910.

Gustav Lilienthal (fig. 27), the brother of the aviation pioneer Otto Lilienthal, was born in Anklam and studied architecture at the Royal Academy of Architecture in Berlin. Together with his brother, he undertook aerodynamic studies that led to the construction of the first glider. They also invented the Anker stone construction set for children. Gustav Lilienthal enjoyed great success with his construction of country houses in Berlin-Lichterfelde in 1890—the so-called castles of Lichterfelde. His outstanding deed as an architect, however, was his founding, along with a few workers, of the building cooperative Gemeinnützige Baugesellschaft Freie Scholle in 1895. He was its first director and architect. In 1898, the cooperative bought forty-four acres of farmland in Tegel. Lilienthal built semidetached houses and groups of three and four houses on the 3,117-foot-long Egidystrasse. He also had other architects (M. Samter, L. Fluth, Schabelski & Keschanowitz, and others) participate in this project. Simple and unpretentious, the houses were typically one story, with additional rooms in the attic. The houses Lilienthal built himself, however, were avant-gardist; he developed a finished parts system for their construction that was a type of Anker stone construction on a larger scale. Moreover, his houses had an ingenious ground plan. The staggering of levels allowed for a great deal of natural light; for example, the kitchen in the middle of the house was lit by windows above the laundry, which lay below it and so on.

There was another innovative element here. In the twelve years between 1899 and 1910, it was primarily the residents themselves who built 71 houses containing 173 apartments, including multifamily dwellings, on the estate. This is a *housing estate*, and not a housing complex; each apartment had a garden.

The multifamily dwellings, with a pub—the Schollenkrug—a bakery, and a grocery store, were built at the intersection of Waidmannsluster Damm/Egidystrasse. After 1918, there was a huge influx of new residents, and the estate was enlarged by Bruno Taut (1925–33). In 1937, after Taut's emigration, the final work on enlarging the estate was completed by the Gemeinnützige Heimstatten Aktiengesellschaft (GEHAG). With a total of 916 apartments on an area of 72 acres, it is Berlin's largest cooperative suburban housing estate.

For the industrial workers in the cooperative, Freie Scholle was a programmatic departure from the *Mietskaserne* in the city, with its real estate speculation and exploitation; theirs became a life in the "open country," free of speculators, free of absurd building regulations, free of oppressive buildings. It was a departure that would ultimately lead to the housing estates of the Neues Bauen of the Weimar Republic—estates that promised its residents new freedom.

Notes

1. Werner Hegemann, *Das steinerne Berlin: Geschichte der grössten Mietskassernen-Stadt der Welt* (Berlin: Verlag Gustav Kiepluhleur, 1930); Albert Gut, *Das Berliner Wohnhaus im 17. und 18. Jahrhundert* (Berlin, 1917); Alfred Schinz, "Das mehrgeschossige Mietshaus von 1896 bis 1945," *Berlin und seine Bauten* teil IV, vol. 8 (Berlin: Verlag Wilhelm Ernst & Sohn, 1974): 1–38; Johann Friedrich Geist and Klaus Kürvers, *Das Berliner Mietshaus*, 3 vols. (Munich: Prestel-Verlag, 1980–84).
2. See Ernst Bruch, *Berlins bauliche Zukunft und Bebauungsplan* (Berlin, 1870).
3. Architekten-Verein zu Berlin, eds., *Berli, und Seine Bauten*, 2 vols. (Berlin, 1877), 1: 440.
4. Ibid., 451.
5. Architekten-Verein zu Berlin and Vereinigung Berliner Architekten, eds., *Berlin und seine Bauten*, 3 vols. (Berlin, 1896), 199–252.
6. Hegemann, *Das steinerne Berlin*, 308–11.
7. Ibid., 298.
8. Julius Posener, *Berlin auf dem Wege zu einer neuen Architektur* (Munich: Prestel-Verlag, 1979), 319.
9. Albert Gessner, *Das deutsche Mietshaus* (Munich: Bruckmann-Verlag, 1909), 139.
10. Walter Curt Behrendt, Review of Paul Mebes' *Um 1800*, in *Neudeutsche Bauzeitung* 4 (1908): 181.
11. Walter Curt Behrendt, *Alfred Messel. With an introduction by Karl Scheffler* (Berlin, 1911).
12. Gemeinnützige Baugenossenschaft Freie Scholle zu Berlin e.G.: *50 Jahre Kampf gegen die Mietskaserne* (Berlin: Selbstverlag, 1947).

Acknowledgments

I would like to thank the following individuals and institutions for their support and permission to reproduce photographs: Landesbildstelle Berlin, Dr. Wilhelm van Kampen, Architekten-und-Ingenieur Verein zu Berlin, Dr. Peter Güttler, the family of Albert Gessner, Landeskonservator Berlin, Professor Helmut Engel, Brigitte Mebes, Beamten-Wohnungs-Verein zu Berlin e.G., Rudolph Mollitor, Plansammlung der Technischen Universität Berlin, Dieter Radicke, Professor Julius Posener, Gemeinnützige Baugenossenschaft Freie Scholle zu Berlin e.G., and Arno Rohr.

On the Uses and Abuses of Air: Perfecting the New York Tenement, 1850–1901

Richard A. Plunz

Richard Plunz is a professor of architecture at Columbia University. He is the author of numerous historical and design studies on housing, including A History of Housing in New York City: Dwelling Types and Social Change in the American Metropolis *(1990).*

As we drew near to New York I was at first amused, and then somewhat staggered, by the cautious and the grisly tales that went the round. You would have thought we were to land upon a cannibal island.
—*Robert Louis Stevenson*
The Amateur Immigrant, *(1895)*

By the middle of the nineteenth century, New York City had achieved its position as the North American metropolis.[1] Between 1820 and 1860, the population grew from 124,000 to 814,000. An additional 267,000 lived in Brooklyn.[2] Rapid growth was heightened toward mid-century by the introduction of steam navigation on the Atlantic, which caused large increases in immigration. Between 1820 and 1860, four million immigrants reached the United States; most through New York. By 1860, 384,000 immigrants had settled in the city.[3] In this period, the dominant characteristics of its present-day culture of housing began to emerge; it became a city not of houses but of housing, with a growing proportion of its inhabitants living in collective accommodations such as could be found nowhere else on the continent. This condition crossed class lines from the tenements of the poor to the increasingly dense rowhouses of the upper middle class.

Fundamentally, the increased physical congestion of New York had substantially altered both the house form and the culture of the colonial city. In 1847, Philip Hone, the famous observer of the New York scene, noted that New York was obtaining certain characteristics of metropolitan Europe in the complexity of its outlook: "Our good city of New York has already arrived at the state of society found in the large cities of Europe; overburdened with population, and where the two extremes of costly luxury in living . . . are presented in daily and hourly contrast with squalid misery and destitution."[4] Prior to this period, Americans tended to see urban health and housing problems as something that they had left behind in Europe. But by the mid-nineteenth century, the heightened contrast between wealth and poverty led to the recognition that American cities had their own problems.[5] New York City as the nation's metropolis became the nexus of this transformation. A debate ensued around the issue of corrective action. On one side were those who saw attempts at reform as an unnecessary interference with natural forces: they argued for nurturing Malthusian corrections that could eliminate social evils without social intervention. For observers on the other side, however, the issue was not so easily resolved. The resulting debate centered around the question of whether the adoption of guarantees for the general public's welfare would conflict with the spirit of laissez-faire capitalism. It was a question that remained unanswered.

The problems of the poor could not be easily isolated, even with the growing physical dimensions of the city. Until the mid-nineteenth century, those aspects of fire and sanitation legislation that affected the poor were intended not only to improve the condition of the poor but to protect the rich from the scourges of poverty as well. At the level of physical proximity, social classes tended to be more intertwined. For example, laws were passed to control fire and disease because these were not easily contained at their origin, and on the occasion

1. Bandits Roost, one of the notorious interior courtyards of Mulberry Bend. Photograph by Jacob Riis, c. 1890. Museum of the City of New York.

of calamity both rich and poor suffered. But as the city grew and ghettos developed on the modern scale, the dynamic became more indirect and abstract, focusing, for example, on the means of production. Productivity in the workplace was affected by the health and housing conditions of its workers. Corrective housing philanthropy was a means of preserving the efficiency of the workforce, and with philanthropy came new ideas for social control. The basis of legislation changed from fundamental safeguards for both rich and poor to more abstract social controls focused primarily on the poor.

The principal design concerns of housing reform in the second half of the nineteenth century were oriented toward increasing amounts of light and air in poorer quarters, while also maximizing the efficiency of the physical layout. While modern medicine had not yet decisively established theories of disease transmissions,[6] empirical data showed an indisputable relationship between dense tenement environments and the spread of disease. As early as 1820 in a report written by Dr. Richard Pennell on the cholera epidemic of the previous year, the link between culture, housing, and health was definitively established. He compared the number of cholera-infected residents who lived in cellars with the number who lived above ground. In one comparison, he found that "out of 48 blacks, living in ten cellars, 33 were sick, of whom 14 died; while out of 120 whites living immediately over their heads in the apartments of the same house, not one even had the fever."[7]

It was not until the mid-nineteenth century in New York City that the case for safeguarding public health through housing reform was championed. Dr. John H. Griscom, a physician who had served as city inspector, became one of New York City's first crusaders for housing reform.[8] He was influenced by the prior work of European researchers and cited the "fearless exposures of Howard, Parent-Duchatelet, Chadwick, Lord Morpeth, and the different sanitary commissions that have been appointed by various governments, [which] have probably done as much for public health, as one half the medicine that has been swallowed since the days of the first mentioned philanthropist."[9] Writing in 1842 about the difficulties of maintaining housing standards for the poor, Griscom identified the landlords as having the responsibility to improve housing conditions. Because he could cite no sound economic reasons, in capitalist terms, for landlords to institute improvements to raise standards above the minimums set by law, he was forced to appeal to their good will. His arguments implied that for all concerned, good intentions would be more profitable than exploitation: the landlords would be duly compensated with "the increased happiness, health, morals and comfort of the inmates, and good order of society, which cannot be estimated in money."[10]

Griscom's writings anticipated the housing issues of the next century in New York. He argued that architectural plans should be subject to the same intensive review as the structural system or the materials[11] and identified the most crucial design issues to be the provision of adequate light and ventilation, a subject that he dealt with at length in his treatise *The Uses and Abuses of Air*. He argued that "impure air is the direct cause of very many, and an aggravation of *all* the diseases

incident to the human frame . . . indeed, one of the scourges of mankind."[12] He upheld the importance of social action in addition to basic medical knowledge, thus setting the stage for the housing activists of the second half of the nineteenth century. Indeed, in New York as elsewhere, issues concerning the provision of light and ventilation continued to dominate housing reform well into the twentieth century, long after the medical imperative had been resolved by the discoveries of modern medicine (fig. 2).

Throughout the first half of the nineteenth century, the predominant forms of housing for the poor in New York were either self-built squatter shacks or reconstructed space that had previously been put to other uses. Former single-family rowhouses were frequently divided into substandard cubicles for poor families—by landlords "who only contrive in what manner they can stow the greatest number of human beings in the smallest space."[13] Before the nineteenth century, new housing was built primarily for the middle and upper classes and consisted almost entirely of single-family houses. Gradually, however, housing construction began to include the tenement.

Of the possible housing options for the poor, the cellar dwelling was both the most ubiquitous and the most hazardous (fig. 3). The cellar inevitably acted as the link between the poor and disease. Overcrowded, filthy, airless, wet, dark, and frequently filled with gases from primitive sewers or with effluent from the outdoor water closets, cellars were the breeding grounds for cholera, malaria, and tuberculosis. The Great Cholera Epidemic of 1849 originated in a cellar on Baxter Street in the Sixth Ward. It was described by the visiting physician, William P. Buell:

At my first visit, on the 16th of May, five human beings, one man and four women, lay upon the floor in different stages of cholera. There was nothing under them but mud and filth, and nothing over them but a few rats of the filthiest description. Civilization and a great city could scarcely afford a parallel to the scene.[14]

In some instances, municipal advancements in sanitation worked to the disadvantage of the poor. An example was the irony of the Croton Aqueduct, which brought pure water into upper-class homes, heralding vast sanitation improvements at that level. At the same time, however, conditions worsened in the cellar dwellings because as individual wells were replaced by the Croton, water tables in the city rose, flooding the cellars.[15] Because cellars represented the worst housing conditions in the city, they were a frequent target of early reformers. Gradually the cellar was replaced by the tenement, which at least eliminated the most subterranean aspect of housing affliction for the poor. The number of cellar dwellings began to decline as early as 1859, when only twenty thousand cellar dwellings were reported, nine thousand less than in 1850.[16]

Of notoriety equal to the cellar was the rookery, a term that also predated the word tenement and held different meaning. Rookeries were not designed to be tenements—usually they were discarded buildings haphazardly reinhabited at tenement densities. Many were wood-frame construction, former single-family houses built before the days of inexpensive brick. Like the cellars, rookeries began to disappear after mid-century and were also common objects of reform, as they tended to burn or fall down easily. The most notorious rookeries in the city were located in the vicinity of Mulberry Bend and the adjacent Five Points in the Sixth Ward, where Worth, Park, and Baxter streets intersected (fig. 1).[17] The Five Points consisted of a cluster of wooden buildings, while Mulberry Bend, one of the city's worst slums, contained both wood and brick structures and had extensive backbuilding. Slum clearance proposals for the area dated from 1829, when the common council contemplated ridding the city of that "place of great disorder and crime."[18] Yet it took the city sixty-seven years to realize that mandate. The descriptions of its horrors are remarkably consistent over that long period (fig. 4).

In 1842, Charles Dickens, visiting the Five Points, wrote in his *American Notes*:

What place is this, to which the squalid street conducts us? A kind of square of leprous houses, some of which are attainable only by crazy wooden stairs without. What lies beyond this tottering flight of steps, that creak beneath our tread! A miserable room, lighted by one dim candle, and destitute of all comfort, save that which may be hidden in a wretched bed. Beside it, sits a man: his elbows on his knees: his forehead hidden in his hands. "What ails that man?" asks the foremost officer. "Fever," he sullenly replies, without looking up. Conceive the fancies of a fevered brain, in such a place as this![19]

James Allaire has been credited with investing in the first substandard new housing, built in the 1840s specifically for poor families. Allaire was an industrialist entrepreneur of some means who appears to have invested heavily in tenement housing.[20] His building, built by Thompson Price, was a four-story house designed for many tenants on Water Street. There is some evidence of an earlier example, dating from the 1820s—a seven-story tenement at 65 Mott Street.[21] Undoubtedly there were numerous other examples around the same time.

The earliest fully documented new project for the poor was Gotham Court, built in 1850 by Silas Wood on Cherry Street.[22] Gotham Court consisted of two rows of six tenements, six stories in height, organized along two narrow alleys intersecting with Cherry Street (figs. 5 and 6). Each tenement contained two dwellings measuring ten by fourteen feet that were subdivided into two rooms, both without cross ventilation. A continuous cellar under each alley contained a long line of water closets and sinks. Small ceiling grates provided ventilation to the cellars. The building facing the alleys of Gotham Court blocked out so much light that on cloudy days lamps had to be used continuously (fig. 7).[23] Gotham Court was a lucrative investment. It was designed for 140 families, but by 1879 it allegedly contained 240.[24] Its overcrowding, filth, crime, and disease made it a notorious New York slum for decades. It became a favorite target of reformers, including Jacob Riis, who succeeded in securing its demolition in 1895 under new provisions added to the Tenement House Law that year.[25]

By the 1860s, new development at tenement densities began to expose some generic problems with the city's gridiron layout. The gridiron was established much earlier, when the city's

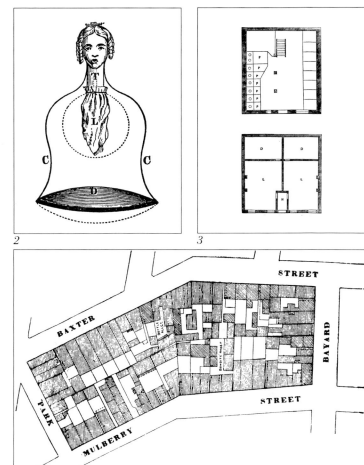

2. *Illustration of a device for demonstrating the functioning of the human lung. From John H. Griscom, M.D.,* The Uses and Abuses of Air *(1854).*

3. *Typical uses for the cellar around 1860: above is a watercloset and below are two dwellings. From Citizens' Association of New York, Report of the Council of Hygiene and Public Health (1865).*

4. *Mulberry Bend in the Sixth Ward of the Lower East Side, said to have been the worst slum in New York City throughout most of the nineteenth century. From the* Review of Reviews, *XII (August 1895).*

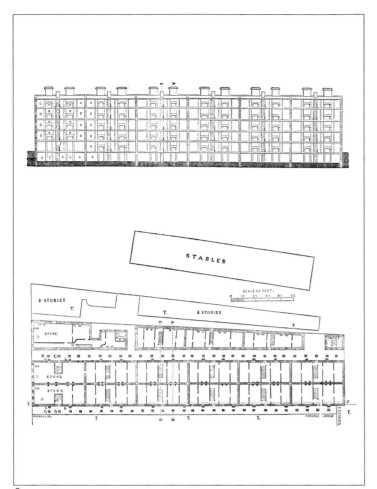

5

6

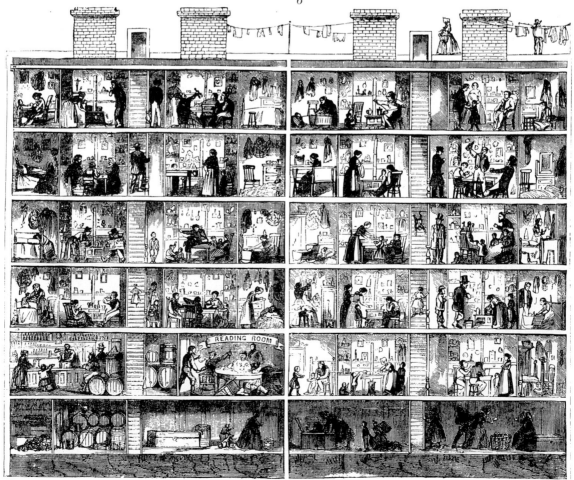

7

population, clustered at the lower end of the island, numbered under one hundred thousand. In 1807, the common council, recognizing that the inevitable growth of the city would require another plan, requested the New York State Legislature to appoint a commission to study the situation.[26] The New York State Commissioners' Plan was adopted in 1811 and became the basis for Manhattan's phenomenal development in the nineteenth century (fig. 8). The Commissioners' Plan organized all of Manhattan real estate above 14th Street into two thousand blocks of two hundred feet by about eight hundred feet. These in turn were subdivided into twenty-five-by-one-hundred-foot lots (fig. 9). The long dimension of each block faced north-south, causing the majority of streets to run east-west between the Hudson and the East rivers. Twelve one-hundred-foot-wide north-south avenues and 155 sixty-foot-wide east-west cross streets were the result.

Even in 1811 the gridiron did not work well. For the small, single-family rowhouse that predominated at that time, the solar orientation of the gridiron was the reverse of the ideal. Had the long dimension of each block faced east-west, both front and rear facades of each house would have received sunlight each day; with the north-south orientation, the south facades received all of the sun. In addition, no service alleys ran through the centers of the blocks, contrary to the usual practice in gridiron planning. The commissioners believed that provision for commercial traffic along east/west streets and maximization of negotiable land through the exclusion of service alleys were more important than adherence to the proven principles of gridiron planning. As a result, the Manhattan grid was substandard. This form, however, remained inviolate for over a century, with the exception of Central Park, for which land was set aside in 1853.

In general, the mechanics of Manhattan land speculation did not permit the removal of potentially salable land from city blocks for the insertion of connector streets. Even if the city doubly reimbursed owners for such a loss of land, the permanent removal of land from the private marketplace would have reduced the potential profits of others in the future. The original gridiron was designed to maximize profits. Land speculation was big business, and the rights of its practitioners were not easily infringed upon. Unfortunately, the flaws of the Manhattan grid were frequently repeated elsewhere, notably in Brooklyn and the Bronx as those boroughs developed. For housing design, it was not until well into the twentieth century that the gridiron was tampered with—in the large government-subsidized projects of the New Deal.

By the 1860s, tenement prototypes had become firmly established for private-market low-income housing. By 1865, as the city's population approached one million, more than fifteen thousand tenements were in use in New York City.[27] The word "tenement" had become commonplace in the technical vocabulary of housing for the urban poor. As a housing type, the tenement's form was generated by the necessity to maximize densities within the constraint of the twenty-five by one-hundred-foot building lot system. The twenty-five-foot width of the tenement was dictated by practical structural constraints such as the maximum span of wooden floor joists and

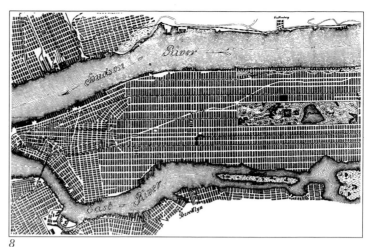

8

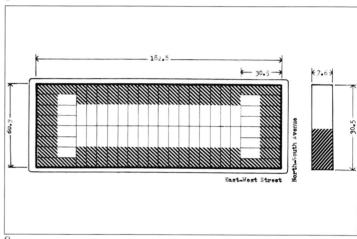

9

5. Gotham Court, completed as an investment by Silas Wood in 1850. Located in the Sixth Ward, it became an example of substandard new housing built for the poor. From Citizens' Association of New York, Report of the Council of Hygiene and Public Health (1865).

6. Block that included Gotham Court in the Alley District of the Lower East Side. From New York Herald (January 23, 1881).

7. Section through Gotham Court "from cellar to garret" in 1879, indicating impossible conditions for adequate light and hygiene. From Frank Leslie's Sunday Magazine V (June 1879).

8. The southern half of Manhattan, showing the commissioner's gridiron of 1811, and Central Park, which was set aside in 1853. From Joseph Stübben, Der Städtebau (1907).

9. System of subdivision of New York City gridiron blocks using twenty-five- by one hundred-foot lots showing pattern of rowhouse development that was prevalent throughout the first half of the nineteenth century.

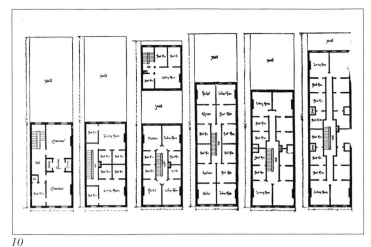

10

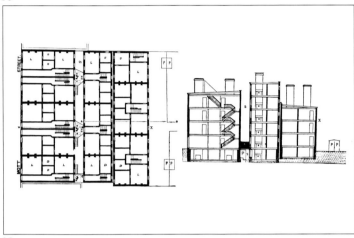

11

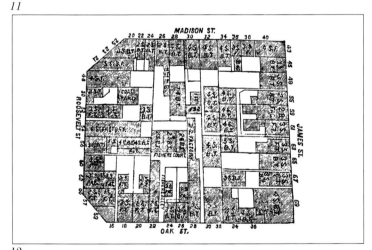

12

10. The evolution of New York City housing prior to the tenement house legislation of 1879 from the single-family rowhouse to the railroad flat. From New York State Assembly, Report of the Tenement House Committee of 1894, Legislative Document No. 37 (January 17, 1895).

11. A notorious tenement of Mott Street known as the Rookery, showing severe conditions of backbuilding with windows entirely obstructed by an adjacent building. From Citizens' Association of New York, Report of the Council of Hygiene and Public Health (1865).

12. Block with extensive backbuilding in the Lower East Side, showing Fishers Alley, a foul interior courtyard where cows and goats were kept. From New York Herald (January 23, 1881).

by the prevalent practice of building only in single-lot increments.[28] The length of the tenement was often more than ninety percent of the one-hundred-foot lot dimension and the height was five or six stories. The long apartments in the tenements were commonly called railroad flats because the rooms were organized like cars on a train. Frequently, older structures were converted to tenements by adding floors and by backbuilding—the practice of filling in rear-yard areas with additional housing. By 1865, hundreds of Manhattan blocks had been overbuilt as tenement housing, with not even minimum standards of space, light, or ventilation.

Figure 10 shows six steps in the evolution of the New York City tenements, from an original single-family rowhouse to a typical railroad flat covering ninety percent of a twenty-five-by-one-hundred-foot lot. In many railroad flats, the rear yard consisted of no more than a few inches, if it was not eliminated entirely.[29] In these tenements, only the rooms facing the street received light. A typical tenement floor often contained eighteen rooms; in the best situations, where the facade of the building had a southern exposure, only two of these rooms received direct sunlight. Unless air shafts were provided, the interior rooms had no ventilation whatsoever. The practice of backbuilding could lead to absurd results, such as the notorious rookery on Mott Street between Bleecker and East Houston streets (fig. 11).[30] Three parallel rows of housing were built on five small lots, with total street frontage of ninety feet. The inner and middle rows had only a foot of air space between them. The windows of one faced the brick wall of the other. The space between the outer and middle rows of housing was six feet wide and filled with privies. In 1865 the Mott Street rookery housed 352 persons, at the extremely high density of twenty-three square feet per person.

Backbuilding was common in every area of Manhattan where high densities were prevalent (fig. 12). In 1882, the New York Daily Tribune placed rear tenements in "a class by themselves" in relation to insalubrity: "Situated in dark courts and approached by narrow, foul smelling alleys . . . their position renders them not only dangerous from a sanitary point of view, but doubly perilous in case of fire."[31] Some interesting formal variations could be found, such as on East 11th Street between First and Second avenues, where the lot lines legislated by the gridiron had become confused with the earlier diagonal system of Stuyvesant Street (fig. 13). An unusual juxtaposition between the orthogonal and diagonal building resulted. Within tenement block interiors, small areas of leftover open space contained the communal water taps and water closets shared by families in one or more of the surrounding buildings (fig. 14). The water closets were either privies or the larger school sinks, the name varying with the method of cleaning: excrement was removed by hand or drained from the vault into the street sewer. Removal was infrequent, and the sewer often became clogged. School sinks were especially infamous as sources of filth and disease.[32]

As late as 1865, the incorporation of small air shafts in tenement housing was an improvement over standard practice—there were not many options for designing tenements. Improvements were minuscule in relation to the standard building practice of the period; for example, a diamond-shaped air shaft might lend an aesthetic touch to an otherwise minimal improvement (fig. 15). The principle of shared air shafts between adjoining buildings was sometimes used to increase ventilation nominally.[33] Figure 16 shows an early version of the shared air shaft for an improved tenement located on Leonard Street. Its generous yard contained a luxurious number of water closets.

By the end of the 1850s, political pressure was building for legal intervention in the tenement house problem. The condition of New York's poor was steadily worsening, a problem reflected in periodic civil disturbances that characterized the vulnerability of the city as a whole. The restive social consequences of the city's newfound metropolitan status were evidenced in riots that began as early as 1849 (fig. 17). The riot of 1849 occurred ostensibly as an outgrowth of a public feud between an English and an American actor, whose differences were symptomatic of the growing schism between European and American cultural norms.[34] But the scale of the riot, which took twenty-two lives and presented in certain terms the consequences of the shifting class structure, indicated that the causes also lay deeper. The city was faced with the volatility of a poor population created by the first great waves of immigration. During the 1850s, insurrection continued, interwoven with a steady pulse of economic and other difficulties. In 1849 the Great Cholera Epidemic took five thousand lives, and another cholera epidemic in 1854 took half that number.[35] By 1857 another major riot left little doubt about the relationship of social unrest to the general urban condition.[36] An initial conflict between the municipal police and the newly created metropolitan police provided the catalyst for a widespread anarchy between ethnic gangs in the slum area of the Sixth Ward on the Lower East Side. On July 4 and 5, 1857, one thousand men and boys fought each other and the metropolitan police; smaller scale conflicts followed in subsequent days in other poor areas, most prominently in the Seventeenth Ward, in the district known today as Chelsea.

In October 1857, not long after that year's riot, the great financial panic brought about the loss of thirty thousand jobs. The widespread severe hardship combined with Mayor Fernando Wood's socialist sensibilities prompted the common council to provide jobs for the unemployed and to distribute food to the poor. This effort, however, provided little relief. By 1858, there were still twenty-five thousand unemployed, who with their families represented one hundred thousand in dire need.[37] The annual reports of the Association for Improving the Condition of the Poor in those years depicted suffering unprecedented in the history of the city, and the state legislature was obliged to take action. The first legislative commission was set up to study the housing problem in 1861, and although it described in detail the pitiable conditions of the tenements, no legislation was advanced.[38] In 1861, the Civil War began, embroiling New York City and the nation at large. Although the New York economy was bolstered by the war effort, social problems persisted, culminating in the draft riot of 1863.

The draft riots were arguably the most traumatic civil disturbances in New York's history.[39] On the surface, they were a re-

13

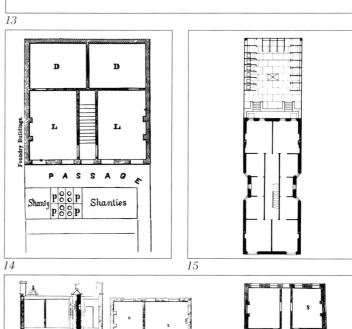

14   15

16

13. A Lower East Side tenement block with an unusual pattern of backbuilding caused by the superimposition of a gridiron on an earlier street pattern. From Jacob Riis, How the Other Half Lives (1890).

14. Typical back tenement on East 28th Street recorded in 1865, showing privies and shacks in the leftover yard area. From Citizens' Association of New York, Report of the Council of Hygiene and Public Health (1865).

15. Early improved tenement on Leonard Street, with a luxurious number of privies in the rear yard area. From Charles F. Chandler, Ten Scrapbooks of Tenement House Plans (1873–1883). Avery Library, Columbia University.

16. Two improved tenements from 1865, so-called because of the provision for minuscule air shafts. From Citizens' Association of New York, Report of the Council of Hygiene and Public Health (1865).

17. Scene from the riot of 1849 depicting the battle at the Astor Place Opera House. From Account of the Terriffic and Fatal Riot at the New York Astor Place Opera House *(1849).*

18. Attack on black residents of Sullivan Street during the Draft Riots of 1863 in a quarter of expanding black population during the Civil War. From Harper's Weekly *(August 1, 1863).*

19. Crowd looting clothing from the Brooks Brothers store on Cherry Street in the Sixth Ward during the Draft Riots of 1863. From Harper's Weekly *(August 1, 1863).*

17

18

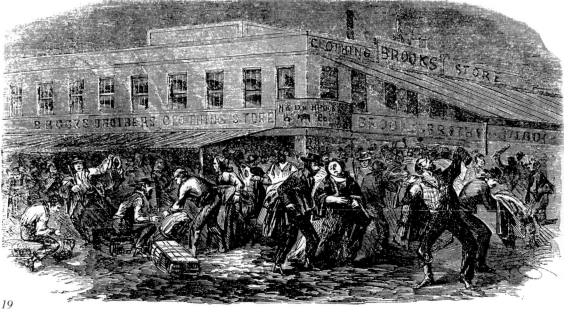

19

action to newly imposed involuntary conscription for military service in the Civil War, which ultimately treated New York's rich and poor unequally; according to rumor, for three hundred dollars one could avoid the draft altogether. As with the previous riots, however, the unrest was also precipitated by the intolerable living conditions of the city's poor and increasing social inequity, even within the poor population itself. Poor whites sought vengeance on the city's growing black population, whose numbers they feared would eventually further reduce their own possibilities of improvement (fig. 18). Tensions were fueled by reasoning such as that without blacks there would be no war, and therefore no draft. The draft riots created the foundation for the dynamic between social class, ethnicity, an environment that has dominated the social unrest of the modern metropolis to the present day. The wretched and diseased population of the tenements, and of the Sixth Ward in particular, poured out into the city streets. Interestingly, women were as prominent as men in the crowds, lending credence to the idea of domestic sources for the unrest (fig. 19). A typical journalistic description captured the incredulous reaction of the middle class:

The high brick blocks and closely packed houses where the mobs originated seemed to be literally hives of sickness and vice. It was wonderful to see, and difficult to believe, that so much misery, disease, and wretchedness can be huddled together and hidden by high walls, unvisited and unthought of, so near our own abodes. Lewd but pale and sickly young women, scarcely decent in their ragged attire, were impudent and scattered everywhere in the crowd. But what numbers of these poored [sic] classes are deformed! what numbers are made hideous by self-neglect and infirmity! Alas! human faces look so hideous with hope and self-respect all gone! And female forms and features are made so frightful by sin, squalor, and debasement! To walk the streets as we walked them, in those hours of conflagration and riot, was like witnessing the day of judgment, with every wicked thing revealed, every sin and sorrow blazingly glared upon, every hidden abomination laid before hell's expectant fire.[40]

Immediately following the draft riots, a group of influential private citizens formed the Citizens' Association of New York to lobby for improvements in the sanitary conditions of the city. The Citizens' Association appointed a subcommittee called the Council of Hygiene and Public Health to undertake a comprehensive survey of conditions. The monumental report, published in 1865, remains a unique document for its scope and thoroughness. Each of twenty-nine Sanitary Inspection Districts was analyzed in detail, with a degree of architectural documentation unknown in previous surveys. Apart from the significance of the study's scope, its analysis prefigured modern sociological methods and began to scrutinize the urban condition with an eye more scientific than in previous surveys. The most sensational statistic cited in the Citizens' Association report related that of a population of more than seven hundred thousand in New York City (excluding Brooklyn), a total of 480,368 persons lived in tenement houses with substandard conditions.[41] One year later, a committee on tenement houses appointed by the state legislature published another report that supplemented the architectural documentation of the Council of Hygiene with physical and social analyses of a number of tenement case studies.[42]

In 1866 and 1867, pressure for serious government legislation yielded the first initiatives with any impact. The state legislature approved a comprehensive law defining standards for building construction in New York City in 1866.[43] The following year, the legislature passed its first comprehensive housing law, the Tenement House Act of 1867, which marked the beginning of its long involvement with raising the standards of low-cost housing design. The tenement was at last legally defined:

Any house, building, or portion thereof, which is rented, leased, let, or hired out to be occupied or is occupied, as the home or residence of more than three families living independently of one another and doing their own cooking upon the premises, or by more than two families upon a floor, so living and cooking and having a common right in the halls, stairways, yards, water-closets, or privies, or some of them.[44]

The purpose of the Tenement House Act was to supplement the newly enacted building construction regulations, giving attention to the problems of tenements. Both documents required increased construction precautions against fire, including mandatory provisions of fire escapes for nonfireproof buildings. The Tenement House Act's hygiene regulations specified a minimum of one water closet for every twenty tenants. Tenement house spatial standards were only slightly improved, with minor attention paid to distances between buildings. The cellar dwelling was prohibited, unless its ceiling was one foot above street level.

The 1860s also saw major advances in the enforcement of building standards, as the first moves were made toward the development of a modern building bureaucracy for New York City. Between 1813 and 1849, building laws had been enforced by city-appointed surveyors; between 1849 and 1860 by fire wardens within the Fire Department. In 1860 the state legislature created the office of Superintendent of Buildings within the Fire Department, with a staff of inspectors to enforce structural safety laws. In 1862 this office was made independent of the Fire Department and renamed the Department of Survey and Inspection of Buildings. All architects' plans were subject to its review, and appeals went directly to the Supreme Court of the city of New York. The legislature created the Metropolitan Board of Health in 1866 replacing the board of health that dated from 1801, which, in 1867, became responsible for enforcing the Tenement House Act. In the same year, the power granted to the superintendent of buildings over tenement houses was also strengthened.[45] This dichotomy between the authority of the so-called health bureaucracy and the design bureaucracy became problematic, however, and the enforcement of tenement legislation was especially affected. For tenements more than any other building type, health and design were inextricably interwoven.

With the growth of enforcing agencies, the review of architectural plans for compliance with building regulations was made mandatory. The 1862 law placed this responsibility within the Department of Survey and Inspection of Buildings, but in 1874, appeals were relegated to a board of examiners instead of the Supreme Court. Under the corrupt conditions of the

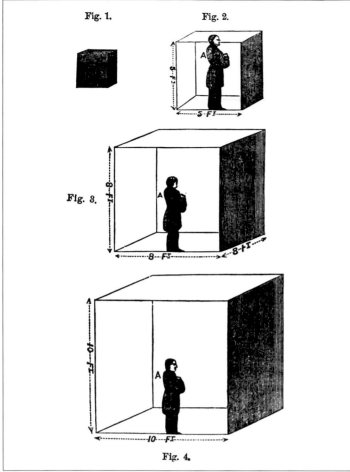

Fig. 1.   **Fig. 2.**

Fig. 3.

Fig. 4.

20

20. Diagram correlating housing density and health pathology. Fig. 1 represents the minimum amount of air needed by one person per hour in order to remain alive, compared with various conditions found in tenements. From Citizens' Association of New York, Report of the Council of Hygiene and Public Health (1865).

21. James E. Ware. The winning entry to the tenement house competition of 1878 sponsored by The Plumber and Sanitary Engineer. From The Plumber and Sanitary Engineer 2 (March 1879).

22. Dumbbell tenement plan devised by James E. Ware and enforced under the provision of the Tenement House Act of 1879. Also known as the Old Law Tenement, it used a coverage of approximately 80 percent. From New York State Assembly, Report of the Tenement House Committee of 1894.

Tweed years, the relationship formed between builders and the city building bureaucracy was adversely affected: appeals were set up entirely outside the judicial system.[46] The mere existence of a building bureaucracy did not guarantee enforcement of the law. One of the most blatant failures involved the provision of fire escapes as mandated by the Tenement House Act of 1867. By 1900, out of a sample of 2,877 tenements, ninety-eight had no fire escapes at all; 653 had only rear escapes.[47]

Typically, architects who were involved with housing for the poor were liberal supporters of housing reform movements not merely design professionals. Architectural innovation came indirectly through legislation, which, in a sense, acted as a buffer between professional ideals and the problems of producing low-cost housing during the zenith of laissez-faire capitalism. But the circumstances surrounding the Tenement House Act of 1879 show that even this level of involvement had its difficulties. The act revised only sections thirteen and twenty-four of the Tenement House Act of 1867, but the revisions were substantial.[48] The most radical provision was that no new tenement house could occupy more than sixty-five percent of a twenty-five-by-one-hundred-foot lot. Other important provisions prohibited the practice of tenement backbuilding except where adequate light and ventilation were maintained, and more water closets were required than in 1867. Unfortunately, the board of health was given discretionary power to enforce the specific provisions. The board yielded to various private interests and the new provisions were in effect nullified. The famous dumbbell tenement, also commonly called Old Law Tenement, was enforced as a kind of compromise. Its coverage was usually at least eighty percent of a twenty-five- by-one-hundred-foot lot, rather than the sixty-five percent stipulated by law.

The design interpretation of sections thirteen and fourteen of the Tenement House Act of 1879 by the board of health bore a curious relationship to tenement house design competition for architects, sponsored in the previous year by an influential new magazine called the Plumber and Sanitary Engineer. The program called for a tenement plan that could be repeated on twenty-five-by-one-hundred-foot gridiron lots. There was to be particular emphasis on improving the typical railroad flat in terms of light, ventilation, sanitation, and fireproofing.[49] In addition, the schemes had to be economically realistic, accommodating enough families for it to pay off as an investment. Of the 209 schemes submitted to the competition, the prize-winning ones were undoubtedly the most conservative, with only minimal modification of prevailing practice in the building of railroad flats.[50] First prize was given to James Ware, a New York architect, who was to become a major figure in tenement design. His design was a variant of the dumbbell-type plan, which covered approximately ninety percent of the lot (fig. 21). Four dwellings on each floor surrounded a central core, which contained a water closet and stairway. Light shafts on both sides of the core could be combined with those of adjacent tenements to increase their effectiveness.

Of the twelve placing entries, most were as conservative as the Ware scheme. Several used innovative approaches, however, going beyond simple rationalization of the status quo. They all attempted to open the center of the building with light courts and external circulation, but at the expense of profitability. The jury was determined to award the prizes to the most profitable designs even if they represented the lowest design standards. When the winning entries were announced, an article in the *New York Times* expressed what came to be widespread popular criticism of the dumbbells:

If the prize plans are the best offered, which we can hardly believe, they simply demonstrate the problem is insoluble. The three which have received the highest prizes offer a very slightly better arrangement than hundreds of tenements now do. They are simply "double houses" front and rear, with the space between occupied by halls and water closets. They have all of the disadvantages of "double houses" which have so often called forth sanitary censure and even adverse legislation. The only access to air, apart from the front, is through the courts in the small spaces between the houses; for the rear, if these plans were generally adopted, would also be closed up by the rear wall of the house in the next street. To add to their ill effects, each suite on the second storey has apparently that old nuisance, a dark bedroom which under the present arrangement, is such a prolific source of fevers and disease. In some of the plans this room ventilates through other rooms, and in others by a small well. The only advantages offered, apparently, over the old system, are in fireproof stairways, more privacy of halls, and the ventilation of the water closets.[51]

The *Plumber and Sanitary Engineer* competition was crucial to the passage of the Tenement House Act of 1879. Several of the competition's organizers founded the New York Sanitary Reform Society, which in turn drafted the legislation and lobbied for its enactment by the state legislature during the winter of 1879.[52] But after enactment by the legislature, the Board of Health was only willing to enforce the standards represented by the winning dumbbell scheme of the competition, in spite of the severe criticism directed against the board (fig. 22). Charles F. Chandler, the respected president of the Board of Health, could not enforce the law because, as the *New York Times* expressed it, he "no doubt feared the political influence which the landlords could bring to bear on the Legislature."[53] The housing bureaucracy was satisfied in that it was ostensibly able to maintain control over tenement building. Real estate interests were undoubtedly satisfied in that no one could argue that the dumbbell was not an improvement over the railroad tenement, yet coverage remained very high, ensuring continued maximum profitability.

In this manner, the 1879 law displayed characteristics that came to dominate housing reform legislation in New York City. First, its implementation reflected the dichotomy between the standards of building law and standards of enforcement, a condition that has been endemic to the growth of the modern metropolis. The level of enforcement simply mirrored or even lagged behind the marketplace, reinforcing rather than challenging norms. Second, through systematic organization of tenement planning, the act made building to high densities easier and more profitable, while paying token respect to the public good. Enforcement was a pragmatic response to reality; dumbbell tenements were efficient and economic and would have happened with or without the law. Increased standards

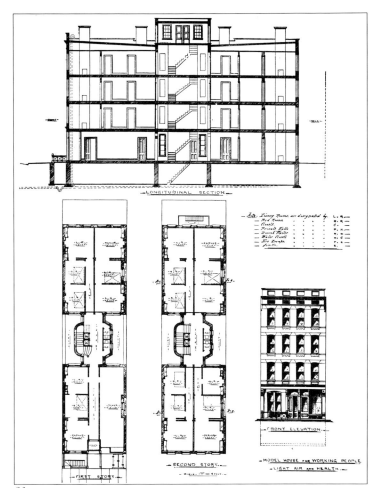

21

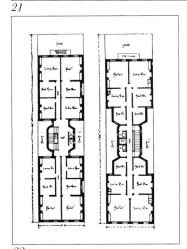

22

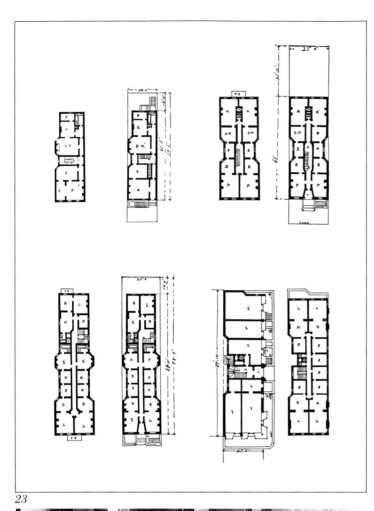

23

24

*23. Typical tenement house plans
that evolved under the Old Law.
From New York state Assembly,
Report of the Tenement House
Committee of 1894.*

*24. Cigarmakers at work in their
tenement quarters. Photograph by
Jacob Riis, c. 1890. The Museum of
the City of New York.*

for light and air—however minuscule in comparison to the railroad flat—brought higher rents and profits, and upwardly mobile tenants of the new dumbbells could afford to pay for improved housing.

By 1900 more than eighty thousand tenements had been built in Greater New York City. These buildings housed a population of 2.3 million, out of a total population of 3.4 million. Approximately sixty thousand tenements had been built after 1880,[54] all of them Old Law, most designed to meet the dumbbell standards that continued to win the approval of the city building bureaucracy until 1901 (fig. 23). No significant advances in tenement standards were made during this critical twenty-year period when the population of the metropolitan area increased from 1.8 million to 3.4 million.[55] Only minor legislative reform was made, much of it unenforceable. The building bureaucracy was reorganized, however, after the enactment of the Greater New York Charter of 1897. The five boroughs of Manhattan, Brooklyn, the Bronx, Queens, and Richmond were placed under the central control of the Department of Buildings.[56]

There were also attempts to unify New York City building legislation beginning with the Consolidation Act of 1882, which created a single document governing building construction laws, in an attempt to remove inconsistencies between various jurisdictions. The building laws for tenements and for general buildings were integrated for the first time while retaining the separate enforcement bureaucracies embodied in the Department of Buildings and the Tenement House Department.[57] The health side of legislation remained with the tenement house laws, although by the turn of the century, bureaucratic transformations had gradually weakened the old dichotomy between design and health enforcement.

In 1884, after considerable reform agitation, the state legislature appointed a second Tenement House Committee (the first having been the committee of 1856–57). The committee reported that the Tenement House Act of 1867 requirement of one water closet for every twenty persons had been largely ignored. They found, in fact, that only thirty percent of the tenements examined had any water closets at all and almost none had running water above the first floor.[58] The committee recognized that scientific criteria for defining sanitary standards would be necessary to legislate the form of the ideal tenement.

The design recommendations of the Tenement House Committee of 1884 were extensive. They included the enforcement of the sixty-five percent coverage specified in the act of 1879, the elimination of all privies, the provision of water supply on each floor, direct light through external windows for all inner hallways and rooms, and the provision of electric street lighting in tenement districts. Unfortunately, the committee had little impact: the tenement house laws were not amended until 1887, three years after the committee released its report. At that time, several enforcement provisions were added, but no additional design controls were imposed.[59]

The lack of substantial new legislation and the recalcitrant attitude toward enforcement were partially caused by the threat

170

of legal recourse on the part of anti-reform interests. These fears were given ample justification by a New York Court of Appeals decision in 1885. The court struck down an amendment to the Tenement House Law passed in the previous year, which had broadened the base for reform by imposing controls on nonresidential uses permitted in tenements. Specifically, the bill had been sponsored by the Cigar-Makers' Union to prohibit manufacturing tobacco products in homes, forcing the manufacturers to assume more responsibility for the workplace (fig. 24).[60] Using the most emphatic language possible, the court found the bill to be a threat to "personal liberty and private property," presumably that of the cigar company proprietors.

Such legislation may invade one class of rights to-day and another tomorrow, and if it can be sanctioned under the Constitution, while far removed in time we will not be far away in practical statesmanship from those ages when governmental prefects supervised the building of houses, the rearing of cattle, the sowing of seed and the reaping of grain, and governmental ordinances regulated the movements and labor of artisans, the rate of wages, the price of food, the diet and clothing of the people, and a large range of other affairs long since in all civilized lands regarded as outside of governmental functions. Such governmental interferences disturb the normal adjustments of the social fabric, and usually derange the delicate and complicated machinery of industry and cause a score of evils while attempting the removal of one.[61]

The court decision was a conservative reaction to previous housing and health reforms and a definitive victory for real estate and manufacturing interests. It cast a pall over the entire reform movement. Public officials had to enforce existing legislation conservatively for fear of inducing further damaging litigation, and the introduction of substantial new bills in the New York State Legislature could only be considered as an uncertain exercise. Theodore Roosevelt, then a New York state assemblyman, later described the severity of the impact: "This decision completely blocked tenement-house reform legislation in New York for a score of years, and hampers it to this day [1914]. It was one of the most serious setbacks which the cause of industrial and social progress and reform ever received."[62]

On the positive side, however, the impasse appears to have simply intensified the determination of the reform movement. During the decades of the 1880s and 1890s, populist reformers became a driving force focusing national attention on the tenements. This movement fully exploited the expanding mass media. New tools, such as photojournalism, added an element of realism and urgency to the documentation of tenement house conditions. Jacob Riis was the giant among the reformers who turned tenement reform into a political crusade. Riis, an immigrant newspaper reporter, published his first impassioned article, "How the Other Half Lives," in *Scribner's Magazine* in 1889, followed by his book of the same title in 1890.[63] Throughout the next decade, he published a series of popular books and campaigned widely for reform, appealing to the moral sensibilities of those he called the "first half." Dr. Stephen Smith, who had been largely responsible for creating the Metropolitan Board of Health in 1866 and served as commissioner of health between 1868 and 1875, launched a campaign for a National Board of Health, which was established by the United States Congress in 1879. Like Riis, his activities helped focus national attention on conditions in New York City, and like Dr. John Griscom before him, Smith helped articulate a scientific imperative for health and housing legislation.[64] In another vein, with the founding of the Charity Organization Society (COS) in 1882, the activities of charitable organizations in the city were centrally coordinated. In general, the COS enlarged the concerns of the Association for Improving the Condition of the Poor.[65]

The Tenement House Committee of 1884 had expressed some frustration with finding an adequate scientific basis for tenement legislation. But these disappointments were soon placated by the moralist outcry that grew with the populist reform movement. In 1885, Charles F. Wingate, who had been a member of the commission, disregarded scientific arguments and wrote instead of the morality of the tenement house problem:

Probably seventy-five percent of the maladies in the cities, which often pass over into the better quarters, arise from the tenement houses. Ninety percent of the children born in these dens die before reaching youth. The amount of sickness is proportioned to the death rate. There is a gradual physical degeneracy. Wasting diseases prevail. Infantile life is nipped in the bud; youth is deformed and loathsome; decrepitude comes at thirty.

Wingate went on to describe the remedy:

What New York wants is a revival of civic pride in her citizens to stimulate them to give their time and thought as well as their money to public duties. Our people are too absorbed in their private affairs and content to delegate responsibilities to ill-paid and harassed officials. Self-interest should teach them, if necessity does not, that a different course of action is imperative. But above all the clergy and all who feel the urgent necessity of mastering and reaching a practical solution of this vast problem.[66]

One aspect of the populist movement was its reaction against the social disruption caused by the massive presence of immigrants, who by 1890 made up forty-two percent of the city's population and occupied almost all of the tenements.[67] Wingate did not hesitate to judge some of them as "ignorant, filthy, and more or less debased, especially the Italians, Poles, Russians and the Bohemians."[68] Others held such views as well, although they were regarded as dangerous by some critics, including Allen Forman, who wrote in the *American Magazine* in 1888:

The Poles, Russians and lowest class of Germans come to us imbued with Anarchistic notions—notions which are fed by the misery and disappointment of their life in this country where they had looked for affluence without work, and fostered by the freedom of speech which is permitted by laws which were framed to govern a people of entirely different character to those who have been pouring in upon us from the slums of Europe.[69]

Moral issues aside, the political containment of the immigrant population did pose obvious practical problems, especially in reference to tenement housing. Two major studies of the tene-

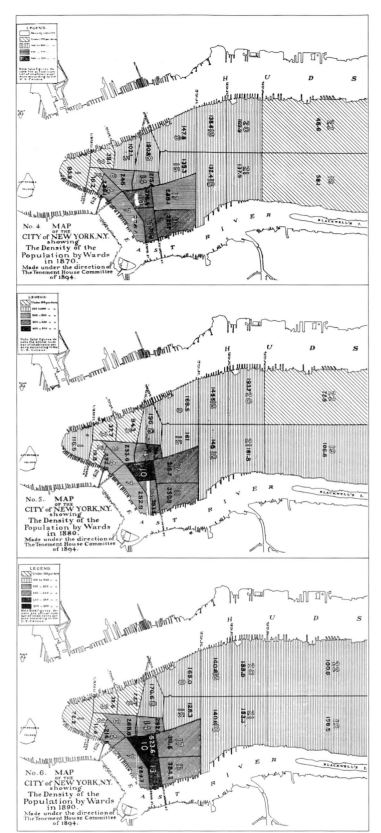

25. *Population densities of Lower Manhattan in 1870, 1880, and 1890 showing the extraordinary Lower East Side agglomeration.* From New York State Assembly, Report of the Tenement House Committee of 1894

ment situation emerged by the mid-1890s. The first was the report of the Tenement House Committee released in 1894. It traced in detail the evolution of tenement house reform and produced unprecedented documentation of conditions, based on a survey of eight thousand houses, occupied by some 255,000 persons. While New York ranked sixth among world cities in population, it was found to rank first in density, at an average of 143 persons per acre. Paris was a distant second with 125 persons per acre. A portion of the Lower East Side was found to have reached a density of eight hundred, surpassing the highest known foreign agglomeration, which was a section of Bombay with 760 persons per acre (fig. 25).[70] The prolific use of such statistical analysis within the report served to push the scientific orientation of the tenement problem to new levels.

The committee's report indicated that more than half of the New York population lived in tenements, and it devoted considerable attention to analysis of tenement design evolution and to discussion of improved plans. It was the first official document to use photography to supplement a written description of tenement conditions (fig. 26). The report was also innovative for the extensive comparative charts and mapping of city-wide conditions—a precedent that contributed to the genesis of the discipline of city planning. The recommendations included increasing the sixty-five percent coverage of the 1879 Tenement House Law to a more enforceable seventy percent, with the elimination of the discretionary power that the board of health had used to circumvent enforcement. Another interesting recommendation was that rapid transit should be developed as quickly as possible to alleviate the overcrowding in tenement districts. As in the case of the commission's report released ten years earlier, the recommendations of the 1894 report had little effect on the Tenement House Act that was passed in the following year,[71] especially in relation to design standards.

In 1895, the federal government produced the second major tenement study of the decade as its first venture into the housing program. The large special report of the Department of Labor, *The Housing of Working People*,[72] used material that had been amassed by Elgin R.L. Gould, economist and housing reformer, who had held a post within the department. It was the first extensive survey of private and public initiatives for housing reform, documenting not only the United States but also England, France, Belgium, Germany, Austria, the Netherlands, Sweden, and Denmark. Previously, the only foreign design initiatives to have been published in the United States were the philanthropic housing projects built in England dating from the mid-century. The Department of Labor report presented critical new information about other European developments, including considerable architectural documentation.

In addition to the numerous European private philanthropic projects, municipalities were beginning to build housing for the poor, and the report of the Department of Labor included examples at Huddersfield and Liverpool in England, at Glasgow in Scotland, and at Duisberg in Germany. These foreign examples did not sway the bias of the report, which expressed

172

its faith in the private sector to house the poor within the limits of government standards. Government abstinence from home building was not due to a lack of lobbying to the contrary, however. Beginning in the 1880s, pressure for serious government intervention had increased from the most progressive sector of the housing reform movement led by Felix Adler and the Society for Ethical Culture. A lecture in Chickering Hall on March 9, 1884 on "The Helping Hand of Government" typified Adler's arguments:

The evils of the tenement house[s] . . . of this city are due to the estates which neglect the comfort of their tenants, and to the landlords who demand exorbitant rents. The laboring classes are unable to build homes for themselves, and the law of morality and common decency binds the Government to see to it that these houses shall not prove fatal to the lives and morality of the inmates. If the houses are overcrowded the government must interfere. It must compel a reduction of the number of inmates, enforce renovation at the expense of the landlord, and where that is no longer possible, must dismantle the houses and remove them from existence.[73]

Such pleas were to no avail. For example, it was not until the crisis of production in World War I that the first government-initiated home-building program was attempted—not for the poor but for wartime factory workers. The government did not take initiatives toward the poor until long after the governments of Europe, during the Great Depression in the 1930s.

The architect Ernest Flagg is generally credited with producing the first comprehensive system of prototypes that could have contributed substantially toward a solution to the light and air impasse of the New York tenement, within the constraints of private production. In 1894, as a recent graduate of the Beaux-Arts, he published his first studies for tenement housing.[74] His prototypes were a clever translation of the courtyard apartment house so prolific in Paris and elsewhere on the Continent into a vocabulary that spoke to the New York tenement dilemma. The Flagg prototypes made ingenious use of the Parisian *porte cochère* and internal courtyard (fig. 27).[75] Four twenty-five-by-one-hundred-foot lots were combined into a single building incorporating an internal central courtyard entered directly through an opening from the street. The building itself was entered from the courtyard, usually by stairs located at each of the four corners. Eighteen-foot-wide light slots opened to the rear, between each one-hundred-foot module. Other plans showed how the model could be modified for seventy-five- and fifty-foot buildings. The one-hundred-foot version was preferred, however, as it redistributed the identical amount of square footage as was typically contained in four dumbbell tenements, but with vastly superior light and ventilation for each apartment.

The influence of Flagg's studies was immediate and widespread. The reasoning articulated by his prototypes was obvious and realistic in response to both the gridiron impasse and the economics of private speculative development. In 1896 he submitted a variation on his studies to the tenement house design competition sponsored by the Improved Housing Council of the Association for Improving the Condition of the Poor.[76] It won first place (fig. 28). James Ware also submitted

26

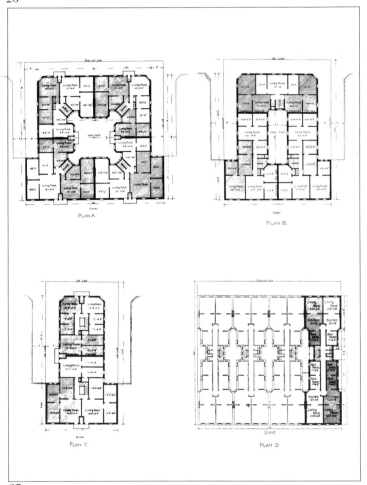

27

26. *The air space between a tenement and its backbuilding, on the Lower East Side block bounded by Canal, Forsyth, Bayard, and Chrystie streets, c. 1895.* From New York State Assembly, Report of the Tenement House Committee of 1894.

27. *Ernest Flagg. Tenement prototypes first published in 1894, using Parisian-influenced central courtyards and* porte cocheres *on multiple lots, compared with a typical dumbbell tenement (Plan D).* From Scribner's Magazine 16 (July 1894).

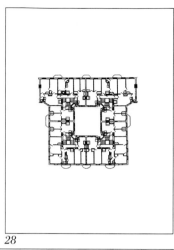

28

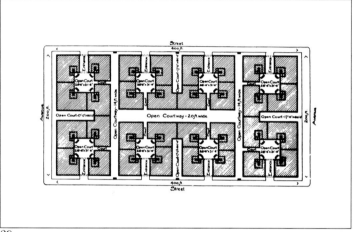

29

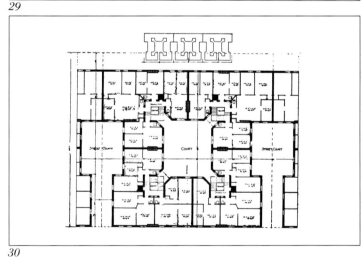

30

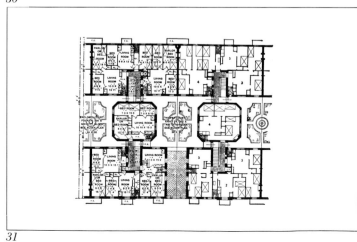

31

a variation on the Flagg plan. He placed second (fig. 29). The same Flagg-type plan dominated a second tenement house competition in 1900, which was sponsored by the Charity Organization Society.[77] Innovative variations were developed, such as the third-place submission designed by Henry Atterbury Smith, which adapted the Flagg-type plan for use with open stairs and toilets vented onto them (fig. 30). The first-prize submission, designed by R. Thomas Short, skillfully manipulated the interior massing to further increase penetration of light over the original Flagg prototypes (fig. 31).

The 1896 competition sponsored by the Improved Housing Council required the design of six-story housing covering not more than seventy percent of a two-hundred-by-four-hundred foot piece of the New York City gridiron. The Charity Organization Society competition in 1900 required the same coverage and height requirements, but with a tighter focus on categories of twenty-five-, fifty-, seventy-, and one-hundred-foot-wide lots. Together the competitions produced a wide range of possible tenement configurations. Both competitions served to develop the architectural vocabulary that was needed to translate tenement studies of the 1880s and 1890s into a coherent, legislatible new form, one that would be more satisfactory than the dumbbell. By 1900 Flagg and Ware had completed building several versions of their 1896 competition entries for the City and Suburban Homes Company, a newly organized philanthropic housing organization.[78] These projects undoubtedly helped focus attention on the practical fabricability of the type.

In 1900 the discourse on the ideal architectural form for the legislated tenement was further developed in an exhibition on tenements sponsored by the Charity Organization Society and organized by reformer Lawrence Veiller.[79] Many recent design studies were shown publicly, including architectural models, more than one thousand photographs, one hundred maps, and many charts and diagrams. A series of conferences was held to discuss different aspects of the tenement house problem. Considerable documentation of model dwellings built in Europe was also presented. A housing exhibition of such size and scope has not been seen since in New York City.

One of the exhibition's architectural models depicted a Lower East Side tenement block, bounded by Chrystie, Forsyth, Canal, and Bayard streets (fig. 32). The two hundred-by-four-hundred-foot block housed twenty-seven hundred persons at an astounding density of fifteen hundred persons per acre, higher than the figures revealed by the Tenement House Commission of 1894. For 605 dwellings, there were only 264 water closets, only 40 were supplied with hot water, 635 rooms faced air shafts, and 441 rooms received no light or ventilation at all.[80] By comparison, a model of a typical dumbbell tenement block was also exhibited, furnishing proof that the 1879 legislation had only succeeded in further aggravating housing conditions (fig. 33). This block, also two hundred by four hundred feet, was said to house more than four thousand persons at a density of more than two thousand persons per acre.

In 1900, under pressure from the Charity Organization Society, the New York State Legislature appointed its fourth Tenement House Commission. Robert DeForest served as chairman, and Lawrence Veiller as secretary. The end product was the classic two-volume study, *The Tenement House Problem*. It provided the most complete survey to that date of the evolution of tenement house legislation and reform, in New York and in other American and European cities. Apart from the report, there were other interesting aspects of the commission's work. For the first time, studies by architects on the design ramifications of alternative tenement controls were seriously considered. Various architects were invited to prepare plans to test the provisions of proposed legislation.[81] Interesting proposals were submitted by Flagg and Phelps Stokes. The Flagg plan was a new fifty-foot prototype that supplemented his 1894 proposals.

In 1901 the state legislature finally passed a definitive legislative response to the agitation of the previous decades. The Tenement House Act of 1901, commonly called the New Law, set the national standard for tenement legislation. Although it has since been modified extensively, its provisions are still the basis for regulation of low-rise housing design in New York City.[82] Its most important provision revised the Old Law coverage requirements that had been established in 1879. The unenforceable sixty-five percent coverage was increased to seventy percent in the New Law, with a mandate for strict enforcement. The minimum dimensions for the dumbbell air shaft were increased to courtyard proportions, which in effect eliminated the enclosed air shaft. The minimum dimensions for interior enclosed courtyards were twelve by twenty-four feet on the lot line and twenty-four by twenty-four feet at the building center, to be increased for buildings over sixty feet high. Minimum dimensions for courtyards opening to the outside had to be six feet wide at the lot line and twelve feet wide at the building center, with increases for buildings over sixty feet high. The rear yard had to be at least twelve feet wide, again with increases for buildings over sixty feet high. No building could be higher than one and one-third of the width of the street it faced. Every apartment had to have running water and a water closet. Every room had to have an exterior window of minimum dimensions, and a series of construction and egress requirements were specified to limit the likelihood of death from fire.

The minimum dimensions established by the New Law could produce only a few efficient floor plans. Figure 34 shows the possibilities allowed for one, two, and three twenty-five-by-one-hundred-foot lot increments, all using the seventy percent maximum coverage. Of the single-lot possibilities, only *B* works at all, and then with a very inefficient plan. Among the double lot possibilities, *E* and *F* work but are also highly inefficient. *B*, *E*, and *F* work better when coverages are reduced to below sixty percent. Only on triple lots can efficient plans be obtained while maintaining the full seventy percent coverage. *G* shows the great affinity of the New Law dimensions for Flagg-type plans. In general, the New Law prevented efficient development from occuring on lots of less than forty-by-one-hundred-foot dimensions. Figure 35 shows a typical New York block, using forty-foot lots, as the majority of speculative developers interpreted the 1901 legislation. The New Law was enforced through organization of a Tenement House Depart-

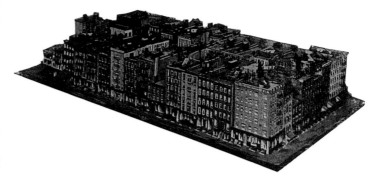

32

33

28. Ernest Flagg. First-place entry to the Tenement House Competition of 1896, sponsored by the Improved Housing Council of the Association for Improving the Condition of the Poor. From James Ford, *Slums and Housing* (1936).

29. James E. Ware. Second-place entry to the Tenement House Competition of 1896, indicating the ideal block configuration. From *Architecture and Building* 16 (January 2, 1897).

30. Henry Atterbury Smith. Third-place entry to the Tenement House Competition of 1900 sponsored by the Charity Organization Society combining the Flagg-type plan with use of open stairs. From William P. Miller, *The Tenement House Committee and Open Stair Tenements* (1912).

31. R. Thomas Short. Winning entry to the Tenement House Competition of 1900 using a variation on the Flagg-type plan with reduced massing at the interior courtyard. From Robert W. DeForest and Lawrence Veiller, *The Tenement House Problem* (1903).

32. Model of a typical Lower East Side tenement block, built for the Tenement House Exhibition of 1900, sponsored by the Charity Organization Society. From Robert W. DeForest and Lawrence Veiller, *The Tenement House Problem* (1903).

33. Model of a typical dumbbell tenement block, built for the Tenement House Exhibition of 1900, showing the definitive increase in density over prelaw tenement housing. From Robert W. DeForest and Lawrence Veiller, *The Tenement House Problem* (1903).

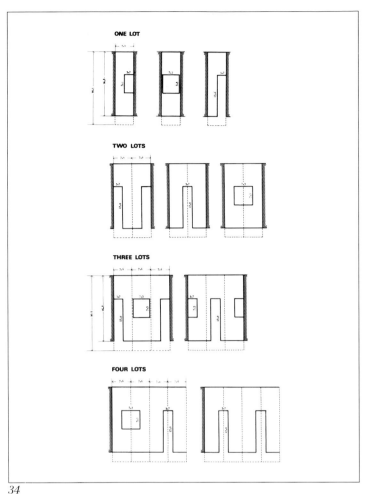

34

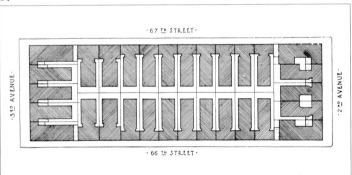

35

34. *Typical tenement configurations permitted under the Tenement House Act of 1901 or New Law, which enlarged the dumbbell airshafts and enforced a maximum coverage of 70 percent; only plans using multiple lots could produce efficient organizations.*

35. *Typical speculative development of an Upper East Side gridiron block under the provision of the New Law, using forty- by one hundred-foot lots. From* Architectural Record *48 (July 1920).*

36. *Typical speculative New Law plan using a fifty- by one hundred-foot lot. From* American Architect and Building News *91 (January 5, 1907).*

36

ment comprising a Bureau of Records, a new Buildings Bureau, and a Bureau of Inspection. With the 1901 legislation, in combination with the political consolidation of the Greater New York Charter of 1897, it was no longer possible to build a blatantly substandard new dwelling in New York City. This increased control, however, when combined with the construction of possible plan types, meant that standards that had originated with the impasse of the high-density areas of Manhattan tended to influence unduly the form of housing throughout the outer boroughs as well, just as the earlier precedent of the commissioners' gridiron for Manhattan tended to be reproduced elsewhere in rote fashion.

The dimensional constraints of the New Law in effect eliminated single twenty-five-foot lot development from the mass market. For higher density tenements, the small developers who built on a lot-by-lot basis could no longer control housing production (fig. 36). Large capital began to monopolize the tenement market. The spatial complexities of the New Law, together with its mandate for larger-scale projects, assured architects a share of this market. Their position had not been so secure under the Old Law, whose requirements could be translated by any builder. For the housing bureaucracy, the New Law firmly established housing control both on paper and in practice. For the general public, it radically improved the quality of tenement housing. In comparison to the Old Law, the New Law managed to achieve a successful balance between real estate interests, the architectural profession, and the building bureaucracy. Ultimately, it was this balance that made the law enforceable (fig. 37).

The legacy of the 1850–1901 era in terms of tenement housing continues to influence heavily the housing stock of New York City today. As of 1987, at least 193,967 Old Law and 574,477 New Law dwellings were still occupied in New York, remaining the largest single representation of dwelling types with the exception of the one- and two-family house (fig. 38).[83] It is a legacy that records the problematic design standards of the more or less unbridled private enterprise of the era (figs. 39 and 40). To be sure, there were many other interesting developments in New York housing during the same period. For example, there was the early high-rise, with its technological innovation that created a dimension of luxury unknown in any other urban setting, and there was the philanthropic housing of the period, which, while minuscule in number in comparison to the private tenements, was still notable for the nonprofit spirit that lay behind its housing ventures. But above all, it is the Old Law tenement that is most often identified with the urban fabric of late nineteenth-century New York. The Old Law tenements, universally criticized as substandard when built, are especially problematic today, as rehabilitation efforts are stalled by seemingly irredeemable plan and massing configurations.

37

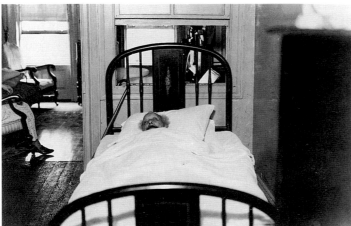

38

39

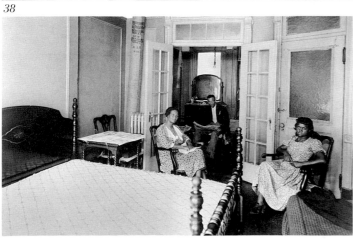

40

37. *View west along East 121 Street from Second Avenue, c. 1937, showing dense walls during the Old Law and early New Law tenements.* Fiorello H. LaGuardia Archives, Fiorello H. LaGuardia Community College, New York.

38. *Interior room in Old Law tenement at 27 West 112th Street, Manhattan, in 1937 prior to demolition for the Stephen Foster Houses public housing project.* Fiorello H. LaGuardia Archives, Fiorello H. LaGuardia Community College, New York.

39. *Evolution of the New York City tenement, from railroad flat, to dumbbell, to a New Law plan.* From City Housing Corporation, Sunnyside and the Housing Problem (n.d.).

40. *Elderly couple in pre-law tenement with interior window, 2294 Eighth Avenue, Manhattan, c. 1937.* Courtesy of Fiorello H. LaGuardia Archives, Fiorello LaGuardia Community College, New York.

Notes

1. See Edward K. Spann, *The New Metropolis: New York City, 1840–1857* (New York: Columbia University Press, 1981), ch. 15. For related aspects of the transformation of the city's popular culture, see Paul Alan Marx, *This is the City: An Examination of Changing Attitudes Toward New York as Reflected in Its Guidebook Literature, 1807–1860* (Ann Arbor, Mich.: University Microfilms International, 1983), parts 3 and 4.

2. Rosenwalke, *Population History of New York City* (Syracuse, N.Y.: Syracuse University Press, 1972), table 19, 63.

3. Ibid., 39, 42.

4. Philip Hone, *The Diary of Philip Hone, 1828–1851*, ed. Allan Nevins (New York: Dodd, Mead, and Company, 1927), 785.

5. This important observation was made in Howard D. Kramer, "The Beginnings of the Public Health Movement in the United States," *Bulletin of the History of Medicine* 21 (May–June 1944): 353–54.

6. See Howard D. Kramer, "The Germ Theory and the Early Public Health Program in the United States," *Bulletin of the History of Medicine* 22 (May–June 1948): 233–47.

7. John H. Griscom, M.D., *Annual Report of the Interments in the City and County of New York, for the Year 1842, with Remarks Thereon, and a Brief View of the Sanitary Condition of the City* (New York: James van Norden, 1843), 166.

8. John H. Griscom, M.D., *The Sanitary Condition of the Laboring Population of New York with Suggestions for Its Improvement* (New York: Harper and Bros., 1845); Griscom, *Annual Report of 1842*; and Griscom, *The Uses and Abuses of Air: Showing Its Influence in Sustaining Life, and Producing Disease, with Remarks on the Ventilation of Houses* (New York: Redfield, 1854).

9. Griscom, *The Uses and Abuses of Air*, 187. Of particular influence was undoubtedly Edwin Chadwick, *Report on the Sanitary Condition of the Labouring Population of Great Britain: A Supplementary Report on the Results of A Special Inquiry into the Practice of Interments in Towns* (London: W. Clowes and Son, 1843), 203.

10. Griscom, *Annual Report of 1842*, 176.

11. Ibid., 175–76.

12. Griscom, *The Uses and Abuses of Air*, 74.

13. Gervet Forbes, "Remarks," in *Annual Report of Deaths in the City and County of New York for the Year 1834* (New York, 1835), 16.

14. Citizens' Association of New York, Council of Hygiene and Public Health, *Report upon the Sanitary Condition of the City* (New York: D. Appleton and Co., 1865), lxiii–lxiv.

15. Griscom, *The Uses and Abuses of Air*, 193–94.

16. New York Association for Improving the Condition of the Poor, *Sixteenth Annual Report* (New York, 1856), 46.

17. Jacob A. Riis, "The Clearing of Mulberry Bend," *Review of Reviews* 12 (August 1895): 172–78.

18. New York City, *Minutes of the Common Council: 1784–1831* (New York: M. B. Browne Printing and Binding, 1917) (April 20, 1829) 18: 11–12.

19. Charles Dickens, *American Notes*, 2 vols. (London: Chapman and Hall, 1842), 213.

20. A brief indication of Allaire's housing activities is given in Moses Yale Beach, *Wealth and Pedigree of the Wealthy Citizens of New York City*, 4th ed. (New York: The Sun Office, 1842). He was described at one time as a "half-millionaire" who owned a foundry and to whom "the mechanic classes in all the upper wards along the East River could point with pride."

21. *Plumber and Sanitary Engineer* 3 (December 15, 1879): 26; and Charles H. Haswell, *Reminiscences of an Octogenarian of the City of New York: 1816–1860* {New York: Harper, 1896), 332.

22. *Evening Post*, August 20, 1850, cited by I.N. Phelps Stokes, *The Iconography of Manhattan Island: 1498–1909* (New York: Robert H. Dodd, 1926). 5 (1829)

23. Citizens' Association, *Report*, 49–55; and "Gotham Court," *Frank Leslie's Sunday Magazine* 5 (June 1879), 655.

24. "Gotham Court," 655.

25. Jacob A. Riis, *The Battle with the Slum* (New York: The MacMillan Company, 1902), 118.

26. John H. Reps, *The Making of Urban America: A History of City Planning in the United States* (Princeton, N.J.: Princeton University Press, 1965), 297–99.

27. Citizens' Association, *Report*, lxix.

28. Tenement construction methods were quite similar to those of the brownstone of the same period. In 1851, Gottfried Semper published an interesting account of these conventions in New York. See Winslow Ames, "New York Brownstone through German Eyes," *Journal of the Society of Architectural Historians* 25 (March 1966), 63–64.

29. Robert DeForest and Lawrence Veiller, *The Tenement House Problem*, 2 vols. (New York: The MacMillan Company, 1903), 1: 293–300.

30. Citizens' Association, *Report*, 135.

31. "Homes of Poor People," *New York Daily Tribune*, January 8, 1882, 10.

32. DeForest and Veiller, *The Tenement*, 1: 306–9.

33. This genre of improved tenements was discussed extensively in Citizens' Association, *Report, passim*.

34. For a general description, see Spann, *The New Metropolis*, 234–41. For an extensive contemporary account, see *Account of the Terrific and Fatal Riot at the New York Astor Place Opera House* (New York, 1849), *passim*.

35. James Ford, *Slums and Housing* (Cambridge: Harvard University Press, 1936), 117, 129; New York City, *Annual Report of the City of New York for the Year Ending December 31, 1854* (1855), 204, 234–35.

36. For a general description, see Spann, *The New Metropolis*, 391–98; and James McCague, *The Second Rebellion: The Story of the New York City Draft Riots of 1865* (New York: The Dial Press, 1968), 39–42.

37. New York Association for Improving the Condition of the Poor, *Fifteenth Annual Report*, (New York, 1858), 17–18.

38. New York State Assembly, *Report of the Special Committee on Tenement Houses*, Assembly Document No. 199 (April 4, 1856); New York State Assembly, *Report of the Select Committee on Tenement Houses*, Assembly Document No. 205 (March 9, 1857). See also New York Association for Improving the Condition of the Poor, *Sixteenth Annual Report* (New York, 1859).

39. For a complete history of the riots, see Iver Bernstein, *The New York City Draft Riots* (New York: Oxford University Press, 1990).

40. Citizens' Association, *Report*, xv–xvi.

41. Citizens' Association, *Report*, lxix.

42. New York State Assembly, *Report of the Committee on Public Health, Medical Colleges, and Societies Relative to the Condition of Tenement Houses in the Cities of New York and Brooklyn*, Assembly Document No. 156 (March 8, 1867).

43. New York State Legislature, *Laws* (1866), ch. 873, 2009–47.

44. New York State Legislature, *Laws* (1867), ch. 980, sec. 17, 2265–73.

45. Joseph D. McGoldrick, Seymour Graubard, and Raymond Horowitz, *Building Regulation in New York City* (New York: Commonwealth Fund, 1944), 49-66.

46. John P. Comer, *New York City Building Control: 1800–1941* (New York: Columbia University Press, 1942), ch. 2.

47. Lawrence Veiller and Hugh Bonner, *Special Report on Housing Conditions and Tenement Laws in Leading American Cities* (New York: Evening Post Job Printing House, 1900), 5–6, 17.

48. New York State Legislature, *Laws* (1879), ch. 504, 554–56.

49. This competition was first announced in "Improved Homes for Workingmen," *Plumber and Sanitary Engineer* 2 (December 1878), 1, 32.

50. Plans of the first eleven winning schemes were published in "Model House Competition: Prize Plans," *Plumber and Sanitary Engineer* 2 (March 1879), 103–06, (April 1872), 131–32, (May 1879), 158–59, (June 1, 1879), 180, (June 15, 1879), 212, and (July 1, 1879), 230.

51. "Prize Tenements," *New York Times*, March 16, 1874, 6.

52. Henry C. Meyer, *The Story of the Sanitary Engineer, Later the Engineering Record Supplementary to Civil War Experiences* (New York, 1928), 14–15.

53. "The Tenement-House Act," *New York Times*, May 25, 1879.

54. DeForest and Veiller, *The Tenement*, 1: 94, 2: 78.

55. Rosenwalke, *Population History*, table 29, 7; table 49, 110.

56. A summary of these changes is found in McGoldrick, Graubard, and Horowitz, *Building Regulation*, 51–56. For a history of the charter movement, see Barry J. Kaplan, "Metropolitics, Administrative Reform, and Political Theory: The Greater New York City Charter of 1897," *Journal of Urban History* 9 (February 1983), 164–94.

57. New York State Legislature, *Laws* (1882), ch. 410, title 5, 125–45.

58. New York State Legislature, Tenement House Commission, *Report* (1885), 42, 44.

59. New York State Legislature, *Laws* (1887), ch. 566, 738–72; and New York State Legislature, *Laws* (1887), ch. 84, 94–101.

60. New York State Legislature, *Laws* (1884), ch. 272.

61. "Matter of Jacobs," in New York Court of Appeals, *New York Reports*

(1885), vol. 98, 114–15.

62. Theodore Roosevelt, *An Autobiography* (New York: The MacMillan Company, 1914), 83. See also Henry Steele Commager, *Documents of American History*, 2 vols. (New York: F. S. Crofts & Co., 1935), 2: 116–18. Commager considered this decision important enough to include in his early editions, but dropped it from later ones.

63. Jacob Riis, "How the Other Half Lives," *Scribner's Magazine* 6 (December 1889), 643–62; and Jacob Riis, *How the Other Half Lives* (New York: Charles Scribner's Sons, 1890). Riis gives ample description of the conditions of the cigarmakers mentioned earlier. See his chapter 12,

64. A good summary of Smith's contribution is found in Gordon Atkins, "Health, Housing, and Poverty in New York City: 1865–1898," Ph.D. diss., Columbia University, 1947, 22–27.

65. For a general history of the AICP and COS, see Lilian Brandt, *Growth and Development of AICP and COS, Report of the Committee on the Institute of Welfare Research* (New York: Community Service Society of New York, 1942).

66. Charles F. Wingate, "The Moral Side of the Tenement House Problem," *The Catholic World* 41 (May 1885), 162, 164.

67. Carrol D. Wright, *The Slums of Baltimore, Chicago, New York, and Philadelphia: Seventh Special Report of the Commissioner of Labor* (Washington, D.C.: Government Printing Office, 1894), 19, 42, 45, 85–86.

68. Wingate, "The Moral Side," 161.

69. Allen Forman, "Some Adopted American," *The American Magazine* 9 (November 1888): 50.

70. New York State Assembly, *Report of the Tenement House Committee of 1894*, Legislative Document No. 37 (January 17, 1885), 11.

71. New York State Legislature, *Laws* (1895), ch. 567, 1099–1114.

72. Elgin R.L. Gould, *The Housing of the Working People: Eighth Special Report of the Commissioner of Labor* (Washington, D.C.: Government Printing Office, 1895).

73. "Tenement House Reform—What the Government Should Do—The Last of Felix Adler's Lectures," *New York Daily Tribune*, March 10, 1884, 8.

74. Ernest Flagg, "The New York Tenement-House Evil and Its Cure," *Scribner's Magazine* 16 (July 1894), 108–17. For an overview of Flagg's work in tenement reform, see Mardges Bacon, *Ernest Flagg, Beaux-Arts Architect and Urban Reformer* (Cambridge: The MIT Press, 1986), ch. 8.

75. Flagg described the French influence in "The Planning of Apartment Houses and Tenements," *Architectural Review* 10 (July 1903): 85–90.

76. The competition program is found in Improved Housing Council, *Conditions of Competition for Plans of Model Apartment Houses* (New York, 1896). For a discussion of placing entries, see "New York's Great Movement for Housing Reform," *Review of Reviews* 14 (December 1896): 692–701; "Model Apartment Houses," *Architecture and Building* 26 (January 2, 1897): 7–10. See also DeForest and Veiller, *The Tenement*, 1: 107–9; Ford, *Slums and Housing*, pl. 7; Anthony Jackson, *A Place Called Home: A History of Low-Cost Housing in Manhattan* (Cambridge: The MIT Press, 1976), 106–8.

77. The competition program is found in Charity Organization Society of the City of New York, Tenement House Committee, *Competition for Plans of Model Tenements* (New York, 1899). For a discussion of placing entries, see Lawrence Veiller, "The Charity Organization Society's Tenement House Competition," *American Architect and Building News* 67 (March 10, 1900): 77–79; "The Tenement House Competition," *Architecture* 1 (March 15, 1900): 104; "Model Tenement Floors," *Real Estate Record and Builders' Guide* 65 (March 17, 1900): 425–55. See also DeForest and Veiller, *The Tenement*, 1: 109–13; Ford, *Slums and Housing*, pls. 8, 9.

78. For a chronology of the City and Suburban Homes Company projects, see City and Suburban Homes Company, *Thirty-Sixth Annual Report* (May 1932): 4. See also United States Federal Housing Administration, *Four Decades of Housing with a Limited Dividend Corporation* (Washington, D.C.: U. S. Government Printing Office, 1939).

79. "Tenement House Show," *New York Times*, February 10, 1900, 7; DeForest and Veiller, *The Tenement*, 1: 112–13.

80. Estimates are from DeForest and Veiller, *The Tenement*, 1: 8.

81. Some of these plans are published in Ford, *Slums and Housing*, vol. 2, pls. 9B, 10A, 10B, 10D, 10E.

82. New York State Legislature, *Laws* (1901), ch. 334, 889–923.

83. Michael A. Stegman, *Housing and Vacancy Report: New York City, 1987* (New York City: The City of New York Department of Housing Preservation and Development, April, 1988), tables 2.43 and 2.44.

References

James Ford, *Slums and Housing*, 2 vols. (Cambridge: Harvard University Press, 1936).

Anthony Jackson, *A Place Called Home: A History of Low-Cost Housing in Manhattan* (Cambridge: The MIT Press, 1976).

Roy Lubove, *The Progressives and the Slums: Tenement House Reform in New York City 1890–1917* (Pittsburgh: The University of Pittsburgh Press, 1963).

Richard Plunz, *Habiter New York: La Forme institutionalisée de l'habitat New Yorkais, 1850–1950* (Liège: Pierre Mardaga Editeur, 1982; rev. and trans. ed., New York, Columbia University Press, 1989).

The Birth Pangs of Modernism

Eberhard Roters

Eberhard Roters was director of the Berlinische Galerie from 1976 until his retirement in 1987. His most important publications include Maler am Bauhaus *(1970),* Europäische Expressionisten *(1971),* Berlin 1910–1933: The Visual Arts *(ed.) (1983),* Galerie Ferdinand Möller *(1984),* E.T.A. Hoffmann *(1984),* Creatio nihili oder Die Herstellung von Nichts: Dada-Meditationen *(1990).*

The term modernism was coined in Berlin by the literary historian Eugen Wolff in September 1886 in a lecture to the members of the literary society Durch.[1] The lecture was held in the back room of a bar in the Alte Poststrasse at the Spittelmarkt. If one were to take the significance of such terms entirely seriously, modernism would now be just over one hundred years old.

Durch (translated literally as "through") is a battle cry that conveys the fighting spirit of a group engaged in a struggle, and it was the motto used by the young writers and literati of Berlin who joined forces in the mid-1880s to bring new life to the stale, academic atmosphere of contemporary literature.[2] This movement has been called naturalism. Its battles were fought in Berlin, and although naturalism enjoyed only a brief florescence, it marked the first stage in the development of modernist art. All of this was determined in Berlin.[3] The contribution of visual art to the development of modernism was as important as that of literature and the theater. It is not a coincidence that the *nom de guerre* was coined by the literati, and its more general use also confirms that artists at this time were highly interested to know what went on beyond the immediate boundaries of their own disciplines. There was clearly a much more intensive exchange of ideas between artists than is the case today. Evidence of this can also be seen in the reciprocal creative stimulation in friendships between artists from different disciplines, such as that between Walter Leistikow and Bruno Wille or between Max Reinhardt and the painter Edvard Munch or between Reinhardt and Christian Morgenstern. This interaction between the different arts, their flexible boundaries, and their reciprocal exchange of discoveries and motives served as a constant incentive for the development and establishment of modernism. This would also be a major stimulus in determining the tenor of the conflict that took place in Berlin. It was therefore necessary that certain forums be found where the artists could meet and engage in spirited discussions of questions, problems, and conflicts surrounding art. This function was served by various meeting places in the city, from the Schwarzes Ferkel[4] and the Nollendorf-Casino[5] to the Café des Westens,[6] and also by the various intellectual journals, from *Pan* to *Sturm* and *Aktion*. The significance of these meeting places of the intellect cannot be overestimated. It was here that the intellectual potency of the avant-garde consolidated itself to a critical force.

Modernism in Berlin emerged between two wars: the Franco-Prussian War of 1870–71, which was won by the German confederation led by Prussia, and the war that began in August 1914 and was eventually lost by the German Empire. This covers a period of four decades. The era's protagonists, who stepped onto the stage of history alongside or immediately after each other, generally belonged to two generations. Consequently the drama of modernism in Berlin is divided into two acts that are then subdivided into a series of overlapping scenes. The plot consists of an unbroken chain of contradictions, misunderstandings, friendships, antagonisms, enmities, brotherhoods, and quarrels. Conflicts that had smoldered for decades, which had been played out through subterfuge and tricks, in the manner of a court intrigue or a comedy of manners, now suddenly came to a head and were fought out in the

1. Ernst Ludwig Kirchner. Belle-Alliance Platz in Berlin, *1912/13. Neue Nationalgalerie, Berlin.*

181

open. The main protagonists are artist, writer, actor or actress, critic, gallery owner, collector, patron, museum director, cultural official, politician, and, as in dramas of the Middle Ages, leading them all is the kaiser himself. The cultivated segment of society provides the extras. Barely visible, however, is the man on the street. He seldom makes an appearance on the stage but turns up all the more frequently in the text. The proletarian plays a role primarily in the recitation. The petite bourgeoisie is the audience. As it is impossible to present the complete play from beginning to end here, a sketch will have to suffice.

Before doing so, however, it is necessary to outline the existing social conditions. Berlin, Europe's youngest metropolis, was very much in the throes of a pubertal acceleration of growth. At the beginning of the nineteenth century it was still the modest residence of the comparatively enlightened kingdom of Prussia. Despite the fact that it was relatively far removed from raw materials, under the influence of the Industrial Revolution, Berlin began to expand rapidly. This growth resulted from intense effort, the extent of which was not foreseen. It was certainly related to the financial support provided by the state for the arms industry at the end of the Napoleonic era. Berlin became the center for the production of heavy machinery, traction engines, locomotives, and railway carriages. The company names Borsig and Schwarzkopff are synonymous with this development. In the absence of professional and economic prospects at home, farmers' sons and daughters, primarily from the distant Eastern provinces, swarmed into the city, becoming Berlin's urban proletariat in the nineteenth century. Under changed but in no way improved working conditions, they would be forced to undergo an intensive and painful process that would lead to the emergence of a new social consciousness, the exemplary consciousness of the big city, that of the working class. The industrial city of Berlin expanded as the working-class suburbs in the north and east spread out far into the Brandenburg countryside—the natural landscape replaced by the gray of tenements. This was how the Colossus of Berlin, the Atlas who was to bear the weight of the great metropolis, grew.

By the middle of the century, at one end of the social scale was a huge proletariat in Berlin that had emerged almost overnight and under quite different historical conditions from those in England or France. This was a class that did not yet have its own history. At the other end of the social scale was a wealthy class incapable of dealing with this explosive development.

This wealthy class was made up of the Junkers and of other Prussian aristocrats in the military or court and state who were incapable of understanding industrial workers as a social class. For them these workers remained the sons and daughters of farm laborers who had escaped to the city instead of remaining at the disposal of the upper class. (Seen from this view, this escape was their first step as potential revolutionaries.) At best they judged them in terms of their suitability as material for the army. Not only was the Prussian aristocracy extremely conservative; the same was true of Berlin's bourgeoisie, which took great pains to emulate the behavior and habits of their aristocratic models. This elitist ideal was reflected in the fervent desire to obtain the title of reserve officer and to wear the Order of the Red Eagle—even if only that of the so-called Fourth Class. Of course, there were exceptions to this conservative norm in Berlin's intellectual circles, personified by such figures as the historian Theodor Mommsen, who was dismissed from Leipzig University for his participation in the liberal movement, or the doctor Rudolf Virchow. These men were a reminder of the deceptive dawn of the Vormärz and had preserved their democratic ideals. Not surprisingly, the general widespread conservatism influenced cultural behavior. During these decades of political regression, every attempt at a creative outburst was hampered by a conservatism that pervaded every aspect of cultural life like sickly sweet perfume. The only genius who was able to assert himself against this was the painter Adolf Menzel, and he was protected by a naturally reclusive nature. The "little excellency," as he became known, was one of nineteenth-century Berlin's most important artists and at the same time a soloist who went his own way and founded no school.

The public forum for artistic activity in Berlin was the Salon.[7] Founded in 1796, this official art exhibition took place biannually until 1876 and thereafter annually. Modeled on the Paris Salon, it was a major artistic and social event where one was seen and sometimes even had one's portrait exhibited. Its reputation did not spread far beyond Berlin, for its exhibition rooms filled to the ceilings with enormous oil paintings and countless classical bronze renderings of "Boys Extracting Thorns" and "Girls Tying Sandals" and other similar figures, revealed nothing except accomplished and routine academicism in the dreariest of genres. In the early seventies, even the art critics, who were as conservative in their views as the rest of Berlin Society, were forced to bemoan the total mediocrity of the Salon.[8]

Artistic activity in Berlin was controlled by two institutions. One of these was the venerable Association of Berlin Artists (Verein Berliner Künstler), which still exists and has become an even more venerable institution, and the other was the Academy of Arts (Akademie der Künste). As part of an administrative reform under its new director Anton von Werner, in 1875, the latter was divided into two sections, an educational institution and a clublike association.

Membership in the academy was considered a privilege. The academy and the association were in constant competition with each other, mostly over who should control the Salon. After Anton von Werner succeeded in being appointed director of both the academy and the association in 1893, however, the steady decline of the Salon left no alternative other than a compromise solution.[9]

The question that now arises is how an atmosphere so bogged down in the rituals of convention was able to provide the impulse which led to Berlin's spirited entry into the modernist era. This question can be answered by first taking another look at existing social conditions and at one aspect in particular which to my mind has not received sufficient attention.

Following the victory over France in 1871, the organization of the German Empire and a period of rapid industrial expansion, the *Gründerzeit*, a new prosperity developed in a city that was now capital of the empire. In the ensuing decades, this led to a hitherto unparalleled expansion in Berlin's economic, industrial, and financial sectors; also, technical, natural, and medical sciences flourished. New technical processes and industrialization were developed in Berlin, whose collective know-how and products were exported all over the world. The first phase of this development was dominated by the establishment of electricity as a form of energy that furthered industrial and economic expansion. The imposing complex of the Siemens works in the northwest of the city grew out of the Telegraphic Institute (Telegraphenanstalt) founded in 1847 by Siemens and Halske. In 1883, the Edison Society was founded by Emil Rathenau, and in 1887, it was renamed AEG (Allgemeine Elektricitäts-Gesellschaft). The second phase of this development, sometimes known as the second *Gründerzeit*, is characterized by the economic exploitation of the new fields in technical processing particularly in the areas of chemistry, chemical technology, chemical therapy, serum chemistry, material testing, and related areas. Thanks to farsighted administrative policy, specialized scientific institutions that worked hand in hand with the new industries were established in the Dahlem and Lichterfelde areas southwest of Berlin.[10] The new prosperity brought new forms of collaboration and interaction. Bankers, industrialists, businessmen, technicians, scientists, and intellectuals depended on each other's cooperation. A new press emerged whose liberalism and broad scope of subjects and opinions greatly improved Berlin's newspaper world. This influential social group, which was amalgamated during the century's final decades, was initially treated with arrogant disdain by the old conservative elite. Mistrust would subsequently replace this attitude, and its members were seen as social climbers and as a source of competition rather than opposition. This new class represented a new type of elite—at least for Prussia. It was made up of personalities from the hard-working middle classes who had come to something as a result of their own efforts. They were self-made, or seen from the more conservative perspective, parvenus. Interestingly enough, within this emerging, urbane social circle, the best example of a dandy was to be found in a man whose origins lay in more worldly, aristocratic circles. This was Harry Graf Kessler, a Paris-born aesthete and diplomat.[11] Berlin's emancipated Jewish bourgeoisie was also an influential, even dominating force in this new social group. Its members placed great emphasis on their Germanness and had become fully integrated into the German language and intellectual tradition. It was important for them to maintain this integration, an assimilation that had only been recently acknowledged in Germany. One of the outstanding personalities among them, Walter Rathenau, whose father had founded the AEG, tried to convince German Jews of the necessity of integration in *Hear, Israel* his famous appeal of 1897: "The state has made citizens of you in order to make Germans of you. You have remained strangers and yet demand that it grant you total equality? You speak of the obligations you have fulfilled: war service and taxes. But more was called for than the fulfillment of obligations, for example, trust."[12] No German can read these sentences today without feeling shame.

In Berlin, the struggle toward modernism, the conflict between the preservation of existing, acknowledged values and the desire to go further, to experiment and change, was fought out between these two elite groups—the old, conservative, traditional elite of the reserve officers dominated by the aristocracy, and the new, cosmopolitan, economically adventurous, liberal bourgeoisie. The latter had to establish an autonomous cultural image for itself. Instead of a hereditary nobility, they could offer a meritocracy. And in its identification with and support for the new directions and movements in art, this elite found a cultural image that reflected its perceptions of itself. The major Berlin collectors came from this elite. It was they who made it possible for art in Berlin to enter the new century, and they established an audience large enough to accommodate this development.

Because they had had to work for their privileges, the members of the new elite instinctively showed greater sympathy for the demands, needs, and sensibilities of the petit bourgeoisie and the workers than the aristocracy had done. This understanding was not accompanied, however, by a corresponding attitude of social or socialist solidarity. On the contrary, by displaying what they had achieved and what they had become, they wished to set themselves apart from the petite bourgeoisie and the proletariat. Nevertheless, the new elite was in a better position to understand the problems of the proletariat. With its energy, social open-mindedness, and interest in professional status, this elite echoed in principle the dreams and wishes of the petite bourgeoisie. It was this, together with the invention of chain stores and office machinery and the resulting automation of working and leisure activities in Berlin, which brought forth a social phenomenon that has formed our ways of thinking and living in the twentieth century. This phenomenon with its dispersive power to level out class barriers was the culture of the white-collar worker.

If the former ruling class had been that of a royal capital, then the new one was that of a metropolis. It was under its influence that Berlin became a metropolis. Naturally, this did not all take place without doubt and suspicion. Like every development, there were certainly opposing factions.

The first phase in the path to modernism in Berlin took place against the background of naturalism. There are certain important dates in the chronology of this development that mark the transition from quantitative to qualitative achievements. One of them is 1889. During a meeting in Café Schiller in March of that year, Otto Brahm, Theodor Wolff, Maximilian Harden, Paul Schlenther, Julius Stettenheim, and Samuel Fischer decided to found the The Free Theater Association (Theaterverein Freie Bühne). The aim of this association was to present new naturalistic drama. This was meant as a deliberate contrast to the antiquated, official court theater associated with Ernst von Wildenbruch. Otto Brahm was appointed theater director; on September 29, 1889, Brahm opened the Freie Bühne with a matinee performance of Henrik Ibsen's *Ghosts*. On October 20, the memorable premiere of Gerhart Hauptmann's *Before Sunrise* took place and ended with the greatest uproar Berlin's theater world had ever experienced. Because of its status as an association, the theater's performances were

2

2. *Lovis Corinth.* Portrait of the Poet Peter Hille, *1902.* Kunsthalle Bremen.

3. *Auguste Renoir.* Afternoon of the Children in Wargemont, *1884.* Neue Nationalgalerie, Berlin.

4. *Edouard Manet.* In the Winter Garden, *1879.* Neue Nationalgalerie, Berlin.

5. *Max Liebermann.* Flax Shed in Laren, *1887.* Nationalgalerie, Berlin.

legally not public events. In staging these sociocritical dramas, the Freie Bühne was, therefore, able to use their unalloyed dialect. On February 26, the Freie Bühne staged *The Weavers* by Gerhart Hauptmann, and the following year when Brahm dared to allow it to be staged in the Deutsches Theater, the kaiser cancelled the royal box.[13] The young artist Käthe Kollwitz was present at the performance, and her graphic cycle *A Weavers' Revolution* was inspired by it.

As was usual with events of this nature in Berlin, the founding of the Freie Bühne was immediately followed by the founding of an opposition group. In 1890, Bruno Wille founded the The People's Free Theater (Freie Volksbühne) with the intention of providing an educational theater of the working classes. In his opinion, the Free Theater was too bourgeois in its aims. The People's Free Theater was immediately torn apart by ideological disputes, and in 1892, Wille withdrew from the association in a sulk and founded the New People's Free Theater (Neue Freie Volksbühne). This concept of a people's theater lives on in Berlin today. The reason for the conflict was that Wille was not a party Socialist. He did not share this party's fundamental recognition that in order for its goals to be achieved, comrades must have a collective standpoint and engage in tactical rituals. Instead, in accordance with humanist ideals of knowledge as power, he wanted to help the workers toward a more developed all-around education.

Wille, who saw himself as a "hermit and comrade,"[14] played a leading role in the ranks of the first Green Party. These were nature lovers and pantheists who united to form the Friedrichshagen circle and moved to the pine heath at the small town of Friedrichshagen situated on a lake (Müggelsee) southeast of the city. There was, however, a direct rail link to Berlin as they ultimately could not live without city air. The brothers Julius and Heinrich Hart belonged to this group as did the monistic popular philosopher and scientific author Wilhelm Boelsche, the poet Peter Hille, the Danish literary couple Olas Hansson and Laura Marholm. The painter Walter Leistikow, the anarcho-socialist Gustav Landauer, the anarchist John Henry Mackay, the poets Richard Dehmel and Max Halbe, and the painter and illustrator Fidus (Hugo Höppener), a supporter of universal social reform, were all occasional visitors to Friedrichshagen.[15] August Strindberg, who came to Berlin as a result of the efforts of the Friedrichshagen group, made his first Berlin home there. His inability to get on with the other members of the group, however, meant that he did not stay very long. The group consisted of individual anarchists and bourgeois sentimental socialists, or as Arno Holz defined them in the title of his malicious dramatic satire of 1896—"Social Aristocrats."

If the literary world caused the first sensation with its modernist dramas, the visual arts were not far behind. Preparation for such a sensation had been under way for some time. On the side of modernism, the protagonists were Max Liebermann and the new director of the National Gallery, Hugo von Tschudi. They were supported by the art trade, in particular by the Cassirer Salon and the collectors. The conservatives were supported by the kaiser, who used his power to enforce his aesthetic views, which were founded on a complete faith in the eternal validity of the artistic ideals of his caste. This side also had the support of his paladin, the official court painter Anton von Werner who in turn had the power of the official institutions behind him—the academy and the Association of Berlin Artists, as he was director of both.

When Werner took over the position as director of the academy in 1875, there were high hopes for what he would do. He was an energetic man with considerable organizational talents, and it was expected that he would bring new life to the stale academic routine.[16] Seen from an administrative point of view, this actually happened. The kaiser and the director of the academy were similar, however, in that the apparent vigor of their personalities could easily hide the fact that their firm belief in technocratic progress was actually rooted in a profound conservatism. The conflicts in the ensuing years were like a game of chess. Every time one party attacked, the other responded with a counterattack, the players almost all belonged to one generation and the kaiser was the youngest amongst them. Werner was born in 1843, Liebermann in 1847, Tschudi in 1851, and Wilhelm II in 1859.

In 1872, Liebermann made his debut at the Berlin Salon, exhibiting *Women Plucking Geese* (National Gallery, Berlin), the first example of his early painting to be shown to the Berlin public. In fact this work is not exactly naturalistic in the sense of a sociocritical or so-called ugly, over-precise, emphatic style of painting. Its objective presentation of the subject is actually closer to the artistic positivism that had already been featured in the work of Menzel. What was important to Liebermann was to explore and present the qualities of a pure style of painting which resulted from a process of observation unencumbered by preconceived notions and that used mundane and trivial motifs, such as everyday tasks. Berlin's shocked art critics labeled him an "apostle of ugliness."[17] In 1877, Liebermann participated in the academy exhibition with the painting *Women Working in the Turnip Field* (Lower Saxony Museum, Hannover), and in 1878, three of his works were included in the Salon. Meanwhile, opposition to his work was growing in Berlin. In 1872, Liebermann went to Holland for the first time, from 1873 to 1878, he was in Paris, and he spent two summers in Barbizon. His encounters with Jozef Israel, Gustave Courbet, and Edouard Manet during the dawn of French Impressionism revealed an inner affinity between himself and these painters, which found expression in his work. Liebermann was, thus, the first to direct Berlin's attention toward the new and exciting developments that were occurring in Europe's visual arts. He thereby succeeded in initiating a breakthrough in the city's self-imposed artistic isolation. The final breakthrough was, however, still a long way off.

The initial impulse for the recognition Liebermann gradually received in Berlin came from outside. The exhibition of the *Flax Shed in Laren* (National Gallery, Berlin) in the Paris Salon aroused the interest of the Paris audience. Liebermann gave the painting to the Berlin National Gallery in 1888; it would not have been possible for the National Gallery to buy it as purchase was blocked by the Regional Art Commission.[18] In the same year, art criticism in Berlin was still talking about the "endless monotony, tedium and boredom" in

3

4

5

6

7

Liebermann's work. The authority the artist already enjoyed, however, meant that he was easily able to take on the role of leader of the young rebels. In 1889, the French government invited European artists to participate in the Exposition Universelle that was being held to mark the centenary of the French Revolution. The European monarchies turned down the invitation but did not prevent participation by individual artists. Liebermann organized a private show by German artists. Despite the Prussian government's repressive attempts to prevent this, approximately forty artists participated. For the first time, and in a foreign country, the German modernists were exhibited as a virtually united front. Even the aging Menzel had not allowed himself to be held back by nationalistic reproaches. The reactions of the French and the independent German press were positive. Among other prizes, Liebermann was awarded the Order of the Legion of Honor for his courageous deed. The Prussian government forbade him to accept it,[19] but Liebermann continued to play a leading role in the politics of the art world; perhaps his strength was bolstered by the government's repressive action. The kaiser's approach to foreign art policy was evident in the presentation of his portrait to the German embassy in Paris in 1890. The official portrait, painted by the court painter Max Koner, was a bombastic, histrionic depiction of the kaiser in an imperious pose. The portrait provoked the exclamation from a senior member of the French military: "Ce portrait là, c'est une declaration de guerre!" ("That portrait is a declaration of war!")[20] The following year, the National Gallery acquired Ferdinand Keller's colossal painting *Kaiser Wilhelm the Victorious*; akin to a high altar to the Hohenzollern, it was a showpiece of excruciating nationalistic kitsch. There was a strong collision of fronts. The mounting pressure of the problem had to vent itself in a crisis. On February 5, 1892, the young artists who represented modernism in Berlin founded the Association of the XI, whose most important members besides Liebermann were Walter Leistikow, Ludwig von Hofmann, and Franz Skarbina. This marked the prelude to the founding of the Secession. On April 3, the XI opened its first exhibition in Eduard Schulte's art gallery on Unter den Linden at the corner of Wilhelmstrasse. Adolf Rosenberg, one of the modernists' main opponents among art critics, opened his furious attack in the *Kunstchronik* with the prediction that having "instigated such a fundamental fiasco this review of the exhibition will probably be their obituary."[21]

The crisis finally erupted at the end of that year, in the course of which the opposing forces had been gathering strength. It was triggered by the Munch affair.[22] The exhibition committee of the Verein Berliner Kunstler had invited the Norwegian to exhibit his work in the circular room of the Berlin Architects' House, which at the time was a very popular venue for exhibitions. The exhibition opened on November 5, 1892. As Rosenberg put it in his review, Munch thereupon sent "fifty-five pieces of canvas and cardboard which had been framed and covered with paint."[23] The conservative art critics were beside themselves with indignation. The majority of the members of the association requested a special meeting which was held on November 12 and chaired by Anton von Werner. A row broke out at this meeting that would shake the Berlin art world to its foundations and led to numerous withdrawals and resignations; it also nearly split the association. The effect was purgative and the energy released provided the first impulse for the founding of the Berlin Secession seven years later. Edvard Munch was not unduly upset by the scandal as he had taken a dislike to Berlin anyway. However, he stayed for the following years (taking extensive breaks in between) and was inspired by and inspirational to Berlin's art scene. He became friendly with Leistikow, made contact with the Friedrichshagen circle, and was a frequent guest at gatherings in the Schwarzes Ferkel, the nocturnal haunt of Berlin's Scandinavian bohemia presided over by Strindberg. In 1894 he began to etch and in 1895, to lithograph, and thus laid the foundation for his brilliant graphic works in Berlin. He painted portraits of some of the more characteristic representatives of the new elite, Julius Meier-Graefe (National Gallery, Oslo), Harry Graf Kessler (National Gallery, Berlin), and Walther Rathenau (Märkische Museum, Berlin). In 1906 he designed the stage decoration for Max Reinhardt's production of Ibsen's *Ghosts* (Museum of Art, Basel), and he created the third version of the *Rheinhardt Frieze* (National Gallery, Berlin) for the foyer of the Kammerspiele Theater.

The first two directors of the *Pan* cooperative were Otto Julius Bierbaum and Julius Meier-Graefe. The latter was a brilliant art commentator and one of the earliest exegetes of Berlin modernism. He attempted to do justice to the new perspective in art by writing about it in an appropriately modern tone.[24] He was also editor of the journal that bore the same title as the cooperative and that made an invaluable contribution to reforms in the art of printing, arts and crafts, and attitudes to art (modeled on the English Arts and Crafts movement). By the time the second issue appeared in 1895, however, a dispute had taken place and the two directors, Bierbaum and Meier-Graefe, resigned before they could be dismissed. The liberal-conservative board of directors, a far too large and unwieldy committee, had been highly indignant at the fact that the two had made the independent decision to include the original of a color lithograph by Henri Toulouse-Lautrec—*Mlle Lender en buste*—in an issue of *Pan*. The page in question had a delicate blend of colors and is now highly sought after by collectors.[25]

If this relatively early—this all happened within months—and perhaps foolhardy attempt to familiarize German audiences with modern French art was doomed to failure, the eventual breakthrough was made possible by the efforts of the hero of modernism in Berlin, Hugo von Tschudi. The son of a Swiss ambassador in Vienna, Tschudi had been Wilhelm Bode's assistant at the Berlin museums since 1872. In 1896 following nomination by Bode, he became director of the National Gallery. He replaced the formidable Wilhelm Jordan, the first director. During his entire tenure, Jordan had had to struggle with the mediocre Regional Art Commission that originated in the heyday of academicism in Berlin. Composed of jealous representatives of group and individual interests, the commission resisted every attempt to introduce an acquisition policy that recognized modern movements.[26] It was this body—which functioned mainly by using its veto—that faced Tschudi when he came to office. Bode was proven wrong in his fears that Tschudi, who until then had had nothing to do with

8

6. *Edvard Munch.* Portrait of Harry Graf Kessler, *1906.* Neue Nationalgalerie, Berlin.

7. *Edvard Munch.* Portrait of Walter Rathenau, *1907.* Märkisches Museum, Berlin.

8. *Henri de Toulouse-Lautrec.* Portrait of Mlle Lender en Buste, *from* Pan, *1 (1895).* Galerie Pels-Leusden, Berlin.

contemporary art, would not be able to muster up sufficient interest for the acquisition activities of the National Gallery. In the year of his appointment, Tschudi traveled to Paris with Liebermann who introduced him to Durand-Ruel, the art dealer for the French Impressionists. This meeting was akin to a revelation for Tschudi. He decided there and then to acquire a representative collection of Impressionist works for Berlin. Back in Berlin, he immediately met with the resistance of the Regional Art Commission that firmly rejected all of his suggestions. In order to avoid being dependent on its consent, he sought patronage from the powerful collectors who belonged to the new elite. This collaboration was extremely fruitful for the National Gallery and to the present its success has been unparalleled. In this way, as early as 1896, Tschudi was able to acquire works by Constable, Courbet, Manet, Monet, Degas, and Rodin. The roster of sponsors reads like a "Who's Who" of Berlin's Jewish patriciate: Eduard Arnhold, Robert and Ernst von Mendelssohn, Hugo Oppenheim, Robert Warschauer, Fritz Friedländer, Isidor Loewe, Oskar Huldschinsky, Georg von Bleichröder. In 1896 James Simon donated Courbet's *Mill Weir* and Karl von der Heydt donated Monet's *View of Vetheuil-sur-Seine* (National Gallery, Berlin).[27] Tschudi continued to pursue this policy during the next few years. In 1898, he even dared to rearrange the exhibition rooms in the National Gallery that were still overflowing with mediocre offerings from Jordan's days. He put the old "junk" in storage and allocated generous space for the new acquisitions. The Regional Art Commission was incensed by this blatant subversion of its authority. With the support of the conservative patriots, the academics mounted the barricades and complained to Wilhelm II. The kaiser responded by passing a decree (1899) that from then on all new acquisitions for the National Gallery, including gifts, would require his authorization. At first, Tschudi complied and the old works were rehung.[28] To his dismay, Wilhelm II found he was unable to check developments in Berlin with demonstrations of power that only revealed his helplessness. He responded to this by placing huge and menacing props at prominent locations in the city. In 1897, the Kaiser-Wilhelm National Memorial by Reinhold Begas was inaugurated on the grounds of the Charlottenburg Palace. And in 1901 the memorials on the Siegesallee, which had been financed by the kaiser's private treasury, were also inaugurated. It was on this occasion that Wilhelm II had his infamous "Gutter Art" speech.[29]

Tschudi's acquisition policy would probably not have been so successful if he had not been able to rely on his group of elite collectors, the bourgeoisie who had a keen interest in art. They had gradually migrated from the western areas of the city to settle south of the Tiergarten in the new districts of Schöneberg and Wilmersdorf and above all along the Tauentzienstrasse and Kurfürstendamm—the artery that ran through the new western area of the city. As early as the mid-eighties, Carl Bernstein, a lawyer from Odessa became the first Berlin collector of works by Liebermann and the French Impressionists.[30] The most important collector, however, was the businessman Eduard Arnhold.[31] At the turn of the century, he changed over from the German Classicists to the Impressionists and acquired, among other paintings and objects, Manet's *Bon Bock* (Philadelphia Museum of Art).

The interest shown by collectors stimulated the art market. Indeed the stimulation was reciprocal. With the opening of Fritz Gurlitt's art salon at 29 Behrenstrasse in 1880, Berlin's art trade began to blossom. In 1883 Gurlitt, the court art dealer, showed Bernstein's Impressionist collection supplemented by works from Durand-Ruel in Paris.[32] In 1897 Keller & Reiner opened their showrooms at 122 Potsdamerstrasse. The Neo-Impressionists were among those who were shown here for the first time.[33] The event, however, that was finally to bring about Berlin's breakthrough on the international art scene was the founding of the Cassirer art salon in 1898. Originally opened by cousins Paul and Bruno Cassirer, the business was soon directed by Paul alone.[34] Cassirer's model was Durand-Ruel, and they worked in close cooperation. The gallery's ledgers bear extensive witness to the development of this collaboration. Among the works exhibited by Cassirer in 1899 was *Déjeuner sur l'herbe* by Manet (Musée d'Orsay, Paris). In 1901 the kaiser expressed anger at the Paul Cézanne exhibition held at Cassirer's salon.[35] In 1904 this was followed by an exhibition of Vincent van Gogh and in 1907 by a group show of Munch, Cézanne, and Henri Matisse. The Cézanne exhibition staged by Cassirer in 1909 was visited by the young Brücke (or "bridge") artists Ernst Ludwig Kirchner and Karl Schmidt-Rottluff, who had come over from Dresden.[36]

The final event that led to the founding of the Berlin Secession was the kaiser's rejection of Leistikow's *Evening Landscape at Lake Grunewald*, declaring that he knew Lake Grunewald and it did not look like that. The collector Richard Israel acquired the painting and presented it—as the Berliners would say *aus Daffke* (for the hell of it)—to the National Gallery.[37] Under the presidency of Max Liebermann, the Secession opened its first exhibition on Whitsun, May 20, 1899. The building it used had been hastily constructed on the Kantstrasse beside the Theater des Westens. The walls were still so damp that as a precautionary measure the paintings had to be taken down at night. The weather was wonderful on the day of the opening. The women wore summer dresses and the men were in tails.[38] The Berlin modernists had achieved their first great victory, and there was nothing to stop them now. Alfred Lichtwark reported an exchange between Tschudi and the kaiser about the Secessionists: "'And then this repulsive cult of the personality,' the kaiser continued, 'it is pure, unadulterated social democracy.' 'On the contrary,' Tschudi replied, 'it is an aristocratic principle.'"[39] Tschudi hit the nail on the head here identifying with a sure instinct the claim that distinguished this new trendsetting social class from the old aristocracy. The kaiser had not understood this, nor was he able to do so.

The court circle in Berlin had not yet recognized that it had long since lost the art war. Its final blow was to fall upon Tschudi. Presuming the kaiser would grant his authorization, Tschudi allowed a number of French paintings to be sent to Berlin, among which were works of the Barbizon school. He had already entered a binding agreement for the purchase. After some vascillation, the matter came to a head in a dramatic argument between Tschudi and Wilhelm II that ended with the kaiser's absolute refusal to go ahead with the purchase. Tschudi felt obliged to resign and left for Munich. His successor in Berlin was Ludwig Justi.[40]

The Secession became an established institution from the day of its opening exhibition. Despite occasional controversies later on, the story of its genesis is far more interesting than its actual history.[41] In fact, it only became interesting again when the founders of the Secession saw that their position of social prominence, attained after such a long hard struggle, was beginning to be undermined by the next generation. Their patronizing attitude toward the new generation was typical of a parent toward a child. They were convinced of the absolute validity of their hard-earned wisdom: they had got it right once and for all, and while they no doubt assumed that their sons would bring a fresh approach to certain situations, they were convinced that however differently the younger generation acted, the general direction would remain much the same, the result of a painstaking process. It is precisely this contradiction that gives rise to the dialectic of the development of social consciousness in a generative cycle. The sons and daughters for their part place great importance on asserting their identity independently of their fathers and on formulating their own concept of culture. In their enthusiasm they often fail to notice just how much the form of their rebellion is dictated by background and upbringing.

From Georg Heym to Raoul Hausmann, from Jakob van Hoddis to Franz Jung, from Franz Werfel to Otto Gross, the members of the next artistic generation, the Expressionists and the Dadaists, were the children of the new elite. This first post-Freudian generation was burdened with a disposition prone to neurosis, and this neurosis had its roots in their upbringing. The intransigent prudery of their authoritarian conservative education was certainly also a contributing factor. Neurosis produces irritations and fissures in the consciousness and is thereby a strong force in the creation of a culture. The creative powers of the Expressionist generation are a particularly good example of this. It is also possible to see a subliminal link between the build up of a conflict of this nature and the outbreak of the First World War, toward which society's center of gravity felt drawn as if by an invisible magnet.

The outbreak of this generational conflict marks the beginning of the second phase of modernism in Berlin. In 1910, the Secession exhibition jury, which hitherto had cautiously tolerated the examples of new directions in art, rejected the work of twenty-seven young artists. Emil Nolde was among them, and he reacted by writing a rather insolent letter to Liebermann. He was subsequently completely excluded from the Secession, albeit against Liebermann's wishes. The latter behaved very decently throughout the entire matter. On the initiative of Max Pechstein and Georg Tappert, the rejected artists got together and formed the New Secession, which exhibited the rejected works in the Maximilian Macht Gallery on the fourth floor of a house at 1 Rankestrasse. The exhibition was mercilessly torn apart by the press. In the *Vossische Zeitung*, Ludwig Pietsch described the female archer on the poster designed by Max Pechstein as "a kneeling, fat, naked person, black on white, inconceivably coarse with broad outlines, painted by a wretched dabbler, a completely formless face from which a pair of swollen, horrible bright red carrotlike lips protrudes."[42] Max Pechstein had come to Berlin in 1908. In 1910 Otto Müller was accepted into the Brücke group in Dresden

9

10

11

9. *Walter Lestikow.* Evening Landscape at Lake Grunewald, *1895.* Nationalgalerie, Berlin.

10. *Max Liebermann.* Artist's Studio on Pariser Platz, *1902.* Kunstmuseum St. Gallen.

11. *Max Liebermann.* Samson and Delilah, *1902.* Städelsches Museum, Frankfurt am Main.

189

12

12. *Emil Nolde.* Pentecost, *1909.*
Neue Nationalgalerie, Berlin.

13. *Ernst Ludwig Kirchner.*
Potsdamer Platz, *1914.* Neue
Nationalgalerie, Berlin, permanent
loan from a private collector.

14. *Oskar Kokoschka.* Herwath
Walden, *1920.* Staatgalerie,
Stuttgart.

15. *Oskar Kokoschka.* Portrait of
Tilla Durieux, *1910.* Museum
Ludwig, Cologne.

16. *Umberto Boccioni.* Street-Life
Forces Itself into the House, *1911.*
Sprengel Museum, Hanover.

from Berlin. The following year, the Brücke artists, Erich Heckel, Kirchner, and Schmidt-Rottluff moved to Berlin. The reason for this decision was mainly the hope that they could achieve more in the capital of the Reich. Over the next few years, Berlin's metropolitan expressionism emerged from the hectic rhythms of the city. Its crowning achievement was Kirchner's portrayal of life on Berlin streets produced between 1912 and 1915. The artists of the Expressionist generation also found their collectors and agents in Berlin. The most brilliant amongst them was Herwarth Walden (Georg Levin) whose first wife was Else Lasker-Schüler. Originally a pianist and composer, in 1904 he had founded the Association for Art (Verein für Kunst). In March 1910 the first edition of the weekly journal *Der Sturm* (*The Storm*) appeared edited by Walden. The rousing title promised cultural revolution as its program. *Der Sturm* became a forum for the literati, poets, essayists, philosophers, and artists of the Expressionist movement, the rebellious children of the new but aging elite. In 1911 *Die Aktion*, a rival to *Der Sturm*, was founded by Franz Pfamfert. Both journals saw themselves as mouthpieces for the struggles of the left-wing bourgeoisie. Whereas the emphasis in *Sturm* lay on artistic and literary events, *Aktion* was mainly political in its scope.

During the following decades, Walden was most successful in promoting the work of the European avant-garde and he revealed a sure instinct when it came to bringing their work to Berlin. In 1912 he founded the Sturm Gallery and opened it with an exhibition of work by the Blaue Reiter—or "Blue Rider," named after a painting by Vassily Kandinsky. At the same exhibition, Oskar Kokoschka was shown for the first time in Berlin. In his second exhibition, Walden was already showing the Italian Futurists, including works by Umberto Boccioni, Carlo Carrà, Luigi Russolo, Gino Severini, and Giacomo Balla. The exhibition was a spectacular success. On some days it had more than a thousand visitors.[43] Its influence on the German avant-garde was immense. Walden's successful attempt at presenting a synopsis of European avant-garde artistic production broadened the horizons of the artists and helped accelerate the development of their style. The term avant-garde is consciously used here as it was Walden's immediate reactions that clearly show just where the avant-garde differed from the modernism and at what point the two diverged. In 1912 Walden displayed the paintings in Sturm that had been rejected by the Cologne *Sonderbund*. These included works by Kandinsky, Alexey Jawlensky, Franz Marc, Gabriele Münter, and Marianne von Werefkin. This was the prelude to Walden's survey of the work of the French, Italian, Russian, Czech, Hungarian, and German Cubist, Futurist, and Expressionist avant-garde that he would present in the First German Autumn Salon in 1913.[44]

In 1913 a new journal entitled *Das Neue Pathos*[45] (*The New Pathos*) appeared in Berlin. It was edited by Hans Ehrenbaum, Paul Zech, Ludwig Meidner, and others. Its title is a reference to the inner motivation of the Expressionists— "heightened sensibility," "emotionalism," "collapse and cry," " awakening of the heart," "appeal and indignation," "love of man," and "pathos."[46] A group of three painters who exhibited in the Sturm Gallery in 1912 called themselves Die Pa-

13

14

15

16

thetiker.[47] Ludwig Meidner, the most important of the three, foresaw the horror of war in his dark, expressive paintings of burning cities and convulsive apocalyptic landscapes that twitched with color. In 1909, a group of young poets and up-and-coming writers founded the New Club, the core of which was made up of the trio of Kurt Hiller, Erwin Loewensohn, and Jakob van Hoddis (Hans Davidsohn). The irregular series of poetry readings held in various Berlin cafés between 1910 and 1912 was entitled "Neo-Pathetic Cabaret."[48] Looking at the photographs of the serious, melancholy schoolboy faces with their profoundly sad expressions, one is moved by the vulnerability of their youth. The club would probably have remained a somewhat insignificant, postadolescent affair if it had not produced two geniuses who were related in the way that they contrasted with each other. These were Georg Heym and Jakob von Hoddis. They both impressed their contemporaries with apocalyptic visions as expressed, for example, in Heym's poem "The War" ("He that slept has risen . . .") and Hoddis's poem, "End of the World," in which sarcasm is used to relieve the pathos ("From pointed pates hats fly into the blue . . .").[49] They were not pacifists, and this should not be overlooked. Rather they were suffering from a profound ennui, a melancholic boredom with civilization. It was under the burden of this boredom that they sensed what was in the air. And whereas on the one hand they feared war, on the other they longed for it; they were caught up in this fatal contradiction and secretly attracted to the horror of the unknown, the apocalypse. This was the generation of Langemarck and that which was to follow. Meidner and Von Hoddis were friends. On long nocturnal wanderings through the bleak suburbs, small, balding Meidner and small, dark tousle-haired Von Hoddis reveled in the autonomous power of the Berlin colossus.[50] Shortly after the outbreak of war in 1914, the Picadilly (an amusement park), which forms the backdrop to Kirchner's *Women at Potsdamer Platz* (private collection), was renamed Haus Vaterland (*House of My Country*).

Georg Heym drowned trying to save a friend on the Havel lake during the winter of 1912. In 1915 Jakob van Hoddis was taken into care due to mental illness; in 1942 he was deported and killed in a mass extermination camp in Poland. In 1916 Ernst Ludwig Kirchner, who was called to the artillery, had a nervous breakdown. Tortured by his clear-sighted, dark predictions, Meidner experienced the outbreak of war in 1914 in Dresden; in 1916 he went to the front as a soldier with the medical corps. Heckel was sent to Flanders with the medical corps where he met Max Beckmann, who was also with the medical corps. Together they visited the old visionary James Ensor in Ostende. In 1916 Beckmann had a nervous breakdown. The shock he suffered released his creative power from its former detachment. From this point onward his penetrating work took on the style of expressive existentialism. Karl Schmidt-Rottluff spent the war on the Eastern front. In 1918 he produced the woodcut *Did Not Christ Reveal Himself to You?*

Notes

1. Jürgen Schutte and Peter Sprengel, *Die Berliner Moderne: 1885–1914* (Stuttgart: 1987 [Reclam 8359], 13 and n. 2, 85. The lecture bore the subtitle "Literary Revolution and Reformation." Schutte and Sprengel prove the origin of the term that for a long time was attributed to Hermann Bahr.
2. As exemplified by the novels of Paul Heyse (Nobel Prize, 1910) and Joseph Lauff and the plays of Ernst von Wildenbruch.
3. The different aspects of this development can be seen particularly clearly in the events in Berlin's theater world. The preoccupations with literature are visualized on stage. In 1894, Max Reinhardt came to Berlin from Vienna. The decisive contrast that soon became obvious between Reinhardt and Brahm illustrates how naturalism, which concentrated on the effect of the spoken word, came to be replaced by the visual and luminous quality of the Impressionist principle. This reveals the differences in attitude between the two different styles. The emergence of these differences was not a gradual process.
4. Eberhard Roters, "August Strindberg," in *Berlin um 1900* (Berlin: Exh. Kat. Berlinische Galerie und Akademie der Künste 1984), 348. Berlin's German-Scandinavian bohemia presided over by August Strindberg met in Türke's wine dealers and bar on the corner of Unter den Linden and Wilhelmstrasse. Discovered by Strindberg, this establishment became their regular haunt. Strindberg gave it its nickname—Black Piglet—on account of the unusually shaped Bessarabian wineskin that served as its sign. An amusing account of the Schwarzes Ferkel circle is provided by the Berlin doctor Carl Ludwig Schleich, in the chapter "Strindberg-Erinnerungen" of his memoirs *Besonnte Vergangenheit* (Berlin: VierFalken Verlag, 1920), 263ff.
5. James Frecot, "Literatur zwischen Betrieb und Einsamkeit," in *Berlin um 1900*, 337ff. From spring 1900 onward the circle of literary friends and supporters Die Kommenden met in the Nollendorf-Casino at Nollendorf Platz. Following the death of the poet Ludwig Jacobowski, this circle was led by Rudolf Steiner. The soirees were attended by Peter Hille, Else Lasker-Schüler, Georg Hermann, Paul Ernst, Erich Mühsam, Käthe Kollwitz, Hans Pfitzner, Herwarth Walden, and Stefan Zweig.
6. The Café des Westens, which was known to the Berliners as Café Grössenwahn (Café Megalomania), was at 18/19 Kurfürstendamm on the corner of Joachimstalerstrasse diagonally opposite the corner where Café Kranzler stands today. Its heyday began in 1899. Regular visitors there included Hans Heinz Ewers, Max Reinhardt, Roda Roda, Frank Wedekind, Ernst von Wolzogen. The Expressionist generation also made their way there. In 1915, the cafe moved to another premises further up the Kurfürstendamm at number 26 that had been opened in 1913. Not least because they missed the familiar, cozy, smoky atmosphere, the regulars moved to the Romanisches Café opposite the Emperor William Memorial Church where Joachim Schmettau's fountain stands today.
7. Nicolaas Teeuwisse, *Vom "salon" zur Sezession: Berliner Kunstleben zwischen Tradition und Aufbruch zur Moderne, 1871–1900* (Berlin: Deutsche Verlag für Kunstwissenschaft, 1987). This laudable publication provides the first detailed account of the prelude to modernism in Berlin and has been a great help to the author of this essay.
8. Teeuwisse, *vom "salon" zur Sezession*, 42ff.
9. Ibid.
10. Erich Engel, "Medizin, Naturwissenschaft und Industrie," in *Berlin um 1900*, 125ff.
11. Teeuwisse, *vom "salon" zur Sezession*, 227ff. The diplomat Harry Graf Kessler lived at number 28 Köthenerstrasse. The apartment, which was furnished shortly before the turn of the century from design plans by Henry van de Velde, was a convivial meeting place for the new elite.
12. Walther Rathenau, "Höre Israel," *Die Zukunft* 5 (1897): 454ff; Schutte and Sprengel, *Die Berliner*, 172ff.
13. On the associations Freie Bühne and Freie Volksbühne see Albert Soergel, *Dichtung und Dichter der Zeit* (Leipzig: 1911), 158ff.; Christel Reckenfelder-Bäumer, "Wissen ist Macht—Macht ist wissen," in *Berlin um 1900*, 407ff.
14. Bruno Wille, *Einsiedler und Genosse* (Berlin: S. Fischer, 1894).
15. Frecot, "Literatur," 327ff.
16. Teeuwisse, *vom "salon" zur Sezession*, 35.
17. Adolf Rosenberg, *Die Berliner Malerschule 1819–1879* (Berlin: 1879); Teeuwisse, *Vom "salon" zur Sezession*, 67.
18. Ibid., 95.
19. Werner Doede, *Berlin: Kunst und Künstler seit 1870, Anfänge und*

Entwicklungen (Recklinghausen: 1961), 51; Teeuwisse, *Vom "salon," :zur Sezession*, 152ff.

20. Emil Ludwig, *Wilhelm der Zweite* (Berlin: Ernst Rowohlt Verlag, 1926), 290.

21. Doede, *Berlin*, 53ff.

22. Werner Doede, "Die Affäre Munch und die Anfänge der Berliner Secessionen," in *Berlin—Ort der Freiheit für die Kunst* (Recklinghausen: Exh. Kat. Nationalgalerie 1960), 7ff; Doede, *Berlin*, 54ff; Peter Paret, *Die Berliner Secession: Moderne Kunst und ihre Feinde im Kaiserlichen Deutschland* (Berlin: Severin und Siedler, 1981), 79ff; Teeuwisse, *Vom "salon" zur Sezession*, 183ff.

23. Doede, *Berlin*, 55.

24. Julius Meier Graefe's main work is *Entwicklungsgeschichte der modernen Kunst (The History of the Development of Modern Art)*, 4 vols. (Stuttgart: Verlag Julius Hoffmann, 1904).

25. Bernhard Maria Holeczek, *Otto Julius Bierbaum im künstlerischen Leben der Jahrhundertwende: Studien zur literarischen Situation des Jugendstils* (Freiburg: Dissertationsdruck Johannes Krause, 1973), 48ff; Eberhard Roters, "Die Kunst des neuen Jahrhundert, in *Berlin um 1900*, 268.

26. Teeuwisse, *Vom "salon" zur Sezession*, 197 ff.

27. Ibid., 201ff.

28. Ibid., 209ff.

29. Ernst Johan, ed., *Reden des Kaisers: Ansprachen Predigten, Trinksprüche Wilhelms II* (Munich: dtv 1966), 99ff; Doede, *Berlin*, 80ff; Schutte and Sprengel, *Die Berliner*, 571ff.

30. Teeuwisse, *Vom "salon" zur Sezession*, 98ff.

31. Ibid., 221ff.

32. Ibid., 104ff. The court art dealer Fritz Gurlitt, who was also Arnold Böcklin's patron, moved to Leipzigerstrasse in 1892. In 1893, he staged the first Lesser Ury exhibition, which met with an outcry in the Berlin press. After his sudden death in 1893, the business was run by his heirs.

33. Teeuwisse, *Vom "salon" zur Sezession*, 236ff. Keller and Reiner specialized in modern arts and crafts. Their salesrooms in 122 Potsdamerstrasse were furnished completely in Jugendstil by Richard Riemerschmid.

34. The Cassirer art salon was in the ground-floor flat of a house in Victoriastrasse in the southern Tiergarten area; the interior was designed by Henry van de Velde.

35. Doede, *Berlin*, 80.

36. Leopold Reidemeister, "Künstler der Brücke in Berlin 1908–1914: Ein Beitrag zur Geschichte der Künstlergruppe Brücke," in *Künstler der Brücke in Berlin 1908–1914*, exhibition catalogue (Berlin: Brücke Museum, 1972), 5.

37. Doede, *Berlin*, 73; Teeuwisse, *Vom "salon" zur Sezession*, 207.

38. Paret, *Die Berliner*, 119.

39. Teeuwisse, *Vom "salon" zur Sezession*, 219.

40. Doede, *Berlin*, 99ff., Teeuwisse, *Vom "salon" zur Sezession*, 218ff. Hugo von Tschudi was appointed director of the Bavarian State Galleries in Munich. As director of the art collection, he was completely independent and accountable only to the Ministry for Cultural Affairs. The purchases that, as a result of the kaiser's interference, he was unable to complete in Berlin were taken over by his family and donated to the Neue Pinakothek gallery in Munich. Immediately after his appointment as director of the National Gallery in Berlin, on the instigation of Bode, Ludwig Justi was placed under direct responsibility of the Ministry for Cultural Affairs. During Justi's era, astute acquisitions were made, and the National Gallery collection was expanded to include major works of the Expressionists. A department for modern art was set up in the Kronprinzenpalais. Justi held his position until he was dismissed by the Nazis in 1937. From the beginning, the position of director of the National Gallery was never without its perils.

41. Literature on the history of the Berlin Secession includes Paret, cf. n. 22; Rudolf Pfefferkorn, *Die Berliner Secession* (Berlin: Haude of Spencer, 1972); Werner Doede, *Die Berliner Secession: Berlin als Zentrum der deutschen Kunst von der Jahrhundertwende bis zum Ersten Weltkrieg* (Berlin: Propyläen Verlag, 1977).

42. Doede, *Berlin, Kunst und Künstler*, 106ff.

43. Ibid., 113.

44. *Erster Deutscher Herbstsalon, Berlin 1913*, exhibition catalogue (Berlin Verlag, Der Sturm); *Der Sturm: Herwarth Walden und die Europäische Avantgarde, Berlin 1912–1932*, exhibition catalogue, (Berlin: Nationalgalerie dem Staatliche Museen, 1961). Among those who participated in the First German Autumn Salon were Paul Klee, Franz Marc, August Macke, Gabriele Münter, Heinrich Campendonk, Alfred Kubin (Germany), Oskar Kokoschka (Austria), Umberto Boccioni, Luigi Russolo, Gino Severini (Italy), Robert Delaunay and his Russian-born wife Sonja Delaunay-Terk, Fernand Léger, Albert Gleizes, Louis Marcoussis (France), Jacoba van Heemskerck (Holland), Albert Bloch and Lyonel Feininger (Germany/America), Vassily Kandinsky, Alexiej von Jawlensky, Marianne von Werefkin, David Burljuk, Natalie Gontscharowa, Michail Larionov, Alexander Archipenko, and Marc Chagall (Russia). The predominance of Russian participants is noteworthy. Walden was the first to present the Russian avant-garde outside Russia as a relatively united force.

45. *Das Neue Pathos*, a new, bi-monthly journal, first appeared in spring 1913 and continued as an annual publication from 1914 to 1919. It was edited by Hans Ehrenbaum-Degele, Robert R. Schmidt, Ludwig Meidner (art), Paul Zech (literature).

46. These chapter titles appear in the first anthology of German expressionist poetry *Menscheitsdämmerung: Symphonie jüngster deutscher Dichtung*, ed. Kurt Pinthaus (Berlin: Ernst Rowohlt verlag, 1920).

47. In 1912, Ludwig Meidner, Richard Janthur, and Jakob Steinhardt founded the painters club Die Pathetiker; they exhibited in the Sturm gallery in October of the same year.

48. Jakob van Hoddis, *Dichtungen und Briefe*, ed. Regina Nörtemann, (Zürich: Arche verlag, 1987), 300ff.; Georg Heym, *Documente zu seinem Leben und Werk*, Karl Ludwig Schneider and Gerhard Burckhardt, eds. (Munich: Verlag C. H. Beck, 1968), 380ff.

49. Pinthus, 39 (Heym) Der Krieg, 3 (Hoddis) Weltende

50. Ludwig Meidner and Jakob van Hoddis in Ludwig Kunz, ed. *Ludwig Meidner, Dichter, Maler und Cafés: Erinnerungen* (Zürich: Arche Verlag 1973), 69ff.

1. Frederick Childe Hassam. Winter
Afternoon, *1900.* Museum of the
City of New York.

The Art World in New York 1900–1919

Patricia Hills

Patricia Hills is professor of art history at Boston University. Her publications include Turn-of-the-Century America: Paintings, Graphics, Photographs, 1890–1910 *(1977),* Alice Neel *(1983) and* John Singer Sargent *(1986). From 1982 to 1983, she held a John Simon Guggenheim Memorial Foundation Fellowship.*

Walked through the interesting streets on the East Side [of New York]. Saw a boy spit on a passing hearse. . . . Doorways of tenement houses, grimy and greasy door frames looking as though huge hogs covered with filth had worn the paint away and replaced it with matted dirt in going in and out. Healthy faced children, solid-legged, rich full color to their hair. Happiness rather than misery in the whole life. Fifth Avenue faces are unhappy in comparison.
—John Sloan, diary entry February 13, 1906[1]

O sun to thee it is to make all visible
under thy rays of light
Lies this great city of cubic form—New York
—Max Weber, Cubist Poems, *1914[2]*

The half century from 1870 to 1920 saw profound changes in the artistic and cultural life of New York City. The post–Civil War years brought unprecedented wealth to the city and a vigorous building boom. Frederick Law Olmsted designed Central Park in Manhattan and Prospect Park in Brooklyn for the new leisure classes, and cultural leaders founded the Metropolitan Museum of Art in 1870 to house the artistic treasures that America's newly rich industrialists and financiers were persuaded to share with the city's citizenry. A new cosmopolitanism marked the 1870s and 1880s for artists, who traveled abroad to study in Paris and Munich and who brought back the latest sophisticated art styles to challenge the traditional history painting, landscape, portraits, and anecdotal genre painting of the previous generation.

Urbanity in those three decades prior to the turn of the century meant a high culture of beauty: elegant villas along Fifth Avenue and in Newport, European-inspired art, and a life of leisure and aristocratic ease. Most ambitious young New York artists, such as William Merritt Chase, Childe Hassam, Julian Alden Weir, and Thomas Dewing, obliged such tastes by providing pictures of beautiful, genteel women posed in sumptuous interiors and surrounded by the eclectic artifacts of an exquisite connoisseurship. The art pleased America's new plutocrats, who were eager to venerate refinement in their own homes and who had no desire to see on the walls of those homes what they saw daily in the workplace. Art critic Samuel Isham aptly described such patrons in 1905:

Life in the country and in the open air is more inspiring than that penned up in city rooms and it has been more painted, but even there the tendency has been to make a thing of beauty rather than to give the "true truth." Not only the artists but their patrons preferred it so. The American man finds enough of prose in the day's work. It does not sadden him; on the contrary, he enjoys it and puts all his energies into it, and when he turns from it he demands that art shall do its duty in furnishing delight and that uncomplicated by too much subtlety. He dislikes problem plays that finish badly and realistic novels that simply give again the life he knows, and he wants his pictures beautiful or at least pretty. He doesn't know anything about art, but he knows what he likes, as he proudly proclaims, and no perfection of craftsmanship is going to make him change his likes.[3]

The hypothetical American patrons conjured up by Isham matched the reality; the working poor of New York would not have appealed as subjects for art to such businessmen. The

195

portrayal of poverty had to be sufficiently removed from the reality of America's industrial proletariat in order to qualify as picturesque; better candidates were the French and Dutch peasants, whom American artists painted when abroad. For pictures of "life in the open air," end-of-the-century patrons looked to Impressionist holiday views by Chase and Hassam, Theodore Robinson, John Henry Twachtman, Lila Cabot Perry, and the European-bred John Singer Sargent, or to poetic evocations of nature by George Inness, Homer D. Martin, Dwight W. Tryon, and Alexander H. Wyant.

In the 1880s and 1890s the National Academy of Design and the Society of American Artists in New York, the Pennsylvania Academy of the Fine Arts in Philadelphia, and the large international exhibitions showed American painting of this genteel persuasion along with older academic art. Such artists influenced the selection of sculpture and murals placed in the neoclassical architecture of the World's Columbian Exposition held in Chicago in 1893; they gratified the yearnings of many for an ideal of classical beauty, of virginal womankind, and of pastoral escape.

Others, however, began to react against the insipidness and unreality of this chic art. Reviewing the American paintings in the Paris Exposition of 1900, art critic Charles Caffin found them as a group a "little fibreless and lacking in marrow." He concluded about American painters:

The necessity of prettiness, of not giving offence to "the most fastidious" and of exploiting the obvious, has been urged upon them, until it is small wonder that a great deal of American painting is characterised by irreproachable table-manners rather than by salient self-expression; by a desire to be amiable rather than convincing.[4]

Caffin aside, visitors to the international expositions took notice more of the advances in technology claimed competitively by each country than of the art. One prominent tourist to that 1900 exposition, the American historian Henry Adams, meditated in the third person on his own fin-de-siècle crisis in *The Education of Henry Adams,* published in 1918. He ruminated about his reservations toward the new technological wonders—the "occult" discoveries and inventions, such as airships, automobiles, radium, X rays, and, of course, dynamos. And he lamented the passing of the era when Venus and the Virgin Mary personified virile powers.

The dynamo became a symbol of infinity. As he grew accustomed to the great gallery of machines, he began to feel the forty-foot dynamos as a moral force, much as the early Christians felt the Cross. The planet itself seemed less impressive, in its old-fashioned, deliberate, annual or daily revolution, than this huge wheel, revolving within arm's length at some vertiginous speed. . . . Among the thousand symbols of ultimate energy, the dynamo was not so human as some, but it was the most expressive.[5]

Adams was not alone in feeling the expressive power of the dynamo. The younger twentieth-century artists also responded to the music of the dynamo's hum and to its ability to revolutionize the lives of people. Some were realists, others, modernists. Some were independently wealthy and university educated, others were self-taught and struggled to make a living.

Some came from families who had lived in the United States for generations, others were recent immigrants. The dramatis personae include Robert Henri, John Sloan, George Bellows, Alfred Stieglitz, Max Weber, Francis Picabia, Marcel Duchamp, and Joseph Stella. Collectively, along with writers, dealers, collectors, art impresarios, and hangers-on, this group established a New York art world that challenged the paintings and sculpture of conventional beauty, of academic high art, of ideal womanhood, and of Grand Tour holiday spectacles. These younger artists drew upon the raw material of city life—the structures of the bridges and the skyscrapers, the energy of the elevated trains and subways, the billowing smokestacks and steam vents, the electric lights at night, and the crowds of anonymous people, the rich and the immigrant poor, hurrying along the avenues.

And it was specifically New York City in the first two decades of the twentieth century that functioned as the source of inspiration and venue for scenes of contemporary life and technological modernity.[6] Indeed, New York, of all metropolitan centers of the world, had achieved a reputation for its ability to assimilate millions of people from diverse ethnic, national, and cultural groups, for its commitment to democratic, social reforms, and for its implementation of the latest technological advances in skyscraper construction, rapid transit, and mass media communication. Whereas the realists focused on the new people of the city (the working classes and the immigrants) and their social relations, the modernists attempted the representation of space, time, speed, and energy—factors that technology and the new forces of production insisted were vital to the political economy. In these two decades, the two groups—realists and modernists—set up the categories of art and defined the terms we use to describe them that have been with us ever since.

Not surprisingly, it was the "forms" of the city (rather than the content of social life or technology) that first entered turn-of-the-century images of New York. Maurice Prendergast in his watercolor *Central Park* of 1901 (Whitney Museum of American Art, New York) represented the spectacle of the park promenade as many spots of color. For *Winter Afternoon* (fig. 1), Childe Hassam introduced the skyscraper but bathed it in the soft focus of tonal painting. Alfred Stieglitz's photograph *The Flatiron* (fig. 2), while sustaining nineteenth-century conventions of pictorial photography, asserted the dynamic presence of that skyscraper, the tallest on the New York horizon in those years. The photograph marks the artist's progression toward the representation of the "new America." Stieglitz recalled:

Watching the structure go up, I felt no desire to photograph the different stages of its development. But with the trees of Madison Square covered with fresh snow, the Flat Iron impressed me as never before. It appeared to be moving toward me like the bow of a monster ocean steamer—a picture of new America still in the making.[7]

Within seven years, Stieglitz photographed New York harbor using a straight photography technique in *The City of Ambition,* 1910 (Museum of Modern Art, New York). The straight edges and clarity of forms, the sparkle of the water and the

196

movement of the steam, depicting all man-made or man-generated forms, better captured New York's energetic commercial enterprise than had his earlier Flatiron photograph, with its romantic contrast of nature (the tree) and technology (the skyscraper).

Stieglitz's most famous photograph is *The Steerage* (fig. 3), today often misinterpreted as an illustration of the welcoming arms of American immigration policy. In fact, the subjects of the photograph are the rejected poor, unskilled, or diseased forced to return to the Old Country. Stieglitz was drawn to depict them not from an inner urgency to join with progressives and implement the American dream of social, economic, and political justice, but because he felt alienated from his wife and the haut monde that she represented. He recalled to his biographer and friend Dorothy Norman the circumstances of the ocean crossing during which he made the picture in 1907:

My wife insisted on going on a large ship, fashionable at the time. Our initial destination was Paris. How distasteful I found the atmosphere of first class on that ship, especially since it was impossible to escape the nouveaux riches. . . . By the third day out I could stand it no longer. . . . Coming to the end of the deck I stood alone, looking down. There were men, women and children on the lower level of the steerage. . . . The scene fascinated me. . . . I stood spellbound for a while. I saw shapes related to one another—a picture of shapes, and underlying it, a new vision that held me: simple people; the feeling of the ship, ocean sky; a sense of release that I was away from the mob called "rich."[8]

Stieglitz's portrayal of the abstract qualities, or shapes, of the modern industrial world portends the later abandonment by modernists of the social content of art; but at that moment Stieglitz's new vision included a romanticized cultural primitivism toward the poor that was grounded in his revulsion against class society.

Stieglitz was a man of his times. Indeed, the twentieth century's first decade witnessed a national preoccupation with the working classes and particularly with the immigrants—who were pouring into Ellis Island and becoming a recognized force in shifting sociological patterns and economic structures.[9] To alienated idealists, which defined Stieglitz at that time, they represented simplicity and a state of innocence. To conservatives, they posed a threat to Anglo-Saxon values. To industrialists, they formed a pool of cheap labor. To reformers, they were living instances of the effects of an inhumane system in sore need of restructuring; but to the realists, they represented a new spirit that promised to infuse American life with fresh vitality.

The life of realist Robert Henri exemplifies one pattern among artists making their mark at the turn of the century. He was born Robert Henry Cozad in 1865 in Cleveland and grew up in the West where his father was a professional gambler. He studied at the Pennsylvania Academy of the Fine Arts in Philadelphia and then spent three years at the Académie Julian in Paris. He returned to teach at the Pennsylvania Academy and was mentor to a group of young newspaper artists—Everett Shinn, William Glackens, George Luks, and John Sloan. In 1895, Henri once more moved to Europe. When he

2. *Alfred Stieglitz.* The Flatiron, *1902–03. 1900.* Museum of Modern Art, New York.

3. *Alfred Stieglitz.* The Steerage, *1907. Reproduced from 291 7-8 (1915).* Museum of Modern Art, New York.

2

3

4

4. *Robert Henri*. Working Man,
1910. Private Collection.

5. *George Bellows*. Cliff Dwellers,
1913. Los Angeles County Museum
of Art.

6. *George Bellows*. Pennsylvania
Station Excavation, *1909*. The
Brooklyn Museum, New York. A.
Augustus Healy Fund.

7. *George Luks*. The Spielers, *1905*.
Addision Gallery of American Art,
Phillips Academy, Andover,
Massachusetts.

returned in 1900 it was to New York City, by now the undisputed artistic capital of America. By 1902, he was teaching at the New York School of Art to an enthusiastic younger generation of realists.[10] Meanwhile, Shinn, Glackens, Luks, and Sloan were all relocating to New York. They had been thrown out of their Philadelphia jobs because the new high-speed presses could reproduce photographs along with the news type, thereby eliminating the need for drawings of news events. In New York, they continued their careers as magazine illustrators while making realist paintings in their spare time.

The young realists were drawn into the orbit of the progressive reform movement, which included philanthropists, sociologists, medical professionals, and journalists seeking to upgrade the living and working conditions of the poor. The motives, and hence the programs, of these progressives were naturally mixed: some were Christian moralists, others were social utopians; some saw poverty as inefficient for an industrial society, others sought to give capitalism a human face in an era of Bolshevik revolutions. Regardless of motivation, the progressives saw the "conspicuous consumption" (Thorstein Veblen's term) of the rich getting out of hand. They pointed out that while the patrons of John Singer Sargent mounted lavish balls in pseudo-Medician palaces, the poor were dying of tuberculosis.[11] The popular magazines that ran articles by the social reformers also hired as illustrators Henri's young artists, who often lived in the same tenements as the poor. Thus, contemporary social attitudes and the artists' own experiences reinforced their decisions to paint urban, working-class New York.

The social documentary photographers of the turn of the century—particularly Jacob Riis and Lewis Hine—served as the link between the reformers of the progressive movement and the young realist painters. Riis, who had emigrated from Denmark and had become a New York City police reporter, took up the camera in order to document better the living and working conditions of the immigrant poor, about whom he lectured to missionary groups. His crusading articles for *Scribner's* were published as *How the Other Half Lives* in 1890. Wisconsin-born Lewis Hine studied sociology at universities before his teaching job at the Ethical Culture School in New York City. He initially used his photographs of Ellis Island in the classroom to teach his students about the pluralism of American culture, but then he quit his job when he was drawn into the reform movement. In 1908, he became staff photographer for the National Child Labor Committee, a group attempting to reform legislation regarding child labor. Such documentary or social photographers as Riis and Hine were not without ambition to create artistic imagery through the manipulation of the subject, cropping, and lighting, since an aesthetic image was a more effective persuasive tool.[12]

The paintings produced during these prewar years by Henri, Sloan, Luks, Glackens, and others such as Jerome Meyers and George Bellows, while not calling for reform per se, heroicized workers in portraiture (fig. 4) and depicted crowded street scenes of working-class life (fig. 5), the building activity that was changing the face of the city (fig. 6), and exuberant children (fig. 7).

5

7

6

8

By this time, the realists had decided that reforming the conservative National Academy of Design was hopeless. In reaction to continual rejections by the exhibition committees of the academy, the group decided to organize its own exhibition at Macbeth Galleries. The exhibition of the five realists in the circle—Henri, Sloan, Glackens, Luks, and Shinn—plus three independents—Ernest Lawson, Maurice Prendergast, and Arthur B. Davies—opened in February 1908 to a howl of protests from critics who dubbed them that "black revolutionary gang." The artists persisted, however, and in 1910 mounted an even larger exhibition of independents.

The most talented of the group was John Sloan, born in 1871 in Lock Haven, Pennsylvania, who left school at a young age to earn money to help support his family. From 1892 to 1894 Sloan studied at the Pennsylvania Academy while working at the *Philadelphia Inquirer* and the *Press.* When he moved to New York in 1904, he supported himself and his politically activist wife, Dolly, on his book and magazine illustrations. Of Sloan, Henri said:

The artists who produce the most satisfactory art are in my mind those who are absorbed in the civilization in which they are living . . . . John Sloan [is one], with his demands for the rights of man, and his love of the people; his keen observation of the people's folly, his knowledge of their virtues and his surpassing interest in all things.[13]

Sloan haunted the city streets and public parks searching out appealing subjects for his art. His diary documents this activity as well as his trips to New Jersey and Coney Island, his impressions of the moving pictures, the Metropolitan Museum's exhibitions, the dancer Isadora Duncan then making a triumphant tour of the United States, and other popular entertainments that the city provided. One typical entry, of June 5, 1907, reads: "Walked up to Henri's studio. On the way saw a humorous sight of interest. A window, low, second story, bleached blond hair dresser bleaching the hair of a client. A small interested crowd about"[14] (fig. 9).

His diary also reveals him to be an artist whose sympathies for the underprivileged and the poor would lead to socialism. Sloan joined the Socialist Party in 1909, read party literature and novels, plays, and essays with socialist themes, attended lectures by Socialist Party leader Eugene Victor Debs, as well as by the anarchist Emma Goldman, participated in strike meetings with his wife, and ran for public office on the Socialist Party ticket. And beginning in 1909, Sloan contributed numerous political illustrations and cartoons to socialist causes and magazines, such as *The Call,* which published his indictment of the tragic deaths in 1911 of 119 seamstresses in a factory fire (fig. 10). From 1912 to 1916, Sloan was a staff member of the socialist magazine *The Masses,* for which he produced both humorous and biting cartoons (fig. 11). The January 1913 issue declared the editorial policy of editor-in-chief Max Eastman and the staff. The magazine was to be:

A revolutionary and not a reform magazine; a magazine with no dividends to pay; a free magazine; frank, arrogant, impertinent, searching for the true causes; a magazine directed against rigidity and dogma wherever it is found; printing what is too naked or true for a money-making press; a magazine whose final policy is to do as it pleases and conciliate nobody, not even its readers.[15]

As strongly as Sloan felt about social issues, and no matter how poignant his cartoons and magazine illustrations, he would not bring the themes of social injustice into his paintings because he felt that art and politics should be kept separate.[16] Like Stieglitz, Sloan would eventually preoccupy himself with the shapes of art when he attempted, unsuccessfully, to blend the two strains of art: realism and modernism.

Alfred Stieglitz's importance for the development of a New York art after the turn of the century was not limited to his photographic studies of the city's commercial vitality. He also functioned as publicist, mentor, and patron to artists and photographers experimenting with new ways of making and thinking about art in the new technological era.

Born in Hoboken, New Jersey, in 1864, Stieglitz came from a wealthy German-Jewish merchant family. In 1882, he traveled to Berlin initially to study mechanical engineering at the Polytechnic; attracted to photography in 1883, he enrolled in courses taught by the photochemist Hermann Wilhelm Vogel. In 1887, Stieglitz won first prize in a competition judged by the photographer and critic Peter Henry Emerson and sponsored by *The Amateur Photographer*, a London publication. Three years later, he returned to New York, and his father helped him set up a photo-engraving business.[17]

Meanwhile, Stieglitz followed the international movement to promote pictorial photography as a fine art. For the New York Camera Club, he began publishing *Camera Notes* in 1897. In 1902, having left *Camera Notes* because of disagreements with other Camera Club members, Stieglitz began *Camera Work*. This quarterly included high-quality, reproductive photogravures by the outstanding photographers of the early twentieth century, including Gertrude Käsebier, Clarence H. White, Edward Steichen, F. Holland Day, Heinrich Kuhn, Alvin Langdon Coburn, Baron De Meyer, Annie W. Brigman, Paul Strand, and Stieglitz himself. It also contained articles on aesthetics and the new modernist art and photography by Edward Steichen, Joseph T. Keiley, Robert Demachy, Charles H. Caffin, Sadakichi Hartmann, Benjamin de Casseres, Marius De Zayas, and Paul B. Haviland, as well as excerpts from the writings of Oscar Wilde, James McNeill Whistler, George Bernard Shaw, Gertrude Stein, Henri Bergson, H. G. Wells, and Friedrich Nietzsche.[18]

In 1905, Stieglitz and Steichen opened a gallery, called the Little Galleries of the Photo-Secession, at 291 Fifth Avenue to exhibit original photography. In 1908, Stieglitz introduced Rodin drawings and Matisse works on paper; Cézanne watercolors and Picasso drawings and watercolors were shown in 1911. In the meantime, he had also begun to exhibit modern American paintings, watercolors, and drawings. Max Weber showed there until he broke with Stieglitz in 1911; Georgia O'Keeffe made her debut in 1916; Arthur Dove, John Marin, Alfred Maurer, Marsden Hartley, and Abraham Walkowitz frequently contributed art until the summer of 1917, when the gallery at 291 Fifth Avenue closed.

10

11

10. *John Sloan*. In Memorium. Here is the Real Triangle, *1911. Published in* The Call *(March 27, 1911).* Delaware Art Museum, Newark. John Sloan Collection.

11. *John Sloan*. Class War in Colorado, *1914. Cover of* The Masses *(June 1914).* Delaware Art Museum, Newark. John Sloan Collection.

The life of the artist Max Weber is paradigmatic of a young American modernist of the period. Born in 1881 in Russia, he and his family emigrated to New York in 1891. He studied principles of design with Arthur Wesley Dow at the Pratt Institute, graduated in 1900, but continued for another year with Dow before teaching four years in Virginia and Minnesota public schools. In 1905, Weber went to Paris where he enrolled at the Académie Julian and was exposed to the new art. He exhibited at the Salon des Independants and the Salon d'Automne, met Dunoyer de Segonzac, Henri Rousseau, and fellow American student Walkowitz, and helped to organize an art class taught by Matisse. In 1909, he returned to New York and, in 1910, was included in Stieglitz's *Younger American Painters* exhibition.[19] For the July 1910 issue of *Camera Work*, he wrote "The Fourth Dimension from a Plastic Point of View," using the language and ideas in currency at the time. He began:

In plastic art, I believe, there is a fourth dimension which may be described as the consciousness of a great and overwhelming sense of space-magnitude in all directions at one time, and is brought into existence through the three known measurements.

And he concluded:

The stronger or more forceful the form the more intense is the dream or vision. Only real dreams are built upon. Even thought is matter. It is all the matter of things, real things or earth or matter. Dreams realized through plastic means are the pyramids and temples, the Acropolis and the Palatine structures; cathedrals and decorations; tunnels, bridges, and towers; these are all of matter in space—both in one and inseparable.[20]

Two themes emerge from Weber's reflections: first, all thoughts and dreams have their realization in the material world, and, second, appropriate subjects ("matter" in space) include the "tunnels, bridges, and towers," that is, the forms of modern New York.

The consciousness of space and time informed the Stieglitz group as it did all of educated society in the decades bracketing the turn of the century.[21] The inseparability of space and time with matter was, of course, at the heart of the new science, just when physicist Albert Einstein was developing the theory of relativity. Physicians such as E. J. Marey studied the physiology of the body in motion; photographers such as Eadweard Muybridge sought to analyze the movements of a galloping horse on film; and scientific management pioneers such as Frederick Taylor and Frank Gilbreth built models of the most efficient paths of motion in factory operations.[22] In order to capture the simultaneous effects of our real-life experience of time, creative writers explored stream-of-consciousness techniques. Ideas about space and matter influenced the look of early cubism where negative space—the shape of the spaces between objects—interlocks with the form of the tangible world the painter wants to represent on canvas. The desire of artists to incorporate the look of time sequences produced the futurist morphology.

It must be emphasized that American artists aimed to represent not impersonal time and space but their own experience

of the vitalization that time and space can give to the forms of modern life. The Italian Futurists' paintings and manifestos surely provided examples of both artistic practice and artistic theory that inspired the Americans, for New York newspapers carried the news of the 1912 Futurists' exhibition held in Paris and of other Futurist activities.[23] One of the English versions of the Futurists' statements, published in 1912 included:

We have declared . . . that what must be rendered is the *dynamic sensation*, that is to say, the particular rhythm of each object, its inclination, its movement, or to put it more exactly its interior force. . . . Every object reveals by its lines how it would resolve itself were it to follow the tendencies of its forces. . . . All objects . . . tend to the infinite by their *force-lines*[,] the continuity of which is measured by our intuition. It is these *force-lines* that we must draw. . . . We interpret nature by rendering these objects upon the canvas as the beginnings or the prolongations of the rhythms impressed upon our sensibility by these very objects.[24]

Such statements stress the role of the artist's consciousness: the subject is ". . . measured by our intuition" and "impressed upon our sensibility." The validity of subjectivity was further reinforced by the theories of the French philosopher Henri Bergson.[25]

New York acted as catalyst to modern artists arriving after a sojourn in Europe where they had come in touch with the new ideas. Joseph Stella saw the work of Cubists and Futurists in Paris but realized the potentiality for his own art only upon his return to New York:

And when in 1912 I came back to New York I was thrilled to find America so rich with so many new motives to be translated into a new art.

Steel and electricity had created a new world. A new drama had surged from the unmerciful violation of darkness at night, by the violent blaze of electricity and a new polyphony was ringing all around with the scintillating, highly colored lights. The steel had leaped to hyperbolic altitudes and expanded to vast latitudes with the skyscrapers and with bridges made for the conjunction of worlds. A new architecture was created, a new perspective.[26]

Similarly, John Marin's statements about his own paintings, watercolors of the dancing forms of the Brooklyn Bridge and the Woolworth Building done after his return from study in Europe, echo the ideas of the Futurist manifestos. To Marin, who came to painting late after a career as an architect, experimentation meant first grasping the essence both of the objective world and of his subjective response to it and then unifying the two. For the catalogue of his 1913 show at Stieglitz's 291 Fifth Avenue gallery, he wrote:

Shall we consider the life of a great city as confined simply to the people and animals on its streets and in its buildings? Are the buildings themselves dead? We have been told somewhere that a work of art is a thing alive. You cannot create a work of art unless the things you behold respond to something within you. Therefore if these buildings move me they too must have life. Thus the whole city is alive; buildings, people, all are alive, and the more they move me the more I feel them to be alive.

It is this "moving of me" that I try to express, so that I may recall the spell I have been under and behold the expression of the different emotions that have been called into being. . . . Feelings are aroused which give me the desire to express the reaction of the "pull forces," those influences which play with one another; great masses pulling smaller masses, each subject in some degree to the other's power (fig. 12).[27]

Marin's "pull forces" were no different from the Futurists' "force-lines," but Marin was living in a city where every year new skyscrapers reached record heights, hourly rumbles were heard from passing elevated trains, and the very ground shook from the subways. Abraham Walkowitz also expressed this inner pulse of the city in his own paintings of skyscrapers.

The new art of the New York realists and emerging modernists made its dramatic public debut at the International Exhibition of Modern Art, familiarly known as the Armory Show, at the Sixty-ninth Regiment Armory in New York from February 17 to March 15, 1913. Organized by Arthur B. Davies, as president of the association of American Painters and Sculptors, and Walt Kuhn, the secretary of the association, as well as leading New York artists opposed to the artistic control held by the conservative artists, the show aimed to showcase the latest European and American art, along with a section devoted to such forerunners of modernism as Ingres, Degas, Seurat, Courbet, Manet, Cézanne, Van Gogh, Redon, and Gauguin. Davies and Kuhn made a whirlwind tour of European capitals in the fall of 1912. In Paris, art critic Walter Pach introduced them to important collections. Back in New York in December 1912, Kuhn wrote to thank Pach:

Today I gave the papers the list of European stuff which we know of definitely. It will be like a bombshell. . . . You have no idea how eager everybody is about this thing and the tremendous success it's going to be. . . . We want this old show of ours to mark the starting point of the new spirit in art, at least as far as America is concerned.[28]

The Armory Show must be considered one of the notorious artistic successes of all time. Some sixteen hundred works went on view, of which 235 were sold in New York. The exhibition traveled to Chicago and Boston, reaching a total audience of about a quarter million people. Stieglitz did not participate in the selection of artworks; but as an honorary vice president of the exhibition, he promoted the show in an article written for the newspaper the *New York American* on January 26, 1913.[29] Former U. S. President Theodore Roosevelt also tried his hand at art journalism in his article "A Layman's Views of an Art Exhibition," written for *The Outlook* on March 29, 1913. He praised the intentions of the organizers to show "the art forces which of late have been at work in Europe, forces which cannot be ignored."

There was not a touch of simpering, self-satisfied conventionality anywhere in the exhibition. Any sculptor or painter who had in him something to express and the power of expressing it found the field open to him. He did not have to be afraid because his work was not along ordinary lines.

However, Roosevelt then cautioned:

Probably in any reform movement, any progressive movement, in any field of life, the penalty for avoiding the commonplace is a lia-

12. *John Marin.* Movement, Fifth Avenue, *1912.* The Art Institute of Chicago. Alfred Stieglitz Collection.

bility to extravagance. It is vitally necessary to move forward and to shake off the dead hand, often the fossilized dead hand of the reactionaries; and yet we have to face the fact that there is apt to be a lunatic fringe among the votaries of any forward movement.[30]

The work singled out by Roosevelt and other critics to ridicule was Duchamp's *Nude Descending a Staircase, No. 2* (fig. 13). Duchamp's painting seemed audacious at the time, but its context includes not only the stylistic and iconographic evolution of Duchamp's own work from decorative Post-Impressionism, but also the motion studies done by photographers, filmmakers, and industrial engineers at the time. In 1912, when the picture was painted, Paris hosted the International Conference on Time, the agenda of which included setting standards for determining an accurate world time.[31] And in the following year, Henry Ford's automobile plant in Highland Park, Michigan, perfected the assembly-line operation whereby a Model T could be built from start to finish in five hours and fifty minutes.[32]

With the knowledge of this world context of the space-time obsession, we are not surprised to note that Duchamp's nude significantly walks with a dangling watch chain, or that Duchamp would explain, within a few years of painting the picture that:

[It] is an organization of kinetic elements, an expression of time and space through the abstract presentation of motion. . . . But remember, when we consider the motion of form through space in a given time, we enter the realm of geometry and mathematics, just as we do when we build a machine for that purpose. Now if I show the ascent of an airplane, I try to show what it does. I do not make a still-life picture of it. When the vision of the Nude flashed upon me, I knew that it would break forever the enslaving chains of Naturalism.[33]

This statement by Duchamp affirms our experiential apprehension of the impersonal space-time continuum. It ignores the conventions of beauty of the academic painters, who saw the world as composed of many static objects. And by rejecting the popular naturalism of Henri and Sloan, who saw the world in terms of the active social relations of people, Duchamp's statement asserts the antipathy that later American modernists and their advocates would have toward the aesthetic visualization of social experience.

Duchamp was not in New York in 1913 to see the Armory Show, but the Cuban-French automobile enthusiast and flamboyant artist Francis Picabia came to view his own entries. Before leaving in April, Picabia called New York "The cubist, the futurist city." "It expresses," he said, "in its architecture, its life, its spirit, the modern thought. You[Americans] have passed through all the old schools, and are futurists in word and deed and thought."[34]

Max Weber was inspired by Duchamp's painting to develop such ideas further. He sought to integrate his thoughts about space and time relationships with his picture making and produced such stunning paintings in 1915 as *New York* (Thyssen-Bornemisza Collection), *Chinese Restaurant* (fig. 14), and *Rush Hour*, which acknowledges the title "*The Rude Descending a Staircase (Rush Hour at the Subway)*" of a newspaper cartoon lampooning Duchamp's famous painting.[35]

Viewers of these works today would hardly know that at the time—1915—Europe was in its second year of a world war. In the United States, the debate over America's neutrality was acrimonious and bitter; the sinking of the passenger ship *Lusitania* by a German submarine in May 1915 tipped public opinion against the Germans. Finally in April 1917, President Woodrow Wilson declared war. Shortly thereafter the United States Congress passed the Espionage Act of June 15, 1917. The Act had relevance to the socialist editors and artists on *The Masses* staff who were forbidden to send the August issue through the mail because of it alleged seditious content. The loss of mail subscriptions forced the magazine out of business; later the government initiated a second suit against *The Masses*, charging a conspiracy to obstruct enlistment, with Art Young's satirical cartoons confiscated as evidence.[36]

Thus, while the months between August 1914 and April 1917 were uneasy for many New Yorkers, there existed a diverse climate of political opinion: John Sloan, although no longer active as a Socialist Party member, along with Robert Henri, maintained antiwar attitudes. George Bellows, also a frequent contributor to *The Masses*, produced some strident anti-German graphics. Photographer Edward Steichen obtained a commission and left for France; Alfred Stieglitz, by background and education pro-German, kept his silence.[37]

While New York harbored American artists with varied views, European artists seeking refuge in the city created a cosmopolitan climate of ideas to challenge the very identity of the work of art. They forged what we have come to recognize as the first American avant-garde, which included the New York Dada group shaped by the ideas of Duchamp, Picabia, and the young American artist Man Ray.[38]

Picabia returned to New York in June 1915, where he rejoined the Stieglitz circle, including Marius De Zayas, Paul Haviland, and Agnes Meyer. The group, with Stieglitz's blessing, issued a little magazine *291*, named, of course, after Stieglitz's gallery. Twelve monthly issues appeared beginning with the March 15 issue. Picabia contributed several so-called machine portraits of his New York friends, including *Ici, c'est ici Stieglitz* (fig. 15) for the July–August 1915 issue; it wittily depicts Stieglitz as a nonfunctional camera, the lens of which points toward the "Ideal."[39] This drawing is typical of the tongue-in-cheek irony of the group, who with artistic wit participated in various anti-art and antibourgeois antics.

When the already famous Marcel Duchamp finally came to New York in June 1915 to avoid the war atmosphere of Paris, the New York avant-garde looked to him for intellectual leadership. He was particularly welcomed by the wealthy collector and amateur cryptographer Walter Arensberg and his wife, Louise, who provided him with housing and commissioned him to make a second version of the *Nude Descending a Staircase*. Duchamp became the centerpiece of the salon evenings held at the Arensbergs' apartment to which poets, writers, and other artists were invited.[40]

On this visit to New York, Duchamp set to work on his ambitious, cerebral, quasi-occult *The Bride Stripped Bare by Her*

13. *Marcel Duchamp.* Nude Descending a Staircase, No. 2, *1912.* Philadelphia Museum of Art. The Louise and Walter Arensberg Collection.

14. *Max Weber.* Chinese Restaurant, *1915.* Whitney Museum of American Art, New York.

15. *Francis Picabia.* Ici, c'est ici Stieglitz, *1915.* The Metropolitan Museum of Art, New York, Alfred Stieglitz Collection.

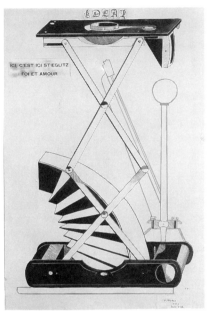

13

15

14

16

17

16. *Marcel Duchamp.* The Bride
Stripped Bare by her Bachelors,
Even (The Large Glass), *1915-23.*
Philadelphia Museum of Art.
Bequest of Katherine S. Dreier.

17. *Man Ray.* The Rope Dancer
Accompanies Herself with Her
Shadow, *1916.* Museum of Modern
Art, New York. Gift of G. David
Thompson.

Bachelors, Even (fig. 16). *The Large Glass,* as the work came to be known, was the culmination and synthesis of a series of paintings of biomechanical figures and anthropomorphized chocolate grinders that seem to have combined alchemical sources and mathematical reasoning (or doodling) with a parody of mechanistic sex. *The Large Glass* was not finished (or, rather, Duchamp did not stop work on it) until 1923. Along the way, he celebrated its chance additions (dust that fell on it in the studio) and accidents (the glass cracked in one of its moves to an exhibition).

Man Ray, a commercial artist from New Jersey whose exposure to the Armory Show radically changed his views of art, was the only American who maintained a Dada stance throughout his life. He allowed chance to dictate the form of the composition of his most famous painting, *The Rope Dancer Accompanies Herself with Her Shadow* (fig. 17). Cutting out pieces of colored paper as a way to stimulate ideas for composition, he noticed the leftover papers that had fallen onto the studio floor and had formed an interesting composition. This accidental chance composition became the basis for his painting. Ray formed a lasting friendship with Duchamp, made movies with him, photographed with mock-seriousness the dust on *The Large Glass,* and moved to Paris in 1920 to live an expatriate life among the Parisian avant-garde.[41]

Just as Stieglitz was terminating *Camera Work* in 1917, art dealer Robert Coady responded to the avant-garde ambience of New York and brought out *The Soil,* a periodical that lasted five issues. Coady, along with his featured writer Arthur Cravan, celebrated American technology and popular culture. In Whitmanesque fashion, Coady catalogued examples of American art in the first issue, dated December 1916:

The Panama Canal, the Sky-scraper, and Colonial Architecture. The East River, the Battery. . . the Tug Boat and the Steam-shovel. The Steam Lighter. The Steel Plants, the Washing Plants and the Electrical Shops. The Bridges, the Docks, the Cutouts, the Viaducts. . . Wright's and Curtiss's Aeroplanes and the Aeronauts. . . . Indian Beadwork, Sculptures, Decorations, Music and Dances. Jack Johnson, Charlie Chaplin, and "Spike" in "The Girl in the Game." . . . Bert Williams, Rag-time, the Buck and Wing and the Clog. Syncopation and the Cake-Walk. The Crazy Quilt and the Rag-mat. The Minstrels. The Cigar-store Indians. The Hatters, the Shoe-makers, the Haberdashers and the Clothiers. The Window Dressers.

And he ends:

—This is American Art.
It is not a refined granulation nor a delicate disease—it is not an ism. It is not an illustration to a theory, it is an expression of life—a complicated life—American life.
The isms have crowded it out of "the art world" and it has grown naturally, healthfully, beautifully. It has grown out of the soil and through the race and will continue to grow. It will grow and mature and add a new unit to Art.[42]

In March 1917, the first exhibition of the Society of Independent Artists was held at the Grand Central Galleries. The guiding principle of the Independents was that no artist was to be rejected if he or she paid the six dollar hanging fee. A scandal occurred when Duchamp, who had been developing his ready-mades and assisted readymades submitted a urinal, which he titled *Fountain* and signed "R. Mutt" (fig. 18). The work was rejected from the exhibition, no doubt to the delight of Duchamp. In the 1917 issue of the little New York magazine, *The Blind Man,* Duchamp wrote about "The Richard Mutt Case":

They say any artist paying six dollars may exhibit.

Mr. Richard Mutt sent in a fountain. Without discussion this article disappeared and never was exhibited.

What were the grounds for refusing Mr. Mutt's fountain:—1. Some contended it was immoral, vulgar. Others, it was plagiarism, a plain piece of plumbing.

Now Mr. Mutt's fountain is not immoral, that is absurd, no more than a bath tub is immoral. It is a fixture that you see every day in plumbers' show windows.

Whether Mr. Mutt with his own hands made the fountain or not has no importance. He chose it. He took an ordinary article of life, placed it so that its useful significance disappeared under the new title and point of view—created a new thought for that object.

As for plumbing, that is absurd. The only works of art America has given are her plumbing and her bridges.[43]

Perhaps in response to Duchamp's challenge, Morton Schamberg, a Philadelphia artist who had been introduced to the Arensberg crowd by the poet/obstetrician William Carlos Williams, constructed his own readymade, called *God*, made up of a miter box and a plumbing trap (Philadelphia Museum of Art).[44]

As for bridges, the Brooklyn Bridge had long been the subject for New York artists and photographers, such as John Marin, as it had been for the poet Hart Crane. With Joseph Stella the Brooklyn Bridge reached its apogee as an icon of America (fig. 19).

When armistice was declared on November 11, 1918, a chapter was already closing on the New York art world. The radical, bohemian, and experimental ambience for artmaking was disappearing. *The Masses* had folded in 1917. Picabia had left for Switzerland in February 1918, and Duchamp had left in August for Buenos Aires. Stieglitz had closed his gallery in 1917 and the same year ended publication of *Camera Work*—devoting himself to his own photography. Edward Steichen entered the world of commercial photography on which he was to have considerable impact in the 1920s and 1930s. Morton Schamberg died of the influenza epidemic in 1918, and Max Weber, already by 1918, was turning away from his experiments with Cubism and Futurism and toward a style of monumental nudes.

The wealthy society matron and talented sculptor Gertrude Vanderbilt Whitney had for some time been supporting the American realists by buying works from exhibitions (she bought four paintings out of The Eight's 1908 show), encour-

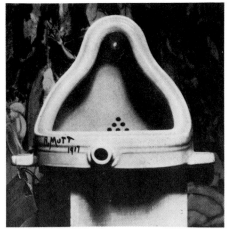

18

19

18. Marcel Duchamp ("R. Mutt"). Fountain, *1917. Reproduced in The Blind Man 2 (May 1917). Photograph by Alfred Stieglitz.* Philadelphia Museum of Art. The Louise and Walter Arensberg Collection.

19. Joseph Stella. Brooklyn Bridge, *1917–18.* Yale University Art Gallery, New Haven Connecticut. Gift of Collection Société Anonyme.

aging her friends to buy American art (she founded the Society of Friends of Young Artists for just such a purpose), and writing checks for causes (she gave a thousand dollars toward the cost of the pine branch festoons to decorate the Armory Show; after 1917, she regularly covered the deficit of the Society of Independent Artists). In 1918, she created the Whitney Studio Club that brought in John Sloan and a younger, less politically radical, crowd of realists who had studied together at the Art Students League.[45] Although radicals such as *Masses* writer John Reed went on to be a founder of the American Communist Party, most art-world types retreated from politics just as an anti-Red sentiment began to sweep the nation with Attorney General A. Mitchell Palmer conducting raids against both foreign born and native socialists, anarchists, and communists.

Today we can justly speculate on how much the art of the realists and semi-abstract modernists related to the issues of the progressive reform movement—a movement with two thrusts: the humanitarian side that campaigned for better housing and better working conditions for the urban working classes, and the efficiency side that promoted scientific management, modernization, and standardization in industry. The realists' concern with people and people's activities pairs them with the humanist ethos of the former group, whereas the modernists' concern with motion studies and with the forms of the city would connect them with the movement to rationalize technology. Both groups saw their own version of the urban future—the promise of egalitarianism or the affirmation of technological modernity.

Art historians in the last four decades have often judged the realists of the Henri group as old fashioned, because in their adherence to a dark, Munich School inspired, painterly figural style, the realists did not challenge the forms of art.[46] Such art historians have pronounced the modernists to be the real revolutionaries in art, because in the matter of pure form, the Stieglitz painters experimented with nonrepresentational genres. This lopsided appraisal denies the radical content of the early twentieth-century realists—which was to reaffirm the tradition of Courbet's socialist art at a time when painting had become the precious mirrors of bourgeois living, and sculpture had become spineless personifications of traditional civic values.

But in viewing the artistic practice of the third group working in New York in the early twentieth century—the Dadaists—we detect a skeptical note: that people and their human relations may not be so compatible with the technology and the forces and structures of capitalist production. Ironic and aloof, and perhaps nihilistic, Duchamp may have recognized that his avant-garde modernism was a modernism with nothing to affirm—a modernism of negation. It is no coincidence that the most recent art historians concerned with identifying the characteristics of the postmodern world are turning to the study of the Dada tradition with renewed vigor.

Notes

1. Bruce St. John, ed., *John Sloan's New York Scene: From the Diaries, Notes and Correspondence, 1906–1913* (New York: Harper and Row, 1965), 13.
2. Max Weber, *Cubist Poems* (London: Elkin Matthews, 1914), as quoted in Percy North, *Max Weber: American Modern* (New York: The Jewish Museum, 1982), 55.
3. Samuel Isham, *The History of American Painting*, new ed. with supplemental chapters by Royal Cortissoz (New York: Macmillan Company, 1936), 500. [First published in 1905; quoted in Patricia Hills, *Turn-of-the-Century America: Paintings, Graphics, Photographs, 1890–1910* (New York: Whitney Museum of American Art, 1977), 11]. The late nineteenth-century preoccupation with beauty is discussed in The Brooklyn Museum, *The American Renaissance: 1876–1917* (New York: The Brooklyn Museum and Pantheon Books, 1979) and The Metropolitan Museum of Art, *In Pursuit of Beauty: Americans and the Aesthetic Movement* (New York: The Metropolitan Museum of Art and Rizzoli, 1986).
4. Charles H. Caffin, *The Story of American Painting* (New York: Frederick A. Stokes, 1907), 343–44.
5. Henry Adams, *The Education of Henry Adams* [1918] (New York: The Modern Library, 1931), 380. For a provocative analysis of Adams' attitudes contained in his chapter "The Dynamo and the Virgin," see Dickran Tashjian, "Henry Adams and Marcel Duchamp: Liminal Views of the Dynamo and the Virgin," *Arts Magazine* 51 (May 1977): 102–12.
6. See Hills, *Turn-of-the-Century America*, and Wanda M. Corn, "The New New York," *Art in America* 61 (July–August 1973): 58–65. A useful cultural history is Arthur Frank Wertheim, *The New York Renaissance: Iconoclasm, Modernism, and Nationalism in American Culture, 1908–1917* (New York: New York University Press, 1976).
7. Quoted in Dorothy Norman, *Alfred Stieglitz: An American Seer* (New York: Random House, 1973), 45.
8. Quoted in Norman, *Alfred Stieglitz*, 75–76.
9. A record 11,745 immigrants were processed on Ellis Island in New York harbor on April 17, 1907; during the peak years of 1910–13 nearly 10.5 million immigrants arrived on America's shores. See Cynthia Jaffe McCabe, *The Golden Door: Artist-Immigrants of America, 1876–1976* (Washington, D.C.: Smithsonian Institution Press, 1976), 59, 61. This exhibition catalogue contains a concise bibliography of American immigration and immigrant artists discussed here.
10. For American artists' biographies, see Matthew Baigell, *Dictionary of American Art* (London: John Murray, 1979). For Henri, see William Innes Homer, *Robert Henri and His Circle* (Ithaca, N.Y.: Cornell University Press, 1969).
11. See Thorstein Veblen, *The Theory of the Leisure Class: An Economic Study of Institutions* (1899) (New York: New American Library, 1953). See also Clyde Griffen, "The Progressive Ethos," in Stanley Coben and Lorman Ratner, eds. *The Development of an American Culture* (Englewood Cliffs, N.J.: Prentice-Hall, 1967), 120–49. A useful bibliography is found in Cecelia Tichi, *Shifting Gears: Technology, Literature, Culture in Modernist America* (Chapel Hill: The University of North Carolina Press, 1987).
12. For Riis, see Jacob A. Riis, *How the Other Half Lives: Studies Among the Tenements of New York* (New York: Dover Publications, 1971). For Hine, see Walter Rosenblum, Naomi Rosenblum, and Alan Trachtenberg, *America and Lewis Hine: Photographs, 1904–1940* (New York: The Brooklyn Museum and Aperture, 1977). Maren Stange's Symbols of *Ideal Life: Social Documentary Photography in America, 1890–1950* (New York: Cambridge University Press, 1989) sets the work of these photographers in historical context; see her discussion on how Riis used the photographs of Richard Hoe Lawrence for his own ends.
13. "New York Exhibition of Independent Artists," *The Craftsman* 18 (May 1910): 162. For John Sloan, see National Gallery of Art, *John Sloan: 1871–1951, His Life and Paintings; His Graphics*, essays by David W. Scott and E. John Bullard (Washington, D.C.: National Gallery of Art, 1971).
14. Quoted in St. John, ed., *John Sloan's New York*, 133.
15. A complete run of *The Masses* can be found in the John Sloan Archives, Delaware Art Museum. For an excellent history, see Rebecca Zurier, *Art for the Masses (1911–1917): A Radical Magazine and Its Graphics* (New Haven: Yale University Art Gallery, 1985).
16. For Sloan's attitudes and his practices, see Patricia Hills, "John Sloan's Images of Working-Class: A Case Study of the Roles and Interrelationships of Politics, Personality, and Patrons in the Development of Sloan's Art, 1905–16," *Prospects* 5 (1980): 157–96.

17. See William Innes Homer, *Alfred Stieglitz and the American Avant-Garde* (Boston: New York Graphic Society, 1977).

18. A sampling of typical essays has been reprinted; see Jonathan Green, ed., *Camera Work: A Critical Anthology* (New York: Aperture, 1973).

19. See North, *Max Weber: American Modern*, for a concise biography.

20. Quoted in Green, *Camera Work*, 202–3. Regarding Weber's interest in the fourth dimension, see Linda Dalrymple Henderson, *The Fourth Dimension and Non-Euclidean Geometry in Modern Art* (Princeton, N.J.: Princeton University Press, 1983), 164–86.

21. See Stephen Kern, *The Culture of Time and Space, 1880–1918* (Cambridge: Harvard University Press, 1983); see also Henderson, *The Fourth Dimension.*

22. Regarding art and the machine, see K. G. Pontus Hulten, *The Machine as Seen at the End of the Mechanical Age* (New York: The Museum of Modern Art and New York Graphic Society, 1968).

23. See John O. Hand, "Futurism in America," *Art Journal* 41 (Winter 1981): 337–42.

24. Dominic Ricciotti, "The Revolution in Urban Transport: Max Weber and Italian Futurism," *The American Art Journal* 16 (Winter 1984): 51.

25. For the influence of Bergson on American artists, see Arlette J. Klaric, *Arthur Dove's Abstract Style of 1912: Dimensions of the Decorative and Bergsonian Realities* (Ann Arbor, Mich.: University Microfilms, 1984).

26. Joseph Stella, "Discover of America: Autobiographical Notes," *Art News* 59 (November 1960): 64–65. I am grateful to Donna Cassidy for bringing this quotation to my attention in her study "The Painted Music of America in the Works of Arthur G. Dove, John Marin, and Joseph Stella: An Aspect of Cultural Nationalism," Ph.D. diss., Boston University, 1987.

27. Exhibition catalogue of John Marin's 1913 show at 291 Fifth Avenue, New York Public Library Papers, roll N53, frame 941; quoted in Cassidy, "The Painted Music of America," 182.

28. Milton W. Brown, *The Story of the Armory Show* (New York: The Joseph H. Hirshhorn Foundation, 1963), 55–56.

29. Norman, *Alfred Stieglitz*, 119.

30. Theodore Roosevelt "A Layman's Views of an Art Exhibition," *The Outlook* (March 29, 1913), 719. Quoted in Roderick Nash, ed., *The Call of the Wild (1900–1916)* (New York: George Braziller, 1970), 185–86.

31. Kern, *The Culture of Time and Space, 1880–1918*, pp. 11–14.

32. Nash, *The Call of the Wild*, 10.

33. Hulten, *The Machine as Seen at the End of the Mechanical Age*, p. 75 and n. 50.

34. Quoted in Arthur J. Eddy, *Cubists and Post-Impressionism* (Chicago: A.C. McClurg & Co., 1914), 96.

35. The cartoon, by J. F. Griswold, was published in the New York *Evening Sun*, March 20, 1913.

36. Regarding America's neutrality, see Barbara W. Tuchman's "End of a Dream, the United States: 1890–1902," in Barbara W. Tuchman, *The Proud Tower: A Portrait of the World Before the War (1890–1914)* (New York: The Macmillan Company, 1966) 133–46.; regarding the fortunes of *The Masses*, see Zurier, *The Masses*, 41–45.

37. For Steichen's World War I photography, see Patricia Johnston, "Edward Steichen's Advertising Photography: The Visual Strategies of Persuasion," Ph.D. diss., Boston University, 1987.

38. Dickran Tashjian, *Skyscraper Primitives: Dada and the American Avant-Garde, 1910–1925* (Middleton, Conn.: Wesleyan University Press, 1975); and Bram Dijkstra, Cubism, Stieglitz, and the Early Poetry of William Carlos Williams: The Hieroglyphics of a New Speech (Princeton, N.J.: Princeton University Press, 1969).

39. Homer, *Alfred Stieglitz*, 190.

40. For Duchamp, see Anne d'Harnoncourt and Kynaston McShine, eds., *Marcel Duchamp* (New York: The Museum of Modern Art, 1973).

41. For Man Ray, see Man Ray, *Self Portrait* (Boston: Little, Brown, 1963).

42. R[obert] J. Coady, "American Art," *The Soil* 1 (December 1916), 3–4.

43. [Marcel Duchamp], "The Richard Mutt Case," *The Blind Man*, No. 2 (May 1917), unpaged. Quoted in Barbara Rose, ed., *Readings in American Art: 1900–1975* (New York: Praeger, 1975), 51–52.

44. William C. Agee, *Morton Livingston Schamberg (1881–1918)* (New York: Salander-O'Reilly Galleries, 1982). The attribution is still under study; see Robert Reiss, "'My Baroness': Elsa von Freytag-Loringhoven," in *New York Dada*, ed. Rudolf E. Kuenzli (New York: Willis Locker and Owens, 1986), 81-101. I am grateful to John Stomberg for bringing this essay to my attention.

45. Roberta K. Tarbell, "Gertrude Vanderbilt Whitney as Patron," in Patricia Hills and Roberta K. Tarbell, eds., *The Figurative Tradition and the Whitney Museum of American Art* (New York: Whitney Museum of American Art, 1980), 10–22.

46. For an example of this view, see Amy Goldin, "The Eight's Laissez Faire Revolution," *Art in America* 61 (July–August 1973), 42–49. On the other hand, in their mastery of public relations and their manipulation of the press, Henri and the rest of The Eight were thoroughly modern; see Elizabeth Milroy, *Painters of a New Century: The Eight and American Art*. Milwaukee: Milwaukee Art Museum, 1992.

Acknowledgments

I am grateful to Kevin Whitfield, my husband, with whom I have discussed these ideas at length, and to Arlette Klaric, my colleague at Boston University, for her helpful editorial suggestions.

1. Bathing at Coney Island.
Museum of the City of New York.

The City and Entertainment: Coney Island and Haus Vaterland

Roger Green

Roger Green writes about art and architecture for the Booth group of newspapers in Michigan. He is the author of Max Papart *(1985) and a regular contributor to* ARTnews *magazine. Haus Vaterland was the subject of his doctoral dissertation in art history at the University of Chicago.*

"Inherent to man," proclaims the 1885 *Handbuch der Architektur*, the definitive German encyclopedia of building terminology, history, and types, "is the longing for revitalization and pleasure, stimulating the heart and soul."[1] This universal yearning, the *Handbuch* decrees, explains the appearance in European and American cities of large public pleasure facilities of manifold kinds.

Both New York and Berlin, being important industrial centers with large populations, had by the late nineteenth century developed prosperous amusement industries, ministering to mass, modern needs for "revitalization and pleasure." In both cities, legions of respectable (and also disreputable) commercial distractions, priced to suit every pocketbook, were handily available to masses of people at dance halls, theaters, cafes, cabarets, restaurants, and bars, to say nothing of wholesome family facilities where sports could be practiced or watched. In both crowded cities, however, a single immense amusement complex—Coney Island in New York, Haus Vaterland in Berlin—stands out historically as having been the most important "safety valve,"[2] catering to the largest number of satisfied customers and developing an international reputation for stimulating mass intoxication over the years.

Coney Island, advertised as "the world's largest playground," occupied (and still occupies) the central section of a five-mile beach, fronting on the Atlantic Ocean in southern Brooklyn. An island in name only, Coney Island originally was separated from the mainland by a tidal creek and a broad stretch of salt marsh, which later were largely filled in. Coney Island was discovered in 1609 by the English navigator and explorer Henry Hudson who, seeking a northwest passage from Europe to the Orient, briefly stopped at the island, trading with its native inhabitants, the Canarsie Indians, before entering New York harbor.[3]

Beginning in the 1830s, Coney Island was developed as a fashionable seaside resort, with hotels, restaurants, and bathing pavilions, constructed at the eastern end of the beach. After the 1870s, when railroads and paved roadways made Coney Island accessible to hordes of distraction-hungry New Yorkers, the area became less exclusive.

In the middle portion of the beach, marked by a three-hundred-foot observation tower,[4] shooting galleries, fun houses, game booths, penny arcades, and other popular, inexpensive attractions began to appear. In 1895, the world's first amusement *park*, Sea Lion Park (whose principal attraction was a troupe of forty sea lions performing aquatic feats) was opened at Coney Island by Capt. Billy Boynton. Two years later Steeplechase, the first of the three much larger amusement parks for which Coney Island became famous, was completed, to be followed in 1903 by Luna Park and in 1904 by Dreamland.

The three parks were key components of an amusement district traversed by Surf Avenue, Coney Island's principal east-west thoroughfare. Steeplechase occupied a site on the south side of the avenue, extending in that direction to the Atlantic Ocean. Luna Park was constructed on the opposite side of Surf Avenue, somewhat to the east, while sprawling Dreamland—

211

2. *Racetrack, Steeplechase Park, Coney Island.* Museum of the City of New York.

3. *Entrance to Dreamland, Coney Island.* Museum of the City of New York.

catercornered from Luna Park—extended, like Steeplechase, south from the avenue to the beach. Encompassing nearly one hundred acres and accommodating hundreds of thousands of guests, the three amusement parks contained scores of extravagant, mechanized thrill rides, and were gorgeously illuminated at night.

In Berlin, the pleasure facility whose popularity most closely matched Coney Island's was a downtown amusement complex known as Haus Vaterland—an enormous domed structure capable of accommodating eight thousand visitors.[5] Haus Vaterland, which opened in 1928, contained on five stories numerous restaurants and bars that faithfully re-created German and foreign locales, combining elaborate decor (including illusionistic light effects and working panoramas) with appropriate music, entertainment and cuisine. In addition to comprehensively simulating a global tour—"The world in one house" was the management's opening night promise to guests[6]—Haus Vaterland contained a first-run motion picture theater, a three-story ballroom and the largest cafe in the world, Cafe Vaterland.

Haus Vaterland differed from Coney Island in many immediately obvious and significant ways. For one, the Berlin amusement complex was markedly smaller than its New York counterpart, occupying a single, freestanding building rather than encompassing a sprawling area. Moreover, while Coney Island was constructed on the outskirts of New York, Haus Vaterland towered mightily above the geographical heart of Berlin: Potsdamer Platz, the teeming intersection on which Haus Vaterland fronted, was the busiest traffic hub in Europe during the 1920s and 1930s, comparable to Times Square in New York.

Because of its construction of downtown location, Haus Vaterland could profitably operate not only during the summer months—like Coney Island—but all year round. Haus Vaterland was primarily a locus for nighttime activities, however, and while reasonably priced, it retained an aura of big-city glamour and exclusivity.

In the face of these and still other conspicuous differences, Haus Vaterland and Coney Island evidence many direct and indirect links—similarities that give symbolic expression to important aspects of industrial modernity as it developed in New York and Berlin. Indeed, Haus Vaterland was indirectly inspired by Coney Island: Haus Vaterland's acknowledged prototype was Berlin's big, "American style" thrill park of 1910, Lunapark, itself self-consciously patterned after the Coney Island parks.[7]

Significantly, multinationalism characterized the attractions at Coney Island, Berlin's Lunapark, and Haus Vaterland, where picturesque or romantic locales in foreign lands were painstakingly re-created. The cosmopolitan character of the three amusement centers is of telling historical consequence, reflecting an atmosphere of internationalism.

By internationalism, one of the hallmarks of Western industrial modernism, is meant global rather than local or national consciousness, ideally extending into concern for cooperation among nations for the common good. Such concern is linked to another distinctly modern phenomenon, urbanization through waves of foreign immigration, which ultimately explains the development of New York and Berlin into world-class metropolises. "If Paris is France," said George C. Tilyou, founder of Steeplechase, "then Coney Island between June and September is the world."[8] Likewise, "a symphony of life . . . embracing and uniting all the nations of the world" was the public image advanced by Haus Vaterland's management.[9]

Haus Vaterland's re-creation of those Coney Island attractions imitating foreign countries admittedly was a superficial expression of internationalism, capitalizing on romantic yet essentially frivolous popular fantasies. However, many of Coney Island's rides and spectacles were genuinely international in the sense that they re-created or directly appropriated attractions earlier introduced at world's fairs, those "festivals of high machine-age capitalism where nation after nation showed off its industrial strength and the breadth of its colonial resources,"[10] but where meaningful cross-cultural fertilization frequently also occurred.[11]

Moreover, by copying Coney Island, Berlin's Lunapark and Haus Vaterland manifested an historically important strain of internationalism in Germany—the *Amerikanismus* or thoughtful imitation of American models that affected countless aspects of German industrial modernization, beginning with unification in 1871 and building to a crescendo during the prosperous years of the Weimar Republic.[12] The United States, widely perceived as the land of unlimited possibilities, captured the imaginations of many forward-looking Germans who sought to pattern their country's development on America's example.

Yet because of financial exigencies and German thoughtfulness and caution generally, the German copies were, like Haus Vaterland, invariably smaller and more prudently conceived than the originals, if frequently also much more highly refined.[13] The aim of this study is to investigate the waves of internationalism made manifest at Haus Vaterland and Coney Island, with special emphasis on *Amerikanismus* as a potent cultural force in Germany.

Certainly Coney Island was a place of superlatives, worthy of attention from Germany and, in fact, the whole world. Already in 1883, one of Coney Island's four grand-luxe hotels, the Brighton Beach Hotel, was described as having "no superior on the Atlantic coast or in Newport or Saratoga."[14] And not just hotel accommodations but the whole spectrum of commercial distractions at Coney Island eclipsed the pleasures available at other resorts.

Besides bathing and other healthy outdoor pursuits (among them fishing, sailing, rowing, and horseback riding), Coney Island offered stimulation at two racecourses, an aquarium, a camera obscura (housed in an octagonal building where moving pictures of the beach were projected on a revolving disk), and at an iron pier projecting one thousand feet into the Atlantic Ocean and accommodating a seafood restaurant with seats for fifteen hundred. On Tuesday, Thursday, and Saturday

4. Shooting the Chutes, Coney Island. Museum of the City of New York.

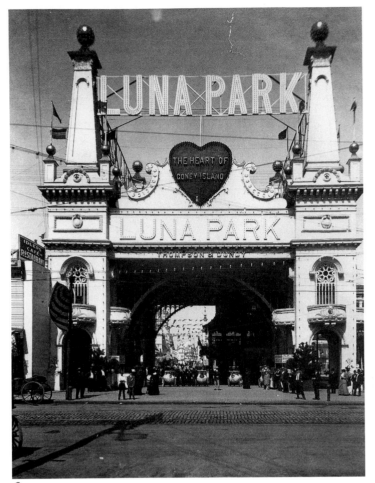

5

6

5. *Entrance to Luna Park, Coney Island.* Museum of the City of New York.

6. *Switzerland Ride, Coney Island.* Museum of the City of New York.

evenings in 1883, displays of fireworks were presented, "augmented by the Grand Naval and Military Spectacle, 'The Bombardment of Alexandria,' featuring 350 drilled and experienced troops."[15]

These and other attractions were supplemented after 1883 by mechanized thrill rides, beginning with the Loop-the-Loop, a railroad track that circled around on itself and caused a rapidly traveling vehicle to cling momentarily to its inner track surface upside down.[16] In 1884, the world's first roller coaster, patented that year by Stephen E. Jackman, was opened, while in 1895, at Sea Lion Park, Capt. Boynton introduced the first Shoot-the-Chute, a toboggan hoisted mechanically to the top of a diagonal incline, from which it rushed toward a body of water.[17] Also constructed at Coney Island was a Scenic Railway, whose meandering tracks passed through portrayals, painted on canvas, of famous landmarks in foreign countries.

The popular thrill ride from which Steeplechase took its name was a mechanized racetrack with iron horses. Described as "a healthful stimulant that stirs the heart and clears the brain,"[18] the serpentine racetrack originally was developed (from the carousel) by William Cawdery of London, then improved by Steeplechase Park's developer, Tilyou. To construct the mechanized racecourse, ninety-six tons of iron and steel plus three hundred thousand feet of lumber were required. Tilyou developed the remainder of the park in imitation of the Midway Plaisance at Chicago's World's Columbian Exposition of 1893; among the rides and attractions he assembled at Steeplechase was the World's Largest Ferris Wheel from the Chicago fair.[19]

Neighboring Luna Park, developed by Frederic Thompson and Elmer S. Dundy, occupied thirty-eight acres and could hold forty thousand visitors, each of whom paid ten cents admission. The principal attraction at Luna Park was a Trip to the Moon on the cigar-shaped airship Luna IV—an illusionistic voyage into outer space that Dundy originally had introduced at the Pan-American Buffalo Exposition of 1901.[20]

During the Trip to the Moon, passengers peering out the airship's windows first saw the earth fade from sight, then the moon grow increasingly large and seemingly close. Eventually, the Luna's windows framed views of the surface of the moon, including "volcanic growths, stalactite drippings, crystallized mineral wonders and all the fairyland magnificence that papier-mache, canvas, paint, artists, electricians and expert stage property men could construct."[21] At this point in the ride, passengers disembarked from the airship, entered the chamber of the Man in the Moon (with walls of green cheese), and then exited.

The architecture at Luna Park, designed by Thompson, was intended to continue the theme of otherworldliness established by the Trip to the Moon. Toward this end, the park was crowded with fanciful towers and minarets, painted in rainbow colors, and outlined by night by more than a million incandescent bulbs. By 1906, the skyline at Lunapark included 1,221 lighted towers, and by the following year, 1,326.[22]

Among the other illusionistic attractions at Luna Park were

7

8

7. Luna Park, Coney Island.
Museum of the City of New York.

8. Iron Pier, Coney Island. Museum
of the City of New York.

20,000 Leagues Under the Sea and Fire and Flames, the latter a mock urban blaze regularly battled by seventy actual firemen, using real fire equipment. Luna Park also included a recreation of a street and marketplace in Delhi, populated by three hundred imported natives of India.

Dreamland, intended by its developer, former New York state senator William H. Reynolds, to eclipse neighboring Luna Park, was considerably larger than the earlier facility, accommodating 250,000 guests. In dramatic contrast to the rainbow-colored buildings at Luna Park, all of Dreamland's fanciful architecture was painted pure white.

The principal attraction at Dreamland, originally introduced at St. Louis's 1904 Louisiana Purchase Exposition, was an illusionistic spectacle called the Blue Dome of Creation; visitors entering the circular structure boarded ships that were conducted through one thousand feet of canals, passing moving panoramas portraying historical scenes extending back in time sixty centuries, concluding with the creation of the earth.[23]

Among Dreamland's international attractions were a gondola ride through the canals of Venice and Coasting Through Switzerland, consisting of twenty-five picturesque Alpine scenes distributed along a mile of track on which sleigh-like cars ran. Two further Dreamland attractions, Fighting the Flames and the Incubator Building, were, like the Creation exhibit, introduced at world's fairs.[24]

Fighting the Flames, a larger and more elaborate version of Luna Park's Fire and Flames, was first presented, by fire chief Charles McCarthy, manager of a team of American firefighting champions from Kansas City, Missouri, at the Paris Exposition Universelle of 1900. The Incubator Building, where most of New York's premature babies were nursed to health, included a Baby-Hatching Apparatus originally introduced at the 1896 *Gewerbe-austellung* in Berlin.

About the thrill rides and spectacles at Coney Island, one observer opined in 1904:

The thing that is furthest from reason, that laughs loudest at the laws of gravitation, is the thing that takes in the Coney Island crowd. To stand any man on his head, whirl him, breathless, through the air, to roll and roast him, to blow away his hat, and to trip up his feet, and to make his eyes bulge and his ears ring, is the object sought by a thousand competitors.[25]

Certainly Coney Island's attractions exhilarated visitors on a mass scale and to a degree of intensity unimagined by the framers of the 1885 *Handbuch der Architektur*. "All is vastness," concluded a visitor to Coney Island in 1917, after marveling at its "infinite capacity" and "immense variety . . . representing an investment of millions of dollars."[26]

Berlin's Lunapark, "a modern amusement park based on American models,"[27] was located on the shores of Halensee, one of the many sparkling lakes that surround the city. The Berlin park included many of the same rides and served the same function as the Coney Island facilities. "Every world

capital needs for its citizens a permanent amusement park," proclaims a Lunapark souvenir book. "It is the great anxiety-breaker, the place where one forgets everything burdensome."[28]

Yet Berlin's Lunapark was constructed at a smaller scale than the Coney Island Parks and excluded the sensational thrill rides such as the roller coaster and Loop-the-Loop, which were considered too dangerous to be permitted in Germany.[29] Instead, attractions that seemed miraculous by virtue of their international flavor were popular lures in Berlin.

A Scenic Railway traveled at ten meters per second on six kilometers of tracks, past some six thousand cubic meters of canvas backdrops, painted with scenes of the Acropolis, American skyscrapers, and the Alps. A re-created Somali village, consisting of primitive huts, was populated each summer by 150 natives of the Egyptian Sudan, among them entertainers and artists charged with continuously demonstrating their customs and skills.

At Haus Vaterland, the international attractions of Lunapark were brought together under one roof by prominent architects and designers, using the newest technology. Like Lunapark, Haus Vaterland was small and restrained by American standards. However, for sophistication and flawless operation, Haus Vaterland was unmatched in Europe and the United States.

The man responsible for Haus Vaterland was a Berlin entrepreneur, Leo Kronau, who had visited Coney Island and who envisioned a gigantic Haus der Nationen (House of Nations) for Berlin.[30] Kronau, who served as Haus Vaterland's first artistic director, providing international entertainment throughout the establishment, sold his idea for the property to the family-owned Berlin restaurant firm Kempinski, which developed and operated Haus Vaterland for many years.

The building occupied by Haus Vaterland, abutting Potsdamer Platz on the southwest, was an extensively reconverted structure, originally erected in 1912, and known for sixteen years as Haus Potsdam.[31] Designed by the architect Franz Schwechten, Haus Potsdam was a six-story office building with a cafe and movie theater built into its lower levels.

Schwechten designed Haus Vaterland in two connected but discretely articulated parts. At the northern end of the building, facing Potsdamer Platz, was a circular pavilion crowned by a copper-covered dome, rising thirty-five meters above the street. Contiguous to the domed pavilion, running south beside the Potsdam railroad station, was a narrow rectangular wing with a mansard roof.

A steel-framed structure faced with two varieties of sandstone, Haus Potsdam was, stylistically speaking, a blend of Wilhelmine historical eclecticism and early modern simplification; the building's rectangular section suggested a Renaissance palazzo in Italy, while the domed pavilion essentially re-created the mausoleum of the Ostrogothic King Theodoric (474–526 A.D.) outside Ravenna.[32]

9

10

11

9. *Haus Potsdam, c. 1912.* Eckhard
Grothe, Berlin.

10. *Cafe Piccadilly in Haus
Potsdam postcard, 1914.* Eckhard
Grothe, Berlin.

11. *Title page of the program for the
opening of Haus Vaterland, 1928.*
Eckhard Grothe, Berlin.

12

13

14

12. *Postcard of Cafe Picadilly in Haus Potsdam, 1914.* Eckhard Grothe, Berlin.

13. *View of main hall in Haus Vaterland postcard, 1942.* Eckhard Grothe, Berlin.

14. *Cafe Vaterland, c. 1912.* Eckhard Grothe, Berlin.

The architect who converted Haus Potsdam into Haus Vaterland, Carl Stahl-Urach, made certain studied changes to the building's exterior, increasing its impression of modernity by covering some planar sections with stucco and by electrically lighting the domed pavilion at night.[33] Arranged in intersecting arcs atop Haus Vaterland's dome were some four thousand electric bulbs that, switched alternately on and off according to an exacting schedule, created the illusion of continuous spinning motion against Berlin's night sky.

"Nobody seeing this vast, flood-lit modern undertaking," exulted a Berlin press reporter about Haus Vaterland's dome, "can escape the impression that here, world-capital life is pulsing."[34] Yet Haus Vaterland's "Babylonian dome"[35] really was an imitation in miniature of the much more ambitious lighting effects at Coney Island.

Stahl-Urach's changes to the interior were more sweeping. While the original cafe and movie theater remained in place on opposite sides of the building, a new entry block containing a grand hall was constructed in the center of the building. Layered vertically on opposite sides of the hall, and accessible from it, were four of Haus Vaterland's principal public rooms.

Facing one another on the third level were the Grinzinger Heuriger, re-creating one of the rustic vintner's gardens outside Vienna, where potent new wine is served, and the Rheinterrasse, which simulated a canopied outdoor restaurant overlooking a picturesque stretch of the Rhine River, between the harbor town of Saint Goar and the Lorelei. Facing one another on the fourth level of Haus Vaterland's grand hall were the Türkisches Cafe, featuring gilded arches and marble floors, and Löwenbräu, a galleried Bavarian beer hall.

The fifth floor contained Puszta Czardas, a Hungarian peasant tavern, the Bodega, a Spanish wine cellar, and the Wild West Bar, a crude frontier saloon in America's Rocky Mountains. The fifth floor also contained the entrance to Haus Vaterland's ballroom or Palmensaal, a stylized re-creation of the Garden of Eden located beneath the big building's dome. The entire sixth floor contained Haus Vaterland's central kitchen, servicing all of the guestrooms below.

By re-creating primitive or exotic countries, many of the rooms continued the internationalism of the thrill parks at Coney Island and of world's fairs. At the same time, Haus Vaterland's top-level kitchen was a transcendent manifestation of the *Amerikanismus* that reached its peak of influence in Germany in 1928, when Berlin was popularly regarded as the most American city in Europe.[36]

Extending to Haus Vaterland's dining rooms from its central kitchen were systems of pneumatic tubes and electric dumbwaiters, the latter connected to one another (at kitchen level) with conveyer belts. Using the pneumatic tubes, waiters sent orders up to the kitchen, from which cooked meals were sent downward via the dumbwaiters; using the same devices, waiters sent dirty dishes back to the kitchen, to be moved by the conveyor belts to special stations for machine washing, drying, and stacking.

*15. Haus Vaterland on Potsdamer
Platz, c. 1930.* Landesbildstelle,
Berlin.

The entire process was developed in imitation of American production line techniques, as pioneered by Henry Ford, and was powerfully influenced by American managerial science, as promulgated by Frederick Taylor. Since the same techniques were used to modernize Germany's factories after World War I, Haus Vaterland's central kitchen was in effect a miniature model of Weimar Germany's revitalized industry, which by 1928 had surpassed pre-World War I production levels.

In fact, all of Haus Vaterland was run like a modern factory,[37] the operations in every department being coordinated with the same exquisitely tuned perfection as the emblematic, spinning play of light on the dome. The Kempinski firm, successful Berlin restauranteurs for some sixty-five years, provided culinary specialties appropriate to the simulated foreign nations and regions of Germany. Hungarian goulash, for example, was available at Pusta Czardas, while sachertorte, prepared according to its "original" recipe—a Kempinski exclusive in Berlin—could be enjoyed at the Grinzinger Heuriger.[38]

As Haus Vaterland's first artistic director, the entrepreneur Kronau arranged entertainment appropriate to the various restaurants and bars. At Löwenbräu, an "original Bavarian band" played *Schuhplattler* music, while on the Rheinterrasse, twenty young Rhine maidens danced among the tables under vine-braided hoops.[39] At the foreign bars the entertainment was more exotic. At Puszta Czardas, violinists played "original gypsy music," while at the Wild West Bar patrons could hear American jazz while black cowboys in full western regalia swung and twirled lassos.[40]

The rich decor in the restaurants and bars completed the kaleidoscopic impression of authenticity. An important feature of the decor were the dioramas and panoramas included in many rooms, most importantly Löwenbräu, and the Rheinterrasse, where illusionistic storms were regularly staged. The diorama at Löwenbräu, framed a painted view of the Zugspitze, the highest peak in the Bavarian Alps. The panorama surrounding the Rheinterrasse, built into Haus Vaterland's domed, circular section, re-created a stretch of the Rhine in papier-mâché.[41]

Haus Vaterland's illusionistic attractions pale almost into insignificance when compared to the much more elaborate rides and spectacles at Coney Island's parks. Yet Haus Vaterland's relatively diminutive attractions delighted legions of young Berliners with limited means, plus crowds of provincial German and foreign visitors to Berlin. In October 1929, scarcely a year after opening, Haus Vaterland welcomed its one millionth guest.[42]

Haus Vaterland's popularity continued through the remaining Weimar and also the Nazi years, when emphasis was placed on the specifically German attractions (although two small foreign bars re-creating Japan and Italy were added, anticipating the 1940 Tripartite Pact among those two countries and Germany). As a result of the Nazi takeover, the Jewish Kempinski family was forced to leave Germany, after first selling Haus

Vaterland to new Aryan owners for a ridiculously small sum of money. During World War II, despite heavy British and American bombing, Haus Vaterland was regularly crowded with customers, who eagerly flocked to any entertainment that would temporarily take their minds off the war.[43]

Haus Vaterland was destroyed by bombs on February 2, 1945, during a daytime air raid. Only the structure's sooty stone walls, surrounding a jumble of broken building parts, remained standing. Yet Haus Vaterland enjoyed many more years of life, first as a symbol of defeated Berlin's will to rebuild itself, then as a focus for new rivalries spawned by the Cold War.

At the end of World War II, when the victorious Allies divided Germany and Berlin into zones of military occupation, Potsdamer Platz was the point from which Berlin's sector lines were drawn. Haus Vaterland, while included in the Russian sector, was connected through two sets of doors to the British and American sectors. Thus it happened that in the postwar confrontation between Russia and the West, Haus Vaterland occupied an uncannily strategic position.

Cafe Vaterland was reopened in the bombed-out and otherwise disused building in 1947. Acclaimed by the Berlin press for representing "the unrestrained will of Berliners to rebuild their father city,"[44] the cafe became a center for espionage, black-marketeering, illegal currency exchange and flight from the Soviets—risky activities precipitated by the cafe's location astride the sector lines. On June 17, 1953, during a violent labor strike in the eastern sector, Cafe Vaterland was destroyed by fire and subsequently closed for all time.

When the Berlin Wall was erected in 1961, Haus Vaterland's ruin was transferred to the East. Yet, remarkably, it was returned to West Berlin in 1972, when the city's senate purchased from East Germany an 8.5-hektar parcel of border land (needed for a new roadway) that included the domed building's ruin.[45] Beginning in the spring of 1976, Haus Vaterland was systematically demolished by the West Berlin construction firm Makri and Losch. By the fall of that year, the shattered amusement palace was reduced to 600 tons of iron and steel, which were sold as scrap.

Compared to Haus Vaterland's demise, the fate suffered by Coney Island—today a seedy, shrunken approximation of its former self—seems unexciting. Not incendiary bombs, but accidental fires and attrition, followed by a program of misguided urban renewal, destroyed Coney Island's glory. Said the writer Mario Puzo, "what a slothful bedraggled harridan it has become, endangered by the violence of its poor and helpless people, as well as by city planners who would improve it out of existence."[46]

In 1911, Dreamland was consumed by flames. In 1944, fire destroyed all but a few of the rides at Luna Park, which ceased operating two years later. In 1966, Steeplechase was closed and razed.

Yet even before Luna Park and Steeplechase disappeared,

16

17

plans for transforming Coney Island were in force. Already in 1938, "a cleaner and more orderly recreation area"[47] at Coney Island was projected by New York City's Park Commissioner Robert Moses, who called for renewed emphasis on sea-bathing at the expense of the midway, prescribing widened beaches and a lengthened boardwalk, landscaped play areas, and public parking lots.

Through the years, through far-reaching programs of demolition and greening, Moses's prescriptions for Coney Island have largely been filled. Today, Dreamland's former site is occupied by the New York Aquarium, an antiseptically modern educational facility with little architectural merit.[48]

Occupying Luna Park's former site are the high-rise buildings of a $123 million public housing project, one of several constructed at Coney Island at the cost of demolishing long-established communities of summer cottages and small, year-round homes.[49] The new public housing exists in a vacuum, lacking the former communities' organically developed amenities and coherence.

The remaining amusements at Coney Island are garish and decayed. Only some isolated landmarks, among them the Cyclone roller coaster and Nathan's Famous restaurant, renowned for its hot dogs since 1916, remind curious visitors of the area's lost glory.

Bleak and dilapidated, Coney Island is no longer "the world's largest playground," the permanent repository of leftover world's fair attractions, the primal model for amusement facilities overseas. Yet the internationalism traditionally reflected at Coney Island today continues, if anything much more meaningfully than in the past, at a neighboring beachfront community, Brighton Beach.

There, some thirty thousand Russian expatriates, who call the area "Little Odessa," have settled in recent years, changing the face of Brighton Beach Avenue with Russian food stores, souvenir shops, and cafes.[50] The presence of these businesses, and of the Russians, testifies, like Haus Vaterland's ruin, to the international reality of the Cold War. Yet the Russian emigres, one of America's latest wave of immigrants, also perpetuate the international character that has traditionally been America's, and particularly New York's greatest strength. While originally created, then, to provide the most lighthearted, even mindless, distractions, both Coney Island and Haus Vaterland accurately if obliquely reflect some of the forces that have given twentieth-century life its distinctive shape.

Notes

1. Josef Durm and Heinrich Wagner, "Oeffentliche-Vergnuegungs-Lokale und Festhallen," *Handbuch der Architektur* (Darmstadt: J.Ph. Diel's Verlag, 1885), vol. 4, 78.

2. Jo Ransom in the essay "Coney by the Sea" describes the amusement district as the "summer safety valve for the most explosively packed metropolis in the world." See Alexander Klein, ed., *The Empire City: A Treasury of New York* (1955; repr., Freeport, N.Y.: Books for Libraries Press, 1971), 169.

3. The name Coney Island is thought to come from the Dutch *konijn eisland* (rabbit island), given to the area because of the many rabbits there. See Rem Koolhaas, *Delirious New York: A Retrospective Manifesto for Manhattan* (New York: Oxford University Press, 1978), 23. Chapter 3 of *Delirious*, "Coney Island: The Technology of the Fantastic," 22–65, provided much of the factual and descriptive information in this study. Equally helpful was one of Koolhaas's principal sources, *History of Coney Island* (New York: Burroughs & Co. Publishers, 1904).

4. According to Koolhaas, *Delirious*, 24–25, the tower originally was constructed for the 1876 Centennial Exposition in Philadelphia, then later re-erected at Coney Island. The Centennial tower is important for prefiguring many later world's fair attractions, including human attractions, subsequently re-created at Coney Island.

5. On Haus Vaterland, see "Haus Vaterland—eine Grossgaststaette in Berlin," *Deutsche Bauzeitung* 62 (May 11, 1929), 337–44.

6. Haus Vaterland opening night program (Berlin, 1928), 1.

7. On Berlin's Lunapark, see "Der Lunapark: eine moderne Vergnuegungsstatte nach Amerikanischem Vorbild," *Die Bauwelt* (1910): 15. That Berlin's Lunapark was not named for New York's Luna Park, but for Paul Lincke's popular operetta *Frau Luna*, is suggested by Jockel Turm, "Damals—auf den Terrassen von Halensee," *Berliner Tagesspiegel* (May 9, 1954): 8. That New York's Luna Park was not named for the airship *Luna IV* but for Dundy's sister Luna in Des Moines, Iowa, is suggested by Edo McCullough, *World's Fair Midways* (New York: Exposition Press, 1966), 57.

8. Ransom, "Coney," 168.

9. Haus Vaterland opening program, 4.

10. Robert Hughes, *The Shock of the New* (New York: Alfred A. Knopf, 1982), 9.

11. For example, the previously little-known Japanese prints exhibited at the Paris Exposition Universelle of 1867 profoundly affected the work of many French artists and, through their endeavors, the development of modern art.

12. On *Amerikanismus*, see Theodore Lueddecke, "Amerikanismus als Schlagwort and Tatsache," *Deutsche Rundschau* (March 1930): 214–19.

13. According to Thorstein Veblen, not inventive genius but the capacity to learn from others' mistakes explains Imperial Germany's phenomenal industrial growth. See his *Imperial Germany and the Industrial Revolution* (1915; repr., New York: The Viking Press, 1954), 194.

14. *The Coney Island Souvenir: An Accurate and Reliable Directory* (Brooklyn, N.Y.: William Patton Griffith, 1883), 49.

15. Ibid., 48.

16. Koolhaas, *Delirious*, 27.

17. Ibid.

18. *History*, 23.

19. Koolhaas, *Delirious*, 30.

20. On the original Trip to the Moon, see Richard H. Barry, *Snap-Shots on the Midway of the Pan-American Exposition* (Buffalo: Robert Allen Reid Publisher, 1901), 37–42.

21. McCullough, *World's Fair*, 55.

22. Koolhaas, *Delirious*, 34–35.

23. Ibid., 44.

24. Ibid., 42–43 and 45–47.

25. *History of Coney Island*, 28.

26. Robert Shackelton, *The Book of New York* (Philadelphia: The Penn Publishing Company, 1917), 341.

27. "Der Lunapark," 15.

28. *Der Lunapark im Jubilaeumsjahre* (Berlin: Lunapark Gesellschaft, 1929), 25.

29. Ibid., 27.

30. According to Haus Vaterland's artistic director from 1935–43, Richard Fleischer, with whom the author spoke several times in Berlin during the winter of 1975–76.

31. On Haus Potsdam, see Otto Sarrazin and Friedrich Schultze, "Der Neubau 'Haus Potsdam' in Berlin," *Zentralblatt der Bauverwaltung* (May 18, 1912): 254–57.

32. Haus Potsdam's architectural symbolism remained intact, even after the building was converted, in the modern style, into Haus Vaterland. The juxtaposition of old and new architectural elements made Haus Vaterland in effect an emblem for the Weimar Republic, which attempted at the ministerial level to be a liberal, reformist democracy but which retained the Kaiser's military, judiciary and civil service more or less intact, despite these entrenched groups' allegiance to conservative ideals.

33. On Stahl-Urach's conversion, see "Haus Vaterland," 337–44.

34. "Haus Vaterland," *Germania* (August 31, 1928): 4.

35. Walter Kiaulehn, *Berlin: Schicksal einer Weltstadt* (Berlin: Bilderstein Verlag, 1958), 228.

36. See Richard Huelsenbeck, "Berlin . . . Endstation," in *Hier Schreibt Berlin: ein Dokument der zwanziger Jahre*, ed. Herbert Guenther (Munich: Paul List Verlag, 1963), 196–99.

37. Fleischer, in interviews with the author, always called Haus Vaterland "my factory."

38. Ibid.

39. Haus Vaterland opening program, 9, 50–51, and 20.

40. Ibid., 15 and 26. According to Fleischer the Wild West cowboys were actual American performers, while most of the other entertainers were Germans in fancy dress.

41. Kiaulehn, *Berlin*, 237, suggests that the real antecedents of Haus Vaterland's Rheinterrasse were not Coney Island spectacles but the many panorama buildings—polygonal structures whose interior walls supported continuous paintings—constructed in Berlin during the nineteenth century. On Berlin panoramas, see *Berlin und seine Bauten* (Berlin: Verlag von Wilhelm Ernst & Sohn, 1896) vol. 2, 534–37.

42. Fleisher, interview.

43. On entertainments in wartime Berlin, see William A. Shirer, *Berlin Diary: The Journal of a Foreign Correspondent 1934–1941* (New York: Alfred A. Knopf, 1941), 207.

44. "Berlins gemeutlischste Waermehalle," *Neues Deutschland* (Berlin), December 23, 1947: 4.

45. See "Bald Baubeginn fuer eine Entlastungsstrasse," *Die Welt* (Berlin), July 20, 1972: 2.

46. Quoted in *Fodor's New York City and Atlantic City* (New York and London: Fodor's Travel Guides, 1987), 144.

47. *The WPA Guide to New York City* (1939; repr. New York: Pantheon Books, 1982), 475.

48. "To be visited for the contents rather than the envelope" is one critical appraisal of the New York Aquarium, designed by architects Harrison & Abramowitz and opened in 1955. See Elliot Willensky and Norval White, *AIA Guide to New York City*, 3rd ed. (San Diego, New York, and London: Harcourt Brace Jovanovich Publishers, 1988), 711.

49. On the housing projects, including some commendable examples, see Ibid., 713.

50. See "Soviet Returnees Anger Emigres in Brooklyn," *New York Times*, January 27, 1987: 27.

Claudia Skoda

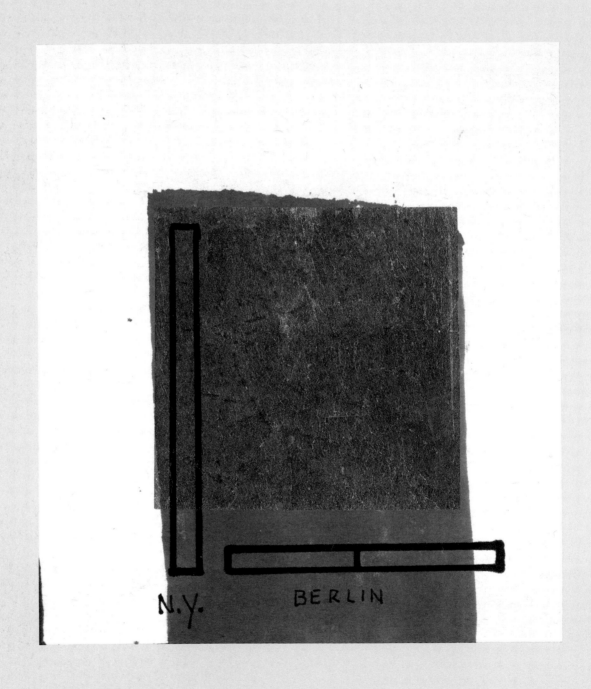

John Russell

There is in me nothing of the oracle, whether Delphic or otherwise. For me to speculate about the future of either Berlin or New York would be ridiculous.

But the alternatives like and unlike have lodged themselves in my mind. How do they apply to the coupling of Berlin with New York? Are these two great cities like one another? Or unlike one another? Or is it that sometimes they are almost like twins, and at other times different beyond all reconciliation?

Good questions. But questions as to which my point of view is distinctly, entirely, and perhaps hopelessly private. Sometimes when I dream of New York, it is as Henry Hudson first saw it when he nosed his ship toward the point at which the ocean meets the great river that now bears Hudson's name. Sometimes when I dream of Berlin, I see it as it was in the reign of Frederick the Great— a city in which an ugly thing was hard to find. (We know from Schinkel's painted panoramas, which are now in his little pavilion in the park of Schloss Charlottenburg, that even in a later Berlin was a city almost without flaw.)

When I move a little bit forward in time, the two cities seem to run in tandem, even if the chronology gets mixed. I see the New York in which Walt Whitman could go to the opera every night of the week and hear voices of a quality undreamed of today. I see Berlin in the mid-1920s with a musical life that could attract Wilhelm Furtwängler, Bruno Walter, Arturo Toscanini, Otto Klemperer, and Erich Kleiber in one and the same week.

Other associations make the two cities seem even more out of step. In no other city have movies been made that were as numerous, as original, and as strongly characterized as was the case in Berlin between the making of *The Student of Prague* and the making of *The Blue Angel*. New York excels as a backdrop for the movies, but as a place in which they are *made*, from the first frame to the last, it hardly exists.

In the matter of criminality, the great

days of the Berlin underworld would be hard to beat. As to the bad behavior of public officials, on the other hand, New York in its plodding way has racked up a very high score in the 1980s. Where affordable public housing is concerned, I look back with tenderness on the social experiments that were made in Berlin at a time when New York lagged far behind.

If we are to think in ethnic terms, there is a difference between the two cities that is huge, ever-present, inescapable. New York derives its life, its energy and its inspiration in large part from its Jewish population. Native Berliners are what they always were— paragons of wit and masters of insubordination— but a great city without Jews risks a terrible dullness.

Like and unlike— the discussion need never end. New York has never had, and never will have, a theater like the Schaubühne of Peter Stein. Its great department stores are in decline, whereas KDW is Babylonian beyond the dreams of Emile Zola. In New York in the 1990s, there is much that is brutal and dehumanizing, but there is also a handmade, unimported cultural life that is almost unimaginably intense. Berlin in that context is still a divided and a mutilated city, no matter how much is done in the way of subsidy and importation.

Unlike, then. But also *like*: these are two cities in which we get a charge of energy, every day of the year, that we get nowhere else. May it always be so!

Thomas Messer

BERLIN	BOTH	NEW YORK
	big	
	arrogant	
	fast	
	with-it	
	crowded	
	impatient	
	loud	
	flashy	
	cynical	
	ill-mannered	
	witty	
	demanding	
	asocial	
river city		harbor
germanic		anglo-saxon
destroyed and rebuilt		rebuilt and destroyed
ex-capital		quasi-capital
	multi-leveled	
	money-minded	
	culture-conscious	
defensive		relaxed
federal		local
	hedonistic	
	sexy	
	gourmand	
burdened by history		ignorant of history
monarchic and liberal		democratic and mafioso
militaristic stigma		commercial image
visionary		narcissistic
dreams of glory		dreams of money
integrated		self-contained
scheisse		shit
	pretentious	
	repugnant	
	perverse	
	insufferable	
	admirable	
	marvelous	
	exemplary	
	essential	

Johannes Fritsche

Ride the New York subway for the first time, and you're caught in a continually vibrating web of noise that suffuses tunnels and stations. Until you get used to it. Look out across the roofs of New York and see antennas, chimney pipes, watertowers, and all the exposed internal organs responsible for the digestion and metabolism of buildings. All unfolds in a free rhythm creating the impression that these things live a life of their own— the impersonal motions and unconsciously produced surplus of a city that has denied all organic mediations and transitions as traditionally defined. Especially in the light of day. New York's sun bleaches out every nuance, buffer, shock absorption between things and human beings. Especially when it comes to the plans of its buildings and streets.

I don't recall which philosopher defined the main purpose of architecture as establishing a harmonious relationship between horizontal and vertical. New York, at any rate, does just the opposite. The horizontal street grid and the truly merciless verticals of the skyscrapers obliterate every relationship between these two fundamental axes of spatial orientation. The grid was designed for pragmatic commercial reasons, and out of the democratic consideration of obviating the centralization and hierarchy of European cities and their distinction of certain places and structures as sacred. The offshoot was a loss of the protective nature of every mediation— and a gain in metaphysical quality.

This was a cause of disquiet to Julius Hardner, an architect who in 1898 envisioned diagonal boulevards to create lines of sight that "would rest on a certain object instead of ending in a perspective of nothingness." The clumsy but useful philosophical formula of keeping nothingness invisible was an effort of history, tradition, and culture. It implied a tying of individuals and things to traditions within which they could transcend their solitary, isolated nature, and become suffused with experience and history. Inanimate things would be brought to life by creating a fine web between them and human beings offering both mutual protection and mutual connection.

Walter Benjamin called this fine web the aura of things, and despite all cultural pessimism, he knew that its dissolution was an ambiguous phenomenon. The aura of European cities historically always involved an element of violence. When this aura is destroyed, violence can emerge in its naked form. But what also emerges is its opposite pole, a second immediacy in which nature reappears transfigured, as for instance in the beautiful animals of New York.

Since it is devoid of aura, New York is unerotic. The term "aura" might be paraphrased by reference to Goethe, who said that "Every living thing generates an atmosphere around itself." Taken literally, meteorologically, this would make New York an extraterrestrial city par excellence, under continual bombardment from both horizontal and vertical directions, bringing it closer to gnosis. Instead of an aura, it's as if an inconspicuous, godless blessing hangs over the city like a perpetual, high-pitched vibration and merges with the pervading fabric of noise like the twittering of birds in the great palm houses of the past century.

Claude Lévi-Strauss once said that the cities of the New World had apparently decayed before they had a chance to grow old. The critic of historical and eschatological thinking was well aware of the theological aspect of this continual fading, and of its reverse: the presence of history as an ageless, transient image. Perhaps it is from this surplus that New Yorkers derive their incredibly friendly alertness and energetic presence.

In brief, New York is a city without atmosphere, and therefore blessed with an ability to act and react in the highest degree. Berlin, in contrast, has to watch out—compared to, say, Paris, it has too little atmosphere to live and, at least as of now, too much to die.

Part Two
1918–1945

1a & b. Contrasting images of the modern megalopolis: public splendor, private misery in New York and Berlin. From Mumford, *The Culture of Cities;* Landesbildskelle, Berlin.

Searching for the New Dimensions of the City

Nicholas Bullock

Nicholas Bullock, a founding member of the Martin Centre at Cambridge University, teaches at the Architecture Association and at Cambridge. He is the author with James Read of The Movement for Housing Reform in Germany and France 1840–1914. *He is currently working on a book on housing and reconstruction in London from 1940 to 1951 entitled* Architecture, Housing, and the Welfare State.

In the 1920s, the large city or *Weltstadt*, such as New York, London, Paris, or Berlin, stood as a compelling image of modernity. To many Germans emerging in the mid-twenties from the turmoil of the postwar years New York represented that modern city. Exciting, brash, ruthless, a mixture of abject poverty and wealth beyond dreams, it represented the most intense symbol of urban society. Conveniently remote yet vividly imaginable, New York appears in poetry, film, and painting of the period; for architects, for musicians, for filmmakers, New York was an inexhaustible source of images of the new age.

Berlin seemed to share many of New York's qualities. It offered something of the same excitement, and it shared many of the same failings—the closing out of nature, the dirt, noise, and misery of high-density tenement housing. Both cities evoked very different responses from individuals who regarded them as the shape of things to come—for better or for worse. Writers such as Oswald Spengler, who saw the *Weltstadt* as symptomatic of the decline of the West, denounced Berlin and New York as terrible symbols of the coming collapse;[1] for others, the city represented an extraordinary concentration of innovation and invention in the sciences, technology, and the arts.[2] More generally, there seemed to be a willingness in the modern city dweller to try something new.

To Spengler and his followers the only solution to the problem of the city was to abandon it, to retreat back to the world of the small market town and to the rural and small-town values of the past. But for those who maintained—despite poor housing, a high crime rate, poverty, and a tendency to choke itself as it struggled to grow—that the city was essential to the civilization of the West, the solution was transformation.

Lewis Mumford, a young New Yorker with knowledge of European planning and whose book *The Culture of Cities* (1938),[3] was to influence the views of many in the United States and Europe, believed that transformation was possible. For Mumford, cities such as New York or Berlin were a product of the failings of the nineteenth century. The previous hundred years had seen the rise of "Coketown," then of "Megalopolis"; to continue down this same path might lead to a "Tyranopolis" or a "Nekropolis." But this was not inevitable. Correctly understood and properly encouraged, he believed, the positive forces in modern society would shape the city afresh in just the same way that the cities of the past had been shaped by their own societies. Looking across the globe, to the few experiments in urban planning in America such as the Greenbelt towns, to Russia, but particularly to Europe, Mumford could point to fragments of this new "biotechnic" order.[4] Concerned with the relationship between society and the city, he had something to say about the way in which a biotechnic society might be organized but could only hint at the forms the new order would take. Were New York or Berlin, with all their obvious inadequacies and failings, to become the norm of an urban society? Or would new forms be created for the twentieth-century city, just as new ways of feeling and thinking had transformed the arts and the sciences?

In 1938, the same year that Mumford's book was published,

2. *Images of the new Berlin: a collage by Martin Wagner. From Wohnungswirtschaft.*

3a & b. *Gideon's* Spirit of the New *in painting and architecture: Picasso,* L'Arlesienne, *1911–12, and Gropius, Bauhaus building, 1926.*

Sigfried Giedion, a young Swiss art historian, was attempting to address a number of related questions. As the Charles Eliot Norton Professor at Harvard University, Giedion gave a series of lectures and seminars, subsequently published as *Space, Time, and Architecture*,[5] in which he set out to explore with his audience what he regarded as the emerging cultural synthesis appropriate to the twentieth century. For Giedion, as for his teacher Heinrich Wölfflin, and for Wölfflin's teacher Jacob Burckhardt, the arts had been a key to understanding the character of an age. Architecture and, by extension, town planning were in Giedion's eyes uniquely qualified to "reflect the inner tendencies of the time" and to serve as a "general index" of the age. More than the other arts, Giedion claimed, "architecture can give us an insight into this process just because it is so bound up with the life of a period as a whole. Everything in it, from its fondness for certain shapes to the approaches to specific building problems which it finds most natural, reflects the conditions of the age from which it springs."[6] To look dispassionately and forensically at the qualities of the new architecture was thus to examine, in a highly selective but manageable way, one of the key strands in the development of a modern culture.

Space, Time, and Architecture was one of the first and most influential accounts of the origins and ideas of the new architecture on either side of the Atlantic.[7] Giedion's task at Harvard was not simply to give a history of recent architectural developments in Europe: he wished to establish the authority of the new architecture as the work of a small coterie of avant-garde architects and as possessing something of the same standing as the great architectural periods of the past. The lectures and seminars were a great success. Who better to act as an ambassador of these ideas in America than Giedion: as a student of Wölfflin and as bearer of the standard of art-historical scholarship exemplified by Burckhardt, Giedion was assured of a sympathetic hearing.

What makes all of this of immediate interest to us is a retrospective look at what were regarded as key developments. From a perspective distanced by fifty years, Giedion's account appears highly selective, albeit in a convincing and, for its time, astonishingly sure-footed way.

Giedion's "Index of the Modern Age"

Giedion saw it as his task "to select from the vast body of available historical material only relatively few facts. History is not a compilation of facts, but an insight into a moving process of life."[8] Working in this way, he hoped to bring together the elements of a "true, if hidden unity, a secret synthesis"[9] that he believed to be emerging in contemporary civilization. By looking at common approaches and "the simularity of methods that are in use today in architecture, construction, painting, city planning, and science,"[10] he argued that he would be able to evaluate the nature of modern culture.

The approach he follows has parallels with those of Wölfflin and Burckhardt: architecture is taken as the index of the larg-

232

er cultural identity of the age and is itself seen as the product not of mere technical concerns but of a synthesis of a variety of different developments. For Burckhardt, perspective and the new sense of space that it implied was a key to understanding Renaissance civilization. For Giedion, a new perception of space as evident in the arts as well as mathematics and the sciences was one of the key elements of the modern age. The fascination with simultaneity lay at the heart of Cubism and Futurism and was one of the attributes of modern life, a fact confirmed by the contemporary physics of Einstein: "Space in modern physics is conceived of as relative to a moving point of reference, not as the absolute and static entity of the baroque style of Newton. And in modern art, for the first time since the Renaissance, a new conception of space leads to a self-conscious enlargement of our ways of perceiving space. . . . The presentation of objects from several points of view introduced a principle which is intimately bound up with modern life—simultaneity. It is a temporal coincidence that Einstein should have begun his famous work, *Elektrodynamik bewegter Koerper*, in 1905 with a careful definition of simultaneity."[11] If Cubism involved a redefinition of ways of seeing space, Futurism, so Giedion claimed, offered a new way of understanding time. Taken together they gave rise to a new simultaneous way of understanding our world in terms of space and time.

This radical perception of space was one precondition for a new architecture; the other was to be found in the extraordinary technological developments of the nineteenth and twentieth centuries. The nineteenth century, dismissed by Giedion as an "Age of Transition," had been immensely inventive in science and engineering, areas of achievement that reflected intellectual abilities. But in the absence of the harmony of thought and feeling, of scientific and artistic understanding, which had been characteristic of the great periods of the past, these achievements had somehow not been sufficient to lead to the establishment of an architecture appropriately expressive of the age. Hence, in Giedion's view, architects' preoccupation with the variety of historical styles and their (general) inability to incorporate technical advances into the mainstream of architecture, so poignantly expressed at St. Pancras Station in London by the separation of Balow and Ordish's train shed and Scott's Great Northern Hotel.

Together, however, the new space-time conception and the advances in technology could produce a new architecture. In buildings such as the Bauhaus and the Villa Savoie and in new approaches to city planning, which exemplified the space-time conception of space and the use of the new technology, Giedion claimed with pride to see emerging the signature of the modern age. Here were achievements that would, in his terms, stand comparison with Burckhardt's Florence or Wölfflin's Rome. Giedion's success in publicizing the cause of modern architecture by providing it with a pedigree comparable to that of the great periods of the past can be seen from the influence that *Space, Time, and Architecture* was to exert over the next twenty or so years. It was a heroic achievement.

But turning aside from the grand sweep of history with the procession of alternating periods of transition and unity that

4a & b. The neues Bauen and new forms of construction: dry construction of Gropius's house at the Weissenhof Siedlung, Stuttgart, and prefabricated to panel system as Ernst May's Roemerstadt Siedlung, Frankfurt. From Bericht ueber die Siedlung in Stuttgart am Weissenhof and Das Neue Frankfurt.

Giedion describes, how sensitive a guide would *Space, Time, and Architecture* have been for those trying to understand the detailed web of debate, ideas, and contacts that lay behind the buildings and projects in a city such as Berlin? The new architecture was certainly more visible in Berlin than in any other major European city: by 1931 there was already a guide book, *Neues Bauen in Berlin*,[12] published in response to popular interest in the subject, which listed well over one hundred individual buildings and larger complexes under construction around the suburbs of Berlin. Was it already possible to see in Berlin the emergence of the new architecture, or *neues Bauen*, which Giedion described and which might harness the advances of the modern age to reforming and reshaping the city?

The Debate over the Neues Bauen in Berlin: Architecture and the Machine

Surveying the central themes of architectural debate in Berlin in the late 1920s, it is possible to recognize many of the ingredients of Giedion's interpretation of the new architecture. Thus one of the central subjects of discussion was the positive benefits that would flow from advances in technology. The case for recognizing the liberating qualities of the machine that had been gradually assembled over almost twenty years before 1925, in the prewar Werkbund debates and in the writings of figures as varied as Frank Lloyd Wright and Theo van Doesburg, was now widely accepted in circles such as the Werkbund, which represented the more progressive elements in design in Germany.[13] Exploited for selfish ends and with no controls to secure the good of the community, industrialization might lead to a megalopolis or New York. But rightly understood and correctly mastered, the new technology could put Mumford's biotechnic order within grasp.

For Walter Gropius, the kind of factory-scale mass production that was being introduced to the automobile industry in America suggested new possibilities for the production of a whole range of goods.[14] The promise of these new methods was that they would enable the designer to break away from the dilemma that had undermined the development of the arts and crafts movement both before the war and in the immediate postwar years when crafts had seemed to offer young radical designers an important alternative form of production. By emphasizing that these new forms of production might exert as significant an effect on form as crafts had done on handicraft production, it was possible for Gropius and others to argue that the machine, correctly used, would continue the tradition of "right making" that lay at the heart of the Arts and Crafts approach. More important, by making it possible to produce large numbers of well-designed objects at a price that was acceptable to the average individual, it would make good design generally available in a way that the Arts and Crafts movement had never been able to.

Equally important in the eyes of those who had responded to Ruskin's and William Morris's call for a change in the position of the worker and a revaluation of the value of work for itself, the new methods of production could now be presented, at

234

least by those who hailed Taylorism and the techniques of scientific management as an impartial and scientific basis for assessing the workload of the individual, as a way of liberating the worker *through* the machine.[15] Writing from the perspective of the mid-thirties in *The New Architecture and the Bauhaus*, Gropius argued: "In the last resort mechanization can have only one object: to abolish the individual's physical toil of providing himself with the necessities of existence in order that hand and brain may be set free for some higher order of activity."[16]

For architects such as Gropius, acceptance of the machine and the new forms of production that went with it would have far-reaching consequences. One of the most important was to strengthen the case for standardization, both in design and in production. For Gropius as for many members of the Werkbund, standardization not only offered economic advantages, it also implied a discipline to design and form that might usefully counter the excesses of individualism or the mindless pursuit of the frivolities of fashion. As in the past, the formal standards of the so-called type form, or Le Corbusier's "objects-types," offered a path to good design: "In all great epochs of history the existence of standards—that is the conscious adoption of type-forms—has been the criterion of a . . . well-ordered society."[17]

For those who saw the task of the designer as providing for everybody, not simply "ministering to the swinish luxury of the rich,"[18] standardization combined with the advantages of mass production also suggested a way of attacking some of the most pressing of social problems. Gropius argued: "The creation of standard types for all practical commodities of everyday use is a social necessity."[19] Standardization, by analogy with the production of Ford's Model-T, would ensure that the general population would be able to afford the well-designed goods that had previously only been available to the affluent. This would be true not only for consumer goods and furnishings but, as many writers in the Werkbund's magazine *Die Form* were to argue, would apply with equal force to architecture, particularly to housing and the production of *Existenzminimum* dwellings.[20]

Complementary to the arguments for standardization was the case made for the rationalization that would be necessary with the introduction of new forms of production. For architects and designers, the fascination with Taylorism and rationalization was as strong (and uncritical) as it was in other parts of German life. In his book on the Bauhaus buildings at Dessau, Gropius emphasized the ways in which design and construction were envisaged to minimize effort and costs in accordance with Taylor's principles; in Taut's book *Die neue Wohnung*, the benefits of rationalization and scientific management were presented as the key to the design of the "new dwelling."[21]

As in the motor industry, where Ford's engineers had achieved at Highland Park remarkable reductions in the time and cost of manufacturing Model-T Fords, so the younger generation of architects believed that the building industry too would be transformed by the process of rationalization. Many argued,

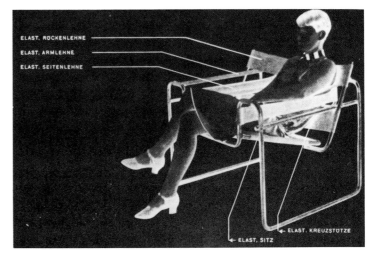

5a & b. Products of the new approach to design: light fixture by Christian Dell and tubular steel chair by Marcel Breuer. From Wingler, Kunstchul-Reform 1900–1933 and Wilk, Marcel Breuer.

der grundriß errechnet sich aus folgenden faktoren

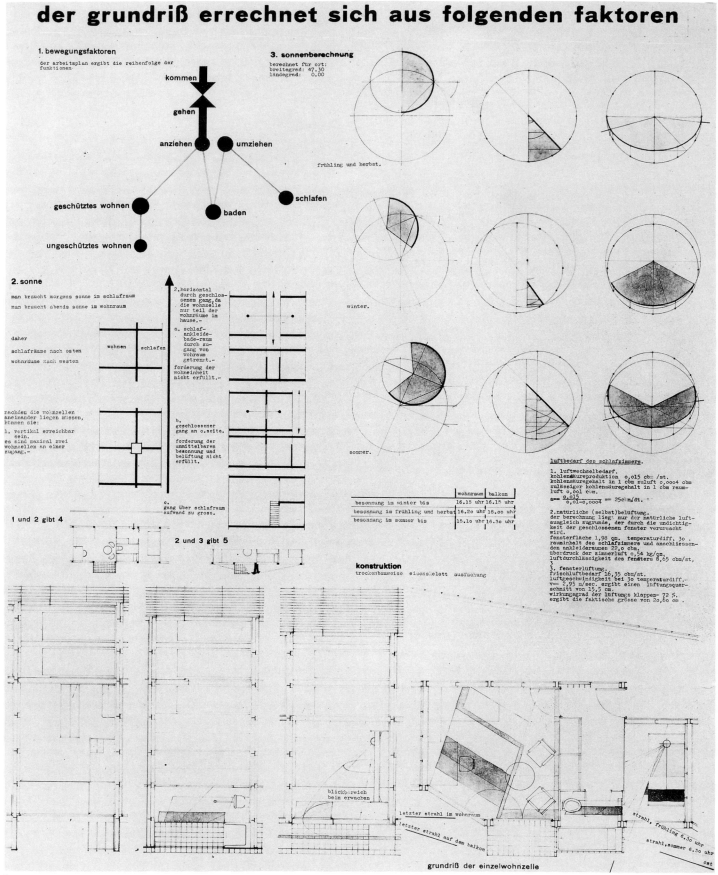

1. bewegungsfaktoren

der arbeitsplan ergibt die reihenfolge der
funktionen

kommen
gehen
anziehen   umziehen
geschütztes wohnen   baden   schlafen
ungeschütztes wohnen

3. sonnenberechnung

berechnet für ort:
breitegrad: 47.30
ländegrad: 0.00

frühling und herbst.

winter.

sommer.

2. sonne

man braucht morgens sonne im schlafraum
man braucht abends sonne im wohnraum

daher

schlafräume nach osten
wohnräume nach westen

nachdem die wohnzellen
aneinander liegen müssen,
können sie:

1. vertikal erreichbar
sein.
es sind maximal zwei
wohnzellen an einer
zugang.-

wohnen   schlafen

1 und 2 gibt 4

2 und 3 gibt 5

2. horizontal
durch geschlos-
senen gang, da
die wohnzelle
nur teil der
wohnräume im
hause.-

a. schlaf-
ankleide-
bade-raum
durch zu-
gang von
wohnraum
getrennt.-
förderung der
wohneinheit
nicht erfüllt.-

b.
geschlossener
gang an o.seite.

forderung der
unmittelbaren
besonnung und
belüftung nicht
erfüllt.-

c.
gang über schlafraum
aufwand zu groß.

konstruktion

trockenbauweise eisenskelett ausfachung

	wohnraum	balkon
besonnung im winter bis	16.15 uhr	16.15 uhr
besonnung im frühling und herbst	16.2o uhr	18.oo uhr
besonnung im sommer bis	15.1o uhr	16.3o uhr

luftbedarf des schlafzimmers.

1. luftwechselbedarf.
kohlensäureproduktion o,015 cbm/st.
kohlensäuregehalt in 1 cbm zuluft o,ooo4 cbm
zulässiger kohlensäuregehalt in 1 cbm raum-
luft o,oo1 cbm.

$$a = \frac{o,015}{o,o1 - o,ooo4} = 25\,cbm/st.$$

2. natürliche (selbst)belüftung.
der berechnung liegt nur der natürliche luft-
ausgleich zugrunde, der durch die undichtig-
keit der geschlossenen fenster verursacht
wird.
fensterfläche 1,98 qm. temperaturdiff. 3o.
rauminhalt des schlafzimmers und anschliessen-
den ankleideraumes 22,o cbm.
überdruck der zimmerluft o,54 kg/qm.
luftdurchlässigkeit des fensters 8,65 cbm/st.

3. fensterlüftung.
frischluftbedarf 16,35 cbm/st.
luftgeschwindigkeit bei 3o temperaturdiff.-
v= 2,95 m/sec. ergibt einen lüftungsquer-
schnitt von 15,5 cm.
wirkungsgrad der lüftungs klappen= 72 %.
ergibt die faktische grösse von 2o,6o cm.

blickbereich
beim erwachen

letzter strahl im wohnraum
letzter strahl auf dem balkon

strahl, frühling 6.3o uhr
strahl, sommer 6.3o uhr
ost

grundriß der einzelwohnzelle

6

like Gropius, that outmoded forms of wet construction would be replaced by dry assembly of factory-produced components; at the Weissenhof exhibition, the houses designed by Gropius and Max Taut set out to demonstrate the advantages in the speed of construction that rationalization of construction might bring.[22] Building on the work of the Deutscher Normenausschuss in rationalizing the design and production of components such as doors and windows during the war, and during the period of austerity building that followed, such architects as Ernst May sought to reduce costs by limiting the number of types and increasing production runs to achieve lower unit costs.[23]

The new forms of construction like those encouraged by government organizations and explored by May at Roemerstadt led to new architectural forms as logical in their reflection of construction as the old forms of vernacular architecture.[24] Using mass production and factory prefabrication, the new building forms were as different from the buildings of traditional construction as the furniture and light fittings of Marcel Breuer or Christian Dell were from the products of the small craft workshop.[25]

The New Architect

The impact of these new methods of production on the role of the architect and designer would also be far-reaching. Industrial production design required the architects and designers to adopt new roles. In the way that filmmakers or photographers such as Carl Meyer or Willi Muenzenberg or poets such as Bertolt Brecht claimed to record the reality of the city as they saw it, responding to the rhythms of urban life and observing them impartially, so architects and designers too looked for a reorientation.[26] In place of the artist/architect who created architecture as a reflection of his or her own fantasy, architects, like the designers of furniture or of household goods, now sought to approach the problems of form in some rational way. In place of the subjective and the personal, there was now an emphasis on the matter-of-fact, the impersonal, the scientific. While stressing the difference between the task of the architect and the engineer, architects were now happy to emphasize the parallels between their work and that of the engineer. Le Corbusier spoke for many German architects when he urged architects to learn from the "Engineers' Approach."[27]

An extreme expression of this pursuit of the objective and the rational in architecture might be found in the approach of Hannes Meyer. Although his designs for the League of Nations building or the St. Peter's School in Basel should be regarded as highly self-conscious and heavily charged with metaphors for what a scientific approach to design might produce, he argued that the architect should proceed with the dispassionate and unsentimental vigor of the engineer. He attempted to show how the design of a student's room could be determined simply by a systematic consideration of what he called functional requirements, such as connections between activities, orientation, and isolation.

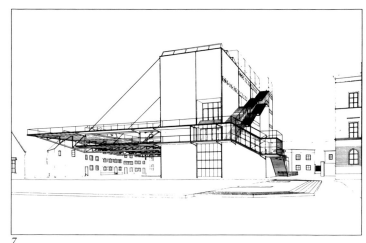

7

6. *The rationalization of design: the layout of a student's room, from Hannes Meyer's course at the Bauhaus.* Bauhaus-Archiv, Berlin.

7. *Hannes Meyer. Project for St. Peter's School in Basel.* Bauhaus-Archiv, Berlin.

Less frantic in renouncing the traditional role of the architect but more serious in their attempt to rethink how the designer might work in the future were such members of the Werkbund as Gropius or Hugo Häring, who saw the architect as the leader of a team bringing together a variety of disciplines—engineers, contractors, and even sociologists and psychologists.[28] With less emphasis on the artistic role of the architect as individual genius, there was now greater architectural interest in solving the pragmatic problems of building and the economic, social, and technical problems that they might involve. Working with the rigor attributed to engineers and scientists, architects began addressing space standards, density, and orientation in a systematic fashion, seeing in them a range of possible determinants of architectural form. At the first two meetings of the Congrès Internationaux d'Architecture Moderne (CIAM), the body founded in 1928 to speak for the new architecture, discussion was dominated by the comparative presentation of research findings from different countries in an attempt to find answers to the pragmatic issues of key importance: housing, the design of the minimum dwelling, and the optimum form of site layout.[29]

Typical of this new interest in the pragmatic problems of architecture was the contribution made by the *Reichsforschungsgesellschaft* (Rfg), established with support of Marie Elisabeth Eueders in 1926, to undertake research into every aspect of housing design and construction, from the layout of the individual dwelling and its components right up to the layout of whole housing estates.[30] Here was an organization (of which Gropius was by 1929 vice chairman) dedicated to sponsoring and encouraging architectural research, coordinating, documenting, and publicizing the results of various experimental housing projects that included among others the Roemerstadtsiedlung in Frankfurt and the Weissenhofsiedlung in Stuttgart. Typical of the studies carried out by the Rfg were comparative studies of different housing layout types that were to result in official support for the *Zeilenbau* layouts favored since 1927 by such architects as Haesler.[31] The same systematic approach is evident in Gropius's study paper "Flach, Mittel oder Hochbau," later presented at the CIAM meeting in Brussels, which investigated the relationship between residential density and building height.[32]

The Forms of the New Architecture

In Giedion's terms the technological achievements of the nineteenth and twentieth centuries had to be complemented by a corresponding development in aesthetic terms, by a new space conception, in order to establish a new architectural language. For Giedion, the shape of this new synthesis was already visible in the work of architects such as Le Corbusier and Gropius, and even before the end of the twenties, broadly similar forms were being explored by a number of architects. It was this similarity of approach that seemed so excitingly evident at the international exhibitions of the new architecture such as the Weissenhofsiedlung of 1927 and the Breslau exhibition of 1929.

Certainly much of the debate among the younger architects of the Werkbund or the Ring group in Berlin focused on the formal properties of the new architecture. These were not to be the product of any preconceived system of forms endowed with the kind of meaning that had seemed to be so important in the past. For most architects, the forms of the new architecture were to reflect the new forms of construction, the new technology, and the new science, and it was this that would ensure that the architecture was appropriate to its age, a refrain in the debate on style since the 1860s. The CIAM manifesto declared: "It is vitally necessary for architecture, abandoning the outmoded conceptions of the craftsman, to rely henceforth on the present realities of industrial technology."[33]

At one extreme there were those such as Ludwig Mies van der Rohe who claimed "to reject all aesthetic speculation" and urged architects to concentrate on the problems of building.[34] A new architecture based on the appropriate use of materials and built with a concentrated dedication to rationality would possess the qualities that were admired in the Doric temple and had characterized the great periods of architectural creativity in the past. As Mies attempted to explain to Walter Riezler in an open correspondence in *Die Form*, form would not be pursued as an end in itself; it was simply the natural outcome of an honest concern with construction.[35] Echoes of this view are to be found in the writings of most of the architects associated with the new architecture: the explanation of the forms of the buildings published in *Die Form, Bauwelt,* or *Das neue Frankfurt* was generally couched in these terms.

But for most architects, there was also a vague sense in which they believed that the forms of the new architecture were a reflection not just of the technology of the age but in some way of the spirit of the age. The feeling that this was bound up with the machine and the way it was changing society was widely reflected in architectural pronouncements and in articles and essays in the pages of journals such as *Die Form*.[36] The idea of a machine aesthetic as something particular to the twentieth century was already well established, as was the application of these ideas to architecture, but it was not so much the form of the machine as the logic that governed the design of the machine that was the most important lesson for the new architecture.

Nevertheless, the forms of modern industrial society, particularly the forms of the big city, still continued to exert a powerful influence over the imagination of architects and to color their view of what a modern architecture might be. For such writers on architecture as Adolf Behne, the appropriate paradigms for the new architecture were those matter-of-fact industrial buildings, factories, bridges, and those anonymous utilitarian buildings that made up so much of the modern city.[37] For many architects these modern images were frequently images of America and of the American city in particular. Cities such as New York suggested what a modern industrial society might be like, where the gramophone, the airplane, and processed food had changed the pattern of everyday life, and where the liberated woman of Helmut Lethen's "Girlkultur" either danced on Broadway or "would every now and then unleash a child from her splendidly trained flanks as if driving a Slazenger ball with her racket."[38]

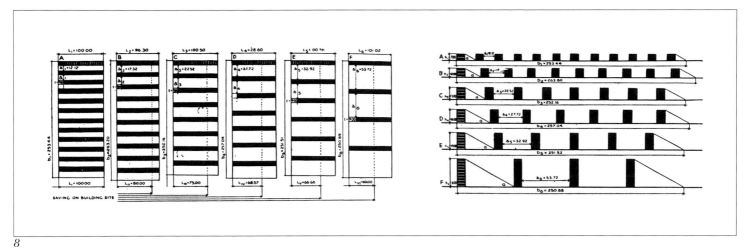

8

9

8. *Walter Gropius. Studies of
lighting densities for residential
layouts.* Bauhaus-Archiv, Berlin.

9. *Weissenhof Exhibition, Stuttgart,
1927.* From Joedicke and Plath,
Die Weissenhofsiedlung.

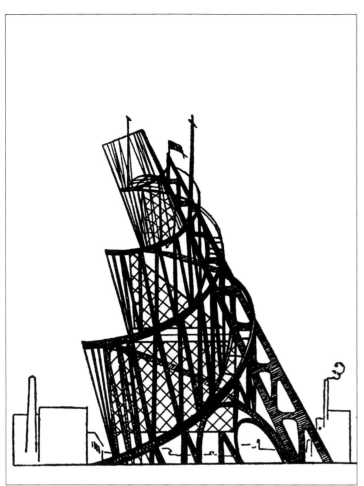

10

10. Image of a new urban
architecture: Vladmir Tatlin.
Monument to the Third
International, 1912. From Behne,
Moderne Zweckbau.

11a & b. Images of a new urban
architecture in America. From
Mendelsohn, Amerika.

To a number of German architects such as Ernst May it was a visit to America that marked the transition to an enthusiasm for the new architecture. One of the most effective evocations of *Amerikanismus* was Erich Mendelsohn's book *Amerika, Bilderbuch eines Architekten* of 1926[39] that illustrated urban life in America and that emphasized in glowing terms the huge industrial power of America, the ruthless economic individualism and its realization in New York—for Mendelsohn, the very embodiment of American life and values.

Even those who claimed to be inspired by rationality and to tread only in the footsteps of the engineer might become misty-eyed by the romanticism of the large industrial city and the pulse of modern life. Hannes Meyer's article "The New World" opens with a series of images of almost futurist intensity: "Motor cars dash along our streets. On a traffic island on the Champs Elysees from 6 to 8 PM metropolitan dynamism rages at its most harshest" and continues with an analogy between the machine and the forms of the new architecture— "Building is a technical not an aesthetic process, artistic composition does not rhyme with the function of a house attuned to its purpose. In ideal and elemental terms the design of our house is like a living machine. The retention of heat, insulation, natural and artificial lighting, hygiene, weather protection, car maintenance, cooking, radio . . . these are the determining lines of force."[40]

The New Architecture and Planning

For young architects in Berlin and for Giedion, the relationship between architecture and planning was crucial to reforming the failings of the megalopolis so evident in both New York and Berlin. In the final section of *Space, Time, and Architecture*, Giedion wrote about town planning, arguing that the approach to the new architecture would of necessity involve thinking at the scale of the city: "Architects today are perfectly aware that the future of architecture is inseparably bound up with town planning. . . . The interrelations between house, town, and country, or residence, labour, and leisure, can no longer be left to chance. Conscious planning is demanded.[41] For the young architects of the *neues Bauen*, it was no longer enough simply to design and build individual buildings, conceived of in the past as isolated and independent monuments: architects now had to look beyond the individual building to the form of the neighborhood and the city.

In the work of a number of Berlin architects, such as Ludwig Hilberseimer[42] or even Bruno Taut,[43] there are a series of suggestions sketching out the relationship between the design of individual buildings and the city as a whole that offer some of the utopian qualities of Le Corbusier's proposals for *A Contemporary City for Three Million Inhabitants*. But it is above all in the ideas of Martin Wagner[44] that we can see an attempt to translate new approaches to planning into a practical program of planning. Using the legal powers provided by the city's *Generalbebauungsplan*, which made it possible to specify key determinants of the form of the city through zoning land use or controlling density, Wagner and his department were able to prepare a strategic plan for the development of

240

the city. His proposals for the expansion of the city's land policy, including the creation of green areas running in from the countryside, and, most important, the siting of the major areas of residential development, did much to shape the strategic decisions underpinning *das neue* Berlin. In Berlin, there had existed not only the potential to make good the most glaring failures of the megalopolis; there was also the determination and the political will to achieve that potential.

The New Architecture and Social Commitment

While Giedion recognized the importance of the links between architecture and planning, many of the younger architects working in Berlin would have been surprised that he should make no more than the most cursory reference in the section on town planning to the social dimension of the new architecture. For many of the younger generation, a concern with social issues, with the provision of good design for basic necessities of everyday life such as simple household goods and housing, was an essential element in the development of the new architecture.

Housing conditions in Berlin had been bad before the war with high densities and a high proportion of small dwellings, many of them shared between two households, in working-class areas such as Wedding and Kreuzberg.[45] In Wedding, for example, where many of the workers in the metal and electrical industries lived—many of them semiskilled or skilled—over eighty percent of all dwellings consisted of one or two rooms only.[46] Densities in this area were higher than the rest of the city with an average of 98.9 people per site, compared with a city-wide average of 77; few of the dwellings had the range of services—running water and a flushing toilet, hot water or central heating—that were commonplace in housing in the more affluent districts.[47]

After the war, Berlin faced a housing shortage of gigantic proportions, which was to be made worse by the rapid rate in the formation of new households, the changing demographic structure of the city, and other consequences of the war such as the arrival of refugees from the occupied territories.[48] Even before the end of the war, the Prussian authorities had already started to provide considerable sums of capital for the non-profit housing sector to encourage house building.[49] But faced with the combined difficulties of a building industry shattered by the war and the impact of the reparations imposed by the Treaty of Versailles, and a constant inflation of labor and material costs, it was impossible to build enough houses to make any impact on the scale of the problem. In 1919, 579 dwellings were built; but by 1921 the number built had fallen to 423. In 1922, the number of completions was up to 3,460, but in 1923 it fell again to 3,059, barely one-fifth the prewar level.[50]

Housing was to remain one of the most intractable of social problems throughout the twenties. Looking back over the period in 1949, Ludwig Preller judged it a sensitive indicator of attitudes to social problems and the direction of social policy.[51] Not until 1927 did the volume of new construction over-

12a & b. Bruno Taut. Gross-Siedlung Britz, 1925–27. From Junghans, Bruno Taut.

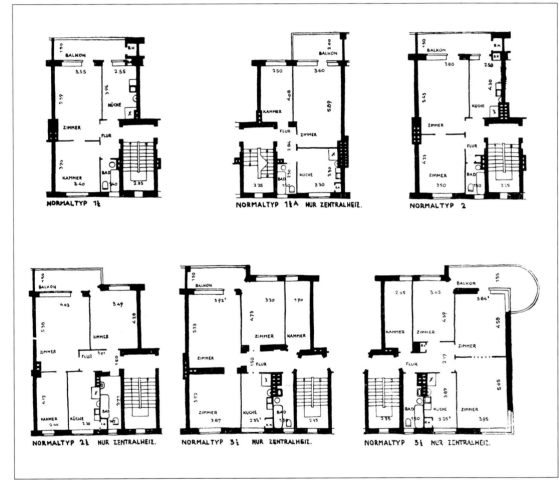

242

take for the first time the rate of formation of new households: in other words, during the nine years between 1918 and 1927, the overall shortage of housing became progressively worse, not better. As the government's housing survey of 1927 revealed unambiguously, housing conditions were worst in the large cities: in Berlin just over ten percent of all households were sharing a dwelling, an index of real housing stress in a city where, overall, dwellings with between one and three rooms accounted for 61.1 percent of the housing stock.[52]

It is against this background that the attempts by state and local government to encourage large-scale housing construction must be seen. In cities such as Berlin, the volume of housing construction dwarfed all other forms of construction. Quantitatively, it was the major architectural challenge of the twenties and of particular interest to many of the younger architects who saw their architectural work as a vehicle for social change. To architects such as Taut or Wagner, here was the real challenge of a socialist architecture.

Working from 1924 as one of the leading architects of the newly formed Gemeinnützige Heimstätten- (Sper- und Bau-) Aktiengesellschaft (GEHAG), Taut was responsible for a wide variety of housing projects that ranged from groups of individual blocks such as the flats at the Normannenstrasse in Lichtenberg to such major housing developments as the Hufeisensiedlung Britz in southwest Berlin.[53] At Britz, one of the largest and best-known of the interwar estates in Berlin, it is still possible to see a reflection, however faint, of those larger utopian themes that had preoccupied Taut in the immediate postwar years and that he still believed were vital to a view of housing as more than the provision of mere shelter.

In these large estates—Die weisse Stadt, Wohnstadt Carl Legien, Grosssiedlung "Onkel-Toms-Huette," Siemensstadt built in the outskirts of Berlin, the new architecture was seen to be set in the service of society.[54] It symbolized the concern for practical social reform that lay at the heart of the German Socialist Party program in such states as Prussia and in such cities as Frankfurt or Berlin.[55] The forms of this architecture reflected the conviction of the younger architects, like the members of the Ring, who believed that an urban and industrial society was the society of the future and that the architecture appropriate to it would be based on new forms of construction and the use of new materials.

The housing programs of the large housing associations[56] such as GEHAG or Deutsche Gesellschaft zur Förderung des Wohnungsbaues Gemeinnützige Aktiengesellschaft (DE GE WO), in Berlin provided a challenging opportunity to show that the new materials and new forms of construction really could provide housing for the mass of the population at a speed and at costs that traditional construction could not. Taut and May believed they could turn this challenge to advantage, demonstrating the strengths and appropriateness of the new architecture for this critical task. In their research into space standards and in their earnest consultations with women on how to plan the interior of the dwelling, including the kitchen—the subtitle of Taut's book *Die neue Wohnung (The New Dwelling)*[57] is "Die Frau als Schoepferin" (Woman as

13a, b & c. Contrasting qualities of pre- and postwar housing: a prewar kitchen; pre- and postwar family life. From Geist, *Berliner Mietshaus* and Nobisch, *Das Wohnungswesen der Stadt Frankfurt am Main.*

243

Creator)—and in the search for ways of reducing building costs and thus rents, and finding better lighting or better orientation, these architects believed that they were reshaping society through the forms of the *neues Bauen*.

Berlin: An Image of the New City?

How far had the young architects of the *neues Bauen* been able to transform the city by 1930 when the Depression put a stop to all but emergency building? Berlin seems to have exercised a particular fascination for a class of cultural historians including Walter Laqueur and Peter Gay because it seemed charged with that vitality of modernism more obviously than any other German city.[58] Does the city deserve its reputation as one of those locations in which the spirit of the age was most concentrated?

At first sight the achievements of the *neues Bauen* in Berlin are most impressive. Stuttgart or Breslau might have groups of exhibition buildings that were of importance in publicizing the *neues Bauen* at home and abroad: in Frankfurt or Hamburg the quality and the volume of new housing were showcased. But it was above all in Berlin that one could see the full variety and vitality of the new architecture. In the center of the city, one could see the glossy Lehninerplatz; there were the office buildings by Wassili and Hans Luckhardt, Emil Fahrenkamps's new Shell-Haus, and new buildings by Peter Behrens at the very heart of the city on the Alexanderplatz. Some of this new building might simply have seemed dressed up in the trappings of modernism, such as the housing built by architectural turncoats Paul Mebes and Paul Emmerich, or the Konjunktur-Kitsch of Heinrich Schaefer, designer of the Karstadt store on the Hermannplatz. But much of what was built reflected the concerns of the architectural debate: much of the new housing was a product of strong convictions about the social role of the *neues Bauen*. Other buildings might have seemed the result of attempts by young architects to work with the supposed rationality of the engineer or to exploit in architectural terms the latest building technology. Above all, however, it was the volume and the quality of the new housing that was particularly striking.

Between 1901 and 1911, the average annual rate of new dwellings completed was around twelve thousand.[59] By comparison during the years 1924–30, the only years in the Weimar era when house building was not seriously disrupted, average production was 19,285, and the average for the last four years was as high as 24,871.[60] Not only was the total volume of housing production high, well over fifty percent was represented by nonprofit housing of various kinds: between 1927–30, this sector built 62.2 percent of all new housing in Berlin. Much of this housing was provided by organizations such as GEHAG or DE GE WO, which, encouraged by Martin Wagner, engaged such young architects as Taut to design their housing, thus reinforcing the connection between social reform and the *neues Bauen*.[61] The large *Siedlungen*, built by these architects around the suburbs of the city, in Zehlendorf, Reinickendorf, or Britz, stand as impressive reminders of the social contribution made by the *neues Bauen* by the end of the

twenties. But how did this affect the housing conditions of the vast mass of the population?

First, despite the scale of the housing program, it is clear that in overall terms the new housing stock represented only a small addition to the city's total housing. Looking at the city as a whole, the great wastes of Hegemann's "Berlin, the world's largest city of housing barracks,"[62] dwarfed the buildings of the *neues Bauen*. Despite the number of new houses built each year, the overall volume of construction during the six brief years of uninterrupted building under Weimar was meager. By 1931, when the economic crisis brought the city's housing program to a halt, the number of dwellings built since 1918 totalled around 210,000, or about sixteen percent of the city's housing stock at the time.[63] Housing conditions and the pattern of domestic life for most Berliners must necessarily have remained very much as they had been in the prewar years.

Second, the social goals that lay so close to the heart of architects Taut, Wagner, and others could not be achieved. The accomplishments of the *neues Bauen* simply did not touch the way of life of the working-class population. The reasons for this are not difficult to understand. Consider the problem of rents. The brutal economic facts of housing costs and rents, to say nothing of the travel costs of living in the suburbs, meant that new social housing was too expensive for all but the most affluent workers.[64] Despite the availability of interest-free second mortgages, rents in the new social housing built during the twenties were very much closer to standard rents than the controlled rents in prewar housing. Rents in prewar housing were relatively well below the rent levels of the prewar years, and this naturally made the rents in new housing seem even higher. By the end of 1927, for example, when rents in old properties stood at 120 percent of their prewar values, the rent for a two-room dwelling might represent sixteen percent of a skilled worker's and twenty-one percent of an unskilled worker's weekly wage.[65] By comparison, rents in new dwellings would have been much higher, more than double the rents for the same type of dwelling in the prewar sector, to say nothing of the higher travel costs and generally higher living costs in the suburbs.

To the white-collar worker and his family, open to the suggestion of upward mobility, the attraction of better housing of the kind provided in these new *Siedlungen* was strong. These were the families that responded to the promise, abetted by women's magazines and publications such as Erna Meyer's *Der neue Haushalt*, that better housing might bring better health, the strengthening of the family, the release of the housewife from physical drudgery, and all the other moral and physical benefits symbolized by the *neue Wohnkultur* and the housing built by architects whose names were associated with the *neues Bauen*.[66]

But for the vast mass of Berlin's working class, the new housing was not only too expensive and located too far from work, it suggested a way of living that was remote from their everyday experience. Although housing in Wedding or Friedrichshain may have been small, densely packed, and poorly equipped, working-class families appear to have been willing to put up with these disadvantages. They did so in order to live in the center of the city where they could enjoy ease of access to work and where rents were low. Perhaps housing conditions here looked less threatening to many of these working-class families than they did to the housing reformers. Indeed the expectations and the experience of housing here must have been much as it was before the war; if anything, the housing crisis of official figures notwithstanding, conditions had improved, with relatively lower rents and fewer people per dwelling than before the war. Perhaps for many working-class families the concern of housing reformers with overcrowding and privacy seemed remote from the attainable realities of housing. Who, when settled in housing conditions to which they had long been accustomed, paying a low rent and living near employment, would want to move to a more expensive dwelling in the suburbs, away from the pub, the neighborhood, family, and friends?

Conclusion

The vision of *das neue* Berlin sketched out by the planners and the architects of the *neues Bauen* was a brave attempt to transform the city. They had tried to modernize the center of the city, they had fought for better (and cheaper) public transportation, better housing, modern schools, open space and recreation areas. The city's plans had been backed both by the Prussian state and by the city government of Berlin; both, under socialist leadership, had displayed a commitment to this vision of a new Berlin. But by 1933, this ideal was far from being realized. With the savage consequences of the Depression for the German economy, the program of improvements had been cut in 1930; with the coming to power of the Nazis in 1933, the plans were abandoned.[67] For the general population, housing conditions and much of the drudgery of day-to-day living barely differed from the prewar years. Even the considerable achievements of the *neues Bauen* were too few.

Nevertheless, in Berlin there had been a real attempt to reshape the city. In a number of suggestive ways, these achievements did indicate, albeit in a fragmentary manner, how to develop new forms for the city free from the glaring failings of the nineteenth and early-twentieth centuries. Perhaps it was just, and indeed still is, not possible to build housing, schools, and hospitals for an entire urban community. But at least the achievements in Berlin did show what could be done with political will and social commitment when the case for planning and a positive role for government was established and accepted. The decay into "Nekropolis" might be avoided. Even Mumford was prepared to praise developments in Berlin such as Britz or Siemenstadt as "setting a new standard in collective planning toward beauty and efficiency." He was willing to take these and other new developments as evidence of the "Signs of Salvage" at the end of his chapter on "The Rise and Fall of the Megalopolis."[68]

But what had been happening in New York during this period? The contrast between the two cities is instructive. As the rich, the wealthy, and the merely affluent struggled to escape the city, taking advantage of the transport network to move into the surrounding boroughs or even to Long Island, Connecticut, and New Jersey, the less fortunate remained crammed into the center at densities generally higher than those in Berlin. The dumbbell tenement block remained a more effective method of packing people onto a plot than even the densest of the Berliner *Mietskasernen*.

It was not that New York was without people who cared for the state of the city. There were a variety of individual initiatives. Housing reformer Edith Elmer Wood continued to campaign for better housing throughout the twenties, as Laurence Veiller had before the war.[69] There were architects with social concerns who, as individuals, or as members of lobbying organizations such as the Housing Study Group, were involved in research on ways to improve tenement design.[70] There was the New York City Housing Authority under Frederick Ackerman, who battled to build better housing for the city and who had close contacts with members of the Regional Planning Association of America.[71] There was the Regional Plan Association, which sought to foster the case for some form of planning in New York. Nor were these initiatives without success; little had been achieved during the twenties, but during the thirties there were a number of individual achievements: housing projects such as the Williamsburg development, the growing influence of the RPA on major planning decisions and increasing involvement in a host of smaller developments.[72] But the commitment to transforming and improving the city as a whole that was to be seen so clearly in Berlin was lacking in New York. The notion that government, whether city or state, should seek actively to plan the city remained alien to New Yorkers until the end of the thirties. The real beginnings of a housing program, backed by the federal government, date only from the Wagner Act of 1937. It was not until 1938 that the New York City Planning Commission actually became an effective planning force.

Nor did New York seem disposed to learn from developments in Europe. As opportunities for the new architecture and planning declined in Europe and the architects and the ideas that lay behind achievements such as those in Berlin started to travel westward across the Atlantic, it seemed to matter less that the social aspirations of the *neues Bauen* and the plans for revitalizing the city as a whole had remained unrealized. The celebration of the new architecture in the two complementary exhibitions organized at the Museum of Modern Art in New York in 1932 may have offered hope to those who wished to explain to Americans that the new architecture was more than just a new architectural style. The combination of the exhibition of the new architecture organized by Henry-Russell Hitchcock and Philip Johnson with the work on housing and planning arranged by Catherine Bauer and Henry Wright seemed to suggest support for a real understanding of the fundamental links between planning and architecture, the social and the formal concerns in these new European developments.[73]

In any event, these hopes were in vain. As the colloquium to discuss the exhibitions demonstrated at the time, architecture and social concerns were to remain largely separate interests in America.[74] The architectural exhibition attracted wide-

245

spread attention, and much of the material on display was published together with an introduction placing heavy emphasis on stylistic issues under the title *The International Style*.[75] Packaged in this way, the new architecture was quickly transformed into the formal plaything of architect Philip Johnson. The exhibition that presented housing and planning was largely forgotten. Perhaps before 1936 Henry Wright might have helped bridge the gap between architecture and housing. But with his death and the growing engagement of people such as Catherine Bauer in the struggle to establish a federal housing program, the possibility of linking architecture and social purpose in America, in the manner of the *neues Bauen*, seemed lost. By the time Gropius and Wagner, freshly arrived from Europe, were in a position to make any contribution to the debate in America, the social purposes of the new architecture seemed all but forgotten.[76]

But the very war that seemed set to obliterate the *neues Bauen* and its achievements was in fact to provide a range of opportunities for realizing the ideals of the *neues Bauen* on a scale undreamed of in the twenties. Amidst the destruction of the war, the debate on the forms of the new city started again with renewed passion. In the mixed fortunes of postwar reconstruction, we can see the real harvest of those visions of the new city that were being explored during the twenties and thirties.

Notes

1. For a discussion of those views opposed to the modern city, see Klaus Bergmann, *Agrarromantik und Grossstadtfeindschaft* (Meisenheim am Glan: Verlag Anton Hain, 1970).
2. For a summary of more positive views of the city between the wars, see Andrew Lees, *Cities Perceived: Urban Society in European and American Thought, 1820–1940* (Manchester: Manchester University Press, 1985), especially ch. 10.
3. Lewis Mumford, *The Culture of Cities* (London and New York: Secker & Warburg, 1938).
4. Ibid., especially ch. 8. Mumford's idiosyncratic terminology was adapted from Geddes's writings.
5. Sigfried Giedion, *Space, Time, and Architecture: The Growth of a New Tradition* (Cambridge, Mass.: Harvard University Press, 1941).
6. Ibid., 19.
7. For comparison, see Niklaus Pevsner, *Pioneers of the Modern Movement* (London: Faber, 1936).
8. Giedion, *Space, Time, and Architecture*, v.
9. Ibid.
10. Ibid.
11. Ibid., 356
12. Heinz Johannes, *Neues Bauen in Berlin* (Berlin: Deutscher Kunst Verlag, 1931).
13. See for example Georg B. von Hartmann and Wend Fischer, eds., *Zwischen Kunst und Industrie, der Deutsche Werkbund* (Munich: Die Neue S, 1975), 33–84; Frank Lloyd Wright, "The Art and Craft of the Machine," in Edgar Kaufmann and Ben Raeburn, eds., *Frank Lloyd Wright: Writings and Buildings* (Cleveland: Meridian, 1960); Theo Van Doesburg, "Will to Style, the Reconstruction of Life, Art and Technology," in Hans Jaffe, ed., *De Stijl* (London: Thames & Hudson, 1970), 148–63.
14. Walter Gropius, *The Principles of Bauhaus Production* (Dessau: 1926), quoted in Tim Benton, Charlotte Benton, and Dennis Sharp, eds., *Form and Function* (London: Crosby, Lockwood, Staples, 1975), 148–49.
15. For a contemporary discussion of Taylorism and "scientific" management, see Ermanski, *Wissenschaftliche Betriebsorganisation und Taylor-System* (Berlin: J.H.W. Dietz & Nacafolger, 1925).
16. Walter Gropius, *The New Architecture and the Bauhaus* (London: Faber, 1935), 33.
17. Ibid., 37.
18. William Morris quoted in William Lethaby, *William Morris on Work, Master* (London: Hogg, 1901), 94.
19. Walter Gropius, *Principles of Bauhaus Production*, 148.
20. For example, Ferdinand Kramer, "Die Wohnung fuer das Existenzminimum," *Die Form* 24 (1929); Haesler, "Zum Wohnproblem," *Die Form* 22 (1929).
21. For a general response to rationalization in Germany, see *Die Bedeutung der Rationalisierung fuer das deutsche Wirtschaftsleben* (Berlin: Tilke Verlag, 1928); for a discussion for the application of these ideas in the field of architecture, see, for example, Walter Gropius, *Bauhausbauten Dessau* (Munich: 1930; new edition, Florian Kupferber Mainz: 1974), especially 153–82; Bruno Taut, *Die neue Wohnung, Die Frau als Schoepferin* (Leipzig: Verlag Klinkhardt & Biermann, 1924), especially ch. 5.
22. The construction of the housing built for the Weisenhof exhibition is discussed in the Rfg's publication *Bericht ueber die Siedlung in Stuttgart am Weisenhof* (Berlin: 1929).
23. Ernst May, "Mechanisierung des Wohnungsbaues," *Das neue Frankfurt* 1 (1926): 33–40.
24. Evgen Kaufmann, "Frankfurter Kleinwohnungstypen in alter und neuer Zeit," *Das neue Frankfurt* 1 (1926): 113–18.
25. A selection of modern furniture, fittings, and interiors is reproduced in the booklet by Wilhelm Lotz, *Wie richte ich meine Wohnung ein? Modern Gut mit welchen Kosten?* (Berlin: Verlag Hermann Reckendorf, 1930); see also articles in *Die Form* such as those on the Weissenhof houses and their interiors, or the frequent articles on furniture and fittings such as "Moebelentwicklung und Typenmoebel," *Die Form* 6 (1928).
26. See John Willett, *The New Sobriety: Art and Politics in the Weimar Period 1917–33* (London: Thames & Hudson, 1978), 105–11.
27. Charles Edouard Jeannert (Le Corbusier), *Towards a New Architecture*, F. Etchells, trans., (London: Architectural Press, 1927), ch. 1.
28. Gropius's views on the subject are set out in *New Architecture and the Bauhaus*, 77–80.

29. The importance of the German contribution to the early CIAM meetings with their emphasis on housing tends to be overshadowed by Le Corbusier's later use of CIAM as a platform to publicize his own ideas on planning; Martin Steinmann, *CIAM, Dokumente 1928–39* (Basel: 1979).

30. For an account of the Rfg see Weber, "Taetigkeitsbericht der Rfg," *Erste Mitglieder-Versammlung* (Mitteilungen der Rfg 12–15) (Berlin: 1928); see also Nicholas Bullock, "First the Kitchen Then the Facade," *Journal of Design History* 1 (1988): 177–92.

31. The strength of support for this form of layout can be gauged from the discussion of housing layouts at the Rfg conference in 1929, *Technische Tagung in Berlin*, Vortraege, Gruppe 4 (Staedtebau und Starassenbau: 1929); see also the articles in *Die Form* on key Zeilenbau developments such as the Dammerstock Siedlung (*Die Form* 6, 9 [1930]).

32. Walter Gropius, "Flach-Mittel-oder Hochbau?" in *Rationelle Bebauungswiesen* (Frankfurt: Englert & Schlosser, 1931), 26–47.

33. CIAM: La Sarraz Declaration, in Steinman, CIAM, 30.

34. Ludwig Mies van der Rohe, "Buerohaus," *G Material zur elementaren Gestaltung* 1 (1923): 3.

35. The exchange of letters is published in Hartmann and Fischer, *Zwischen Kunst und Industrie*, 214–16.

36. For example, Curt Ewald, "Die Schoenheit der Maschine," *Die Form* 6 (1925); "Schmuck und Maschine," *Die Form* 8 (1928); Roger Ginsburger, "Eisenbahnwagons, Flugzeuge und Automobile," *Die Form* 25 (1929); Franz Ludwig Habbel, "Formen in modernen Flugzeugbau," *Die Form* 7 (1930).

37. Adolf Behne, *Der moderne Zweckbau* (Munich, 1926; new edition, Frankfurt and Vienna: Bauwelt Fundament; Friedrich Vieweg & Sohn, 1964).

38. Quoted in Willett, *The New Sobriety*, 103.

39. Erich Mendelsohn, *Amerika, Bilderbuch eines Architekten* (Berlin: Rudolf Mosse Buchverlag, 1926).

40. Hannes Meyer, "The New World," *Das Werk* (Bern, 8 1926), quoted in Benton et al., *Form and Function*, 107–8.

41. Giedion, *Space, Time, and Architecture*, 25.

42. Ludwig Hilbersheimer, *Berliner Architektur der 20er Jahre* (Mainz and Berlin: Florian Kupferberg, 1967), ch. 8.

43. Taut produced number of overall plans for Magdeburg, but his most extensive project in Berlin was the Berlin-Britz Siedlung, which was conceived as part of Martin Wagner's overall plan for Berlin: see Kurt Junghans, *Bruno Taut, 1880–1938* (Berlin: Elephanten Verlag, 1971), 52–66 and 77–95.

44. Besides the official documentation of his plans for Berlin, Wagner presented his ideas in a series of articles in *Wohnungswirtschaft*, of which he was editor from 1924 to 1926, and *Das neue Berlin, Grosstadtprobleme*, which he co-edited with Adolf Behne; see Homann, Kieren, and Scarpa, eds., *Martin Wagner 1885–1957, Wohnungsbau und Weltstadtplanung, Die Rationalisierung des Gluecks* (Berlin: Akademie der Künst, 1985).

45. Nicholas Bullock and James Read, *The Movement for Housing Reform in Germany and France 1840–1914* (Cambridge: Cambridge University Press, 1985), 187–206.

46. See the results of the 1925 survey of housing in Berlin: *Statistisches Jahrbuch der Stadt Berlin*, vol. 4 (1928), table 44.

47. *Mitteilungen des statistischen Amts der Stadt Berlin*, vol. 4, Heft 5, table 8.

48. The postwar housing crisis in Berlin is described in *Geschichte der gemeinnuetzigen Wohnungswirtschaft in Berlin* (Berlin, 1957), 88–92.

49. For a summary of postwar housing policies, see Albert Gut, *Der Wohnungsbau in Deutschland nach dem Weltkriege* (Munich: Callney, 1928), and Waldemar Zimmerman, ed., "Beitraege zur staedtische Wohn-und Siedlwirtschaft," in *Schriften des Vereins fuer Sozialpolitik* 177 (Leipzig, 1930).

50. *Geschichte der gemeinnuetzigen Wohnungswirtschaft*, 92.

51. Ludwig Preller, *Sozialpolitik in der Weimarer Republike* (Stuttgart: Ferank Mittelbach Verlag, 1949), 483–94.

52. *Statistisches Jahrbuch der Stadt Berlin*, vol. 4 (1928), table 42.

53. For a general discussion of Taut's Berlin housing work, see Junghans, *Bruno Taut*, 77–95.

54. For a survey of the housing built in Berlin during the 1920s, see Ernst Heinrich and Karl K. Weber, eds., *Berlin und seine Bauten*, Teil IV Wohnungsbau, Band A (Berlin: Verlag Wilhelm Ernst & Soan, 1990).

55. Barbara Lane, *Architecture and Politics in Germany 1918–45* (Cambridge, Mass.: Harvard University Press, 1968); see also Christian Engeli, *Gustav Boess, Oberbergermeister von Berlin* (Berlin, 1971); and Dieter Rebentisch, *Ludwig Landmann, Frankfurter Oberbeurgermeister der Weimarer Republik* (Wiesbaden, 1975).

56. *Geschichte der gemeinnuetzigen Wohnungswirtschaft*, 103–16.

57. Taut, *Die neue Wohnung, die Frau als Schoepferin*.

58. Peter Gay, *Weimar Culture* (Harmondsworth: Penguin, 1969); Walter Laqueur, *Weimar: A Cultural History 1918–33* (London: Weidenfeld & Nicholson, 1974).

59. Bullock and Read, *Movement for Housing Reform*, 197.

60. Heinrich & Weber, *Berlin und seine Bauten*, 26–28.

61. Ibid., 268–391.

62. Hegemann, *Das steinerne Baerlin*, has as its subtitle "Die groesste Mietskasernestadt der Welt."

63. *Geschichte der gemeinnuetzigen Wohnungswirtschaft*, 102.

64. Nicholas Bullock, "New Housing and The Housing Market in Berlin in the 1920s," forthcoming.

65. *Statistisches Jahrbuch der Stadt Berlin*, vol. 4 (1928), 108–14 and 51, table 61.

66. For a discussion of the *neue Wohnkultur*, see Bullock, "First the Kitchen," 180-88.

67. *Berlin und seine Bauten*, 27–28; Petsch, *Baukunst und Stadtplanang im Dritten Reich* (Munich: 1976), 98–113.

68. Mumford, *Culture of Cities*, 260.

69. Roy Lubove, *The Progressives and the Slums: Tenement House Reform in New York* (Pittsburgh: University of Pittsburgh Press, 1962); and Gerald Daly, *Housing Policy and Pressure Groups: The Impact of Central-Local Government Relations and Reformers on American Housing Policy 1933–53* (Ph.D. diss., Cambridge University, 1985).

70. Richard Pommer, "The Architecture of Urban Housing in the United States during the Early 1930s," *Journal of the Society of Architectural Historians* 37 (1978): 249–56.

71. For an account of the development of the ideas of the RPAA circle and their engagement with housing see Roy Lubove, *Community Planning in the 1920s: The Contribution of the Regional Planning Association of America* (Pittsburgh: University of Pittsburgh Press, 1963).

72. Kenneth T. Jackson, "The Capital of Capitalism: The New York Metropolitan Region, 1890–1940," in Anthony Sutcliffe, ed., *Metropolis 1890–1914* (London: Mansell, 1984), 337–43.

73. Pommer, "Architecture of Urban Housing," 235–36.

74. The colloquium was reported in some detail in *Shelter* 2 (April 1932): 3–9.

75. Henry-Russell Hitchcock and Philip Johnson, *The International Style: Architecture Since 1922* (New York: W. W. Norton, 1932).

76. Pommer, "Architecture of Urban Housing," 260–64.

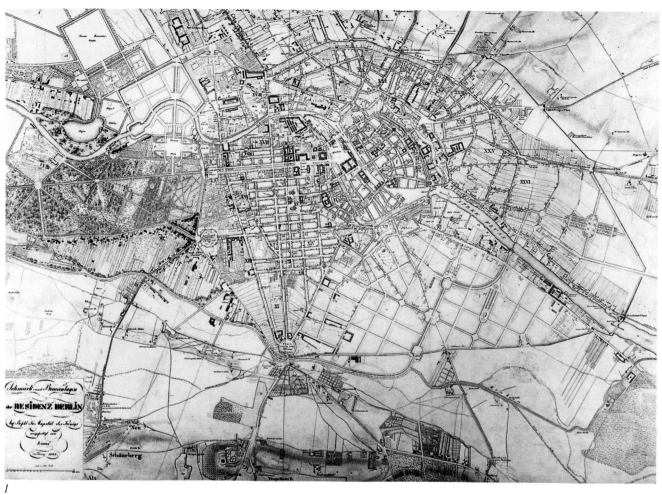

1

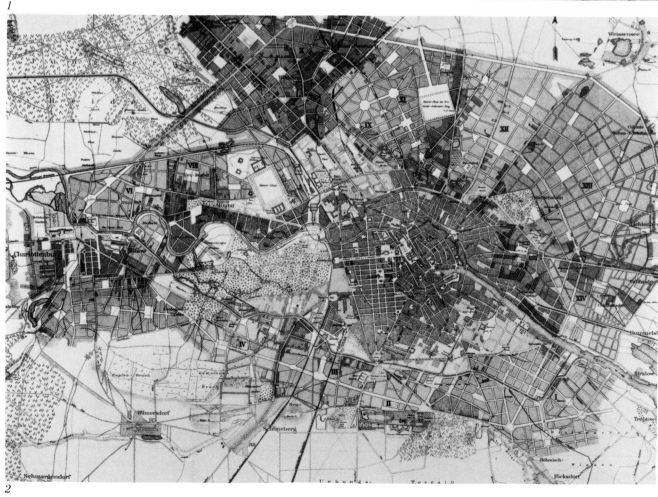

2

Modernism and the Metropolis: Plans for Central Berlin 1910–41

Vittorio Magnago Lampugnani

Vittorio Magnago Lampugnani is director of the German Architectural Museum and professor at the Stadelschule, both in Frankfurt am Main, and an adviser to Domus. *Lampugnani also was an adviser to the International Building Exposition in Berlin and visiting professor at Harvard University. He has received grants from the German Academic Exchange Service, the American Council of Learned Societies, and the Institute for Advanced Studies, Berlin. Formerly deputy editor of* Domus *and editor of* Casabella, *he is the author of numerous publications, including* Encyclopedia of Twentieth-Century Architecture *(1986),* Architecture of the Twentieth Century in Drawings *(1982), and* Architecture and City Planning in the Twentieth Century *(1980).*

1. Peter Joseph Lenné. Plan for the royal capital, Berlin, 1845. Landesbildstelle Berlin.

2. James Hobrecht. Overview of plan for Berlin, 1862. Landesbildstelle Berlin.

From the Greater Berlin Competition to the Mächler Plan

The most remarkable urban planning schemes developed by German architects during the late Wilhelmine and Weimar periods (1910–33) were inspired by the city of Berlin.[1] The Prussian capital had expanded with ever-increasing speed during the latter half of the nineteenth century, from just fewer than two hundred thousand inhabitants in 1817 to more than a million in 1877. A plan advanced by James Hobrecht in 1862, based on the considerations of Peter Joseph Lenné (figs. 1, 2), was accordingly cut out for a city of four million, an estimate that turned out to be very close to the mark; by the early years of the twentieth century, the population of greater Berlin, including suburbs, had burgeoned to 3.8 million.

So it was by no means farfetched that a competition held in 1907 for the planning of greater Berlin should have been conceived for a city of at least five million. Launched by the Association of Berlin Architects, the Competition for the Development of a Basic Plan for the Construction of Greater Berlin was designed to bring every aspect of the proliferating city under the planners' control, aiming to find "a broad and consistent solution both as regards the demands of transportation and as regards those of beauty, hygiene, and economic efficiency."[2] A further if more implicit aim of the competition was, of course, to bring the city up to the standard expected of the capital of a belated world power. Entries were to cover three essential planning phases: a basic building plan for a residential area of about twelve hundred square miles, a partial plan for a typical inner-city area, and suggestions for individual construction projects. Solutions were to be presented for an improvement in the execrable living conditions of the lower social strata, for the creation of green areas, and for the alleviation of downtown traffic problems. A reorganization of the railway system with its eight large terminals was considered to be a prime prerequisite of bringing the runaway expansion of Berlin under control.[3]

Twenty-seven plans were submitted, and it was not by accident that they concentrated on the area bordered by the Spree River and the Landwehr Canal. Joseph Brix and Felix Genzmer, whose first-prize entry was sponsored by the Elevated Train Corporation (Hochbahn-Gesellschaft), envisioned a rail line tunneling beneath a monumentally redesigned Königsplatz and connecting Lehrte Station with Potsdam and Anhalt stations. Hermann Jansen, whose plan was likewise awarded a first prize, limited himself to several new streets through existing built-up areas between Potsdam Bridge and Kemperplatz (fig. 3). At least this was an alternative to filling up the Landwehr Canal and turning it into an automobile thoroughfare, a suggestion that was being seriously discussed at the time.[4] The entry by Rudolf Eberstadt, Bruno Möhring, and Richard Petersen (third prize) focused particularly on Königsplatz, which they redesigned with a grand gesture. They also created Neuer Opernplatz on Königgrätzer Strasse (now Stresemannstrasse). Finally, Bruno Schmitz and Otto Blum, in conjunction with the firm of Havestadt & Contag (fourth prize), conceived a sweeping urban sequence extending from a gigantic parade and sports field in southern Berlin to a new southwest central station, and from a museum district

249

*3. Hermann Jansen. Plan for
Greater Berlin, major traffic
arteries, 1909. Landesbildstelle
Berlin.*

*4. Otto Blum and Bruno Schmitz
with Havestadt and Contag. Entry
for Competition Greater Berlin,
1907–10. From Josef Ponten,
Architektur die nicht gebaut wurde.*

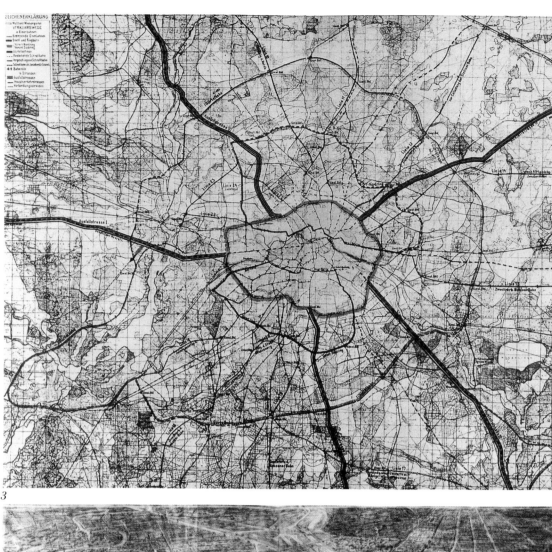

3

4

in Friedrichsvorstadt through Königsplatz to a Forum of Arts on the Spree River, a New Monumental Quarter, and a northwest central station (fig. 4).

None of the winning entries of the Greater Berlin Competition, which were awarded in 1910, were ever realized. Still, they were displayed that year by Werner Hegemann in an exhibition held in Berlin's Royal Academy (Königliche Akademische Hochschule für Bildende Künste) and had considerable influence on the international urban planning discussion of the period.

A still greater and more immediate influence, however, was reserved for the plan that Martin Mächler presented in 1917 and revised in 1919 (fig. 5). The aims of the plan were certainly high, envisioning Berlin as nothing less than a manifestation of "the relationship of the German Empire to the world, as a metropolis."[5] Mächler suggested that all the foreign ministries and embassies that were scattered around the city be concentrated on or near the Platz der Republik. He conceived of a great World Fairgrounds that would "forge a link between the German people, as represented by their labor, and the world."[6] Mächler's plan also foresaw a replacement of Anhalt and Potsdam stations by a new railway terminal in the vicinity of Tempelhof, which would be connected by subway with a cross-shaped Central Station named for Friedrich List located on the site of Lehrte Station.[7] To facilitate traffic flow, he suggested that Jägerstrasse continue through the Ministry Gardens, where a new opera house was to be located. Above all, Mächler envisaged a grand north-south axis, which apart from its functional purpose of connecting Berlin's northern and southern districts had an eminently symbolic function to fulfill—that of demonstratively crossing what he and others considered the absolutist east-west axis of the city. It was no accident that in Mächler's plan, both the Siegesallee and the Siegessäule, an avenue and a column commemorating the Prussian victory over the French in 1871, were eliminated.

The plan, which Mächler detailed in 1920, was never realized. This was not due to its content but was a result of the precarious economic (and political and social and ideological) situation of the German Reich, which following the debacle of World War I had ventured onto shaky ground with the Weimar Republic. Still, the idea of a north-south thoroughfare connecting the districts of Moabit and Wedding with Schöneberg and thus filling a longstanding and serious gap in the city's transportation network, continued to attract attention, in Erwin Gutkind's forceful advocacy of a broad north-south axis during a conference on the competition for an expansion of the Reichstag Building in 1929.[8] The idea was to reach a sinister apotheosis a few years later in the plans of Albert Speer.

The Third Dimension in Urban Planning, or the Germanization of the Skyscraper

The skyscraper as a building type eminently suited to the big city—and especially to Berlin—had been a prime subject of discussion among German architects since before World War I. The models in this regard, of course, were Chicago and New

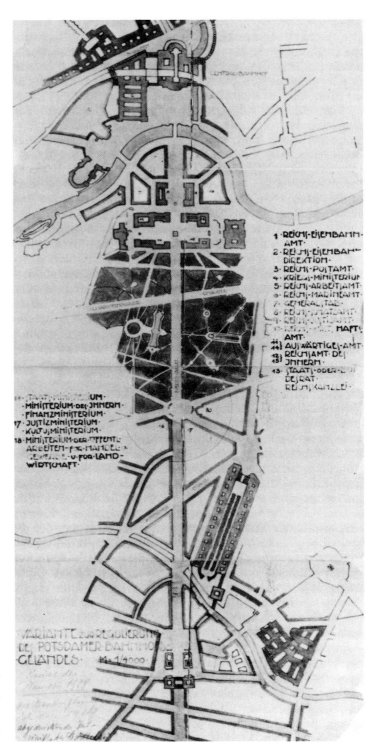

5. Martin Mächler. Detail from plan for Greater Berlin, 1919. From 750 Jahre Architektur und Städtebau in Berlin (exhibition catalogue, Stuttgart, 1987).

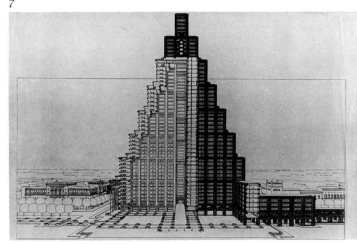

York, though it was generally agreed that these should undergo a "Germanization."[9]

As early as the Greater Berlin Competition, a monumental high-rise had been projected for Potsdamer Platz by Bruno Schmitz and his committee. In 1912, the daily newspaper *Berliner Morgenpost* conducted a survey on the subject of the skyscraper, the results of which were published in a brochure entitled *Berlin's Third Dimension.*[10] Many well-known politicians, businessmen, and architects contributed to the survey, including Peter Behrens, who strongly advocated a development along North American lines for Berlin and emphasized the aesthetic and symbolic potential of the skyscraper.[11] The year 1913 marked the publication of Otto Rappold's *Der Bau der Wolkenkratzer,* an investigation of the technical and functional aspects of skyscraper architecture based on American examples.[12]

That same year, the Dresden architect and watercolor artist K. Paul Andrae rendered the first plates for *Das grössere Berlin* (1913–16), a series of studies of skyscrapers and monumental buildings (fig. 6) for which he chose suggestive musical captions such as "Allegro tanto" and "Andante maestoso."[13] In plate eight, he projected an immense high-rise city that in many respects anticipated Hugh Ferris's visions of New York in *The Metropolis of Tomorrow.*[14] Andrae's skyscraper studies, conceived for an imperial Berlin as capital of a victorious German empire, were shown in 1919 at the "Exhibition of Unknown Architects" organized by the Working Council for Art (Arbeitsrat für Kunst), where they were promptly misunderstood as modern signposts of a "freer and stronger future."[15]

Serious discussion of the skyscraper really did not begin in Germany until about 1920. The ground was prepared in a 1918 study by Paul Wittig, president of the Berlin Building Association, in which he advocated skyscraper architecture "only for the purpose of creating urban beauty in world capitals, including of course Berlin."[16] Wittig provided examples in the shape of his own, earlier projects. In May 1920, the first German skyscraper competition was announced in Danzig, and the architect responsible for the invitations gave a lecture on "High-Rise Buildings as a Means of Alleviating the Housing Shortage."[17] This was to anticipate the strange if highly effective argument that Max Berg was to develop a short time later in two essays that attracted a great deal of attention and provoked a flood of reactions.[18]

Above all, however, there was a spate of more or less concrete projects for tall buildings. Between 1920 and 1921, Bruno Möhring created designs for about twenty towers to be located at carefully selected sites around Berlin, including Askanischer Platz, Lehret Station, and Friedrichstrasse Station (fig. 7). By means of this relative dispersion, Möhring hoped to avoid both the chaotic proliferation of skyscrapers characteristic of American cities and the isolated tall building, which, though it "certainly lent interest to the aspect of a city," could not convey "that certain impression" characteristic of modern cities.[19]

Otto Kohtz, another architect who designed high-rise projects for Berlin in 1920, aimed to create "a series of architectural centers of interest in the dull if turbulent sea of Berlin's buildings by means of well-placed and harmoniously designed towers" that would provide "a focus and a direction for the eye."[20] Like Möhring, Kohtz selected a number of prominent sites for his projects, even locating one of them on the illustrious Königsplatz. During the war, he had already envisioned a Hall of Victory on that site, but in the absence of victory, there was no reason for the hall and so he made do with a Reichshaus, which was to further no less a cause than "welfare, health, morals, law, vigor, spirit, and beauty."[21]

Kohtz's geometric City Crown, erected on a square plan with sides 427 feet in length, was to rise to a height of 626 feet, tapering upward like a ziggurat; inside, it was to have an immense cruciform hall bathed in a mystic light falling through the colored glass of its tracery facade. Like Berg, Kohtz also believed that high-rises could help alleviate the city's housing shortage, though he arrived at this conclusion by a convoluted path, arguing that if all the government offices scattered around Berlin were concentrated in his new project, the two thousand or so apartments they had appropriated would again become available for tenants.[22] What is more, he viewed the huge construction site and the rationalized labor the project would entail as a gigantic public relief project that would help lower unemployment. In 1921 Kohtz designed a second, more unwieldy version of the building for the same site, which struck Le Corbusier as so gauche that he published it in *L'Esprit Nouveau* as a typical (and highly welcome) example of bad German architecture.[23] It was not until well into the 1940s, when Albert Speer's plans for a Great Hall had irrevocably superseded the Reichshaus, that Kohtz finally abandoned his idea of raising a monumental structure on the most prominent lot in the imperial capital.

Still in the year 1920, several other skyscraper projects for Berlin were advanced, including German Bestelmeyer's ten-story circular building for the Imperial Debts Administration on Oranienstrasse (which would have been built if the Department of Building Control had not rejected it); Joseph Reuter's unconventional and prototypical skyscraper for the Charlottenburg district; and Hans Kraffert's American-style office building on Blücherplatz. None of these projects was realized; but a year later, a sensational competition was launched to garner ideas for an office high-rise on a triangular lot located adjacent to Friedrichstrasse Station,[24] and initially it had very good prospects of actually being built.

Berlin Skyscraper Competitions, 1921–29

The sponsors, who appropriately called themselves the Tower Corporation (Turmhaus Aktiengesellschaft), gave the entrants only six weeks to prepare their idea sketches, but the project proved so challenging to Berlin architects, who were as good as unemployed anyway, that they submitted more than 140 designs. Although such celebrities as Hans Poelzig, Hans Scharoun, Hugo Häring, and Ludwig Mies van der Rohe submitted designs of a very high quality, all of which, in one way or another, anticipated a new urban architecture, the selection committee—made up of such influential conservative architects as Bestelmeyer, Ludwig Hoffmann, Heinrich Straumer, and Hermann Billing—gave the awards to conservative designs. There was one exception—second prize went to Hans Luckhardt, Wassili Luckhardt, and Franz Hoffmann, who, thanks to a tenacious press campaign on the part of Adolf Behne, were invited to develop their project in more detail.

Their work eventually ran aground on the sandbars of indifference; it turned out that the corporation had launched the entire competition for publicity reasons alone. They had already, in the spring of 1921, secretly commissioned Möhring, Kohtz, and Kraffert for the project, which they actually intended to build and for which they now had the League of Tower Friends (as the trio named themselves) prepare final plans. But luck was not on their side either, and the whole enterprise subsequently collapsed on account of delayed building permits and resulting financing difficulties.

The excitement caused in Berlin architectural circles by this first skyscraper competition had hardly abated when a second was announced in late summer of 1921. This time, the lot lay on Kemperplatz. The nominal contractor was a group called the Reconstruction Corporation for the Erection of Tall Buildings, chaired by the same man who headed the Tower Corporation; the sponsor of the competition was the Association of Berlin Architects, who invited its own members, and no one else, to participate. Though more than seventy designs were submitted, the results were so mediocre that the corporation launched yet another competition before the year was out, this time inviting six other architects, including Peter Behrens, Erich Mendelsohn, Hans and Wassili Luckhardt, and Bruno and Max Taut. Not least on account of the tight stipulations, none of them designed a real skyscraper: Behrens's modest nine-story corner building was the highest. Again, none of the avant-garde projects managed to reach the building stage, an honor reserved for a dull design by Heinrich Kaiser and Eduard Jobst Siedler that had received third prize in the initial competition.

In 1924, the competition for the redesign of Unter den Linden was won by Cor van Eesteren with a sequence of medium-height towers and slabs. Third prize was shared by Alexander Klein and Georg Salzmann. Adolf Meyer submitted a noteworthy design.

In spring 1929, the Tower Corporation, nerve-racked and financially bled by nine years of the tough if not always aboveboard struggle to build on its Friedrichstrasse Station lot, sold the property to the newly established Berlin Transportation Corporation (Berliner Verkehrs-Aktiengesellschaft). By the end of the year, this group had launched a limited competition to which they invited five prominent architects and firms: Alfred Grenander, Heinrich Straumer, Paul Mebes and Paul Emmerich, Erich Mendelsohn, and Mies van der Rohe. The Berlin Transportation Corporation required a large office building for its management. The jury, which included Otto Bartning and Martin Wagner, decided to award two first prizes, to Mendelsohn and to Mebes and Emmerich.

9. Hans Poelzig. Design for skyscraper on Friedrichstrasse, view from north, 1921. Plansammlung der Universitätsbibliothek der Technischen Universität, Berlin.

10. Hugo Häring. Skyscraper on Friedrichstrasse, 1921. Bauhaus-Archiv, Berlin.

11. Hans Scharoun. Skyscraper on Friedrichstrasse, 1921. Bauhaus-Archiv, Berlin.

9

10

11

Once again, this time on account of the Depression, no actual building resulted. Still, this competition was not a complete failure since it served the purpose of developing new conceptions of tall urban buildings and bringing them to the precise and detailed design stage.

Within just less than a decade, German architects had indeed explored the entire gamut of potential urban planning and architectural solutions with regard to the tall building, and, at least on paper, they achieved remarkable results. In the first competition for an office high-rise at Friedrichstrasse Station, the late-expressionist, three-facade structure by Poelzig (fig. 10), the gigantic biomorphic design by Häring (fig. 11), the complexly articulated consumer cathedral by Scharoun (fig. 12), Soeder's prismatic composition, and above all Mies van der Rohe's sharp-cornered, crystalline tower (see page xx), constituted radical solutions to the problem of the tall building that freed themselves from American patterns and established a new, autonomous tradition. In the second competition for the same site, it was primarily Mendelsohn (fig. 14) with his daring combination of a cubic volume with a dynamically rounded form, Grenander with his solitary structures (fig. 15), and Mies with his magnificently proportioned glass-walled designs (fig. 16), who expanded and ramified this new tradition. Their designs became fixed stars by which modern architecture was to navigate for decades.

The Mythology of Transportation and Urban Architecture

In early 1924, a number of avant-garde Berlin architects formed a group they called the Ring to represent their professional and cultural interests. Just two years later, the group accomplished its main objective: Martin Wagner became *Stadtbaurat*—the director of the city's Department of Urban Planning and Development. Until 1923 this office had been held by the conservative and authoritarian Ludwig Hoffmann and thereafter by interim appointees. Wagner, who had devoted himself to the problem of city-center renewal since the first postwar years, not only initiated a huge house construction program for various sites on the city's periphery but immediately tackled the reorganization of downtown Berlin.[25]

Wagner's first priority in this regard was traffic and transportation. This was not only in response to a real problem in Berlin, whose traffic chaos had necessitated putting a traffic light right in the middle of Potsdamer Platz (1924) and whose north-south connections were still woefully inadequate; it was a reflection of the mythology of the era. For the 1920s, the phenomenon of dense, rushing, metropolitan traffic was a fascinating symbol of modern life itself. In Walter Ruttmann's revolutionary documentary film *Berlin, Symphonie einer Grosstadt* (1927), the movement of human beings and vehicles through the city streets obviously plays the lead role. And in Friedrich Wilhelm Murnau's *Sunrise* (1927), a passionate kiss indulged by a country boy and girl standing in the middle of a city street causes a spectacular traffic jam.

The architects were by no means immune to this fascination. For Mächler, traffic represented the metabolism of the urban

254

organism,[26] a well-chosen metaphor in that it pinpointed transportation as the driving force behind a city's economic growth. For Wagner, the private automobile amounted to a pair of "seven-league boots" that anyone could don and within a few minutes be relaxing in a peaceful countryside or enjoying the "pulsating" life of downtown.[27] Mendelsohn even went a step further, deriving from motorized traffic and its dynamic nature a special architectural style, which he first demonstrated in his conversion of the Rudolf Mosse Building (1921–23). In connection with this project, Mendelsohn explicitly pointed out that his building was no longer to play the role of "innocent bystander" with regard to the traffic flow but at last had become a "receptive, participating element in [its] movement."[28]

With this conception, Mendelsohn had invented that specific but international big-city architecture whose program was to be articulated—if with quite different aesthetic implications—in Ludwig Hilberseimer's 1927 book *Grosstadtarchitektur*: "Big-city architecture is a new kind of architecture with its own form and laws. It represents today's socioeconomic situation. It seeks to free itself of everything that is not straightforward, aims at reduction to essentials, the greatest possible development of energy, the most extreme tension, and constant precision; it corresponds to our contemporary lifestyle and is an expression of a new sense of life whose nature is no longer subjective and individual but objective and collective."[29]

Apparently Hilberseimer had profited from a reading of Georg Simmel's brilliant essay, "Die Grosstädte und das Geistesleben" ("Big Cities and Intellectual Life") in which, as early as 1903, the metropolis was characterized as a place where "culture has transcended every personal aspect" and "the mind has become impersonal."[30]

Metropolitan Berlin Projects and Buildings, 1927–31

The first results of Martin Wagner's city-center renewal policy were not long in coming. In 1927, the Ring architects presented designs for the Platz der Republik and a new thoroughfare through the embassy gardens as the Grosse Berliner Kunstausstellung. Their suggestions were based on the plan by Mächler, which was exhibited alongside other historical projects that had influenced them (including one by Karl Friedrich Schinkel of 1840). Hugo Häring adopted Mächler's north-south axis and renamed it Strasse der Republik (fig. 17), reduced the size of the square by adding rows of monumental ministry buildings, placed offices for the Reichstag president axially across from the Reichstag Building, on the far side of a straightened stretch of the Spree River, and moved the Victory Column to the great traffic circle known as Grosser Stern, which was later actually carried out by Speer in 1939. Hans Poelzig's plan (fig. 18) envisioned an enlarged Platz der Republik quietly enclosed by ministries. Peter Behrens composed the urban space with more freedom, envisaging a skyscraper as a counterpoint to the Reichstag Building. Hilberseimer submitted an elegant yet functional design for the junction station, which he conceived as a simple structure of

12

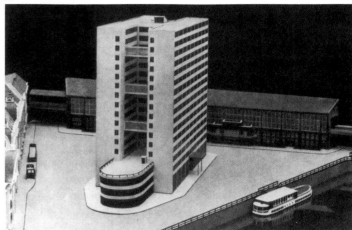

13

14

12. Erich Mendelsohn. Model of skyscraper on Friedrichstrasse, 1929. Staatliche Museen Preussischer Kulturbesitz, Berlin, Kunstbibliothek.

13. Alfred Grenander. Model of skyscraper on Friedrichstrasse, 1929. From Der Schrei nach dem Turmhaus (exhibition catalogue, Berlin, 1989).

14. Mies van der Rohe. Skyscraper on Friedrichstrasse (drawing on photo), 1929. From Der Schrei nach dem Turmhaus (exhibition catalogue, Berlin, 1989).

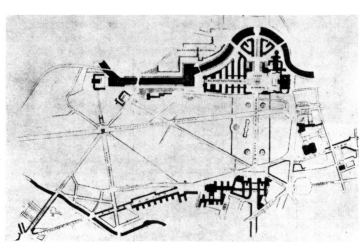

15. *Hugo Häring. Redesign of Platz der Republik, 1927.* From Vittorio Magnagno Lampugnani, *Architektur als Kultur.*

steel and glass. Also exhibited were projects for the continuation of Französiche Strasse and Jägerstrasse by Peter Behrens, Adolf Rading, Heinrich Tessenow, and Hans Scharoun. All in all, these projects represented a ramification and focusing of Mächler's ideas, and their authors self-confidently hoped to create new "spiritual values" through architecture and urban planning.[31]

In a less centrally located yet by no means peripheral area of Berlin, Erich Mendelsohn was concurrently beginning a much more ideologically modest project that would turn out to be his chef d'oeuvre (fig. 19): the Woga complex on Kurfürstendamm (1927–31) named for the contractor, Wohnhausgründstücks-verwertungs-Aktiengesellschaft. Designed to fulfill a multiplicity of functions, this little city within the city is a masterpiece of volumetric composition. It mediates wonderfully between the architectural scale of the street and that of the pedestrians, who feel invited, but not coerced, to enter the square and the shops just beyond. The brusqueness of the Mosse Building and the futuristic pathos of the Schocken Department Store in Stuttgart are overcome; a lively but respectfully restrained urban architecture encloses a complex and unprecedented sequence of public spaces, dialectically continuing and complementing those of nineteenth-century cities.[32]

The year 1927 also brought the commencement of a housing development on Tempelhofer Damm, designed by Eduard Jobst Siedler. Its two five-story parallel buildings are connected by stairwells that give rise to a linear sequence of small courtyards. The ground floor is treated as a monumental socle and set off from the upper floors by a continuous cornice.

Still more metropolitan were Scharoun's Berlin projects of the same period. In 1928–29, he collaborated with Georg Jakobowitz on an elegant apartment house on Kaiserdamm (fig. 20), stacking up a series of small, luxurious flats to produce a very original and dynamic architectural configuration that is a virtuosto contribution to big-city mythology. In 1929–30, there followed, likewise in collaboration with Jakobowitz, the six-story apartment house on Hohenzollern-damm, which contains only one-room flats and accents the corner of Mansfeldstrasse with a sequence of tiered semicircular balconies.

Rudolf Fränkel's large apartment block on Schöneberg City Park with its four hundred flats dates from the year 1931. The austere, flat-roofed building, finished in light yellow stucco, is articulated by means of indented stairwell windows. The verticality of the windows provides an effective contrast to the horizontality of the loggias, which, placed in pairs, are linked by a small cornice with the horizontal corner windows of the living rooms to form a unified motif that determines the character of the street facade. The load-bearing concrete pilasters between the loggias are finished in a roughened stucco and the wooden window frames in clear varnish. The ground floor, faced with dark brown fire-brick, gives the effect of being a socle. In the courtyard, there is an underground garage whose roof has a lawn; storefronts extend along the Meraner Strasse side.

16

17

16. *Hans Poelzig. Redesign of Platz der Republik, 1927.* Plansammlung der Universitätsbibliothek der Technischen Universität, Berlin.

17. *Erich Mendelsohn. Woga complex on Kurfurstendamm, 1926–28.* Staatliche Museen Preussischer Kulturbesitz, Berlin, Kunstbibliothek.

18. *Hans Scharoun. Apartment house on Kaiserdamm, 1928–29.* Akademie der Künste Sammlung Baukunst Berlin.

18

Traffic Flow, Business Interests, Architecture: The Debate on the Redesign of Alexanderplatz

In 1929, while the Woga complex was still under construction, three projects for central Berlin fueled the debate over the design of big-city squares—redesigns of Alexanderplatz, Potsdamer Platz, and Leipziger Platz, and an expansion of the Reichstag and design of the Platz der Republik.

For Alexanderplatz (the first installment of Alfred Döblin's famous novel of that name would appear in September 1929), a competition was launched in February 1929 in which six architects were invited to participate. The description was based on a plan worked out by Wagner himself. He summed up its principles in "Das Formproblem eines Weltstadtplatzes" ("The Form of the Metropolitan Square"), published in *Das neue Berlin* a month after the invitations were sent out. The latter, he wrote, was essentially an "almost continually filled traffic sluice, the clearing point for a network of main traffic arteries," from which he concluded that "an uninterrupted flow of traffic" was the prime consideration in such a square's design and "formal criteria . . . of only secondary significance."[33] Increases in traffic density, however, could be predicted for a period of twenty-five years at most. Therefore, the size of a metropolitan square should be based on predictable traffic density and its shape on traffic flow, and after twenty-five years, when the functional conditions had changed, the square could be demolished and rebuilt.[34]

Wagner's conception of a metropolitan square was almost exactly the same as that of Döblin. Rosenthaler Platz, a busy intersection in eastern Berlin, is described by Döblin as nourishing itself. The city's public space has transformed itself into an autonomous and complex but faceless living creature that devours people and vehicles, swishes them around, and then spews them out again in all directions.[35] And in the famous description of Alexanderplatz, where the blows of a steam hammer repeatedly punctuate and drown out the street noise, Döblin relates that:

Where Jürgen's stationery store used to be they've torn down the building and put up a hoarding in its place. An old man sits there with a doctor's scale: Check Your Weight, 5 Pfennigs. Oh dear brothers and sisters swarming over Old Alex, stop a minute to take in this view, look through the hole in the fence next to the scale, consider the rubble-strewn vacant lot where Jürgen's once flourished, and consider too Hahn's Emporium, vacated, emptied and gutted. . . . This is how Rome was done for, Babylon, Niniveh, Hannibal, Caesar, all done for, oh, remember that. About which let me remark that, first, all of these cities are now being excavated, as we learn from the pictures in last week's Sunday supplement, and second, that these cities have fulfilled their purpose and we can now start building new ones. You don't cry over your old trousers when they wear out and fall apart, you buy a new pair—that's what makes the world go round.[36]

This view that cities were doomed to rapid obsolescence, held with melancholic irony by Döblin and with cool realism by Wagner, had profound consequences for the competition to redesign Alexanderplatz. Since the life-expectancy of its architecture was as limited as that of Franz Bieberkopf's trousers, the projected new buildings were to have no "permanent economic or architectural value."[37] Still, they required enormous capital and were expected to pay for themselves in less than twenty-five years. This meant that the buildings had to be efficient yet attractive in order to catch the eye of passersby—potential customers. This could be achieved, again according to Wagner, in two ways. First, they should be adapted not only to the "flow lines" of motorized traffic but to the "walking lines" of pedestrians ("buying power," Wagner calls them) in order to draw them into the shops, department stores, restaurants, and offices. And second, although the structures should be inexpensively built, they should be striking enough in design. As Wagner put it:

Forms of the utmost lucidity that retain their characteristic aesthetic effect during both daytime and nighttime hours are fundamental prerequisites for the metropolitan square. *In*flowing light by day and *out*flowing light by night change its aspect absolutely. *Color, form,* and *light* (advertising signs) are the three main construction elements.[38]

In view of this precise conception, it is no wonder that the first prize in the competition went to the entry that reflected it most precisely. Hans and Wassili Luckhardt, in collaboration with Alfons Anker, actually presented little more than a more detailed version of Wagner's own plan (fig. 21). The edges of the square, which follow the lines of an ideal traffic flow, are closed off by tall, sweeping buildings whose ground floors conform to the hypothetical walking lines of ambulatory buying power. Two of the streets that lead into the square are bridged by structures in Wagner's General Plan. The largely homogenous facades, a simplified version of the so-called Mendelsohn style, consist of alternating layers of strip windows and wall surfaces designed to carry advertising. The entire square is a metaphor for the ebb and flow of traffic, a gigantic decoration that openly celebrates modern life (not to mention capitalism).

The other proposals, including that of Peter Behrens (fig. 22), were also reinterpretations of Wagner's plan. An exception was Mies van der Rohe's project (fig. 23), which presented eleven freestanding buildings, sharp-edged prisms of glass and reinforced concrete, set back from the ideal circumference line of the square. The focus of the project is a seven-story office building with six shorter buildings arranged one behind the other at right angles to it. Corresponding to the foremost building, set flush with the square, are four others placed at intervals around it, buildings of the same type but with dimensions adapted to the varying lot size. In the middle lies the open space of the square with its circular road and intersecting tramlines. "Of all the designs presented," wrote Hilberseimer with a not unbiased glance at the five others, "Mies van der Rohe's is the only one that breaks with this rigid system [of frontages conforming to traffic flow] and attempts to arrange the square regardless of traffic lines, which run in accordance with their function, solely in architectonic terms through the use of individual buildings."[39] Mies's design was promptly relegated to last place, and Behrens, after his plans had been considerably altered and reduced, was commissioned to build on Alexanderplatz.

19

20

21

19. Hans and Wassili Luckhardt
and Alfons Anker. Model for
competition for redesign of
Alexanderplatz, Berlin, 1928.
Bauhaus-Archiv, Berlin.

20. Peter Behrens. Model for
competition for redesign of
Alexanderplatz, Berlin, 1928.
Bauhaus-Archiv, Berlin.

21. Mies van der Rohe. Aerial
photograph with drawing submitted
for competition for redesign of
Alexanderplatz, Berlin, 1928.
Bauhaus-Archiv, Berlin.

259

22

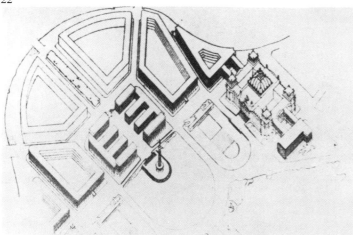

23

22. *Martin Wagner.* Carousel,
*redesign of Potsdamer Platz and
Leipziger Platz, 1929.* Akademie
der Künste Sammlung Baukunst
Berlin.

23. *Emil Fahrenkamp and Heinrich
de Fries. Redesign of Platz der
Republik and extention to the
Reichstag Building, 1929.* From
Heinz Raack, *Das Reichstags-
gebäude in Berlin.*

Plans for Potsdamer Platz and Leipziger Platz

The problem of redesigning Potsdamer Platz and Leipziger
Platz was almost identical with that of Alexanderplatz: the reconstruction of a metropolitan square was necessitated by the
growing demands of traffic. The discussion began as early as
1928, and Mendelsohn made a series of sketches projecting a
unified design based on grouping several skyscrapers on the
most prominent corner sites. This time Wagner did not organize a competition. Instead, he worked out his own project in
collaboration with Felix Unglaube: a three-story carousel with
a subway station in the basement, an almost purely trans-
portational structure whose neon-sign facades were meant to
celebrate capitalist consumption (fig. 24).

The same principle provided the basis of Marcel Breuer's alternative design, in which traffic was also distributed among
various levels (but without the carousel) and the facades lining the square were again little more than glorified billboards.
For Breuer, too, the drama of the big city was motion: "The
drama reaches its climax at the main intersection! Seen in
modern terms, downtown squares are nothing other than the
culmination of streets."[40] He thought that the architecture of a
large city should be characterized by great reserve: "buildings
in their simplest form . . . whose exterior merely sets a basic
rhythm for the incessantly changing, surprising, individually
varied colors and lights of the city. They are the naked body
which the course of time clads in ever new and different
ways."[41]

Even if modernists were excited by the metaphors for speed
and commercialism, they did not completely lose sight of the
principles of classical and monumental architectural composition. This was revealed in the competition for the expansion
and landscaping of the Reichstag Building on the Platz der
Republik.

Paul Wallot's Reichstag Building had soon proved to be too
small for the administration of the new republic. Apart from
hundreds of new offices, archives, a library, and reading
rooms were required. A first competition for an extension was
announced in 1927; its sole result was the insight that "no
construction task associated with the Reichstag can be tackled without considering the design of its surroundings, that is,
the Platz der Republik."[42] Therefore, in the second, invita-
tional competition, launched in 1929, the square itself was included in the project description.

First prize went to a design by Emil Fahrenkamp and Heinrich de Fries (fig. 25). Close runners-up were projects as diverse as those of Bestelmeyer and Poelzig (who arranged ten
huge prisms in a gloriole that followed the meanderings of the
Spree River), Georg Holzbauer, and Franz Staff. Honorable
mention went to drawings by Behrens, Häring, Wilhelm Kreis,
Paul Schmitthenner (who proposed an astonishing tower more
than 197 feet high), and Eduard Jobst Siedler. The main task
was an expansion of the Reichstag Building on the adjacent,
almost triangular site extending to the Spree; but in the end it
would be questions dealing with urban design that would take
priority. So numerous and extensive were the proposals for the

redesign of "this square without space, this area without a square"[43] that, paradoxically, an attentive observer gained the impression that the sole defect of this nineteenth-century square was its paltry landscaping: "If this is really changed, then comparatively minor architectural alterations would be enough to make the Platz der Republik into one of Europe's most magnificent squares."[44] And Hegemann, who published the results in *Wasmuths Monatshefte für Baukunst*, also took the liberty of advancing his own idea—a slender 328-foot-high skyscraper that would temporarily provide the needed space until the square was definitively redesigned and that could be demolished as soon as the permanent structure was finished.[45]

The End of Metropolitan Dreams

Such modesty was not the rule at the time, nor did it seem adequate to meet the task at hand. Karl Scheffler, in *Die Architektur der Grosstadt*,[46] had conjured up a vision of enormous cities with a diameter of thirty-six to sixty miles, monumental beehives of activity. In connection with the Platz der Republik project, Mendelsohn now demanded, however, that Berlin at last be given squares that could match the Place de la Concorde. In taking Paris as a model, he was firmly within a Berlin tradition. Nor was Mendelsohn immune to the nationalistically tinged local patriotism that was in the air, stating that "Berlin, as a world center that represents the German empire, must break its small-town chains."[47] To which Häring polemically replied, "Any architect for whom the arrangement of objects in space has any real meaning would have . . . continued the broad Strasse der Republik from Alsen Bridge to Kemperplatz in order, first of all, to draw a firm, clear line through this axis of the autocrats."[48] With this declaration, Häring was of course giving verbal support to his own project of 1926 with its north-south axis borrowed from Mächler. Seen within this historical context, the plan for the north-south axis (Grosse Strasse) developed between 1936 and 1941 by Speer, general building inspector for the redesign of the imperial capital, represents a logical, if megalomaniacal, continuation (fig. 27). Its predecessor was above all Mächler's plan; its ideals were Paris and Vienna, which, however, were planned to pale into insignificance beside Hitler's Berlin (which in the meantime had passed the four-million population mark). Unlike the 1.2 miles of the Champs Elysées, Berlin's grand avenue was to run a full 4.2 miles, 394 feet wide. Planned for its northern end, on the banks of a lake obtained by widening the Spree, was a Grand Hall, or Hall of the People. As a southern termination, before the street reached South Station, a triumphal arch measuring 384 feet high and 558 feet wide was projected, beside which the Arc de Triomphe in Paris, at 230 feet high, would have looked dwarfish. On the 2,624-foot-long plaza between Speer's comparatively modernist station building and the elephantine arch, an avenue of trophies, with captured tanks and artillery, was to have been built. The street itself was not really a north-south connecting road at all but a largely self-contained, elongated parade ground for troops; there was in fact no link between the Grand Hall and the working-class districts in the city's north. It would have been flanked for almost its entire length solely by monumental gov-

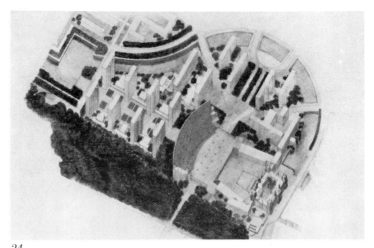

24

25

24. Hugo Häring. Redesign of Platz der Republik, 1929. Akademie der Künste Sammlung Baukunst Berlin.

25. Albert Speer. Model for the north-south axis, Berlin, 1936–41. Landesbildstelle Berlin.

ernment and business buildings—among others, the Ministry of the Interior, the Opera House, the AEG administration building designed by Peter Behrens, the offices of the Hermann Goering Works, the Allianz Insurance Building, a structure projected by Wilhelm Kreis for the Army High Command including Soldiers' Hall, Speer's Reich Marshal's Office, his complex comprising the Grand Hall and the Führer's Palace, the Reichstag Building, Police Headquarters, the War Academy, the building for the Navy High Command by Paul Bonatz, City Hall by German Bestelmeyer, and finally North Station. All of these structures were to be erected without the aid of private speculation, as part of a comprehensive plan in the style of that carried out by Georges-Eugène Hausmann under Napoleon III in Paris. A consortium of companies was formed in 1941; but before the year was out, Speer forbade all work not essential to the war effort, and the immense project, which for obvious reasons had been kept secret from the public, died in the planning stage.[49]

Notes

1. Some of the plans discussed in this paper are found in *Die Bauwerke und Kunstdenkmäler von Berlin, Bezirk Kreuzberg, Karten und Pläne*, ed. Manfred Hecker (Berlin: Gebrüder Mann, 1980); see especially Hecker's essay "Stadtplanerische Entwicklung des Bezirks Kreuzberg," 19–35.
2. Quoted in Albert Hofmann, "Gross-Berlin, sein Verhältnis zur modernen Grosstadtbewegung und der Wettbewerb zur Erlangung eines Grundplanes für die städtebauliche Entwicklung Berlins und seiner Vororte im zwanzigsten Jahrhundert," *Deutsche Bauzeitung*, Beilage für Wettbewerbe 28 (April 2, 1910): 198.
3. Ibid.
4. "With this radical solution," Jansen notes with regard to filling in the Landwehrkanal and paving it over, "one of our thorniest problems might possibly be solved were it not for the fact that the Landwehrkanal with its elegantly curved banks is one of the most charming features that Berlin has, to say nothing of the suburbs, which already have such a dearth of lovely views. Before sacrificing such a characteristic feature—which would happen as soon as the low-lying watercourse were replaced by a promenade at street level—no other conceivable measure should be left untried. The prime aim of the competition, after all, is not to shorten the journey from center to periphery by a few minutes but above all *to create and retain beauty!*" Quoted in Hofmann, "Gross-Berlin," 235, 236.
5. Quoted in Max Berg, "Der neue Geist im Städtebau auf der Grossen Berliner Kunstausstellung," *Stadtbaukunst alter und neuer Zeit* 8 (June 20, 1927): 41.
6. Ibid.
7. In Mächler's plan, all of the Berlin railway terminals were eliminated—Lehrter, Stettiner, Potsdamer, Anhalter, and Görlitzer Bahnhof.
8. *Baugilde*, 1929, 2,001.
9. The term *Germanization* occurred in the subtitle of an essay on the Danzig Skyscraper Competition of 1921: "Das Danziger Hochhaus. Eine 'Germanisierung' des Wolkenkratzers," *Vossische Zeitung* 2nd supplement, "Umschau in Technik und Wirtschaft" 40 (October 7, 1921). See also Rainer Stommer, "'Germanisierung des Wolkenkratzers'—Die Hochhausdebatte in Deutschland bis 1921," *Kritische Berichte* (Giessen) 10 (1982): 36–53.
10. *Berlins dritte Dimension*, ed. Alfred Dambitsch (Berlin: Ullstein Verlag, 1912).
11. "In terms of urban design a city should be conceived as a unified architectural configuration. No city that has grown all out of proportion is much helped, as regards the aesthetics of space, by creating squares, admirable as this may be. Nor can a church steeple have much effect in an overall picture characterized by flatness and overextension; a city laid out in the horizontal plane demands voluminousness, which can be achieved only by adding compact, vertical masses." Peter Behrens, in *Berliner Morgenpost*, November 27, 1912. Quoted in Fritz Hoeber, *Peter Behrens* (Munich, 1913), Moderne Architekten, vol. 1, 227ff.
12. Otto Rappold, *Der Bau der Wolkenkratzer* (Munich, 1913).
13. See Kurt Hager, "Architekturskizzen des Architekten K. Paul Andrae, Dresden," *Das Bild* (1937): 243.
14. Hugh Ferriss, *The Metropolis of Tomorrow* (New York: Ives Washburn, 1929).
15. See Walter Riezler, "Revolution and Baukunst," (1919; repr. in *Arbeitsrat für Kunst: Berlin 1918–1921*, exhibition catalogue, Akademie der Künste, Berlin, 1980), 96.
16. Paul Wittig, *Über die ausnahmsweise Zulassung einzelner Turmhäuser in Berlin* (Berlin, 1918), 14.
17. See "Der erste Wolkenkratzer in Europa?" in *Baugewerbs-Zeitung* (1920), 188.
18. Max Berg, "Der Bau von Geschäftshochhäusern in Breslau zur Linderung der Wohnungsnot," *Stadtbaukunst alter und neuer Zeit* 1 (1920–21): 99–104, 115–18; Reprinted with a slightly altered conclusion under the title "Der Bau von Geschäftshochhäusern in den Grosstädten als Mittel zur Linderung der Wohnungsnot, mit Beispielen für Breslau," *Ostdeutsche Bauzeitung* 18 (1920): 273–77. After a look at the North American skyscraper, Berg rather melodramatically exclaims, "What Acropolis of Labor, what an intelligent expression of American enterprise, might not have resulted if builders instead of engineers [*Tektonen statt Techniker*] had been at work here, if the will to socially aware design had been given the chance to unfold. . . . Only a socially organized people, suffused with a sense of social labor, will be able to lend a corresponding artistic expression to the works in which its labor is embodied. Germany comes closest to meeting this chal-

lenge. Just as it will lend form to the socialist state, Germany will take the lead in molding human labor. . . . To gain an idea of the architectural aspect of future cities you have to imagine that today's high buildings, monumental in comparison to those of the Middle Ages, will be over-shadowed by the huge modern buildings, temples of human labor, of the business districts."

19. Bruno Möhring, "Über die Vorzüge der Turmhäuser und die Voraussetzungen, unter denen sie in Berlin gebaut werden können," *Stadtbaukunst alter und neuer Zeit* (1921): 353–57, 370–76, 385–91; the quotation is on 371.

20. Otto Kohtz, *Büroturmhäuser in Berlin* (Berlin, 1921).

21. This was a part of his plan's title.

22. Otto Kohtz, "Das Reichshaus am Königsplatz in Berlin. Ein Vorschlag zur Verringerung der Wohnungsnot und der Arbeitslosigkeit," *Stadtbaukunst alter Zeit* 1 (1920–21): 241–45 (expanded version published under the same title by Verlag Der Zirkel, Berlin, 1920).

23. Le Corbusier, "Curiosité?—non: anomalie!" *L'Esprit Nouveau* 9 (June 1921): 1,017.

24. See *Der Schrei nach dem Turmhaus: Der Ideenwettbewerb Hochhaus am Bahnhof Friedrichstrasse Berlin 1921/22*, exhibition catalogue (Berlin: Argon, 1988).

25. See Ludovica Scarpa, *Martin Wagner e Berlino: Casa e città nella Repubblica di Weimar, 1918–1933* (Rome: Officina Edizioni, 1983; German ed., *Martin Wagner und Berlin: Architektur und Städtebau in der Weimarer, Braunschweig und Wiesbaden: Republik, Vieweg, 1986).

26. See Scarpa, *Martin Wagner* (German ed.), 84.

27. Martin Wagner, *Wirtschaftlicher Städtebau* (Stuttgart, 1951), 139.

28. "Die internationale Übereinstimmung des Baugedankens oder Dynamik und Funktion" (1923) in Erich Mendelsohn, *Das Gersontschaffen des Architekten, Skizzen, Entwurfe, Bauten* (Berlin 1930), 28.

29. Ludwig Hilberseimer, *Grosstadtarchitektur* (Stuttgart, 1928), 98.

30. Georg Simmel, "Die Grosstädte und das Geistesleben," *Die Grosstadt: Vorträge und Aufsätze zur Städteausstellung* (Dresden, 1903), 188–206.

31. Hugo Häring, "Die Sonderausstellung städtebaulicher Projekte Gross-Berlins in der Grossen Berliner Kunstausstellung, veranstaltet von der Architekten-Vereinigung 'Der Ring,'" *Stadtbaukunst alter und neuer Zeit* 8 (June 20, 1927): 50–55.

32. See Norbert Huse, *"Neues Bauen" 1918 bis 1933: Moderne Architektur in der Weimarer Republik* (Munich: Heinz Moos Verlag, 1975), 113–19.

33. Martin Wagner, "Das Formproblem eines Weltstadtplatzes," *Das Neue Bauen* 2 (Berlin, 1929): 33-38. The entire passage is worth reading in context: "A metropolitan square is not a small-town square. The design of a small-town square, a marketplace, can be based on purely architectural criteria and still not come in conflict with the occasional demands of traffic (as on market days). The metropolitan square is an almost continually filled traffic sluice, the clearing point for a network of main traffic arteries. Now, one can say the ensuring an uninterrupted flow of traffic through this clearing point is the primary and essential factor, and formal criteria, functional form, are of only secondary significance. Nevertheless, no city planner will be able to separate the one from the other, and a closer scrutiny of the problem will lead to the result that purpose and form, ground plan and elevation, square area and street walls will all enter an organic unity. Metropolitan squares are organisms with a characteristic formal aspect. To this day Europe has yet to see organically designed metropolitan squares."

34. Ibid.

35. See Alfred Döblin, *Berlin Alexanderplatz*, ed. W. Muschg (Olten Freiburg, 1961); and Volker Klotz, *Die erzählte Stadt: Ein Sujet als Herausforderung des Romans von Lesage bis Döblin* (Munich: Carl Hanser Verlag, 1969), 372–418.

36. Döblin, *Berlin Alexanderplatz*, 181.

37. Martin Wagner, "Das Formproblem," 33–38.

38. Ibid.

39. Ludwig Hilberseimer, untitled article ("Das Projekt Mies van der Rohes im Wettbewerb für die Umgestaltung des Alexanderplatzes"), *Das Neue Berlin* 2 (1929): 39–41. It is noteworthy that although Hilberseimer approved of Mies's concept, he did so only in this particular case and by no means as a general principle: "It used to be that architecture forced itself upon traffic; nowadays, the opposite seems to be the case. It is nevertheless conceivable that a harmony could exist between the two that leaves both complete freedom. In the projects for a redesign of Alexanderplatz, necessary for traffic reasons, this harmony would initially appear to be present, with architecture and traffic having equal rights. When you look into the problem more deeply however, it turns out that the architecture is merely a facade architecture that has nothing to do with the building organisms that lie behind it. The circular form necessitated by traffic has been transferred to the frontages, which are also built over the street, so that in the classical style the square is enclosed. The aim has been to make a solid architectural configuration out of the loose grouping that Alexanderplatz is. Here the question arises whether the building line must run parallel to the traffic or whether both are relatively independent of one another. Ideally, of course, they should be in conformance. In this special case, however, it would appear that this architectural form does violence to the organism of buildings and streets, and that, for ostensibly architectural reasons, it destroys the architectural configuration."

40. Marcel Breuer, "Verkehrsarchitektur—ein Vorschlag zur Neuordnung des Potsdamer Platzes," *Das neue Berlin*, 136-41; quotation on 136.

41. Ibid, 141.

42. Ludwig Hilberseimer, "Reichstagerweiterung und Platz der Republik," *Die Form* 5 (1930).

43. Martin Kiessling, "Der Reichstagwettbewerb," *Das neue Berlin*.

44. Ibid.

45. Werner Hegemann, "Turmhaus am Reichstag?" *Wasmuths Monatshefte für Baukunst* (Berlin, 1930): 97–104.

46. Karl Scheffler, *Die Architektur der Grosstadt* (Berlin: Bruno Cassirer, 1913).

47. Erich Mendelsohn, "Zum Platz der Republik," *Das neue Berlin*.

48. Hugo Häring, "Herrn Mendelsohn zur Erwiderung," *Das neue Berlin*.

49. See Lars Olof Larsson, *Die Neugestaltung der Reichshauptstadt, Albert Speer Generalbebauungsplan für Berlin* (Stuttgart: Gerd Hatje Verlag, 1978).

*1. Clarence Stein. Phipps Gardens
Apartments, 1931. Court. From
Architectural Record 71 (March
1932).*

Neighborhood Block and Garden Court: New York City Housing between the World Wars

Richard Pommer

Richard Pommer is the Sheldon H. Solow Professor of the History of Architecture at the Institute of Fine Arts, New York University. His publications include "The Architecture of Urban Housing in the United States in the early 1930s," Journal of the Society of Architectural Historians *(1978), "Mies van der Rohe and the Political Ideology of the Modern Movement in Architecture," in* Mies van der Rohe, Critical Essays, *ed. Franz Schulze (1989), and* Weissenhof 1927 and the Modern Movement in Architecture *(with Christian Otto, 1990).*

The life of the community focuses on the great court or central park. All units are entered from it, most living rooms face it, balconies are turned towards it. —Clarence Stein, 1931[1]

The urban street block has long been the true locale of the "neighborhood," the identifying social unit of New York City, in the districts of the poor as well as the middle class. It is the turf over which gangs fight, the domain of the block captain corralling votes for the Democratic machine, and the setting of the block party on the Upper West Side or the Lower East Side. The predominance of the block came in no small measure from the totalitarian grid of Manhattan, which provided an automatic identity to every resident within it.

The same commercial pressures that established the grid for the convenience of builders and speculators guaranteed that no alternative to the urban block could readily become the basis of low-income housing. As the *Siedlungen* of Berlin spread out into the suburban fields and forests after World War I, most of the housing projects of New York were still squeezed into the more densely populated quarters of the central city. The periphery of Berlin, Frankfurt, and other German cities had been legally regulated and acquired in large parcels by the powerful municipal governments to prevent speculators from controlling the outlying land. On this ring of fields and forests, the cooperative building societies proceeded with the support of the municipal governments to establish the pattern of the new *Siedlungen*: low houses, separate or in long rows, set in ample open tracts, as in Bruno Taut's Falkenberg *Siedlung* of 1912–14 or Martin Wagner's project of 1918 in the Lindenhof suburb of Berlin.

But in New York City, real estate speculators wanted the suburbs for future middle class subdivisions, and no municipal administration had the power to stop them. Labor unions and philanthropic societies seldom provided the money to buy more than an occasional parcel, nor could they expect help from the city treasuries. The price of the outlying land rose so high that housing projects had to be built in densities not much lower than the speculative blocks of five- and six-story walk-up apartment houses filling the outer reaches of Manhattan, Queens, and the Bronx. The few housing projects built downtown where the poor congregated near their jobs usually required slum clearance, which the owners of the adjacent properties and their political allies expected as the price for their support. Under such circumstances, housing for those with small incomes—large in scale and low in density—was all but impossible to build.[2]

Public as well as private housing in New York was therefore forced into the confines of the gridded block. Yet even this could not be established as a coherent social unit with its own amenities: the demands of the speculators forced the block's subdivision into the twenty-five by one-hundred-foot lot, which restricted the development of townhouses and tenements for more than a century. At the end of the nineteenth century, the nascent movement for philanthropic and limited-dividend housing could offer no better arrangement for model tenements than plans one-hundred by one-hundred feet with narrow light courts (fig. 2).[3] By that time, the Berliner Spar-

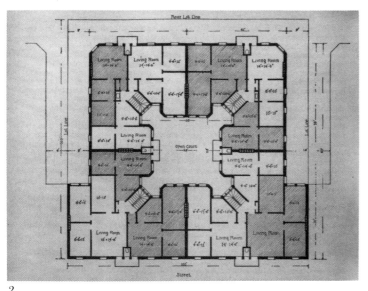

2. *Ernest Flagg. Model tenement plan, 1922.* From *Scribner's Magazine* 16 (1984).

3. *Andrew J. Thomas. Metropolitan Life Houses, Queens, 1922. Project.* From *Architectural Forum* (July 1922).

und Bauverein had built several projects by Alfred Messel of entire blocks opened by huge garden courts and playgrounds within a perimeter of well-ventilated apartments.[4]

The architects of the philanthropic and limited-dividend housing, such as I. N. Phelps Stokes and Ernest Flagg, usually had been trained at the Ecole des Beaux-Arts, or the American schools of architecture modeled upon it, to lay out the new housing with the small square courts, ample stairs, symmetrical plans, and a *marche* toward a *pointe de vue* of the Parisian *maison de rapport*. The court also resembled on a smaller scale the courts of European palaces and the New York apartment buildings for the extremely wealthy, such as the Dakota.[5] It was therefore a fitting representation of the philanthropic hand-me-down approach to housing in New York, which was entirely in keeping with the trickle-down arrangement through which the poor obtained much of their housing in America by moving into the decayed residences of the rich.

But the apartment plans of the philanthropic buildings had to be far more ingenious than on the Continent because of higher standards in New York for plumbing, ventilation, privacy, and construction, even in model housing. Toilets and running water in every apartment, ample closets, entrance halls, direct access to most rooms, corner exposures, tiled staircases, and exteriors of good brick and stone—such were amenities commonly provided in New York housing at the end of the century. The combination of French beaux-arts design, the English institution of limited-dividend and philanthropic housing, the high standards of New York apartment planning and construction, and the squeeze of the New York grid—constricted further by the weakness of the American housing movement—set the terms for New York housing in the 1920s and 1930s, except for the perimeter blocks and garden courts introduced after the war.

World War I brought the federal government into housing, as into other areas of American life, transforming its ambitions, scale, and form over the next two decades.[6] The war workers' housing built by the U.S. Housing Corporation and especially by the Emergency Fleet Corporation enabled American architects to plan for the first time on a scale larger than a portion of a block. Instead of the small courts of philanthropic housing, they were encouraged to open up the buildings in U-shaped blocks set on larger sites. Even more important for later housing, the architects and reformers came to admire English garden city planning and its goal of establishing entire communities.[7]

Many of the leaders of American housing, particularly in New York City, emerged from these wartime government offices. They included Robert J. Kohn, later the housing director of the Public Works Administration; Frederick L. Ackerman, who was to become the first technical director of the New York City Housing Authority; Henry Wright, a future collaborator with Clarence Stein; and Andrew J. Thomas, an apartment house specialist who developed the so-called New York garden apartment.[8]

After the war, Thomas grouped the U- and H-shaped blocks together around large gardens and playground courts the full length and width of the city block (fig. 3).[9] Next he linked the units to produce an almost continuous but deeply indented perimeter, notably in two projects sponsored in 1926 by John D. Rockefeller, Jr.—the Paul Laurence Dunbar Apartments in Harlem and the Thomas Garden Apartments in the Bronx (figs. 4 and 5).[10] Ample apartments, many with a large dining room as well as a living room, several outside corner exposures, a full bath, and an entrance hall, distinguished this housing from its meaner London prototypes and the minimal, standardized apartments of the Berlin *Siedlungen*.[11] The recessed perimeters, which became a hallmark of housing in New York and other cities in the later 1920s and early 1930s, provided light, air, and corner views as well as more apartments in each block, and became the chief articulation of the simple brick elevations. With their axially organized and carefully landscaped gardens, the courts became the cynosure of the housing blocks, the view of choice in photographs and presentation drawings of the period (figs. 1, 4).

In his development of the full court, Thomas followed the example of nineteenth-century English philanthropic housing, which hollowed out the urban block to a thin perimeter of flats around large courts in order to reduce the population densities and to bring light and air into the tubercular urban fabric.[12] He was able to demonstrate to the satisfaction of the philanthropic businessmen and himself that it was possible to lower land coverage with the perimeter plan and still increase returns on investment.[13] The court was also an instrument and emblem of community for utopian planners from Charles Fourier and Jean Baptiste Godin to Clarence Stein. Because social status was so uncertain and therefore dependent on place of residence in New York City, even more than in smaller American cities, the courtyard house offered a *private* communal space, protected from the insecurities of the city, both for the rich in their luxury apartments and for the workers or lower middle class in their garden apartments.[14]

What was most striking in postwar New York housing, however, was not so much the court itself but rather, as the name of the new apartment houses indicated, the garden. In the United States, and particularly in New York City, the park was the only social space the public could agree on. Before the mid-nineteenth century, Manhattan was notorious for failing to set aside public spaces except for cemeteries and parade grounds—Washington Square exists only because it was first a potter's field and then a military parade ground—prior to opening up its relentless grid for Central Park. Few public squares were built in America, yet the park movement was able to reserve large urban tracts for parks and parkways in the later nineteenth century. Similarly, the City Beautiful movement came closest to realizing its ideal programs when it set its buildings on a park, such as the lakefront of Chicago or the mall in Washington, D.C.

It was the garden city movement in England, however, that promoted the communal function of the garden court in residential quarters, particularly through the work of Raymond Unwin who, in his projects for Hampstead garden city, adopt-

4

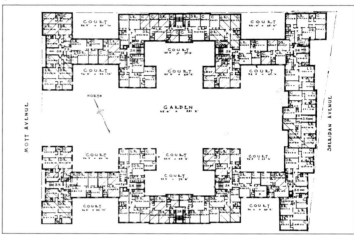

5

4. *Andrew J. Thomas. Thomas Garden Apartments, Bronx, 1926. Courtyard view.* From *Architectural Record* 63 (1928).

5. *Andrew J. Thomas. Thomas Garden Apartments, Bronx, 1926. Plan.* From *Architectural Record* 63 (1928).

ed the green monastic quadrangles of Oxford and Cambridge as a models for community.[15] The English garden city program left an early mark on the federal wartime planners but exerted its chief influence through the Regional Planning Association of America (RPAA) after the war.

The RPAA was founded in New York City in 1923 by Kohn, Ackerman, Wright, Stein, Lewis Mumford, and a few other admirers of the Fabian socialist ideals of the garden city founders and the cost-cutting site planning of Raymond Unwin.[16] In a series of projects, Stein opened out the garden courts on an increasingly larger scale and restudied the indented perimeter, sometimes in collaboration with Henry Wright, with an empirical rigor unmatched earlier in the United States and seldom in Europe. At Sunnyside Gardens in Queens, Stein and Wright arrayed low houses around the commons, as Stein called them, derived from the new larger blocks recommended by Unwin; in the adjacent Phipps Gardens elevator apartment, Stein turned the block entirely in upon its garden (fig. 1), and at Hillside Homes in the Bronx, he attempted for the first time to expand beyond the confines of the city block (fig. 6).

Through the propaganda of the RPAA, the example of Thomas's work, and the influence of Stein, the garden court within an indented perimeter block became the preferred design for urban housing in New York City when the state and then federal government began to support larger housing projects in the late 1920s and early 1930s.[17] With the backing of the New York State Housing Law of 1926, which promoted limited-dividend corporations, the Amalgamated Clothing Workers Union began to build larger projects with extensive cooperative facilities, notably the Amalgamated Houses near Van Cortland Park South in the Bronx. The architects of the projects, George Springsteen and Albert Goldhammer, adopted the indented perimeter plans used by the earlier philanthropic housing, thereby conferring more progressive social and political connotations on the New York garden apartment.[18]

In the Depression year of 1932, President Herbert Hoover unintentionally initiated the continuing intervention of the federal government in public housing by authorizing the Reconstruction Finance Corporation (RFC) to issue loans in support of limited-dividend housing.[19] The following summer, the Roosevelt administration ordered the new Housing Division of the Public Works Administration (PWA) to take over the RFC program, and within a year the PWA made loans for seven projects with about 3,100 rooms. Hillside Homes, planned in 1932–33 with an RFC loan was an ambitious and paradigmatic project of the first federally supported housing programs in New York City.[20] Clarence Stein first wanted to close most of the traversing roads and array the buildings on an open, sloping site five blocks wide, as superblocks in large crankshaft patterns around long and broad greens following the lay of the land. Had he been able to carry this project out, it would have come closer to the successful expansion of the New York housing block to a large parklike site than any earlier attempt. But when his application was made to the PWA in the summer of 1933, Stein was required to restore the roads and close the courts in an arrangement more typical of New York.

Despite Stein's concessions to the PWA, Hillside Homes was far more aesthetically successful than Knickerbocker Village on the Lower East Side (fig. 7), the only project built entirely with RFC funds.[21] Two blocks near the Manhattan Bridge were torn down under the provision of the slum clearance act to make room for the project. The architects, John S. Van Wart and Ackerman, arrayed the perimeter blocks around two landscaped courts, but in order to house two thousand middle-class families on such costly land and still make a profit, they raised the building twelve stories and added a penthouse in an unbroken wall, shutting out light and air and requiring costly elevators. For these reasons, Knickerbocker Village was derided by the RPAA and other housing reformers for whom the walk-up garden apartment remained the model for urban public housing in the early 1930s.[22]

Just when these reformers began to leave their mark on New York City's public housing, the new architecture and planning of the European modernists arrived to challenge and disorient their approach. The confused reception of European modernism was immediately evident in the exhibition of modern architecture at the Museum of Modern Art in the spring of 1932, which split the works into separate exhibits, one on architecture, arranged by Philip Johnson and Henry-Russell Hitchcock, and the other on housing, planned by the RPAA inner circle of Stein, Wright, and the young Catherine Bauer.[23] The architectural exhibition paid no attention to social issues, and the housing section displayed the example of Radburn, New Jersey, by Stein and Wright, with its small, wooden, pitched-roof houses, alongside others by Ernst May and Otto Haesler, without regard to differences in form. Yet for most European architects of the modern movement, housing was the chief purpose of the new architecture and could no more be divorced from the new forms than form from function, or urban planning from architecture.

Bauer was instrumental in organizing the housing section of the exhibition,[24] and Mumford wrote the separate catalogue introduction to it.[25] They were among the few New Yorkers to understand the new housing both as planning and as architecture and to welcome its vast new scale in the organization of communities and of urban space.[26] After a tour of the German *Siedlungen* and other European housing in 1930, Bauer published an article in *Fortune* magazine that was the first to recognize both the formal and the communal rationales of modern European housing, especially as represented by the huge *Siedlungen* of Ernst May in Frankfurt.[27] After the exhibition at MOMA, Mumford himself came around to a more balanced comprehension of European modernist architecture, though always with more emphasis on its social and functional sides.[28] In her monumental study *Modern Housing* (1934), Bauer began to see, as few other Americans did, that the housing of the modern movement was not simply a reform of capitalist housing, in the fashion of the garden city movement and the RPAA, but a drastic critique meant to supplant it.[29] She came to understand that the new housing had to be supported on a vast scale by the government as a social right, not by a handful of well-intentioned reformers and capitalists as an act of benevolence, and that the new open planning of the European modernists was the sign of this break with the hand-me-

6

7

*6. Clarence Stein. Hillside Housing,
1934.* From *Architecture* 71 (May
1934).

*7. John S. Van Wart and Frederick
Ackerman. Knickerbocker Village,
Lower East Side, Manhattan, 1934.*
From *Architectural Record* 75
(1934).

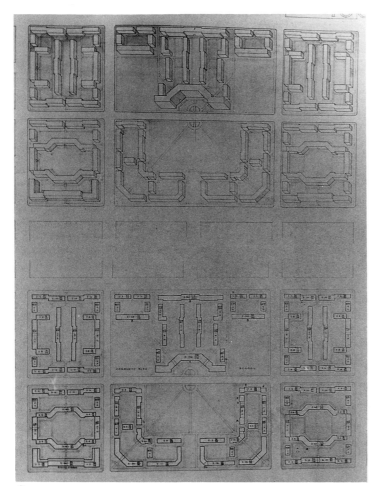

8

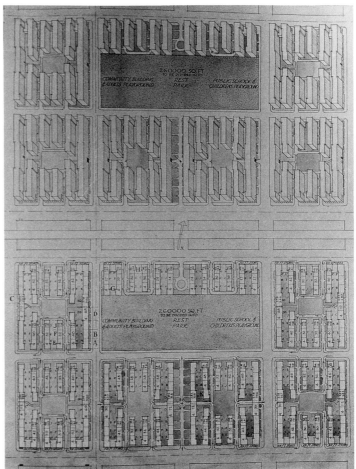

9

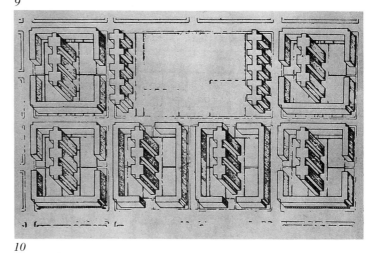

10

8. Electus Litchfield, New York City
Housing Authority competition
project, 1934. Avery Library,
Columbia University.

9. John W. Ingle. New York City
Housing Authority competition
project, 1934. Avery Library,
Columbia University.

10. Stephen Hedrich. New York City
Housing Authority competition
project, 1934. From James Ford,
Slums and Housing, with special
reference to New York City-
Cambridge, MA., 25E.

11. William Lescaze. Chrystie-
Forsyth Houses, Manhattan, 1931.
Project. Lescaze Archives, George
Arents Research Library, Syracuse
University.

11

down attitude of the philanthropists symbolized by the garden court.

But Bauer and Mumford were writers, not architects, and their comprehension of European housing was based on broad considerations. A third member of the RPAA, Henry Wright, looked upon himself as a planner and cost accountant as well as an architect[30] and accepted European modernist housing for pragmatic reasons, without concern either for its ideological or formal character. Wright spent four months in the winter of 1932 studying housing in Europe and turned his notes into the concluding chapter of his book *Rehousing Urban America*, completed in 1933 though published only in 1935.[31] Still he ignored the formal design, technology, and utopian ideology of European housing in favor of its practical advantages.[32] Together with Mumford and a younger housing architect, Albert Mayer, Wright established the Housing Study Guild in New York in the summer of 1933 to train architects in the new methods of research, cost analysis, and planning.[33] In his role as an adviser to the PWA, Wright exerted considerable influence on the assimilation of the indented perimeter plan to aspects of European modernist housing.[34] But neither he nor the other advocates of modernist planning had much of a direct voice in the housing program of New York City, which was still dominated by the beaux-arts architects and the urban grid.

The differences among the approaches of the RPAA, the beaux-arts architects, and the young modernists emerged in the critical event in New York City's initial housing program, the New York City Housing Authority competition held in June 1934 to select the architects for the projects to be financed by PWA loans.[35] Ackerman, who had worked with Stein and Wright at Sunnyside and Radburn and had been appointed the technical director for the housing authority, wrote and supervised the competition, assisted by a committee of architects nominated by the New York architectural societies. The competition, which was conceived as the initial step towards the design of Williamsburg Houses in Brooklyn, the largest and most costly of all the PWA projects, called for the clearance of sixteen blocks of slums and their rebuilding as six superblocks with a large area for parks, a school, and a community center.

Many of the surviving entries for Williamsburg Houses followed the indented perimeter plan developed by Stein for Hillside Homes (fig. 6), including Stein's own entry. Beaux-arts architects such as Electus Litchfield, who had built the formally planned Yorkship Village in Camden, New Jersey, for the U.S. Shipping Board in World War I, submitted grandiose arrangements, reminiscent of Versailles and comparable to recent French town plans, which would have overwhelmed the mean streets of Brooklyn (fig. 8). Several younger entrants offered modifications of the German *Zeilenbau* scheme of parallel straight rows or played with strange combinations of tall towers ringed by lower perimeter blocks, provincial parallels or derivatives of recent French and Dutch designs (figs. 9 and 10). None of the known designs, however, broke free of the block, fully taking advantage of the amplitude and openness of the site.

The disjunction between modernist planning and the conditions of New York, and between social issues and architectural form, became most sharply evident in the New York City work of the Swiss architect William Lescaze, who ultimately designed the Williamsburg Houses project. Lescaze was the chief purveyor of recent European design on the East Coast, rivaled only by Richard Neutra on the West Coast.[36] Lescaze had come to the United States in 1920 after studying with the modernist sympathizer Karl Moser in Zurich and thus stood outside the main European developments of the decade. Though he could easily reproduce the varieties of Continental modernism, Lescaze had little interest in the political ideologies or comprehension of the design of the European modernists.

In December 1931, Lescaze, in nominal partnership with George Howe, submitted a proposal for the Chrystie-Forsyth Houses in New York (fig. 11).[37] The project was designed by Lescaze's office in New York, with most details the work of the young Swiss architect Albert Frey who had worked from 1928 to 1929 in the atelier of Le Corbusier.[38] The site was a long corridor in a dense slum on the Lower East Side that was flanked and traversed by heavily traveled streets. On this difficult site, Frey disposed an ingenious adaptation of the crankshaft arrangement of apartment houses from Le Corbusier's City of Three Million project in order to open up the site for playgrounds while retaining the cross streets and a suggestion of the city block. Galleried slab towers developed by Walter Gropius in the late 1920s housed cross-partitioned apartments one major room deep that opened to the sun and could be flexibly arranged; the galleries and minor rooms could be turned toward the noisy street and the living rooms and bedrooms toward the courts.[39] Yet in its display of functional ingenuity, the design contradicted the formal and ideological principles of European modernism on which it was based. The orientation of the rooms and the slabs was not uniform, as was preferred in Europe as an index of *sachlich*—hygienic and egalitarian planning. Because the crankshaft arrangement of Le Corbusier's City of Three Million scheme made systematic orientation impossible, it was hardly ever imitated. The galleried plan had been developed in Germany for two-room apartments, not the four or five necessary on the Lower East Side, so that in Lescaze's project large hallways had to be provided within the apartments for access to the rooms, wasting precious space and blocking cross ventilation. Open corridors would have been as impractical in New York as they proved to be in Germany during the winter. The desire for humane variations in housing that would complement the New York city block diminished the formal logic of European modernist planning without achieving a significantly more livable arrangement.

Another Lescaze project, which Frey worked on in its initial stage (it was not carried much further), is also an eclectic mix of European modernism and New York housing design. The project, called River Gardens, was planned for a vast site on the Lower East Side flanking the approaches to the Williamsburg Bridge (fig. 12).[40] Derived from the cross-shaped office towers of Le Corbusier's city plans, Frey's towers were varied drastically in height in an attempt, as the architect later said, "to re-

12

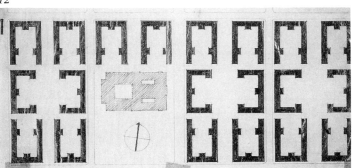

13

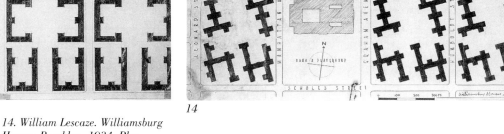

14

12. William Lescaze. River Gardens
Housing, Manhattan, 1931. Project.
Lescaze Archives, George Arents
Research Library, Syracuse
University.

13. William Lescaze, after proposed
plan by the New York City Housing
Administration, Williamsburg
Houses, Brooklyn, 1934. Lescaze
Archives, George Arents Research
Library, Syracuse University.

14. William Lescaze. Williamsburg
Houses, Brooklyn, 1934. Plan.
Lescaze Archives, George Arents
Research Library, Syracuse
University.

late [the towers] to the human scale and avoid a stereotyped monotony."[41] The design also preserved a vestigial reference to the enclosures of the recessed perimeter block. But the compromise between Le Corbusier and New York succeeded only in destroying the hierarchical system, rational order, and open sweep of Le Corbusier's city along with the old scale and closure of the tenemented grid around it.

The éclat of these projects led Richmond Shreve, who had helped run the competition and the team of architects chosen to build Williamsburg, to bring in Lescaze to design the housing project. As the chief architect of the Empire State Building, Shreve presumably wanted a more experienced modernist than the competition had provided. Lescaze had to take into account a schematic plan (fig. 12) developed by Ackerman's office on the basis of the competition designs, which disposed the buildings in small U-shaped courts around larger central courts on four superblocks, a scheme derived from the layout of Hillside Homes (fig. 6). Lescaze turned the long blocks fifteen degrees from the north-south grid to the northwest and connected them with crossbars in a semblance of small courts around a central court, with spurs for a more extensive perimeter (fig. 14). In the elevations (fig. 15), the concrete floor plates were brought to the surface and turned up in wide spandrels to carry the pinkish brick. The result at a distance gives the effect of *Zeilenbau* blocks in echelon formation, detached from the city around it. But up close the courts and projections of older American housing become predominant. As one critic noted in 1938: "The reasons for the change of angles [from the street grid] seem obscure. . . . The present layout converts the courts into perfect channels for our most vicious Northwest winds." Mumford remarked that the T-unit plans of the apartments, adapted though they were to the court and spur pattern, oriented many of the rooms incorrectly in this angled layout. It was characteristic of Lescaze to seek the dramatic aesthetic of a pseudo-*Zeilenbau* system perhaps at the cost of its meaning and function.[42]

The remaining projects developed by the housing authority in 1934–35 were then apportioned among the other winners of the Williamsburg competition.[43] Harlem River Houses for Negroes was planned in accordance with the separate but not equal policy of the PWA, and at the same time as Williamsburg. Red Hook in Brooklyn and Queensbridge Houses were both broached in 1934 but postponed to the following year because money had to be diverted for emergency relief. None of these projects shows much evidence—if any at all—of European modernist influence.

Harlem River Houses (fig. 16) was the work of a team headed by Archibald Manning Brown, a beaux-arts society architect, but was largely the design of Horace Ginsbern, one of the ablest and most prolific apartment house designers in New York City (and therefore in the United States) during the 1920s and 1930s.[44] The architects were given a wedge-shaped site cut in two unequal parts by Seventh Avenue. On the larger segment they placed the main group of buildings around a large sunken rectangular court, with playgrounds and cobblestone walks; the court was bisected with a wide walkway that continued 152nd Street east to a deep court in

15. William Lescaze. Williamsburg Houses, Brooklyn, 1934. Lescaze Archives, George Arents Research Library, Syracuse, New York.

16

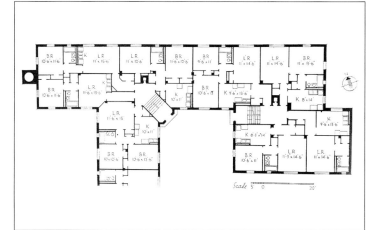

17

16. *Archibald Manning Brown and Horace Ginsbern. Harlem River Houses, Manhattan, 1935. Bird's-eye view.* New York City Housing Authority.

17. *Archibald Manning Brown and Horace Ginsbern. Harlem River Houses, Manhattan, 1935. Apartment plans.* From *Pencil Points* 19 (May 1938).

18. *Electus Litchfield. Red Hook Houses, 1935. Bird's-eye view.* New York City Housing Authority.

18

the smaller group of buildings across Seventh Avenue, an idea first proposed by Stein in Hillside Houses but never executed because of the expanse of the Harlem River. In its simplified form of beaux-arts design, the project has the largeness usually reserved for civic monuments, and the spaciousness is brought inside by the ample corner staircases and apartments—the larger ones circumambulated from room to room (fig. 17).

The Wagner Housing Act of 1937 established the U.S. Housing Authority which provided federal funds to local housing authorities.[45] Although intended to encourage greater local control, the act gave bureaucrats more power over the initiatives of architects and sponsors. The law placed a limit on construction costs of $1250 per room in cities with populations of more than five hundred thousand and required the elimination of an equivalent amount of slums, harsher regulations that significantly increased the height of the buildings and altered the site planning of urban projects. This remained the basic program until after World War II.

The Wagner Act revived the dormant Red Hook and Queensbridge housing projects, but with much severer costs restrictions. Red Hook in Brooklyn had been worked out in detail in 1935 (fig. 18)[46] by the chief designer Electus Litchfield, who, as in his design for the 1934 New York City Housing Authority competition, emulated the grand plans of the French. At Red Hook, Litchfield proposed three boulevards leading to the apartment buildings, all three or four stories high in early PWA fashion. Revising the project in 1938 to meet the new regulations, he had to raise the blocks to six-story elevator buildings and narrow the boulevards. But a grassy walkway still swept down the center—Mumford compared it to the canal at Versailles—towards a *pointe de vue* that Litchfield is reported to have hoped might be a tower, as in the recent French project of Villeurbanne near Lyons.

The Queensbridge project (fig. 19) was open to the modernism admired by the Housing Study Guild.[47] It was located on part of a site in Astoria advocated by the guild for its low cost and accessibility.[48] The chief architect was William F. R. Ballard, who had worked with the guild and in Stein's office on Hillside Houses, assisted by a team including Henry S. Churchill, an apartment-house architect who had participated in the Astoria study and who was responsible for the elevations of Queensbridge. Its tall towers and low site coverage were analogous to Le Corbusier's City for Three Million and its Y-shaped towers to those developed by Le Corbusier in the 1930s. But the project's architects admitted only to a limited interest in European modernism and thought that their work was merely a pragmatic response to the new U.S. Housing Authority regulations and not an adaptation of Corbusian models. Despite the European parallels, the disposition of the partly linked towers in zigzags around large courts still reflected the indented perimeter arrangements of earlier New York housing.

By comparison to Harlem River and Williamsburg Houses, the costs per room in these two projects were almost halved.[49] But densities rose significantly, by more than a third at Queensbridge over Harlem River, for example. Mumford in

19. William F. R. Ballard. *Queensbridge Houses, Astoria, Queens, 1935. Bird's-eye view.* New York City Housing Authority.

20. *Lewis Davis and Samuel Brody.
Riverbend Houses, New York City,
1967. Court view.*

1940 thought that the sites had been overcrowded, leading to excessive standardization of the dwelling units, with the result that "both projects are unnecessarily barrackslike and monotonous." For him they represented a drastic falling off from earlier standards.

Despite or perhaps because of the technical excellence required to meet the new federal guidelines, the projects after Queensbridge began to assume the dreary appearance for which all public housing of the 1930s in the United States would soon be known. The empiricism advocated by Wright and the Housing Study Guild served only to undermine their garden city ideals when the architects were confronted with the restrictions of the new housing laws. Instead of attempting to change the regulations or merely to denounce them, the reform architects simply called upon their technical ingenuity to reduce costs as best they could, exactly as their predecessors had done in the apartment houses, tenements, and philanthropic housing of New York City.

The ground was now cleared for the invasion of modernist towers, the Corbusian slabs and crosses standing free on superblock parks of postwar housing in New York.[50] With the housing bureaucracy well established and more funds available, it was possible to acquire sites large enough to present the illusion of a European modernist scale, but once again, it was the parks that helped make the housing politically acceptable. Only with the rising criticism of modernist urban planning and housing in the 1960s did the trend begin to slacken. In her book *Death and Life of Great American Cities* (1961), the New York journalist Jane Jacobs took the model of her own neighborhood in Greenwich Village to advocate the virtues of the New York block with low-rise apartments facing out onto the crowded streets of Manhattan's grid. Soon architects were again planning open-courtyard blocks related in scale to the adjacent brownstones, such as those of the New York garden apartment building—for example, Riverbend Houses near Harlem River Houses by Lewis Davis and Samuel Brody (fig. 20). Now the chief attraction of the court, however, was not its utopian evocation of social solidarity but rather its advantage for mutual surveillance, as Jacobs had emphasized in her analysis of the street as a place to see and be seen by neighbors and intruders. Nor is it surprising that the court is paved and without much greenery, for the sake of easier maintainance.[51]

In the more recent plan for Battery Park City by Alexander Cooper and Stanton Eckstut (fig. 21),[52] the New York block and grid have been fully restored, but the open communal courts of the garden apartment and early public housing have been dropped by most residential architects in favor of narrow backyards behind buildings turned out to the street (fig. 22). But only the very rich can afford this kind of housing, those who have their emblems of community in the athletic clubs within their buildings, and can do just as well without the garden courts. Neither the garden apartment block of the housing reformers—despite postmodernist polemics favoring its revival[53]—nor the slabs and towers of the modernists seem to have had more than a fragmentary and passing effect on the filled-in blocks and grid of the speculators' city.

*21. Alexander Cooper and Stanton
Eckstut. Battery Park City.*

Notes

This essay was written in 1988, and later studies could not be cited. It was written chiefly for German readers.

1. Clarence Stein, *Towards New Towns for America*, 2nd ed. (New York, 1957), 88

2. On New York City's housing in the inter-war period, see especially James Ford, *Slums and Housing, with Special Reference to New York City*, 2 vols (Cambridge, Mass., 1936); Richard Plunz, "Institutionalization of Housing Form in New York 1920–1950," in *Housing Form and Public Policy in the United States*, ed. Richard Plunz (New York, 1980), 158–200; Anthony Jackson, *A Place Called Home: A History of Low-Cost Housing in Manhattan* (Cambridge, 1976).

3. I.N. Phelps Stokes in Ford, *Slums and Housing*, II, 870, plans by Ernst Flagg of 1894, pls. 7c, d. Flagg's plan helped shape the Tenement House Law of 1901.

4. Nicholas Bullock and James Read, *The Movement for Housing Reform in Germany and France 1840–1914* (Cambridge: 1985), 132ff.; Tilmann Buddensieg, "Messel und Taut: Zum 'Gesicht' der Arbeiterwohnung," *Archithese*, 12, 1974: 23–29.

5. On courts for the rich and poor in New York, see Robert A.M. Stern "With Rhetoric: The New York Apartment House," *Via, 4* (1980), 78–111.

6. United States Shipping Board, Emergency Fleet Corporation, Passenger Transportation and Housing Division, *Housing the Shipbuilders* (Philadelphia, 1920); *Types of Housing for Shipbuilders...* (Philadelphia, 1919); Henry Wright, *Rehousing Urban America* (New York, 1935), 64–75; Roy Lubove, "Homes and A Few Well-Placed Fruit Trees," *Social Research*, 27 (1960): 469–486. NA, United States Shipping Board, General Records of the Design Branch, RG 32, Box 45, July 8, 1918, list of architects and their responsibilities.

7. Roy Lubove, "Homes."

8. Robert A.M. Stern "With Rhetoric: The New York Apartment House."

9. "Metropolitan Life Houses in Queens," *Architectural Forum*, July 1922: 30. Thomas had proposed a similar plan in 1919 for the New York State Reconstruction Commission: New York State Reconstruction Commission, Housing Committee, Report, Albany, 1919, 47–52; cited by Plunz, "Institutionalization of Housing Form in New York City," 158.

10. "The Paul Lawrence Dunbar Apartments, New York City," *Architecture*, 59 (January 1929): 5–12 On Thomas see also Robert A.M. Stern, Gregory Gilmartin, and Thomas Mellins, *New York, 1930: Architecture and Urbanism between the Two World Wars* (New York, 1987), 419–21, 439–41, 479–86, and Stern, "With Rhetoric."

11. John Taylor Boyd, "A Step Towards Slum Clearance: The Garden Tenement of the Empire Mortgage Company on the East Side of New York," *Architectural Record*, 58 (March 1925): 204–216, claimed that the supervisory architect of the London County Council "pronounced our housing standards as seen in the garden tenements of the Metropolitan Life Insurance Company and Bayonne Housing Corporation superior technically to the more recent British housing." The architect for both was Thomas.

12. J.N. Tarn, *Five Percent Philanthropy, An Account of Housing in Urban Areas between 1840 and 1914* (Cambridge, 1973).

13. New York State, Reconstruction Commission, Report, 47–52, cited by Plunz, "Institutionalization of Housing in New York," 158.

14. On the function of the apartment house in establishing status see Richard Pommer, "High Rise Living," in *Cities, the Forces that Shape Them*, ed. Lisa Taylor (New York, 1982), 28, 77. Stern, "With Rhetoric," discusses the parallels between the courtyards of New York apartment houses for rich and poor.

15. Raymond Unwin and Barry Parker, *The Art of Building a Home*, (London, 1901); Raymond Unwin, *Nothing Gained from Overcrowding* (London, 1912). See Walter Creese, *The Search for Environment: The Garden City, Before and After* (New York, 1966), 240–243; Creese, *The Legacy of Raymond Unwin, Human Patterns for Planning* (Cambridge, 1967).

16. Roy Lubove, *Community Planning in the 1920s: The Contribution of the Regional Planning Association of America* (Pittsburgh, 1963).

17. The New York State Board of Housing, which administered the New York State Housing Law of 1926, recommended Thomas' Metropolitan Life apartments as a model for the new housing. (Lubove, Community Planning in the 1920s, 79; Stein had been the chairman of the New York State Commission of Housing and Regional Planning from 1923 to 1926, and his reports "paved the way for New York State's intervention in the housing Field

(Lubove, *Community Planning in the 1920s*), and Plunz, "Institutionalization of Housing Form in New York 1920–1950."

18. Using the model of the European housing societies, the union worked through the Amalgamated Housing Corporation; its cooperatives included Amalgamated Houses in the Bronx and Amalgamated Dwellings (now Hillman Houses) on Grand Street. The first block of the Amalgamated Houses in the Bronx were begun in 1926 and have been torn down. See E. Rachlis and M.E. Marqusee, *The Landlords* (New York, 1963) and Abraham Kazan, *Fifty Years of Amalgamated Cooperative Housing*, 1927–1957 (New York, 1958).

19. *Urban Housing: The Story of the PWA Housing Division* 1933–1936, Federal Emergency Administration of Public Works, Bulletin No. 2, Washington, 1936; National Records Center, Suitland, MD, Record Group 196; R. M. Fisher, *Twenty Years of Public Housing* (New York, 1959).

20. Clarence Stein, *Towards New Towns for America* (New York, 1957); Henry Saylor, "The Hillside Housing Development," *Architecture*, 71 (May 1935): 244–252.

21. "Knickerbocker Village Housing Project," *Architectural Record*, 75 (February 1934): 122–124; "Knickerbocker Village," *Architectural Forum*, 61 (December 1934): 458–464. The large court and tall buildings can be traced directly back to English nineteenth-century examples, which Ackerman had studied, and have little directly to do with Amsterdam South and other European models of the 1920s, as claimed by Stern, Gilmartin and Mellins, *New York, 1930*, 418.

22. Albert Mayer, "A Critique of Knickerbocker Village," *Architecture*, 71, (January 1935): 5–10.

23. Philip Johnson and Henry-Russell Hitchcock, *Modern Architecture: International Exhibition*, Museum of Modern Art, New York, 1932. Information from Johnson, Hitchcock, and Elizabeth Mock Kessler.

24. A point confirmed by Johnson and by Hitchcock in communications to me.

25. Johnson and Hitchcock, *Modern Architecture: International Exhibition*, 179–189.

26. Mary Susan Cole, *Catherine Bauer and the Public Housing Movement 1926–1937*, Ph.D. Dissertation, George Washington University, 1975; *Shaping an Urban Future, Essays in Memory of Catherine Bauer Wurster*, eds. B.J. Frieden and W.W. Nash (Cambridge, 1969), 205–211, for bibliography of Bauer's writings. Lewis Mumford's "Form in Modern Architecture," in *Architecture*, 1929 and 1930, especially 62 (July 1930): 1–4; *Lewis Mumford: A Bibliography 1914–1970*, ed. Elmer S. Newman (New York, 1971). On the liaison between Mumford and Bauer see his *Sketches from Life, The Early Years* (New York, 1982), 459–466.

27. Catherine Bauer, "Art in Industry," *Fortune*, 6 (May, 1931): 94–110.

28. Following a trip to Europe with Bauer, Lewis published "Machine for Living," Fortune, 7 (February 1933): 78ff; "Notes on North Sea Architecture," Yale Review, 22, Spring 1933, 513–24, and "Planned Community," *Architectural Forum*, 54 (April 1933): 252–74.

29. Catherine Bauer, *Modern Housing* (Boston and New York, 1934): 147–49, 212–23.

30. Henry Wright Papers, Cornell University; Records of the Graduate School of Fine Arts, University of Pennsylvania, where he had only superficial training as an architect.

31. Columbia University, Avery Library, manuscript of *Rehousing Urban America*.

32. "My primary interest in housing," Wright wrote early in the 1930s, "is not as a social need by as an opportunity to begin to apply careful thought and planning to the detailed development of the community and provide opportunities for releasing pent up skill and enthusiasm heretofore suppressed by the influence of narrow business objectives and existing credit overload." Henry Wright Papers, Cornell University, autobiographical notes.

33. Lubove, *Community Planning in the 1920s*, 126; *The Letters of Lewis Mumford and Frederick J. Osborn*, ed. M.J. Hughes (Bath, 1971), Mumford to Osborn, Oct. 4, 1966.

34. Richard Pommer, "The Architecture of Urban Housing in the United States in the Early 1930s," *Journal of the Society of Architectural Historians*, 38, 4, (1978): 235–64.

35. Pommer, "The Architecture of Urban Housing in the United States in the Early 1930s," 249ff; Ford, *Slums and Housing*, II, 897, 921–923, pl. 25; Columbia University, Avery Library, Vertical File (now lost), and Ware Library, NYCHA Housing Competition. Office of Horace Ginsbern, New York, Frederick Ackerman to Electus Litchfield Nov. 30, 1934.

36. William Lescaze, *On Being an Architect* (New York, 1942); Robert A.M.

Stern, *George Howe* (New Haven, 1975). Lorraine Welling Lanmon, *William Lescaze, Architect* (Philadelphia, 1987).

37. *Shelter*, II (April 1932): 21–23; Stern, *George Howe*, 101–104, 248, includes the project in the works attributed to both Howe and Lescaze, but the only indication of Howe's interest in housing is a paper by him on "Planning Low-Cost Housing" in his records at Avery Library, Columbia, dated by Stern c. 1931 (225) which is brief, vague and pertains to Philadelphia. Lescaze ran an office in New York effectively separate, for most projects, from Howe's in Philadelphia.

38. Frey wrote me in 1973–74 that he had been largely responsible for the design and Lescaze for the program.

39. On the history of housing with external galleries see Martin Steinmann, "Das Laubenganghaus," *Archithese*, 12 (1974): 3–13. Another assistant of Lescaze's, the German-trained Alfred Clauss, developed a galleried slab with Corbusian duplexes for a project in Zeilenbau formation: *Architectural Record*, 71 (March, 1932): 196–197.

40. Lescaze papers, Job. no. 336. The birds-eye view (fig. 10) is signed by Lescaze and dated Oct. 4, 1932. Frey in a letter to me recalled that he had proposed the varying heights of the buildings, but that his proposal had been altered in detail in the birds-eye view.

41. Letter to me of Jan. 18, 1974.

42. Williamsburg Houses, A Case History of Housing, (Federal Emergency Administration of Public Works) Washington, DC, 1937 NYCHA Archives, Central W-399, "Program of the Williamsburg Project...Dec. 24, 1934; and W-395-I. The NYCHA scheme was approved June 26, 1935. Lescaze Papers. Job. no. 388; Talbot F. Hamlin, "New York Housing: Harlem River Homes and Williamsburg Houses," *Pencil Points*, 14 (May 1938): 281–89; Lewis Mumford, "The Skyline," *The New Yorker* (Feb. 26, 1938): 42–44.

43. Langdon Post, *The Challenge of Housing* (New York, 1938): 190, NRC, RG 196, H-1300.702; NA, RG 48, Department of the Interior, Central Files, Emergency Housing Corporation, New York General 483, Hoopingarner to Ickes, Dec. 21, 1934; NYCHA archives, Central W-395-1, Vol. IV.

44. Harlem River Houses (Federal Emergency Administration of Public Works), Washington, DC, 1937. Drawings and documents in the Office of Horace Ginsbern and Associates, including a memo of Brown, July 9, 1935, and "Tentative Set-up for Slum Clearance Project # 3 NYCHA," establish beyond reasonable doubt that Ginsbern, assisted by Will Rice Amon, was the chief designer, despite claims by others. Ginsbern, who had no architectural degree, had designed eighty-eight multiple dwellings by April 1934, chiefly in the Bronx. See also Donald Sullivan and Brian Danforth, *Bronx Art Deco Architecture*, exhibition catalogue, Hunter College, New York, 1976, and my review in *Art in America*, May-June 1976, 54–55. John Louis Wilson, a black architect from Harlem, designed the communal facilities, according to Roy Strickland and James Sanders, "The Harlem River Houses," *Harvard Architecture Review*, no. 2, (Spring 1982): 48–59. According to Frederick Ginsbern, a son and the successor of Horace Ginsbern, Wilson was put on the team at the last moment for political reasons by Harold Ickes, the administrator of the PWA.

45. R.M. Fisher, *Twenty Years of Public Housing*, Thomas McDonnell, *The Wagner Housing Act* (Chicago, 1957).

46. NYCHA, Fifth Annual Report, 1938, Fortune 21 (April 1940): 82–89; Lewis Mumford, "Versailles for the Millions," *The New Yorker* (Feb. 17, 1940): 42. NRC RG 196, H-1202, Boxes 75, 76. information from Alfred Easton Poor and Arthur C. Holden.

47. NYCHA, Fifth Annual Report, 1938; Mumford, "Versailles for the Millions," Letters to me in 1975 from William F. R. Ballard, Frederick G. Frost, Jr. and Burnett C. Turner.

48. "Realistic Re-planning," *Architectural Forum*, 61 (July 1934): 49–55.

49. NYCHA, Sixth Annual Report, 1939, 10–11. Total cost per room and persons per gross acre were: Harlem River, $2,170.32; ppa, 182.2; Williamsburg, $2,296;ppa, 207; Red Hook, $1,160.99; ppa, 235.8;Queensbridge, $1,079.35, ppa, 256.5

50. A starting point for a study of this development from an architectural viewpoint in Plunz, "Institutionalization of Housing Form in New York City, 1920–1950l," 183–195.

51. The courts and play areas of another project of the mid-1960s, Richard Meier's Twin Parks Northeast, were also made concrete.

52. Alexander Cooper Associates, Battery Park City, New York, 1979 (Mimeographed).

53. Stern, "With Rhetoric."

1. Adler & Sullivan. Rendering of a highrise for the Fraternity Temple Association. From *New American Architecture,* 1926.

Between America and Germany: Werner Hegemann's Approach to Urban Planning

Werner Oechslin

Werner Oechslin is a professor of the history of art and architecture at the Eidgenössische Technische Hochschule in Zurich and director of its Institute for the History and Theory of Architecture. Previously, Oechslin was visiting professor at Harvard University and has held professorships at the University of Geneva and at the University of Bonn. Oechslin also taught at the Freie Universität, Berlin, and at the Massachusetts Institute of Technology, Cambridge. His numerous publications concentrate on eighteenth-century architectural history in Italy, France, and southern Germany; architectural theory from Leon Battista Alberti to the modern era; festive architecture; the architectural history of the modern era; and architectural criticism.

In the spring of 1926, the exhibition "Neue Amerikanische Baukunst" ("New American Building") was shown in the Regional College of Applied Arts in Hamburg. The event was a timely one; owing to various competitions and the general discussion concerning the greater Hamburg area, the question of architecture and city planning was very much in the foreground. In his brief preface to the catalogue, Richard Meyer, the director of the college, commented:

Of all German cities, Hamburg is most interested in staging this exhibition. As in New York the trend here has been to crowd large office blocks into the small area in the center known as the "City." The intellectual and business links between Hamburg and America span the ocean like a bridge reaching out into the New World. In both places artists and architects share the will to create a form of their own which lends expression to intellectual life. In America too those who feel responsible for the expression of life in art are also keen to break free from historical styles.[1]

At the time, most architects were trying to express themselves in this or a similar way. There was widespread admiration for New York office blocks and skyscrapers. The "will to art"[2] and the emphasis on finding expression for an intellectual milieu, however, were typical of the German attitude, in spite of having become, by this time, meaningless and hackneyed. The idea of a desire to "break free from historical styles" on the other hand can only have been wishful thinking and corresponded more to standard formulae than to reality. The exhibition had as many classical–historical exhibits as modern ones. McKim, Mead & White were displayed alongside Hood and Saarinen; Corbett was placed with Sullivan. This was anything but a presentation of liberated architecture.[3] It was more a broad representation of architecture in America. Thus, Meyer went on to qualify his claim: "Architects in the New World are struggling with the task of expressing exclusively American ideas. For this reason alone the exhibition should not be interpreted as an example for us to imitate in our approach to architectural tasks in Hamburg." Instead, he pointed out, it would suffice to see the exhibition as "an overview of architectural aims" where "historical and modern tendencies are clearly struggling to find expression." And the entire exhibition should inspire "understanding of the two great nations, the German and the American people."[4]

The preface to the catalogue was also courteously reticent on the question of German-American relations. "The American world is still far away across the water. People on both sides of the Atlantic continue to harbor many misconceptions about each other—some of these are natural misconceptions which can be explained by the differences in the development of the two nations and some are quite unnatural ones fed by the general trends."[5] What is actually being described here is a difficult, prejudice-ridden relationship. The exhibition was intended to be seen as paying homage to Sullivan, who had died in April 1924, and in this way it was intended as a vehicle for certain trends.[6] A summary in German of Sullivan's 1906 essay "What is Architecture? A Study of the American People" with its rousing plea for simplicity, philosophy, poetry, and the art of expression was included in the catalogue. Sullivan's essay should have helped to indicate the difficulties that faced America on its entry into the modern era.[7] In contrast, an es-

281

say by Tallmadge originally published in the *Atlantic Monthly* entitled "Forwards in Architecture," which followed Sullivan's essay in the catalogue, pointed to the areas in which post-1893 American architecture had caught up with or even surpassed achievements in European architecture.[8] Tallmadge informed the reader that "before 1893 we had no buildings which were equal to those in the mother countries let alone surpassed them,"[9] but then the Woolworth Building and the bank buildings brought together "the glory of Rome with American big business." The "understated, pure beauty" of the Lincoln memorial in Washington would put to shame "the excessive affectation of its pompous rival," Rome's monument to Vittorio Emanuele. New York's Pennsylvania Station could only be compared with the ancient Roman thermal baths of Caracalla. And "in some parts," at least, Sullivan's auditorium in Chicago "comes close to" Garnier's Paris Opera House.[10]

Tallmadge was declaring that it was time "for a new era, an era when—in addition to other miracles—the United States would take its rightful place in the sun"; he was conjuring up visions of a challenge to "the majesty of the Periclean era and the ecstasy of the thirteenth century." The organizers of the Hamburg exhibition, however, were a lot more reticent, if not to say unsure, about making such claims.[11] Too little was known about American architecture, especially its intellectual background. The only available comprehensive account of this nature was Lewis Mumford's *Sticks and Stones*, published in 1924.[12] Tallmadge made a passing reference to the "great influence of the so-called Chicago School on German and Dutch architecture."[13] Contrarily the catalogue's editors had the following comment to make on the various texts by American contributors: "None of the writers has anything to say about a German influence."[14] Thus, hidden behind the immediate reason for the exhibition "New American Architecture" were attitudes ranging from careful probing to covert suspicion. The only basis for a direct comparison with German architecture could be found in the "American imagination's" strong roots in the Gothic style.[15] Just how awkwardly the development of modernism was viewed even in this context is illustrated by the example of Bertram Grosvenor Goodhue. Goodhue, who was once counted as the "best exponent of Gothic" until he "suddenly threw off the chains of tradition and declared his allegiance to Modernism" with his design for the Nebraska Capitol, was cited as the best illustration of the transformation undergone by American art at the time.[16]

The 1926 exhibition in Hamburg illustrates how sketchy knowledge about the United States was and vice versa. Moreover, the ideas, such as they were, were formulated in very vague terms. Richard Neutra's two decisive publications on the modernist interpretation of America were not yet available.[17] That their appearance quickly changed the image of America in Germany can be seen in the comments and expectations expressed at the time. In 1927, the year *Wie baut Amerika?* (*How Does America Build?*) was published, Richard Neutra wrote in a letter, "I have produced the most radical thoughts in a polite way."[18] Neutra's second volume, which Joseph Gantner introduces with the comment, "This is the voice of today's young generation," was published as part of the series Neues Bauen in der Welt (New Architecture in the

World).[19] The publisher introduced the volume with the following remark: "The author of the second volume is Richard J. Neutra, an architect who lives in Los Angeles and who is the leading figure in America's first modernist school of architecture: it can therefore with justification be defined as an architectural *portrait of unknown America*."[20] This was the situation in 1930. In a preface to the first volume of the series, written the previous year,[21] Gantner declared that its aim was to invite the "collaboration of some of the leading figures in the new movement" and to illustrate "for each country, the constructive, formal and economic elements, which had inaugurated, supported and ultimately brought about the breakthrough of the new architectural movement."[22] The revised view of America, the revelation of the "unknown America" would, in other words, proceed from the tendentious perspective of the New Architecture: the price of reaching any understanding at all would be to adopt a one-sided view based on these premises. It was then merely one small step to the propagandist notion of the International Style with modernism furthermore seen as expressly derived from American precursors.[23] In this way the question of historical origins was dealt with for both countries—at least for the representatives of the modern movement. The uncertainty that made them shrink from direct comparison during the Hamburg exhibition in 1926 had been overcome. Also at an end, however, were the variety of arguments that would have sustained a more differentiated view and that went beyond straightforward, strictly modernist ideology—a multifaceted view such as that held by Werner Hegemann. Put simply, the often chauvinistic, nationalist prejudices were just being overcome through improved knowledge on each side, when the modernist view, based on selective criteria, added a new variation to the one-sided image of America. It is impossible to imagine the America-Germany discussion without these peculiar paradoxes. In comparison, Hegemann's comprehensive, informed, objective presentation *Amerikanische Architektur und Stadtbaukunst* (*American Architecture and Urban Planning*), published in 1925 and 1927, lacked, atypically, this ideological appeal.[24]

A direct contrast to this was Erich Mendelsohn's book *Amerika*, which also appeared in 1925 and relied heavily on the fascination inspired by first impressions and photographs.[25] Mendelsohn may have commented critically on the fact that "Europe tends to look with admiration rather than carefully at the U.S.A.," but on the other hand "this romantic bias" also found eloquent expression in the briefly commentated pictures in his own book.[26] *Amerika* is presented as an architect's picture book, and the commentary is provided by Mendelsohn himself in terms reminiscent of Expressionist texts, such as "frenzy" and "the ecstasy of perspective."[27] The Manhattan skyline, the Brooklyn Bridge, the skyscrapers, and the silos are presented as the embodiment of the "typically American." The pictures provide a similarly exaggerated and sweeping portrayal of "civilization in its extreme forms," "the gigantic" and "the grotesque."[28] Yet as he did in his later book *Russland, Europa, Amerika*,[29] Mendelsohn sometimes used a more sober form of expression when describing the new and imminent and using formulas such as the following: "Clarity begins to emerge with regard to a distinct character," and "Building in New York today is undertaken with logical and technical

2

(Erbaut 1908—13.) Architekten: McKim, Mead und White. Ganz im Vordergrund ragt in das Bild ein Stück des kleinen Kuppelturmes des sehr schönen alten Rathauses (erbaut 1803; vgl. Abb. 124—25), dessen Nord- (d. h. Rück-) Seite ursprünglich in unbehauenen Steinen errichtet wurde, weil man es für unwahrscheinlich hielt, daß der Bau von Norden her viele Betrachter finden würde. Heute baut sich der weitaus größte Teil der Neunmillionen-Stadt (einschließlich des neuen Rathauses) nördlich des alten Rathauses auf. Beim Beurteilen der ästhetischen Wirkung des schmalen Turmrathauses mit dem neuen Rathaus muß berücksichtigt werden, daß die vorliegende Abbildung aus der Höhe gemacht wurde, während der Entwurf des Turmes für die Ansicht von der Straße berechnet ist. Vgl. Abb. 122 und 123.

3

AMERIKANISCHE ARCHITEKTUR & STADTBAUKUNST

EIN ÜBERBLICK ÜBER DEN HEUTIGEN
STAND DER AMERIKANISCHEN BAUKUNST
IN IHRER BEZIEHUNG ZUM STAEDTEBAU

760 ABBILDUNGEN AUSGEWÄHLT UND ERLÄUTERT VON

WERNER HEGEMANN

ZWEITE AUFLAGE: 1927
ERNST WASMUTH A.-G. BERLIN, MARKGRAFENSTR. 31
IM VERLAGE DER MONATSSCHRIFT: „STAEDTEBAU"

2. Bertram Grosvenor Goodhue.
Prize winning entry for the State
Capitol in Lincoln, Nebraska.

3. Werner Hegemann,
Amerikanische Architektur und
Stadtbaukunst. *Second edition,*
Berlin 1927.

4. Erich Mendelsohn, Russland, Europa, Amerika. *Berlin, 1929.*

precision."[30] Both statements offer a strange contrast to the aphoristic approach described above, which however is characteristic for most of the propagandist literature of the modern movement. This is true of Le Corbusier just as it is of Mendelsohn's famous picture books, and it prompted Mendelsohn to interpret the New York zoning laws as a sign of the *"will to the new,"*[31] an expression based on Werkbund terminology.

Although presented as "of utmost contemporary significance"[32] and ultimately conforming to the formal architectonic aims of the New Architecture, Mendelsohn's image of America also remained more or less true to the stereotype that had been consolidated and passed down in a long tradition reaching back to the work of Walter Rathenau.[33] This perpetuation of existing attitudes meant that the veil of unknown America was barely lifted and potential conflicts were not defused, particularly when it came to issues where Germany insisted on its cultural uniqueness.

Rathenau described the American as an "unusual person," "clear-sighted, objective," of "considered yet shrewd judgment" and with "a matter-of-fact confidence about himself and his opinions" and "a surprising certainty and objectivity concerning his own desires."[34] However, when it came to the declared German values such as spirit and ethical values, he had sharp criticism for America.[35] "If one comes closer to this spirit (America's) one sees that it is natural and healthy but soulless."[36] Rathenau similarly concluded: "Yankee intelligence is clear and consistent, but banal. They are as unfamiliar with a personality of thought as they are with individuality."[37]

Attempting to counter such prejudices successfully was not always an easy task. Hans de Fries resorted to harsh words to do so, basing his argument on the example of Frank Lloyd Wright. In 1926, the year of the Hamburg exhibition where Wright's absence was recognized as a serious shortcoming,[38] de Fries published a brief monograph on Wright entitled *Frank Lloyd Wright: Aus dem Lebenswerk eines Architekten* (*From the Life's Work of an Architect*). From the beginning, de Fries drew attention to the fact that in using the term "disciple of the Gothic," precisely what Wright meant was the *spirit* that determined architectural forms.[39] He used Wright's own words from the essay in which Wright defined America as a "frame of mind."[40] Thus armored, de Fries attacked "intellectual architecture, of which we are blessed with an abundance here in Germany," describing it as "bungled" and saying it was high time that "this nonsense about the will to style, functional form, the spirit of the absolute idea, etc., should come to an end." He goes on to speak of "empty talk," "egocentric coryphaei," and the "architecture of afternoon tea, horn-rimmed spectacles and the utterly inflated ridiculousness of a supposedly cultivated class."[41]

Just as the discussion about architecture in Germany displayed diversity and confusion, so, too, did the debate over America. The idealized image of a modern civilization stood in contrast to old, national German prejudices, and all in all, the "romantic bias" diagnosed by Mendelsohn made a more objective portrayal seem less interesting and less attractive.

These attitudes must be taken into consideration if Hegemann and his academic work and writing are to be properly evaluated. Any attempt at a historical account of architecture that takes its orientation from the ideals of the New Architecture or its individual aspects will almost be forced to overlook the figure of Hegemann. He does not fit nicely into the modernist perspective. His activities and interests are too closely linked with complex contemporary events and their many entanglements. In contrast to the picture books put forth by Gropius and Mendelsohn, Hegemann's books overflow with information. His use of objective, descriptive language and demonstrative information stands in stark contrast to the aphoristic style favored by the modernists in their architectural writing. To a certain extent, this difference can be attributed to Hegemann's character and personality, but it also owes much to the recognition of urban planning as a separate discipline, which occurred, at the latest, with the first issue of *Der Städtebau* (*Urban Planning*) in January 1904, in which the scientific character was officially claimed.[42]

Hegemann's impartiality was confirmed on more than one occasion. Nevertheless, in 1926, when he was in his second year as editor of *Der Städtebau* and had worked for some time on *Wasmuth's Monatshefte für Baukunst* (*Wasmuth's Architecture Monthly*), some of his opinions were considered one sided or unfounded. De Fries, who that same year had published his book *Junge Baukunst in Deutschland* (*Young Architecture in Germany*),[43] which in a polemical and acerbic vein had dismissed all the famous names and egocentric approaches, accused Hegemann of "not taking enough responsibility for the sociopolitical tasks of the present." With these arguments, de Fries contested Hegemann's candidacy for *Stadtbaurat* (director of the city's Department of Urban Planning and Development).[44] In this era, so rich with conflicts and important decisions, Hegemann was now obviously somebody in a powerful position, which for de Fries meant that he had to be attacked. A few years earlier, in 1920, the situation had been so different that de Fries had nominated Hegemann, who was still in America, for the post of director of urban planning in Berlin with the following recommendation: "There is no doubt that Hegemann would like to return to Germany and assume important tasks in his field. He is not the candidate of any political party, does not belong to any clique, nor does he represent any particular interests. Until now he has not even been a candidate, although on the basis of his knowledge of urban planning and the technical requirements for housing in cities in the entire world, he is particularly qualified to deal with the ailing organism which is Greater Berlin."[45] Statistics on the housing accommodation situation in Berlin provided by Hegemann were presented to corroborate the argument that "a person of truly great stature" was required for this post.

Thus, from de Fries's point of view, Hegemann was impartial in the best sense of the word prior to his return to Germany in 1921. Given his experience in both Germany and America, it is unlikely that Hegemann would have had any difficulty in accepting the picture of developments in America as correct in spite of the confusion presented in the 1926 exhibition in Hamburg.[46] His background predestined him to see things from a perspective of exceptional breadth.[47] Born in 1881 in

5. *"New York: A look into the future in 1890." Erich Mendelsohn,* Russland, Europa, Amerika. *Berlin, 1929. The picture illustrates the European idea of the chaotic American city at the turn of the century.*

WERNER HEGEMANN

DAS STEINERNE BERLIN

GESCHICHTE DER GRÖSSTEN MIETKASERNENSTADT

DER WELT

MIT DREIUNDSECHZIG TAFELN

UND ZAHLREICHEN ABBILDUNGEN IM TEXT

VERLAG VON GUSTAV KIEPENHEUER IN BERLIN

6

7

8

*6. Werner Hegemann, Das steinerne
Berlin. Geschichte der grössten
Mietskasernenstadt der Welt.
Berlin, 1930.*

*7. Photograph (model) of the
structural framework for Erich
Mendelsohn's planned conversion of
the Herpich House. From Der
Städtebau.*

*8. Erich Mendelsohn. Herpich
House after its conversion. From W.
Hegemann, Reihenhausfassaden,
Geschäfts- und Wonhäuser aus alter
und neuer Zeit.*

Mannheim, he came to Berlin to study, where later he also became a relative of Otto March.[48] The time and the place—Berlin—were ideal for concentrating on the newly established discipline of urban planning. The situation can best be understood by examining the arguments advanced by Theodor Goecke and Camillo Sitte in the foreword to the first issue of *Der Städtebau*.[49] They considered it "unbelievable" that no such organ yet existed and explained this circumstance by pointing out that "the liberation of urban planning from the completely mindless realm of outlining ordered street patterns" had only recently emerged as a clear objective. Urban planning should now be evaluated according to its claim of a separate discipline. "All of its activities should be directed toward clearly perceived aims." Technicians, artists, economists, health officials, social policymakers, administrative officials, and members of legislative bodies were named as the key figures in this "great discipline," a discipline that was also described as a science and an art, "unifying all technical and applied arts."[50]

As Hegemann was beginning his studies, which were based on this interdisciplinary approach, urban planning was indeed enjoying its first real success as an independent discipline. In 1903–04, Hegemann moved from Berlin to Paris, where he studied economics with Charles Gide and art history with Henri Lemonnier.[51] His study of economics first led him to America to the University of Pennsylvania and finally to Strasbourg and Munich, where he finished his doctorate in 1908. It was then that he began to travel back and forth between America and Europe. The conception of his profession as he later developed it would be impossible to understand without taking this traveling into account. His knowledge of America was a source of inspiration for his activities in Germany and vice versa. A major feature of his work was his constant attempt to explain the opposing position. The "Boston 1915" exhibition of 1909 inspired the urban planning exhibitions of 1910 and 1912, which, like that of Greater Boston were concerned with Greater Berlin and Greater Düsseldorf. This international dimension to urban planning certainly owed something to Hegemann's educational background. In the final analysis, however, it developed as a consequence of the new demands made by the discipline of urban planning. As an economist, Hegemann assigned less importance to cultural differences than, for example, New York–born Wilhelm Dunkel. In his doctoral thesis on the development of urban planning in the United States, written under Gurlitt in Dresden and published in 1917, Dunkel spoke of the "poverty of the cultural legacy in urban planning" and drew a direct correlation between this poverty and the "spirit of Americanism" with "its misleading ideals of freedom."[52] Whereas Dunkel referred to a stultified capacity for development and even spoke of the "thousands of hindrances posed by a Medieval age which have not yet been overcome,"[53] Hegemann had no qualms at all about investigating, in both Europe and America, his ideas on urban planning. Indeed, he was impartial in the true sense of the word. He was interested in facts and developments and registered and organized thousands of them.

What is immediately striking about Hegemann's first major

publication, the two-volume report of 1911–13 entitled *Der Städtebau nach den Ergebnissen der allgemeinen Städtebau-Ausstellung in Berlin* (*Urban Planning after the General Urban Planning Exhibition in Berlin*), is also a characteristic shared by his later works, the *American Vitruvius* and *Amerikanische Architektur und Stadtbaukunst*. Hegemann did not argue using theories but instead presented detailed facts. Although they appeared to be only a casual accompaniment to titles and quotations, they were carefully placed, and in their range and volume, the complexity of urban planning became readily apparent. Hegemann thereby familiarized the reader with the complicated processes and developments that had to be viewed as a whole to produce a scientifically correct perspective of the problems faced by urban planning. Through paying close attention the patient reader will find the references and quotations that Hegemann provided in addition to statistics, details that reveal him to be an extremely committed and knowledgeable exponent of his discipline. They can be found, for example, in his characterization of the three-class electoral system of 1849 as the reason for the poor living and tenancy conditions in Berlin,[54] or in his comparison, using a quotation from Lujo Brentano, of the greater volume of air space enjoyed by inmates in Bavarian prisons with the smaller volume of air space in approximately forty-six percent of apartments in the east end of Munich.[55] A summarized manifesto-like account of Hegemann's credo does not exist, however, and it is impossible to divide his convictions neatly into categories. It is this difficulty that made Hegemann such an irritating and misunderstood figure, right up to and even after the publication of *Das Steinerne Berlin* (*Berlin: City of Stone*). His arguments are too diverse to be reduced to a common denominator, and thus, as in the case of the *American Vitruvius*, the impression made is one of an enormous thesaurus[56] that has little instructive use.

Hegemann therefore differed from most commentators writing after 1918, who increasingly dominated the discussion with catchy headlines and reductive formulas. De Fries's comments of 1920 and 1926 on Hegemann are typical in this respect.[57] What de Fries overlooked is that being impartial is by no means the same as having no opinion. That Hegemann's approach was often irritating can surely be explained by his lack of contact with developments within German architecture, which, at the time, were dominated by modernism. Hegemann had been absent from the European scene for too long to have been familiar in 1921 with the arguments in vogue with the modernists, who were actually not much younger than he.

Several examples illustrate this unfamiliarity. In 1924–25, Mendelsohn's project for the conversion of the Herpich building in Leipziger Strasse was a source of controversy. In an attempt to overcome the excessive delay caused by the protracted wrangling among the building supervision authority, the committee of experts, and the mayor of Berlin, Mendelsohn appealed to twenty-three experts for their help. Of the twenty-three, Hegemann was the only one who refused his support. He gave his reasons for doing so in his journal *Der Städtebau*.[58] It was not that he wanted to defend the action taken by the various officials. On the contrary, in a spirit akin to that of Mendelsohn's criticism of the delay, he condemned the may-

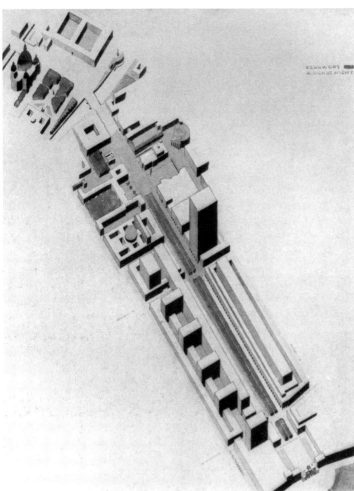

9. *Cornelius van Eesteren. Prize-winning entry for the redesign of Unter den Linden.* From Der Städtebau, *1926.*

or's tactics and described them as indicative of "a kind of despotic regime in the style of Frederick the Great!" Nevertheless, he also criticized Mendelsohn's design. Previously, in a study on the "street as a unity," which appeared in the May/August issue of the journal, he had actually praised the structural framework of the Herpich House (basing his observations on a 1:1 model). He had considered it to be a bold demonstration of the possibility of "buttressed porticos with a good angle of incidence for light."[59] In particular, he praised the way in which the recessing of the upper stories "in two different scales" made it possible to harmonize the building with the historical context, and he hailed Mendelsohn as "one of the most brilliant of the modern architects."[60] A few months later, however, Hegemann refused Mendelsohn his support because in the meantime, side oriels, which had not been visible in the structural framework, appeared on the model. Hegemann commented: "To me these oriels look like a ridiculous legacy from the time when Leipziger Strasse was still a residential street and was filled with particularly tasteless buildings."[61] He was against all the dominant horizontal articulation, for despite all other reservations one might have about the Wertheim building, he said, Messel had marked out "a vertical rhythm which he had introduced in a superb manner." He would only accept this horizontal emphasis if at least the oriels were abandoned. "I think the building supervision authority would be doing you a service as an artist if they forced your client to reject these oriels."[62] Thus, using his own aesthetic criteria, Hegemann refused his support to Mendelsohn on an issue concerning administrative procedure and publicized his reasons for doing so in *Der Städtebau.* There was nothing halfhearted in the way that Hegemann expressed his provocative criticism: "I don't take exception to the fact that Mendelsohn's facade would like to be modern but rather to the fact that these oriels make it seem old-fashioned and are reminiscent of the bad taste of the [18]80s. In view of this most important issue of the distribution of mass, the individual details (whose style evoke something of a battleship and tank turret) appear to me to be less important."[63]

There can be no doubt that Hegemann irritated his contemporaries with comments of this nature. Calling the distinctive feature of Mendelsohn's style—the curved edges of his buildings—oriels and comparing them with forms of the 1880s must have provoked much consternation. The cutting remark about battleship and tank turret, a far too obvious allusion to the Einstein tower, also shows that Hegemann was in no way above becoming involved in the architectural squabbles of the day. It can hardly be described as Solomonic to vote at the same time against both the building authority and the architect. On the other hand, the example illustrates the extent to which the criteria of urban planning form the basis of Hegemann's arguments and how blind he was to the development of the modern movement in architecture, which was then reaching its zenith in Germany.

For this reason, it would be somewhat overhasty to interpret Hegemann's support of van Eesteren's project for the redesign of Unter den Linden as a decisive change in his attitude toward a radical, modern project. Here, too, his position was oddly balanced. It can even be seen as demonstrating his attempt to remain independent of all contemporary trends in order to maintain a scientific, urban planning approach. Hegemann's arguments again found expression in *Der Städtebau* (1926), and once again he devoted an undue amount of space to distinguishing between his arguments and those made by others.[64] Shortly beforehand, Hegemann had discussed Mario Labò's competition design for Greater Genoa and praised him for making an honest attempt at "solving important urban planning tasks" but added a reservation concerning the bombastic and thus unacceptable architectural style characteristic of all of Italy.[65] Italian architecture was too academic for the modernists, and traditionalists saw it as ridiculing tradition. This time Hegemann expressed his middle-of-the-road approach as follows: "Perhaps as early as a few decades from now an unprejudiced observer will see only congenial manifestations of the same tasteless *Zeitgeist* in the excesses of Italian academic and Dutch modernist architecture."[66] For the modernists, this statement without doubt went too far. How could the most retrogressive and progressive styles possibly be mentioned in the same breath?

Walter Curt Behrendt, who had been editor of the journal *Form* since 1925 and was thus Hegemann's direct opponent, must have felt particularly affronted by such comparisons. Hegemann's association with the slightly younger Behrendt was based not only on their joint emigration to the United States in 1933 but also on their early involvement in the new problems connected with urban planning. In his book *Die einheitliche Blockfront als Raumelement im Stadtbau (The Uniform Block Facade as a Spatial Element in Urban Planning)*,[67] Behrendt thanked Hegemann and named him, with Brinckmann, Goecke, Mebes, and March, as a source of inspiration. And still in 1930, Behrendt's review of Hegemann's *Der Städtebau nach den Ergebnissen der Städtebau-Ausstellung in Berlin*, which originally appeared in *Kunst und Künstler (Art and Artists)*, was reproduced in *Das Steinere Berlin*. There, Hegemann's early work was particularly praised, "because the author is up to the demands of his task not only academically but also personally which is no less important in this case."[68] Behrendt's development, however, took a different course from that of Hegemann. He sided with the modernists. That he did so is already evident in the titles of his later publications, *Der Kampf um den Stil im Kunstgewerbe und in der Architektur (The Conflict of Style in Arts and Crafts and in Architecture, 1920)*, and *Der Sieg des Neuen Baustils (The Triumph of the New Architecture, 1927)*.[69] What Behrendt shared with Hegemann was a historical approach and extensive reference to developments in America. Behrendt was also among those who were preoccupied with defining the architectonic approach of the New Style. As to this, hardly any other German critic placed greater emphasis on the importance of the Dutch influence.[70] As late as 1937, in a chapter of *Modern Building* dealing with international leaders, he wrote that "the first place is due to J. J. Oud."[71] That Hegemann could launch his attack on "modernist Dutch excesses" and at the same time support van Eesteren's project, which was in fact awarded first prize in the Unter den Linden competition, had to provoke Behrendt's criticism. Hegemann's reply in *Der Städtebau* gave no indication, however, that he had been chastened by this criticism:

Hasty judges of the Linden competition (as for example, the previously far more astute Walter Curt Behrendt), whose understanding of "form" has recently been weakened by an unrestrained admiration for the aberrations of Amsterdam architecture, felt justified in accusing the editor of inconsistency because, as a jury member, he awarded a prize to a Dutch architect even though he had campaigned against the "Dutch style" in his writings.[72]

In a defiant vein, Hegemann described these as:

. . . superficial judgments which cannot distinguish between Amsterdam kitsch and Rotterdam severity. Van Eesteren himself wrote to the editor, "I agree with you when you attack the Amsterdam School and I am very displeased when undiscerning observers classify me as belonging to it."[73]

Yet Hegemann was not interested in distinguishing between the various streams of Dutch architecture. Once again, he was intent on demonstrating how only objective criteria—and not prejudices based on taste or fashionable preferences—should be used in judging architecture.[74] He did not refer at all to avant-gardism but instead concentrated on urban planning:

The undersigned at least did not support this design because of its artistic and asymmetrical aims but rather because it presents a potentially usable and economically viable method of reducing the height of private buildings on Unter den Linden to four stories.[75]

To illustrate his point, Hegemann referred to an earlier argument already familiar to the competition entrants—that of the two different scales.[76] This argument, which he had used in the case of Mendelsohn's Herpich building, was also divorced from stylistic and aesthetic considerations. Hegemann obviously felt that his point of view thereby provided a solution to modern requirements. The repetition of the scale of the old building line achieved by the "strong low cornices" guaranteed integration and adaptation; "the other scale allows the height to be raised through the addition of extra stories." Hegemann thought that if these additional stories were "pushed back far enough into the interior of the block, one could hope to achieve new effects, as it were from a fourth dimension, which, however, would do no serious harm to the dignity of the old buildings, Berlin's greatest architectural treasures."[77] Such were the arguments presented by Hegemann in his "Evaluation of Van Eesteren's Design." The example and the justification were taken from an area in which Hegemann's authority cannot be questioned—American urban planning. "The idea of recessing the upper stories in the gradual extension of height has become familiar through the New York zoning law of 1916. Since 1921, the editor has supported the idea of exploiting this concept not only for the purposes of providing better light but also to achieve aesthetic ends."[78] If one follows Hegemann's bibliographical notes on this question, one comes upon Hegemann's and Peets's own suggestions for the "grouping of public buildings" in the context of "city plazas"[79] in *Amerikanische Architektur und Stadtbaukunst* (1925). In both cases, the aesthetic evaluation of the zoning law principle cannot be understood as anything other than the aesthetic of volumes, an aesthetic that had been familiar since the French *embellissement* theory of the eighteenth century.[80] Thus while this urban planning approach

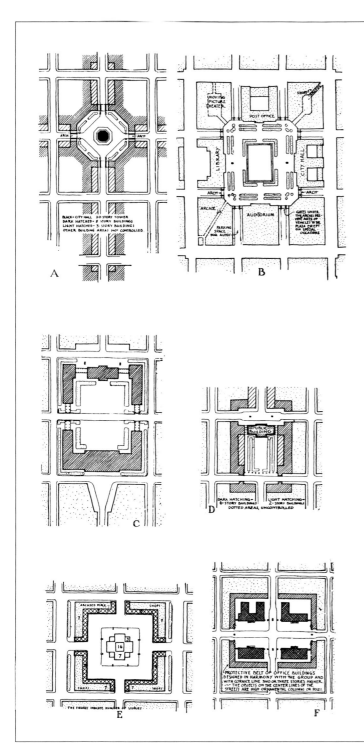

10. *Werner Hegemann and Werner Peets. "Six Plans for Grouping Public Buildings." "Administration Forum with Traffic Circle." From Amerikanischer Architektur und Stadtbaukunst.*

contained the seed of a convergence with the aesthetic views of modernism, the actual aesthetic issue of style was still ignored.

Like the majority of German critics, Hegemann castigated the random erection of skyscrapers in New York. Even Hilbersheimer quoted him and took this position as his main argument in the discussion of the chaos of American urban planning in his book *Grosstadtarchitektur (Metropolitan Architecture)*, which was published in 1927.[81] Hegemann's criticism, however, never degenerated into anti-Americanism. Instead, once again his interest lay in revealing both sides of the coin. Despite the criticism of their misuse by speculators,[82] he was convinced that the zoning law regulations represented a means of design that could harmonize not only the different scales of existing and new building volumes but old and new architecture in general. The deliberate reference to *Amerikanische Architektur und Stadtbaukunst* reveals the context in which Hegemann placed his arguments. In the book, Hegemann used the premise of the "skyscraper as a source of traffic problems"[83] to propose the introduction of multilevel transport facilities. Once again, his solutions were taken exclusively from the area of urban planning, and he supports his case with examples ranging from Leonardo to Courbet. In the final analysis, he used a pragmatic approach just as he had previously used the principle of recessing for the preservation of scale.[84] It was a perspective that explained the origin of Hegemann and Peets's proposal for city plazas, which Hegemann calls the "adaptation of Renaissance ideas to modern American conditions."[85]

The development of Hegemann's approach, which led to such "applications of practical modern developments,"[86] can be traced via *Amerikanische Architektur und Stadtbaukunst* to the *American Vitruvius* and clarifies also the relationship between these two distinct but frequently confused publications.[87] In 1922, in the *American Vitruvius*, Hegemann took his examples from the history of European urban planning (frequently referring to material from his first major work of 1911–13, *Der Städtebau nach den Ergebnissen der allgemeinen Städtebau-Ausstellung in Berlin*) for the purpose of instructing America. In *Amerikanische Architektur und Stadtbaukunst* of 1925 he used American examples to propagate his ideas in Berlin and Germany. The lists of frequently reused but newly organized examples were adapted to suit the new readership. A residential block on Central Park by McKim, Mead & White was concisely described in 1922 as "an example of the horizontal subdivision of a high building, a principle accommodating varied functions in plaza and street designs."[88] In the 1925 German version, this principle was more clearly expressed, and the exemplary nature of the solution was suggested as "a typical example for the effective alignment of facades which is a necessary condition for the control of wide streets and squares by high walls."[89] Hegemann added to this, "At the same time" the block provides "an example of the successful adaptation of old forms to new functions."[90] The Madison Park building by Warren and Wetmore was presented as a "type of planning" that was a direct result of the New York zoning law, and its positive effects for lighting were stressed.[91] In the German edition of 1925, he added that such planning made a repetition of the horrifying conditions in New York impossible.[92] Topographical proximity led Hegemann to a short digression on the construction of train stations, ending with a recommendation for Berlin: "It is to be hoped that in the planning of new districts (i.e., around the Berlin railway stations), greater planning wisdom will prevail than was the case when the great electric railway and suburban rail stations of the New York Central Railroad were built."[93]

Thus Hegemann repeatedly attempted to put forward suggestions for improvements in urban planning and to persuade his audience of the feasibility of these solutions. There was also another side to the discussion beyond the preoccupations of architectural modernism, which reached a culmination in 1938 in the third volume of City/Planning/Housing. (This volume, however, was no longer edited by Hegemann himself but by William W. Forster and Robert C. Weinberg.) In this work, such contrasting architectural statements as Luckhardt's project for Berlin's Alexanderplatz and Paul Ludwig Troost's redesign of Munich's Königsplatz were presented as alternative but equally valid solutions to the same problem.[94] In the discussion of the adaptation of old squares to modern traffic conditions, contradictions between modern and historical-classical architectural patterns (and, of course, the corresponding ideological backgrounds) were completely overlooked. The main argument was again the dual-level transport-system—in analogy to Hegemann's own proposal for Leipziger Platz. To this proposal was added what was then defined as the "third approach": the complete elimination of traffic taken from the Munich example.[95]

Because of his objectivity, for Hegemann stylistic differences were only of a secondary or even incidental importance. This attitude is also the only way that his misunderstandings with de Fries and Behrendt can be explained.

The conflict with Le Corbusier reveals another aspect of Hegemann's pragmatic[96] approach and once more indicates the varying degrees of topicality in his position before and after 1914–18. The Berlin urban planning exhibition was one of the events that most influenced the young Jeanneret on his visit to Germany in 1910. Indeed, it can be assumed that it was through Hegemann, who had studied with Lemonnier in Paris,[97] that he first heard of the great French urban planning tradition and the embellissement theories.[98] This circumstance would certainly account for the fact that in 1922 Le Corbusier sent his project for Ville Contemporaine to Hegemann.[99] Hegemann's reaction was negative from the outset. As usual, he returned to his criticism at a later date in an article in Der Städtebau (1927) entitled "Critique of Le Corbusier's City Redevelopment Plan" and pursued it further in Das Steinerne Berlin (1930) and even in the posthumously published City/Planning/Housing (1938).[100] With the developments in real estate speculation in New York in mind, Hegemann feared that Le Corbusier's plan could end up being realized.[101] He added somewhat sarcastically that this would occur not "because they [the skyscrapers] are desirable, healthy, beautiful, and reasonable from the perspective of urban planning but because they are theatrical, romantic, unreasonable, and generally harmful, and because it is part of the money-making ac-

tivities of a metropolis, in what is literally the world's most international city, Paris, to serve the need for sensation and the vices of native and imported fools."[102] The statement is worth noting in the light of Hegemann's own career: during his stay in Buenos Aires and Rio de la Plata in 1930, he could have discovered very concretely that greater attention could be attracted through grand rhetorical gestures and verbal virtuosity.[103] In the light of Le Corbusier's statement "Il faut tuer la 'rue-corridor'" however, with which, ten months previously, in October 1929, he had prefaced his suggestions for the adaptation of his Plan Voisin[104] to Buenos Aires, Hegemann's suggestion that speculation and undesirable developments should be avoided through the introduction of regulations was actually quite unspectacular.

Hegemann's arguments in Der Städtebau were far from visionary. All he could find to put forward against Le Corbusier's disarming statement "Nettoyons d'abord le terrain"[105] were figures and calculations, which, even if mathematically correct, have failed to persuade to the present day. This, although in the same year (1927) the Free German Academy of Urban Planning[106] and Ludwig Hilberseimer (Grosstadtarchitektur)[107] both detected the same mistakes in Le Corbusier's plan. As had been the case with Mendelsohn, Hegemann went too far in his aggressive commitment to the discipline of urban planning, defining Le Corbusier's plan as "a logical continuation of Haussmann's overrated work." He maintained that Le Corbusier's plan, like Haussmann's, was essentially retrospective and did not do justice to new possibilities. Hegemann did not choose to formulate his arguments diplomatically:

For much the same reason I would now like to suggest that Le Corbusier's plan is only vieux jeu, that the desire to introduce the American skyscraper motif on such an extensive scale seems powerful enough but is far from representing the generous realization of a truly modern urban planning concept.[108]

Just how much the two sides in this discussion were at cross-purposes and how two advocates of ultimately European approaches could accuse each other of naive and blind Americanism becomes clear with a comment made by Le Corbusier early on in Vers une architecture. Le Corbusier included and commented on Hegemann's picture of the Spreckel building in San Francisco,[109] which the latter had described in the American Vitruvius as impressive in what he called its effective contrast: "Ecoutons les conseils des ingénieurs américains. Mais craignons les architects américains. Preuve."[110]

Even disregarding their shared early interest in French embellissement, both Hegemann and Le Corbusier belonged to a European tradition that was familiar with regulated proportions and principles of order. Hegemann could also have legitimized Le Corbusier's idea using the image of medieval Siena ("spaced far apart on a small area"). He had already used this image once in support of the zoning law and against the jungle of American skyscrapers.[111] Facts and figures, however, were more important to him. Moreover, soon he would be hearing that he was still thinking in pre-1914 architectonic forms and that he was only willing to accept conformist modern solutions.

291

Even today, it is difficult to evaluate Hegemann's position, particularly for the time he spent in Germany during the Weimar Republic. But some things can be established or at least assumed. Although Hegemann was only a few years older than the founding figures of postwar modernism, his attachment to the prewar era was much deeper. Thus, the principle of continuity and the recognition of great historical achievements were important to him just as avant-gardist or tabula rasa hysteria was alien to him. He believed in the solidity of a systematic approach and reasoning. The rise and triumph of urban planning as a science and discipline coincided with Hegemann's studies and the beginning of his professional activities. This experience no doubt influenced him for the rest of his life and bound him to that historical phase and its ideals. Even in the line he adopted as a writer and as the editor of *Wasmuth's Monatshefte für Baukunst* and *Der Städtebau* and despite all the political interruptions, his fight for Berlin was based on the perpetuation of the idea of the *Grosstadt*. In the final analysis, this idea is where Hegemann's thinking was rooted. In *Berlin ein Architekturdenkmal: Ein Programm für die Zukunft* (Berlin—An Architectural Memorial: A Program for the Future), which was published in the *Berliner Architekturwelt* (*Berlin's Architectural World*) in 1905, Ernst Schur had the following to say: "Berlin is a city which is aiming to expand beyond the organism of the 'state' to that of 'world.' It should join the ranks of world metropolises which reach beyond the separating barriers to unite the world, which are the centers of more expansive, wider circles."[112] Hegemann was guided by such perspectives and was able to accept the American challenge and engage in a critical comparison. In *Das Steinerne Berlin*, written in 1930, the idea of Berlin's expansion still very much set the tone. This "legacy" was dedicated to "the memory of Hugo Preuss" and introduced with a quotation: "It was Hugo Preuss who gave form to the Berlin idea of building the new *Grosstadt*." Hegemann's manifesto was then followed by a resigned and accusatory comment on the contemporary situation: "It is a German illusion to believe in the possibility of creating an intellectual capital as long as the so-called educated people are almost proud of their inadequate understanding of urban planning."

For Hegemann the outcome of this misconception was the "largest city of housing barracks in the world," which he wrote about in 1930.[113] And in his eyes, the reason for it was the failure to understand the norms of urban planning. His life's work was devoted to establishing the objective basis and scientific nature of the subject. So doing cost him an understanding of and involvement in the ideas and demands of the postwar modernists, but his work should not be merely interpreted as antimodernism. For it was precisely in his rejection of the stylistic approach that Hegemann wished to stress the primacy of urban planning. His approach, however, remained architectural and had nothing to do with the later unfortunate division between transport planning and architecture. He believed first and foremost that urban planning must take on the public and representative tasks of architecture, and this belief was always implied in the concept of civic art (the subtitle of the *American Vitruvius*) and in the dual concept of *Architektur und Stadtbaukunst*. Looking from today's perspective at the painfully slow course taken by the development of modern ar-

chitecture with respect to its representative tasks—right up to Le Corbusier's defeat in the Völkerbundspalast competition[114]—it is easier to understand Hegemann's insistence on the turn-of-the-century proposals and approach of urban planning. Hegemann certainly did not want these early achievements to be forgotten. And thus in an essay marking Hermann Jansen's sixtieth birthday in 1929, he could ascertain "with satisfaction" that those "urban planning methods" that had been "quietly put into practice" had had their effect, for example, in providing a framework for the Spandau-Haselhorst competition.[115]

Hegemann did not remain entirely without a position on the transformation of architectural style into modernism. Unlike many exponents of urban planning, he did not make an absolute of formal appearance;[116] however, in his urban-planning analyses, the building and its mass always played a role. It could almost be said that Hegemann's architectural taste was located in the abstraction of ornament and stylistic additions, in reductionism and in the so-called *plan de masse*, factors that again were completely in tune with the approach established before 1914 in Berlin and that were still valid in America in the 1920s and 1930s. Hegemann's judgment that Goodhue's competition entry for the Nebraska Capitol in Lincoln was influenced by the "effective grouping of aligned masses"[117] could well indicate the perspective from which these interests originated.

Hegemann shares also a middle-of-the-road stance in the urban planning debate. On the one hand, he defended Camillo Sitte both against accusations of romanticism and against those who wished to appropriate him. In the debate surrounding the Münsterplatz in Ulm, he therefore suggested that "the so-called Fischer school" proudly acknowledge its "Romanticism of 1890–1910."[118] On the other hand, any form of extremism was anathema to Hegemann. In a court settlement with Martin Wagner, he was forced to retract his statement that the *Stadtbaurat* restricted his activities primarily to finding commissions for a group of extremist architects who were his close friends."[119]

Because Hegemann never sided with the modernist camp, his position is difficult to define. From today's vantage point this in-between position makes him particularly interesting and instructive, at least for those who have finally rejected a concise, linear account of architectural modernism. Nonetheless, it is anything but new.

On February 11, 1948, a symposium entitled "What is Happening to Modern Architecture?" was held in the New York Museum of Modern Art.[120] A text by Lewis Mumford, published in the *New Yorker* in the previous autumn, was used as a starting point for the discussion. Mumford had said that Le Corbusier's dictum of the *machine à habiter* (machine for living in) had become old hat and that Sigfried Giedion, the former "leader of the mechanical rigorists," had now turned to the monumental and symbolic. Alfred Barr opened the colloquium with the observation that "it is hard for two old soldiers to remember a campaign in exactly the same way," and he attempted to liberate the International Style from dogmatism. In reply, Henry-Russell Hitchcock pointed out how numerous the representatives and supporters of the modern movement had become. Gropius reacted to the reproach of "old hat" by maintaining that the concept of functionalism had always been taken too literally; the "rigorists," he said, could be found not only among modernists but also among the representatives of the Beaux-Arts, and Giedion, incidentally, had always fought against the "Swiss rigorists." The symposium continued on this level of intrigue and excuses. Mumford closed the meeting, concluding, "What is happening to modern architecture? None of us has yet found out." Instead of aiming to present clear architectural solutions, he preferred to demand "greater humanism and universalism" as the sole basis of a new civilization. There can be no doubt that Werner Hegemann, the universalist who rejected the dictatorship of architectural trends, would have agreed with him.

Notes

1. See *Neue amerikanische Baukunst*, exhibition catalogue (Hamburg: Staatliche Kunstgewerbeschule, 1926).
2. The *Wille zur Kunst* (will to art) as the way forward was one of the mottos of the Werkbund. See, for example, P. Jessen, "Die Werkbund und die Grossmächte der deutschen Arbeit," in *Die Durchgeistung der deutschen Arbeit: Jahrbuch des deutschen Werkbundes 1912* (Jena, 1912), 2ff. (*Wille zur Qualität* [will to quality], 3; *Wille zur Kunst*, 5).
3. See *Neue amerikanische Baukunst*: the 597 listed exhibits (23–66) and the comprehensive list of contributors (77–83) actually do provide a broad comprehensive view of the American situation. The internal American crisis of 1893 is dealt with by presenting various and contradicting aspects.
4. Ibid.
5. Ibid., 1.
6. Ibid.: "We would like to thank Louis Henry Sullivan for providing the initial inspiration for our exhibition. It was he who suggested the title 'Progressive American Architecture' as a guideline. . . . But the visionary, who could sense the approach of a new art in the desert of old Chicago, can help us today in showing the path towards an understanding of the problems of modern American architecture."
7. Ibid., 9ff.
8. Ibid., 16ff.
9. Ibid., 19. That this assessment of the development of American architecture cannot be corrobroated by Sullivan's fate need not be explained here.
10. Ibid., 20.
11. Ibid., 22. Hamburg was also familiar with such euphoric claims to world-wonder architecture. Rudolf G. Binding has at least suggested such a comparison in his commemorative publication on Höger's Chile House. See Oechslin, "Zu Rudolf G. Bindings Hymnus auf das Chile-Haus in Hamburg," in Für Ulrich Conrads von Freunden (Braunschweig, 1988), 128ff.
12. Ibid., 2. Lewis Mumford confirmed this opinion in the preface to the Dover edition of *Sticks and Stones* (New York, 1955): "When this book was first published, in 1924, no history of American architecture as a whole had yet been written."
13. *Neue amerikanische Baukunst*, 21.
14. Ibid., 2.
15. Ibid.
16. Ibid., 3, 4. Due to the harmonization of height and the balancing of mass and free space, Hegemann also approved of Goodhue's solution for Lincoln, Nebraska (see Hegemann, *Amerikanische Architektur und Stadtbaukunst* [Berlin, 1925], 38). See below.
17. See Richard Neutra, *Wie baut Amerika?* (Stuttgart, 1927), and *Amerika: Die Stilbildung des Neuen Bauens in den Vereinigten Staaten* (Vienna, 1930).
18. See Neutra, ed., *Richard Neutra: Promise and Fulfillment 1919–1932* (Carbondale, 1986), 168.
19. See Oechslin, "Neues Bauen in der Welt," (Rassegna, 38, 1989): 6-9.
20. From the commentary on the dust cover of the series.
21. Hegemann had already distanced himself from Gantner in a critique of the latter's book *Schweizer Stadt*. The *Frankfurter Zeitung* qualified Hegemann's polemic a "differentiated but all too sparing rationalism"; this judgment was used as an advertising slogan in *Der Städtebau* 2 (1926: s.p., before 17).
22. See Gantner, "Vorwort des Herausgebers" (October 1929) in El Lissitzky, ed., *Russland, Neues Bauen in der Welt, Band 1* (Vienna, 1930), 7.
23. See Oechslin, "Neues Bauen," and Hitchcock and Johnson, *The International Style: Architecture since 1922* (New York, 1932), 25: "But it was in America, that the promise of a new style appeared first, and up to the War, advanced most rapidly."
24. See Hegemann, *Amerikanische Architektur und Stadtbaukunst* (Berlin, 1925; rev. ed., 1927) Ein Überblick über den houtigen Stand der amerikanischen Baukunst in ihrer Beziehung zum Städtebau. (Preliminary title: Der Städtebau nach den Ergebnissen der internationalen Städtebau Ausstellung Gothenburg. First Volume: Amerikanische Architektur & Stadtbaukunst) (Berlin, 1925; second edition: 1927). In terms of style and method this work by Hegemann is similar to Hegemann and Peets, *The American Vitruvius: An Architect's Handbook of Civic Art* (New York, 1922). However, with regard to content, it differs considerably (see below and also the later, in part posthumous, three-volume publication *City/Planning/Housing*.
25. See Mendelsohn, *Amerika: Bilderbuch eines Architekten* (Berlin, 1926).

26. Ibid., vi.

27. Ibid., ix.

28. The quotes are taken from some of the chapter headings, which in turn reflect a stereotypical image of America.

29. See Mendelsohn, *Russland, Europa, Amerika: Ein architektonischer Querschnitt* (Berlin, 1929).

30. Mendelsohn, *Amerika*, 33, in reference to Equitable Trust Building as an example of the "second phase of the skyscraper," and *Russland, Europa. Amerika*, 196, in reference to Medical Center 1.

31. Mendelsohn, *Russland, Europa. Amerika*, 212, in reference to Medical Center 2. On the term *Wille zum Neuen*, see above and note 2. This example also serves to illustrate Hegemann's contrasting unemotional opinion of the zoning law, which is based on his perspective as a professional city planner. Hegemann rejects the concentration of mass of the type in Mendelsohn's examples and sees the zoning law as a way to overcome such mistakes. See Hegemann, *Amerikanische Architektur*, 56: "The belated American zoning law should prevent the repetition of such conditions."

32. See Mendelsohn, *Russland, Europa, Amerika*, 5.

33. See Rathenau, "Vier Nationen," in *Reflexionen* (Leipzig, 1908), 118.

34. Ibid., 125.

35. Ibid., 130.

36. Ibid., 126.

37. Ibid.

38. See *Neue amerikanische Baukunst*, 3: "Frank Lloyd Wright, Sullivan's favorite pupil is missing"; "Authorization has been given for an additional exhibition at a later date."

39. See de Fries, *Frank Lloyd Wright: Aus dem Lebenswerke eines Architekten* (Berlin, 1926), 9. De Fries adds critically: "We would have to bend the truth if we were to see the constructivist gestures of our young architects, some of whom are extremely capable, as much more than a new type of plastic ornamentation. The profit which may have derived from Wright and others and from their own intellectual capacities has resulted in nothing more than a modernistic variation of a purely formal gesture."

40. Ibid., 15: "And 'America' is a frame of mind which is not exclusive to this continent but which is establishing itself all over the civilized world."

41. Ibid., 31–32. Similar criticism can be found in de Fries, *Junge Baukunst in Deutschland: Ein Querschnitt durch die Entwicklung neuer Baugestaltung in der Gegenwart* (Berlin, 1926), 7.

42. The preface entitled "To Our Readers" signed by Theodor Goecke and Camillo Sitte (*Der Städtebau* 1 [1904]: 1–4) opened with the programmatic declaration: "EVERY SCIENCE has always tried to establish absolute clarity with regard to the aims of the entire spectrum of its activities, to reveal the historical development of its field, to assemble everything which will aid in the promotion of its further development and to establish appropriate boundaries with related disciplines."

43. De Fries, *Junge Baukunst*, 7.

44. See also Hegemann's "Eine Berichtigung zur Stadtbauratfrage," in *Der Städtebau* 2 (1926).

45. Ibid.

46. See *Neue amerikanische Baukunst* and Hegemann, *Amerikanische Architektur*.

47. The best, most recent accounts of Hegemann's life and development can be found in C. Crasemann Collins, "Hegemann and Peets: Cartographers of an Imaginary Atlas," in A. J. Plattus, ed., Hegemann and Peets, *The American Vitruvius* (repr., New York, 1988), xii–xxii, and "A Visionary Discipline: Werner Hegemann and the Quest for the Pragmatic Ideal," *Center: A Journal for Architecture in America, University of Texas, Austin* (New York, 1989). The author would like to thank Christina Crasemann Collins for access to proofs and manuscripts.

48. Hegemann's first magnum opus *Der Städtebau nach den Ergebnissen der allgemeinen Städtebau-Ausstellung in Berlin* (Berlin, 1911) is dedicated to "the promoter of the idea of Greater Berlin Dr. Otto March, engineer and city architect." Vol. 2 has a further dedication to "Members of the Propaganda Committee 'For Greater Berlin'" including Hermann Muthesius and Werner Weisbach, "and the men and women of Greater Berlin who supported the aims of the Propaganda Committee in word, letter, advice, and action."

49. Goecke and Sitte, "To Our Readers," 1–4.

50. Ibid. A further key sentence: "Urban planning is a science, urban planning is an art with quite distinct research aims and quite distinct, onerus practical tasks."

51. On Hegemann's studies with Gide, see Crasemann Collins, "Hegemann

and Peets," xii. (A more detailed account of Hegemann's personal biography and educational background is deliberately omitted here as it can be obtained from the studies by Crasemann Collins.)

This phase in Hegemann's education should not be underestimated in the consideration of the Berlin urban planning exhibition and the mass of information about the history of urban planning in Paris that it provided: Hegemann reveals his sources in a list of thanks (*Der Städtebau* 2 [1913]: 162 n. 126. Among these is Henri Lemmonier, professor of art history, Sorbonne (whose seminar the author attended for one year). This is of additional interest because the detailed treatment of French urban planning history and the French *embellissement* theory would appear to have inspired Le Corbusier—whose drawings after Patte are known—during his visit to Berlin.

52. See Dunkel, *Beiträge zur Entwicklung des Städtebaus in den Vereinigten Staaten von Amerika* (Dresden, 1917), 49.

53. Ibid., 105.

54. See Hegemann, *Der Städtebau* (1911): 15–16.

55. Ibid., 81.

56. Hegemann himself defines his aim in the preface as the "compilation of a thesaurus." See Crasemann Collins, "Hegemann and Peets," xii and xvii, where the author correctly comments on the eclectic nature of the collected material.

57. See de Fries, *Junge Baukunst*, passim.

58. See Hegemann, "Eine wichtige Berliner Stadtbaufrage: Erich Mendelsohn's Herpich-Umbau in der Leipziger Strasse, *Der Städtebau* (1925): 156–7.

59. See W. Hegemann, "Die Strasse als Einheit," *Der Städtebau* (1925): 95 and 106. Later too, Hegemann delivered a decidedly positive judgment on the Mendelsohn building: "The vertical articulation of the Wertheim building is counteracted on the same street by the horizontal articulation of the new Herpich House (figs. 427–29). And despite everything that can be said against the details of this building, such as the play of the cornices ('lit cornices' beneath the windows in the central building, decorative cornices above the windows of the oriel), this building is the most beautiful one on Leipziger Strasse and one of the most beautiful buildings of our time" (Hegemann, *Reihenhausfassaden, Geschäfts- und Wohnhäuser aus alter und neuer Zeit* [Berlin, 1929], 27).

60. Ibid., 106 and 107.

61. See Hegemann, "Eine wichtige Berliner," 156.

62. Ibid.

63. Ibid., 157.

64. See Hegemann, "Zur Beurteilung des van Eesternschen Entwurfes," *Der Städtebau* (1926): 27–28.

65. See Hegemann, "Gross Genoa" *Der Städtebau* (1926): 8.

66. Ibid., 9. On Hegemann's attack on the Dutch avant-garde's "chamber of horrors" see Oechslin, "Die Talsuisierung des russischen Beitrages zur modernen Architektur," in *El Lissitzky. Der Traum vom Wolkenbügel*, exhibition catalogue (Zurich, 1991), 9, 16, 17.

67. See Behrendt, *Die einheitliche Blockfront als Raumelement im Stadtbau: Ein Beitrag zur Stadtbaukunst der Gegenwart* (Berlin, 1911), 10.

68. See Hegemann, *Das steinerne Berlin* (Berlin, 1930), appendix: "Städtebauliche Schriften desselben Verfassers" (s.p.).

69. See Behrendt, *Der Kampf um den Stil im Kunstgewerbe und in der Architektur* (Stuttgart, 1920), and *Der Sieg des Neuen Baustils* (Stuttgart, 1927).

70. Behrendt's particular interest in Dutch culture is also apparent in his book *Die Holländische Stadt*.

71. See Behrendt, *Modern Building: Its Nature, Problems, and Forms* (New York, 1937), 152.

72. See Hegemann, "Zur Beurteilung," 28.

73. Ibid.

74. If the categories for the various groups of "Opponents of the New Architecture," which Behrendt defines in *Der Sieg des neuen Baustils* (11), are applied to Hegemann, he would emerge not as one of these ("hopeless") opponents who misinterpret the concept of tradition but as a member of the "benign" group whom Behrendt defines as follows: "They see the work of the New Architecture as harmless artistic folly and as one of the many new artistic fashions which have emerged in rapid succession in recent years."

75. See Hegemann, "Zur Beurteilung," 27.

76. See Hegemann, "Die Strasse," 95 and 106.

77. See Hegemann, "Zur Beurteilung," 27.

78. Ibid.

79. See Hegemann, *Amerikanische Architektur*, 58–60: the relevant chapter, following the one on zoning, is headed "Transport Circle" and contains sketches on grouping of public buildings by Hegemann and Peets. These already appear in the *American Vitruvius* (1922) where they are contained in the comprehensive chapter "The Grouping of Buildings in America."

80. In the *American Vitruvius*, Hegemann and Peets presented sketches of various ground-plan solutions of the French *embellissement*, for example, Blondel's proposal for Strasbourg (1768) (77) and different proposals by Patte for a Place Louis XV (80, 81, and 83).

81. See Hilberseimer, *Grosstadtarchitektur* (Stuttgart, 1927), 10. Hilberseimer refers here to Hegemann's essay "Das Hochhaus als Verkehrsstörer" which appeared in *Wasmuth's Monatsheften* (1924, pp. 296). Hegemann gives this problem more detailed treatment in *Amerikanische Architektur*: Das Hochhaus als Quelle von Verkehrsschwerigkeiten (p. 44).

82. Despite the accusation of possible abuse through speculation—this argument receives rather one-sided emphasis in Ciucci, et al., *La Città americana dalla guerra civile al "New Deal,"* (Bari, 1973) (240, 246–47, and 471– Hegemann also notes "surprising artistic effects . . . most of which, however, did not get beyond the purely picturesque." Referring to his own sketches, Hegemann draws attention to the possibilities which present themselves when the regulation of skyscrapers is put to use for artistic intentions in the design of squares" (See Hegemann, *Amerikanische Architektur*, 55).

83. See Hegemann, *Grosstadtarchitektur*, and *Amerikanische Architektur*

84. Recessing and the multiplication of traffic levels (interaction) are presented as the new methods compatible with traditional urban-planning principles. Hegemann made a practical suggestion for doubling the transport levels at Potsdamer Platz (see W. Hegemann and O. Lange, "Potsdamer Platz-Phantasien," *Der Städtebau* (1925): 176–77, *Das steinerne Berlin* (Berlin, 1930), 271–72, and *City, Planning, Housing*, 37, fig. 239). This solution can be compared with analogous attempts in Berlin, for example, with Martin Wagner's proposals for Alexander Platz (L. Scarpa, *Martin Wagner und Berlin* [Braunschweig, 1986], figs. 43, 44). After his trip to America in 1929, Wagner reacted (104) similarly to Hegemann and Hilbeseimer in reference to American skyscrapers and traffic problems.His *Städtebauliche Probleme* in amerikanischen Städten und ihre Rückwirkung auf den deutschen Städtebau (Berlin, see above) pays sufficient attention to this point of view. (10.).

85. Hegemann, *Amerikanische Architektur* p, 59, figs. 196–201: Hegemann expressly referred to these plans in his explanation of his position on van Eesternen's project. The Renaissance aspect does not appear to have disturbed him at all here. The corresponding formulation in *American Vitruvius*, 148: "adaptation of various Renaissance motives to modern conditions."

86. This can be found in the commentary to the sketches in question (Hegemann, Amerikanische Architektur, 59).

87. The example dealt with here demonstrates how particularly in the lists of illustrations Hegemann's concern is to provide a comprehensive explanation for his German audience. In the layout, these extended texts frequently lead to the elimination of an illustration (as is the case in the example shown here).

88. Hegemann and Peets, *American Vitruvius*, 136.

89. Hegemann, *Amerikanische Architektur*, 57.

90. Ibid.

91. Hegemann and Peets, *American Vitruvius*, 145, fig. 611.

92. Hegemann, *Amerikanische Architektur*, 56, fig. 188.

93. Ibid.

94. Hegemann, *Urban Planning*, III, 37: The title and subtitle are Public Squares, and The Replanning of Plazas for 20th-Century Traffic respectively.

95. Ibid. The complete passage reads: "A third approach is illustrated in the recent redesign of Königsplatz in Munich, where the traffic problem is solved by simply eliminating all traffic and replacing the former central geensward with a paved enclosure for National-Socialist military display."

96. In her study of Hegemann, C. Crasemann Collins uses the term "pragmatic ideal" (Crasemann Collins, *Hegemann and Peets* p.).

97. See *Der Städtebau* 2 (1913): 162 n. 126.

98. See Oechslin, "Allemagne: Influences, confluences et reniements," in *Le Corbusier—une encyclopédie* (Paris, 1987), 33, and "Le Corbusier und Deutschland: 1910–11," in *Le Corbusier im Brennpunkt*, ed. Oswald and W. Oechslin (Zürich, 1988), pp. 28, and 40–41.

99. See Crasemann Collins, *Hegemann and Peets*, p. xix. Collins correctly draws attention to the fact that Hegemann failed to discover the affinity between his own views and those of Le Corbusier.

100. See W. Hegemann, "Kritik des Grosstadt-Sanierungs-Planes Le Corbusiers," *Der Städtebau* (1927): 69 and *Das steinerne Berlin* (Berlin, 1930), table 62. Id., *City, Planning Housing* ed. R. N. Anshen, II, (New York, 1938) p. 272. In the following passage it becomes clear why at this point Hegemann still held fast to his early criticism and to the comparison with Haussmann:
"Since that time—i.e. 1927—Le Corbusier has publicly admitted (for instance in his lecture given at Columbia University in November, 1935) that large parts of his proposed towers are badly lighted. He has made new proposals for towers which are much lower (i.e., much less "economical") and which do not suffer from the ugly light shafts of his former plans. After, however, having made all these reasonable concessions, Mr. Le Corbusier calmly proceeded to show lantern slides illustrating his old proposals of badly lighted towers and discussed them as if they could still be taken seriously."

101. Hegemann, "Kritik," 69: "No one who has carefully observed how the incredible increases in rents in the business quarter in New York allow and even encourage the building of skyscrapers in a metropolis should doubt that the plan will soon be realized even if it involves economic and health problems for the general public."

102. Ibid., 70.

103. See Liernur, Juncal y Esmeralda, Peru House, Maison Garay, "Fragmentos de un debate tipologico y urbanistico en la obra de Jorge Kalnay," in (Borghini/Salama/Solsona) 1930–1950. *Arquitectura moderna en Buenos Aires* (Buenos Aires, 1987): 109; 114–15. For further information on Hegemann's comparatively unspectacular appearances in Buenos Aires, the author would like to express his sincere thanks to Pancho Liernur.

104. See Le Corbusier, *Précisions sur un état présent de l'architecture et de l'urbanisme* (Paris, 1930), 167.

105. Ibid. Both rhetorical statements introduced Le Corbusier's ninth lecture on October 18, 1929, in Buenos Aires.

106. See Adler, "Wissenschaftlicher Städtebau auf der Hamburger Tagung der Akademie," *Der Städtebau* (1927): 126–27.

107. Hilberseimer, *Grosstadtarchitektur*, 13. (Hilberseimer was at least willing to give detailed treatment to Le Corbusier's suggestions at first place under the heading "Schematic Attempts at Solutions."

108. Hegemann, "Kritik," 70.

109. Hegemann and Peets, *American Vitruvius*, 150, and Hegemann, *Amerikanische Architektur*, 57.

110. See Le Corbusier, *Vers une architecture* (Paris, 1923), 29.

111. Hegemann and Peets, *American Vitruvius*, 145, and Hegemann, *Amerikanische Architektur*, 56. To emphasize this it is perhaps interesting to recall Le Corbusier's famous sketch for his ninth lecture in Buenos Aires (*Précisions*, 203), in which the *paradoxe pathétique* of New York is compared with the *destinée d'une ville neuve*, represented by the Buenos Aires skyscrapers planned at great distances from each other.

112. *Berliner Architekturwelt* 81 (1905): 1.

113. Hegemann, *Das steinerne Berlin*, 9–10.

114. See Oechslin, *Le Corbusier und Pierre Jeanneret, Das Wettbewerbsprojekt für den Völkerbundpalast in Genf 1927* (Zürich, 1988), passim.

115. See Hegemann, "Hermann Jansen zu seinem sechzigsten Geburtstag," *Der Städtebau* (1929): 269.

116. A. E. Brinckmann.

117. See Hegemann, *Amerikanische Architektur*, 38.

118. See Hegemann, "Camillo Sitte und die 'Fischerschule,'" *Der Städtebau* (1925): 39.

119. Court settlement between Martin Wagner and Werner Hegemann in *Der Städtebau* (1929): 56.

120. See "What Is Happening to Modern Architecture? A Symposium at the Museum of Modern Art," *The Museum of Modern Art Bulletin* 15 (Spring 1948): 2, 5, 11, and 18.

1. Othmar Amman. George
Washington Bridge, Manhattan.
3,500 feet clear span.

Moses and Ammann: Notes on the Modernization of the Empire State

Kenneth Frampton

Kenneth Frampton, an architect and architectural historian, is the Ware Professor of Architecture at Columbia University, New York. He has written numerous articles and books of which the most well known is his study Modern Architecture: A Critical History. *From 1972 to 1982 he was a member of the Institute for Architecture and Urban Studies in New York and co-founder of the journal* Oppositions *published by the IAUS over the same period. He is currently finishing two books,* Labor, Work and Architecture *and* Studies in Tectonic Culture.

They are the same people, only further from home
On freeways fifty lanes wide, on a concrete continent
spaced with bland bill boards
illustrating imbecile illusions of happiness
The scene shows fewer tumbrills but more maimed
citizens in painted cars and they have strange license
plates and engines that devour America

—Lawrence Ferlinghetti
A Coney Island of the Mind, *1955*

Robert Moses: Origins and Early Career

Born in 1888, a second-generation American of German Jewish origin, Robert Moses (fig. 1) was given a secular upbringing by his strong-willed mother, Bella Moses, who was responsible for moving the family from New Haven to New York in 1897. His father, Emanuel Moses, had been a prosperous New Haven store owner but was compelled to retire at the age of forty-six after the family moved to the city. Aspiring to be part of the New York Jewish elite, the Moses children were all educated at the non-religious Society for Ethical Culture School in New York, and Bella Moses spent much of her later life in charitable work on behalf of the newly migrated Eastern European Jewry of the Lower East Side. Yet she was devoted to civic improvements as well; one of her most memorable achievements was the building of a permanent summer camp for the Madison House Settlement.

For someone who would eventually have such a public polytechnical career, it is odd that Robert Moses should have had such a literary education, particularly since he excelled in the humanist subjects at Yale University. He achieved a reputation as a Latinist and a poet, and went to Oxford in 1909 with the aim of taking a doctorate there, but the study of history aroused his interest in the British Civil Service, and he promptly turned his thesis into a dissertation on the subject. After a short stint studying political science at the University of Berlin, Moses returned to New York and enrolled at Columbia University in 1912 to finish his doctorate. In 1913 he entered New York's Training School for Public Service at the bureau for Municipal Research and thereafter joined its research unit. Moses seems to have inherited a reformist zeal from his mother and, with an unfailing sense of destiny, gravitated toward civil service reform. Research made him impatient, however, and in 1914, he joined New York's Municipal Service Commission hoping to act on his ideas. After four more years of fruitless work, Moses, frustrated by the obdurance of the Empire State's bureaucracy, had the good fortune to be hired by the newly elected governor of New York state, the legendary brown-derby hatted, cigar-smoking Al Smith.

Smith was a Lower East Side street kid and reform Democrat. It was his adviser, the social reformer Belle Moskowitz, who would be responsible for Moses's initial rise to power and his subsequent enactment of civic works.[1] Moses's first achievement along these lines was the elimination of traffic crossings over rail at grade, which were prevalent everywhere in New York state when Smith became governor.

By 1923 the new industrial methodology of Taylorization had

297

2. Robert Moses. 1939. Courtesy of
the Special Archives, Triborough
Bridge and Tunnel Authority.

3. Othmar Amman. 1945.

reduced the average working week to one-third of its 1914 level. The corresponding increase in leisure time, plus the invention of Henry Ford's Model T automobile in 1909 and the initiation of its mass production and ownership between 1919 and 1923, served as the joint rationale for Moses's *State Park Plan for New York* of 1923, in which he first began to think in terms of state parks and beaches. His acknowledged masterpiece, Jones Beach, built on a reclaimed barrier reef, was projected around this time, along with the Southern State Parkway, which would prove to be the only efficient means for reaching the beach from New York City. Thus, as early as 1923, Moses was already projecting the forty thousand acres of parks and 124 miles of parkway that he would eventually build on Long Island, and in 1924, he was appointed by Smith to head up the newly created Long Island State Parks Commission.

Moses's concept of the parkway was based on the fifteen-mile Bronx River Parkway, built between 1912 and 1925 by engineer Leslie G. Holleran and landscape architect Gilmore Clarke. This was an extended version of the sunken traverse roads that Frederick Law Olmsted had devised for crossing Central Park but scaled to the region and to the automobile. Indeed the very term "parkway" had been coined by Olmsted and Calvert Vaux who first used the term for the Eastern and Ocean parkways in Brooklyn and the famous Fenway in Boston.[5]

Hermann Ammann: Railroads, Bridges, and Roads

Othmar Hermann Ammann (fig. 2) was born of Swiss-German parentage in Schaffhausen in 1879. The son of a straw hat manufacturer, Ammann was heir to a prosperous bourgeois family of painters, physicians, lawyers, clergymen, and merchants. Determined to become an architect, he was the top student in mathematics in the Kantonschule in Zurich, but by the time he entered the university he had changed his field to engineering. Ammann was trained, like the great Swiss engineer Robert Maillart, at the engineering school of the Swiss Federal Polytechnical Institute in Zurich (ETH); both men were among the last students of Wilhelm Ritter, a professor in bridge design. Ritter possessed a critical and lucid command of American bridge technology (*Der Bruckenbau in den Vereiningten Staaten Amerikas*, 1895), but in his lectures, he concentrated on elegant detailing, statical logic, and tectonic rationality. Of Ritter's influence on Maillart and Ammann, David Billington has written:

As every bridge designer knows . . . overall form means nothing if the details are not well done. All the pieces must fit together and none must be structurally weak. To the watch-making Swiss, details are an esthetic part of design because they require great care. About one third of the entire text and illustrations in Ritter's book were given over to a detailed review of joints, connections, eyebars and rivets. Many of the drawings are elegant and Ritter criticized others as not elegant. He proceeded from overall form to detail and emphasized both....Overall Ritter's book was a unique work in the [Carl] Cullmann tradition, and Maillart's notes reflected his teacher's international study. Almost certainly this American focus stimulated Ammann as well and helped him decide to make his career in the United States.[2]

Ammann graduated from ETH in 1902; two years later he emigrated to the United States, where he at once began to work on the construction of steel railway bridges. In 1905 he joined the Pennsylvania Steel Company under chief engineer Frederic C. Kunz. It was in this capacity that Amman eventually came to work on the 1,182-foot, quasi-cantilevered Queensboro Bridge in New York City, built between 1906 and 1909 to the designs of Austrian engineer Gustav Lindenthal. In 1907, at the age of twenty-seven, Ammann was called by the engineer C. C. Schneider to investigate the disastrous failure of the Quebec cantilevered bridge then under construction over the Saint Lawrence River. In 1912 he came back from Pennsylvania to New York to work as chief assistant to Lindenthal on the design and supervision of the Hell Gate four-track railway arch built over the East River in 1916 (fig. 5). Lindenthal had been preoccupied since the early 1890s with the idea of building a mammoth span across the Hudson, and in 1920, he proposed such a crossing at 57th Street. Lindenthal's multiple-decked bridge was to have been suspended from four cables, braced in pairs, and hung from two monumental gateway towers. Joseph Gies's account of the design affords a remarkable picture of the ambitious scope of the proposal.

The plan originally envisioned six railroad tracks and was later modified to permit addition of even more. In its final form, Lindenthal's design is the most ambitious suspension bridge ever proposed. It called for two decks each of the fantastic width of 235 feet. The lower deck was to carry twelve rapid transit tracks, two trolley tracks, two bus lanes and two fifteen foot sidewalks. The upper deck was to carry sixteen passenger-car lanes. Eventually the proposed junctions of Lindenthal's grandiose bridge was [sic] taken up by a whole complex of sub-acqueous tunnels.[3]

While Ammann had faithfully assisted Lindenthal in the construction of Hell Gate, he objected to the gargantuan Hudson River project, arguing that the design should be lighter and restricted to vehicular and pedestrian traffic. Lindenthal's insistence on a grandiose multitransit bridge led to an eventual split between the two men—but also to Ammann's subsequent triumph.

Upon leaving Lindenthal's employ, Ammann persuaded the newly constituted Port of New York Authority to build a lighter but wider span between Washington Heights and Fort Lee, connecting into the Manhattan grid at 179th Street. Early in 1924, Ammann was charged by the authority to design such a span, then known as the Fort Washington Bridge. This crossing over the Hudson, later renamed the George Washington Bridge, was a 3,500-foot clearspan suspension structure carrying eight vehicular lanes on the upper deck and four mass-transit lines below. Fully detailed by 1926, this mammoth structure took five years to complete. In this remarkable work, Ammann increased the previous maximum span for suspension construction by a magnitude of three and improved the aesthetic of such structures by eliminating the stiffening trusses at the level of the roadbed. In this instance, he calculated that the deadweight of the bridge was sufficient to maintain its sideways stability against wind and sympathetic vibration.

After the 1929 stock market crash, Ammann was obliged to

introduce certain economies into the finish of the George Washington Bridge, among them the elimination of Cass Gilbert's original stone cladding for the 650-foot-high steel latticework towers at either end of the bridge. Since these towers had been designed with a falsely arched form in order to give the semblance of a stone arch, this omission provoked considerable controversy. While Ammann supported the stone encasement of the towers, he nonetheless considered that the proportioning of the pylons was such as to permit the latticework to remain exposed (fig. 3).

In 1928, Ammann was appointed to the post of chief engineer for bridges to the Port Authority and two years later, at the age of fifty, was appointed chief engineer, a post he held until 1937 when he became director of engineering. In passing from the Hell Gate railway arch of 1916 to the George Washington Bridge of 1930, Ammann's career covered the transition from the rail- to the road-building era.

Parkways and Parks

The year 1925 saw Robert Moses negotiating with the farmers of southern Long Island in order to purchase rights of way for his Southern State Parkway (fig. 4). Soon after, he was engaged in the same activity for the Northern State Parkway, but this time his deals were made with robber barons, not farmers—the Vanderbilts, Morgans, Phipps, and above all the financier Otto Kahn—who had long since staked out their claim to the northern half of Long Island.

Moses was as aggressive with this so-called "landed" aristocracy as he had been with the farmers on the southern shore. He had succeeded in surreptitiously incorporating expropriation rights in the New York State parkway legislation that he had drafted in Albany; thus, should he fail in purchasing easements at a reasonable price he would enact their mandatory acquisition by the state under New York's newly acquired appropriation powers.[5] A long and bitter fight ensued with the Long Island gentry, who were capable of defending themselves against the state where the relatively poor agricultural populace could not.[6] That this fight should carry both Smith and Moses to the point of political destruction was hardly surprising given the forces arrayed against them. Many delays occurred, and both parkways were not to get fully under way until a compromise had been reached in which the northern route would only be constructed along a path approved by the barons.[7] Although Moses lost this short-term battle, he succeeded in winning the war. Thus as Robert Caro writes of Moses's suit against the Taylor Estate:

Moses had never stopped developing the Taylor Estate—as if its acquisition were a *fait accompli*. By the Spring of 1927, he had laid concrete for the access roads and parking fields, set out scores of stone fireplaces and picnic tables, erected wooden bathhouses with showers and lockers and finished renovating the mansion and out buildings at a total cost of hundreds of thousands of dollars. During the summer of 1927 it had hundreds of thousands of visitors. By the time the higher courts came to rule on the question whether the Taylor Estate was a park, it *was* a park [the Heckscher State Park].[8]

4

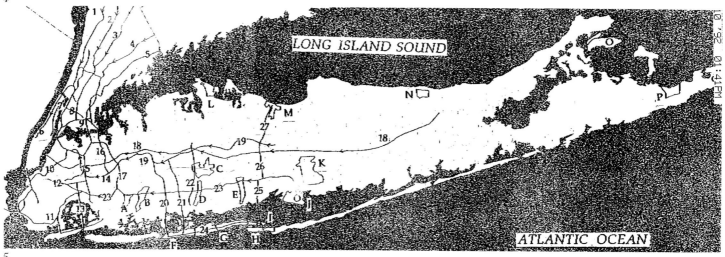

5

4. Robert Moses, Gustav Lindenthal,
and Othmar Amman. Astoria Pool
(1936) and Hell Gate railway
bridge (1916). The pool was
designed by Aymar Embury.

5. Robert Moses. A schematic map of
Manhattan, Bronx, and Long
Island showing the parks and
parkways built under his
jurisdiction between 1926 and
1945.

Key to Streets
1. Saw Mill River Parkway
2. Sprain Parkway
3. Bronx River Parkway
4. Hutchinson River Parkway
5. New England Thruway
6. Henry Hudson Parkway
7. Harlem River Drive
8. Cross-Bronx Expressway
9. Bruckner Expressway
10. Brooklyn-Queens Expressway
11. Shore Parkway (Belt)
12. Atlantic Avenue
13. Marine Parkway
14. Grand Central Parkway
15. Van Wyck Expressway

16. Clearview Expressway
17. Cross I. Parkway
18. Long Island Expressway
19. Northern State Parkway
20. Meadowbrook Parkway
21. Wantaugh State Parkway
22. Seaford-Oyster Bay Expressway
23. Southern State Parkway
24. Ocean Parkway
25. Robert Moses Causeway
26. Sagtikos State Parkway
27. Sunken Meadow State Park

Key to Parks
A. Valley Stream Park
B. Hempstead Lake State Park

C. Bethpage State Park
D. Massapequa State Park
   (Undeveloped)
E. Belmont Lake State Park
F. Jones Beach State Park
G. Gilgo State Park
H. Robert Moses State Park
I. Captree State Park
J. Heckscher State Park
K. Connetquot State Park
L. Caumsett State Park
M. Sunken Meadow State Park
N. Wildwood State Park
O. Orient Beach State Park
P. Hither Hills State Park
Q. Montauk Point State Park

Moses himself understood this triumph as a public relations victory: "As long as you are on the side of the parks, you're on the side of the angels. You can't lose."[9] Later, he was fond of saying, "Once you sink that first stake, they'll never make you pull it up."[10] Moses pursued this last principle with superhuman daring and tenacity, using the fifteen million dollars allocated by the state for parks to begin building ten parks. Thus by 1926, work had commenced on Montauk Point, Hither Hills, Wildwood, Sunken Meadow, Belmont Lake, Hempstead Lake, Valley Stream, Fire Island, and his masterpiece, Jones Beach. He would add to this such works as the Astoria Pool of 1936 (fig. 5) built in conjunction with the Triborough Bridge complex and Jacob Riis Park, completed on Long Island in 1938 (fig. 6)

Despite the advisory presence of the architect Harvey W. Corbett and the landscape architect Gilmore Clarke, Moses designed Jones Beach on his own. According to a surviving member of Moses's original team we learn:

On [one] trip to the beach Harvey Corbett suggested that the water tower be designed as an Italian campanile, or church bell tower. There were many different types, Corbett said, and started to reel them off. As he was reeling he mentioned the one in Venice. "Venice! I like the one in Venice best," Moses said. According to one of the men there, "he pulled out another one of his envelopes and sketched the campanile in Venice right there—and that's how the water tower was done. And that's the way most everything was done. He had the architects and engineers there, but he was the architect and engineer of Jones Beach. He was more responsible for the design of Jones Beach than any architect or engineer of all of us put together."[11]

Knowing that Al Smith would be compelled to relinquish the governorship in 1928, Moses worked at a breakneck pace between the Park Commission's 1926 budget allocations and the end of Smith's term two years later. By then, the parks were partially complete, the Southern State Parkway was underway, and Jones Beach was basically in place. The bathhouse, campanile, restaurant, and two ten-thousand-car parking lots were completed by the end of 1929, and the attendance at Jones Beach doubled over the next two years to some three million per year. The press lauded Moses's achievement as a true accomplishment for the people of New York.

Franklin D. Roosevelt succeeded Smith as governor, and the old populist patronage was gone; without Smith, Moses had little chance of prevailing over the Long Island elite. While Roosevelt would not do battle with the New York establishment, he was willing to keep Moses supplied with money. By 1930, Moses was able to complete Ocean Parkway which linked Jones Beach to Fire Island, and in 1931, he started work on the compromise route for the Northern State Parkway. At the same time, he took further steps toward expanding the infrastructural network of the New York hinterland, initiating new parkways in the midst of the Great Depression. Included were the Belt Parkway (then known as Marginal Boulevard), the Grand Central Parkway, the Hutchinson River Parkway (fig. 7), and the Henry Hudson Parkway (fig. 8), which was designed to link up with the state-sponsored Saw Mill River Parkway. In announcing these projects in February 1930,

6. Robert Moses. Jacob Riis Park, Long Island, New York. 1938.

7

8

7. *Robert Moses. Hutchinson River Parkway, 1936.*

8. *Robert Moses. Henry Hudson Parkway, 1936.*

Moses anticipated his imminent collaboration with Ammann, especially on the Bronx-Whitestone Bridge. This second generation of parkways, built between 1930 and 1939, was conceived by Moses to culminate in the swan song of his prewar career, the 1939 New York World's Fair. Ammann's services were now essential: Moses needed to get his motoring public across the water to the fair.

Bridges: A Lifelong Collaboration

The creation of the Triborough Bridge Authority (TBA) in 1933 received the immediate backing of the Roosevelt Administration, which put a $37 million, twenty-year loan in the hands of the TBA—essentially in the hands of Moses, its sole director from 1934 to 1968. Characteristically, Moses organized the Triborough Bridge Authority as a state within a state with its own emblem, flag, and police force. He saw to it that the empowering act, ostensibly created to build the bridge alone, had wide ramifications that went well beyond the simple construction of a bridge. From the outset, the Triborough Bridge was conceived as something far more complex than its main suspension span. Moses saw it as a regional traffic machine that would link Eastern Boulevard in the Bronx to the Randall's Island interchange, with traffic crossing the Triborough Bridge into Grand Central Parkway headed east to Long Island. The Triborough Bridge was in effect four bridges connected by a continuous viaduct of which Ammann's Hell Gate cable suspension span at 1,380 feet (120 feet longer than the Brooklyn Bridge) was by far the most spectacular (figs. 9–13).

Under [the architect Aymar Embury's] and Ammann's guidance the traditional granite expression of the anchorages as well as the vaguely Gothic handling of the suspension bridge towers evolved into a fresh astylar essay in Modern Classicism that borrowed from the streamlining of such industrial designers as Norman Bel Geddes, Raymond Loewy and Walter Dorwin Teague. Granite gave way to exposed steel, painted blue-grey and to warm beige poured concrete. A happy device of V-shape arrises was brilliantly orchestrated to control cracking while creating rhythmic concrete surfaces; the steel was meticulously detailed down to the last bolt to make out of structural necessity, the pleasing visually logical patterns of architecture.[12]

Following completion of the Triborough Bridge in 1936, Moses and Ammann built the 2300 foot clear span Bronx Whitestone Bridge (fig. 14, 15) in April 1939. Then the third largest suspension bridge, the Whitestone stretched technology to the limit. Ultimately, Ammann stiffened its form after completion, for psychological rather than technical reasons. Using only low plate girders at the side of roadbed, Ammann and Embury achieved a lean design that was publicly praised by Moses and Talbot Hamlin, among others. Needless to say, the bridge was enormously popular with the motoring public. Over six million vehicles crossed it during the first year of operation, and this success soon led to as much congestion on the bridge and its approaches as anywhere else in Moses's expanded infrastructure. For the first time, traffic engineers (and Moses with them) faced the now familiar paradox that the more a highway network is amplified and extended, the

9

12

10

13

9. Othmar Amman and Aymar Embury. Triborough Bridge, 1933. Aerial view of entry complex looking north from Queens.

10 & 13. Amman & Embury. Triborough Bridge, 1933. 1,380 feet clear span.

11. Amman & Embury. Harlem River Lift Bridge, one segment of the in Triborough Bridge complex, 1933.

12. Amman & Embury. Triborough Bridge, 1933. Detail of cable anchorage joint in the main suspension span.

11

14

15

14. Othmar Amman. Bronx
Whitestone Bridge, 1939. 2,300 feet
clear span.

15. Othmar Amman Bronx
Whitestone Bridge, 1939. Night
view showing the cable suspension
illumination installed in 1989.

16. Othmar Amman. Throg's Neck
Bridge, 1961. 1,800 feet clear span.

17. Othmar Amman. Verrazano-
Narrows Bridge, 1959–1969. 4,260
feet, linking Brooklyn and Staten
Island. The bridge at mid-span clears
the mean high water level by 228 feet.

16

17

greater the amount of traffic drawn into the system—a paradox now recognized as the solution becoming the problem.

Despite discouraging traffic jams, Moses remained committed to highways and bridges throughout his life, and in this respect his response to increasing traffic congestion bordered on the irrational, along with his lifelong ideological opposition to all forms of mass transit. For Moses, as for Henry Ford, the private ownership of an automobile represented the quintessence of American freedom, and it is this, among other considerations, that led him to oppose the construction of a mass transit line down the central median strip of the postwar Long Island Expressway. (Had he not opposed such a provision, New York City travelers would now perhaps possess a relatively traffic-free, rapid means of getting to and from Kennedy Airport.)

By the late thirties, Moses was obsessed with the construction of bridges. In 1939, Moses and Ammann proposed a Brooklyn-Battery megabridge. The anchorage and approaches on the Battery side would have been as high as a ten-story building, and the roadbed running over Battery Park at a height of one hundred feet would have been wider than Fifth Avenue. When the then Secretary of War finally opposed the project on security grounds, Moses shifted his energies overnight to the construction of the Brooklyn-Battery Tunnel. Designed by Ole Singstad, the nine-thousand-foot tube was not completed until 1950, due to wartime restrictions

Only briefly sidetracked by this subaqueous triumph, in 1965 Moses and Ammann went on to build the 1,800 foot clear span Throg's Neck Bridge (fig. 16) crossing Long Island Sound, completed in 1961 and the Verrazano-Narrows Bridge linking Staten Island and Brooklyn fully completed in 1969 (figs. 17–19). With its 4,260-foot span the Verrazano is still the longest suspension bridge in the world, exceeding the Golden Gate Bridge in San Francisco by sixty feet.[13] The proliferation of tolls on the Triborough Bridge system transformed the Triborough Bridge and Tunnel Authority from a traffic machine to a money machine, with each successive project financing the next. Even in the mid-1960s when Moses was seventy-seven and Ammann was eighty-five, the two were still proposing megabridges, including a seven-mile Oyster Bay Bridge, running from the village of Bayville in Nassau County to the city of Rye in Westchester. At the end of his life, Ammann was convinced that new forms of high-tension wire cable would eventually permit spans of up to two miles.[14] Of this unrealized vision, Moses wrote: "The Verrazano-Narrows Bridge is as light as anything monolithic spanning a channel can be. The Sound Crossing will by comparison be a gossamer thread over an arm of the sea.[15]

The 1939 New York World's Fair

The 1939 New York World's Fair, masterminded by Moses, was not only the apotheosis of his personal popularity; it was also the swan song of that form of accessible modernity that underlay the ethos of the New Deal (fig. 20). The World's Fair site was intended by Moses to become a permanent regional

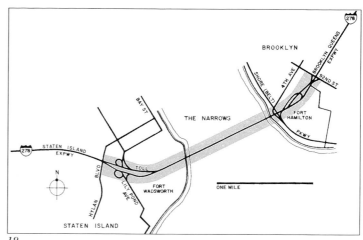

18

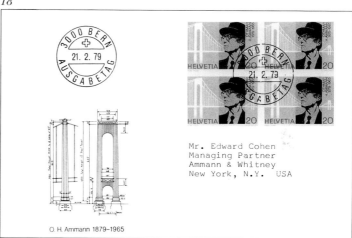

19

18. Othmar Amman. Verrazano-Narrows Bridge. Schematic plan showing bridge approaches. Total length including access ramps, 13,700 feet.

19. Othmar Amman. First issue of a commemorative stamp printed by the Swiss Postal Service in 1979. The official envelope shows elevations of the Verrazano-Narrows towers rising 690 feet above the mean high water level.

20

21

20. *Views of the New York World's Fair, 1939. Official catalogue.*

21. *Albert Kahn. Ford Motor Co. Pavilion, New York World's Fair, 1939.*

22. *Albert Kahn. Ford Motor Co. Pavilion, New York World's Fair, 1939.*

23. *Albert Kahn. Ford Motor Co. Pavilion. Road of Tomorrow Exhibition. Garden and lower level designed by Walter Dorwin Teague.*

24 & 25. *Walter Dorwin Teague. U.S. Steel Pavilion, New York World's Fair, 1939.*

park, equivalent at a regional scale to Manhattan's Central Park. Moses cleared the Flushing Meadows swampland, then known as the Corona Dump, and remade it into a landfilled site. Landscape architect Gilmore Clarke was brought into the picture to design and supervise its upgrading. In 1938, Moses alluded to the fact that the Corona Dump had been the "valley of ashes" of F. Scott Fitzgerald's novel *The Great Gatsby*. With pathos, he wrote in the *Saturday Evening Post*:

In another quarter of a century, old men and women will be telling their grandchildren what the great Corona Dump looked like in the days of F. Scott Fitzgerald, how big the rats were that ran out of it . . . and how it was all changed overnight. But none of them will get as much of a thrill out of their remembrance as those who had an active part in the translation of the great meadow from Dump to Glory.[16]

That this was an achievement of lasting significance there can be no doubt, just as the Fair itself remains a utopian memory in the minds of those children fortunate enough to have visited it in the last moments of peace before World War II. As an architectural model for a brave new world, however, the fair was an ambiguous demonstration, and Lewis Mumford was one among a number of critics who attacked the vaguely Beaux-Arts layout, and its relation to the individual buildings. In retrospect, instructive comparison may surely be made between the New York fair of 1939 and the Paris World Exhibition of 1937, above all because they both exuded the same Art Deco, modernized classical aura (fig. 21). While European totalitarian states exploited this vaguely classical manner in Paris to give monumental weight to their national and ideological identities, a similar ideology was surely detectable in the form of the American Hall of Nations designed by the architects of the Fair board.

This official manner did not however prevent the idea of a liberative modernity from displaying itself, as we may judge, for example, from Oscar Niemeyer's brilliant Brazilian pavilion and William Lescaze and J. Gordon Carr's Aviation Building. Many other individual contributions sustained the exuberant mood of the fair, ranging from Alvar Aalto's imaginative interior to the various contributions made by leading American industrial designers, such as Raymond Loewy, Gilbert Rhode, and Donald Desky. These quite varied works expressed an enthusiastically functionalist attitude toward the machine forms of the future. Thus beyond the official art deco line, the fair produced a kind of latterday futurism also evident in Albert Kahn's Ford Pavilion and Road of Tomorrow (figs. 24, 25) Wallace K. Harrison's Trylon and Perisphere and in Walter Dorwin Teague's U. S. Steel Building (figs. 26, 27). These particular works surely represented the kind of popular modernity Moses and Ammann would have appreciated.

Critical Reaction to the Moses Empire

Altogether, the sum total of Robert Moses's achievement during forty years of autocratic power amounted to twelve bridges, thirty-five autoroutes, 627 miles of roads, 130 miles of expressways, two subaqueous tunnels, 658 playgrounds, seven-

22

23

24

25

26

27

28

*26 & 27. Robert Moses and New
York State Power Authority
Engineers, Robert Moses Power
Dam, St. Lawrence Seaway, 1958.*
Courtesy of the New York Power
Authority.

*28. Robert Moses and New York
State Power Authority Engineers,
Robert Moses Niagara Power Plant,
Niagara River Gorge, 1960.*
Courtesy of the New York Power
Authority.

ty-five state parks, and five million acres of parkland. His civic projects of a more urban nature ranged from the refurbishing of the Central Park Zoo in 1934 to the building of Lincoln Center between 1960 and 1965. As director of the New York Power Authority from 1954 to 1963, Moses oversaw the construction of a control dam and two hydroelectric dams along the banks of the St. Lawrence as well as the large-scale landscaping that these projects necessarily entailed (figs. 26–28). The inauguration of the Robert Moses Massena Power Dam in 1960 was but a culmination of his long association with this part of New York region, where the Empire State runs into Canada. He first worked there was in 1928 when he was engaged in the landscaping of Niagara Falls.

Despite his soft-spoken humility, Ammann's achievements and indeed his sense of self were no less Faustian. In his later years, he had a telescope installed in his private suite on top of the Carlyle Hotel in New York City, and there he could survey the skyline replete with all the bridges that he had achieved in his career as an engineer. The crossings with which he had irrevocably transformed the landscape and the life of the region ranged from the hump-backed profile of the Bayonne Bridge built between New Jersey and Staten Island in 1931 to the Verrazano-Narrows filigree linking Brooklyn and Staten Island in 1965 (fig. 29). Ammann's total oeuvre amounted to some ten major bridges, built in fifty years of service, among which three had been record spans at the time of their erection.

Robert Moses was a populist, and he suffered from many of the ideological contradictions that populism brings in its wake: while he distanced himself from New Deal socialism and maintained an elitist attitude toward those whom he regarded as subject peoples, he nonetheless remained committed to popular reform and to the American ideal of the universal pursuit of health, wealth, and happiness. In this regard, Moses and Henry Ford complemented each other: Moses helped to provide an infrastructure for the popular Model T Ford. He applied time-study methods to industrial management and in this manner he attempted to Taylorize New York's civil service. In addition while Moses initially opposed the socially concerned, liberal Republican Fiorello La Guardia, he turned around in 1933 and endorsed La Guardia as candidate for mayor in a Democratic town. It was in part through such opportunistic stratagems that Moses was able to realize his global aims, comparable in so many respects to the modernization programs then being pursued by European totalitarian states, above all by the National Socialist government of the Third Reich.

Despite manifest ideological differences, Ford's and Moses's accomplishments were much like those of Porsche and Fritz Todt. It is obvious that Ferdinand Porsche's KDF Wagen, his "Strength Through Joy" car that after 1945 became Volkswagen (fig. 30) was intended to be Germany's answer to the challenge of Ford's Model T, and similar comparisons may be drawn between Moses's parkway network and Todt's autobahn system in Germany. The swimming pools, parks, and sport facilities built under the auspices of the Third Reich parallel, in many respects, Moses's equally comprehensive program for

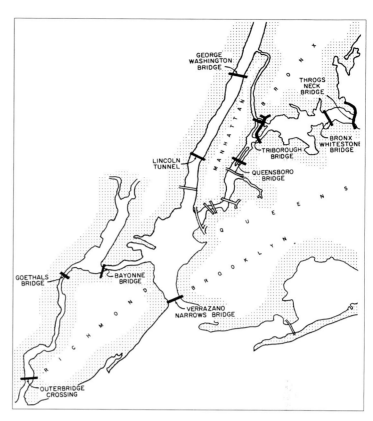

29. Othmar Amman. Bridge Construction 1909–69. With the exception of the Hells Gate rail bridge, this schematic map shows all of the New York regional crossings for which Amman was responsible between the Lindenthal Queensborough Bridge of 1909 and the Verrazano-Narrows Bridge of 1969.

30. Ferdinand Porsche, KdF
Wagen, Germany 1937. Hitler's
answer to the Model T Ford as
depicted in a propaganda poster of
the period.

upgrading recreational facilities in New York State. In words
that could be applied almost as easily to Moses, Robert Taylor
speaks of Todt's autobahnen as the workings of an imperious
demiurge. Of Todt himself, Taylor writes:

The highways were technology become architecture . . . [He] found
the building of highways an artistic commission. Not only were they
architecture, but they were "community" architecture as well. In the
construction of the highways, he said, engineers and architects had
learned to forget the follies of the liberal era and, as a team, to produce "genuine community work."[17]

Todt apparently saw himself as a unique combination of engineer and artistic genius who assisted German technology to
transcend its earlier materialist and capitalist formulations.

The characteristic of the Autobahnen, most often cited by the writers, is their harmony with the German landscape. The effort to preserve the countryside from the destruction by modern engineering
found praise throughout Europe, and this is what attracted non-Nazi
architects, such as Paul Bonatz to participate. Tight control was exercised on the design of all buildings near the highways and only gas
stations were permitted to stand close to the road. The new roads
were justifiably praised by critics for their successful integration
with the human and natural landscape and because they opened up
new areas of the Fatherland for city dwellers. For Bonatz, the highways led to a "rediscovery of Germany."[18]

Purged of their mystical nationalism, similar appraisals could
no doubt be made of Moses's parkway and its attendant amenities. Indeed, who has not felt within the confines of Jones
Beach that one has inexplicably entered into the oceanic domain of a utopian socialist state. Even today, we are awed by
the monumental calm of this great collective space. This, as
Marshall Berman has put it with sympathetic irony, was
Moses's masterpiece: the giant Rosebud of Citizen Kane.[19]

Moses's civic art was both rigorously modern and disarmingly
popular. Like Todt's autoroutes and Bonatz's bridges, Moses's
works were always topographically grounded and brought into
subtle harmony through sensitive landscaping. As Moses put
it, he wanted to scale down the "architecture to the size of a
good time."[20] In that sense, it was not an architecture of modern abstraction, but rather a civic art that was lean and agile
where it had to be. Elsewhere, it was an *architecture parlante*,
often built of traditional materials. In this regard Moses seems
to have been particularly fond of a mixture of Barbizon brick
and Ohio sandstone, articulated to seem futuristic and yet feel
parodoxically familiar. The stone-faced, randomly coursed
arches of Grand Central Parkway and the multicolored, lumi-
nescent rainbow arches of Radio City Music Hall, succeed in
being modern and popular at the same time. In retrospect,
both the parkways and Rockefeller Center evoke that *joie de
vivre* of the 1930s that we have never been able to recover,
even though these forms came into being in the midst of the
Depression.

Like the liberative promise of the popularly priced automobile, the images that Moses created through his architecture
had an enormous impact, as much on industrial designers as
on architects. No one responded more enthusiastically to

310

Moses's exemplification of a popular modernity than the industrial designers Walter Dorwin Teague and Norman Bel Geddes, both of whom wrote books indirectly acclaiming Moses's work as a new egalitarian form of environmental culture. One may say that Teague even tried to rival Moses in his "Road of Tomorrow" exhibit designed for the Ford Motor Company in the 1939 New York World's Fair. In much the same spirit Teague's book, *Design This Day*, paid direct homage to both Moses and Ammann. Thus, Teague gave prominence to the entire gamut of Ammann's achievements from the Triborough Bridge to the Bronx-Whitestone Bridge. In a similar vein he gave equal space to the Henry Hudson Parkway and the Hutchinson River Parkway together with Jacob Riis and Astoria parks, as though they all embodied the very quintessence of modernity. Bel Geddes took a parallel attitude in his book, *Magic Motorways*, in which he featured the West Side Highway, the George Washington Bridge, and the Bulkley plan that projected superhighways across the entire American continent. Not to be outdone by Teague's Ford exhibit, Bel Geddes also designed a new prototypical city plan, the so-called Futurama, for the General Motors Pavilion at the New York World's Fair.

Within the unfolding polemical history of the modern movement, Sigfried Giedion was one of the first historians to canonize Moses's vision in his 1939 Charles Eliot Norton lectures given at Harvard University and published later as *Space, Time, and Architecture*. Giedion was particularly taken with Moses's parkways and included within the last pages of his influential study air views of both the Randall's Island interchange and the Henry Hudson Parkway, which was realized as a linear park and boat basin between 1934 and 1937. Giedion also included an aerial shot of the so-called pretzel intersection along the Grand Central Parkway where the parkway feeds into Union Turnpike, the Interboro Parkway, and Queens Boulevard, built by Robert Moses in 1937. In contrast to disorganized ribbon development Giedion appraised the parkway in the following terms:

Why may the parkway be called an element of the city which is now in the building? For one thing it fulfills a fundamental law of the nascent town; it separates the intermingled functions of vehicular and pedestrian traffic. At the same time it delivers the death blow to the notion that the highway is an isolated track running through the countryside but unrelated to it. It is conceived in terms of its surroundings, being itself a part of nature. Perhaps most important of all, it is controlled in its entire layout by regulations governing all construction along its borders, even limiting the number of gasoline service stations. . . . Entirely forbidden are residences, business houses and factories. Property owners have learned that their civil rights are not infringed when they are not allowed direct access to the parkway, but that is useful in a wider sense to them as well as to the community. . . . Finally, the parkway is the forerunner of the first necessity in the development of the future town; the abolition of the *rue corridor*.[21]

In his book *Can Our Cities Survive* (1947), Jose Luis Sert was more circumspect. While he cited Moses's work with qualified approval, he remained nonetheless critical of the kind of city sprawl that Moses's parkways had facilitated. Today we can have no doubt that the speculative suburbanization of southern Long Island acquired its initial impetus from the introduction of the parkway system. Like the Triborough Bridge that was supposed to draw traffic away from the congested Queensboro Bridge, the results were the reverse of the desired effect.

The Postwar Years

Nothing was quite the same after World War II, and during these years Moses's bad press began to accumulate. The previously optimistic and naive belief in the benefits of techno-scientific progress was fundamentally shaken by the war and by the apocalyptic events that brought it to an abrupt close. Faith in the possibility of synthesizing progressive technology with significant cultural form was broken by the instrumental ruthlessness of mass culture. The postwar reconstruction of Europe and America not only entailed de-Nazification and the Marshall Plan in Germany but also the rise of the oil and automobile lobbies in the United States, which succeeded in creating the federal and state subvention of the postwar freeway construction program. What Moses had demonstrated at a state scale was now put into practice on a continental scale. Unfortunately, Moses's parkway was stripped of its civic and natural amenities to provide a simple way of getting from *A* to *B*. The all-but-total subsidy of the freeways, the GI Bill, and FHA mortgage regulations indicated quite clearly that the railways would be allowed to deteriorate and that the postwar population would be dispersed into new, privatized suburban infrastructures, wherein constant commutation would be the order of the day and where the supermarket and the strip would become the commercial and civic substitute for the traditional main street.

In all this Moses's lifelong antithetical attitude to mass transit played a salient if indirect role. So much so, in fact, that General Motors was to exploit Moses's own methods in bringing about the closure and demolition of Los Angeles's highly efficient suburban transit system which ran throughout a large part of the city; the same right of way was then used for the ubiquitous expressway. In the mid 1950s Los Angeles lost, once and for all, a viable mass transit system. In exactly the same climate, colored by McCarthyism, the new towns of the New Deal era were sold back into private ownership, and virtually at the same time, flourishing provincial towns throughout the United States were deprived of their lifeblood: the railroad and the main street that it had always served. The symbiotic triad of the expressway, the suburb, and the supermarket filled the ensuing void.

With the loss of his idealism after 1945, Moses's postwar career was largely a matter of expediency. The neologism of the expressway superseded the parkway, and the change in terminology was of the utmost significance. Moses's postwar proliferation of throughways, clover leafs, and interchanges was to be just as bereft as the interstate highways of the amenity and elegance that characterized his prewar work. It became an economic means to an end—a swirling concrete barrenness emanating from Manhattan over the entire region.

An equally positivistic attitude prevailed when Moses took charge of the New York City Housing Authority in the late 1940s. As chairman of the mayor's Slum Clearance Housing Committee, his modus operandi was ruthless site clearance, followed by maximized economic production of steel-framed, brick-faced *caserne* blocks; that is to say, by twenty-story apartment towers and slabs spaced at regular intervals. Despite their fulfillment of an urgent need and their provision of certain public amenities, the old public/private structure of the New York City street grid was largely destroyed by these developments. However well-built and upgraded their space and lighting standards, these new blocks and towers totally disrupted the old social intimacy of the nineteenth-century city fabric. Equally absent was Moses's "scaled down architecture of a good time" together with his former feeling for material quality and richness of detail. All of this was suppressed by the single-minded economic constraints of his new reductive attitude. It was now a matter of "on-line" production, a question of piling one floor on top of another and of adding one identical steel framed punched window to the next. While some 800,000 people were rehoused in the process, against the 550,000 who were displaced, we need to set this favorable balance against the socio-sensual deprivation involved in such a blank approach to mass housing.

Moses's former ability to transform a valley of ashes into a utopian landscape deserted him after the war. From then on, his more heroic moments were restricted to the megatechnocratic projects, to Ammann's Verrazano-Narrows crossing, and to the power dams that he built in upstate New York. Although he was aware, in his old age, of the ecological problems that would attend the mass ownership of the automobile, he was unable to return to the well-rounded spirit of his youth. This tragic shift in perspective has been well characterized by Marshall Berman in his book *All That Is Solid Melts Into Air* when he writes of the postwar Cross-Bronx Expressway as a perverse, self-destructive desecration of the humanistic modernity of Moses's prewar vision:

I can remember standing above the construction site for the Cross-Bronx Expressway, weeping for my neighborhood (whose fate I saw with nightmarish precision), vowing remembrance and revenge, but also wrestling with some of the troubling ambiguities and contradictions that Moses' work expressed. The Grand Concourse, from whose heights I watched and thought, was our borough's closest thing to a Parisian boulevard. Among its most striking features were rows of large, splendid 1930's apartment houses: simple and clear in their architectural forms, whether geometrically sharp or biomorphically curved; brightly colored in contrasting brick, offset with chrome, beautifully interplayed with large areas of glass; open to light and air, as if to proclaim a good life that was open not just to the elite residents but to us all. The style of these buildings, known as Art Deco today, was called "modern" in their prime. For my parents, who described our family proudly as a "modern" family, the Concourse buildings represented a pinnacle of modernity. We couldn't afford to live in them—though we did live in a small, modest, but still proudly "modern" building, far down the hill—but they could be admired for free like the rows of glamorous ocean liners in port downtown. (The buildings look like shell-shocked battleships in drydock today, while the oceanliners themselves are all but extinct.)
As I saw one of the loveliest of these buildings being wrecked for the road, I felt a grief that, I can see now, is endemic to modern destruction not merely of "traditional" and "pre-modern" institutions and environments but—and here is the real tragedy—of everything most vital and beautiful in the modern world itself. Here in the Bronx, thanks to Robert Moses, the modernity of the urban boulevard was being condemned as obsolete, and blown to pieces, by the modernity of the interstate highway. Sic transit![22]

Two fundamental strategic precepts governed Moses's lifelong obsession with the provision of a comprehensive infrastructure. The first of these was to universalize the garden city idea as advocated in Ebenezer Howard's *Tomorrow: A Peaceful Path to Real Reform* of 1898: namely, a strategy of decanting the dissatisfied, overcrowded metropolitan populations into the surrounding countryside, first on the basis of weekend leisure trips and later through daily commutation by car. The second precept was even more ideological, namely to supersede the railway with a universal system of autoroutes. Like Frank Lloyd Wright in his Broadacre City of 1932, Moses believed in the egalitarian destiny of the automobile and his opposition to mass transit would stem from this preconception.

It is ironic that while Moses's entire life was dominated by exurban considerations: he never learned to drive (he was always chauffeured around) and he remained committed to the profoundly patrician, cultural institutions of Manhattan that were the ultimate origin of his own elitism. Moses's career was suffused with a kind of manic, displaced imperialism, in which he had to content himself with New York's Empire State rather than with Africa, and with the transformation of small-scale agriculture into the petit-bourgeois dream of a continuous recreational park rather than with the building of the Suez Canal. The low, eleven-foot headroom of his parkway bridges testifies to the fact that he thought his idyllic rainbow world should not be made too available to the natives: the low headroom excluded not only trucks but also the buses of the urban poor. This perverse ideology meant that Moses was opposed not just to fixed rail transit but to all forms of public transport. As a lifelong admirer of Moses, Roosevelt's Secretary of Labor Frances Perkins noted that, like his mother, Moses did not love people. On the contrary they both saw them as a rebellious anarchic mass that had to be bathed, aired, and recreated simply to make them into a more serviceable and manageable public.

While Moses's patriarchal pastoral vision has been overwhelmed by consumerism, its suggestion of an alternative modernity still persists, illuminating the past and warning us against the rapacity of a hyper-technocratic future.

Notes

1. For Belle Moskowitz's role in New York's reform movement, see Robert A. Caro, *The Power Broker: Robert Moses and the Fall of New York* (New York: Vintage Books, 1975), 91–93. I am indebted to this mammoth study for much of the factual information about Moses's career.

2. David Billington, "William Ritter: Teacher of Maillart and Ammann," *Journal of the Structural Division, Proceedings of the American Society of Civil Engineers* 106, no STS (May 1980), 1112, 1113.

3. Joseph Gies, *Bridges and Men* (New York: Grosset & Dunlap, 1963), 223.

4. Frederick Law Olmsted made his first designs for the Boston Parkway system in 1881. "Olmsted separated different types of traffic (through and local) and used the connecting ways between different parts of his park system as parks themselves and, indeed, as organic parts of the whole 'Emerald Necklace.'" See Julius Gyu Fabos, Gordon T. Milde, and V. Michael Weinmayer, *Frederick Law Olmsted, Sr., Founder of Landscape Architecture in America* (Amherst: The University of Massachusetts Press, 1968).

5. Caro, *The Power Broker*, 174.

6. Ibid., 182, 183.

7. Ibid., 182.

8. Ibid., 216.

9. Ibid., 218.

10. Ibid.

11. Ibid., 223.

12. Robert Stern, Tom Mellins, and Gregory Gilmartin, *New York 1930* (New York: Rizzoli , 1987), 686.

13. Although a board of four engineers including Ammann, himself, Joseph Strauss, Leon Moisseiff, and Charles Derleth, it now seems that the basic design dating from 1925 was the result of close collaboration between Moisseiff and Ammann.

14. See John M. Kyle, Jr., "Tribute to Othmar H. Ammann," in *The Engineer and His Works: A Tribute to Othmar Hermann Ammann* (The New York Academy of Sciences, September 29, 1967), 743. Kyle writes: "Several years ago it was my privilege to attend a meeting between Mr. Ammann and the great Italian architect-engineer, Pier Luigi Nervi. Their discussions centered on the method of designing and constructing a bridge across the challenging Messina Straits. Mr. Ammann had definite ideas as to how this could be done, and as a matter of fact, told Dr. Nervi that he saw no reason why a span of two miles should not be achieved."

15. Harvey Aronson, "The Man and His Monuments," *The Newsday Magazine*, December 4, 1988, 9.

16. Robert Moses, "From Dump to Glory," *Saturday Evening Post* 210, January 15, 1938, 12–13.

17. Robert Taylor, *The Word in Stone*, 200.

18. Ibid., 202.

19. Marshall Berman, *All That Is Solid Melts Into Air* (New York: Penguin Books, 1982), 298. Berman's reference is, of course, to the *leitmotif* of Orson Wells's cinematic masterpiece, *Citizen Kane*.

20. Caro, *The Power Broker*, 221, 222.

21. Sigfried Giedion, *Space, Time, and Architecture* (Cambridge, Mass.: Harvard University Press, 1954), 3rd edition enlarged, 735, 736.

22. Marshall Berman, *All That Is Solid*, 295.

Acknowledgments

I am indebted to the following persons without whom this text would have never been written: Roy Strickland, J. P. Kleihues, Karla Britton, David Billington, Dr. Margot Ammann, Barbara Richardson of the TBTA, and above all Edward Cohen of Ammann and Whitney.

Manhattan Transfer: The New York Myth and Berlin Architecture in the Context of Ludwig Hilberseimer's High-Rise City

Fritz Neumeyer

Fritz Neumeyer is chairman of the History of Architecture Department at the University of Dortmund. He taught at the Southern California Institute of Architecture, at Harvard University and at the Technische Universität, Berlin, and was a research associate at the Getty Center for the History of Art and the Humanities. Neumeyer's numerous publications deal with architecture from the eighteenth to the twentieth centuries and include Großstadtarchitektur *(with Hans Kollhoff, 1989),* Mies van der Rohe: Das Kunstlose Wort *(1986), and* Das Haus Wiegand von Peter Behrens *(with Wolfram Hoepner, 1979).*

1. *Berlins Dritte Dimension (Berlin's Third Dimension). Cover of the brochure of* Berliner Morgenpost, *1912.* Kunsthistorisches Institut Universität, Bonn.

Towers Loom on the Horizon

New York, metropolis of the New World, has played a role in the architectural imagination of our century that is similar to that played by Rome, metropolis of the Old World, in the minds of eighteenth-century European architects. To Piranesi, the ruins of Rome left the viewer guessing whether the dank, ancient vaults had once housed workshops or torture chambers; New York has fueled similarly ambivalent and disquieting fantasies of a future that is as fascinating as it is horrifying. Ever since the turn of the century, European architects have been tantalized by New York, whose mythical growth has inspired some with unparalleled urban optimism and caused others to turn their backs with a shudder on this modern Babylon.

The first industrial boom of the young century, culminating in World War I, prepared the ground for Americanism in Europe. With the dissemination of American production and organizational methods, the spirit of commercialism and applied technology triumphed over the retarding forces of the nineteenth century. "Taylorism," "trust-building," "city-development"— such were some of the magic words in a formula that was to lead to modernization on an international scale.

The new era found its architectural landmarks in engineering structures, silos, and factory buildings, and above all in the skyscraper. The first to discover the dramatic potential of modern functional architecture were the Italian Futurists around 1910. In their renderings of the *Città Nuova*, a hypermodern civilization with its silos and skyscrapers celebrated its triumph over the architecture of the past. A short time later, Le Corbusier, in his *Esprit Nouveau*, saluted American engineering structures as the "glorious progenitors" of a new age that, in America, had already become an architectural reality: "The American engineers and their calculations are crushing moribund architecture beneath them."[1]

The skyscraper, based on a systematic application of modern machinery and construction methods, the result of hardboiled business thinking, was the most salient symbol of the period. No other modern creation more clearly reflected the radical change in cultural parameters that had taken place during the age of materialism. That the relationship between tradition and innovation had entered a critical stage was nowhere more strikingly illustrated than in the transformation of the New York skyline. Within the space of a few decades, the city's topography, at first defined by brownstones, had soared into the third dimension. New York had changed more than any other city in the world; while "others developed, New York exploded."[2]

The alarm that this transformation of the urban scene caused on the other side of the Atlantic would be worth a historical investigation in its own right. The higher the New York skyscrapers grew, competing for business and air space, the more lurid the myth surrounding them became and the longer the shadow they cast across the horizon.

By about 1910, this shadow had reached Europe, and with it, Berlin. That year the Berlin building code was revised. Reading the discussion today, one has for the first time a sense of skyscrapers looming in the background. The question of whether Berlin's much-touted advance to the status of metropolis might not be furthered by allowing residential buildings to have six stories rather than the previously prescribed five was enough to invoke terrifying visions of New York conditions on the Continent.

"Skyscrapers or Six Stories in Berlin?" asked the concerned author of an article in the journal *Berliner Architekturwelt* in 1909.[3] As soon as "the first concession was made" and an attic story allowed, he feared, Berlin would irrevocably succumb to the same high-altitude fever that gripped New York. Manhattan's "pleasant monsters" could not help but appeal to Berlin speculators, who felt their "skin tingling with delight" when they thought about the profits such buildings would bring. An ounce of prevention is worth a pound of cure, the author reminded his readers, for as soon as "the first concession was made, this would be the thin edge of the wedge and the trend to the 'skyscraper' would be almost impossible to reverse."[4]

From that point on the discussion of "Berlin's third dimension"[5] (fig. 1) stood in the shadow of New York, about which little was known apart from the shape of its striking silhouette. Only a handful of architects, including Peter Behrens, H. P. Berlage, Adolf Loos, and Otto Wagner, were able to form an opinion on site during the years before World War I and contribute criticisms that helped make the debate more objective. The general mood, however, remained negative, even into the next decade, when skepticism with regard to the skyscraper continued to influence the younger generation of architects. Although they admired the technical accomplishments of American builders, they had little good to say about the aesthetic and urban design results. The avant-garde standpoint was summed up in the famous postscript that Le Corbusier added to his famous "Three Reminders to Architects" of 1922: "Let us listen to the advice of American engineers, but be wary of American *architects*."[7]

The statements that emerged from the first heated debate among Berlin architects in 1909 continued to hold, by and large, for the 1920s: "Despite the flourishing of industry," declared Felix Rütter, "we would certainly wish our cities to express German attitudes rather than American ones."[8] Nonetheless, the skyscraper represented a sign of hope to a people "exhausted, starved, and drained" by the war, for as another author enthused, "If our hopes could build, they would raise houses—bigger and more beautiful skyscrapers!"[9] What was implied by the commonly used term *Turmhaus* (tower building), reminiscent of medieval cities, was a Germanic variant of the skyscraper. Although the skyscraper is American in origin, its reformulation was an expression of longing for a contemporary equivalent of the Gothic cathedral to crown the modern city.[10]

Yet even such an outspoken advocate of the high-rise city as Ludwig Hilberseimer could attack Manhattan, calling its uncontrolled vertical growth unplanned and reckless, with each building robbing the next of daylight. Citing Lewis Mumford and Henry Ford, both of them great opponents of the modern industrial metropolis and its architecture, Hilberseimer, writing in 1926 in the avant-garde magazine *G*, prophesied the imminent demise of this "artificial product" born of the "spirit of speculation," as he called New York, along with everything else that was artificial in the modern world.[11] Hilberseimer concluded his article with an aerial photograph of Manhattan (fig. 2) that bore the caption: "So—*Le fin de la cité?*" The answer to this question was not revealed until the next page, where the reader was told, *"NON! Mais le fin de la cité fondé sur le principle de la spéculation"* ("But it is the end of cities based on the principle of speculation, the end of cities that have been unable to free themselves from the city of the past and find their own inherent legitimacy).[12]

How an alternative, proper Manhattan, designed in accordance with its "inherent legitimacy," would look was indicated by a perspective rendering from Hilberseimer's own hand, a mathematically regular "high-rise city" (fig. 3) in which chaos was held in check by schematically rigorous uniform block frontages set in straight rows. With this ostinato of monotonously regular, stripped slabs placed at equal intervals, Hilberseimer sounded the final, programmatic chord of his critical discussion of American architecture.

Hilberseimer's design for a high-rise city, though more a theoretical statement than an actual plan, was informed by a new attitude to urban design. It was an attitude that had found its first and perhaps most passionate expression in Karl Scheffler's influential study of 1913, *Die Architektur der Grosstadt* (*Big-City Architecture*). Modern cities, wrote Scheffler, suffered from "inward and outward formlessness" and had once again taken on "the traits of arbitrary settlements." It was time to bring them up-to-date, define their form in truly contemporary terms. Such a "consciously metropolitan architecture," he felt, "could only be enriched by a rigorously established uniformity" of cityscape and skyline.[13] In Hilberseimer's high-rise city, this "will to uniformity," which Scheffler considered typical of the age, was taken to its "logical conclusion"[14] to the extent that the plan recognized the typical and universal traits of modern civilization and raised uniformity to the first principle of urban design. Viewed in the context of the plan's publication, during the time when American architecture was being widely and harshly criticized as undisciplined, its intention and direction become clear. Unlike most skyscraper designs produced in Germany at that period, its functionalist pathos did not attempt to reinterpret the skyscraper as a dramatic object lending neoromantic interest to the city skyline, but to encourage the logical application of modern principles of labor and organization to architecture.

In this case, as the polemical structure of the essay indicates, the design was a matter of presenting no less than a rational alternative to New York. Hilberseimer's soberly deployed high-rise city of uniform blocks, which has since become known as one of the "standard illustrations of the horrors of modern urban design,"[15] was clearly directed against the chaotic complexity of the metropolis, as epitomized by New York. His stereotypical city represented Berlin's demonstrative answer to Manhattan.[16]

2

3

2. Ludwig Hilberseimer,
"Architecture Americain" in G:, 4,
March 1926.

3. Ludwig Hilberseimer,
"Architecture Americain" in G:, 4,
March 1926.

A Fruitful Perspective: Broadway on Friedrichstrasse?

In spite of the criticism and predictions of Manhattan's demise, its vitality and attractiveness remained undiminished. Its soaring mass of buildings and deep canyons, what Hilberseimer reviled as the grotesque planlessness of its design and the pomposity of its false fronts, continued to exert a magical influence on European architects.[17] From the mid-1920s, when American dollar credits helped stabilize the German currency and economy, a procession of architectural pilgrimages to the United States took place. For modern architects who dreamed of renewing their art by an infusion of rationality in construction and organization, a trip to New York became well-nigh obligatory.

New York even began to outstrip the classical centers of European education. "America, the land of unlimited opportunities," wrote Paul Westheim in *Das Kunstblatt* in 1926, "attracts all those who make architecture or meditate on architecture in our antiquated world. Manhattan Island with its picturesque panorama of skyscrapers is today what the Acropolis was for the art connoisseur of a hundred years ago."[18]

That his was a widespread sentiment may be seen from the books on America published by European architects during the 1920s. Whereas the prewar years had seen only a single German publication on American architecture,[19] by the mid-1920s, book after book had appeared, and in large editions.[20] There was even an *American Vitruvius*, written by Werner Hegemann.[21]

"America and its skyscrapers are the great art fad at the moment. Among young and even older architects it is considered good form to take a jaunt to the United States. They photograph America, write books, hold lectures—an exhibition of American architecture has even been shown at the Academy," noted *Das Kunstblatt* in 1926, marking the contemporary "America fad" and "skyscraper fetishism"[22] that was being fueled in particular by Berlin journalists and publishers. In 1924, for instance, the Rudolf Mosse publishing house had financed a trip to the United States for Erich Mendelsohn, who had just converted the firm's building and had gained a reputation as an avant-garde architect with his Einstein Tower near Potsdam. The directors hoped in return to publish a book by Mendelsohn or a series of articles in the *Berliner Tageblatt* and were amply rewarded with a volume of seventy-seven photographs, mostly taken by Mendelsohn himself and reproduced in photogravure, published in 1926 under the title *Amerika: Bilderbuch eines Architekten*. Probably as a sideswipe at Mendelsohn, *Das Kunstblatt* sneered in 1927, "Many a Berliner went to New York for a few weeks or months and then wrote his book about the whole United States."[23]

Nevertheless, Mendelsohn's book was a tremendous success and, as the definitive photographic documentation of America, made architectural history in the Weimar Republic.[24] Bertolt Brecht considered *Amerika* one of the best books of 1926. "Excellent photos," he wrote, "all of which you could really hang individually on the wall and which create the impression—which is surely misleading—that big cities are habitable."[25] By 1927, the number of books on America published in Germany had multiplied to such an extent that the journal *Literarische Welt* thought it necessary to publish a selected bibliography of travel books alone.[26]

Although the points of view from which architects of the 1920s discussed American life and architecture were as different as their personal interests, they tended to agree on the reservations they felt about the country's overall urban design. Still, their involvement with American conditions was not without its effect on their own development, in terms of both architectural ideas and conceptions of urban planning. El Lissitzky's *Wolkenbügel* (cloud hanger), Friedrich Kiesler's concept of a horizontal skyscraper, Mendelsohn's elegant and complex big-city architecture of the late 1920s, and Richard Neutra's Rush City are only a few examples that emerged more or less directly from a confrontation with the architecture of America's big cities.

In Berlin architectural circles, the creative involvement with the phenomenon of New York, which especially preoccupied the Dadaists, had been set in motion in the early 1920s by Ludwig Mies van der Rohe and Hilberseimer. Their projects individually reflected themes in American architecture long before doing so became an art fad. The famous statement with which Mies made his debut in 1922 describes the American skyscraper as the impetus for the modern, entirely glass-walled high-rise structure that was to ring in a new architectural epoch: "Only skyscrapers under construction reveal the daring structural idea, and at this stage the impression of the soaring steel skeleton is overwhelming. When the masonry fronts go up this impression is completely destroyed, and the structural idea, the necessary basis for artistic design, is destroyed."[27]

Ten years before Mies's conception of the "skin-and-bones building" in which the new "structural idea" of the skyscraper found expression, Peter Behrens had returned from America with a similar sense of the aesthetic promise of this building type. "What made the greatest impression on me aesthetically, and in general, for that matter," wrote Behrens in the daily *Berliner Morgenpost* in 1912, was "without a doubt the extremely tall commercial buildings . . . [whose] audacious construction bears within it the seed of a new architecture."[28] Mies, a Behrens pupil, was to take his mentor at his word and make this seed sprout into a new generation of steel-and-glass skyscrapers.

In view of Mies's intention to strip the skyscraper of its trivial ornamentation and his argument that on a triangular lot the proper solution would be "a prismatic form adapted to the triangle," an obvious parallel comes to mind:—the famous Fuller Building on Broadway at the corner of Fifth Avenue. Built to the plans of Daniel H. Burnham in 1901 and likewise on a triangular lot, its unique shape soon earned it the nickname the Flatiron Building (fig. 4).

No other New York skyscraper could match the sense of dramatic energy exuded by the Flatiron Building, which made

4

6

4. Flatiron Building, New York, c. 1903.

5. Die Neue Jugend (The New Youth). *Title page, June 1917.*

6. *Edward Steichen.* Flatiron Building, Evening, *1904.* Metropolitan Museum of Art, Alfred Steiglitz Collection.

5

7

8

history as "the sensation of its day."[29] Although its fame as New York's tallest structure was short-lived—Times Square soon boasted taller ones—it continued to fascinate the public as well as artists for many years. No other office building of the period was so frequently represented in paintings and photographs, not to mention cartoons and caricatures.[30]

The Flatiron Building became a symbol and trademark of New York in Europe as well. In his *American Travel Notes* of 1913, H. P. Berlage—Mies's next, decisive mentor after Behrens—gave precedence to the Flatiron in his illustrations of skyscrapers because, as he declared, it provided the clearest expression of "American brutalism."[31] The German avant-garde was on familiar terms with the striking features of this New York monument, as it was reproduced, for instance, in June 1917 on the cover of *Neue Jugend*, a monthly review published by the Berlin Dadaists (fig. 5).

Only a short time later, in the winter of 1921–22, this structure underwent an architectonic reincarnation. Stripped of all superfluous decoration, with a nearly identical number of stories, it now stood at Friedrichstrasse Station in Berlin. Transformed into a sheer glass prism, it, too, was a disconcerting presence in its surroundings, and this distanced, out-of-place quality gave the building its specific, utopian aura. The mood was captured by both Edward Steichen's famous color photograph *Flatiron Evening* of 1904 (fig. 6) and Mies's no less famous charcoal rendering of 1922 (fig. 7). In these two genre pictures of twentieth-century skyscraper architecture, the building is seen in a mysterious evening twilight, further transforming it into a mystical object.[32]

Islands of Order: Objective Urban Architecture

A similar ritual of abstraction, aesthetic purification, and architectonic reincarnation of one of the icons of the metropolis may be inferred from the design submitted by Hilberseimer, Mies's friend, for the Chicago Tribune Competition of 1922–23 (fig. 8). This time it was not the Flatiron but the Equitable Building in Manhattan (fig. 9) to which one of the high priests of the Berlin avant-garde applied the procedure of elementary design, stripping it of all individuality, such as depicted in the buildings in George Grosz's Dadaist paintings of the period (fig. 10). It is surely no coincidence that Hilberseimer's extensive activities as an art critic (which have yet to receive the scholarly appreciation they deserve) include essays on Dadaism written around 1920 in which the "broad scope of its activity" is praised as an "enlivening element" in art.[34]

This radical relinquishment of ornament had already been deemed a necessity as early as 1913 by Karl Scheffler. It was the only way to achieve "noble uniformity," he said, as the basis of a new design that would truly earn the appellation "modern." Building firms in the future, Scheffler declared, "would have to simply tear down today's big city and shave its execrable, dishonest, pompous architecture [*Gründerarchitektur*] smooth by the square mile."[35]

9

10

7. *Mies van der Rohe. Skyscraper at Friedrichstrasse Station, 1922.* From *Rassegna* 27, 1986.

8. *Ludwig Hilberseimer. Design for the Chicago Tribune Building Competition, 1922.* From *Rassegna* 27, 1986.

9. *Ernest R. Graham. Equitable Building, New York, 1912–15.*

10. *George Grosz,* Untitled, *1920.* Kunstsammlung Nordrhein-Westfalen, Düsseldorf.

MERZ 18/19

LUDWIG HILBERSEIMER
GROSSTADTBAUTEN

11

12

13

*11. Merz 18/19, January/April
1926. The Getty Center for the
History of Arts and Humanities.*

*12. Ludwig Hilberseimer, in front of
a skyscraper tower built from the
model of his "welfare city," 1927.
From* In the Shadow of Mies.

*13. Pennsylvania Hotel, New York,
1915–20. Photograph published in*
Wasmuths Monatsheften für
Baukunst 5, *1920/21, H. 7/8. Used
by Hilberseimer as an illustration
for his essay "Das Hochhaus."*

The lesson Hilberseimer taught American architecture from the either-or viewpoint of early modernity could not have been clearer. It is hard to imagine a more drastic illustration of the desire for new, objective design with an uncompromising functionalism and a military uniformity, a design with which the avant-garde took revenge on the past. The naked window openings in Hilberseimer's Tribune Building were ranged one above the other like vertical columns of rectangular zeroes. The familiar decorative facade was replaced by unadorned reality—the reality of numbers, financial calculations, the true basis of modern business.

In a world exclusively determined by hardheaded considerations, it was enough to inset slightly one of the zeroes on the ground floor to mark architectonically the entrance to the building. This approach was the ultimate message of the credo of *Das neue Bauen*, as proclaimed by Mies in 1923: "The office building is a building of labor, organization, clarity, economy."[36] Hilberseimer's rendering underlined that proclamation of absolute sobriety: architecture was now the emptiness of a black square on a white background. "Questions of a general nature" had become the focus of art, whether painting, sculpture, or architecture.[37]

Hilberseimer's architecture had taken refuge in objective means of design that corresponded to those developed by Grosz in his early imagery. There, human beings and buildings alike were reduced to stereotypes to give "an absolutely realistic picture of the world." And as a "guiding image" for this reality, an engineering drawing with its "neutrality and clarity" was far superior to "uncontrollable babbling about kabbala and metaphysics and saintly ecstasies."[38]

Much the same could be said of Hilberseimer's architecture, which, like Dada, declared war on sentimentality and ideology and negated style with the shocking dryness of an engineering drawing. Indeed, "compass and ruler," as Grosz would have wished, had driven out "the soul and metaphysical speculations."[39] Not surprisingly, Hilberseimer's skyscraper, completely purged as it was of all metaphysical speculation, earned the approval of the Dadaists. His Chicago Tribune Building design graced the cover of *Merz*, a Dada journal edited by Kurt Schwitters, whose double issue 18/19 for January–April 1926 (fig. 11) was devoted to Hilberseimer's tract, *Grosstadtbauten*.[40]

The salient question as to the actual architectural character of the skyscraper had been raised as early as 1911 by Berlage. On a lecture tour through the United States, he asked the Municipal Art Society in New York, "Ought not, after all, the character of these titanic buildings be that of a mass grouping, with omission of everything that can detract from this expression? For here we certainly have the concentration of modern business life, and, therefore, also its architectural expression, so that these buildings could establish the architectural forms for the whole of modern architecture."[41]

The skyscraper gave rise to complex functional and symbolic issues that were fundamental to the definition of modern architecture. For the task of building a skyscraper could not be approached by what Mies called aesthetic speculation with received, historical forms and styles; it had to be approached by elementary design, whose principles and concepts derived from the nature of the task. A good skyscraper could not result from the "expediency," as Hilberseimer termed it, of applying decoration to the facade or from, he said, "piling up materials," which produced only "false monumentalization. Rather, it resulted from a design process based solely on considerations of function, space, and volume. As a building, the skyscraper, like any other building type, required composition in terms of a rhythmical arrangement of geometric solids.

Seen from this point of view, the architectural competition of false fronts in Manhattan and the chaotic aspects of the cityscape, whether in New York, or elsewhere, had to be condemned as an expression of arbitrariness and incompetency. The observation that speculation with skyscrapers in Manhattan had produced something out of a fairy tale was by no means a compliment. "It is only in the Orient that one can still find cities of such unrestrained capriciousness," concluded Hilberseimer[42] in a narrow-minded verdict which almost seems to anticipate the later disparagement of the Weissenhof Housing Estate by nationalists, who in 1941 dismissed this icon of modern architecture and urbanism as an "Arab Village."[43]

Although rejected generally as "academic achievements that bear no value for the future," New York's buildings included two that managed to pass Hilberseimer's tough test. One, already mentioned, was the Equitable Building of 1912–15, by Graham, Anderson, Probst & White; the other, the Pennsylvania Hotel of 1915–20, designed by the renowned firm of McKim, Mead & White.[44]

Hilberseimer found words of praise especially for the Equitable Building, whose volume and floor space—almost thirty times that of the lot area—had led to great resistance culminating in the Zoning Regulation of 1916.[45] In an essay entitled "American Architecture," coauthored in 1920 with the critic Udo Rusker, Hilberseimer had drawn a distinction between "corrupted" and "true" America. In architectural terms, that distinction relied on whether "the building's mass" had been successfully designed to form a "monumental organism" that lent the building "inner consistency and logical cohesion," or whether architecture had continued to play its old role, that of a "badly fitting mask." To Hilberseimer, only one example of New York high-rise architecture in 1920 fulfilled the former criterion: "In the entire mountain chain of the New York business district, there is only one [structure], Ernest Graham's Equitable Building, with its vertically articulated, cubic masses, that represents an attempt to realize logically these new ideas. The others continue to be haunted by Palladian misunderstandings à la Parisienne or other historical frippery."[46] Mendelsohn held a similarly high opinion of the Equitable Building. Placing it in the "second skyscraper period," he noted in 1925 that its "Gothicism [had been] freed of adornments and self-deceptive romanticism. It marks the beginning of the removal of the irrelevant and of a clarity about our nature and the meaning of the age."[47]

But above all, it was the "type of mass articulation" based on the "wing-system of the ground plan" that led Hilberseimer to call the two buildings "valuable and new"[48] in his astonishing evaluation of 1922. One can easily imagine what must have appealed to him about these ground plans: their right angles and regular proportions. With their forecourts and side wings, these ground plans possessed the lucidity and legibility of capital letters,[49] otherwise found only in the U, H, or E forms of classical, symmetrical plans.

Lucidity and regularity—these were the high aims to which Hilberseimer's urban architecture aspired. Just as the Pennsylvania Hotel or the Equitable Building[50] embodied simplicity and clarity in a chaotic cityscape, emerging like islands of order from an ocean of forms and signs, elementarist architecture aimed at a conscious articulation of space. Its regularly placed volumes, which structured an entire block in a uniform rhythm of masses and intervals, represented an attempt to curb the amorphous confusion of the cities of the day.

Hilberseimer's skyscraper essay of 1922, which was illustrated only with a photograph of the Pennsylvania Hotel (fig. 13) and the Monadnock Building in Chicago, outlined the two essential steps in his strategy to transform his New York models. Once one had followed Dadaist strategy and gotten rid of the bourgeois values represented by "Palladian misunderstandings" and "historical frippery," he declared, "the naked functional structure [would] be revealed." This was the first necessary step in the process of purification, which according to Hilberseimer would "surely be an advantage, though not in itself a solution."[51]

The design solution he envisaged became apparent in the second step. It aimed at reducing the geometric shape of the building volume—which in the case of the skyscraper seemed automatically to demand "powerfully delineated contours,"—to the most "concise, necessary, general" terms. "When geometrical figures become proportioned bodies," wrote Hilberseimer, "the result is architecture. Diversity of form coupled with the greatest possible unity. Details subordinated to the generative, principal line. Against the concise, cubic configuration, details recede entirely. What counts is the general design of the masses, the laws of proportion that govern them."[52]

Uncompromising utility plus proportion—this, then, was the basic formula of elementary design. It aimed at what Scheffler called a kind of monumental prose, an architecture in which rigorous functionality was combined with the Italian ideal of architecture, the art of creating pleasing relationships of space and plane. In the conception of a modern, skin-and-bones neoclassicism, said Hilberseimer, "the problem of all architecture" had "finally been recognized as cubic and rhythmic in nature and had to be solved a new way, with reference to all existing conditions."[53]

The foundation for that approach had been laid by Behrens in his prewar industrial classicism, which had been strongly influenced by Schinkel. This classicism would provide a basis for the work of the next generation of architects. Indeed, in a 1912 discussion, Behrens admitted the practical advantages and structural audacity of the American commercial building but found it necessary to remind American architects that "proportion is the alpha and omega of all artistic creation." He suggested that when it came to the proportioning of the sky-scraper, they could do worse than look at the campanile of Florence Cathedral.[54] Behrens was in the best of society; Schinkel had long before referred to Giotto's structure in his project for a tower at the end of Leipziger Strasse.

In his essay "On the Question of the Skyscraper," published ten years later, Behrens expanded his discussion to include considerations of urban design. Starting with the formula that "architecture is the design of solid bodies," he stated that the "stereometrical task" consisted in creating a "consistently or-ganized whole . . . in which every plane and every individual dimension have a regulated dependence on the proportions of all the other parts and of the entire city."[55]

This new aesthetic ideal of the urbanism of uniform blocks un-derlay the "cubic articulation of the building volume" that Hilberseimer praised in his two American exceptions. A the-oretical outline for this modern "architecture of the city" had been provided by Walter Curt Behrendt in 1911, in a disserta-tion dedicated to Scheffler and entitled, "The Uniform Block Front as a Spatial Element in Urban Construction."[56] Behrendt anticipated the open forecourts of Hilberseimer's wing system, suggesting that they were the most effective way of lending a powerful and uniform rhythm to the frontage of a city block. "A carefully balanced proportioning" of the ele-ments and an "attuning of the mass of the relief" to the "over-all proportions of the block frontage" were necessary, he said, to ensure that the "recurring rhythm" of mechanically repeat-ed building elements could be given a monumental overall effect.

Behrendt's discussion boiled down to the imperative: "Not the individual building but the rhythmical sequence of buildings within a block, the architecturally unified block frontage, rep-resents the spatial element in the art of designing cities to-day."[57] The task of modern urban construction was "to form unified block frontages in order to obtain elements of spatial composition" and "by repeated employment of certain consis-tent types . . . [to lend] the block frontage that unity of propor-tion so important for the general impression."[58] And not with-out reason, when he recapitulated his ideas about the modern big city in 1920,[59] Behrendt referred to the industrial build-ings of Behrens as a model, citing their grouping of volumes, the rhythm of their column arrangements, the force of their masses, and their striking contours. They represented, he said, an architectural and urban design configuration whose elemen-tal formal power had the expressiveness of a primeval form.

Against this background, the wing-system plans so favored by Hilberseimer appear as building blocks in the city. A formal element of order had been found that was suitable for use as an "element of spatial composition" in both a functional and an aesthetic sense; it had proven both its economic effectiveness and its ability to organize in the merciless jungle of Manhattan.

Liberated from the capitalist conditions where it first arose, this element could also play a crucial role in the city of the fu-ture, the so-called Welfare City. The plan for such a city, which Hilberseimer worked out on the drawing board for the *Wohlfahrts-Ausstellung* (Welfare Exhibition) in Stuttgart in 1927, supplied a unified block frontage for a city whose relief structure was basically modeled on the baroque ideal. On a plan arranged symmetrically around a central axis, the topog-raphy of this ideal modern city included a downtown area on whose square terrain twenty-four examples of Hilberseimer's building blocks were arranged in an orderly pattern (fig. 14). With its fourteen stories and four wings, the building block, as a volume, bore an astonishing similarity to the Pennsylvania Hotel. If one takes away the hotel's historicized socle and its Palladian upper portion, what remains is a plain, rather somber building, which also has fourteen stories. With its square, regularly spaced openings, it looks as if Hilberseimer himself could have designed it (fig. 15).

This basic example of a stylized urban architecture was as in-terchangeable and universal as the big city itself. With the emergence of a world economy all differences began to disap-pear, including differences in the world capitals, which, as Walther Rathenau had predicted in his famous essay, "Kritik der Zeit" of 1911, were fast becoming identical in terms of structure and function.

The building block, conceived for the purpose of lending uni-ty to cities and their architecture, could also be used theoreti-cally—or more correctly, as a model—to build a skyscraper, as indicated by a photograph of Hilberseimer in front of a tow-er consisting of six of his fourteen-story model units for the Welfare City stacked one on top of the other (fig. 12). Yet since he was out to dissolve the modern metropolis[60] and propagat-ed its decentralization, Hilberseimer was basically suspicious of the skyscraper. His high-rise city had nothing to do with the high-rise as an architectonic and urbanist landmark. Instead, it was planned in terms of multistory row buildings, which permitted a certain urban density while ensuring some open space. In short, his conception was based not on the metropo-lis but on the housing estate.

With the aid of a photo collage, Hilberseimer illustrated what such a high-rise housing estate of modern office and commer-cial buildings would look like in the middle of Berlin. It was the same polemical device that the dadaists had employed to reflect the chaos of modern civilization.

While Mies had spliced his alternative to the New York sky-scraper into the Berlin cityscape at the northern end of Friedrichstrasse, Hilberseimer pasted his alternative, orderly Manhattan into the southern part, at the intersection of Friedrichstrasse and Unter den Linden (fig. 16). Camillo Sitte, advocate of romantic urban design, tried to save calm areas of tradition in the modern traffic-dominated city; Hilberseimer, the apostle of this very type of functional city, imposed a cold but modern apparatus onto the old city's body, which, like a heart-lung machine, would supply it with air and economic vi-tality. This mechanical transformation of the traditional city introduced its own axis, which ran at right angles to the *via tri-umphalis* of feudal Berlin, Unter den Linden, and extended from the triangular area at Friedrichstrasse Station in the

14

15

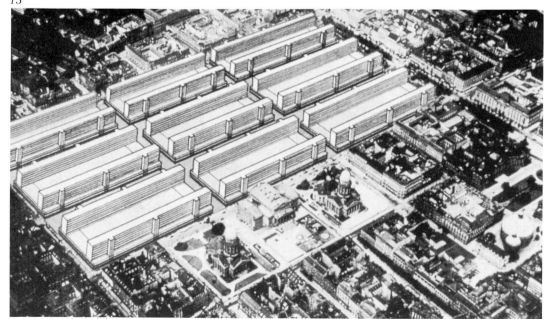

16

17

18

17. *Ludwig Hilberseimer. High-Rise City, Nord-Süd Strasse, (street running from north to south), 1924. From* Rassegna 27, 1986.

18. *Ludwig Hilberseimer. Proposal for the development of city office and commercial buildings for the High-Rise City in Berlin's Friedrichstadt. From* In the Shadow of Mies.

19. *Peter Behrens. AEG high-voltage plant, 1909. From* Tilmann Buddensieg, Industriekultur.

19

north to the roundel of the Belle-Alliance-Platz (fig. 18). It was a route that had already been traced out underground by a subway line.

It was probably not a coincidence that Hilberseimer's island of modernity had cast its anchors at the Gendarmenmarkt in immediate proximity to Schinkel's Schauspielhaus. The remark "Better from Schinkel to Schinkel," made a 1914 unpublished manuscript entitled "Die Architektur der Grosstadt" ("Big-City Architecture") in which Hilberseimer criticized the "errors and endless aberrations" of the nineteenth century, indicate where historical points of reference ought to be.[61] His preference for classicism extended to Schinkel's urbanism of blocks as well as Behrens's large-scale structures. It was particularly the organizational pattern of the latter—from their combination of multiple stories and large halls to the exterior stairwells—that he found exemplary (figs. 19, 20). Ultimately, Schinkel, Alfred Messel, and Behrens, for whom he found words of praise and respect,[62] represented that authentic tradition from which modern Berlin architecture derived its abstract language of volumes and proportions, a language that was then applied on a larger scale, as an ordering principle, to the city itself.

Later, in a moment of self-criticism, Hilberseimer admitted that the "new Berlin," somber in its row upon row of uniform buildings (fig. 21) bore more resemblance "to a necropolis than to a metropolis."[63] It was a city in which the feared chaos of modern life had been frozen into an abstract mechanical rhythm that was itself frightening. The maelstrom of modern city's street perspectives as expressed in Mendelsohn's dynamic designs, the provocative unrest of the great city and the chaos of modern civilization as captured in the metropolis collages of dadaists like Hanna Höch and Paul Citroen—nothing like this was allowed a presence in Hilberseimer's "new Berlin." Here, modern life had been buried beneath the "modernistic gravestones" of a "row-built cemetery."[64]

That the vibrancy of a metropolis might derive from its uncontrollable instability and continual conflicts seemed hardly conceivable to Hilberseimer, who swore by objectivity. One of the few who saw New York through subjective eyes was Herman Sörgel, architectural theorist, author,[65] and editor of the Munich journal *Die Baukunst*. To him, the disharmonious, irregular, and arbitrary character of New York "especially [as regards] the artistic aspect of its urban design," made it "perhaps one of the most interesting" of cities[66] precisely because it had emerged "completely unintentionally, straight from life," without "the depressing intention of making 'art.'" Behrens, as Hegemann reports, apparently took a similar position around 1926.[67]

Sörgel pushed aside the entire debate on the correct design of the skyscraper with the salient argument that, regarding "the overall rhythm of a city it is quite irrelevant whether one architect builds in a Gothic style, the next in Renaissance, and a third in a modern idiom; the individual forms are submerged in a larger whole. . . . As architecture, New York cannot be grasped in terms of isolated, detail views, but must be seen as a continually running film."[68]

Obviously having in mind the sterile order generated by the type of urban architecture Hilberseimer promoted as an alternative to Manhattan, Sörgel wondered what New York City would look like if turned over to this kind of modern design: "Imagine Broadway as a 'unified block frontage!' Or what would happen if one were to give Times Square to an urban-planning seminar in Germany to work it over and bring harmony and 'order' into the confusion—it would be dead with one blow, its nerve cauterized, its rhythm and pulsation would cease, and the continually self-renewing life of six million people would be reduced to nothing but a model in a museum."[69]

Paul Morand, whose 1929 book on America is one of the most impressive literary achievements of its kind, would surely have agreed with Sörgel's opinion about the city. Comparing New York to a perpetual storm, Morand concluded that "if it's insane to live in a city, then at least New York is an insanity that makes it worthwhile."[70]

Notes

1. Le Corbusier, *Vers une Architecture*, 2nd ed. (Paris, 1924), 20.
2. Paul Morand, *New York* (Vienna, 1930), 119.
3. Felix Rütter, "Wolkenkratzer oder sechs Geschosse in Berlin?" *Berliner Architekturwelt* 9 (1909): 242–44.
4. Ibid., 244.
5. *Berlins dritte Dimension: Stimmen von Städtebauern für eine bessere bauliche Ausnutzung der Berliner City* (Berlin, 1912).
6. Peter Behrens, "Beitrag zu einer von der Berliner Morgenpost veranstalteten Umfrage über die bauliche Entwicklung der Berliner City unter dem Titel 'Berlins dritte Dimension,'" *Berliner Morgenpost*, November 27, 1912. I am indebted to Tilmann Buddensieg for kindly providing the Behrens article and permitting me to use the cover illustration of this brochure.
7. Le Corbusier, *Vers une Architecture*, 29.
8. Felix Rütter, "Wolkenkratzer,": 244. Especially relevant in this connection is the argumentation of Martin Mächler, "Zum Problem des Wolkenkratzers," *Wasmuths Monatshefte für Baukunst und Städtebau* 5, nos. 7/8 (1920–21): 191–205, 260–74.
9. Richard Herre, "Hochhäuser für Stuttgart," *Wasmuths Monatshefte für Baukunst* 6 (1921–22): 375.
10. In this connection, see Rainer Stommel, "'Germanisierung des Wolkenkratzers'—Die Hochhausdebatte in Deutschland bis 1921," *Kritische Berichte* 3 (1982): 36–53. Of contemporaneous opinions, the most interesting are Paul Wittig, *Studie über die ausnahmsweise Zulassung einzelner Hochhäuser in Berlin*, Denkschrift (Berlin, 1918; 2nd ed., 1920); and Bruno Möhring, *Über die Vorzüge der Turmhäuser und die Voraussetzungen, unter denen sie gebaut werden können*, Denkschrift (Berlin, 1920).
11. Ludwig Hilberseimer, "Architecture Américain," *G* 4 (March 1926): 4–8.
12. Ibid., 7, 8.
13. Karl Scheffler, *Die Architektur der Grossstadt* (Berlin, 1913), 10, 38.
14. Ibid., 35ff. See also in this connection Otto Wagner's description of "strict simplicity," which he considered a remedy for the "hopeless disorder of our street frontages": "If the work in progress is to be a faithful reflection of our age, the simple, practical, or one could even say military character of our approach must be given full and complete expression" (*Moderne Architektur* [Vienna, 1896]; quoted in Otto Antonia Graf, *Otto Wagner, Das Werk des Architekten*, vol. 1, 1860–1902 [Vienna, 1985], 274). See also Otto Wagner's essay, *Die Grossstadt* (Vienna, 1911).
15. Richard Pommer, "A Necropolis Rather than a Metropolis," *In the Shadow of Mies: Ludwig Hilberseimer, Architect, Educator, and Urban Planner* (New York, 1988), 17.
16. Previous analyses of this well-known Hilberseimer project have overlooked the New York connection. This is true even of Pommer's *In the Shadow of Mies*; see my review, "In the Shadow of Mies—Irritations about a Shadow," *Design Book Review* 17 (1989): 62–63.
17. See Ludwig Hilberseimer, "Das Hochhaus," *Das Kunstblatt* 6 (1922): 525–31; and Hilberseimer and Udo Rusker, "Amerikanische Architektur," *Kunst und Künstler* 18 (1920): 531–45.
18. Paul Westheim, "Frank Lloyd Wright," *Das Kunstblatt* 10 (1926): 426ff.
19. F. Rudolf Vogel, *Das amerikanische Haus* (Berlin, 1910).
20. Werner Hegemann, *Amerikanische Architektur und Stadtbaukunst: Ein Überblick über den heutigen Stand amerikanischer Baukunst in ihrer Beziehung zum Städtebau* (Berlin, 1925; 2nd ed., 1927); Erich Mendelsohn, *Amerika: Aus dem Bilderbuch eines Architekten* (Berlin, 1926; 6th revised and expanded ed., 1928); Walter Curt Behrendt, *Städtebau und Wohnungswesen in den Vereinigten Staaten: Bericht einer Studienreise* (Berlin, 1926; 2nd expanded ed., 1927); Richard Neutra, *Wie baut Amerika?* (Stuttgart, 1927) and *Amerika: Die Stilbildung des Neuen Bauens in den Vereinigten Staaten* (Vienna, 1930); Martin Wagner, *Amerikanische Bauwirtschaft* (Berlin, 1925) and *Städtebauliche Probleme in amerikanischen Städten und ihre Rückwirkungen auf den deutschen Städtebau* (Berlin, 1929). See also Bruno Taut, *Die neue Baukunst in Europa und Amerika* (Stuttgart, 1929); and Erich Mendelsohn, *Russland, Europa, Amerika: Ein architektonischer Querschnitt* (Berlin, 1929).
21. Werner Hegemann and Elberts Peets, *The American Vitruvius: An Architects' Handbook of Civic Art* (New York, 1922); and Hegemann, *Das Steinerne Berlin* (Berlin, 1930).
22. "Die Amerika-Mode," *Das Kunstblatt* 10 (1926): 165–67.
23. "Die neue deutsche Kunst in Amerika," *Das Kunstblatt* 11 (1927): 379.
24. Herbert Molderings, "Amerikanismus in der deutschen Fotografie der Zwanziger Jahre," *Camera Austria* 22 (1986): 32.
25. Bertolt Brecht's reply to a survey conducted by the Berlin magazine *Das Tagebuch*, inquiring as to the best books of the year 1926; quoted in Molderings, "Amerikanismus," 38.
26. *Literarische Welt* 3, no. 41 (1927): 12; cited by Helmut Lethen, *Neue Sachlichkeit 1924–1932: Studien zur Literatur des Weissen Sozialismus* (Stuttgart, 1970), 187. Among the most significant of the travel books that deal only in passing with built reality and the skyscraper is Paul Morand's *New York* (Vienna, 1930). See also Gerhard Venzmer, *New Yorker Spaziergänge: Eindrücke und Betrachtungen aus der Metropole der neuen Welt* (Hamburg, 1925); Rudolf Hessel, *Amerika* (Dresden, 1929); Franz Westermann, *Amerika, wie ich es sah: Reiseskizzen eines Ingenieurs* (Halberstadt, 1925); Paul Rohrbach, *Amerika und wir: Reisebetrachtungen* (Berlin, 1925); Otto Moog, *Drüben steht Amerika: Gedanken nach einer Ingenieurreise* (Braunschweig, 1927); Adolf Halfeld, *Amerika und der Amerikanismus: Kritische Betrachtungen eines Deutschen und Europäers* (Jena, 1927); M. J. Bonn, *Die Kultur der Vereinigten Staaten von Amerika* (Berlin, 1930); Graf Hermann Keyserling, *Amerika, Der Aufgang einer neuen Welt* (Stuttgart, 1930). On Americanism in general, see Peter Berg, *Deutschland und Amerika 1918–1929: Über das deutsche Amerikabild der Zwanziger Jahre* (Lübeck, 1963).
27. Ludwig Mies van der Rohe, "Hochhäuser," *Frühlicht* 1, no. 4 (1922): 122–24.
28. Peter Behrens in *Berliner Morgenpost*, November 27, 1912.
29. Earle Schultz and Walter Simmons, *Offices in the Sky* (New York, 1959).
30. See Merill Schleier, *The Skyscraper in American Art, 1890–1931* (Ann Arbor, Mich., 1986).
31. H. P. Berlage, *Amerikaansche Reiseerinneringen* (Rotterdam, 1913), 9, fig. 3.
32. Further aspects of Mies's skyscraper designs are discussed in Fritz Neumeyer, *Mies van der Rohe: Das kunstlose Wort* (Berlin, 1986), 236ff. On the reception of the skyscraper in American art and the depiction of the Flatiron Building in the photographs of Alfred Stieglitz and Edward Steichen, as well as in painting, see Schleier, *Skyscraper*.
33. See Grosz's paintings, *Der schöne Fritz*, 1920; *Republikanische Automaten*, 1920; *Berlin C*, 1920.
34. Ludwig Hilberseimer, "Anmerkungen zur neuen Kunst," *Kunst der Zeit* 1–3 (1923): 52–57. See also "Merzmalerei," *Sozialistische Monatshefte* 26, no. 14 (1920): 625; and "Dadaismus," *Sozialistische Monatshefte* 26, no. 25/26 (1920): 1120–22. An initial investigation of Hilberseimer's activity as a critic is found in Agnes Kohlmeyer, "Apollio e Dioniso: Hilberseimer critico d'arte," *Rassegna* 27 (1986): 27–33.
35. Scheffler, *Die Architektur der Grossstadt*, 130.
36. "Bürohaus," *G* 1 (July 1923): 3.
37. "Man is no longer depicted in individual terms, with penetrating psychology, but as a collective, almost mechanical concept. The individual's fate is no longer important. . . . Lines are drawn unindividually, photographically; modelling is achieved through construction. A return to stability, structure, utility" (Georg Grosz, *Zu meinen Bildern* [1921]; quoted in Uwe M. Schneede, ed., *Georg Grosz: Leben und Werk* [Stuttgart, 1975], 66). "The demands of the age for frankness and utility must be fulfilled. . . . Interest is focused on questions of a general nature. The significance of the individual is constantly decreasing; his fate no longer interests us. The crucial achievements in all fields possess an objective character" (Ludwig Mies van der Rohe, "Baukunst und Zeitwille!" *Der Querschnitt* 4, no. 1 (1924): 31–32.
38. Grosz, *Zu meinen Bildern*; quoted in Schneede, ed., *Grosz*, 66.
39. George Grosz and Wieland Herzfelde, *Die Kunst ist in Gefahr: Ein Orientierungsversuch* (Berlin, 1925), 11: "The compass and ruler have driven out the soul and metaphysical speculations."
40. Hilberseimer's "Grosstadtbauten" had been published a short time previously, in 1925, by Aposs-Verlag, Hanover, who were also the publishers of *Merz*. *Merz* 18/19 was conceived as the first volume in a series on the New Architecture, the second volume of which, by Dr. Mahlberg and U. Kosina, on transportation structures, was announced but never appeared. Hilberseimer's relationship to dadaism has yet to receive much attention in the literature. Apart from his personal contact with leading members of the movement, such as Hans Richter, the issue of dada architecture has yet to be broached at all.
41. H. P. Berlage, "Modern Architecture," *Real Estate Record and Guide* 88 (December 1911): 920; quoted in Robert A. M. Stern, Gregory Gilmartin, and John Massengale, *New York 1900: Metropolitan Architecture and Ur-*

banism 1890–1915 (New York, 1983), 177. Berlage's lectures were published under the title *Een Drietal Lezingen in Amerika gehouden door H. P. Berlage Bouwmeester te Amsterdam* (Rotterdam, 1912).

42. Hilberseimer, "Das Hochhaus," 525.

43. Ibid., 527.

44. Kenneth Turney Gibbs, *Business Architectural Imagery in America, 1870–1930* (Ann Arbor, Mich., 1985), 141. See also Thomas A. P. Leeuwen, *The Skyward Trend of Thought: Five Essays on the Metaphysics of the American Skyscraper* (The Hague, 1986), 16.

45. Hilberseimer and Rusker, "Amerikanische Architektur," 542.

46. Mendelsohn, *Amerika*, 33.

47. Hilberseimer, "Das Hochhaus," 527.

48. In this connection, see the volumetric analysis of skyscrapers by Steven Holl, *The Alphabetical City*, Pamphlet Architecture no. 5 (New York, 1980).

49. In *Groszstadtarchitektur* of 1927, which incorporated an expanded version of a 1922 text, Hilberseimer added a third example to these two, writing "For all the significance these buildings have, particularly Ernest R. Graham's Equitable Building, McKim, Mead, & White's Pennsylvania Hotel in New York, and perhaps the General Motors Building by Arthur Kahn in Detroit, they are really only academic achievements that bear no value for the future. The only valuable and new thing about them is their articulation of masses. . . . The great majority of skyscrapers, however, are a far cry from these and similarly tasteful buildings" (*Groszstadtarchitektur* [Stuttgart, 1927], 64).

50. Hilberseimer, "Das Hochhaus," 528.

51. Ludwig Hilberseimer, "Der Wille zur Architektur," *Das Kunstblatt* 7 (1923): 133ff. The argumentation is identical to that in his essay "Das Hochhaus."

52. Ibid., 528ff.

53. ". . . the commercial buildings, due to their audacious construction, bear the seed of a new architecture within themselves. I am not saying that they are monuments of modern architecture worth emulating; in them, too, the immature American need for ornamentation found an opportunity to apply Gothic or Greek or Roman ornament instead of aiming at proportion foremost, such as that found in perfection in the campanile of the Florence Cathedral. Still, the ornament shrinks to insignificance beside the constructional lines of this building, and it lends the city a silhouette" ("Berlins dritte Dimension," *Berliner Morgenpost*, January 27, 1912).

54. Interestingly, Werner Hegemann, in the context of a critique of skyscraper architecture, recalled this project of Schinkel's, in which it seemed to him that Schinkel "wanted to discover the 'tower per se'" ("Das Hochhaus als Verkehrsstörer und der Wettbewerb der Chicago Tribune: Mittelalterliche Enge und neuzeitliche Gotik," *Wasmuths Monatshefte für Baukunst* 8 [1923–24]: 304).

55. Peter Behrens, "Zur Frage des Hochhauses,": *Stadtbaukunst in alter und neuer Zeit* 24 (1922): 370.

56. Walter Curt Behrendt, *Die einheitliche Blockfront als Raumelement im Stadtbau. Ein Beitrag zur Stadtbaukunst der Gegenwart* (Berlin, 1911).

57. Ibid., 82.

58. Ibid., 83, 85.

59. Walter Curt Behrendt, *Der Kampf um Stil in Kunstgewerbe, Malerei und Architektur* (Berlin, 1920), 217ff.

60. See in this connection Richard Pommer's rather sweeping statement, "Hilberseimer obviously hated the city—he spent a lifetime not so much thinking about it as trying to exorcise it" (Pommer, "Necropolis," 36).

61. "Errors and endless aberrations resulting from the search for style in the nineteenth century. Until Jugendstil. Better from Schinkel to Schinkel. Schinkel never forgot to derive his principles from the object itself. That makes him modern. Despite antique reminiscences" (Ludwig Hilberseimer, "Die Architektur der Grosstadt," MS, 1914; Hilberseimer Papers, The Art Institute of Chicago). This text also contains appreciative analyses by Alfred Messel and Peter Behrens.

62. Ibid: "And finally, as a solution, or at least a preliminary one: Messel's Wertheim Building. . . . The prototype created by Messel . . . finds its most lucid expression in Peter Behrens's A. E. G. Small Motor Factory, on Voltastrasse, Berlin, which at the same time points up the monumental potential of [Messel's] tall buildings. Style derived from the essence of the object."

63. Ludwig Hilberseimer, *Enfaltung einer Planungsidee* (Berlin, 1963), 22.

64. Richard Pommer, "Necropolis," 36.

65. Herman Sörgel, *Einführung in die Architektur-Ästhetik. Prolegomena zu einer Theorie der Baukunst* (Munich, 1918; 3rd expanded ed., *Architektur-Ästhetik*, Munich, 1921).

66. Herman Sörgel, "New York: Ein Amerikanisches Stadtbauproblem," *Die Baukunst* 2 (January 1926): 2.

67. In his introduction to an article entitled "Should Berlin Build Skyscrapers" of 1928, Hegemann wrote, "After Peter Behrens expressed his unqualified admiration for the chaos of the New York business district in a Berlin lecture two years ago, it should come as no surprise that the fantastic skyscraper depictions by the talented American artist Hugh Ferris are finding imitators in Germany and that the romantics of the high-rise forest consider well-founded resistance to skyscrapers outmoded and retrograde" ("Soll Berlin Wolkenkratzer bauen?" *Wasmuths Monatshefte für Baukunst* 12 [1928]: 286). Behrens's "Zur Frage des Hochhauses," 369, already contains indications of a critical reconsideration of the generally accepted verdict that New York was merely "chaotic." Still, the "higher artistic principle of the architectural art," which he sensed in this "chaos," seemed to him merely a result of chance: "But in all the confusion and arbitrariness, an impression of the opposite crops up, if more by chance."

68. Herman Sörgel, "New York," 2.

69. Ibid.

70. Paul Morand, *New York* (Vienna, 1930), 270.

Art Deco Skyscrapers: Towers of Modern Babel

Rosemarie Haag Bletter

Rosemarie Haag Bletter is a professor of architectural history at the City University of New York Graduate Center, where she is also coordinator of the Interdisciplinary Program in Modern German Studies. She is the author of numerous publications, including El Arquiteco Josep Vilaseca i Casanovas *(1977),* Venturi, Rauch and Scott Brown: A Generation of Architecture *(1984), and* Skyscraper Style *(with Cervin Robinson, 1975).*

The biblical story of the Tower of Babel is the archetypal tale about the power of tall buildings over social structure. According to current research, the tower may have reached no more than ten stories,[1] though in later lore it assumed larger and larger proportions. In the Old Testament,[2] its construction became a sacrilegious attempt to reach the heavens. Divine punishment for this arrogance was the imposition of diverse tongues, the resulting babble making collaboration among the tower's workers impossible.

In the twentieth century, Vladimir Tatlin used an inversion of this morality tale about human presumption as one of the paradigms for his projected Monument to the Third International of 1920. Not only would his project rival the Eiffel Tower in height, but in his utopian expectations it was to be a reverse Tower of Babel that would unify the multifarious languages of the Soviet Union.[3] Both in the biblical story and in Tatlin's politicized fantasy, the tower makes or breaks an entire society through the presence or lack of communication. The modern skyscraper as invented in the United States does not quite as directly refer to spoken language. Rather, it incorporates an immense vocabulary of visual communication, the primary language of advertising, that has become the lingua franca of the contemporary world.

The skyscraper, among the many new building types of the nineteenth century and perhaps the most perplexing building type to define, made its most drastic impact on the cityscape on a visual and social level. A museum is consistently referred to as a museum, no matter how idiosyncratic its external architectural expression might be; most building types for that matter, except the skyscraper, are wholly determined by their designated internal function. On the other hand, while most early skyscrapers may have been office buildings, we cannot say that all office buildings were necessarily skyscrapers. Some twentieth-century skyscrapers are residential buildings, contain educational institutions, or have mixed uses. The definition of a skyscraper depends on height alone. Yet height in a skyscraper is not seen in absolute terms. We cannot claim that a fifteen-story building is a skyscraper but a ten-story structure is not. What was tall in 1880 had been absorbed by the urban context by 1900 and what was tall in 1900 was no longer so by 1930. This dependence on relative surroundings for the definition of the skyscraper has produced innumerable disagreements and confusion about its origins.

Because of the skyscraper's dependence on relative height in a constantly shifting urban context, it is more useful to rely on comparative height within a given time rather than absolute number of stories to distinguish it from the ordinary tall building. Some historians have tried to place the exact origin of the skyscraper by dating the first use of that term.[4] The problem with this method is that the term was applied to tall buildings only after their invention (an earlier term, "elevator building," did not persist in general usage, because elevators came to be used in many building types and because it does not suggest the same powerful image as the word *skyscraper*). At any rate, the word *skyscraper* itself had undergone several changes of meaning: before it was applied to tall buildings in the late nineteenth century, it variously referred to a triangular sail

331

*2. Cass Gilbert. Woolworth
Building, 1911–13.* The New-York
Historical Society.

(also known as "moon-raker"), a tall person, a high horse, or, most interesting, a tall tale.

Recently, Thomas van Leeuwen, in a fanciful and unconvincing attempt to write a religious-mystical history of the skyscraper, has used the word *skyscraper* to distinguish the American conception of this building type from the European one.[5] He cites the German *Wolkenkratzer* and Dutch *Wolkenkrabber* (literally "cloudscraper") to bolster his claim that the European notion was not as grandiose as the American image. He neglects to mention, however, that, for instance, the French *gratte-ciel*, the Spanish *rascacielos*, or the Italian *grattacielo* copied the American term. In fact, one could make a better case that for European architects, who did not build skyscrapers in the first half of the twentieth century, the tall building played a larger mythological role than it did for American architects who were familiar with the compromises encountered in actual construction.

Fritz Lang was inspired by the Manhattan skyline when he saw it as a dark, indistinct silhouette one evening in 1924 while he was briefly detained on a boat as an enemy alien. Later he would reuse this dramatic image, intensified to a more ominous scale, in his film *Metropolis* of 1926.[6] When Le Corbusier visited New York nearly a decade later, in 1935, the romance of the American skyscraper was destroyed for him, if not the desire for larger towers. He wrote:

Monday morning, when my ship stopped at Quarantine, I saw a fantastic, almost mystic city rising up in the mist. But the ship moves forward and the apparition is transformed into an image of incredible brutality and savagery. Here is certainly the most prominent manifestation of the power of modern times. This brutality and this savagery do not displease me.[7]

And then, of course, Corbusier went on to say with his accustomed *braggadocio* that New York skyscrapers were too small.

The best-known American histories of the skyscraper have expended much effort in defining which one came first.[8] Winston Weisman, for example, proclaimed Gilman & Kendall and George B. Post's Equitable Life Assurance Company Building (1868–70) in New York to be the one. But at 130 feet with five or seven floors (not satisfactorily clarified in his text) this building was barely taller than the Palazzo Farnese in Italy or the Crystal Palace in London. Since the notion of the skyscraper depends on exceptional height, a building that is just somewhat taller than average buildings will not do. Also, the definition of what makes a skyscraper, aside from great height, depends on a large number of categories that are, however, not all given the same importance by various historians. Some stress structural, others formal, compositional factors.

The need to find a first skyscraper, a pursuit eventually abandoned by Carl Condit, though not by Weisman, ought to be questioned as a worthwhile enterprise. Can there really be a first example in a building type as inconsistently defined as the skyscraper, whose extremely complicated features are also interrelated? William H. Birkmire in his *Skeleton Construc-*

tion in Building of 1893 correctly pinpointed the unusually interdependent factors behind skyscraper construction. While he concedes that high land values are in part responsible for the rush to build tall, he goes on to say that "the effect has in some measure become the cause."[9] Cause and effect can be turned upside down: because there are tall buildings, land values are high.

Lewis Mumford in *The Brown Decades* of 1931, by applying a social analysis to the skyscraper, put height and the steel frame into a broader context that placed little importance on the issue of the first skyscraper.

The priority for the invention of steel frame or skeleton construction has been disputed; it was claimed by, among others, L. H. Buffington, Minnesota architect, who applied for a patent; but the whole question becomes a little absurd when one remembers that the traditional American frame house is based on an exactly comparable method of construction. The new elements were the fireproofing of the component materials, and the more exact calculations made possible through the use of steel, along with the opportunity of increasing the height of the structure, which was limited only by the strength of the foundations and the expense of vertical transportation. Socially the skyscraper gave encouragement to all our characteristic American weaknesses: our love of abstract magnitude, our interest in land-gambling, our desire for conspicuous waste: it did this to such an extent that it is almost heresy to call attention to the defects of the tall building: the dubious economy of vertical transportation at the magnificent maximum rate of nine miles per hour: the waste of cubage in the unused sections of express elevator shafts—to say nothing of the shutting out of sunlight and air, and the intensification of congestion on the streets and in the subways.[10]

American architectural historians for the most part have tended to stress physical data (engineering and design) in analyzing the skyscraper. An exception is Kenneth Gurney Gibbs's *Business Architectural Imagery* (1976), an unusually detailed economic differentiation of construction financing between New York and Chicago skyscrapers. His study goes beyond an obvious discussion of the tall office building as a visible symbol of capitalism.[11] He suggests that New York skyscrapers were initially more conservative than those in Chicago because business in the East was constrained and made more accountable by an established public morality. Business practices in the Midwest tended to be freewheeling by comparison. New York buildings were more likely to be erected by individual companies, whereas in Chicago the financing was commonly undertaken by outside investors, making them both more anonymous as clients and, again, less accountable.

The steel frame, the elevator, high land values, and prevailing business practice all contributed to the growth of the skyscraper. But there is an additional psychoeconomic ingredient that made for an intense competition for pre-eminence, particularly in New York where skyscrapers were commonly financed and associated with a single firm: prestige and public relations. The advertising potential of the skyscraper was already fully exploited in Cass Gilbert's Woolworth Building (fig. 2; 1913). At fifty-five stories it became the tallest enclosed building in the world until it was eclipsed by the Chrysler and Empire State buildings more than twenty-five

years later (up until 1930 the Eiffel Tower was the tallest structure in the world, but because of its open iron framework it was considered a glorified observation platform and not a skyscraper).

While the Woolworth Building was being planned, Frank W. Woolworth, the self-made millionaire and creator of the five-and-ten stores that bear his name, was told that he might never receive a full return on his investment. He nevertheless gave the approval to proceed; he intended to turn the building into the biggest advertisement for his company's success. To start with, the opening ceremony was a public relations event. At an agreed-upon moment, President Woodrow Wilson in Washington pushed a remote-control button that turned on the Woolworth Building's dynamos, and eighty thousand electric lights suddenly illuminated the structure. Outside, the thousands who had awaited this event "first gasped, then shouted their admiration," according to a Woolworth publication of the time. Inside, the twenty-eighth floor had been transformed into a banqueting hall, where eight hundred guests in black tie were served an opulent dinner that started with caviar, oysters, and turtle soup. A Boy Scout choir and several high-minded speeches reminded them of the patriotic significance of the occasion.

The Woolworth Building has twenty-eight elevators that would stretch, if placed end to end, a distance of two miles. It rises 792 feet, but it also extends 115 feet below ground. In addition to offices (it has thirty acres of floor space), it originally featured an observation platform and a swimming pool. At the time it was erected, the building was used by thirty-five thousand people daily.[12] The skyscraper had become a city within the city, an urban beehive whose economic influence, both positive and destructive, reached far beyond the building proper.

The image of the Woolworth Building became not only identified with the Woolworth Company, but a representation of the Woolworth Building as a logotype began appearing on many of the company's products. A friend of Frank Woolworth's, the Reverend S. Parkes Cadman, had called the building a Cathedral of Commerce, an appellation that found favor with the building's owner and that is apt for skyscrapers in general.

Although the neo-Gothic style is today identified with the Woolworth Building, an early alternate design by Cass Gilbert shows a neoclassical version.[13] The Beaux-Arts approach to design that had been dominant in New York encouraged coherent, usually symmetrical massing with a wide range of choices for the envelope. Neo-Gothic and neoclassical styles became competing alternatives for the skyscraper, depending on whether the architect used the cathedral and its verticality or the more ubiquitous but low-slung public building as his prototype. Within view of the Woolworth Building is McKim, Mead & White's classicizing Municipal Building, completed in 1914, a year after the Woolworth Building. Such a flexible notion of appropriateness was not only characteristic of New York's early twentieth-century skyscrapers but extended to their interiors as well. While the public spaces of lobby and hallway usually follow the building's overall style, the private

3

3. *Ernest R. Graham. Equitable Life Assurance Building, 1913–15.* The New-York Historical Society.

4. *McKenzie, Voorhees & Gmelin, Barclay-Vesey Building, 1923–26.* Cervin Robinson.

4

offices of the owner not infrequently reveal a different personal conviction.

Woolworth's office, for example, was done in French Empire Style. The presence of an oversize portrait of Napoleon took this interior beyond the realm of exotic decor, making overt political associations. This stylistic and ideological disjunction between the public and private spheres, however, is not an innovation of American capitalism. In ancient Rome at the point when republic became empire, Augustus commissioned works of art in divergent styles, revealing or concealing political intent, depending on their public relations value. In the Ara Pacis Augustea, a public marble altar, he is shown as a benign paterfamilias and all the figures occupy a common space; whereas in the small private Gemma Augustea, he is depicted hierarchically as a divinity in apotheosis above conquered enemies, the space layered conceptually in a style usually associated with the Middle Ages. The exterior of the modern skyscraper is geared to a presumed public acceptance, while the office is a somewhat closer reflection of private taste, just as the Gemma Augustea is a truer indication than the Ara Pacis of Augustus's personal ideals.

Architects had begun to propose some municipal control over the rapid growth of the skyscraper since the 1890s;[14] however, politicians responded only when pressure was exerted by the real estate industry once it perceived a threat to existing holdings. The tremendous height of the Woolworth Building and, even more important, the sheer elevation of Ernest R. Graham's Equitable Building of 1915, which rose thirty-nine stories without any setbacks, finally spurred the establishment in 1916 of New York's zoning law requiring setbacks for tall buildings (fig. 3).

Few skyscrapers that might exemplify the 1916 zoning law were completed during the economic slump after World War I and into the early twenties. The comparatively small but exquisite American Radiator Building by Hood and Fouilhoux of 1924 and the huge Barclay-Vesey Building by McKenzie, Voorhees & Gmelin of 1923–26, which impressed European architects because of its massive hulk, are exceptional (fig. 4). The skyscrapers most characteristic of the Manhattan skyline were not planned until the later twenties when the economy had heated up to a speculative intensity, and many were completed in 1929, the year of the stock market crash. Some, especially those that were already under way, were not finished until 1930 or 1931. Only when the Depression settled in with full force did construction come to a virtual halt.

New York's skyscraper boom coincided with the popularization of Art Deco, which was based on an eclectic amalgam of contemporary styles seen at the Paris exposition of 1925, an exhibit initially organized to help French designers compete with German avant-garde design.[15] When this mode was adopted for skyscrapers, it did not displace the traditional symmetrical Beaux-Arts massing but was used as a fashionable veneer over the more conservative aspects of an American commercial style. For most companies, it was good public relations to display a degree of modernity without the alienating aspects of an avant-garde approach. The 1925 exposition displayed official pavilions that were classicizing with a nod at least in the ornamental detailing to Cubism, Futurism, Expressionism, and especially the Wiener Werkstätte (Le Corbusier's l'Espirit Nouveau pavilion and Melnikov's Soviet pavilion were exceptions). The New York Art Deco skyscraper stylistically occupied the same middle range between tradition and the avant-garde.

Whether these skyscrapers contain watered-down allusions to the vestigial classicism of the Wiener Werkstätte or the crystalline angularity of German expressionism, they suffered no lack of popular appeal (fig. 5). Nearly all have startlingly idiosyncratic terminations and large-scaled ornamentation that define the setbacks, which can be seen from a great distance (fig. 1). The tactile definition of the lower floors, made for the close-up view of the passerby, is continued in a clearly marked entry (fig. 7) and an inviting, lushly decorated lobby. Based on an older crafts tradition, polychrome terra cotta, patterned brick, varicolored marbles, sculpted reliefs, mosaics, and metal work appear in exotic abundance (fig. 8). As skyscraper towers, they are easily remembered, and in their lower zones, they are sensuous and have an immediate visual appeal. These buildings had become part of the new mass culture that has its roots as much in film and advertising as in an architectural tradition. Advertising, in fact, became sophisticated in the twenties with the largest firms centered in New York; the public relations power of the skyscraper with a strong mnemonic feature had already been realized by Woolworth, but in the period from 1928 to 1932, companies used their skyscrapers to compete against one another and found ways to make their buildings stand out against the other remarkable towers that were filling in an increasingly crowded skyline.

Dramatic and filmic devices often incorporating lighting techniques provided the competitive edge, placing the skyscraper squarely in the center of the urban stage. Diaphanous building tops were lit at night—often in changing colors—and lobbies were made more theatrical by indirect lighting. Light beacons placed inside and behind the open lacework of the upper tower of the Gothic RCA Victor Building (later renamed the GE Building) by Cross & Cross (1930–31) created a fantastic silhouette at night, giving the effect of a high building without a massive structural center (fig. 1). Equally effective was the lobby of William Van Alen's Chrysler Building (1928–30) (fig. 10) with its indirect lights placed in a vertical series suggesting a raised curtain or the lobby of the News Building by Howells and Hood (1929–30) with a globe that seemed to float on a pool of light reflected over and over like a cosmic galaxy in the Expressionist faceted black-glass ceiling (fig. 11).

Both late modernists and postmodernists look back to Art Deco skyscrapers as models that are still worth emulating. The design of uncommon terminations such as in Hugh Stubbins's Citicorp Building (1978) or in Philip Johnson's AT&T Building (1984) are intended as such nostalgic references, as is the AT&T Building's whole three-part composition with its strongly defined entry meant to be a reconstitution of Art Deco and Beaux-Arts composition.

5

6

7

8

5. *Ely Jacques Kahn, Bricken Casino Building, 1930–31.* Cervin Robinson.

6. *Ely Jacques Kahn. The Park Avenue Building, 1927.* Cervin Robinson.

7. *Raymond Hood. The News Building, entry, 1929–30.* Cervin Robinson.

8. *Raymond Hood. McGraw-Hill Building, 1930–31.* Cervin Robinson.

9

10

9. Associated Architects, RCA Building, Rockefeller Center, 1931–35, later renamed the GE Building. Cervin Robinson.

10. William Van Alen. Chrysler Building, 1928–30, lobby. Cervin Robinson.

11. Raymond Hood. News Building, black glass ceiling in the lobby. Cervin Robinson.

11

What is memorialized in such postmodern designs, however, is a highly idealized version of a classical composition with beginning, midsection, and top that can exist today only in architectural models and renderings. In reality, vantage points that would have allowed a full view of such buildings were already by the late twenties being occluded by other tall towers. Art Deco architects seemed to have sensed this fracturing of views in the dense urban context by addressing the pedestrian's close-up view and the distant panorama of the skyscraper's top seen from several blocks away as separable elements. Architects of the period occasionally implied this disintegration of the complete perception of a structure by reconstituting the skyscraper as a miniature image. Thus a small-scale version of the skyscraper might appear as a sculpture, a relief, or a mural above the entrance or inside the lobby. With its several setbacks and great height, much of the building's termination was obscured from below, but the miniature version appended to the building near street level could make its general schema visible, albeit in an abstracted version. Instances of such miniatures occur in the Chrysler Building, Shreve, Lamb & Harmon's Empire State (1930–31) and 500 Fifth Avenue (1930–31) buildings, and in Clinton & Russell's 60 Wall Tower (1930–32) (fig. 12).[16] These small-scale versions of New York skyscrapers that attempt to evoke perceptual integrity despite the actual visual dislocation are comparable to gargoyles in a Gothic cathedral, where the medieval sculptor offset, though only in a marginal way, the overwhelming program of the church.

The disjunction between model and perceptual reality over which the architect had no control was then repeated on a different plane in the not infrequent break between the overall design (the advertised quasi-modernism of Art Deco) and the owner's own taste. While the exterior of the Chrysler Building employed stainless steel and displayed abstracted images of the automobile—hub caps, mudguards, and radiator ornaments—Walter Chrysler's own office was executed in a neo-Renaissance style, as if he were a European merchant prince. Both the disjunction imposed on our perception by urban density and the discontinuity of style between the public building and its private space have only intensified since World War II. Though most aspects of the interior design of Eero Saarinen's CBS Building (1965) were controlled by the architect, the office of chairman of the board William Paley was the exception: it was a wood-paneled, eighteenth-century English lord-of-the-manor realm. This type of public/private discontinuity is not unique to skyscrapers. Witness Richard Rogers's Lloyds Building in London (1986) where, despite the futuristic display of high technology, the board of directors hired a French decorator, Jacques Grange, to do its private offices in a pseudo-traditional style.

While it is rather common to deal with the individual skyscraper as an instance of good or bad design, its economic impact on existing buildings needs further amplification. One of the few publications that contains a general economic critique of the causes that fueled construction in the twenties is a book sponsored by a real estate lobby, the National Association of Building Owners and Managers, Earle Shultz and Walter Simmons's *Offices in the Sky* (1959). Just as real estate's support for the zoning laws had signaled self-preservation of an industry rather than urbanist ideals, so the National Association of Building Owners and Managers has its own protection at heart. Nevertheless, its statistics marshaled against overbuilding are worth considering. According to Shultz and Simmons, between 1925 and 1931, New York increased its office space by a dramatic ninety-two percent. During the same time period, office vacancies increased from 5.5 percent to seventeen percent.[17] The National Association of Building Owners and Managers blamed the oversupply of office space on boom financing through real estate bonds. This method of financing large construction projects had actually been conceived in the 1890s. Thus, when money could not be raised from a single wealthy investor or through a single mortgage, the mortgage was divided into small portions and sold as bonds to the public. This comparatively novel method of financing allowed small investors to participate in the real estate market, which reached speculative intensity in the later twenties when bond houses offered extremely high interest rates. The president of the National Association complained in 1926 that "Buildings were being put up entirely through the endeavors of bond houses to sell bonds, whether the buildings were needed or not."[18] Bond houses had become large institutions that encouraged the overproduction of speculative office space in order to perpetuate their own profits.

The National Association fought the overproduction of office space and real estate bond issues throughout this period but without much success. Shultz and Simmons refer to the "kidnapping of tenants" from the older buildings in order to fill new ones. While this sort of fevered speculation was in effect halted by the Depression, it has reappeared on several occasions after World War II. When Minoru Yamasaki's World Trade Center (1962–76), consisting of two 110-story towers, was completed, seven times the floor space of the Empire State Building was suddenly dumped on the market. The towers, erected by the Port Authority of New York and New Jersey, a public agency, were not fully rented for some time after their completion. At the behest of then Governor Nelson Rockefeller, one of the projects's prime movers, a number of state governmental offices were relocated into the World Trade Center.

Some skyscraper histories have taken for granted an almost Darwinian adaptation in insisting that skyscrapers were built as a direct response to needed office space.[19] But just as the relationship between high land values and the skyscraper could be turned upside down, as Birkmire noted as early as 1893, the relationship between needed office space and construction is not necessarily one of cause and effect. Rather, the economic machine is driven by speculative greed, often leading to overproduction of needed space and to the subsequent loss of tenants among the older buildings. One might perhaps see this in the light of the more aggressive Darwinian analogy: the survival of the fittest—but the analogy is superficial because commercial fitness in this case does not contribute to the survival of society at large.

When the Empire State Building (figs. 14, 15) was inaugurated in 1931 as the newest tallest building, the ceremony resembled the hoopla that had surrounded the opening of the

12

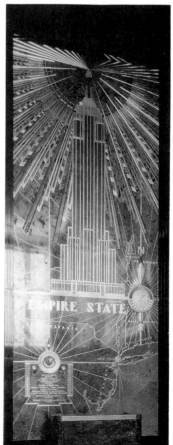

14

13

12. Clinton & Russell. 60 Wall Tower, 1930–32. Cervin Robinson.

13. William Van Alen. Top of the Chrysler Building. Cervin Robinson.

14. Shreve, Lamb & Harmon. Empire State Building, lobby, 1930–31. Cervin Robinson.

15. Shreve, Lamb & Harmon.
Empire State Building, 1930–31.
Cervin Robinson.

Woolworth Building in 1913. President Hoover pushed a button in Washington to turn on its lights, and Governor Franklin Roosevelt and Mayor James Walker gave speeches on the radio. It was completed in one year through labor-saving devices. To move the work force of thirty-five hundred men, temporary construction elevators were installed, and to feed them efficiently, rolling kitchens followed the crews upward.[20] The romance of the tall building and technological know-how were still intact.

The Empire State Building, however, unlike the Woolworth, Chrysler, News, or McGraw-Hill buildings, no longer advertised the self-made businessman or an individual company. It typified instead speculative construction with the names of the inventors not known to the general public. An earlier scheme for a smaller tower by the promoter Floyd De L. Brown had failed when he was unable to raise enough money for the project. He was bought out by a syndicate that consisted of Louis G. Kaufman, president of the Chatham and Phoenix Bank, Ellis P. Earle, president of the Nipissing Mines Company, John J. Raskob, former director of General Motors and of the Democratic National Committee, and Pierre S. du Pont, chairman of the board of E. I. du Pont de Nemours. Further, this group of investors arranged for a loan from the Metropolitan Life Insurance Company and made Alfred E. Smith, the well-liked former governor of New York State and unsuccessful Democratic nominee for president of the United States in 1928, president and spokesman for the so-called Empire State Company.[21] The name chosen for the building, the Empire State Building, refers to the popular name for New York State, implying a political connection that was exploited as a public relations device as had been the hiring of Smith, who was paid a Hollywood-style salary of $50,000 a year. The Empire State Company was the patriotic disguise for a syndicate of real estate speculators. Despite the Empire State Company's efforts to promote the building, it had difficulties filling its forty acres of new office space throughout the thirties. It was completed at a time when there had already been too much overbuilding, a factor made worse by the stock market crash and the subsequent Depression, which began to make an extensive impact on the economy by 1932. Office vacancies in New York reached twenty-five percent in 1934.[22] By this time, Rockefeller Center had added even more difficult-to-rent space in midtown Manhattan. Despite up-to-date services and superior public relations methods, as well as sophisticated research to identify tenants whose leases were about to expire in other buildings, even Rockefeller Center had a vacancy rate of twenty percent in early 1935.[23]

The speed with which new office space came on the market during the late twenties encouraged an intraurban mobility among the tenants of skyscrapers. While the Woolworth Company and the *Daily News* are still housed today in the skyscrapers associated with them, they have become the exception. The McGraw-Hill Company moved from its distinctive building designed by Hood, Godley & Fouilhoux (1930–31) to a much larger, but not better, skyscraper in the sixties. By contrast, the Chrysler Corporation has not been in the Chrysler Building for some time now. Though the Chrysler Building has had several recent owners, the building is still known to everyone as the Chrysler Building. In this case the association with a company name became so powerful that the name survived the change of ownership. This was not often true, however. The original RCA Building by Cross & Cross (1930) lost its major occupant to the RCA Tower (1931–33), the anchor of the Rockefeller Center complex. Symbolism, such as vibrating Victrola needles, became meaningless when the former RCA Tower was occupied by General Electric. In 1933, John D. Rockefeller unsuccessfully tried to get GE to move to Rockefeller Center as well. The Radio Corporation of America even agreed to changing the RCA sign atop the tower to GE. An ironic footnote to such rapid dislocations is that General Electric, which recently took over RCA, changed the name of the RCA Tower at Rockefeller Center to GE Tower (fig. 9).

In the typical skyscrapers of the late twenties that had been erected by individual owners and had become identified with them, the building's name and the company with which it became associated could become detached, assuming separate histories. Such an uncoupling of name and occupant, however, will never become an issue for the Empire State Building. Since it was speculative from its inception and its name for that reason was never an advertisement for a specific company, its generic, geographic name will remain as meaningful—or meaningless—as it was in 1931.

Notes

1. Alan Cowell, "Iraq Is Working to Resurrect—Some Say Massacre—The Ruins of Babylon," *New York Times*, September 27, 1987, 14.
2. Genesis 11:1–9.
3. Gail S. Harrison Roman, "Vladimir Tatlin's Project for a Monument to the Third International: A Paradigm for Russian Revolutionary Thought" (Ph.D. diss., Columbia University, 1981), 163–64. More formalist references to the Tower of Babel's importance for Tatlin are cited in Christina Lodder, *Russian Constructivism* (New Haven: Yale University Press, 1983), 62.
4. Winston Weisman, "New York and the Problem of the First Skyscraper," *Journal of the Society of Architectural Historians* 12 (March 1953): 13–21, and J. Carson Webster, "The Skyscraper: Logical and Historical Considerations," *Journal of the Society of Architectural Historians* 17 (December 1959): 126–39. For a more detailed discussion of conflicting histories of the skyscraper, see Rosemarie Haag Bletter, "The Invention of the Skyscraper: Notes on Its Diverse Histories," *Assemblage* (February 1987): 110–17. This is an expanded and revised version of "La possibile storia del grattacielo," *Casabella* (April/May 1980): 57–60.
5. Thomas P. P. van Leeuwen, *The Skyward Trend of Thought: Five Essays on the Metaphysics of the American Skyscraper* (The Hague: AHA Books, 1986), 1.
6. Peter Bogdanovich, *Fritz Lang in America* (New York: Praeger, 1967), 15.
7. Le Corbusier, *When the Cathedrals Were White*, trans. Francis E. Hyslop (New York: McGraw-Hill, 1964), 34.
8. Carl W. Condit, *The Rise of the Skyscraper* (Chicago: University of Chicago Press, 1952), and his revised, expanded version, *The Chicago School of Architecture: A History of Commercial and Public Buildings in the Chicago Area* (Chicago: University of Chicago Press, 1964); and Winston Weisman, "A New View of Skyscraper History," *The Rise of American Architecture*, ed. Edgar Kaufmann, Jr. (New York: Praeger, 1970), 115–60.
9. William H. Birkmire, *Skeleton Construction in Buildings* (New York: John Wiley, 1900), 7 (this book was first published in 1893).
10. Lewis Mumford, *The Brown Decades: A Study of the Arts in America 1865–1895* (New York: Dover, 1959), 138–39.
11. Kenneth Gurney Gibbs, *Business Architectural Imagery: The Impact of Economic and Social Changes on Tall Office Buildings 1870–1930* (Ann Arbor, Mich.: University Microfilms, 1976).
12. Edwin A. Cochran, *The Cathedral of Commerce: The Highest Building in the World* (New York: Woolworth Co., 1917; Montgomery Schuyler, *The Woolworth Building—1913* (New York: privately printed, 1913); and H. Addington Bruce, *Above the Clouds and Old New York* (New York: Woolworth Co., 1913).
13. The neoclassical rendering of the Woolworth Building is among the Cass Gilbert holdings in the library of the New-York Historical Society.
14. Donald Hoffman, "The Setback Skyscraper City of 1891: An Unknown Essay by Louis H. Sullivan," *Journal of the Society of Architectural Historians* 29 (May 1970): 186; and Francisco Mujica, *History of the Skyscraper* (New York: Archaeology and Architecture Press, 1929), 45.
15. More on the economic competition behind the planning of this exhibition can be found in Cervin Robinson and Rosemarie Haag Bletter, *Skyscraper Style: Art Deco New York* (New York: Oxford University Press, 1975), 44–48.
16. Rosemarie Bletter, "Metropolis Réduite," *Archithese* 18 (1976): 22–27.
17. Earle Shultz and Walter Simmons, *Offices in the Sky* (Indianapolis: Bobbs-Merrill Co., 1959), 162–63.
18. Ibid., 143ff.
19. See for example Heinz Ronner, "Skyscraper: A propos Oekonomie": *Archithese* 18 (1976): 44–49.
20. Shultz and Simmons, "Offices in the Sky," 168.
21. Ibid., 165ff.
22. Carol Herselle Krinsky, *Rockefeller Center* (New York: Oxford University Press, 1978), 76 and 88.
23. Ibid., 77.

1. Hannah Höch, A Slice with the Kitchen Knife: Dada through Germany's First Weimar Beer Belly Era, *1919. Neue Nationalgalerie, Berlin.*

Post-Expressionism: Notes on Dada, Neue Sachlichkeit, and Bauhaus

Wieland Schmied

Wieland Schmied is professor of art history at the Akademie der Bildenden Künste in Munich. From 1978 to 1986 he was director of Berlin's Artist Program (DAAD). During the 1970s he was at the National Gallery in Berlin and directed the 15th European Art Exhibition. He has published extensively on twentieth-century art.

Berlin's heyday was the 1920s, the twenties, the golden or roaring twenties—the decade in which the city came into its own. Today when we speak of Berlin's former greatness and past glory, we are not referring to the Berlin of the German Empire (1871–1918), nor do we mean the Berlin of the *Gründerjahre*, the years of rapid industrial expansion from 1871 to the turn of the century. What we are referring to is the Berlin of that brief, hectic, controversial, optimistic, and ultimately tragic period between 1918 and 1933, between the end of World War I and the beginning of the Third Reich.

The Weimar Republic was essentially a Berlin Republic. Berlin was the scene of its conflicts and the place where its destiny was fulfilled. The contradictions of the age were lived out here; they were voiced in the literature, acted out in the theaters, and they found a form in the new medium of film. They dictated the rhythm of the music and could be seen and understood on painters' canvases.

Between 1890 and 1914 before the decline of the Habsburg empire, Vienna had competed with Paris for the position of Europe's major metropolis. In the 1920s, it was Berlin that provided the challenge, claiming to be Europe's most important city. And indeed the artistic and intellectual forces of the twenties were to succeed where the political and military efforts of the Wilhelmine empire had failed or had only had a limited success. Berlin became the focus of (at least) intellectual Europe's undivided attention. In retrospect, it would be easy to misrepresent the Weimar Republic (or as I've referred to it here, the Berlin Republic) in the numerous symposiums and publications as an exemplary model for community life in the industrial age.

When, for this reason, the Council of Europe in Strasbourg decided to stage its fifteenth art exhibition in 1977 in Berlin, there could be no doubt as to the topic or period in art history Berlin would choose for the exhibition. Four related exhibitions, dealing with different aspects of this era, were united under the general title of "Trends in the Twenties." The development "From Constructivism to Concrete Art" was traced by Dieter Honisch in the National Gallery. At the Academy of the Arts, Peter Pfankuch presented an outline of European architectural projects entitled "From the Futuristic to the Functional City." Also in the academy, Eberhard Roters presented "Dada in Europe" in all of its diverse, anarchic, and enthusiastic, philosophical, and political varieties. And in the Orangery of the Charlottenburg Palace, the author of this essay had the honor of presenting the section "The New Reality—Surrealism and Objectivity" in which Surrealism and Neue Sachlichkeit, above all the French and German varieties, were contrasted using often surprisingly related motifs. There was no better place in Europe for the most excellent artistic works produced in the twenties to be assembled with the aim of reviving the discussion—half a century later—concerning the era in which they originated.

Three Central Experiences

There were three central experiences that the artists of this era

341

2

2. Max Beckmann, The Night,
1918–19. Kunstsammlung
Nordrhein-Westfalen, Düsseldorf.

3. Rudolf Belling, Sculpture 23,
1923. Neue Nationalgalerie, Berlin.

were trying to come to terms with: the horror of World War I, the experience of the modern city, and the fact that the avant-garde seemed to have reached the end of the road.

The war was a decisive experience that changed lives and not only the lives of those who fought in the trenches. Even those who were spared the experience of fighting at the front were confronted with the futile loss of life, the total annihilation of received values, and the collapse of the familiar order. Some of the most talented German artists fell in the war: Macke in 1914, Weisgerber in 1915, Franz Marc in 1916, Morgner in 1917. Oskar Kokoschka was badly wounded; Hans Beckmann, Kirchner, Grosz, and Lehmbruck had nervous breakdowns. Of all the German artists who were to survive more or less intact, it was Otto Dix who went on to produce the most horrific paintings and drawings of the victims: the dead lying in the trenches, the mutilated and the crippled, despised social outcasts condemned to waste away for the rest of their lives. George Grosz formulated the most passionate, venomous indictments against those who had accelerated the approach of war and then profited from it. In contrast, Max Beckmann recorded the atrocities he witnessed in the form of disquieting allegories whose complexity and destructive elements evoke the dimensions of classical tragedy.

The experience of the modern city had already been a disquieting topic for the Expressionists; Kirchner had seen the dark narrow streets of Berlin as a type of jungle, a world through which coquettes prowled like predatory cats. Whereas the faces in Kokoschka's portraits show the city as a force with the power to inspire and to destroy, the prescient Meidner projected the detonation of an imminent apocalypse onto his portraits. After the war and its catastrophes, the city became a place of alienation and the scene of contemporary conflicts. The Expressionists had perceived the city as an entity, albeit a dangerous and sinister one. Now it was shattered into hundreds of different facets, like the kaleidoscope of a technological civilization where each individual aspect is opaque and alien, in which pleasure all too easily changes into exploitation, security becomes paralysis, and small-scale affluence turns into large-scale inflation.

The great dynamic movements of the prewar years—Fauvism, Futurism—had lost their original impetus and their infectious energy; their protagonists appeared to have lost their élan. Crystalline Cubist structures suddenly seemed fragile, no longer capable of bearing their load. People had grown tired of experiments. A sense of insecurity spread. The mixing of styles and stylistic pluralism became the predominant modes of the era. Cubo-Futurism and Cubo-Expressionism were only two of the hybrid forms that emerged at the time. In continuing to paint works of a Cubist nature along with neoclassical works, Picasso was to become the first exponent of stylistic pluralism. Nowhere is this development more clearly seen than in the work of the Novembergruppe that was founded in late autumn 1918 in Berlin. Its very name was synonymous with revolution, and it was in this spirit that the group set out proclaiming: "The future of art and the grave nature of the present situation oblige us, the intellectual revolutionaries (Expressionists, Cubists, Futurists), to unite." But all that grew out of this claim was a loose association for the purpose of organizing shared exhibitions. The Novembergruppe never became a coherent artists' movement. Belated Expressionists and moderate Cubists, abstract and semiabstract painters, committed realists, tolerant constructivists, and renegade Bauhaus members existed more or less (usually less) peacefully, side by side and with each other. If there was a predominant style in this Babylonian mix, it was a hybrid style, which borrowed from the different isms, and which could be integrated into the individual concepts to create something new out of the Expressionist and Constructivist, realistic and Cubist elements. *The Musician* (1921) by the Russian emigrant Iwan Puni was an example of the way this tension and harmony actually combined on occasion to produce an original homunculus out of New Objective Realism and Synthetic Cubism.

Crossroads and Magnet

Just as the most varied forces and talents came together in the Novembergruppe, in the twenties, the whole of Berlin became the center where the most diverse paths crossed and where the different movements met, mingled, or kept apart. The city had a magnetic attraction for the most contrary of spirits. It offered hundreds of possibilities for people to meet, and it was big enough for people to be able to keep out of each other's way, the ideal place to experiment with coexistence. Artists came to Berlin from all parts of Germany: from Dresden and Düsseldorf, from Karlsruhe and Munich. It was a meeting place for Scandinavians and Austrians, French and Eastern Europeans, Russians, Poles, Czechs, and Hungarians. For years, Berlin was the preferred interim refuge of Russian emigrants—painters, sculptors, writers—who were on their way to Paris, in flight from the bureaucratic terror in the aftermath of the October Revolution. They were all sidetracked there for a while and stayed on (nearly always in the zoo quarter) in the hope that the situation at home would improve and permanent exile would prove unnecessary after all. Chagall and Lissitzky, Puni and Babij, Naum Gabo and Antoine Pevsner, Nabokov and Schklovsky: for all of them, Berlin became a temporary home and a place of intensive productivity.

The role assumed by Berlin as crossroads, and to a certain extent melting pot, made it possible for the late Expressionists and Cubo-Expressionists, Dadaists, and Constructivists, the Magic Realist painters, militant Verists and Neue Sachlichkeit artists to develop side by side without one group dominating to the exclusion of the others.

In retrospect it is possible to say that of all the movements and hybrid forms that thrived there, two in particular substantiate Berlin's claim to be the artistic capital of Europe in the twenties. These are Dada and Neue Sachlichkeit, or to be more precise, Dada in all its variations and Neue Sachlichkeit in all its varieties. Both of these movements in Berlin had a politically committed wing and one which was more interested in purely aesthetic questions. Dada politician George Grosz and Dada mentors Heartfield, Wieland Herzfelde, and Walter Mehring created a vehicle for radical social criticism with the Malik publishing house, and the journals *Jedermann*

3

343

4

5

sein eigener Fussball (Everyone His Own Football), Die Pleite (The Crash) and *Der blutige Ernst (Deadly Serious)*. Meanwhile the other wing with Superdada Baader and Dadasophs Hausmann, Hannah Höch, and Richard Huelsenbeck concentrated more on the destructive energy and shock effect of the individual work and action. This polarity was later reflected in the two wings of Neue Sachlichkeit, with the critical Verists on one side and the politically more indifferent (if not conservative) Magic Realists on the other.

Indeed there was a direct link between the radical politicization of Dada by George Grosz and John Heartfield and the committed social criticism of the Verists. Many of the painters we are familiar with as Neue Sachlichkeit artists first went through a Dadaist phase. And this is not only true of George Grosz, it also applies to Rudolf Schlichter and Otto Dix. The same can also be said of Christian Schad. As a result of his Dada period in Zürich, however, he was predestined for the right wing of Neue Sachlichkeit, that is, Magic Realism, rather than for any form of political activity.

Paris

At this point it would be interesting to take a brief look at events in Paris. In Paris, Dada evolved into Surrealism. This can be seen in the way Max Ernst's art developed. In Berlin, it was Neue Sachlichkeit that evolved out of Dada, and here George Grosz is our example. In both cases, something of the *pittura metafisica* spirit of artists such as Giorgio di Chirico and Carlo Carrà combined with the Dada delight in experiment and collage to give birth to something new—Surrealism in one case, Neue Sachlichkeit in the other.

In spring 1919, Max Ernst and George Grosz discovered the work of de Chirico and Carrà almost simultaneously from reproductions published in *Valor Pastici*, a Roman art journal that was quickly distributed in Germany. However, they each reacted to the *pittura metafisica* in a completely different way. Whereas Max Ernst transposed de Chirico's petrified scenery into a dream world, George Grosz translated it to the contemporary experience of the metropolis. Whereas Max Ernst allowed de Chirico's rigid, virtually immured figures to be roused to a dreamlike state, Grosz interpreted de Chirico's and Carrà's Renaissance architecture as modern commercial and industrial buildings and their tailor's dummies as war cripples with artificial limbs or as robots obeying commands. Rudolf Schlichter reacted in much the same way to the *pittura metafisica* world of stage scenery and dummies. His watercolor *Roof Atelier* (1920) depicts tailor's dummies, men with artificial limbs, puppets and mannequins in various rigid poses, and like Grosz's *Republican Automatons* of the same year, it very clearly marks the transition from Dada to Neue Sachlichkeit.

There is another factor that links Dada and the painting of Neue Sachlichkeit. The world presented to us in the work of both these movements does not come from merely one mold as in Expressionism. It is heterogeneous, fractured, and fragmented. Even if the Neue Sachlichkeit painters made a more concerted effort than the Dadaists not to accentuate the fragments but rather to join them together to produce a coherent picture, both realities are artificial. Incidentally, this applies equally to the Magic Realists and to the Verists who were directly inspired by Dada. The collage technique developed by the Dadaists and particularly by Max Ernst, and the photomontage technique promoted by the Berlin Dadaists Hausmann, Höch, and Heartfield were important in showing the painters how they could transpose the moment of collage and montage into a painting and produce or mount a synthetic reality from painted fragments of reality. In addition to the Dada techniques, de Chirico and his *pittura metafisica* also came to their help once again. In de Chirico's world, not only are individual objects to be found within a strange environment, the cohesion of the whole has been disturbed in a mysterious way. The first impression is deceptive. What we have in front of us here is not the familiar Renaissance perspective. Instead we are presented with a range of contradictory perspectives. Each building has its own alignment, and the alignments do not meet. De Chirico completely abandons the so-called technique of degradation (the "clouding" of the atmosphere against the background of the painting like a sfumato). As a result, his three-dimensional sage resembles a glass-enveloped vacuum. The spotlight throws hard shadows. Distant details often seem unrealistically clear, near, and disproportionately reduced. De Chirico's clarity has a disturbing quality. In his paintings, even ordinary objects seem strange. Classical harmony is lost. There is, however, a hidden force that brings together the strangest phenomena and perspectives.

It was here that the Neue Sachlichkeit painters found a technical means that allowed them to move beyond Dada and helped them to find a new order for their fragmented world. It was as important to get over Dadaism as it had been to get over Expressionism. I referred earlier to the fact that the avantgarde had reached the end of the road. No matter how spectacular they might once have seemed, many of the avantgarde's attitudes were no longer convincing in the skeptical mood of the twenties. And this mood was perhaps nowhere quite so dispassionate, so skeptical as in Berlin. In the aftermath of the devastation caused by the Great War and in the spirit of restoration that followed the confusion and attempted revolutions of the immediate postwar period, the Neue Sachlichkeit painters were concerned with recovering the object, presenting a new experience of the world of objects, and finding a new source of orientation in the visible world. They knew instinctively that nineteenth century realism was the least suitable means to achieve this (even if some lesser talents did resort to it in the twenties). They were aware that their points of reference had to be more substantial and complex if they were to be used in creating a new image of reality and if they wanted to mount this reality from diverging details. Thus, apart from the so-called grand realism of Henri Rousseau (a term coined by Kandinsky), Fernand Léger's conceptual realism, the object world of de Chirico seen from a metaphysical perspective, and the neoclassicism of Picasso and Derain, there was little for them to choose from in this century. Although, with few exceptions, they seldom attained the stylistic heights of these models, in using them (and the great masters of previous centuries who were most important for Dix, Schad,

6

4. Rudolf Schlichter, Bert Brecht, *1926*. Städtische Galerie in Lehbachhaus, Munich.

5. George Grosz, Untitled, *1920*. Kunstsammlung Nordrhein-Westfalen, Düsseldorf.

6. George Grosz, Pillars of Society, *1926*. Neue Nationalgalerie, Berlin.

7

8

7. *Raoul Hausmann,* The Spirit of
Our Times, *1921.* Musée National
d'Art Moderne, Paris.

8. *George Grosz,* The Engineer John
Heartfield, *1920.* Museum of
Modern Art, New York. Gift of A.
Conger Goodyear.

and Schrimpf) for orientation, their focus was sharpened and
their methods radicalized.

Where and to What Extent Can Modernism
Be the Art of the Metropolis?

In identifying Berlin with two movements, Dada and Neue
Sachlichkeit, and neglecting the wide range of other creative
impulses that existed there, it was not my intention to present
Berlin as a synonym for Germany in the Weimar Republic.
Berlin here represents the modern city with four million inhabitants, the European metropolis, the political, economic,
and intellectual center of the German Republic, the place
where artists could experience the city as a self-contained
world. It is, therefore, no coincidence that is was here that
Dada and Neue Sachlichkeit were able to thrive and had a
particular topicality.

Dada is, perhaps, the first of the modern movements that is
entirely the product of the metropolis. The entire modern
movement is, of course, marked by the spirit of the industrial
age, by the radical changes in the scientific worldview, by a
civilization that encompasses all areas of human life (and
sometimes also the flight from it). In order to intensify their
perception of nature and as a result develop their art, however, the Impressionists actually left Paris and made their pilgrimage to the light of the Ile de France. Much the same can
be said of the Expressionists. Expressionist painting gives an
incomparable sense of modern man who is an integral part of
the city but is nevertheless drawn back to nature in search of
himself. Expressionist artists experienced the rapture of being
at one with nature—Van Gogh in the midday heat of Provence,
Edvard Munch in the evenings on the beach at Assgaard.
They also experienced a deep alienation from nature and were
frequently torn between the two extremes of communion and
alienation.

Similarly, German Expressionism is no child of the metropolis; it grew in the smaller provincial centers. The art of Die
Brücke—or Bridge—originated in the area between Dresden
and the Moritzburg lakes, that of the Blaue Reiter (the Blue
Rider) between Munich and Murnau. Paula Modersohn
worked in Worpswede, Christian Rohlfs in Hagen, Soest, and
Weimar, Emil Nolde on the island of Alsen, in Ruttebüll,
Utenwarf, and later in Seebüll. Nolde may have spent his win-
ters regularly in Berlin from 1909 onward, but he remained a
stranger in this city, and his art was hardly influenced by it at
all. This is basically also true of the Brücke painters who
moved to Berlin after 1910. Karl Schmidt-Rottluff and Otto
Müller essentially remained painters of landscapes and people in landscapes. The same can be said—with certain reservations—of Erich Heckel and Max Pechstein. Again, it was
landscapes, groups of figures, and interiors that dominated
their paintings. If the move to the city is in any way reflected
in their work, it appears less in the form of a change in theme
(the Berlin motif appears only in individual pictures) than in a
new sharpness and brittleness.

How the Expressionists and Futurists Experienced the Metropolis

The one exception here—and indeed an overwhelming one—is E. L. Kirchner. And it is he who first comes to mind when we speak of the metropolitan experience in Expressionist art. Of all the Brücke painters, only his work has that vibrating, nervous tension that is a reaction to the hectic activity and staccato rhythms of the city. His encounter with the city of Berlin released energies that led to the uncompromising achievement of his unique style. Among the Expressionists, there is only one other genuine metropolitan painter, whose early work is characterized by the same vibrating, nervous tension: Oskar Kokoschka. Down to the last wrinkle and vein, all of the faces he paints are city faces. However, after intense periods of experiencing the city and following the turning point marked by World War I, even people like Kirchner and Kokoschka were drawn back to nature—Kirchner to the solitude of the Davos Mountains and Kokoschka on endless journeys through Europe. This new experience of nature presented them both with numerous new motifs and ultimately led to a change in their styles.

Even in their city paintings, the Expressionists were looking for a link with nature. This is as true of Kirchner as it is of Macke or Meidner. The Futurists present an altogether different case. Despite the underlying illusionist concepts, both the content and the style of their paintings are shaped by the technological world, by the euphoria of the machine, the ecstasy of speed and the rhythms of the city. In metaphoric terms, the Blauer Reiter mounted the bicycles, motor cars, or trains of Boccini, Balla and Carrà in order to move ahead more quickly. The Futurists, however, are the romantics of the machine age, uncritical admirers of technology and the metropolis. Gradually, all traces of nature also disappeared in the contemporaneous *pittura metafisica* works of de Chirico. Here, nature's disappearance is accompanied by a sense of grief and lament. De Chirico shows us an ossified world that is empty of people, a world that has become architecture. His "Italian Squares" are surrounded with arcades, walls, and factories that offer no way out. It is a place where neither trees grow nor flowers blossom.

Dadaist Art as a Product of the Metropolis

Whereas the Futurists (and in his own way Chirico) systematically eliminated nature from their pictures, from the outset Dada was the art of the metropolis, and it was so in a much more radical sense. Man now appears as products of his environment—no longer nature's being but instead civilization's being. Yet, it is not only the way in which the feeling for life in the city is expressed by Dada, it is not only Dada's often ironic interest in what's in the air and on the street, it is above all the technical methods Dada employs that make this art a product of the metropolis. Using the stylistic techniques of collage and photomontage that are totally in tune with the time, the Dadaists presented our world as one capable of being totally manipulated. At the same time, these stylistic methods reflected the reality of the city and the way it is presented in the mass media—in the newspapers, magazines, and films. The stylistic techniques of collage and photomontage are essentially akin to the strange, unconnected juxtaposition of a variety of realities that change continually as they unfold to a passerby or to a bus driver on the Kurfürstendamm, or as they stare up at the reader from the page of the *Vossische Zeitung*, as they are presented on Piscator's stage or in a film sequence from *Metropolis*. Anyone who decides to work with these models cannot escape the spirit of the modern metropolis.

Of course, this radicalism was not peculiar to Dada from the beginning. When Dada originated in 1916 in Zürich and first appeared as a visual phenomenon in Hans Arp's wood engravings, this particular metropolitan dimension had yet to appear. Arp's reliefs may have had a collage character about them, but it was other features of his work that classify it as Dada. These were the element of chance in the determination of individual forms and total composition, the use of the simplest materials and worn-out castoffs, the complete negation of all art's functions within bourgeois society and its value system, the liberation from the necessity of making sense. From now on, sense, no sense, and nonsense had the same value in art. There is a direct link between Arp's work and *Merz* art developed by Kurt Schwitters in Hannover almost three years later. It was in Berlin, however, that Dada first became the art of the metropolis.

Richard Huelsenbeck, who came from Zürich to Berlin in 1917 and joined the groups connected with the *Freie Strasse (Open Road)* and *Neue Jugend (New Youth)* journals, including Franz Jung, Grosz, Hausmann, Heartfield, and Wieland Herzfelde, perceived Berlin as a "city of tightened belts . . . where hidden rage was channeled into a boundless greed for money, where people were ever more concerned with their bare existence. Whereas living in Zürich was like being in a health resort . . . in Berlin one didn't know if one would have a hot midday meal the next day."[2]

A further element, both thematic and structural in nature, which was accentuated in the collage technique and which led to the invention of photomontage, soon emerged in Berlin. This was the mechanization and automation of the individual that was inspired by the dummylike figures of de Chirico and Carrà, and its pendant, the assumption of anthropomorphous, robotlike features by the machine. The transformation in the artist's understanding of himself as one who is bound up in the myth of creativity to the self-image as mechanic or builder was indelibly linked with the mechanization of the image of the human being and its culmination in the vision of *l'homme machine*.

Evidence of the Dada techniques such as collage and montage, the obsession with the dummy and the rejection of the myth of creativity can, of course, be found elsewhere, for example, in Max Ernst's work in Cologne. One aspect is unique to Berlin and that is its politicization. In Berlin, the attitude of utter social indifference, which was often considered typical of Dada and the Dada dandy, was transformed into total involvement and socially critical aggression. It was here that the anarchic energies unique to Dada lost their random irrational nature and became the vehicle of harsh political satire. For the Herzfeld brothers, Grosz and Schlichter, Dada was a weapon in the class war. But this weapon was still too closely associated with eccentricity and irrationality, too much delight was taken in actions that shocked the bourgeoisie for it to survive for very long. In July 1919, the Dadaists threw an anti-Weimar leaflet into a meeting of the Weimar National Assembly signed by the Dadaist Central Committee of the World Revolution (Baader, Hausmann, Tzara, Grosz, Huelsenbeck, Jung, and others). The pamphlet declared: "We will blow Weimar up, Berlin is the place, da . . . da . . . Nobody and nothing will be spared."[3] But Weimar was not to be overthrown in this way. No one realized this sooner and more clearly than Grosz himself, and he drew the consequences from this by concentrating on an unadorned, Veristic style of painting and drawing. In a manifesto entitled *Art Is in Danger*, which he wrote in 1925 with Wieland and Herzfelde, he summarizes his change in attitude toward art. He still defends Dada for what it had achieved: "To the accompaniment of bawling and jeers it had broken with a narrow, arrogant, and overrated milieu." He says of it that "this movement has made all isms in art into petty affairs of the atelier which took place the day before yesterday."[4] By 1925, Dada was a part of the past. It is not only for Grosz that it belongs to yesterday. The future, as Grosz would like it to be interpreted, belongs to "art with a purpose, art in the service of the revolutionary cause." It belongs to the realistic artist "who describes and criticizes . . . the face of our era." At the same time, "as the propagandist and defender of the revolutionary idea and its supporters, he takes his place among the army of the oppressed."[5] Admittedly, Grosz would abandon this aspiration all too soon.

The New Realism: A Machinelike Structure

The broad range of Neue Sachlichkeit—from Verism as a left wing, to Magic Realism as a right wing—does not allow one to identify it as the realization of Grosz's programmatic demand for art with a purpose. Grosz was certainly right about one of its aspects, however, and it is one which, at least until the mid-twenties, is by no means insignificant: the political aspect, that of being involved in and witnessing events.

But this aspect was not the only one that made Neue Sachlichkeit into an essentially metropolitan art form. Its origins in Dada and *pittura metafisica* are just as urban as its fascination with the conceptual realism of artists such as Fernand Léger, in which Dada's obsession with machines lives on as a perspective of the future with a more positive slant. It was perhaps with an eye to Léger and certainly to French artists such as Auguste Herbin and Jean Metzinger, that Franz Roh, the first herald of Magic Realism, described the *Gegenständlichkeit*, the perspicuity of the Magic Realists, as a "machine-like structure" and contrasted it with the Expressionists' "organizational conception" of the figure.[6] In his book, *Post Expressionism*, the first account of Neue Sachlichkeit in book form, which was published in 1925 parallel to the exhibition in the Kunsthalle in Mannheim that aimed at providing an overview of German painting since Expressionism, Roh presented a schematic outline of twenty-two points in which Ex-

pressionism and Post-Expressionism were in diametrical opposition. The individual differences distinguished by Roh are of less importance to us here than the basic fact that ever since the two first appeared in the early twenties, such art historians as Roh or Hartlaub (the director of the Kunsthalle in Mannheim) had interpreted Neue Sachlichkeit and Magic Realism as Post-Expressionism, as movements that set about replacing Expressionism and that also represented the greatest conceivable contrast to it. Contemporaries saw the influence of earlier movements on this new form of realism, particularly that of the "Dada phase," as comparatively insignificant. Even today we cannot reach a complete understanding of Neue Sachlichkeit, and consequently of the 1920s, without taking a look at the art of the Expressionist movement for purposes of comparison. Two distinctions that Roh considered to be of little or no importance, are of particular interest to us here. Both of these relate, directly or indirectly, to the concept of a specifically metropolitan form of art.

The Difference between Expressionism and Neue Sachlichkeit

The artists of Neue Sachlichkeit were quite different from the Expressionists not only in the way in which they saw and interpreted their subject but also in the techniques and means they employed. Expressionists artists were essentially painters, whereas drawing was the primary medium of the Neue Sachlichkeit artists.

As a result, the latter saw themselves more directly and exclusively confronted with reality, with external reality. The expressionists were at home in their own individual reality and in the reality of art; the artists of Neue Sachlichkeit were only at home in reality and, as is evident in all of their paintings and drawings, they certainly did not consider this to be a real home.

The Expressionist thought in color, the Neue Sachlichkeit artists used the language of the line. We are, of course, familiar with an abundance of powerful and elaborate, sketched and composed drawings by Kirchner, Von Heckel, and Schmidt-Rottluff. We also have these three artists to thank for the renaissance of the woodcut.

And of course, the paintings by the Neue Sachlichkeit artists should not be overlooked. These include Otto Dix's *Big City Triptych* and *The Match Seller*, Grosz's *Dedication to Oscar Panizza* and *Pillars of Society*, Conrad Felixmüller's *Death of Walter Rheiner*, and the gallery of the faces of well-known and unknown contemporaries painted by Dix, Grosz, Christian Schad, Rudolf Schlichter, and George Schrimpf, the industrial world of Carl Grossberg, the celestial landscapes of Franz Radziwill, and finally the sculpted still lifes of Alexander Kanoldt and Eberhard Viegener.

The drawings by the Expressionists that are familiar to us are the drawings of painters, whereas the paintings by the Neue Sachlichkeit artists are paintings by artists whose main medium is drawing. For all of them, from Dix to Schlichter and from

Grosz to Schad, the drawing, the line, the contour, the outline was the main constitutive element of the picture. All of the energy came from the line; color only helped it, lending support and emphasis. The line provided the framework and structure of the picture, color added mood and atmosphere or in some cases did not add it, excluded it, conspicuously omitted it. The stringently formed space, composed in the manner of a collage, vacuumlike and devoid of all atmosphere, has repeatedly been named as one of the most important aspects of Neue Sachlichkeit painting.

Of all artistic means, it is the line that best lends itself to be used as a weapon, a weapon for attack and defense. In choosing the line as the instrument most appropriate for their purposes, the artists of the twenties were part of a German tradition in which drawing had played a role in a combative, committed humanism and had depicted the active and suffering individual. Albrecht Dürer, Jörg Ratgeb, and Hans Baldung Grien all belong to this tradition. Observation and declaration, note and message, witticism and reproach—everything could be reproduced by graphic means and had found expression in them in the course of the centuries.

The Expression of the Zeitgeist

Yet another important distinction can be made between Expressionism and Neue Sachlichkeit. This concerns our concept of Neue Sachlichkeit and its definition in its contemporary context. Neue Sachlichkeit mirrored its *Zeitgeist* to a far greater extent than Expressionism had ever done. In its oscillation between ecstasy and apocalypse, between vision and experience, in its fascination with the urban experience and its emotional response to nature, Expressionism certainly revealed the mood of an era. Its connection to this era, however, was never as direct and concrete as that of Neue Sachlichkeit to the 1920s. The pictures and drawings by the artists of the Neue Sachlichkeit read like an account of events in Berlin during the Weimar period. They depict its desires, ideals, and disappointments, its evasions, conflicts, and shortcomings. A line in the chorus of a popular song at the time went "There's something in the air called objectivity."[7] The fetishes of the new era—airships, airplanes, cars, electricity, radio, records—are sung of in a callow, flippant tone. At the same time, values such as love and sensitivity were mocked. They seemed to be little more than the ballast of a past era and could only hamper one in the effort of coping with life in a mechanized world:

Out with stucco and details!
Houses now have smooth facades!
By tomorrow it's quite clear
These facades will all disappear

With cynical delight, the line of the song pursues this thought to its logical conclusion:

Out the door the furniture goes
Out with everything whose pace is wrong
In our opinion, which no mercy shows
Everyone who's there just doesn't belong.[8]

9

10

9. George Grosz, Portrait of the Writer Max Hermann-Neisse, *1925.* Städtische Kunsthalle Mannheim.

10. Otto Dix, The Match Seller I, *1920.* Staatsgalerie, Stuttgart.

349

11

12

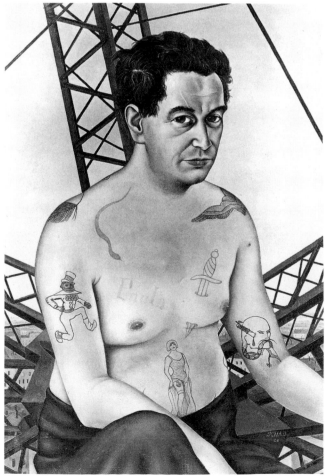

13

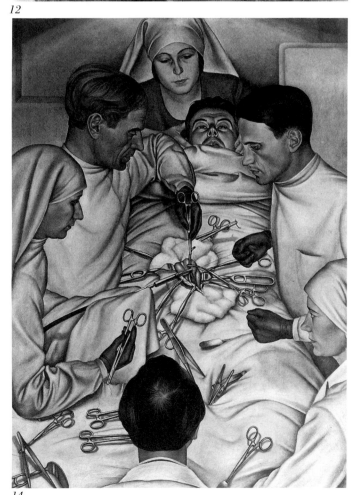

14

The artists of the Neue Sachlichkeit painted this feeling that they said was in the air. At the same time by painting it, by translating it into the vacuumlike space of their paintings, they defended themselves against it. They used objectivity in the attempt to protect themselves, to shield themselves against an era that was all too objective. They were well aware that they themselves were among the people who didn't belong and they tried to come to terms with this. They were familiar with the contemporary callow and cynical tone, they and their art were exposed to it daily. They responded to this tone, but did not entirely adopt it. They hid their sensibilities behind the objects and they themselves remained invisible. Objects cannot be as cynical as people—and they weren't as easily hurt. For this reason they clung to their objects and were hesitant about allowing people into their pictures.

The Expressionists enjoyed painting nudes. In contrast, Otto Dix almost always portrayed the naked person as mutilated, or ravaged by old age, sickness, vice, and debauchery. In the case of Schad, the naked body of a woman appears as an object, a thing that is available, which can be possessed and manipulated. Dix and Schad liked painting tattooed skin: the tattoo represented a desperate hope that the body's inevitable decay could be postponed, and at the same time, it is like a suit of armor.

"Man is good," the Expressionists had proclaimed. "Man is an animal,"[9] countered Grosz at the beginning of the twenties. This cynical declaration, however, was soon replaced by recognition of the fact that humans needed help and protection. They needed to be shielded from the capitalist exploiter and the bloodthirsty militarist, from the threatening, anonymous forces of technology and the metropolis, from progress, from the world of the machine.

None of them believed in visions. Grand visions had brought disaster. This disaster had been accompanied by grand concepts and words. They distrusted them. They rejected them. With the exception of Max Beckmann, who in certain respects did not really belong to the movement, the artists of Neue Sachlichkeit created no new vision. This distinguishes them from the Expressionists and the Bauhaus artists; their political commitment focused more on concrete, attainable aims than on new visions or utopias. It was more of a sympathy with the deprived, or a rage aimed at institutional cynicism. It didn't last. Toward the end of the twenties, and long before they were labeled degenerate by the Nazis, their anger had dissipated, their strength was exhausted, their commitment gone. Their view of reality had lost its terse power. The contours lost their sharpness. Instead of continuing to confront contemporary conflicts, these artists withdrew to idylls. Instead of painting cacti (around 1925 the favorite still life subject), they painted flowers; instead of city streets they painted landscapes. Increasingly, these landscapes reveal the absence of that objectivity and precision that once made them so fascinating. After 1933, many of the best painters, including Dix, took the step that had been foreshadowed in their art some years earlier: they went into inner exile—in reality, this meant moving to the provinces. Berlin ceased being the lively metropolis it had been. Berlin itself became provincial.

15
11. *Otto Dix*, Portrait of Sylvia V. Harden, *1926*. Musée National D'Art Moderne, Paris.

12. *Christian Schad*, Egon Erwin Kisch, *1928*. Hamburger Kunsthalle.

13. *Rudolf Schlichter*, Egon Erwin Kisch, *c. 1928*. Städtische Kunsthalle, Mannheim.

14. *Christian Schad*, Operation, *1927*. Städtische Galerie in Lehbachhaus, Munich.

15. *Max Beckmann*, Self-Portrait in Tuxedo, *1927*. The Busch-Reisinger Museum, Cambridge, Massachusetts. Photograph courtesy of Fogg Art Museum, Harvard University.

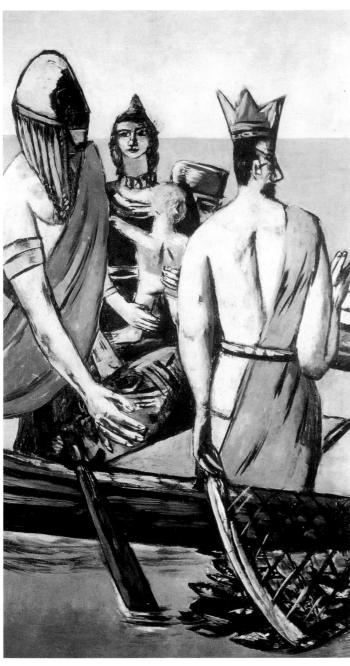

16. Max Beckmann, Departure,
1932–33. Museum of Modern Art,
New York. Photo courtesy of
Bildarchiv Preussischer
Kulturbesitz, Berlin.

This may be the reason why Beckmann went in the opposite direction. Having lost his professorship at the Städel School in Frankfurt am Main, he moved to Berlin where he had already lived before World War I. The anonymity of the big city seemed to offer him better protection than the smaller city of Frankfurt. It was here that his confrontation with his era found a more radical and intensive expression in his pictures—even if this was done using the code of mythical metaphors. In 1933, the year that he moved to Berlin, he painted *Departure,* the first of his large, allegorical triptychs so rich in allusions. Later on, Beckmann laconically announced the theme of this painting to be the liberation from "life's torments" and the "deceptive appearance," the break away to "freedom," the "new beginning," and the "essentials."[10] In *The Night,* which he painted at the end of World War I, he had attempted to ward off the unleashing of the forces of evil. He managed to stand four more years of life in Berlin. Then, just as the exhibition "Degenerate Art" was opened, in which twelve of his paintings were exhibited, he left to live in exile in Amsterdam.

George Grosz is a different case. He had left Berlin at the beginning of 1933, and pursuing the "American dream" of his childhood, he began to build a new life as an artist and teacher in New York. In contrast to Beckmann, he was burned out artistically. He no longer had the sharpness that had inspired his best pictures and drawings, the anger at injustice and hatred of its perpetrators. In contrast to Berlin, the New York scene was not a world stage where the era's history was being made and where he could accuse or warn. In New York, he was attracted to its homey, endearing, and sentimental aspects. In Manhattan's sea of houses, his sure eye discovered the provinces.

The Bauhaus

If we maintain that the concern of the Neue Sachlichkeit painters, and particularly of its Verist wing was skepticism and sobriety and that they were not interested in the grand vision, or far-reaching utopia (a claim from which we have only excluded the special case of Beckmann), it must also be said that this distinguishing feature of twenties realism is particularly evident in Berlin. The Berlin climate has always been conducive to realism. The delight in acute observation, in minimal characterization and telling detail is as much part of Adolph Menzel's work as of Liebermann's and even an Expressionist such as Kirchner cannot avoid it in the pictures of street scenes and cafés he painted during his Berlin years.

This type of realism was sometimes only expressed as a sober registering of facts, but it usually had an emphatic, aggressive, occasionally somewhat melancholy tendency that was indebted to Dada in its skepticism toward high-flown visions and utopias. Can this tendency be understood as the general failure of Weimar culture in the 1920s? This is open to question, and it is here that a distinction must be made. We established at the beginning of the essay that the Weimar Republic was essentially a Berlin Republic. It was in Berlin that the most active forces in the visual arts could be found. The most important galleries and collectors were in Berlin, and it was there that the leading art journals were published. But Berlin was by no means the only center. It was constantly challenged by many other smaller centers that had their own artistic traditions. These included cities such as Dresden, Düsseldorf, Cologne, Karlsruhe, Hannover, Munich, Weimar. Of all these cities it was Weimar that posed the greatest challenge to Berlin in its role as a magnet and melting pot.

In 1919, Walter Gropius founded the State Bauhaus and thereby created a place for utopia, although it must be admitted that at the beginning the exact shape this utopia should take remained vague. Expressionist and Constructivist visions overlapped. This center, a home for vision and utopia, contrasted sharply with the analytical spirit of Dada and the synthetic spirit of Neue Sachlichkeit and the way in which they had developed in the Berlin climate.

It would be an oversimplification to understand Berlin culture and Weimar culture of the twenties as being in diametrical opposition. Weimar refers here not only to the town where the Constitutional Assembly first met in 1919 and gave the young republic its name, but also to the home of the Bauhaus, which originated in the same year in Van de Velde's School of Applied Arts. Weimar spirit can be summarized as representing all of the concepts for a potential future that were conceived within the Bauhaus circle. In contrast, the Berlin spirit was characterized by a concentration on the here and now. It was utopia versus reality.

Berlin and Weimar: Opposite Poles

A political parallel for this Weimar-Berlin contrast can be found in the ideal modern republic as envisaged by the Constitutional Assembly and in the ensuing reality of a political life that became even more exhausted and splintered. In both social and aesthetic terms, Weimar represented a view back to the past, to the best German traditions; at the same time, it represented the view forward to a utopian concept of the future in all areas of human existence. Berlin represented the lived present. This view was also expressed by Oskar Schlemmer in his Bauhaus manifesto of 1923, which although compiled with the agreement of the Masters' Committee at the Bauhaus, was never made public. While Schlemmer's programmatic concept of the so-called cathedral of socialism to be built by everybody referred to an original aim of the Bauhaus, as early as 1929 this concept no longer seemed generally applicable to the work of the Bauhaus. Thus, Oskar Schlemmer's idealistic visions never obtained a consensus. They give an exact description, however, of the uninhabited enthusiasm for utopian ideas associated with the early days of the Bauhaus. Taking up a quotation from Goethe, Schlemmer wrote:

[It is a question of] the synthesis, the certification, the intensification, and the concentration of all positive elements toward a strong center. The idea of the center, divorced from half-measures and weakness and understood as the balance and equilibrium, will become the idea of German art. Germany, the country at the center, and Weimar at its heart are not for the first time the chosen sites for intellectual decisions. What is important is the recognition of what

is appropriate for us, so that we do not lose our direction and goal. There should be a counterbalance between contrasting poles, revering the distant past and the distant future, rejecting both reaction and anarchy. An idealism of activity that encompasses, penetrates, and unites art, science and technology, and is effective in research, teaching, and work, will make the artistic construction of mankind possible. It is a construction that is simply a reflection of the global construction.[11]

In 1923, the year he wrote this, Schlemmer also painted his programmatic work *Paracelsus—The Legislator*. If we compare this to Dix's well-known *Portrait of the Art Dealer Alfred Flechtheim*, which he painted in Berlin around 1926, a clearly defined picture of the two extremes of the art of the 1920s emerges. In Schlemmer, we have the concept of an imaginary center that is born of the spirit of Weimar and the Bauhaus and symbolically represented by a historical figure. Dix, on the other hand presents us with the realistic eccentricity of a contemporary who is representative of Berlin during this era. Schlemmer combines a romantic vision with geometric, calculated construction; in Dix, pitiless, sharp observation is combined with the technical precision necessary to realize it. Schlemmer attempts to present a type, a general human law valid beyond all time, but Dix insists on the individual, the individual in his or her singularity and uniqueness. In Schlemmer, the focus is on a figure conceived as a coherent whole; in Dix there is a deliberate use of selected, succinct details. In Schlemmer, there is the projection of an ideal image rooted in the intellect, in Dix, a statement of the artist's perception of himself as witness of his time.

The intellectual range of this era reveals itself in such exemplary contrasts. For Schlemmer, Weimar represented the striving toward an imaginary center. As we have seen, Dix, insisted on the perceptible eccentricity of an era that did not find a respite or even seek it. If Weimar and Schlemmer were concerned with counterbalancing contrasting poles, the work of Dix, Grosz, Schad, or Schlichter exemplified the impossibility of achieving this. Weimar and Schlemmer were attracted toward both the distant past and the distant future; toward the dream of the union of all creators in a medieval workshop and the ideal of a new social order with no class distinctions. In all of its aspects, Berlin stood in contrast to this, for it represented a present that was fragmented and devoid of all illusions.

Berlin finally won out in this competition of ideas embodied in the names of Weimar and Berlin; reality conquered vision. The different phases in the development of the Bauhaus, marked not least by the move from Weimar to Dessau in 1925 and finally to Berlin in 1932, show that it was not only shaken by internal conflict and harassed by unsympathetic and malevolent politicians, but that it was deliberately treading a path from dream to reality. This path led from Expressionism to Functionalism, from the cathedral of socialism to the machine for living, from the vision of a unity in the arts to an increasingly practical orientation and an interest in high-quality industrial design. It was not a coincidence, therefore, that in the course of its move toward the present, the Bauhaus also moved geographically from Weimar toward Berlin. Dessau, where it moved to halfway through the decade, is almost exactly halfway between Weimar and Berlin. It was not a coincidence that the Bauhaus could not flourish in the Berlin climate (particularly in the years 1932–33). In order to develop its visions, it needed the isolation and the protection of the provinces and with this a certain distance from the immediate present. It is only possible to imagine the Tolstoy disciples and the reformers, the itinerant preachers and nature freaks who were attracted to the Bauhaus in the early days like moths to a flame in the atmosphere of Weimar. The soft rolling hills of Thuringia took on something of Monte Verità of Ascona. Oskar Schlemmer was right when he wrote in 1923, "The crisis of the era was also one of the intellects. A cult of the unconscious, the inexplicable, a leaning toward mysticism and sects originated in the search for ultimate things, which a world of doubt and disunity threatened to deprive of their meaning . . . A fervor for the means of expression emerged as on the altar pictures." However, three years later in 1926 in Dessau (and almost exactly halfway through the history of the Bauhaus), Schlemmer noticed a radical change: "The atmosphere here with regard to art is so far removed from everything that is not topical and timely in its effects. Dadaism, circus, variety shows, jazz, tempo, cinema, America, airplane, car. These are the present concepts."[12] The Bauhaus had moved more than halfway to Berlin.

Chicago: A Synonym for Berlin

"Variety shows, jazz, tempo, cinema, America, airplane, car"—this sounds exactly like Bertolt Brecht's Berlin. And this is how he appears in the portrait painted by Rudolf Schlichter in 1926, the year of Schlemmer's diagnosis of the new situation in the Bauhaus. The writer as mechanic, wearing a leather jacket, which reflects the city's neon lights, in the background his newly acquired car (radiator and wings can be seen), the favored cigar in his hand, looking at the world with a skeptical laugh; nothing can shake his equanimity. When Brecht speaks of Mahagonny or of Chicago and its slaughterhouse in his plays, he is actually talking about Berlin. For him Mahagonny and Chicago were synonymous with Berlin, just as Berlin was a synonym for the modern metropolis. In his play, *In the City Jungle*, images of New York, Chicago, Detroit, and Berlin melt to form the vision of one single, enormous, man-eating Moloch.

Three Works as Resumés of an Era

If we look for parallels in the visual arts, which also represent the character of the modern metropolis and the spirit of the era when the city began to form each individual detail of human life and its art, three names come to mind—Max Beckmann, Otto Dix, and George Grosz.

There are three major works or cycles in which these artists evoke the twenties using the image of Berlin and its inhabitants, in which they capture its look, taste, and smell. They are Beckmann's *Hell*, ten oversize lithographs created in 1919 and his most important graphic work, Grosz's unfinished triptych of 1926 with the central piece *Eclipse of the Sun* and the right-hand panel *Pillars of Society*, and Dix's *Big City Triptych* of 1927–28.

In *Eclipse of the Sun* and even more so in *Pillars of Society*, Grosz draws on his numerous cycles of critical works from *Ecce homo* to *Reckoning Will Follow*. Here we encounter once again all of the types he had so cruelly and precisely depicted, the representatives of the bourgeoisie, military, church, press, and parliament, complete with their distinguishing attributes and characteristics. Whereas Grosz used his drawings to form a large tableau, Beckmann built his lithographical cycle *Hell* around the transformation of his painting *Night* into graphic form. Beckmann places his people in a cosmos of good and evil; Grosz removes them from all natural or metaphysical contexts. Beckmann saw his figures as subject to transcendent forces; in Grosz, the representatives of power play their own game and are subjected to no other rules than to those of their own class.

Like Grosz, Dix bases the panorama of his *Big City Triptych* on many individual observations; as opposed to Grosz, however, Dix's panorama is not the accusing illustrative construction of one of the era's great critics but a calm report by an eyewitness who enjoys sharp contrasts and crass confrontations and combines them with the staccato rhythms of the jazz band to form a crazy dance. Grosz's *Eclipse of the Sun* is a construct with visionary elements, Beckmann's *Hell*, and Dix's *Big City Triptych* combine events and the atmosphere of the twenties with personal experiences. The lithographs of the *Hell* cycle have been experienced and suffered right down to the last detail. The same applies to the work of Dix, particularly his *Big City Triptych*. In the same way that Beckmann showed what befell him on his visits to Berlin and how in reaction to these shocks he repeatedly tried to determine anew his place in this world, *Big City Triptych* can also be read as a chapter in Dix's biography with a tension between the dance halls and the prostitutes, the carefree amusement and confused shock.

More than any other works of their time, these three by Beckmann, Dix, and Grosz bear witness to life in Berlin in the twenties. And here Berlin is a city where life vibrated day and night, in which everything seemed possible even if there was no time for dreams. A city that produced many things but believed in very little. Art and civilization, creative forces and technical media cooperated in a new way, and during all this time an evil force was spreading and a seed germinating that would blossom into something horrific.

Notes

1. Uwe M. Schneede, ed., *Künstlerschriften der 20er Jahre*. Documents and manifestos of the Weimar Republic (Cologne, 1986) 100: Novembergruppe, newsletter of December 13, 1918.

2. Richard Huelsenbeck, *En avant dada* (Hannover/Leipzig, 1920), 20.

3. Pamphlet, "Dadaisten gegen Weimar," Berlin, February 6, 1919, reproduced in the catalog of the exhibition, "Tendencies of the Twentieth Century," (Berlin, 1977), 3/180.

4. Uwe M. Schneede, ed., *Künstlerschriften*, 154 ff.

5. Uwe M. Schneede, ed., *Künstlerschriften*, 165.

6. Franz Roh, *Nach-Expressionismus. Magischer Realismus. Probleme der neuesten europäischen Malerei* (Leipzig, 1925).

7. Quoted by Matthias Eberle, *Otto Dix und die Neue Sachlichkeit* in Chr. Joachimides, N. Rosenthal, W. Schmied, eds., *Deutsche Kunst im 20. Jahrhundert* (Munich, 1986), 447. English edition: *German Art in the 20th Century* (London/Munich, 1985).

8. Eberle, *Otto Dix*, 447.

9. George Grosz, *Statt einer Biographie* (1925) in Uwe M. Schneede, ed., *Künstlerschriften*, 62.

10. Max Beckmann, letter to Curt Valentin, February 11, 1938, Museum of Modern Art, New York, Archive Painting and Sculpture Department.

11. Oskar Schlemmer, "Das Staatliche Bauhaus in Weimar," manifestos 1923, in Uwe M. Schneede, ed., *Künstlerschriften*, 211.

12. Oskar Schlemmer, *Letters and Diaries*, Tut Schlemmer, pub. (Munich, 1958). Also see Eberhard Roters, *The Painter of the Building* (Berlin, 1965).

1. Peggy Bacon. Frenzied Effort
(The Whitney Studio Club), *1920.*
Whitney Museum of American Art,
New York.

The New York Art World During the Interwar Years

Garnett McCoy

Garnett McCoy, a graduate of the University of Virginia, served as senior curator of the Archives of American Art at the Smithsonian Institution until his retirement in 1988. His books include The Artist in America *(1967),* David Smith *(1973), and* Reliable Sources *(1987). He has written many articles and reviews on American art history and is currently editor of the* Archives of American Art Journal.

Two succeeding forms of patronage determined the development of the New York art community in the interwar years. Just as the period itself breaks neatly into two decades, each with its own distinct character, so does the artistic support system exhibit two sharply divergent patterns in the 1920s and 1930s. At precisely midpoint between the armistice in 1918 and the onset of World War II, the entire art world structure built up over a hundred years collapsed in a welter of confusion and despair. Thereafter the search for solutions to the crisis of production and consumption turned the Depression period into a massive and altogether unique experiment in public patronage.

The New York art world after the armistice took a strong interest in modernism introduced in the previous decade. A receptive mood, more hospitable to new forms of expression, became evident in the 1920s—a combination of postwar optimism, fashionable disillusionment, and eager acceptance of up-to-date cultural trends. Expanding prosperity and extensive publicity built up the market for School of Paris production, a market still heavily dependent on European, especially French, authority in art matters. The earlier triumph of Impressionism supported a growing belief among both buyers and critics that Post-Impressionism had equally lasting merit.

In 1921 the impeccably conservative Metropolitan Museum of Art sponsored a Post-Impressionist exhibition. Bending to the persuasive powers of the American painter Arthur Bowen Davies, the collectors John Quinn and Lizzie Bliss, and Bryson Burroughs, its own curator of paintings, the museum organized a show of 126 paintings representing a range of French art from Manet and Monet to Matisse and Picasso. All were borrowed from private American collections.[1] Unlike the Armory Show eight years earlier, the Metropolitan exhibition met a neutral reaction in the art press and a feeble if vituperative protest from the old guard. A pamphlet issued by the Committee of Citizens and Supporters of the Museum hurled the now familiar accusations of degeneracy, insanity, and fraudulence, and, capitalizing on the recent red scare, substituted bolshevism for anarchism; however, its anonymous character diminished its effect and exposed it to ridicule. "Its vulgarity is equalled only by its cowardice," Quinn stated in a widely published response. "No one argues with anonymous libelers."[2]

World War I had relatively little direct effect on American art, but postwar prosperity stimulated a significant expansion in the thriving New York art market. By 1919, the number of galleries handling the work of contemporary American artists had quadrupled over that of only twenty years earlier. Far from being a herald of a change or new beginning, however, the end of the war introduced an era in which continuity with the preceding decade prevailed.

In some respects, indeed, a regressive tendency is evident. The battle against convention and sterility in art having been won, the high excitement attending a rising avant-garde declined. With few exceptions, most notably that of Stuart Davis, New York artists lost interest in the outer reaches of formal or expressive experimentation and seemed content to modify and assimilate the advances recently made in Europe. The generation that came to maturity in the 1920s lacked dominant figures such as Robert Henri, Arthur B. Davies, and Alfred Stieglitz. As beneficiaries of the successful revolution, younger men and women, especially those inspired by Kenneth Hayes Miller's classes at the Art Students League, came to the fore without a strong compulsion to explore new ground. The most conspicuous aspect of the postwar period lies not in the innovative vigor of its art but rather in the active development of societies, journals, museums, collectors, and other components of the art world structure.

New artists' societies sprang up to encourage and exploit a growing public interest in contemporary art. The New Society of Artists, the Salons of America, the New Gallery, Inc., the Whitney Studio Club, and the Société Anonyme all appeared between 1918 and 1922, each including at least some representatives of what was still called "the new art." Organized chiefly to hold exhibitions of their members' work, they supplemented and broadened the more limited exposure available in commercial galleries. The New Society of Artists and the Whitney Studio Club took on a social dimension as well, although the former, the most conservative of the groups, succumbed to the institutional tendency to grow overly respectable. In an indignant letter of resignation over a restrictive ruling on dinner invitations, the modernist sculptor Elie Nadelman protested the view "that the members should not be trusted to invite their friends to the dinner given by the society on the grounds that their friends may not be desirable guests."[3]

The proliferation of art galleries that marked the immediately preceding period continued after the war. Alfred Stieglitz, unwilling to stay on the sidelines after the demise of his Gallery 291, reasserted himself and his circle with the Intimate Gallery in 1925 and expanded it in 1929 as An American Place. In 1924, the German dealer J. B. Neumann opened the New Art Circle, where he promoted both German and American modern artists. Edith Halpert's Downtown Gallery began operations in 1926 with a stable of progressive Americans and remained a major force in New York until well into the 1960s.

One decided change that did take place after the war was the shift in leadership away from artists and toward patrons, dealers, and writers. Ten years earlier, the dominant figures of the New York art world were men such as William Merritt Chase, Robert Henri, and Arthur Davies—charismatic figures who attracted followers, impressed collectors, and knew how to manipulate the art press. The success of Henri and Davies's campaign to break the power of the National Academy of Design and bring new exhibiting opportunities to younger artists had the unintended effect of giving commercial galleries new power in the art community. Modernism itself, with all its attendant publicity, inspired growing public interest in contemporary art while wartime and postwar prosperity brought an expanded class of collectors into the market. As the number of galleries grew—at least a dozen were established between 1912 and 1920 and several more in the ensuing decade[4]— and new buyers appeared, art critics increased their influence as well. The vacuum created by the absence of commanding

leading artists among the rising generation was filled by a group of patrons whose activities and benefactions set the direction of the New York art world in the postwar period.

Unlike such energetic collectors as Quinn and Isabella Stewart Gardner, these new patrons aspired to roles larger than that of merely acquiring works of art and helping individual artists. Several were themselves moderately talented artists. Hamilton Easter Field, heir to a modest fortune, studied in Paris, fell under Picasso's sway, conducted classes, established a gallery, painted, collected, wrote criticism, contributed to the support of several artists, and served on the board of the Society of Independent Artists.[5] A Quaker and an incurable idealist, he considered the society's practice of giving special notice to its prominent participants in publicity releases a denial of egalitarian principles. After arguing the point for several years, he withdrew and founded a rival group, the Salon of America, which held annual exhibitions of work by artists with advanced views.

In 1920 Field launched *The Arts*, a monthly journal of opinion and reviews which soon attracted a considerable audience among artists and the art public. The magazine, much of it written by Field himself, affected a tone of objectivity and evenhanded treatment toward the various stylistic tendencies, but in fact it favored a cautious form of modernism represented by Cézanne and Picasso and by such Americans as Davies and John Marin. The more retrograde academic work on the one hand and nonobjective efforts on the other were simply ignored.

When Field died unexpectedly in 1922, *The Arts* fell into the hands of one of its contributors, Forbes Watson, who persuaded Gertrude Vanderbilt Whitney to give it financial backing. With her seemingly inexhaustible funds and matching willingness to spend them in support of American art, Whitney was already the most open-handed patron in the city. Like Field, she was a working artist, in her case a sculptor, and in her earlier years, she dabbled in bohemianism while maintaining her high-society respectability. Having access to two fortunes, she indulged an impulse to charity on a grand scale. She bought and commissioned works of art, subsidized artists, and turned her Greenwich Village studio into a club and exhibition center.[6] After 1917, she became the chief financial supporter of the Society of Independent Artists. In an inspired act of perceptive judgment, she hired the formidably self-assured Juliana Force as her secretary and general assistant, and later appointed her as her deputy in the handling of art-related activities. Thereafter, in all but matters of critical importance, Force made the decisions and Whitney signed the checks.[7]

The Whitney Studio Club, an organization formed by Whitney in 1918 and directed by Force, became their most active medium of patronage. It held exhibitions of work by its members, primarily young artists, over the next ten years. Membership was relatively open, although applicants had to meet Force's approval. The club's exhibitions, which always received prominent advertising and favorable notices in *The Arts*, promoted advanced, but not too advanced, tendencies.

Stuart Davis was given a retrospective show in 1926, but the general tone was dominated by such established figures as Edward Hopper, Glenn Coleman, and, among the rising generation, Alexander Brook, Yasuo Kuniyoshi, and Reginald Marsh. Force bought several works from each exhibition to add to Whitney's collection, which eventually became the basis of the Whitney Museum of American Art.[8]

Katherine Dreier, another artist-patron, had a more single-minded aim—the social and spiritual elevation of the American public through modern art. A propagandist rather than a philanthropist, she passionately believed in the uplifting quality of the school of Paris and later of the German and Russian avant-garde. Her family background—prosperous, German-American, and politically progressive—gave her the financial security, independent mind, and stubborn determination she needed to pursue her goal. A strong association with the Theosophical Society and with Marcel Duchamp influenced her views on modernism's regenerative potential. Lacking Whitney's vast resources, she concentrated on a single venture, the Société Anonyme, an organization she founded in 1920 with advice and help from Duchamp and Man Ray. Their own interests were reflected in its first large exhibition, a Dadaist show, but when they left the country soon afterward, she turned her attention to Kandinsky and constructivism. The Société Anonyme's collection, actually Dreier's own, never occupied more than two or three rented rooms, although it sometimes had the use of larger gallery or museum space. Its program consisted chiefly of occasional lectures, a few publications, and a series of loan exhibitions. One notable accomplishment was a large and surprisingly comprehensive international show of current European and American artistic trends, the most important one since the Armory Show. Held in 1927 at the Brooklyn Museum, it failed to achieve the impact its quality deserved because the location was considered inconvenient.[9]

From the beginning of her enterprise, Dreier hoped to turn the Société Anonyme into a museum of modern art. She could not support such an institution alone, however, and her dictatorial behavior and unconventional views prevented cooperation from richer, more staid patrons. After the Brooklyn show, her organization suffered a prolonged decline. In the end, she donated the collection to Yale University.[10]

The idea of a public museum devoted to contemporary art gained new adherents with the dispersal of Quinn's immense collection in a series of auction sales in 1926. Forbes Watson, who had intermittently suggested such an institution in *The Arts* for several years, used the occasion to renew the campaign. "Heaven send New York a museum of modern art, so that folks may see what is going on in the world," he wrote in the May 1926 issue.[11] His editorials were supported by the critic Henry McBride, a champion of modernism, in his *Dial* and *New York Sun* columns after the Société Anonyme's Brooklyn show. Together, they persuaded the art writer and collector A. E. Gallatin to give his substantial Post-Impressionist and Cubist collection to New York University in 1927 as the Gallery (later the Museum) of Living Art.[12] While it was well maintained and open to the public with no admission fee,

2

3

2. Edward Hopper. Night Windows, *1928.* The Museum of Modern Art, New York. Gift of John Hay Whitney.

3. Yasuo Kuniyoshi. Nude, *1929.* Hirshhorn Museum and Sculpture Garden, Wahington, D.C.

4

5

4. *Stuart Davis.* Egg Beater,
Number 2, *1927.* Whitney
Museum of American Art, New
York.

5. *Louis Guglielmi.* Wedding in
South Street, *1936.* Extended loan
to the Museum of Modern Art, New
York, from the United States WPA
Program.

its limited scope and academic setting failed to satisfy what
had by then become a burgeoning movement.

By the time the Gallery of Living Art opened, the opposition to
modernism had little remaining force. "Modern art has made
phenomenal progress toward universal popularity," Watson
wrote. "In the field of pure painting and sculpture the liberals
are winning the honors." He also touched on sure proof that
the "new art " had become fashionable.

Not only has the business of many galleries been transformed in
character and the great department stores begun to be "art conscious"—the whole advertising world pours out its heart in modernistic printing and designs. Small powers of discernment are required to trace the derivation of the modernism which had spread
through the decorative trades and advertising. In color, texture and
design, it has come from modern painting and modern sculpture.[13]

In 1929 the requisite combination of wealth, respectability,
and commitment came together when Lizzie Bliss, long a willing slave to Davies's persuasive powers, discussed the subject
of a museum during a chance meeting abroad with Mrs. John
D. Rockefeller, who then took it up with another dowager, Mrs.
Cornelius J. Sullivan. All three women were collectors of Post-
Impressionist work and all were eager to have their judgment
confirmed by the authority a museum could provide. On their
return to New York, they formed a committee that included the
art historian and Harvard professor Paul J. Sachs, whose
banking family background gave him added solidity. This
group agreed to establish a museum to be called the Museum
of Modern Art, and on Sachs's recommendation it hired his
former student Alfred H. Barr, Jr., to serve as director. The
first exhibition, a loan show of works by Cézanne, Gauguin,
Seurat, and Van Gogh, opened in November 1929 in temporary quarters.[14] Lloyd Goodrich observed in a review the following month that the museum represented for America "the
first apotheosis of modernism and its acceptance by respectable society."[15]

Earlier that same year, Whitney, increasingly occupied by
her society responsibilities and lacking sufficient exhibition
space, decided to abandon her active role in the art community. Having already transformed the Whitney Studio Club into
the less participatory Whitney Studio Galleries and now willing to give that up as well, she offered her entire collection of
more than six hundred works by American artists to the Metropolitan Museum. At a meeting with Force, the director rejected it out of hand. That very afternoon the two furiously indignant women began to plan their own museum. They announced their intentions at a press conference on January 3,
1930, less than two months after the opening of the Museum of
Modern Art, but organizational and building delays postponed
the museum's official inauguration to November 1931.[16]

The economic depression that followed the stock market crash
of 1929 had a shattering impact on the New York art community. Its most direct consequence, the collapse of the market
for works by living artists, threatened to destroy the liveli-
hoods and aspirations of an entire generation of young
painters and sculptors."I am stranded in Gloucester," Stuart
Davis wrote his dealer on September 20, 1933. "I have every

360

respect for the fact that your gallery is doing very little business and that it is impossible for you to make any payments. However, if you can develop some dough it is a matter of the first importance to me."[17] The indirect effects of the Depression were complex and far-reaching. Artists began to feel a new sense of identification with the society at large and especially with people suffering from unemployment and privation. "The early 1930s were coldly sobering years," the painter Louis Guglielmi wrote later. "Faced with the terror of the realities of the day, [the artist] could no longer justify the shaky theory of individualism and the role of spectator. . . . The time has come when painters are returning to the life of the people once again and by so doing are absorbing the richness, the vitality, and the lusty healthiness inherent in the people.[18]

In these circumstances, an accessible art of social content reflecting current realities took on new significance. Urban and industrial themes, depictions of downcast or defiant victims of capitalism's dislocations, and scenes of oppression and social conflict expressed artists' efforts to confirm their solidarity with the working class. Most of them pursued variations on a realist style as the best way to project meaning and commitment to an audience lacking aesthetic sophistication. Meyer Schapiro, then in a high Marxist phase and a lecturer at the radical John Reed Club and writer for the Artists' Union journal *Art Front*, promoted this view in 1936:

Before the levels of art which the artist values can become available to the masses of people, two conditions must be fulfilled—that the art embody a content and achieve qualities accessible to the masses of the people, [and] that the people control the means of production and attain a standard of living and a level of culture such that the enjoyment of art of a high quality becomes an important part of their life.[19]

Mounting anger, bewilderment, and frustration drove the art world to the political left in the years after 1929. Even before the Depression's onset, indications of such a movement were apparent. The *New Masses* magazine began publication in 1926 as a Comunist Party cultural organization, with sharp satirical cartoons and decorative illustrations by William Gropper, Hugo Gellert, Louis Lozowick, Glenn Coleman, Stuart Davis, Peggy Bacon, and Adolf Dehn, George Grosz's leading American disciple. Indeed, socialist and anarchist sympathies were held by a number of artists as far back as the early part of the century, an aspect of the more general bohemian culture that flourished in Greenwich Village before and during the war. *The Masses* and its successor, the *Liberator*, provided an outlet for artists with a social conscience in those years, and the Peoples Art Guild of 1915 and 1916 made a valiant attempt to promote a more democratic market than the one served by commercial galleries.

The nature of the current crisis, however, called for different kinds of efforts. Deep political discontent and growing demands for explanations and solutions provided an ideal climate for the views offered by the John Reed Club, founded in the fall of 1929 by a group of writers and artists associated with the *New Masses* and named after the famous journalist,

poet, and revolutionary who had died in Moscow eight years earlier. Several of its artist members were already committed radicals in the days of the old *Masses* and *Liberator*, and others such as Anton Refregier and Raphael Soyer were younger converts. They soon created an art school, organized thematic exhibitions open to the public, and sponsored lectures and discussion groups on the theory and practice of art and art history from a Marxist point of view.[20] With rapidly growing numbers of disillusioned artists in search of a solution to their plight, the club's approach attracted widespread attention. Its stimulating educational programs and its confident belief in a socialist future in which artists would be treated with honor and respect appealed to men and women eager to learn and willing to act. On his return to New York from Europe in 1931 the young painter Max Spivak heard about the new organization. "People who were more left had joined the John Reed Club," he recalled later. "They were much more socially aware, they had meetings there. There were fights and arguments and so forth in the club. This attracted you to the fact that something was happening."[21]

True to the Marxist belief in the necessity of both theory and practice, members of the club formed special rallying groups. When Diego Rivera's Rockefeller Center mural was destroyed in 1934 because it included a portrait of Lenin, the Artists Committee for Action organized protests. Led by Hugo Gellert and Stuart Davis, the committee also agitated for a New York municipal art gallery to be controlled by artists rather than by a committee of patrons and officials. Another spin-off, the Unemployed Artists' Group, successfully demanded publicly funded employment programs for artists. The Unemployed Artists' Group also called for expanded, more democratic projects and then reorganized itself as the Artists' Union to protect the rights of the employed.[22]

Organized activity became a normal condition for many New York artists. The Artists' Union, a much broader and less explicitly ideological organization than the John Reed Club, held exhibitions and discussions. It marched under its own banners in May Day parades, distributed leaflets, held innumerable meetings, passed stern resolutions, and took to the streets at every threat to the federal art programs. Its monthly *Art Front*, one of the best art magazines of the period, carried articles by a remarkable array of talented figures, including Meyer Schapiro, Harold Rosenberg, Stuart Davis, Philip Evergood, Max Weber, and Fernand Léger. The Artists' Union swiftly gained strength, established branches throughout the country, and remained an active presence in the art community for the rest of the decade.[23] As one youthful participant described it years later:

You belonged [to the Artists' Union] simply because issues that were vital to your well being and your job were discussed there and it was a great place because it was full of artists. It was a mixture of tremendous seriousness, political awareness, great leadership and very unexpected things that would happen. You went to a meeting very innocently . . . and suddenly you found that your were in a sit-in and that you were going to be there for two days. It was all very exciting and you had the feeling that you were changing the world.

The Artists' Union was only partially given over to a discussion of job issues. There were also lecturers and discussion groups that were associated with the Union. . . . It was always such a great pleasure to go. You met before the meeting, you had the meeting and you discussed business, and then you went to a cafeteria to have coffee and to argue some more. It was marvelous.[24]

The John Reed Club's final achievement was the creation of the American Artists' Congress in late 1935. Unlike the Artists' Union, essentially a pressure group for job protection, the congress stood for more abstract ideas—peace, cultural freedom, antifascism. As a Popular Front organization representing the broadest possible coalition of liberal and radical elements, it reflected the Communist International's turn from a revolutionary policy to one of cooperation with all democratic forces in the common struggle against fascism. American artists were well aware of the fate their German colleagues had suffered under the Nazi regime and were equally conscious of the potential threat to artistic freedom posed by powerful reactionary movements in America. The Artists' Congress was designed to draw in prominent figures whose standing would lend weight and substance to the cause.

The first meeting of the congress, held at Town Hall in February 1936, was an unqualified success. About 360 members heard papers given by Lewis Mumford, Rockwell Kent, Margaret Bourke-White, Paul Manship, Meyer Schapiro, José Clemente Orozco, and twenty-nine others. They passed resolutions and established an executive committee to carry out policy and plan future activities. Stuart Davis, its chief organizer and chairman, served as national secretary for the next four years.[25]

The federal government's art projects during the Depression filled the vacuum created by the collapse of the art market. Between 1933 and 1943, a series of agencies assured the continuation of art production by paying artists to work at their trades. Well over two thousand artists working in all media and every stylistic persuasion received a small but living wage together with the supplies they needed and the independence they craved. In effect, the state established itself as an art patron on a grand scale. Hundreds of public buildings throughout the city, from prisons to schools to hospitals, acquired well-executed murals, sculpture, easel paintings, prints, and craft objects. If the quality was inconsistent, the subject matter often pedestrian, and the manner of expression sometimes unadventurous, the wholesale exercise in public art consumption nevertheless achieved impressive results. By 1943, when the last project closed down, some 300 murals, 2,000 pieces of sculpture, 12,000 paintings in oil, watercolor, gouache, and pastel, and 7,500 prints had been completed in New York alone. In addition to creative productivity, an ambitious educational program was pursued through the organization of community art centers, innumerable art classes, and hundreds of exhibitions held at schools, libraries, union halls, museums, galleries, hospitals, and prisons.[26]

The first of these ventures, the Public Works of Art Project (PWAP), began in December 1933 and lasted just six months. Experimental in nature and regarded as a purely temporary expedient, artist selections were based on a quota system and

the judgment of advisory committees. With four thousand applicants for New York's quota of five hundred openings and with the strong-minded Juliana Force of the Whitney Museum in charge there, an inevitable bias in favor of reputable figures took place. Administrators in both Washington and New York saw ability and talent, as well as need, as the standard to uphold. As Edward Bruce, director of the PWAP, stated, "One phase of this work, of course, is to put men to work, but I think that we ought all remember that we are putting artists to work and not trying to make artists out of bums."[27]

With an eye to public acceptance for such a novel use of taxpayers' money, Bruce and his assistants took a cautious approach to subject matter and style, an attitude faithfully followed by Force. A successful businessman turned landscape painter, Bruce favored representational work and had little sympathy for experimental work. Abstract artists such as Byron Browne found themselves frozen out. "The PWAP does not help the real creative artist," he wrote, "In the first place the subject matter is dictated to the artist. As my work contains little or no emphasis on subject matter, I was ignored for a long time after the PWAP began to function and then cut off after a period of four weeks."[28]

Washington's insistence on quality and prudence soon came into conflict with the widespread view among New York artists that the PWAP was primarily a relief program, an opinion articulated and acted on by the Unemployed Artists' Group. When the project closed in June of 1934, its legacy comprised several hundred works of art, a precedent for further government action, a rising chorus of demands for increased employment and greater freedom of expression, and a much strengthened Artists' Union.

An altogether different kind of program, the Treasury Department's Section of Painting and Sculpture, began in October 1934. This too fell under the direction of Edward Bruce. Operating with a system of juries and competitive awards, this program conformed to Bruce's penchant for decorating new federal buildings—chiefly post offices—with murals and sculpture of assured quality and safe subject matter, while avoiding uncongenial paintings by abstract artists. Relatively few works sponsored by the section were undertaken in New York but nearly three hundred local artists received commissions to embellish buildings in other parts of the country. The Treasury Department also established the Treasury Relief Art Project as a supplementary venture for the decoration of the older federal structures. Its most successful accomplishment in New York was a series of custom house murals painted by Reginald Marsh.

The Federal Art Project, one of several cultural agencies of the Works Progress Administration (WPA), was by far the largest and best-known example of government art sponsorship during the Depression. At its peak in 1936, it employed more than five thousand artists throughout the nation, of whom nearly half were in New York City. Its subdivisions included art production in all media, a design laboratory, photography workshops, community art centers, and a visual recording of American crafts design extending back to the eighteenth cen-

6

7

6. Reginald Marsh. The Coast Guard Cutter "Calumet" Meeting the "Washington." *Study for mural in the Custom House, New York City, 1937.* National Museum of American Art, Smithsonian Institution, Washington, D.C.

7. Moses Soyer. Artists on the WPA, *1935.* National Museum of American Art, Smithsonian Institution, Washington, D.C.

tury. This ambitious undertaking, an immense expansion of the short-lived PWAP, was explicitly conceived and carried out as a relief project to provide work for indigent artists, but its scope greatly exceeded such a mechanical formula. It became instead a concerted effort to raise public art consciousness on a national scale. As its director, Holger Cahill, wrote, "The aim of the project will be to work toward an integration of the arts with daily life of the community, and an integration of the fine arts and practical arts."[29]

This democratic, even populist conception reflected the basic New Deal impulse as well as Cahill's own vision of the role of art in society. A writer, exhibition organizer, and authority on American folk art, he had close personal relations with many New York artists and a clear understanding of their needs. The Federal Art Project in New York was headed by Audrey McMahon of the College Art Association staff, which had been administering state and federal relief funds. Like Force, McMahon was a strong, determined administrator but had a more evenhanded approach and better political skills.

Project artists in New York received an average pay of twenty-five dollars a week. Easel painters were expected to turn in a finished product every few weeks. Working conditions under the Federal Art Project were remarkably benign considering the fact that in New York at least, the project authorities exercised minimal supervision, took an enlightened view of artistic freedom, and conscientiously avoided favoritism.[30]

Such a satisfactory arrangement did not last. Within a few months, a gathering conservative assault on the WPA found expression in newspaper attacks on, among other things, artists living on taxpayers' money and painting subversive pictures. In an effort to deflect congressional criticism, the entire WPA operation in New York was placed in the hands of Colonel Brehon Somervell, whose military training and prejudices were ill-suited to dealing with a highly politicized art community. A series of reductions in project funding met excited resistance among artists led by a militant Artists' Union, which organized work stoppages, picket lines, and sit-ins. McMahon found herself caught in the middle:

I walked this tightrope. I was a buffer state between these two quantities. The purely administrative which had very little concept as to what we were really about . . . and the artists who wanted more, more, more, more and when the Artists' Union got moving they pressured me and I was a buffer state between them and the administrator because . . . if they had gotten at him, since he didn't know what they were talking about at all, they would have been clobbered.[31]

In 1939 and 1940, congressional investigators and FBI agents conducted interrogations to gather information on union membership and political views. A sister agency, the Federal Theater Project, came to an end in 1931, a victim of charges of left-wing propaganda, but the Federal Art Project survived, albeit on a much reduced basis, until 1943. A final report outlined its achievements in New York:

Some 200 murals have been allocated to hospitals, schools, colleges, libraries, armories, court houses, and penal and welfare institutions.

Approximately 2,100 individual pieces of sculpture, both free standing and architectural, were produced . . . and allocated to various public institutions. Over 12,000 oils, watercolors, gouaches, and pastels, more than 75,000 prints from 3,000 original plates, 14,670 poster designs printed in 750,000 copies per year, and over 6,000 plates of the Index of American Design were produced and allocated.[32]

In the postwar period, the New Deal art projects were harshly criticized for the low-quality work and emphasis on socially conscious expression in the work produced and for operational bureaucracy in the programs themselves. Many of the participating artists looked back with mixed feelings—on the one hand a desire to forget the fact that they had been recipients of relief funds and on the other a nostalgia for the collective sense of purposefulness and gratitude for the opportunities offered. As Cahill wrote in response to an attack made in 1954:

My decision to try to give you another angle was made after a recent conversation I had with Willem de Kooning. When I read Bill your sentence (without naming the source) "From the point of view of quality, the results of federal patronage of the arts were negligible," he replied at once the writer "Vas all vett," with strong Dutch emphasis. Then he told me of his own experience on the project. He was then a resident alien and was employed for a year until Congress passed a law barring alien employment. . . . The single year of painting made him determined to give up working for decorators and devote himself exclusively to painting, no matter how difficult. He says the project gave him the courage to do that and made him, for the first time, feel that he was a part of American life and that he had something valuable to contribute.[33]

In New York City, the Federal Art Project under McMahon imposed no rules on subject matter or style. Abstract easel paintings, sculpture, prints, and even murals were produced and accepted as readily, if not as frequently, as those done with a traditional or modified realist approach. Indeed, despite the greater popularity of the latter among both artists and public, the modernist impulse continued to thrive throughout the decade. Jan Matulka at the Art Students League and Hans Hofmann at his own school exerted a strong influence on dozens of students attracted to abstract art, and Stuart Davis and John Graham persuasively asserted its validity as the only appropriate form of twentieth-century expression. Neither camp respected the other's position; each accused the other of holding reactionary views. Debates and polemics—sharp but not overtly hostile—were part of the discourse of the period, featured at Artists' Union discussions and in the pages of *Art Front*. But through their organizations, the antagonists presented a united front in the face of threats to job security and freedom of expression.

A resurgence of modernism occurred in 1937 with the formation of a coherent group of nonobjective painters and sculptors, the American Abstract Artists. Its organization came as a reaction to two large-scale abstract art exhibitions in New York—a 1935 Whitney Museum show of abstract work by Americans, most of whom were regarded by pure abstractionists as "stalled in various ill digested ferments of impressionism, expressionism, and half-hearted cubism," and a 1936

Museum of Modern Art exhibition, "Cubism and Abstract Art," which excluded Americans.[34]

The American Abstract Artists held its first show in 1937 and annually thereafter. By 1939, it had fifty-three members, including Josef Albers, A. E. Gallatin, Balcomb Greene, Ibram Lassaw, Ad Reinhardt, David Smith, and Vaclav Vytlacil. Many had studied with Hans Hofmann, and several played a role in a concerted attack on Communist influence in the American Artists' Congress.

The strains endured by the Popular Front alliance reached a crisis with the Nazi-Soviet Pact of August 1939. Liberals were thrown into a welter of confusion and disillusionment, and Communists and their loyal followers were forced into a defensive stance that effectively isolated them from mainstream opinion. A small but energetic group of Trotskyists and anti-Communist liberals seized the opportunity to destroy party influence in its chief center of strength, the Artists' Congress. They were abetted in this effort by other artists who felt constrained by the continuing hold of social realism on the art expression of the time. Led by Ilya Bolotowsky and the art historian Meyer Schapiro, the dissidents organized themselves as a caucus or faction within the congress and demanded that the leadership state its position on the war. At a raucous meeting held in April 1940, the executive board set forth a policy of neutrality, and when the attending members approved it by a large majority, the opponents resigned in a body. So did Stuart Davis, the executive secretary, followed by such other prominent but inactive figures as George Biddle, William Zorach, and Lewis Mumford. The congress lasted another three years, but its vitality and sense of purpose were gone. The socially conscious approach to art that was such a conspicuous feature of the New York art world throughout the 1930s never recovered.[35]

Notes

1. Russell Lynes, *Good Old Modern* (New York: Atheneum, 1973), 40–41.
2. Ibid., 45.
3. Elie Nadelman to the New Society of Artists, n.d. Geri Melchers Papers, microfilm roll 1182, Archives of American Art, Smithsonian Institution.
4. *American Art Annual* (Washington, D.C.: American Federation of Arts, 1912–20).
5. Henry McBride, "Hamilton Easter Field's Career," *The Arts* 3 (January 1923): 3.
6. B. H. Friedman, *Gertrude Vanderbilt Whitney* (New York: Doubleday & Co., 1978).
7. *Juliana Force and American Art* (New York: Whitney Museum of American Art, 1949).
8. Ibid. See 64–66 for a list of exhibitions held by the Whitney Studios (1914–27), the Whitney Studio Club (1918–28), the Whitney Studio Galleries (1928–30), and the Whitney Museum of American Art (1931–49).
9. Ruth Louise Bohan, "The Société Anonyme's Brooklyn Exhibition, 1926–1927: Katherine Sophie Dreier and the Promotion of Modern Art in America" (Ph.D. dissertation, University of Maryland, 1980).
10. Ibid., 290.
11. Forbes Watson, Editorial, *The Arts* 9 (May 1926): 240.
12. Watson, Editorial, *The Arts* 12 (November 1927): 239.
13. Watson, Editorial, *The Arts* 12 (December 1927): 293.
14. Russell Lynes, *Good Old Modern*, 60.
15. Quoted in Ibid., 57.
16. *Juliana Force and American Art*, 23–24.
17. Stuart Davis to Edith Halpert, 10 September, 1933, Downtown Gallery Papers, Archives of American Art, Smithsonian Institution.
18. Louis Guglielmi, "After the Locusts," in *Art for the Millions: Essays from the 1930s by Artists and Administrators of the WPA Federal Art Project*, Francis V. O'Connor, ed. (Greenwich, Conn.: New York Graphic Society, 1973), 113.
19. Meyer Schapiro, "Public Use of Art," *Art Front* 2 (July–August 1936): 5.
20. Virginia Marquardt, "*New Masses* and John Reed Club Artists, 1926–1936: Evolution of Ideology, Subject Matter, and Style," *The Journal of Decorative and Propaganda Arts* 12 (Spring 1989): 70–72.
21. Max Spivak, *tape-recorded interview*, n.d., 18. Archives of American Art, Smithsonian Institution.
22. Gerald Monroe, "Artists as Militant Trade Union Workers during the Great Depression," *Archives of American Art Journal* 14 (1974): 7–10.
23. Patricia Hills, *Social Concern and Urban Realism: American Painting of the 1930s* (Boston: Boston University Art Gallery, 1983), 16.
24. Abram Lerner, *Tape-recorded interview*, December 1975, 27–30. Archives of American Art, Smithsonian Institution.
25. Mathew Baigell and Julia Williams, eds., *Artists Against War and Fascism: Papers of the First American Artists' Congress* (New Brunswick, N.J.: Rutgers University Press, 1986).
26. Francis V. O'Connor, *Federal Art Patronage: 1933 to 1943* (College Park, Md.: University of Maryland, 1966).
27. Quoted in Francis V. O'Connor, "The New Deal Art Projects in New York," *American Art Journal* 1 (Fall 1969): 59.
28. Quoted in Ibid., 68.
29. Ibid., 70–72.
30. Quoted in Ibid., 63.
31. Richard D. McKinzie, *The New Deal for Artists* (Princeton, N.J.: Princeton University Press, 1973), 105.
32. Audrey McMahon, *Tape-recorded interview*, November 1964, 17, Archives of American Art, Smithsonian Institution.
33. Quoted in O'Connor, "New Deal Art Projects," 78.
34. Holger Cahill to Edgar Richardson, June 30, 1954, in "Document," *Archives of American Art Journal* 24 (1984): 22.
35. George L. K. Morris, "The American Abstract Artists," *American Abstract Artists 1939* (1939).
36. Garnett McCoy, "The Rise and Fall of the American Artists' Congress," *Prospects* 13 (1989): 336–37.

1. *Michael Blackwood, 1986.*

Berlin and New York: A Personal Involvement

Michael Blackwood

Michael Blackwood was born in Breslau and moved to Berlin with his family in 1936. In 1949 they immigrated to the United States and settled in New York. He began work on his first documentary film, Broadway Express, *in 1957 and was a producer and a director for German Television between 1961 and 1965. On his return to New York, he founded his own documentary film production company to make films about cultural and social issues. In 1970, he began an open-ended series of documentaries about contemporary art and artists and later expanded the series to include architecture, dance, and music.*

In 1936 I arrived in Berlin at the age of two, from Breslau, with my parents of course. Breslau had traditionally provided fresh blood for Berlin. Every fourth successful Berliner was from Breslau, just as every fourth New Yorker is from New Jersey or the Midwest. Berlin had been the place of the future ever since the 1830s, the same time New York was beginning its golden age. So, migrating to Berlin was not unusual, except that in 1936, at least for my parents, it had a very different meaning. Hitler's regime was three years old and life in the provincial cities of Germany had become unbearable for anyone who was either opposed to the regime or Jewish. Since people greet each other rather obsessively in Germany, there was a constant refrain of "Heil Hitler." While at that time no one could imagine the future Holocaust, the incessant Heil Hitlers alone seemed oppressive. And anyone who did not participate became suspect. In Berlin, Heil Hitlers were exchanged only among functionaries and at government offices. Ordinary people still said "Morgen" or "Mahlzeit," as they always had, being genuine big-city folks, although one relative reported to my freshly arrived parents that the delivery boy at Passover clicked his heels at their door with a friendly smile, saying crisply, "Heil Hitler, I am bringing the matzohs." Many people flocked to Berlin in those days, not so much because it had a future but as a last refuge. In 1936 Berlin was in the throes of the Olympic Games. To real Berliners, Jesse Owens was the hero of the season, Hitler, I am sure, much less so, even though these were still relatively harmless times. Later, during the years of destruction from the air, his popularity in Berlin diminished much more.

My parents settled in and so did I. I remember getting lost in our cavernous basement (which later protected us during the Allied air raids and the final assault on Berlin by the Russians) and taking walks in the Tiergarten with my Jewish grandmother (my father's mother). My mother's parents were not Jewish, an important factor for future survival, as the Nazis were obsessed with the religion of one's grandparents—the fewer Jewish, the better off you were. Later, in 1938, my mother traveled to Brazil for six months to see whether we might be able to retreat there, *im Falle eines Falles* (in case of the worst). I remember walking with my father in Kurfurstendamm, looking at the many splendid neon advertisements and movie marquees. On the surface, the old glitter of pre-Nazi times was still there, but it must have been a pretty hopeless time, no sign of a brighter future except for those who actually believed in Hitler. Things in New York were not all roses either, because of the Depression. The future of both cities was uncertain, something that changed soon thereafter due to political decisions made in Berlin—Germany's attack on Europe and later its declaration of war on the United States. New York became one of the biggest centers of the war effort.

My mother returned in 1939, and soon it was too late to leave. My Jewish grandmother, suffering from senility, was unwanted by Brazil or any other country that still offered Jews a possible haven (Cuba, Dominican Republic, Shanghai, etc., but not the U.S., Canada, Australia, or any other English-speaking country). My father was not willing to leave her behind and so unwittingly risked the life of his family, not to mention his own.

2

3

2. *Blackwood at the Berlin Zoo,*
1938.

3. *Blackwood at Timmendorfer*
Strand, 1940.

I inherited heaps of wonderful toys from the children of our friends and relatives who were departing. Naturally, toys had to stay behind, as did books and other cultural baggage. In 1940 my mother arranged to have me baptized into the Lutheran Church by Father Pfarrer Gruber. Although this was a highly illegal act under the 1935 Nuremberg Laws, she thought that it might help me. I remember my baptism in the then still intact Emperor William Memorial Church, and I also remember the brave Pfarrer Gruber who fortunately survived the war. While the baptism did not change my legal status, as I was still considered Jewish because I did not receive this baptism before the Nuremberg Laws went into effect in 1935, it helped being in contact with the church, which had established a small network of homes for children of mixed marriages. One of them was at the Baltic Sea; soon after my baptism my mother persuaded me to accept this opportunity for a vacation, "a delightful summer camp for kids." She did not tell me that she was, in fact, hiding me from the Gestapo. With every succeeding war year, I went for longer and longer periods. In the fall of 1940, I started going to the local *Volksschule* (public school) at Joachimstalerstrasse, another illegal situation that my mother perpetrated by simply registering me as someone whose religion is "mosaisch," another way of saying "Jewish" but a term not commonly known in Germany. At least not at that school, where no one blinked an eye at this description. Had she written "Jewish," they would have directed her to take me across the street, where the only Jewish school in Berlin was located. Of course all the children and youngsters attending that school were in constant danger of being picked up by the Gestapo. For my mother, breaking the law seemed like the smaller risk.

In 1941, the war came to Charlottenburg, where we lived. In Carmerstrasse, off Savignyplatz, a building received a direct hit and burned to the ground. I stood there watching all day, and I remember the skeptical faces of the Berliners who watched with me. While they might have been misled by Hitler and his henchmen to believe that Germany could conquer the world, in Carmerstrasse they began to understand that the world would not let itself be conquered. The future seemed very bleak; by 1942, it was even bleaker.

The schools were semiclosed that year, since most kids and teachers had been sent to the countryside for the remainder of the war as air raids, now also in broad daylight, made life in Berlin quite dangerous. I do not know why I was allowed to continue at the school in Joachimstalerstrasse, because I did not qualify for evacuation to the country. Maybe they really thought that being mosaisch was being a member of some strange but permitted cult. School consisted of *Appell* which meant endless singing of the patriotic Nazi song material (I remember aping my fellow classmates when we raised our right arms in the Nazi salute by putting my left hand under my outstretched right arm to prevent it from falling down in exhaustion). We also had to write *Aufsätze* (compositions); one had as its theme "Der Fuhrer und die deutsche Reichspost" ("Hitler and the Postal Service"). Also we were asked to draw heroic action scenes from the front lines, based on reports in newspapers. My mother helped me accomplish these during endless air raids at night. Often we would not go down to the basement and instead huddled around a candle in the darkened kitchen. Later this became impossible, and we even went to the basement of a larger office building farther down on Uhlandstrasse, which was much more substantial and provided better shelter.

That year a children's bunker was instituted by either the city or the Hitler Youth Organization in a huge office complex named after Hermann Göring near the Tiergarten S-Bahn station. Here youngsters were supposed to be able to sleep through the air raids, protected by thick concrete reinforcements and antiaircraft batteries on the roof. I went there for about two weeks but did not like the authoritarian atmosphere. One had to be there at 6 PM and strip for a quick physical examination (they wanted to avoid epidemics). The bunker was for kids six to sixteen years of age, boys and girls, and while I was intrigued by the bared female forms, I was also worried about being teased for my different looking penis. (My parents had never gone into much detail with me about Jewish customs in order not to make me self-conscious and in hopes that I would have a normal everyday life.) Although the examining doctors wore SS uniforms under their white hospital garb and the nurses were also either military or otherwise quite official, no one ever questioned me about my penis for political or any other reasons. Neither did my fellow bunkermates. After a quick, free dinner, it was bedtime in the double-decker dormitories, so that we would be well asleep by the time the air raids started, usually around 9 or 10 PM.

It was a generally out-of-control scene. The younger kids played crazy games, climbing around and tricking each other, while the older kids fornicated. We indeed did not have to worry about the air raids, although no one could bear the rumble of bombs and antiaircraft fire in the roof. This all changed one night when an immense attack befell Berlin, which raised such a fire cloud over the city that the light of day was almost invisible the next morning. We all lay in our beds sobbing, mortified by the continuous thunder of heavy antiaircraft fire and exploding bombs. No one was allowed to go home in the morning unless he or she was picked up by a relative or neighbor, as there was the fear that many people had not survived this raid. In fact quite a few Berliners died that night. I was incredibly relieved when I saw my father's smiling but ashen face in the doorway around 10 AM, and we walked across Tiergarten und Bahnhof Zoo to our building, which was unharmed. The sky over the entire city was bright red and black from all the fires and smoke. The streets were littered with the debris from damaged dwellings, felled trees, fragments of bombs, parts of shot-down planes, and whole sections of collapsed buildings. Ever since that day I had a sense of privilege to be able to witness the destruction of one of the major cities of the world. Berlin's future was rapidly sinking below zero, while New York's future must have been rising in those days a notch up for each one that Berlin's dropped.

In July 1942, a week before my eighth birthday, a new member joined our family. I was excited to inspect my baby brother at Martin Luther hospital in Berlin, where he was baptized without questions asked the day after his birth. My mother chose Christian as his name for extra protection, but under German law he was nevertheless considered Jewish. In her dedication to the survival of the family, she believed that my father and I would have better chances if aside from her there was another Christian family member. She may have been right, as the persecution of the Jews by the German authorities was a totally unemotional and purely bureaucratic affair. Some clerk might have gotten confused by the balanced look of the family: two Jewish and two Christian members, and therefore have delayed the deportation of the two Jews for the time being. Little Christian, after much initial illness, grew into a strapping boy, looked after until the end of the war to a large extent by me, as our mother worked regular hours every day.

In 1943 I was playing with some friends in front of our building and accidentally smashed the plate-glass windows of the front door, which had miraculously survived the air raids so far. The janitor's wife came rushing out and, as she was fond of me, invoked the help of God that an air raid would occur that evening, so it, instead of me, could be blamed for this tragedy. Her husband, who worked the late shift at the gasworks, could only leave his job at the end of an air raid. I joined her in praying to our common Lutheran God and we succeeded. An air raid was announced just before the end of the janitor's shift. While it was probably the most uneventful one of the whole war, several extremely large bombs were dropped directly on our neighborhood just before the raid was over, nearly killing us all.

I felt greatly relieved, but when the "all's clear" was sounded and we came out of our cellar, the whole front part of our building was demolished (Berlin's traditional apartment buildings are grouped around a courtyard in four parts: main building, side wings, and rear garden wing), including the janitor's apartment. Of course there was no longer any trace of the glass door which I had broken that afternoon. I never mentioned the incident to my parents at the time. Trying to live an ordinary boy's ordinary life, I was afraid of reproach and punishment. Perhaps I only subconsciously sensed the real danger of my deed. Had the janitor found the damage and reported it negatively to the authorities, "damage caused by a member of a part-Jewish family," we could have all been deported at once to the concentration camps.

A similar incident occurred when a policeman discovered me and several other boys at play in the ruins of the synagogue in Fasanenstrasse, which had been burned down in the Reichskristallnacht of 1938. It was a dramatic place in which to play, quite mysterious and one of our favorite hangouts. Several of the boys were half-Jewish without fully being aware if it, like myself. Maybe that is why we were attracted to this once holy place. When the policeman suddenly descended on us, everyone got away but me. He walked me one block over to Uhlandstrasse by my ear to hand me over to my father, who happened to be home on sick leave from his forced labor job at Pertrix, Berlin's leading flashlight battery maker, loading batteries on trains headed for the front lines. The policeman was a typically old-fashioned Berlin *Wachtmeister* (cop), who while winking at my father told him that next time he would have to take me to the police station and put me under arrest. I was really scared and my father was glad that this would not have greater repercussions. (A similar typical Berlin cop told me some years after the war, when I complained to him that the man just passing us had been following me for the past half hour: "mach dir mal keene Sorge Kleener, det is wohl bloss een Schwuler"—"Don't worry kid, it's just a queer.")

After that sick leave, my father was assigned to Berlin's sanitation department until the end of the war. He was part of a group of four hundred fifty Jewish workers who survived because their boss insisted to the authorities to the very end that he could not keep his rounds without them. When the Russians were nearly at the door of the sanitation depot, he sent his Jewish workers home saying something like, "Take care of yourselves, as we will really be busy once this is over in a few days." Minutes later, an SS commando arrived with orders to shoot this treasure trove of Jews, and when the sanitation boss told him of his orders to his Jewish workers, they shot him as a traitor to the German people and their Führer.

The last months of the war I spent in the country at the Evangelisches Kinderheim near Lubeck at the Baltic Sea, where the British arrived as liberators. Not long before they came, I had sent my parents an envelope full of leaflets telling about the impending end of the war that had been dropped by Allied planes. It got through the mail all right: if it hadn't it would have meant the end of us, as there was the death penalty for those who picked up Allied propaganda leaflets. I also sent them a carton of cabbages, which arrived just before the Russians surrounded the city. It helped them survive. VE day in New York and Berlin must have been as different from each other as night and day, but there were some similarities. In New York there was understandable euphoria but also in Berlin, not only among all those who had waited twelve long years for this day but also among the many more who had only recently realized what Hitler had wrought on Germany.

The first few years after the war, although immensely difficult, continued to be extremely positive for us in Berlin. There was hope of a new Germany and a renewed Berlin. With the beginning of the Cold War and the deepening of the East-West conflict, this hope faded. Instead of a new Germany, two countries emerged, and Berlin reflected this situation most dramatically. As a cultural entity, Berlin was made to bear the brunt of the World War II: it was cut in half, lost its hinterland, lost its position as the German capital, lost many of its best citizens (in two waves: one under Hitler, the second when the blockade and later the wall made clear the city's helplessness and vulnerability). West Germany became a provincial country without a major cultural center, a country without a real capital.

In 1949, I arrived in New York, at the age of fifteen, with my parents and my brother, Christian. On December 12, we alighted from the *General McRae,* a troop transport, at a pier in midtown Manhattan and were offered free donuts and coffee by the United Service for New Americans, which had sponsored us. I had known an artist in Berlin who painted portraits of American army officers in exchange for donuts, and here they were free. I was impressed with the normalcy of the city compared to Berlin. Food was plentiful and very cheap, al-

though we soon realized that most tempting looking fruit and vegetables had also very little taste. Department stores and supermarkets were crammed with things that seemed within everyone's reach. Unlike other immigrants, I had no interest in my fellow countrymen, neither the Germans nor the Jews. It was hard to find the right kind of Germans—people who had left Germany before the war because of Hitler—and I did not find the German Jews my parents knew very inspiring. I could not exactly relate to the rest of the Jewish community. New Yorkers seemed to live in great comfort, had automobiles, and could afford many things, most of which did not exist in the postwar Berlin I knew. I am of course talking about the middle-middle class in both cities—the people between the lower- and upper-middle classes. While this class is still very much in evidence in Berlin today, it is heading for extinction in Manhattan.

Manhattan at the end of the 1940s was physically unchanged from the 1920s and 1930s, with all its neighborhoods still intact. The movement to the suburbs was still at its inception and the impact of Robert Moses's surgery on the city yet to be felt. The jet age did not begin for another ten years, and New York was very much a part of mainland America and in many ways provincial. New Yorkers, like all other Americans, believed that there was only the "American Way" and looked down on the rest of the world. The impending Cold War, the un-American activities investigations, and the ascendancy of Dwight Eisenhower all contributed to a gloomy decade of small mindedness, during which New York began to change dramatically toward the corporate-headquarters city it has become today. The Puerto Ricans and southern blacks, who came to the city during that time to perform menial tasks, hoping to succeed like the Italians and Jews before them, were never accepted and became a permanent underclass. They served the landlords mainly as replacement tenants for the departed lower-middle and middle-middle classes, who had been lured away to lifeless new suburban communities. Today, as the city is no longer "a place of opportunity for all," they have been replaced largely by yuppies, the landlords having changed course from creating slums to creating gentrified co-ops and condominiums. But even the ranks of the yuppies have thinned due to the persistent recession.

To exchange bombed-out Berlin for postwar Manhattan in mid-teenage years was a very positive experience for me. Just as I had enjoyed walking around the destroyed city, I spent much time doing the same in New York, getting to know Manhattan intimately. I had in fact been tempted to take an after-school job as a messenger but settled for a more pragmatic position in an Irish-American restaurant where I also got free meals. While New York prides itself on being a melting pot, in those days people stayed essentially with their own kind, particularly the WASP establishment which felt infinitely superior to all. While today newly arrived foreigners from industrial countries are welcomed with open arms as potential investors, the immigrants of those years were essentially ignored, unless they had some especially heart-rending persecution tales to tell. I had relatively few problems assimilating, as I soon spoke English fluently, except that no one could pronounce or spell my name, Schwarzwald. It was very helpful to be young, nevertheless people were not yet ready to meet someone German, nor could they understand how someone Jewish could have survived Germany. No one who did not spend these years in Germany can fully understand all the nuances and fine points of being half-Jewish, and it was quite impossible to explain all that to an "innocent" American. When I became a citizen in 1955, I decided to translate my name to Blackwood. While Schwarzwald was not a bad name in Germany, conjuring up the majesty of the Black Forest, it sounded ugly when Americans tried to pronounce it. Beyond that I wanted to get away from being associated with Germany, at least on first encounter. It never occurred to me that by changing my name I was also distancing myself from my Jewish background. My Judaism was always a private, personal matter to me. Generally I thought of myself as a German, or better a Berliner, which later changed to feeling like a New Yorker, not necessarily an American. Had I arrived thirty years later, all this would not have been necessary, as attitudes toward Germans had changed and people are much better at dealing with difficult names. Thirty years later, in retrospect, I would have wanted to keep my original name in order to connect myself more closely to my German and Jewish background. But then, thirty years later we would not have immigrated to the United States.

After high school I soon decided to become a documentary filmmaker and was apprenticed to Isaac Kleinerman, a first-rate film editor at the time. By 1957 I was making my own films, the first being a portrait of the New York subways at night, titled *Broadway Express*. With the end of the Eisenhower years, New York began to awake from its stupor to a lively art scene. Contacts increased with foreign corporations and individuals who slowly began to discover the city as a place of opportunity. While Europe was rebuilding its war-torn cities, New York was busy destroying neighborhoods and characteristic quarters of the city in the name of progress and development. Berlin was not exactly rebuilt when I returned there for the first time in the summer of 1959, ten years after my departure. I was very glad to be back and spent an entire week walking the streets I knew so well, in both East and West Berlin. To me, there is no city in the world as wonderful as Berlin in summer, and so I did not allow the general sense of doom in both parts of the city to get me down. On leaving, I realized things had not changed since we left in 1949. Only a miracle could save Berlin.

In the 1960s, I spent much time in Berlin, both in East and West. In 1964 I made a documentary film portrait of Walter Ulbricht, the head of state of East Germany, and later a film about Felsenstein, the genial director of East Berlin's Komische Oper. In West Berlin, I spent time at the Deutsche Oper making a film about Henze's opera *The Bassarids*, which had a libretto by Auden. Later I filmed part of a documentary about Thelonius Monk in West Berlin. Monk had never been to East Berlin so I agreed to show him around. He felt that it was "ahead of our time, because you hardly see any cars." When we returned through Check-point Charlie, the East German guards decided to search Monk. They found a $1,000 bank note, which he had not declared on entry. It fell to me to explain that Monk kept this brand-new bill as a good-luck

4. *Blackwood, Berlin, 1946.*

5. *Blackwood, New York, 1954.*

4

5

371

6. *Blackwood, Munich, 1962.*

7. *Blackwood, New York, 1974.*

6

7

charm. I was very worried that they would not let him go, and I appealed to them to make an exception, saying that blacks have enough trouble in their own land. After some time, by now late in the night, they agreed to let him pass and returned his talisman. While East Berlin was repulsive for its own reasons, West Berlin, reminiscent in many ways of a Las Vegas surrounded by a dour East Germany, had its own negative aspects. A hopeless situation.

New York during the Kennedy years and thereafter until the fiscal crisis of the mid-seventies experienced its cultural heyday but also heightened development, which really meant more and more ugly buildings in the so-called late modernist style. Artists moved into the lofts of lower midtown and SoHo, producing pop art, minimal art, postmodern dance, and all sorts of other innovative ideas. Midtown and Lower Manhattan began to shrink, and prizes for real estate and rents, as well as for art, rose. I had started a documentary film production company in 1966 and was busy documenting many of the activities in the arts. By the mid-seventies, art, like Manhattan real estate, had become a form of investment. Much of the real estate boom was fueled by foreigners who wanted to acquire second homes in the city, in case of right-wing revolutions or left-wing election victories in their own countries. For many it was a good way to squirrel away money and to this day Manhattan real estate is still a bargain compared to many cities in Europe or Tokyo. Under hapless Mayor Koch, who mostly served real estate interests, the city's infrastructure had deteriorated dangerously, causing it to resemble a city in an underdeveloped country. His successor, David Dinkins, New York's first black mayor, seems even less capable and presides over a continuously widening disaster that is like a cancer slowly devouring the city. Few of the rich, talented, and powerful want to get involved in this tragedy, considering New York only one of their many bases and outposts in the United States and abroad.

There is no longer any cheap space in Manhattan for experimenters or immigrants with little money. The success stories of the past, for which New York is famous, would be impossible today. By catering exclusively to powerful corporations and service industries that feed on these corporations, New York is cutting its own throat. There will be fewer and fewer new ideas and far less fresh blood seeking their fortune, trying a new idea, working their way up from the bottom of some enterprise to provide employment to talented and resourceful people.

Ordinary people and with them the lower-middle class and a good part of the middle-middle class will no longer have a place in Manhattan, as costs are too forbidding and steadily rising. Families are particularly affected as public schools are unsuitable and private schools too costly and often inaccessible. Young artists are no longer able to afford lofts in Manhattan and older, successful artists spend much time away from the city or are thinking of relocating due to the harshness and tension of Manhattan life these days. The streets are covered with litter and with homeless people. Crime is rampant, city services poor, corruption pervasive. Making the largest profit possible seems to be on everyone's mind, rather than thinking about the continuity of the city, making a plan for the future.

Needless to say, unless a miracle happens, I think New York is headed for disaster, if not immediately, certainly within the first or second decade of the new millennium. The day will come when this corporate tower of Babel will collapse, when there are no more profitable deals possible and nothing else will be there for the city to fall back on.

While New York continues to destroy itself, Berlin seemingly has been rescued from its fifty-year coma. In a matter of months, Eastern Europe declared its independence from the Soviet Union in 1989. East Germany under Honecker held out to the last moment, reminiscent of Germany under Hitler during the last months and weeks of World War II, as the Allies advanced. A giant demonstration in East Berlin led by many responsible people, among them artists, intellectuals, and clergy, who had long been fed up with the absurd and brutal Honecker, signaled the final hours of the regime. On November 9, the anniversary of Kristallnacht fifty-one years earlier, the Wall was breached and West Berlin became flooded for weeks by speechless East Germans gaping at "the bananas on every street corner," just as in May 1945, as people emerged from basements after the last shots of World War II had been fired in the western and southern parts of Germany, to admire the chocolate bars of the American soldiers.

The overnight change was not all positive. Right-wing groups suddenly rose all over East Germany; West Germans led by Chancellor Kohl moved in to grab the political and economic spoils while the people who had slowly built up a resistance to the regime over the years and wanted a meaningful union with West Germany were swept aside, leaving the field to all sorts of opportunists. Within weeks the character of the Berlin we knew for all these postwar years had changed. The atmosphere and stimulation of the city being an outpost or enclave of another world had given way to an ordinariness, a city half stuck in the past that would take decades to reclaim and half built for a future that had been canceled. Although Germany, now united, decided to declare Berlin its capital again, the great metropolis it once was cannot be ordered by vote of parliament. Had the two German states found a way to gradually unite as two sovereign nations, Berlin would have grown together in a more natural way. Today the unification of the city is all politics, speculation, grabbing advantages, court cases, claims, and witch hunts. Nevertheless Berlin has a future, as it now has come to the end of its destruction, its ordeal. Berlin's future, its restoration as a true metropolis, is largely uncertain, but possible. Much depends on what will happen in Eastern Europe in the coming years. If all these new republics prosper culturally and economically, Berlin will prosper culturally also, as the East-West gateway, the beacon on the road. If the economy in Eastern Europe experiences prolonged hard times, Berlin may just be the quiet administrative center of Germany for a long time, Europe's biggest building site trying to house the one hundred thousand bureaucrats who will eventually arrive from Bonn. At least there is concern about Berlin; Germans generally want it to succeed and prosper and do not begrudge it substantial amounts of their taxes.

New York, by contrast, is left to a great extent to its own devices. Americans may enjoy visiting, shopping, and entertaining themselves in the city but otherwise do not care to support it as a national treasure if it costs them actual money. Mitterand's Grands Projets for Paris are the sort of injection New York could use as America's cultural capital. But even more than Grands Projets, what is needed in New York is a broad scheme for its future that would bring it from the nineteenth century into the twenty-first, orchestrated by truly inspired people who are not motivated by anything but the city's plight. Only through very radical new solutions will New York have a chance for a future. Maybe Tokyo could serve these planners as a model. It is a large metropolitan region headed by a governor, with an economy equal to that of France and a sizable surplus in its treasury. A similar approach for New York would provide it with the tax base it deserves, but it would also mean that sizable parts of Connecticut, New Jersey, as well as several New York state counties such as Westchester, would have to become part of this New York metropolitan region. There are of course many other solutions, but as far as I can see all would require radical change if this city is to stand a chance for a brilliant future.

I myself plan to continue as an ardent observer of the fate of the two cities, hoping to hold out in my small vantage point in Manhattan.

Observations

John Hejduk

BERLIN LOOMS

the vanished can
still be felt
banal stanchions
of rusting concrete
envelop the outline
stretched wire produce
the void
air can be blue
the smoke geometric
ice cream licked
from the rafters
the obelisk was moved
on axis
the dry bark of
linden trees split
across the street
the moist shadow
of barges rippled
october ash felled
the pharmacist's cough
drops bought
for a mark
the black eagles swept
the boulevard clean
the canal became
a gelatin
the plan had been
erased.

CU1947

Swedish torment and Horn and Hardart
Entwistle sipped from the vested straw
Felt fedoras and winter coats
Pencil stubs accounting credits
Her teeth fell from her mouth
upon the couch
Beauregards frame and Bible House
Irving Place and Newman Club
The Priest's confessional breath blew
swinging tits and bobby socks
Dylan Thomas and Alex Nevsky
Mott Haven leads straight for
Saint Mary's Park
Old man Fetig wraps the carp
Pluck the chicken salt the pail
Tub butter hardens in oak vats
It's the Greeks who have the concession
on Sassetta Franks
Darby Dent swept the court
The smock of Delaney revealed
the pigeon's neck
was swiftly cracked and dropped into
a shoe-shine box
Pointy shoes and blunted brush
Black trench coat and blue ear muff
Temperas black and white
That one in the pin stripe suit
is a mother-fucker
I always thought so
Not that one the other
Slushed snow under rotting Els
The Ginny Lind fish are to be
moved to Brooklyn
The booksellers dispossessed
Cincinnati Dancing Pig
Bowery drones Mac trucks
Cheese blintzes finish your soup
The church of All Nations
Third Rome.

Georg Baselitz

Georg Baselitz. Theme: The House.
1988. Photograph by Frank Oleski,
Cologne.

Georg Baselitz. Garden Fence,
1988. Galerie Michael Werner,
Cologne.

Georg Baselitz. "N.Y.", *1988.*
Galerie Michael Werner, Cologne.

Georg Baselitz. "Still No Snow,"
1988. Galerie Michael Werner,
Cologne.

Irene Dische

Chapter One: The Man Who Called the City Mommy

Illustration of an impulse solution to urban problems

Everyone blamed Giorgio Limbardo for what John Wheeler did. It was Giorgio who encouraged John to call the city Mommy, Giorgio who celebrated John as the most honest of the aesthetes that crowded the Paris bar. Giorgio and John were opposites. Giorgio was famous, John unknown. Giorgio from the south—Parma—John from the north—Detroit. John was tall, strong and condescending. Giorgio was short and delicate, and of natural modesty and tolerance others would have found impossible to retain after becoming professor.

Giorgio was considered an infallible judge of any question of taste. When Giorgio was seen paying for a tin of ravioli at a supermarket, the hitherto exorbitant value of fresh ravioli crashed on the bourse of public opinion. Giorgio elevated John to superior status by associating with him. He found his urban problem interesting.

John's problem was this: he adored Berlin, and at the same time he was fed up with it. Yet he didn't leave because he had a beautiful apartment in the best neighborhood, and he could not bear the thought of someone else living there. The flat was small, furnished with hand-me-downs left by another tenant, but it looked out on the Ku'Damm, Berlin's main street.

John knew that as soon as he moved out, the landlord would allow someone else to move in, and that he said, "would be like seeing Mommy with another man; I would be unbearably jealous." Often John went to see Giorgio at his regular table at the Paris Bar and complained: his future was tied up, he was locked into Berlin life against his will, by his jealousy.

John had come to Berlin to write a serious play about the fifties. In the eighties, artists with work problems often came to Berlin, many on fellowships. Wheeler did not stand out

in that crowd, he was rather ordinary, a playwright without a play. He had spent three years not writing the play in New York. He had grown thin on fashionable drugs that help writers work, and then in Berlin he grew tubby on tension-relieving junk food. Nothing relieved his inability to move words from his head down to the paper. When he tried to write a line and it wouldn't come, he felt an unbonded hatred that attached itself to the nearest individual.

He enjoyed his own bad moods because he saw how they impressed people. For a while his bad moods were the consolation for having to write the beautiful dialogue he expected of himself. Later, they became all that he expected of himself.

Giorgio Limbardo took John Wheeler's jealousy seriously. In the first place, he believed in an aesthetic solution to all problems, including emotional ones. "You can't bear the idea of someone living in your apartment," mused Giorgio. "But it's no solution to hang on to it for life, because someday, you'll die and then someone else will live in it!"

Perhaps he should have known that the weak, arrogant Wheeler would take any advice that justified his own impulses. Nevertheless, one afternoon Giorgio told him, "You'll have to destroy the object of your jealousy. You could burn it down."

Long-term consequence of impulse solution: memorials (excerpt from City Planners Yearbook, 2009)

The committee decided that despite the time and money invested in the international competition, a memorial to Wheeler would not serve the needs of the public now. The memorials to World War Two have all been taken down at terrible public expense, and we do not want to saddle the next generation with the same burden of removing negative monuments. Even now, the word "Wheeler" means nothing anymore to the average abiturient, who assumes the Ku'Damm was always a side street. Gellert's winning design for a museum in the shape of an *Altbau*—a tenement—will be implemented as the new geriatric wing in the state hospital.

Analysis: the prisoner sees himself #1 (from the Warden's memoirs)

The prisoner was given a small hand mirror after a year of good behavior. He used it to check on his teeth and on the condition of his complexion. His first wrinkle appeared in about 1995. He inquired about the rights of prisoners to have plastic surgery and was indignant that they had none at all. After ten years, he was allowed to have an additional mirror so that he could see the back of his head. He sent the first years of the century pulling out white hairs as they grew. He kept himself almost bald and never had to see the barber. After another ten, the prisoners helped pitch together to buy him a full-length mirror, which a delegation delivered to Wheeler. The prisoner became interested in clothes again, and spent the money his mother sent him on clothes ordered from Armani.

Anecdote: The Help

The jail help was very fond of John Wheeler because he was so polite. Then he told a newspaper reporter that he came from a poor family, and therefore he identified with the maids. This got back to them and annoyed them. They felt that Wheeler was too childish to come from a working-class family: that is, he was messy and not at all interested in rehabilitating his reputation.

Analysis: From the brochure "Screening Classrooms for Children with Early Signs of De Lassaulx Syndrome"

It is the obligation of the teacher to recognize and report the potential De Lassaulx child. As Dr. De Lassaulx pointed out in his ground-breaking work of 1989, symptoms of De Lassaulx syndrome should be evident in the earliest school years. These include the child's obsessive relationship to his or her mother, towers, hard surfaces, and potholes. J. Ritchie reported a case in Boston of

a boy who was followed up after an alert teacher reported he was inordinately attached to his mother and had started organizing his blocks into what he called fairyland. He was on the police files as a potential offender and subsequently identified as the Subway Bomber of Boston. The man's problems began after the combat zone was moved into the former Sachs department store and each floor allocated to a different perversion, He was motivated by shame and anger at Mommy's interference and expressed his rage by hitting the city in the bowels.

Reference to:
Folk songs (genre: hard rock) 1990s

"Metropolitan Mommy"
What is the city but a personal friend
Lend me a penny, big city
What's all that brick worth if you cannot depend
It will melt buttersoft for a gentleman
A city can be pretty
A city can be fun
But what a city has to—
Is support a city son.
Metropolitan Mommy
Give me electricity
Give me water, all my fill
And take away the heating bill

Analysis: Wheeler about his childhood (from the court records)

I was a wonderful child. Always quiet. Always polite. I never once raised my voice. I hate children who are loud and impertinent. I was quiet because my mother was perfect and one has to be quiet in the presence of perfection.

Reference to:
(from *Time*, August 2005)

"Giorgio Limbardo, the vice president of Cooper Union has been appointed as curator of the Met's new department of Architectural Sketches. Asked about his maiden exhibit he replied, "I will focus on Destructionalism."

Analysis: The prisoner sees himself #2 (from a letter to his social worker)

I am not untidy. I always close my cupboard after opening it. No, I don't have a cupboard in here. I'm speaking

about (gestures to his pants) and about life in general. I'm not one to procrastinate and leave a cupboard open for no reason.

I don't know what envy feels like. I was happy when Albert was released from prison early. Everyone knows he slept with the prison director to get out. I am not at all competitive either. I wrote Gerling a note of congratulations when he had his prison memoirs published, even though the book was a tad superficial.

Analysis: The arson specialist is interviewed on TV

The specialist achieved controversy by arguing that Wheeler should be treated as a conventional arsonist. The following quotes are form a television talk show.

"There are male and female pyromaniacs. The female fire is bowl shaped and made with nylon stockings. The male fire is conical and made with toilet paper."

"But in case of Wheeler, we had an amateur who resorted to twigs and newspaper in the first day of the winter sales when everyone was out shopping. The idea to use twigs can probably be traced to the time he served with the Boy Scouts. No, I can't rule out that the man would have used an atomic bomb if he knew how to obtain one."

"Would that be a male or a female fire? You know Bob, you've just suggested a new species of arsonist, the global politician. I'll have to work on the classification."

Anecdote: Barbara Schmidt (from an interview with here)

B. Schmidt was hired as a social worker specializing in De Lassaulx Syndrome. No doubt she was very suited for this task, having had a history of architecture in her own family. She was warmhearted and respectful and always referred to herself as the inmates' "personal assistant." Wheeler was very famous, of course, which made it hard to deal with him normally. She always saw interviews coming. She never spoke a word about her relationship to John beside denying that it was of a romantic nature. She said, "It's none of your damn business." His relationship to the city was a matter of great concern to her because she realized that he still loved and desired it and wanted it all for himself.

Anecdote (or analysis?): The prisoner works on his play
(according to Dr. Turna, prison psychiatrist)

The prisoner borrowed a pen from the warden. When the warden looked away, Wheeler took some white paper from his desk. When the warden received a telephone call, Wheeler helped himself to some chocolate visible in an open drawer. The warden smiled, put his hand over the mouthpiece and said, "Why don't you buy yourself what you need at the prison shop? You have enough money." Wheeler replied, "I don't pay for my food here. Why should I pay for paper?"

Back in his cell, the prisoner sat down at his desk and arranged the paper and the pen and the chocolate in various patterns. He picked up the pen and set it point down on the page. Immediately, an image came into his head: of a white expanse that was time immemorial. He wrote his name on the page.

He put away the pen and paper and switched on his television.

Forecast: The prisoner imagines his release
(from his unpublished diary [as supplied by B. Schmidt])

It will come as a great surprise. The mayor will come to my cell door with a scroll. The guards will open the door. Hopefully, I will be doing something decorous. He will smile and say I can pack my books—he will admire their number—and then he will read the pardon. I will fall around his neck and sob into his ear. He will be deeply touched. Then, when I pull away, he will see that I have only been pretending to cry and he will feel a fool, and cut the ceremony short. I will go directly to the airport and fly to New York.

My friend Giorgio will be living there in impeccable style—a co-op on Central Park North. He will have a spare bedroom. I will dirty his cashmere and silk and use up his hand cream and q-tips. I will complain about the smallness of the room and the narrowness of the bed. German jail cells are more spacious. My mother will visit us, I will recognize her after all these years, and the two of them will chatter about me.

When he dies, I will stay on his flat. When my mother dies, I shall inherit the earth.

Daniel Libeskind

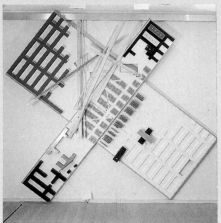

NEW YORK

The cyclopes could see double because the gods recognized their shortsightedness. Offenders against these rare giants from Sicily valued theories about zero population growth and the progress of optometry. Above all, humanity was attempting in those early years—like superman today—limited development of fascism. False curtain calls, spectacles with animals performing nocturnes, even Japanese soldiers manipulating computers with involuntary reflex action could not bring back this type of extravaganza again.

While new, funfilled beings take their place—shoring up dusty monuments, reconstructing dinosaurs, amputating limbs—it's the end of primitive choreography skipping over the trap.

Wilted flowers eased the fall of the Roman Empire. And this culture suspends each eagle's impressive beak from the curved sanctuary in order to caricature the inadequacy of humanistic morality.

The point of being is precisely this: to transform human perspective into the world's, a custody in which apes animate a few chairs by stacking and unstacking them in liquid air, while the birds oppress the low-sinking heart.

BERLIN

Variation in series—solace to terms in the Talmud. Your text is correct but gullible. Muse unfit.

The statue of humanity that ingeniously decorates the dark alley of the mind acts like Cellini's gold Perseus: casts a shadow by fueling envy. It's easier instead of a cape, unscrew Hercules's nameplate without using an axe than to acknowledge the genius of the departed—their right to sell the world to the unborn.

Threatened with extinction through competition, the hand engages in cultural terrorism: grasps whatever it can (Italian tutti-frutti), squeezes the fluid out of the lungs by treating the neck as a sponge.
In just the same way, our hopeless precision is a delusion of alchemists in search of metallic novelty based on perjury. Universal blindness will emerge when sculptors have finished the ultimate work: carving water to represent solid matter enraged by summer heat.

Gupta's melancholic atmosphere in which, here and there, an infant could be reared, is not inferior to our suffering Pierrots.

Part Three
1945 to the Present

1. *General view of Urbino.*

2. *Typical housing within walls of Urbino.*

Collage and Chaos

Peter Blake

Peter Blake is a professor of architecture at Catholic University in Washington, D.C., and an architect practicing in New York, Boston, and Washington. He was curator in the department of architecture and industrial design at the Museum of Modern Art (1948–50) and editor of The Architectural Forum *and* Architecture Plus. *From 1975 to 1979 he was chairman of the department of architecture and planning at the Boston Architectural Center. He is the author of* The Master Builders *(1960),* God's Own Junkyard *(1964), and* Form Follows Fiasco: Why Modern Architecture Hasn't Worked *(1977) and is a frequent contributor to magazines and journals. He was awarded the Architecture Critic's Medal from the American Institute of Architects in 1975 and a Distinguished Designer Fellowship from the National Endowment for the Arts in 1984.*

A personal note: I was born in Berlin, went to school in England, and then lived in the United States. I returned to Berlin in an American uniform, driving a jeep, a day or two before the city surrendered to the Allies in May 1945; I have visited Berlin ever since, almost once a year—it is my home.

I have a second home, and it is New York. (I actually live in a suburb of New York, called Washington, D.C., but that is neither here nor there.) I have lived in New York most of my life, and most of my friends and relatives live there. Berlin•New York is not an abstraction for me.

If you were to identify the most important issue in urban architecture and design in the nineteenth and twentieth centuries, you would have to say that it has something to do with the image of a democratic, egalitarian city.

Western cities, prior to the political and industrial revolutions of the nineteenth century, were built in the image of autocracy: they were built by and for emperors and kings and popes and princes, and they were extraordinarily and beautifully expressive of what was what and who was who. If you look at Urbino, for example, even today, you see an image of a fortress capped by the two symbols of power—the cathedral and the palace (fig. 1). If you look at any city in the West that has survived from the Middle Ages and the Renaissance, you will see those two symbols of who is who and what is what, regardless of where you stand—the cathedral and the palace. And if you looked closely enough, you would see the houses of ordinary people, of the governed, lined up in identical fashion along identical streets, with brick or stucco walls, tile roofs, small windows and small doorways, and sometimes small walled courtyards or gardens—all contained within the protective as well as restrictive city walls (fig. 2). The image of Urbino in the days of Federico da Montefeltro—indeed, the image of Urbino today—comes to mind again. It is the absolutely perfect expression of who was who and what was what. It is the image that still excites tourists and filmmakers and architects and other spinners of dreams.

It is an extraordinarily powerful image. After all, what could be simpler than a massive fortress dominated by the two instantly recognizable symbols of temporal and religious power? And what could be easier to translate into grand skylines and spectacular silhouettes? And, finally, what could, more unmistakably, express the subservient position of the serfs? No wonder architects loved the simplicity of the message; no wonder image makers of the past as well as the present found these simple, expressive skylines ideally suited for grand, panoramic murals and equally grand, equally panoramic travelogues .

But then, about two hundred years ago, all that began to change. What happened, of course, was that the old centers of power—the palace and the cathedral—collapsed and were replaced. In Washington, D.C., Charles L'Enfant attempted to create a new image by replacing the duality of palace and cathedral with the duality of the Presidency and the Congress, the White House and the Capitol. (He never quite figured out what to do about the third center of power in the emerging

American democracy, the judiciary; and so the Supreme Court was put in cold storage, somewhere on Capitol Hill.) It was a noble effort but not terribly convincing. For example, it became increasingly clear that popular democracy was not a triad but a sort of quadruped, with the fourth center of power being the dollar (or the yen, the mark, or simply money). Indeed, it has become evident, in the United States at least, that money is not only one of the four legs of a democratic society but in fact the most important of the four, the one that often dominates the other three.

How on earth do you translate those facts into architectural and urbanist images? The answer, to date, is that nobody really knows (fig. 3). Robert Venturi, who has clearly given a great deal of thought to the question, seems to feel that the image of this sort of society is mediocrity, compromise, laissez-faire—in short, Main Street, USA. Kallmann & McKinnell, who won the Boston City Hall competition in 1966 (and built their massive concrete fortress in the image of Corbusier's La Tourette) believed that the appropriate image was a monument to popular democracy (fig. 4). And others, such as Jane Jacobs, seem to feel that an appropriate image of an egalitarian participatory democracy is no center at all, but a series of decentralized community meeting places, like storefronts behind which neighbors can meet and discuss their differences (fig. 5).

In New York, the effort to create an urban image of a free society has been almost totally undirected. The only visible motivation in the building of New York—and I am referring, principally, to Manhattan—has been greed. Whenever altruism or some other softhearted or softheaded goal seemed to stand in the way of greed, the power of money invariably has won out. (I am not saying this in anger; a fairly good case can be made, and has in fact been made, for greed as a more creative motivating force than altruism, though not, I confess, in my own mind.) The forces that have shaped Manhattan architecturally in the past seventy-five years are quite crude and unsophisticated, and there has been very little effort to conceal the crudeness. For example, there has been no effort to conceal the real power of money and greed in the making of Manhattan: the skyline of the island, reading from south to north, is clearly and crudely dominated by a dozen or more architectural symbols that spell out, precisely and quite unmistakably, who is who and what is what (fig. 10). The south end of the island is dominated by the temples of the downtown Rockefellers: Chase-Manhattan, built when David Rockefeller controlled that bank, and the World Trade Center (fig. 6), built when David's brother Nelson was the governor of New York; the midtown skyline is dominated by Rockefeller Center (fig. 7), built by the patriarch himself; and the northern stretches are dominated by Lincoln Center (fig. 8), built by David's oldest brother, John D. Rockefeller, 3rd. Farther north, the Cloisters and Fort Tyron Park were also built by the Rockefellers.

While the Rockefellers were acquiring virtual control of the city, they acted like Medicis: their palaces and cathedrals are often in good taste and occasionally (as in the case of Rockefeller Center) quite remarkable. Those who followed them—a motley crew of nouveaux-riches, cutthroat developers, and other exploiters—have created their own vulgarities up and

3

4

5

386

6

7

8

8. Wallace K. Harrison. Lincoln
Center, West Side, Manhattan,
1962–68.

9. Park Avenue, Manhattan, c.
1970. View north from Pan Am
Building at about 45th Street.

9

down the island, often with the active help of venal architects who preferred making money to making art.

Admittedly, there were and are fairly complex zoning regulations that govern the heights, setbacks, bulk, and various other aspects of New York's new (and recycled) buildings. There are regulations as to their usage and landmark preservation laws and agencies charged with enforcing them. But the stakes are so high that private developers spend vast sums bending and breaking those rules in the courts and millions of dollars supporting the election campaigns of politicians likely to be flexible in interpreting those rules. It is fair to say that since the end of World War II private developers in Manhattan have almost always had their way and that there are very few recorded instances when the general public or a local community has won out over a developer willing and able to spend vast sums in the courts and in the political arena (fig. 9).

Despite the fact that Manhattan's post-World War II skyline was shaped primarily by greed, the resulting urban image is remarkably successful. Unlike the Federal Triangle in Washington, D.C., for example, which was shaped primarily by regulation and compromise—and which, as a result, is one of the most boring cityscapes since Albert Speer's designs for Berlin—the new Manhattan is a wonderfully chaotic mess. Nothing aligns with anything else; nothing matches anything else; nothing conforms or contextualizes with anything else. Architecturally, the new Manhattan is sheer anarchy and an almost perfect image of a totally untrammeled free society. It is virtually impossible for a typically modern or traditional architect to walk down a Manhattan street and not despair; nothing that you subscribe to as a fundamental principle of urban design seems present or holds true. Chaos is everywhere, and the result is absolutely wonderful (fig. 10).

Rockefeller Center, to cite a specific example that has fascinated me for some time, is now more than fifty years old and still admired by most architects as a successful case history of modern, urban design on a skyscraper scale (fig. 11). This complex has recently grown to about two dozen skyscrapers, with a gross floor area of around twenty-five million square feet and a daytime population of around fifty thousand people. (That figure, including visitors, messengers, and service personnel, may be much higher.) It is a well-composed, largely unified city-within-a-city, replete with stores, restaurants, theaters, exhibition spaces, and, of course, corporate headquarters and other offices.

Some twenty years after Rockefeller Center was planned and built under the benevolent direction of the Rockefellers, a very similar complex (in size, at least) of skyscrapers, stores, hotels, and other amenities began to take shape just a couple of blocks to the east of the Rockefeller complex, on a stretch of roughly ten city blocks, between 50th and 60th streets east and west of Madison Avenue. This complex probably contains just as much office space and just as many other amenities as the original Rockefeller enclave. But unlike the latter, this ten block stretch was not planned by anyone. It conforms, more or less, to the prevailing zoning laws despite the fact that each builder tried, in one way or another, to obtain a special excep-

10. Times Square at night, Midtown Manhattan, 1970s. View north. Robert Rauschenberg called Times Square America's greatest work of art.

389

11

11. *Rockefeller Center, axial view.*
Rockefeller Center; © Rockefeller
Group, Inc.

12. *Philip Johnson and John
Burgee. AT&T Building, night view
from the west, 1984.* Timothy
Hursley.

tion or variance from the authorities in order to make his sky-scraper taller or fatter and—in any event—different from its neighbors.

The result is a collection of some of the most bizarre buildings erected anywhere since World War II. They include a sky-scraper shaped like a huge Chippendale grandfather clock (fig. 12), a skyscraper shaped like a ski jump, a skyscraper with a cantilevered corner so terrifying that pedestrians scurry across the street to avoid having to walk in its shadow, and many others. This collection also contains two new Renaissance *palazzi*, a glass-enclosed botanical garden, the rear end of a neo-Gothic cathedral, a couple of fairly respectable Art Deco buildings from the 1930s, and a sprinkling of five-story townhouses with walk-up apartments.

From a city planning point of view, the ten-block stretch is a disaster area. Yet—despite monumental traffic jams, the inadequacy of subway lines that skirt the district—this part of Madison Avenue is a wonderful place to visit, to work, to shop and window shop, and to watch the passing parade. It is the sort of street that makes New York a place unlike any other in the world. And it makes absolutely no sense at all, architecturally or urbanistically.

It would be irresponsible to suggest that the kind of chaos and untrammeled greed represented by post-World War II Manhattan is an ideal to be emulated elsewhere—or even to be tolerated in New York. The picturesque chaos that is Manhattan has its price, and it is a price being paid by the poor and by people with only moderate incomes.

Those who once created most of Manhattan's special ambience of many nationalities and many cultures have been driven out of Manhattan. The beautiful lofts created by Manhattan's artists—and without any help whatsoever from architects and planners—have been turned into residences for rich lawyers and stockbrokers who find it chic to live in SoHo, while the artists have been driven away into Queens and New Jersey. And the fringes of Manhattan that were once Little Italy and Chinatown and French and Spanish quarters now boast more and more flashy condominium towers for more and more flashy developers, and their lawyers, bankers, and psychiatrists.

In short, the argument initially advanced for the Manhattan skyline as an image of a totally free society is turning out to be an illusion, and a cruel one. For the image that we see today is not so much the image of freedom but the image of a social order consisting of the nouveaux riches and the nouveaux pauvres (with batallions of police protecting the former from the latter).

In contrast to such developments in New York, during the 1980s in what was then West Berlin a conscious attempt was made to create a new urban image of a free society. This was the work of the International Building Exposition (IBA).

Josef Paul Kleihues, whose ideas have largely shaped the New IBA—the new structures designed for and built on infill

390

13. *Ludwig Hilberseimer. Project for High-Rise City, Berlin 1928.*

14. *Housing project, Pecs, Hungary, 1982.*

15. *Charles Moore. Housing complex at Tegel Harbor, Berlin (International Building Exposition) 1985–90.* Archiv der Internationalen Bauausstellung.

16. *Peter Eisenman. Residential and commercial buildings, Kochstrasse/Friedrichstrasse, Berlin, (International Building Exposition).* Archiv der Internationalen Bauaustellung Berlin.

17. *Aldo Rossi. Residential and commercial buildings, Wilhelmsstrasse/ Kochstrasse, Berlin (International Building Exposition).* Archiv der Internationalen Bauausstellung.

13

14

15

sites throughout the city and on bombed-out city blocks left barren since 1945—clearly believed that the best way to create a vital, vibrant, and colorful new city was not to assign large tracts of land to one specific architect or developer but to commission many different architects to design relatively small projects on adjacent lots. The resulting urban collage—a term coined by Colin Rowe and Fred Koetter in their important book *Collage City*—would create the kind of visual free-for-all that one might expect in a laissez-faire society. Admittedly, the free-for-all, or collage, would be artificial rather than the result of free-market forces, as New York developers would call them. It would be close enough to the urban image of a populist, participatory democracy to represent a new urban form very different from that bequeathed to the West by autocracies of the past.

Stylistically, and in every other respect, the IBA's new buildings are a colorful architectural mixture—sometimes, perhaps, not colorful enough, and at other times not mixed enough. But they represent a truly extraordinary attempt, especially when compared with earlier efforts in twentieth-century planning and urban design. For, in effect, what Kleihues and his associates created is the very antithesis of the so-called ideal cities proposed by Le Corbusier, Ludwig Hilberseimer (fig. 13), and others that formed most of our thinking of the past half century (fig. 14). Unlike those ideal cities that placed a premium on unity, on repetitive modularity, and on other images of regimentation, the image created by the IBA is one of deliberate variety, of color, sometimes even of chaos. The buildings look as if they had been commissioned by different clients and designed by different architects (quite true) and built under different sets of rules (which is not).

One might fear that there would be a certain Disneyland element in some of this artificially created color, but there is surprisingly little of it. Even in such clearly charming complexes as Charles Moore's apartments in Tegel there are very real elements of Berlin's architectural tradition—klutziness and all—rendered sensitively and with a highly observant eye (fig. 15). But in most of the new structures commissioned by the IBA, there is no effort to create an artificial past or a colorful present; most are straightforward buildings by architects with different points of view, and the result, more often than not, is the sort of variety that makes cities interesting—the sort of variety that makes much of Manhattan interesting, too.

16

17

1. Joesph Paul Kleihues with Mirko
Baum, Ludger Brands, and Walther
Stepp. Master plan for the
International Building Exposition,
Berlin 1974 Demonstration areas:
Southern Tiergarten and Southern
Friedrichstadt within its urban
context.

From the Destruction to the Critical Reconstruction of the City: Urban Design in Berlin after 1945

Josef Paul Kleihues

Josef Paul Kleihues is an architect and urban designer in Berlin. Since 1973 he has been professor of architectural design and theory and since 1986 professor of architectural design and planning at Dortmund University. He was the Irwin S. Chanin Distinguished International Professor at Cooper Union from 1986 to 1990 and a visiting professor at Yale University in 1987. He was director of planning for the International Building Exposition in Berlin and has been responsible for numerous exhibitions. His publications include The Museum Projects *(1989) and* Berlin Atlas zu Stadtbild und Stadtraum *(1971–73). He is also the editor of* Dokumente und Projekte. Die IBA Neubaugebiete *(since 1984),* Die Dortmunder Architekturhefte *(since 1975), and* 750 Jahre Architektur und Städtebau in Berlin *(1987).*

But it is the fate of most ideas to run through our lives in fetters. Many people who gaze longingly after them and cannot understand why they do not spread their wings and fly, do not know where these fetters lie. This is why the first step in a struggle for ideas is to release their fetters. This release of fetters constitutes cultural policy, as we understand it.
—Felix Schumacher

In 1945, Berlin lay in ruins. It was an hour of extreme need and despair and of renewed hope in a new start. Yet even in this first hour, Berlin's fate as a city between two worlds was foreshadowed. For the population, this preordained ideological polarization was at first of no relevance since its concern was solely with day-to-day survival.

On another level, however, the scant three years between capitulation and division of the city were characterized by an embittered political struggle over the positions advanced by two opposing ideological camps. And urban design projects in postwar Berlin were affected by this polarization from the very beginning.

Doubtless, professional and idealistic attempts were made during these years to develop coherent approaches to rebuilding the devastated city as a unity. Yet instead of taking place in a common organizational context, these attempts were made at various places and supported—or hindered—by various group or party interests. Planners did not even wait until the first elections in 1946 to see what the government might advance in the way of programs or goals. The competing plans began to take shape as early as the summer of 1945, in groups headed by Hans Scharoun in the Berlin town council and by Walter Moest in the southwestern residential suburb of Zehlendorf. The result was the Collective Plan and the Zehlendorf Plan, both of which, after heated and subjective discussion, were presented to the public in 1946 (fig. 1).[1]

For all their differences, the two plans shared one thing in common—a projection into the future that largely overlooked the realities of the day. In a sense, they were early examples of that planning lingo, which has since become so familiar, including zoning and utilization distribution, statistics and transportation management, but little consideration of the volume, space, and images that make up the experience of the city. Both plans were far removed from reality in another regard as well. As the homeless Berliners were sifting the ruins of their dwellings and patching them up as best they could to keep out wind and rain, neither of the planning committees felt it necessary to advance a program of reconstruction, basing their projects instead on further demolition to make way for a gigantic street system and extensive rezoning measures (fig. 2).

Complaints are often made about the unrealized hopes and missed opportunities of the post-Hitler period of reconstruction. This is particularly the case with respect to the Collective Plan—Scharoun's conception of an urban landscape that, running like a zoned strip city in the east-west direction, would have been oriented to the topography of the Spree and Havel River Valley. Actually, the plan consisted largely of an

2. As women in Berlin sifted through the debris of the destroyed city in search of stones that could be used for the reconstruction, architects were planning further demolition and utopian models for the city. Landesbildstelle Berlin.

evocative description of Scharoun's idea, which he detailed only at certain key points. One of these exemplary details was a plan for the Charlottenburg district on either side of the east-west axis and around Charlottenburg city hall. It clearly reveals where the thrust of the Collective Plan lay—in a total demolition of the war-damaged areas and their complete redesign. This is quite obvious from the model, in which only Charlottenburg Palace and the dense built-up area to the south have been retained, while the rest of the district has been cleared to make way for alternating high-rise slabs and groups of single-family houses that demonstrate the then-progressive idea of the open city (fig. 3).

The rationalism of this plan, however, seemed all too mechanical, and as a model attempt to continue the intellectual and artistic ideals of the 1920s, it could not help but fail. This can also be said of Scharoun's subsequent contribution to the Hauptstadt Berlin competition, which, though more expressive, must be considered a conceptual ramification of the earlier Collective Plan, in which the city is conceived and defined in terms of its permeation by forests and lakes.

This well-intended new start was not the only seed of that completely misconceived modernism that set out to do away, once and for all, with the historical city as a principle and with the city of stone as social injustice incarnate. In the ensuing years, it would largely succeed on both accounts.

Hence the fate of these early plans and their offshoots are by no means of marginal significance in comparison to actual developments, that is, the razing of entire blocks and districts of Berlin that began in the early 1950s. They are highly interesting both as theoretical models and as revealing documents of a school of thought that had a not inconsiderable influence on the political decisions of the following years.

Essential aspects of the Zehlendorf Plan were initially adopted by Karl Bonatz, *Stadtbaurat* (director of the city's Department of Urban Planning and Development) in postwar Berlin's first elected town council (fig. 4). The traffic and street plan, which played a dominating role, was defined more precisely and brought into closer conformance with the stipulations of the Collective Plan. The revised Zehlendorf Plan was submitted at the end of 1947. A year later, in December 1948, the city was divided, sealing the fate of the Collective Plan, which after being initially supported by the East Berlin town council, was then modified and eventually, in summer 1949, officially adopted as the Reconstruction Plan.

The following year brought criticism of previous planning on the part of Walter Ulbricht. An independent building policy for the German Democratic Republic (GDR) was proclaimed; after initial difficulties in orientation had been overcome, the new policy went into effect with the laying of the cornerstone of Stalinallee in February 1952. The ideological confrontation in architecture and urban planning in Berlin had begun.

3

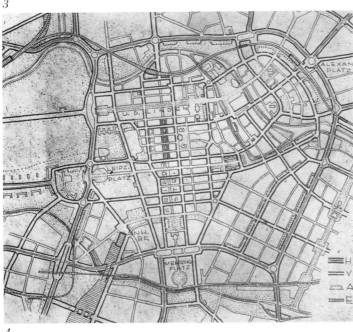

4

3. Hans Scharoun. "The New Principles in a Destroyed Area of the City," 1946. In contrast to the "city of stone," in the "open city" highrise slabs would contrast with groups of single family housing.

4. The Bonatz Plan, 1947. The traffic-oriented city is already evident in the early plans for the redesign of Berlin. From Walter Most, "Karl Bonatz," *Neue Bauwelt*, (Berlin, 1947).

5. *Stalinallee, 1952–56. This example of socialist realism in architecture and urban design also acknowledged elements of the city's architectural history.* Ullstein Bilderdienst, Berlin (Klaus Lennartz).

6. *The Hansaviertel, 1954–1957. In its function as a symbol of free, democratic architecture, the Interbau was in obvious contrast to the more grandiose Stalinallee.* Landisbildstelle Berlin.

5

6

The Progressive Tradition of Socialist Realism

As a basis for reconstruction in the eastern half of the city, sixteen guidelines were issued by the Ministerial Council of the GDR on July 27, 1950.[2] By this date, most of the original members of the planning collective, all of whom figured as advocates of the Charta of Athens, had already moved to West Berlin. The general political reasons for their move were accompanied by professional considerations arising from the antithesis between the new East German principles of urban design and the Athens Charter.

From a contemporary point of view, the fifth of the sixteen new commandments might seem entirely up to date: "City planning must be based on the organic principle and take account of the historically developed structure of the city while eliminating its deficiencies." And although the sixth commandment bears strong overtones of Stalin's dicta on urban planning and architecture, proclaiming that "the squares in the city center" would be the site of "political demonstrations, marches, and celebrations of national holidays," who would deny the statement that the key issue of urban planning and the city's architectural design is indeed "the creation of an individual and unique face for the city."[3]

Still, most of these guidelines, and the ideological formula that the content of architecture must be socialist and its form national, or that the most important and monumental buildings should be erected at the city center, were hardly compatible with the ideas and hopes of the so-called Whites, the vanguard who remained devoted to the Bauhaus heritage and to the CIAM.

Interbau versus Stalinallee

Thus there emerged on either side of the Wall in the mid-1950s those two emblematic examples of antithetic approaches to architecture and urban planning: Stalinallee in the East and the Hansaviertel in the West. While Stalinallee was the key symbol of a propaganda campaign that celebrated the national reconstruction program and the new doctrine of socialist realism in architecture and city planning (fig. 5), the Hansaviertel in West Berlin was the keystone of modern inner-city reconstruction, a symbol of free, democratic building and a reply to the officially ordained pomp of Stalinallee (fig. 6).

After initial difficulties in interpreting the GDR's sixteen building guidelines, Hermann Henselmann demonstrated a pragmatic skill in meeting Ulbricht's requirements and ideas. In its own way, the concept underlying Stalinallee recalls the constituent elements of urban design. This is by no means limited to the longitudinal and latitudinal axes of the city plan, whose dominating element, a mile-long avenue, is enlivened by urban spaces of various forms. In addition, the planning reveals a precise conception of the geometry and the outward aspect of the city.

A differentiated geometry, consisting of an alternation of relatively uniform blocks parallel to the street with towerlike cor-

ner buildings and structures located in the intersection squares, was intended to express both national and Berlin architectural traditions, as well as symbolizing the "steadfastness of the populace of the new state."[4] The neoclassical style of the architecture and its stately ornamentation were meant, on the one hand, to recall the tradition of Berlin neoclassicism (the window formats, for instance, being based on Schinkel's Feilner house) and on the other hand to lend elevated aesthetic expression to the heroism of the working class and its new consciousness. The underlying aim of Stalinallee was to contribute to an aesthetically pleasing cityscape.[5]

Naturally, this cityscape could not but seem suspect to those members of the vanguard who had remained in East Germany and who were eager to reinstate the modern tradition that had been quashed by Hitler. And this despite the fact that they knew full well that the animosity of the USSR with respect to the Charter had become clear even before its final definition—one of the main reasons why the CIAM, which was originally to be held in Moscow, was moved to Athens.

Thus it was that architects in the western half of the divided city attempted to make good what had been declared unacceptable in the eastern half. The Bauhaus, functionalism, and the rediscovered Athens Charter were looked upon as manifestos of a modern urban design and *Neue Sachlichkeit* architecture that had been buried under the ruins of war. The rationalism of the 1920s was to serve as the point of reference for the *neues Bauen* of the postwar period. Apart from being a theoretical maxim, this amounted to a moral demand, a reparation of past evils that was owed to the nation and to the world.

Yet in practice, there was to be no return to the rigors of the International Style proclaimed in the 1920s. The Hansaviertel, presented to the public in 1957 under the auspices of the Interbau competition, was simply a medley of diverse ground plans and building types, structural approaches, and materials. This corresponded to the openness of the site layout that had emerged from a competition.[6] Moreover, this plan was completely altered by the final, seemingly random placement of the individual apartment buildings with regard to height, width, and depth. The diverse structures of the Hansaviertel indeed seem to have been built more or less by chance (figs. 7, 8, 9).[7]

As early as 1960, Leonardo Benevolo named the Hansaviertel as a prime example of the indifference of modern European urban planning and design, declaring: "The disunity apparent in the Interbau quite faithfully mirrors the processes underway in European cities, where one is confronted with the most diverse streams and has difficulty perceiving the unity of the modern tradition, which is concealed beneath an abundance and multiplicity of solitary phenomena."[8] All the same, Benevolo greeted the experiment and the international comparison it involved among various ground plans and approaches to architecture in the field of housing construction.

Generally speaking, the Hansaviertel at least deserves credit for being one of the most popular inner-city residential areas in Berlin. Part of its popularity certainly derives from its

7

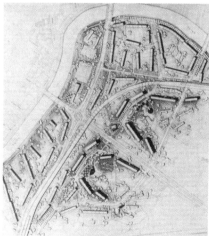

8

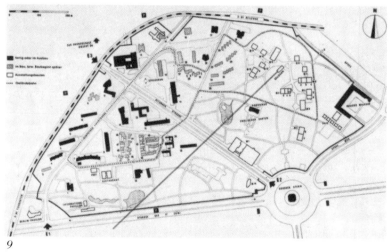

9

7. The Hansaviertel before its
destruction. In the Interbau's
official catalogue, it was announced
that "Berlin's foremost architectural
responsibility lay in abolishing this
unacceptable building's density and
opening up the city."
Landisbildstelle Berlin.

8. Original design for the Interbau.
During the planning stages it was
completely altered. From Berlin und
seine Bauten, IV

9. The official plan of the Interbau.
Influenced by the Chartar of Athens,
the aim for a more "open" city is
also evident in this plan. From
Berlin und seine Bauten, IV.

favorable location opposite the Tiergarten, as well as from the fact that its spacious and open configuration is firmly anchored in the plan of the city by the densely built-up neighborhoods to the west and north, which survived the war largely intact.

Both projects, Stalinallee and the Hansaviertel, were symptomatic of the politically and theoretically antithetic approaches that characterized the architectural and urban-design development of postwar Berlin. Yet they proved to be ineffective as examples. It was the mass-housing construction of the period that was to determine the urban planning of the ensuing years. And the result, at least in East Berlin, was a reduction to the level of the economically feasible.

From the Ideological to the Technocratic Model

Hardly had Stalinallee been completed and the general plan of 1955 been developed in conformance with the sixteen guidelines on urban planning when the East German debate over principles began anew. It was fueled, in the first place, by the political question as to why the hypotheses and existing architecture that had been developed in the interest of a new, socialist society had not found a satisfactory echo among the working populace.[9] Even more crucial was the issue of economic conditions and technological possibilities and aims. The "struggle against ugly, antinationalistic, unaesthetic, and spiritually debilitating constructivism"[10] had simply become too expensive; the cost of Stalinallee is reported to have exceeded that of normal housing of the period by almost fifty percent. In the East German *Handbuch für Architekten*, published in 1954 and still entirely faithful to the sixteen guidelines, "the fundamental problem in industrializing housing construction" was still seen to be a "creative application of completely industrialized building methods" (fig. 10).[11]

Yet soon, all aesthetic scruples were thrown to the wind, and again, the initiative came from Moscow.[12] This time it was Kurt Liebknecht who, citing Nikita Khrushchev, proclaimed in early 1955 that there was no need to transform a "modern apartment building . . . into a church or a museum."[13] Apart from this allusion to the ornamentation of Stalinallee, for which he himself was largely responsible, Liebknecht pilloried its high costs of construction.

This marked the emergence of a new building policy in the GDR. Ground and floor plans were standardized, and a rationalization of initially still conventional construction methods eventually led, by way of a semi-industrialized large-block masonry construction, to the industrialized large-panel construction in reinforced concrete.

The look of the prefabricated housing that since the late 1950s has become ubiquitous in the eastern half of Germany and Berlin is a cogent embodiment of the purely technocratic principles on which not only ground plans and facades but the design of entire cities were based (fig. 11).

Compared to this building program, the maintenance and re-

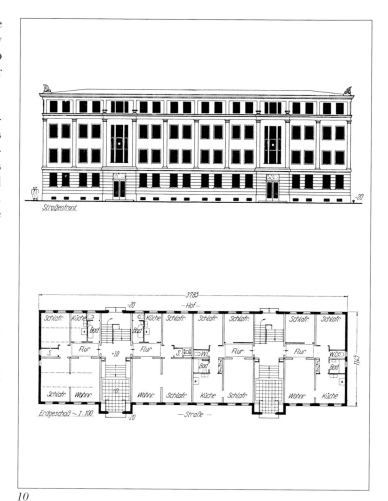

10

11

10. Apartment house with large panel construction in reinforced concrete. Elevation and floor plan. From *Handbuch für Architekten*.

11. An example of the anonymity of housing construction in the 1950s and 1960s in which functional and economic considerations played dominating roles. Landisbildstelle Berlin.

12. *Aerial view of the Friedrichstadt after its destruction in World War II. For twenty-five years, housing policy and urban design in Berlin was not a question of reconstruction but rather of demolition and new construction. From Senatsverwaltung für Bau- und Wohnungswesen, (Berlin, 1954).*

pair of the prewar buildings that still existed in great numbers in East Berlin had hardly any visual impact, since costs had to be kept low and materials were scarce. Important as it was both in sociopolitical terms and for the maintenance of an amenable urban environment, even modest rebuilding proved too ambitious and costly, completely overtaxing the precarious budget of the then-GDR.

The International Competition, Hauptstadt Berlin

In the wake of the popularly successful Interbau competition (in which Hans Scharoun was not invited to participate), West Berlin, with the support of the federal government, again launched an attempt to call attention to the urban situation of Berlin—East and West. In the context of an international competition held in 1959, the unity and visual coherence of Berlin as a potential capital were to be emphasized, at least in the form of plans and despite the city's political division. The planning region for the competition bordered on the north by the Spree River and on the south by the Landwehr Canal, extended in the east-west direction from Alexanderplatz to the Grosser Stern Square.

About one hundred fifty designs were submitted, which, for all their diversity, shared one negative characteristic—a veritably abysmal ignorance with respect to historically developed structures and even with respect to the neighborhoods that had survived the war largely intact and had yet to be demolished (fig. 12). Another point on which the participants seemed tacitly to agree was the radically altered traffic network that the competition organizers had declared to be binding (fig. 13). All of them apparently adhered more or less to the concept of the open or disaggregated city.

In Scharoun's design, an urban landscape of the type he had been propagating for years and that had been prefigured in the Collective Plan, only a handful of public buildings in East and West remained as a reminder of historical Berlin. Yet unlike most of the other participants, he at least recalled the trio of city squares associated with the gateways of the baroque town and its expansion: the square-shaped Pariser Platz, the octagon of Leipziger Platz, and the circular Belle-Alliance-Platz (now Mehringplatz). Such reminiscences, however, could by no means excuse the wholesale destruction of the city's center that was foreseen by most of the plans, including Scharoun's (fig. 14). Morally speaking, the longing reflected here to transform a big city into a Garden of Eden may be legitimate. Yet the consequence of such an illusion would have been to wipe out historical traces even more thoroughly than Albert Speer's planned north-south axis with its grandiloquence could have done.

The illusion of Berlin both as capital and as urban landscape were shattered for what then seemed an interminable period on August 13, 1961. Thirty years have passed since the last attempt was made to plan for Berlin as a whole. Still, the Hauptstadt Berlin competition was not to remain the only effort to set an example in the field of architecture urban planning.

13

14

*13. Competition area for the
International Competition,
"Hauptstadt Berlin," 1958. From
Senator für Bau- und
Wohnungswesen, (Berlin 1954).*

*14. Hans Scharoun. Detail of a
design submitted in the
International Competition,
"Hauptstadt Berlin." It was
awarded second prize. Berlin,
Ergebnis der Internationalen
Stadtebaulichen Ideenwettewerb
'Hauptstadt Berlin', ed., Senator für
Bau- und Wohnungswesen, (Berlin,
1960).*

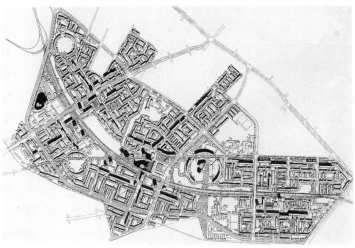

15

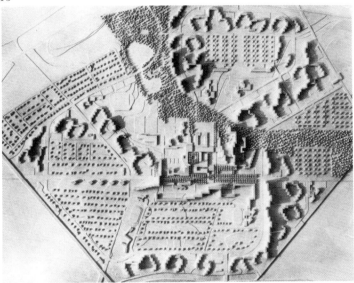

16

15. *The TAC-II Plan for the apartment complex in Britz-Buchow-Rudow, 1963. It made a cautious attempt to reclaim the street for the city.* From *Berlin und seine Bauten, IV.*

16. *The Markisches Viertel. Commencement of building, 1963.* From *Berlin und seine Bauten, IV.*

Caprice, Routine, Ambitious Individualism, and First Signs of Historical Awareness

The first signs that Berlin was beginning to recall the tradition of the European city came in 1960, with the return of one of the great protagonists of modern architecture, Walter Gropius. With the Architects Collaborative, Gropius developed an overall plan for the huge apartment complex in Britz-Buchow-Rudow that now bears his name and that represents an attempt to reclaim for the urban experience at least one key element of the historical city—the street. This attempt was made, moreover, without jettisoning the hypotheses and principles of the AthensCharter.

Gropius's first, revised design, which has become known as the TAC II plan, reflects this conception very clearly. Its slabs of various lengths and heights, set parallel to the longitudinal and latitudinal axes of the plan, give rise to streetlike spaces of varying degrees of continuity. However, there are no closed corners or square or block configurations of the traditional type. The geometric pattern remains abstract; it is lent focus by three circular areas of green surrounded by structures (an homage to Taut's Hufeisensiedlung), as well as by an extended green belt, which with the subway tracks forms the backbone of the development (fig. 15). If it had been realized in this form, the plan would have been a landmark among those few projects that, since the 1960s, had begun to show a resurgence of historical awareness. Instead, Gropius's conception was ignorantly and arbitrarily watered down. The western section of the TAC II plan was sacrificed to the mundane building routine of the public housing contractor, GEHAG, and its architects under Wils Ebert. In the eastern part, the DE GE WO, one of the largest city housing corporations, gave free rein to individual architects' interpretations of Gropius's design. Only here and there does one see evidence of their attempts to do justice to his intentions.[14]

The planning idea of the Märkisches Viertel development, in contrast, was put into practice with a greater degree of fidelity. This was doubtless due to the fact that its three original architects (Werner Düttmann, Georg Heinrichs, and Hans-Christian Müller) retained artistic supervision and contributed materially to the construction process with projects of their own.

In terms of conception, the Märkisches Viertel is a typical example of the urban-planning approach of the early 1960s. While retaining an obligation to the open building method defined in the Charta, its authors no longer felt it necessary to adhere to the rationalistic stringency of row construction, which they considered too functionalist, monotonous, and cold—and above all, too unimaginative. Instead, they relied more on the effects of a sweeping artistic gesture with which their structures fraternally embraced the weekend garden plots that existed on parts of the site. The resulting architectural configuration corresponded to an alternation of building heights that by the same token was inspired not so much by rational considerations as by emotions and visual ideas (fig. 16).

The aesthetic thrust of the project was underscored by the employment of particularly artistically committed architects at various phases of construction. Yet in consequence of having aimed so high, the Märkisches Viertel sunk all the lower in the estimation of its critics, whose frequently exaggerated and ideologically aggressive attacks only served to divert public attention from the much worse, purely technocratic housing projects of the period. Despite the legitimacy and goodwill that characterized the enormous effort necessary to realize it, the Märkisches Viertel ultimately came to figure as the incarnation of the failure of modern urban planning in many respects (fig. 17).

Reassessment of the Historical City

As early as 1964, immediately after the planning decision for the Märkisches Viertel, Wolf Jobst Siedler published a book entitled *Die gemordete Stadt* (*The Assassinated City*),[15] in which he accused "modern urban planning of premeditated, collective murder."[16] His brilliant visual and verbal comparisons of the new housing developments with those of historical Berlin amounted to a sweeping indictment of the urban planning of the day and its manifold sins.

Just two years later, a theoretical underpinning for the elements and characteristics of the historical European city were provided by the Italian architect Aldo Rossi, in his *L'Architettura della citta*.

The first conscious return to the traditional configurations of city blocks and public spaces in Berlin was marked, in 1967, by a plan I developed with Hans Heinrich Moldenschardt for the Ruhwald area. Even at that comparatively late date, a conception of this kind was considered a provocation directed against the established routine of modern urban planning, which indeed was part of the intention (fig. 18). Yet routine continued to dominate the scene, and this led to increasingly vocal criticism of a functionalist architecture that was seemingly reducing itself to more and more purely technocratic terms. Cities, it was lamented, were growing increasingly unlivable and losing their identity. In Berlin, this criticism was directed primarily at the continuing policy of demolition and reconstruction, and it culminated in the late 1960s in connection with the social unrest of the student movement.

The *ultima ratio* of the bitterly committed architecture students of the day was "stop building!" For one thing had become clear about the razing and rebuilding that was going on in Berlin—it alleviated only certain problems related to negative living conditions. The new housing, with its standardized floor plans and building intervals designed to provide more light, air, and sun, was ill suited to reconstituting the old neighborhoods and the intimate atmosphere and close social ties that had been so recklessly abandoned. Still, as unpolitical and technocratic as the sweeping urban renewal methods then being applied in many German cities were, the first project designed to retain the aspect of a traditional neighborhood, on Christstrasse in Charlottenburg, seemed merely romantic, a partial social surrogate for a citywide loss of identity. This initial attempt to conserve the cityscape, which eventual-

17

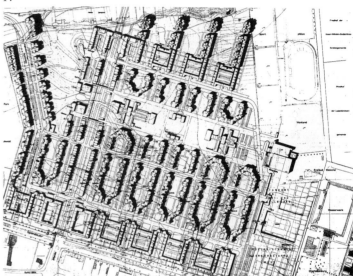

18

17. The Markisches Viertel. It has often been criticized as a prime example of the failings of modern urban design. Ullstein Bilderdienst Berlin.

18. Josef Paul Kleihues. The Ruhwald Project developed in 1967 by the author in partnership with Hans Heinrich Moldenschardt.

ly led to the declaration of the old Charlottenburg district as a renewal area, nevertheless proved popular and served as an example for many similar, more or less successful projects.

Ever since, the nostalgic coddling of old neighborhoods and milieus had been considered good form in Berlin architectural circles. Yet there was more at stake in projects of this kind— the development of a new awareness of and approach to history, based on the insight that the social, functional, and technical interrelationships of big cities and the specific qualities of life dependent on them are related to architectural patterns that cannot be recklessly ignored or destroyed. Concretely, it was a matter of saving what was left of Berlin, formerly the world's largest tenement city, as exemplified by the Luisenstadt and SO-36 districts.

Daily life in these two sections of Kreuzberg was anything but idyllic in the late 1970s and not very much has really changed since. Urban renewal efforts are still primarily determined by the social situation of those concerned, to which only methodically differentiated and sensitive renewal projects can do justice.

So it was certainly an altered consciousness, tempered by a nostalgic backward glance at the intact cityscape of the great prewar capital, that led to increasing criticism of postwar housing and urban planning policy in Berlin, and eventually to the idea of a project, perhaps along Interbau lines, to show that things could be done differently. What emerged was a program of comparatively modest scope, the International Building Exposition, limited to the area of the former diplomatic quarter at the southern edge of the Tiergarten, whose foremost aim was to exemplify the potential of modern public housing.

Living in the Inner City

Against the background of Berlin's architectural and urban development since 1945, it soon became obvious that there could be no simple repetition of the 1957 Interbau in the former diplomatic quarter.[17] The new building exhibition would have to be devoted to an integrated treatment and solution of issues and planning tasks of a very diverse nature.

And, equally obviously, it would be no easy matter to develop new models of "the inner city as an amenable place to live." Models of this kind—not merely verbal but actual, practicable examples—faced a conflict of orientation and aims since they were to be devoted to a rediscovery and development not only of individual and regional solutions but of generally applicable approaches as well. Nevertheless, the Berlin International Building Exposition in 1987 was widely acclaimed as a success for the social and cultural development of architecture and urban planning. There were two, mutually complementary, aims of the exhibition.

In the renewal districts covered by the exhibition, the demonstration areas of Luisenstadt and SO-36, first priority was given to preserving the largely surviving architectural substance

from the nineteenth and early twentieth centuries. Hardt-Waltherr Hämer, who was responsible for the renewal area, characterized the work required and the high degree of social commitment it entailed as sensitive urban renewal and defined a number of guidelines to refurbish these areas in close cooperation with their inhabitants. Models for the healing of such moribund areas, in which new building was largely limited to infrastructural improvement (schools, for example), were familiar from a number of European cities, including Bologna, Rotterdam, Stockholm, and Helsinki. Yet the exhibition areas faced very special problems, since they were densely built-up with five- and six-story apartment buildings with extremely narrow courtyards, and their inhabitants were for the most part underprivileged and of non-German citizenship (largely Turkish).

Work in the areas of new construction in a sense posed a problem of even greater complexity. The three inner-city demonstration districts—southern Friedrichstadt, southern Tiergarten, and Prager Platz—had not only suffered heavy war damage. Their real destruction had set in after the war, with the radical razing not merely of ruined and rebuildable but of largely intact structures. These are facts to which I have already referred; they are well known, and they represent one of the saddest chapters in Berlin's architectural history.

They also help to explain why the exhibition was devoted to reconstructing the ruined city, an admittedly rather sweeping aim that could easily give rise to misunderstanding. It really goes without saying that no one involved in the project was out to reconstruct Berlin as it was in the eighteenth or nineteenth century. The principal aim was to reestablish a link with the better side of Berlin's tradition, as a city of the Enlightenment and the principles of humanism, while taking modern requirements into account. This is why the concept of a critical reconstruction of the city was a theme of the work, in the hope that this historical view might prevail.

Critical reconstruction involved a recognition of the elements that constitute a city in both the intellectual and the formal, aesthetic sense, and a retention of those historical traces that embody the sufferings, hopes, and disappointments of past generations in order to be in a position to enrich the identity of the city in terms of social and artistic criteria.

Critical Reconstruction of the City

Perhaps I should speak of traces of the past recalled, which influenced the work but did not determine it. By comparison to more strongly reductive theories in which the relationship to tradition is more direct, the notion of a critical reconstruction was more open-ended and receptive to experimentation. With an eye to an urban whole that was not superficially harmonious but dialectically complex, the architects devoted themselves to a conscious involvement with conflicting standpoints as aim and method.

Modern involvement with the city as a historical phenomenon is intrinsically dialectical in any case. The question of how to bring the classical dialectical argument to bear on the present in a meaningful way and without becoming retrograde was in a sense the issue at hand, and I believe it is an issue that no one in the future will be able to avoid. After all, modernity is part and parcel of our biographies and cultural history; this means that any conception of historicity that does not wish to be accused of the old, characteristic repressions will have to remain aware not only of a complex and internally contradictory tradition but of the modern protest against this tradition as well. Compared to the aims of what has come to be known as classical modernity, this is an expanded and more highly differentiated demand. For the modernity of the 1920s, as much as it set out to storm the bastions of authoritarian convention with a strange dialectic of enlightenment, nevertheless still dreamed of a unity, a new stance based on progress and technology that ran counter to history and that was to find expression in an international style.

By taking an uncompromising stance against historicism, the classical modern architects brought only the first term of the dialectical process into play—that of simple negation. It was no coincidence but practically the causal result of this negative stance with respect to tradition that modernity sought its categories for the most part in objectifiable experiential factors. The simple negation of this naive functionalism, as Aldo Rossi has termed it, meant that as far as the possibility of emancipation was concerned, it remained within the restricting frame of reference of a defensive stance. This frame of reference was restricting for the simple reason that any defense mechanism, in order to form and maintain itself, requires the image of an antagonist, someone or something that must be engaged in battle and destroyed—yet which cannot be destroyed without jeopardizing oneself and above all one's self-liberation. This latent, unreflected dependence on tradition in which modernity remained entangled throughout its violent struggle with tradition is in fact the source of the magic that surrounds classical modernity; at the same time, it represents the weak point at which attacks are so often directed, based on simplified versions of Max Weber's argument that enlightenment has deprived the world of all magic.

Perhaps this may help explain the working title "A Critical Reconstruction of the City," which was intended to encourage a dialogue between tradition and modernity rather than emphasize the contradictions between the two, which would have been much too simplistic.

I was concerned to find an approach that, instead of striving for a higher unity based on the dissolution of different or conflicting interests, would aim at solving a merely apparent contradiction, by encouraging the free, and in a sense even autonomous, development of the separate elements of the city (building, block, street, square) while ensuring their integration into a larger whole, an order made recognizable by the history of the city and its genius loci.

Although this did not presuppose any priority of urban planning with respect to the individual architectural object in the sense of a value system, it did presuppose the importance of the logic of planning decisions. On any other basis, the particip ation of far more than one hundred architects could hardly have led to the enrichment of the city by buildings or originality but would probably have resulted in a self-serving exhibitionism on the part of diverse architectural theories and artistic capabilities.

The priority of the plan and configuration of the city thus defined were and remain a methodological constituent of the theoretical concern with a critical reconstruction of the European city, for which the demonstration districts of the new construction area of the Berlin International Building Exposition in 1987 provided a first, experimental field. Principal importance was attached to a precise planimetric and stereometric definition of the urban layout, though other architectural aspects—particularly those relating to functional organization—were also discussed in very early phases. This methodological stringency arose from the conviction that the culture of the European city, whatever development it may take, cannot afford to waive the methodical organization of an urban design based on certain, binding goals. This was brought home to us in an unforgettable way during years of debate in an attempt to reach the right decisions.

The extent and conception of an order of this kind, in which particular interests manifest themselves as diverse elements of the city, cannot be satisfactorily defined in terms of the classical statement that the whole is more than the sum of its parts, unwilling as I was to sacrifice this ideal from the outset. But as a closer look at the individual projects indicates, the notion of critical reconstruction permitted a greater degree of functional, social, and aesthetic autonomy to each part of the whole than did the historical city with respect to its public buildings, or even the classical moderns with respect to their program of architectural autonomy. This is in fact the source of the attribute classical, because today we cannot be concerned with the reconstruction, either relatively speaking or in the figurative sense, of the *status quo ante*. Critique (*kritiké*) stands as a challenge to judge, to weigh, and to evaluate, in the face of arbitrariness or dogmatism from whatever camp. Critique, finally, implies the claim of modernity to possess an awareness of crisis while retaining a positive attitude to life.

Modernity, defined as a vital awareness of history and a vitalizing awareness of crisis, can never be as clear-cut or absolute as the classical modern architects still thought it could be. Modernity today is a consciousness of crisis, existential, lived through. The demise of the classical belief in a universal regulative cannot be interpreted as a temporary political symptom. The early moderns lived through a period of crisis, and their thinking was shaped by it. There is no way to avoid our obligation to face the work they produced and the suffering they went through. The step we can attempt to take is thinkably small—and when I say "thinkably," I mean it literally, in the sense that the step can be conceived.

The temptation is great to escape from an awareness of crisis into the perfect world of a neoclassical or historical order or, in the course of a fanatical pursuit of new creations, to succumb to what Nietzsche called a frenzy of originality.

With the aid of a critical reconstruction, we attempted to re-
discover Berlin, a city that since the Enlightenment, since
Gilly and Schinkel, had developed in constructive opposition
to classical unity by emphasizing the vital uniqueness of its
parts as parts of a vital whole. On the day when Berlin was re-
united, this aim took on expanded significance and the chance
of realizing it became greater than ever before.

Notes

1. The entire project of the collective headed by Scharoun was exhibited in the White Room of the Berlin Palace under the title "Berlin Plans—First Report." Scharoun described the planning in detailed form in a lecture held on September 5, 1946. The following citations may serve to characterize his approach:

What remained after the bombing raids and Battle of Berlin had torn the city apart, created a mechanical disaggregation? The remnants present an opportunity to design an urban landscape on their basis. For the city planner, the urban landscape is a principle of design by means of which extensive housing areas can be brought under control. It is a way to divide up the outsized and gigantic into comprehensible, humanly scaled parts and relate these parts to another like the woods, meadows, mountains and lakes are interrelated in a beautiful landscape.

As regards urban structure and traffic system, Scharoun remarked with special reference to Berlin that "the system of radial and ring streets previously employed in big cities is outmoded, since it was predicted on the existence of a center point—once formed by marketplace and church—whose disappearance had made the converging streets meaningless." Then he goes on to say, "Instead, we would suggest a parallel arrangement of business and housing units which would permit an organic development from each individual nucleus."

This structural idea of a zoned urban landscape corresponded to what Scharoun called the basic units of the new housing developments he conceived: "The residential areas are divided into basic units for four thousand to five thousand inhabitants each. These are fundamental cells that approximately correspond in size to the core of the Siemensstadt development and that are scaled such that they can be experienced by a child and represent a world to a child. They reflect the unity of life, life as a coherent structure." Projected onto Berlin, this notion led to the conception of a belt city: "The overall street system follows the configuration of the primordial river valley, with the Barnim and Teltow, the Spree and the Havel, and in shape and direction is vitally integrated in this valley and the topographical conditions, which today have become completely blurred and well-nigh obliterated to sight" (Hans Scharoun, *Berlin plant—erster Bericht* [Berlin, 1946], 156ff.).

2. *Handbuch für Architekten* (Berlin: VEB-Verlag Technik, 1954), 101ff.

3. The final quotation is taken from the fourteenth of the sixteen "principles of urban planning" (*Handbuch für Architekten*, 101ff.).

4. Frank Werner, *Stadtplanung Berlin: Theorie und Realität*, part 1 (Berlin: Kiepert, 1976), 152.

5. See especially Frank Werner, *Städtebau Berlin-Ost*, (Berlin: Kiepert, 1969), 56.

6. First prize in the competition for the rebuilding of the Hansa Quarter went to Gerhard Jobst and Willy Kreuer. The actual construction plan, however, was drawn up by a committee headed by Otto Bartning, and it bears very little resemblance to the award-winning plan. See especially *Berlin und seine Bauten*, part 4, vol. A (Berlin: Wilhelm Ernst und Sohn, 1970).

7. The Interbau competition enjoyed the patronage, as is usual in such cases, of the federal president, who at the time was Theodor Heuss, a man knowledgeable in the fields of architecture and urban planning. He was one of the few who, despite critical reservations, defended the Hansa Quarter and attacked the widespread demolition that was then official policy. In his catalogue introduction Heuss wrote: "Political absurdity has wiped out landmarks of Berlin history after the war, a process that has taken place only in this city and that was prompted by stupidity and maliciousness. Still, at the edge of the Tiergarten a building project has been completed that, documenting the midpoint of the twentieth century, bears a definite obligation to the demands and the principles of a future era" (*Interbau Berlin 1957*, official catalogue of the International Building Exhibition, Berlin, 1957).

8. Leonardo Benevolo, *Geschichte der Architektur des 19. und 20. Jahrhunderts*, vol. 2 (Munich: Callwey, 1964), 444.

9. Werner, *Stadtplanung Berlin*, 160.

10. Ibid., 148.

11. *Handbuch für Architekten*, 543.

12. Werner, *Stadtplanung Berlin*, 160ff. In his chapter on the second "turning point in East German building policy" in 1954–55, Werner described the role of Liebknecht and Collein as follows: "The advocates of the previous building policies, particularly Liebknecht, put themselves in the first ranks of the critics, regardless of the obvious contradictions this involved them in. Those responsible, including Collein and Liebknecht, remained on top, and in 1954 and 1958 became candidates for the central committee of the SED [Socialist Unity Party]. While the changeover initially concerned building technology foremost and only later extended to urban planning, even then it had hardly any adverse consequences for these men. (This may well have been just insofar as the first changeover only came about when pressure was placed on the responsible experts.)"

13. Werner, *Stadtplanung Berlin*.

14. Jan Rave remarked on this in his essay for *Berlin und seine Bauten*: "With the pedestrian street, Horst-Caspar-Steig and its flanking three-story structures by Kleihues and Moldenschardt, Gropius's fundamental idea was put into practice at least at one point" (Jan Rave, "Die Wohngebiete 1945–1967," in *Berlin und seine Bauten*, part 4, vol. A, 216).

15. Wolf Jobst Siedler and Elisabeth Niggemeyer, *Die gemordete Stadt* (Munich and Berlin: F. H. Herbig Verlagsbuchhandlung, 1964).

16. Wolf Jobst Siedler and Elisabeth Niggemeyer, *Die gemordete Stadt*, 2nd ed. (Munich and Berlin: F. H. Herbig Verlagsbuchhandlung, 1978). The quotation is from one of the press responses (*Die Zeit*, Hamburg) excerpted on the dust jacket.

17. Initially, the then-director of the Berlin Senate Building Agency, H. C. Müller, strongly advocated limiting the 1980s building exhibition to the relatively small area of the former diplomatic quarter.

18. To counter the idea of an isolated building exhibition, Wolf Jobst Siedler and I initiated a publicity campaign in the daily *Berliner Morgenpost* in 1977, under the title, "Models for a City." In conjunction with talks with leading politicians, this led to a revision of the decision to limit the exhibition to the erstwhile diplomatic quarter and to the establishment of key aims for the new program.

Manhattan Montage: The Art of Spatial Restructuring 1945–88

M. Christine Boyer

M. Christine Boyer is an architectural preservationist and city planner. She has written critically on the history of American urban planning and is the author of Dreaming the Rational City: The Myth of American City Planning *(1983),* Manhattan Manners: Architecture and Style 1850–1900 *(1985), and* The City of Collective Memory: Its Historical Imagery and Architectural Entertainments *(forthcoming). She is professor of urbanism at the School of Architecture, Princeton University.*

Sergei Eisenstein, the great Russian film director, claimed that the streets of New York were extraordinarily difficult for a stranger to remember. The streets being numbered rather than named, they failed to produce images in his mind calling forth the complex sensations that characterized each street. Consequently, he had to fix in his memory a set of objects such as theaters, stores, and buildings. At first, with the mention of 42nd Street, for example, only with difficulty could he enumerate elements belonging to that street. Eventually, however, all the elements began to fuse dynamically and assemble into a single recognizable image of the street. Such was the spectator's experience of montage as a single view congealed out of associated elements.[1] Had Eisenstein returned often to New York, he would have seen that the characteristics he had committed to memory were reassembled time and again, for change and fragmentation are enduring characteristics of New York City's streets.

Perhaps the story began fifty years ago when an independent city planning commission was first created to guide the city's physical development. Much to Mayor La Guardia's displeasure, such a government agency would have encroached on his territorial powers. Thus he decided to impede the commission's potency by appointing a commissioner from each New York borough and including on the panel of experts nonpolitical professionals such as an architect and an engineer. Rexford Tugwell was selected as the first planning chairman from 1938 to 1941, but confronted with the furious opposition that met his proposed comprehensive plan for the physical appearance of the city, he realized that city planning in New York City was an impossibility and resigned. His arch rival, Robert Moses, took over as the promoter of ad hoc projects, reducing city planning forever to a marginal activity of the government. No one in New York would propose again a physical plan to guide the city's development.[2] Moses wanted New Yorkers to turn their attention to practical and immediate projects, not woolly-eyed long-range plans. He asked the architectural firm of Skidmore, Owings, and Merrill in 1944 to design a postwar planning exhibition. From a semicircular ramp, spectators gazed down upon Moses's map of New York on which were placed toy-sized models of elementary schools, health centers, hospitals, police stations, fire houses, and sewage treatment plants. As one critic noted, this was far from a city plan and more like a building replacement scheme that would cost the city $1.27 billion.[3]

A fragmented city view was not just the product of Moses's vision but belonged as well to the spatial conceptions of the modern architect. Sigfried Giedion praised Moses's parkway system, whose meaning and beauty, he felt, could not be grasped from any single point of observation but instead was revealed only to the traveling eye. Yet this magnificent parkway, Giedion criticized, ends where the massive body of the city begins. "It has not been able to penetrate the city because the city has persisted in remaining an inflexible structure, tightly bound within itself and immovable."[4] Nevertheless, he argued, the parkway eventually would begin to restructure the city on a new and massive scale—the kind of scale that Rockefeller Center had introduced for the first time into Manhattan. This complex of fourteen buildings, Giedion declared,

1. View north on Park Avenue from Grand Central Station.

411

2

2. *United Nations Headquarters, 1947–53.*

3. *Skidmore, Owings & Merrill. Lever House, 1952.*

4. *Cesar Pelli & Associates. Museum Tower, 1985. Cervin Robinson.*

could be "grasped from no single position nor embraced in any single view. There becomes apparent a many-sidedness in these simple and enormous slabs which makes it impossible to bind them rationally together."[5] "At Rockefeller Center the human eye must function similarly [to stroboscopic photographic studies]; it has to pick up each individual view singly and relate it to all the others, combining them into a time sequence. Only thus are we able to understand the grand play of volumes and surfaces and perceive its many-sided significance."[6] So a consensus seemed to arise among architects and planners who agreed that it was far better to plan the huge metropolis of New York in well-defined districts and artful fragments and to forget about how one related to another. And thus it remains today, a city constantly restructured as a montage of assembled views and devoid of a compositional arrangement.

The Restructuring of Midtown Manhattan

One of the more spectacular redevelopment schemes in postwar New York was of course the 1946 decision to locate the headquarters of the United Nations on a site donated by Rockefeller along the East River where tenements and slaughterhouses once stood. As the scheme for the U.N. developed, however, it was apparent that its surrounding district now lay in the direct path of the ever-expanding business and retail section that was spreading north from Grand Central Station and overflowing from the hotel and shopping district along Fifth, Madison, and Park avenues. Zeckendorf, the developer who had initially assembled the U.N. site, suggested that a new master plan and street realignment be designed in the area north of the U.N. site—from 46th to 49th streets and between First and Third avenues—so that the area could be restructured in superblocks for the future location of hotels, theaters, convention halls, concert halls, and press and communication offices. The city, however, said no. Consequently, the New York chapter of the American Institute of Architects (AIA) undertook a modified plan, but this too was rejected. In a spectacular piece of architectural surgery, the AIA designed a grand new east-west boulevard that would have connected the U.N. site with the Grand Central Station zone, cutting through the blocks between 46th and 47th streets from Lexington to First avenues.[7] But New York was in no mood to plan a grand new international center, and it would be left for private enterprise in subsequent years to establish the character of the place.

Between 1920 and 1960, however, more than 92 million square feet of office space were built in Manhattan south of 60th Street, especially during the building boom of the 1950s. Because of this burst of office development, primarily in the midtown section around Grand Central Station, attempts were made as early as 1951 to rezone the city, reducing its residential allotments and easing up on the restriction of office location. The civic dignity of Park Avenue below 60th Street had been destroyed in 1937, when its two or three consecutive miles of splendid hotels and apartments were rezoned to allow commercial development. Although this elegant avenue above 42nd Street had achieved distinction only in the decade after 1914, it received its first wedding-cake stepped-back office

412

tower—a product of the 1916 zoning envelope—when the Universal Pictures Building was located on the east side of the avenue between 56th and 57th streets in 1947. This development was soon followed by two more elegant and appropriate structures: Lever House on the west side between 53rd and 54th streets in 1952 and the Seagram Building on the east side between 52nd and 53rd streets in 1958. The architectural low point of the avenue was reached, however, in 1963 when the fifty-nine-story Pan Am Building was erected over the annex of Grand Central Station, between 44th and 45th streets, completely usurping the view.

Both Lever House and the Seagram Building, on the other hand, had much to teach New Yorkers about skyscraper decorum. Rather than being greedy commercial developments absorbing the full expanse of their zoning envelops, they instead discretely sculptured out space about their towers and welcomed the pedestrian into their plazas. Pulled in from the edges of its site, the slab tower of Lever House was visible from three sides and rose from an elegant two-story pedestal that opened onto its adjoining streets; the Seagram Building made a minimal statement intended to contrast with the traditional composition of Park Avenue by beautifully balancing a detached tower on a raised podium. These buildings were daring innovations offering the serene and aloof effect of pure mute space so absent from the hustle and bustle of the contemporary city. Yet no one could project that these silent insertions would be mimicked banally again and again until barren plazas and artless towers destroyed the street wall and voided the city's texture in countless places.[8]

When the 1916 zoning ordinance was created, the only skyscraper north of 23rd Street was the Times Tower designed by Eidlitz and MacKenzie in 1904 on the triangular plot of land above 42nd Street alongside Broadway. Even though the area around Grand Central Station was expected to generate development and was zoned accordingly as a business district, no planner foresaw how quickly cheap real estate prices and the expansion of rapid transit would turn the district into an overdeveloped midtown office center. An early zoning revision of 1943 lowered the height of the building facades along 42nd Street but allowed Babylonian ziggurats that displayed a terraced and pyramidal look on every side street in the district. The entire midtown area became strangled with traffic and inflated real estate values and filled with nondescript architectural filing cabinets while the fringes of the district, east of Third Avenue and west of Eighth Avenue, where office towers might have been welcomed, lay fallow and underdeveloped.[9]

Finally, after careful negotiations, a new zoning ordinance was put into place in 1961. The old 1916 tripartite distinction that divided the city into use, height, and area districts became instead districts in which allowable uses were specified, bulk and density requirements spelled out, and parking regulations determined. Floor Area Ratios (FARs) became the dominant tool to control the height and bulk of skyscrapers, and eventually appeared to be the only planning instrument the city retained in the 1970s and 1980s. Embedded in the 1961 zoning controls lay an architectural consensus that Manhattan could benefit from the lessons of Lever House and the Seagram

3

4

Building: developers were offered FAR bonuses in return for the provision of such public amenities as open plazas and freestanding towers, arcades and subway entrances. Unfortunately, no one was able to predict how frequently these bonuses would be used and how quickly midtown Manhattan would become superdeveloped as a result.[10]

Copying these design requirements, Sixth Avenue above 42nd Street soon was transformed into a bleak and overpowering canyon of office towers, and not a single planner's voice could be heard over the roar of the construction cranes. When the elevated railway was removed in the early 1940s, a random assortment of decrepit apartment houses, stores, and lofts were suddenly revealed, but not for long. The New York Hilton erected its ugly head on the west side of the avenue between 53rd and 54th streets in 1963 while the CBS Building arose on the northeast corner of 52nd Street in 1965 and a series of colorless towers and empty plazas, such as the Time-Life, Sperry-Rand, McGraw-Hill, Exxon, and Celanese buildings, tried to steal some luster from their neighbors at Rockefeller Center.

Since postwar Americans continued to demonstrate their fascination with the automobile, it could be expected that railway passenger revenues would decline, making the New York Penn Central real estate holdings in the Grand Central district a promising source of new revenue. The Pan Am building was already an intruder, absorbing the sky space over Park Avenue. In 1968, another controversy erupted when plans were announced to erect a fifty-nine-story air-rights tower designed by Marcel Breuer and Associates directly over the station's waiting room. Once again the villain was the city, for no plan existed to prevent the defacing of such a worthy landmark and regulating the ad hoc development of office towers in an already overcrowded district. Grand Central Station was one of the city's recently designated landmarks, having received that distinction in 1967 over the objection of its owners. The New York City Landmark Commission, itself a newly created legislative body formed only in 1965, denied permission to erect a tower atop the terminal. The issues were settled in court after the United States Supreme Court in 1978 recognized the legal right of New York to regulate urban space in its three dimensional envelope. Thus the hole in the sky created by the low ceiling boundaries of the station and the tower walls that surround it came under public control. This ruling also allowed the station's development rights (TDRs) to be transferred to contiguous but more appropriate sites. Grand Central Station would be back in the news in 1986 and the future of its densely built-up blocks once again at stake. Penn Central Transportation Company now was proposing to transfer its development rights underground along the railway tracks to the block between 46th and 47th streets and Madison and Vanderbilt avenues. On that small site, First Boston Corporation planned to squeeze a gigantic seventy-four-story retail and office tower. New Yorkers cannot have it both ways, developers argued: if they want to save the low-scale ambience of historic landmarks, such as the Grand Central Station, then they have to expect superdevelopment in other locations.

With the benefit of development rights transferred from land-

mark structures, megastructures have sprouted in the oddest arrangements. Some towers have grown out of their historic bases, such as the Palace Hotel over the Villard Houses on Madison Avenue between 50th and 51st streets or the gigantic new tower looming over the low-rise Coty-Rizzoli facades on the west side of Fifth Avenue and 56th Street. Other towers were built to the side or in back of a landmarked structure, such as the towers behind Saks Fifth Avenue opposite Saint Patrick's Cathedral on Fiftieth Street between Fifth and Madison, the Metropolitan Tower next to Carnegie Hall on West 57th Street, or the Trump Tower on Fifth Avenue and 56th Street. In general, however, as New York recovered from near bankruptcy in the mid-1970s and as faith in Manhattan as a prestigious address renewed, a new era saw expansive office headquarters shoehorning their towers onto overcrowded midtown blocks on the East Side: the AT&T Building, the IBM Building, and the Equitable complex began the trend. By 1988, some fifteen additional skyscrapers were nearing completion.

The city was concerned in the early 1980s with this East Side megadevelopment and proposed zoning incentives to permit bulkier structures to rise on the underdeveloped West Side blocks between 40th and 57th streets, an area that includes the theater district and Times Square. But here, too, development went out of control, and by 1988 fifteen hotel and office projects had been erected. Perhaps the biggest blockbuster of all was the Worldwide Plaza covering the entire city block between 49th and 50th streets and Eighth and Ninth avenues. The real center of this West Side restructuring is the Times Square area, where four towers designed by Philip Johnson and John Burgee were planned to form Times Square Center on both sides of Broadway between 41st and 43rd streets, and at least ten other straight-edged towers now fill the next ten blocks to the north. Finally, a sharp controversy lingers over the scaled-down version for a skyscraper complex to arise on the west side of Columbus Circle over the old Coliseum site, where it would cast its shadow over Central Park.

The city responds to this process of ad hoc development with special district controls wherever a neighborhood's ambience is threatened or in need of strengthening, such as in Lincoln Square, Greenwich Street in Lower Manhattan, and Union Square. By the late 1960s, for example, the special quality of a luxury retail district along Fifth Avenue between 36th and 59th streets was threatened as one bank and airline office after another opened, entryways to office towers punctured the continuity of the street wall, and some of the larger department stores, such as Best and Co., experienced financial difficulty. A special Fifth Avenue zoning district was created to protect the street wall on both sides of the avenue, and developers were given extra FAR bonuses if a mixture of residential, office, and retail space was provided. In addition, buildings with arcades that ran from side street to side street received additional bonuses. The designs of the Olympic and Trump towers have implemented these new controls, offering a mixture of uses and developing the twenty-four-hour pedestrian arcades in exchange for their loftier spaces. Historic preservation adds another layer to district controls. Since 1965, the New York City Landmarks Commission has frozen large areas of Manhattan from future development unsympathetic to historic appearance: the SoHo/Cast-Iron historic district south of Houston Street; Greenwich Village historic district; a Ladies' Mile historic district from 14th to 23rd streets between Sixth Avenue and Broadway; a large Upper East Side historic district covering most of the blocks between Fifth and Park avenues from 59th Street north to 79th Street; and a newly created West Side historic district, an attempt to stop the explosive growth above 59th Street by designating a section of the city a block or two in depth along Central Park West from 62nd to 96th streets.

Residential Restructuring

From the New Deal to the late 1960s, New York experienced an unprecedented postwar economic boom, and the city's problems seemed centered around social welfare, obsolete housing, inadequate transportation, neglected community services, racial segregation, poverty, and crime. Government subsidies were allocated predominantly to private corporations, often for luxury development with the hopes of creating a trickle-down effect of economic development. Direct government subsidies for low-income housing and social-welfare reforms declined by the late 1960s while tax credits and targeted allotments increased, again an attempt to stimulate private real estate development, and the city's focus on the urban crisis evaporated or was transformed into broader issues of economic growth and market vitality.[11] Targeting money for the expanding sectors of the economy, however, meant disinvesting other sectors, and in the mid-1970s, New York faced a fiscal crisis. As a result, New York in the 1970s and 1980s experienced increasing economic inequality as the poor and less privileged were displaced from the residential areas of Manhattan and from the focus of public attention. Now the city seems recovered from these economic problems, and Manhattan once again became a world command center for international banks and transnational corporations with an expanding financial, legal, and advertising service base. This growth in the 1980s spawned new office and commercial development and created a lively demand for luxury residences, sophisticated entertainment, and shopping complexes.

In the 1940s, New York suffered financially as a result of deteriorating housing and depreciating land values. The homogenous 1811 grid pattern of streets—criticized for its textual monotony—was thought to be the cause of New York's postwar slums, thirteen of which had been scheduled for clearance and redevelopment with low-rent housing units by the city's planning commission in 1940.[12] By 1943, New York State was one of the first in America to pass urban redevelopment legislation enabling corporations to condemn private property and offering them property tax exemptions for redeveloping the land as a neighborhood unit.

A new building type, the residential tower set in an asphalt park and bounded off sharply from surrounding areas by chain-link fences, began to emerge throughout the city. New York had become so fixated on housing as the route to urban redevelopment and neighborhood restructuring that few looked at the issue with an eye to improving nonresidential properties or promoting harmonious community development. New York was preoccupied with the removal of blight and its substitution with low-income housing projects and by the mid-1960s generated project after project with absolutely no way of creating a linkage between disparate sites.[13]

Stuyvesant Town was emblematic of the city's approach to housing. This massive palisade of thirteen-story red-brick apartments was erected in 1948 by the Metropolitan Life Insurance Company on the East Side between 14th and 20th streets to house twenty-four thousand tenants on sixty-one acres. Although there was no guarantee that only low-income tenants would be accepted, the city still offered the developer twenty-five years of property tax abatements, a subsidy amounting to approximately fifty-three million dollars.[14] Lewis Mumford complained in 1950 that at various intervals all along the East River in Manhattan from the Brooklyn Bridge to 155th Street could be found these inflexible, oblong ten- and twenty-story housing prisms standing against the skyline like so many children's building blocks in H-, T-, and Y-patterns. Mumford warned that this type of low-income housing would create "urban disabilities" more difficult to solve than the small-scale slums they so wantonly replaced.[15]

Perhaps no neighborhood suffered more from urban renewal than the west side of Central Park between 59th and 97th streets. Once an economically and socially integrated neighborhood with rows of townhouses and family-style apartment houses, the Upper West Side had been losing its middle-class population since the 1920s. As the exodus created a vacuum, landlords took advantage of this loss—often quadrupling their profits—by converting single-family houses into apartment and rooming houses to accommodate low-income groups and turning large, family apartments into smaller units and furnished rooms. Conditions on the West Side continued to deteriorate as crime rates increased, fire and health hazards grew, and minority groups generated new social problems for the district. The Upper West Side now held an outer shell of wonderful apartment buildings along Riverside Drive and Central Park West, but its center had been deteriorating for years.[16]

Mayor Robert Wagner announced in 1955 that he would request the designation of certain slum areas and deteriorating blocks of the West Side as an Urban Renewal Area and thus open the floodgates for federal aid to finance new public housing projects and to subsidize the rehabilitation of still-viable structures. In response, a twenty-block area between 87th and 97th streets, from Central Park West to Amsterdam Avenue, was declared blighted, a proclamation that cleared the way for its complete redevelopment. In the meantime, the city soon realized that sound neighborhood restructuring meant achieving a mixture of incomes and classes and began to make a concerted effort to attract the middle class back to the Upper West Side. Consequently by 1957, the Mitchell-Lama Slum Prevention Law had its pilot run in this renewal area. Under this act, low-interest loans were offered to developers for middle-income housing projects. Also, in order to save existing structures from demolition and to spur voluntary rehabilitation work, the city decided to resell many of the rowhouses it had recently condemned and acquired, requiring that new buyers remodel or rehabilitate the structures. Between 1963 and 1973, more than twelve hundrd row houses were renovated on the West Side between 59th and 90th streets.

Soon after the first urban renewal project was announced, another site was selected to the south: the Lincoln Square urban renewal project would turn 59th to 70th streets from Amsterdam to West End avenues into a new Cultural Center for the Performing Arts. Selective clearance of a nine-block area between 83rd and 86th streets and Amsterdam Avenue to Riverside Drive stabilized that district, and Mayor Wagner declared a war on blight from 79th to 104th streets, selecting 84th Street as a community improvement district. Called the most troubled block on the West Side, the *New York Times* reported in 1961 that it was the scene of deplorable living conditions where violent clashes often took place between blacks and Puerto Rican residents. Within six months, seven hundred of the one thousand so-called problem families were removed, four slum buildings were razed, and a new drug rehabilitation center had opened. Similar plans were announced to rehabilitate 85th Street between Riverside Drive and West End Avenue, while 80th Street was being renovated by private developers.

These plans would not go forward without citizen complaints, however. Fingers were pointed at property owners who profited immensely from government-sponsored redevelopment. A West Side Tenants Committee referred to the 87th Street to 97th Street project as "one of the largest real estate grabs the city has ever known." The committee objected to plans that destroyed the neighborhood scale and tradition of the Upper West Side by razing all the buildings along a ten-block stretch of Amsterdam Avenue and rebuilding the street with a setback that gave it a shopping mall effect. A similar plan for Columbus Avenue also was denounced as equally extraneous to the architectural and neighborhood quality of the Upper West Side. In addition, it was correctly projected that new apartments provided by urban renewal entrepreneurs would be too expensive and too small for most of the families threatened with relocation and displacement and that neighborhood businessmen and storekeepers would not be able to afford the new rental spaces.

By 1965, the West Side renaissance was well underway. Since the southern border of the Upper West Side below 67th Street was secured by the Lincoln Center for the Performing Arts, its northern border was stabilized above 87th Street where redevelopment had surged ahead, and luxury housing along Central Park West and Riverside Drive had never been lost, the interior area seemed ripe for restructuring. Within this bounded area that Mayor Wagner already had partially redeveloped, tax incentives in the 1970s underwrote private market rehabilitation. In fact, as the city slid toward its fiscal crisis during the mid-1970s, at a time when the doors of the municipal bond market were closed and there was no federal money available to continue neighborhood restructuring, tax incentives became the only real-estate game in town, and developers eagerly took advantage of them to garner windfall profits by renovating abandoned structures, run-down hotels, underutilized

office buildings, as well as row houses and luxury apartments and even restoring facades on historic landmarks.

A City Planning Commission report has claimed that in the 1970s, seventy-five hundred people between the ages of twenty-five and forty-four moved to the West side between 70th and 86th streets, representing forty-seven percent of the area's population. Today new restaurants and specialty stores have sprung up all along the avenues of the Upper West Side. While rents have soared, townhouses for sale are just about unheard of, and commercial rents for boutiques and restaurants have reached a peak more typical of luxurious locations on the Upper East Side. A few years ago, the commission also listed more than 132 Upper West Side sites that were soft or ripe for development, many of these along the major avenues and occupied by small-scale structures. By the late 1980s, rampant development had been roaring up the spine of Broadway, turning every sleepy two-story structure into a mammoth new apartment house in emulation of those along Central Park West. The extremely tall spire of the Park Belvedere, visible from all over the Upper West Side, has dared to raise its head over the Natural History Museum and Manhattan Square at Columbus and 79th Street while a cluster of new luxury apartments and television studios adorn the Lincoln Center district. To the south lies the controversial development on the old Coliseum site and to the west, extending along the Hudson River below 72nd Street, stand the air rights over seventy-six acres of Pennsylvania Railroad yards that the developer Donald Trump currently controls. In addition, there are many churches scattered throughout the neighborhood whose congregations have dwindled over the years, and some of these churches intend to retain the option to sell their development rights to speculators who would erect tall towers over their sanctuaries.

Of course many of the old-time residents of the Upper West Side have opposed these new transformations. Active citizen protest has driven more than one developer to modify his plans and to erect more community-oriented structures, but these voices cannot stop the thrust of development. Faced with the failures of planning, the creation of a large historic district appears to be the only approach to channel the real estate market and preserve the architectural ambience and residential quality of the Upper West Side. The City Planning Commission has responded too late and too weakly by tinkering with zoning so that it currently prohibits high-rise structures on the mid-block townhouse sections below 96th Street. It appears that New York's residential districts have few resources to combat speculative real estate growth that slowly eats away at a neighborhood's integrity, reducing its more spontaneous mixture of economic classes and land uses until its original residents are displaced and a homogenized luxury enclave appears.

The gentrification of the Upper West Side, or the so-called natural process of filtering up to more productive uses, is not an isolated event. Harlem, the Lower East Side, and the East Village are experiencing various stages of the same process. Without a plan, this systematic gentrification fits nicely into the overall process of the spatial restructuring of Manhattan's office districts, financial centers, entertainment zones, and retail complexes in fragmented patterns across the city. The center of metropolitan New York during the 1970s and 1980s has been transformed increasingly into a residential and working enclave for the professional and managerial elite. Polarized between the very rich and the extremely poor, New York in the late 1980s continued to underwrite the real estate market with tax incentives and zoning allowances while withdrawing from subsidized low-income housing and its former welfare commitments.

Restructuring Lower Manhattan and the Waterfront

The old office district of Lower Manhattan was not going to take a back seat in this restructuring game and simply watch midtown capture its former glory. It was apparent to downtown interests, as early as 1950, that the undisputed center of financial and commercial capital below Fulton Street in Lower Manhattan was entrenched. Beginning in the 1920s, its supremacy had been challenged by the Grand Central district, and another setback came when Rockefeller Center opened in the 1930s. Except for the Brooklyn-Battery Tunnel and a nearby public parking garage, Lower Manhattan development was static while uptown was thriving on United Nations activity, transportation terminals, and postwar office development. So a plan was proposed to connect its transit system with commuter lines, develop more garages, widen the narrow maze of streets near the East River to ease the flow of traffic, and generally enhance the accessibility of Lower Manhattan so that it could compete successfully with the uptown office center near the major nodes of transportation. Since 1948, moreover, studies had been made to test the feasibility of constructing an elevated crosstown expressway to connect the Holland Tunnel on the west with both the Manhattan and Williamsburg bridges on the east.[17]

The district eventually was restructured through plans proposed during the 1950s for an expanded Civic Center near Foley Square and with ideas developed by the Citizens' Committee on Lower Manhattan Redevelopment and a Rockefeller-sponsored Downtown Lower Manhattan Association. New approaches were built to the Brooklyn Bridge, and with the removal of the elevated railway Park Row became a broad thoroughfare as far north as Chatham Square. Pearl Street, too, was widened between Franklin and Fulton streets so that its blocks of substandard structures and narrow meandering streets south of the Brooklyn Bridge and close to the East River were ready for redevelopment. There was also a proposal to condemn six blocks on the southern edge of Battery Park as an urban renewal site and build luxury apartment towers so that financial workers could walk to Wall Street.[18]

A Rockefeller-sponsored report noted in 1958 that the financial district in Lower Manhattan was forced to reach skyward because it had no land on which to expand horizontally. At the same time, it was completely hemmed in by decaying and underutilized districts. In the very shadow of the financial district, on approximately ninety-seven acres of land north of Fulton Street, the old meat, fruit, vegetable, butter, and egg market sat along old decaying piers on the Hudson River in rows of deteriorated structures more than a hundred years old. Since the Washington Market no longer delivered produce primarily intended for Manhattan, it could be relocated outside of the city in modernized and efficient structures and its former location redeveloped more profitably with housing. Over on the East River, the congested narrow lanes south of the Brooklyn Bridge were the logical path of expansion for the financial district. The plan was to relocate the Fulton Fish Market and demolish the waterfront piers and build a helicopter port and an airstrip for commercial planes. Since the Fulton Fish Market no longer received its major shipments by sea, but relied instead on truck distribution, it too could benefit from relocation and its area redeveloped with housing.[19]

As if to show good faith toward the financial district, David Rockefeller's Chase Manhattan Bank soon announced plans to erect a new office tower including a gratuitous plaza. By 1960, a building boom had been created, and sixteen new office towers could be counted along the narrow streets of Lower Manhattan. In the early 1960s, the twin 110-story towers of the World Trade Center were built, Pace College began to expand, the Civic Center grew, and Beckman Hospital built a downtown annex. Still the waterfront, barricaded behind a ring of highways around the periphery of the financial district, continued to decline as cargo shipping and wholesale marketing either moved away or was removed. Regional planners even in the 1930s had recognized the waterfront as a lost opportunity, noting that one of the city's "most striking architectural feature is its mass of high buildings as seen from the surrounding areas of water, which give it the benefit of open space from which its buildings can be seen. It is on the frontage of these water areas that its greatest opportunity lies for creating beauty of buildings."[20]

A respectable body of citizens formed a mayor's task force in 1967 to talk about the threatened city and its abandoned waterfront. What New York needed, they agreed, was a new civic identity and grandeur of style in its architectural statements. So they reported: "Usually it is in the long view that grandeur is realized, but sometimes it seems that New York is officially numb to these possibilities."[21] Since development took place in fragmented districts, no designer was able to secure a vista to enhance each project. Vistas were possible from the four corners of Central Park, but, these citizens warned, they were likely to be overpowered by clumsy designs such as the Coliseum, a routine structure already sitting on its southwest corner in 1955. The United Nations was a successful place in itself, but the grand avenue once planned to link it with Grand Central Station had never been completed. Lincoln Center was another development project that had failed to get a vista opening onto Central Park. In addition, the waterfront clearly needed to be restructured and made available or at least visible to the citizens of New York. So the report concluded: "The city's largest sweep of nature by far is its harbor and rivers. The city is almost twenty-five percent water, with no less than 578 miles of waterfront within the city limits. This presents opportunities for both lyricism and liveliness which has largely been neglected."[22]

*5. Benjamin Thompson &
Associates. Pier Pavillon, Pier 17,
South Street Seaport, 1984.*
Steve Rosenthal.

*6. Plan for development of Lower
Manhattan.* New York Public
Library.

By the late 1980s, however, a spectator could pass along the waterfront of Manhattan following a sequence of visual enclosures, both real and imaginary—from Riverwalk on the East River to South Street Seaport, South Ferry, Battery Park City, the Hudson River Center, Television City, or some facsimile to come and a grand ribbon of green stretching between Riverside and Battery parks—and experience a surprising compositional effect that both pulls these diverse scenes together and sets them apart from each other. South Street Seaport is a typical story of waterfront restructuring, where the dynamics of buying and selling not only determined its origin but controlled its future as well. The last vestiges of New York's mercantile district, an eleven-block area of four- and five-story late-eighteenth- and nineteenth-century commercial structures, was imperiled in the 1960s by a Wall Street building boom and the relocation of the 1822 Fulton Fish Market. From an urban redevelopment viewpoint, the area contained only shabby structures, dilapidated piers, marginal enterprises, and squatters. It deserved to be officially designated a slum. In 1966, the Lower Manhattan Plan, noting that the financial district was running out of space, proposed that office and luxury residential towers be built on landfill extending out to the pier line along the entire waterfront from the Brooklyn Bridge on the East River to Battery Park on the Hudson River. Six residential communities were planned to house between ten and fifteen thousand people each, with each centered on a plaza located on the waterfront axes of Wall, Broad, Chambers, and Fulton streets and the World Trade Center.

But there were disagreements in the 1960s about how to implement this scheme. Since shipping activity on New York's waterfront was declining, what a splendid time to recapture its glory by building a maritime museum! Consequently, a bill was passed in the state legislature in 1966 to locate such a museum on Schermerhorn Row, which contained twelve counting houses (1810–12) erected by Peter Schermerhorn on Fulton Street, even though this row was right in the center of one of the proposed new residential communities. The newly formed Friends of South Street Seaport had intended to build a living outdoor museum recreating the ambience of the so-called street of ships on four blocks of the old mercantile district along the East River with Schermerhorn Row as its centerpiece. Their plan was to develop a mixture of residential, retail, office, museum, and pedestrian spaces in restored and reconstructed buildings. The City Planning Commission in 1968 created the Brooklyn Bridge Southeast Urban Renewal Plan in order to carry out some of the new development that the Lower Manhattan Plan called for and some restoration activity that the Friends of the South Street Seaport envisioned.

And then began a long negotiation game in which parcels of land were traded back and forth between a number of players; the city's glut in office space during the early 1970s, its fiscal crisis of the mid-1970s, and its reemergence as a world-class city and financial center with an expanding white-collar employment base in the 1980s played important roles. A part of this restructuring game, the South Street Seaport became a historic district in 1977, but a new public-private partnership sprung up as well. The meaning of preservation would be stretched beyond protecting the rich history of New York's

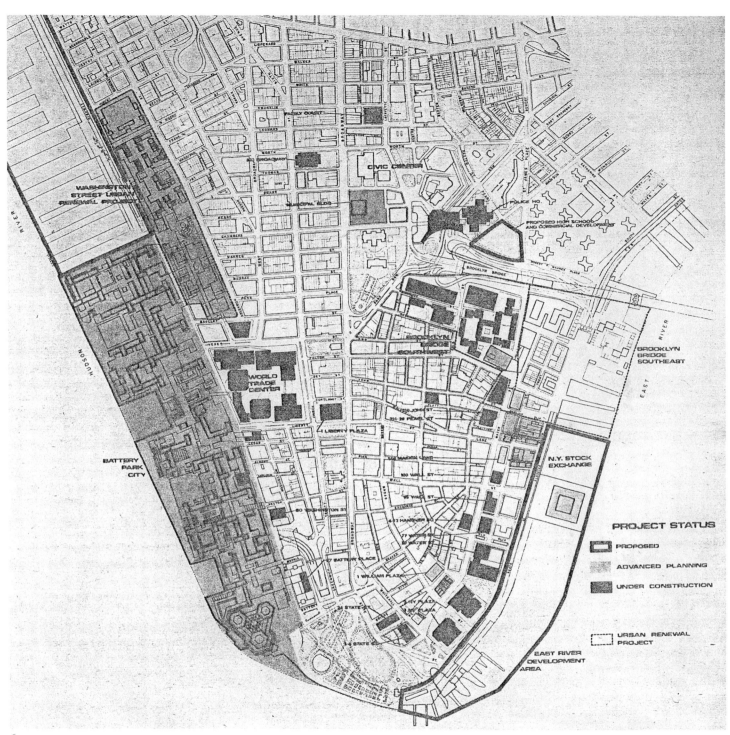

WASHINGTON
STREET URBAN
RENEWAL PROJECT

BATTERY
PARK
CITY

WORLD
TRADE
CENTER

1 LIBERTY PLAZA

N.Y. STOCK
EXCHANGE

CIVIC CENTER

POLICE HQ.

PROPOSED HIGH SCHOOL
AND COMMERCIAL DEVELOPMENT

BROOKLYN BRIDGE

BROOKLYN
BRIDGE
SOUTHWEST

BROOKLYN
BRIDGE
SOUTHEAST

EAST RIVER
DEVELOPMENT
AREA

PROJECT STATUS

☐ PROPOSED

▨ ADVANCED PLANNING

▧ UNDER CONSTRUCTION

⬚ URBAN RENEWAL
PROJECT

HUDSON RIVER

EAST RIVER

nineteenth-century maritime development to include the creation of a twenty-four-hour-a-day tourist attraction with sustaining residential and commercial development. In 1979, the Rouse Company jumped into the fray, offering with the aid of the Urban Development Corporation to turn South Street Seaport into a festival place based on the model of Boston's Faneuil Hall and Quincy Market and Baltimore's Harborplace. By the time South Street Seaport officially opened in 1983, three-quarters of its museum exhibition space had been reassigned to Cannon's Walk, an interior arcade lined with shops. Besides the museum, whose cultural program had yet to be financed, a few ships rehabilitated and reberthed at its slips, and a multiscreen adventure film *The Seaport Experience*, cultural resuscitation stalled while redevelopment gained an advantage. The new Fulton Market Building opened in 1983, and new pier pavilions and a thirty-four-story office tower called Seaport Plaza opened in 1985. To put it another way, New York's maritime culture had become a valuable commodity.

On the other side of Lower Manhattan, there arose yet another fragmented piece in the contemporary game of spatial restructuring—Battery Park City. Once linked by the 1966 Lower Manhattan Development Plan to the rest of the waterfront, Battery Park City was presented in the 1980s as an autonomous neighborhood and a spectacular symbol of New York's return to its rightful status as a world-class city. But like South Street Seaport, Battery Park City—built on ninety-two acres of landfill—is a historically constituted and structured compositional space. Here one can find a reflection of the city's prewar apartment houses combined with the views and atmosphere of Brooklyn Heights, the reproduction of Central Park lampposts and benches, and images drawn from the private enclave of Gramercy Park as well as the great landscapes of Olmsted's parks. This urban dream is based on a master plan created in 1979 that used design guidelines based on elements and styles from the city's best residential sections, its original grid-iron street pattern, and the more subtle effects of its lighting, signage, and colors.

Battery Park City was not designed as a single-use project, like the red-brick housing complexes that dotted the East River, the cultural capital of Lincoln Center, or even the international headquarters of the United Nations. Instead, it is a multi-use city within the city, incorporating apartments and offices, museums and schools, parks and theaters, hotels, restaurants, and shops. As a business center of worldwide importance, New York's financial district needed room to expand and places to house its workers. Two years after plans for the World Trade Towers were announced, the city proposed using soil excavated in the development of towers for landfill along the derelict Hudson waterfront. The key to this new development lay in the creation in 1968 of a quasi-public Battery Park Authority empowered by the state to sell bonds in order to finance its landfill operations, remove the decadent piers, and complete the necessary infrastructure.

By 1976, however, Battery Park City was a barren landfill unable to attract development interest. The intervening years were of course exactly the period when New York slid toward bankruptcy. In such financially gloomy times, the Battery Park City Authority was unable to sell additional bonds and thus could neither raise the money for development loans nor attract development interest. As New York's office market began to recover in 1977, and its image as a glittering world city reemerged, the need arose for corporate support services, communication centers, entertainment spaces, and luxury housing to complement its expanding white-collar employment. The World Trade Center was becoming a dominant force in the restructuring of Lower Manhattan, and this new transportation, tourist, and commercial hub lay directly opposite the Battery Park City site and was in fact pushing the office center of Lower Manhattan toward the west and the river.

To the north of the World Trade Towers, the old Washington Market had been removed, allowing Tribeca to achieve a lively pace of luxury residential loft conversions. It was reasoned then that if the master plan for Battery Park City was reorganized to allow more flexible and smaller-scale development and that if the ideal of middle-income residential communities in Lower Manhattan could be abandoned, the barren landfill of Battery Park City might appeal to local developers. The time seemed ripe for restructuring the view of waterfront development. Discarding the superblock megastructure mentality of the modernist 1966 plan, the revised master plan of 1979 followed Manhattan's street pattern, creating smaller rectangular blocks; conventional building lots and streets with sidewalks would enable block and lot development to prevail. The street would once again become the major organizing force for urban design, reintroducing shopping arcades, street-level crossings, and vehicular traffic. In addition, a variety of park and landscape designs, public amenities, and street furniture would exploit the natural potential of this waterfront property. Since the success of the new plan was dependent upon commercial development, the business district of this new town was shifted to the center of the site just opposite the World Trade Towers. Transfer of development rights from site to site enabled a large-scale complex to arise.

Gateway Plaza, the first residential development in Battery Park City, opened in 1982. Previously, in 1981, Olympia and York Properties began construction on the four towers of the World Financial Center, and the Battery Park Authority designated eight development teams for its Rector Place residential community. By 1983, the first segment of the waterfront esplanade was opened, and within a few years, the World Financial Towers, some of the parks, and Rector Place were completed. And there is more to come.

One writer has noted, "If this newest part of Manhattan were a movie set, New Yorkers would laugh at its impossible concentration of city landmarks in reality,"[23] for this compositional form explicitly relies on a series of familiar, undisturbing, and comfortable views—now called consensus architecture—taken from New York's architectural past. Commenting upon Battery Park City, the architectural critic Paul Goldberger claimed that this triumph of urban design is "close to a miracle" for being "the finest urban grouping since Rockefeller Center."[24] Goldberger also remarked that he, like other New Yorkers, agreed that there was nothing wrong with Manhattan

420

as it appeared and that "most of the attempts by architects and planners to rethink the basic shape of the city [since 1945] have resulted in disaster."[25]

Conclusion

And so the landscape of contemporary Manhattan appears, a montage composed of discontinuous parcels and specially designed insertions that annihilate the in-between spaces and cut away the contradictions inherent in the process of restructuring. No coordinating device rises to hold the fragmented composition together nor to modify the inequality that sets poor and abandoned areas against luxury and profitable districts. Of course, every architectural structure is buffeted about by regulatory controls that suggest its form, land prices that determine its location, and economic conditions that set its value. But real estate capital within these rules is allowed to be both flexible and independent: withdrawing and reinvesting as seems profitable, yet slowly and systematically revitalizing the whole. If we began in the postwar boom to assail the grip of tradition and permanence that failed to materialize an open and mobile city, then we end with a view reevaluating the values of time and place that our modern vision has plundered. If we focused on poverty and blighted neighborhoods in the expansive postwar decades, then the 1970s and 1980s have seen us contract to consider only profitable real estate investments, economic development projects, and neighborhood gentrification. Yet the process of spatial restructuring with its language and logic of economic growth and vitality underwrites all of these endeavors. Economic expansion ushers in on its coattails geographic expansion, slowly and somewhat invincibly transforming the landscape of Manhattan into an enclave for the elite.

Notes

1. Sergei Eisenstein, *The Film Sense*, trans. Jay Leyda (New York: Harcourt Brace, 1942) 15–16.
2. Mark I. Gelfrand, "Rexford Tugwell and the Frustration of Planning in New York City," *American Planning Association* 51 (1985): 151–60.
3. "Planning with You," *Architectural Forum* 80 (June 1944): 87; and "New York Gapes at Its Future," *Architectural Forum* 80 (May 1944): 57.
4. Sigfried Giedion, *Space, Time and Architecture* (Cambridge: Harvard University Press, 1941; 13th ed., 1962), 735.
5. Ibid., 752.
6. Ibid., 755.
7. Frederick J. Woodbridge, *East Midtown Manhattan: A Comprehensive Plan for Development* (New York: American Institute of Architects, 1948); William Zeckendorf, "New Cities for Old," *Atlantic Monthly* (November 1951); and Robert C. Weinburg, "A Comprehensive Plan for East Midtown Manhattan," *Journal of the American Institute of Architects* 12 (July 1949): 13–19.
8. Lewis Mumford, "House of Glass," *The New Yorker* 27 (August 9, 1950): 48–54; and "The Lesson of the Master," *The New Yorker* 34 (September 13, 1958): 141–52.
9. Lewis Mumford, "The Sky Line," *The New Yorker* 30 (October 23, 1954): 132–38.
10. Jerold S. Kayden, *Incentive Zoning in New York City: A Cost-Benefit Analysis* (Cambridge, Mass.: Lincoln Institute of Land Policy, 1978).
11. Michael Peter Smith and Dennis R. Judd, "American Cities: The Production of Ideology," in Michael Peter Smith, ed., *Cities in Transformation* 26 (Beverly Hills, Calif.: Sage Publications, 1984).
12. Sylvia W. Stark, *Ailing City Areas: Economic Study of Thirteen Depressed Districts* (New York: Citizens' Housing Council of New York, 1941).

13. David Crane, *Planning and Design in New York: A Study of Problems and Processes of Its Physical Environment* (New York: The Study Group of New York Housing and Neighborhood Improvement, September 1966).
14. Lewis Mumford, "Prefabricated Blight," in *From the Ground Up* (New York: Harcourt, Brace, and World, 1956), 108–14.
15. Lewis Mumford, "Red-Brick Beehives," *The New Yorker* 26 (May 6, 1950): 92–98. The 1949 federally funded housing act simply added fuel to the urban renewal fire razing section after section of the city. Within ten years, Manhattan planned to redevelop the following Title 1 projects: Corlears Hook, Harlem, North Harlem, West Park (Manhattantown), Morningside-Manhattanville, Columbus Circle, South Greenwich Village, Washington Square South East, Bellevue, Seward Park, Lincoln Square, Park Row, Pennsylvania Station-South/Riverside-Amsterdam, Gramercy Park, Cooper Square, and Park Row Extension.
16. The story of the West Side's gentrification is condensed from M. Christine Boyer, "The West Side Renaissance" (unpublished monograph, 1983).
17. James Felt and Co., Inc.; Voorhees, Walker Foley and Smith, *Recommendation for a Redevelopment Study of Lower Manhattan South of Fulton Street* (June 12, 1950).
18. Report by Hulan E. Jack, borough president, *Manhattan Civic Center Development* (1957).
19. David Rockefeller and John D. Butt, *Lower Manhattan Recommended Land Use Redevelopment Areas, Traffic Improvements* (New York: Downtown-Lower Manhattan Association, Inc., 1958).
20. Thomas Adams, *The Building of the City, Regional Plan*, vol. 2 (New York: Regional Plan of New York and Its Environs, 1931), 75–76.
21. William Paley, James M. Clark, Jr., Joan K. Davidson, Eli Jacobs, Philip C. Johnson, George Lindsay, Mrs. Albert A. List, Walter McQuade, I. M. Pei, Jaquelin Robertson, Robert A. M. Stern, and Walther N. Thayer, *The Threatened City: A Report on the Design of the City of New York by the Mayor's Task Force* (February 7, 1967), 26.
22. Ibid., 30.
23. Michael deCourcy Hinds, "Shaping Landfill into a Neighborhood," *New York Times*, March 23, 1986; section 8, 1, 18.
24. Paul Goldberger, "Battery Park City Is a Triumph of Urban Design," *New York Times*, August 31, 1985.
25. Ibid.

In Dialogue with Witnesses to the Past: The Architecture of West Berlin

Peter Rumpf

Born 1941 in Wattenscheid, Peter Rumpf studied architecture at the Technische Hochschule in Munich and the Technische Universität in Berlin. Until 1971, he worked in the architectural offices of Robert Tepesch and Professor Peter Lehrecke in Berlin. He then became an editor of Bauwelt and has been its editor-in-chief since 1987.

West Berlin was an odd sort of place where everything was always a bit different from anywhere else. The image that the city liked to project of itself was that of a fairground: the Brandenburg Gate and the Radio Tower, the Kongresshalle (with and without its hat brim), the Internationales Congress Centrum and the Bierpinsel, the Europa-Center with the Mercedes star, and the Ku'Damm with a demonstration. West Berlin was open around the clock The city was much more than this, however, and when one went into the side streets one began to understand its fascination for so many people. There it became clear that the artificial situation in which the city found itself also allowed for the kind of experiments and exceptions that elsewhere would have had difficulty withstanding the harsh glare of a political and economic spotlight. At a safe distance from this spotlight, creativity could flourish.

This had not always been true of Berlin's architecture. During the 1920s Berlin was the place where the renewal of architecture and the renewal of society through architecture had been attempted in a more radical manner than in any other city. Within a decade, however, the level of its architecture had sunk far below that which it had once represented and was submerged in an intellectual morass of provincialism while claiming world domination. In the immediate postwar period, therefore, there was a very strong desire in the city to prove that the process of reconstruction really would be divorced from the recent past.

This position was motivated more by political than by ethical considerations. It perceived every form of antihistoricism as progressive, and every form of continuity, no matter how carefully formulated, was decried as reactionary and left by the wayside. This was a position which was shared equally by politicians, intellectuals, and narrow-minded citizens, and it would mark the city more deeply than the 1920s, the Third Reich, or even the war's bombs had done. This was as true for the eastern as for the western part of the city.

Characteristic of this "new start" in the city's postwar architecture was a hypertrophic radicalism in the way its urban structure should be reordered, even though the bare necessities of life were hard to come by. On the other hand, perhaps hardship was exactly the reason for such hypertrophy. Loss is liberating. At the time it was thought that the greater the loss, the greater the freedom from constraints, be they spatial or physical. It was also a "zero hour" with respect to the people who made the decisions concerning architecture. These young architects saw themselves as the successors of an interrupted modernism. Often, however, they only appropriated modernism's formal codes and adapted them to a large scale for the huge task of reconstructing the city. On the opposing side, they were faced with an influential group of people centered around Hans Scharoun, the head of Berlin's Department of Building and Housing.

Even if each came from an entirely different direction, both schools had the same goal. Berlin should be prepared for the year 2000. It should have fresh air and green spaces, be adapted to traffic and divided according to functions. It should be manageable and modern—whatever one meant by the lat-

1. Ruin of the Memorial Church of Emperor William with Egon Eiermann's new structure (1961), 1966. Landesbildstelle Berlin.

423

2

3

ter term. Above all, it had to be different from the Berlin that had come to an end with the kaiser and with Hitler. This goal was most apparent in the attitude toward buildings that had managed to survive the war or had not already been sacrificed to the reordering of the city. Whenever it was considered necessary to widen or curve a street or to construct new autobahn routes, there was no hesitation about cropping or even demolishing the buildings that stood in the way. Such operations, which over large areas had a decisive influence upon the architecture, continued into the 1960s and 1970s. Although they had the support of all of the leading authorities; today, everybody agrees that they were disastrous for the urban structure and for the development of a sense of identity on the part of Berlin's citizens. No Berliner will now admit that he or she ever played a role in this fateful development.

If one wants to discover individual examples of architectural nonconformity behind the mass production, one has to look at the challenges that faced architects, who had to deal with what had been left over. Their responses give a far stronger impression of the city's attributes than do the spectacular individual buildings that can still be found on countless postcards and that, very early on, formed Berlin's reputation as an architectonic revue. These responses were certainly less spectacular than such highlights but they have had a more lasting effect (at least in the western part of the city). Perhaps they even paved the way for the subsequent rejection by the IBA (International Building Exposition) of ruthless urban renewal and its recognition of the importance of continuity.

Around 1960

Not coincidentally, it was the construction of churches that provided conflicting architectural trends with a formal experimental field and an architectonic sphere of action. The church was probably the institution whose traditional self-image had been most seriously shattered; it was also the most open to all attempts to view society in new forms. This was true of both denominations. A striking example of the ecumenical fresh start can be found on the edge of what remained of the city, in Schöneberg. Within the framework of the neighboring construction on land between Dominicusstrasse and Hauptstrasse, across from the town hall, architects Hermann Fehling and Daniel Gogel made full use of the language of the Scharoun school in their virtuosic stacking of expressive inner and exterior spaces upon each other. The Catholic Church, St. Norbert's (fig. 2), and what remained of the churchyard after it was lopped off to widen a street, represent an attempt to create a new street front between high gable walls through the use of ascending and descending concrete slabs. At the other end, the Paul Gerhard Church (fig. 3) recedes from the street line, thereby creating a dynamically articulated square in front of the old Schöneberg village church. Despite the contradictory nature in which this architecture indicates its recognition of an existing situation, it displays great sensitivity in the manner in which it incorporates its neighbors into its lines.

Elsewhere in 1961, the construction of another church also demonstrated how one could take the past seriously and at the same time express the desire for a fresh start. In the case of the Emperor William Memorial Church (fig. 1), a further circumstance played a role. The construction of the Wall on August 13, 1961, meant that this church was foreseen as the center of free Berlin, both spiritually and in terms of urban design.

As the focal point of a junction of five important streets, where the surrounding buildings had been completely cleared away and replaced with widely spaced new constructions of varying quality, Egon Eiermann's architectonic ensemble can be seen as the first postwar attempt to give form to the inner city. (Housing estates such as Charlottenburg North in 1957 and the Interbau in the same year were situated on the city's borders.) The later decision to include the ruin of the tower belonging to the church of 1898—a building of questionable architectural merit—also marked the first significant attempt to face the architectural and ideological legacy of an era that had come to an end. It was faced in an appropriate manner; appropriate as the compositional pivot and central point of a configuration of simple geometric buildings and as the manifest reminder of a recent past. The image was immediately comprehensible. It was where and how the clock had stopped.

A third example of how one could come to terms with the legacy of a bygone architectural era can be found on the Kurfürstendamm, in the stories built onto the Hotel am Zoo (fig. 4). There does not appear to be anything spectacular about this hotel, and it goes unnoticed by passersby who are accustomed to flashier attractions. Yet at a time when it was the norm to knock to stucco off facades and to standardize the appearance of houses from the reactionary Wilhelmine era so that they would better suit a democratic, postwar era, Paul Baumgarten made use of exactly this tension between the two eras. He restored the facade of the hotel, built by Alfred Messel at the end of the nineteenth century, and added two stories of his own composition that incorporated the proportions and rhythm of Wilhelmine-era architecture. Set back by barely thirty-nine inches, the stories place little structural burden upon the older building. On the contrary, they actually relieve it of some of the heaviness common to Wilhelmine-era buildings. Nowhere in Berlin during these early years was there a comparably successful attempt to connect the old with the new.

Such confrontation with the immediate past, however, would remain the exception. During these years, those of the Willy Brandt era, headlines were made by larger projects, such as the Hansaviertel (1957; fig. 5), the Unité (Le Corbusier, 1958), the German Opera House (Fritz Bornemann, 1961; fig. 6), the Philharmonic Hall (Hans Scharoun, 1963; fig. 7), the Europa-Center (fig. 8), or the planning of the Märkisches Viertel (fig. 9). There was no evidence of the least desire to consider the past. On the contrary, such projects expressed a desire for the bright new beginning, free of the shadows cast by history. The change came in 1968. It did not come from the politicians and certainly not from the established and successful architects. It came from the students.

Paradoxically, rebellion in the universities—against traditions that were considered antiquated and downright

4

2. Carl Köhn. St. Norbert's Church, Schöneberg (1916), 1987. Badly damaged during World War II, the new tower and facade were designed by Hermann Fehling in 1966. Landesbildstelle Berlin.

3. Hermann Fehling and Daniel Gogel. Paul Gerhard Church, Schöneberg (1962), 1987. To the right is the old Schöneberg village church. Landesbildstelle Berlin.

4. Hotel am Zoo, Kurfürstendamm, Charlottenburg, 1982. Landesbildstelle Berlin.

5

5. *Hansaviertel, Tiergarten
(1955–57), 1962.* Landesbildstelle
Berlin.

6. *Fritz Bornemann. German
Operahouse, Bismarckstrasse,
Charlottenburg, 1963.*
Landesbildstelle Berlin.

7. *Hans Scharoun. Philharmonie at
Kemperplatz, 1963.*
Landesbildstelle Berlin.

8. *Europa-Center on
Tauentzienstrasse, Charlottenburg,
1966.* Landesbildstelle Berlin.

6

7

mildewed—directed attention toward the value of that which still existed and centered on the danger of its removal. Urban renewal had been born and with it—albeit inadvertently—nostalgia in all of its forms.

Around 1970

At this time, the legacy of the not-so-good old days was given its due. In buildings with impressive, turn-of-the-century facades, young people lived in flats and communes amid their junk-shop furniture. Also, there was growing awareness of the historical nature of a city such as Berlin. Naturally, the construction of so-called satellite towns on the outskirts did not cease, and plans continued to be made for future traffic rings. But the word history had now taken on a different, new ring. The legacy of the late nineteenth century and contemporary social conditions rather than unclad concrete and demolition now played roles in critical and informed attitudes to architecture. Glass blocks, roughcast plaster, strip windows, and flat roofs were abandoned for wooden window frames, fairfaced masonry, colored facades, and stucco. The barely perceptible trails that had been laid in the 1960s now expanded into broader paths.

A pioneer on these paths was indubitably Hardt-Waltherr Hämer. With like-minded colleagues, he undertook the hitherto unpopular attempt to renovate the legacy of Hegemann's city of housing barracks. He did so by bringing light and air into the dark and stuffy courtyards and by saving old buildings from the demolition crane through the carefully budgeted renovation of their flats and the installation of new balconies, baths, kitchens, and central heating. Architectural considerations only played a secondary role here. The primary issue was one of cost, for until this point it had been the accepted premise that demolition and new construction were more profitable than modernization.

That it did not have to be this way was demonstrated in a model attempt with houses on the Putbusser Strasse in Wedding (fig. 10). Improvisation and organization rather than architectural considerations played the primary role here. The architect exchanged the role of artist for that of a social worker. Political concepts replaced formal discussions.

The model attempt of 1972–74 was followed by similar attempts at renewal in other areas with old buildings. Soon, one could see the effects on entire blocks. Dozens of socially committed architects transposed the experience gained from the pilot attempts to Charlottenburg's Klausenerplatz, Kreuzberg's Mariannenplatz, Brunennstrasse in Wedding, and the area between Nollendorfplatz and Dennewitzplatz in Schöneberg. Their efforts did not always meet with approval from those with an eye to social developments, for even socially committed architects could not get around the fact that any renovation, no matter how careful with costs, would lead to an increase in rents. The conflict was unavoidable and ended in a wave of house squattings. Today, this, too, is history.

What was considered significant was not appearance but content. The demand for social relevance rested on a deep con-

8

9

9. *Märkisches Viertel, Reinickendorf (1962–68), 1976.* Landesbildstelle Berlin.

10. *Modernization of old apartment houses on Potbusser Strasse in Wedding (1972–74), 1974.* Landesbildstelle Berlin.

10

viction shard by a generation of young architects. Influenced by the universities, which understood themselves as progressive, these architects believed that their responsibility lay in the social sphere. Questions of form and structure were relegated to the background. Even so, there are a few examples from the 1970s that show that there were other possibilities and that the requirements of flat dwellers could be combined with quality architecture.

A good case in point can be found on the periphery of the Hansaviertel in the Tiergarten. Rebuilt by the Interbau in 1957, the Hansaviertel was meant to reflect a new vision of urban dwelling. Two houses from the late nineteenth century survived the bombs of the war and demolition. The Planning Collective No. 1 (fig. 11)—comprising the architects Geist, Maier, Moldenschardt, Voigt, Wehrhan, Göpfert, and Spangenberg—added a new structure to the fire protection wall of one of the houses. Although this addition made clear use of the architectural language of the 1970s, it also formed a valid conclusion to these houses. Inside, the older and newer flats were dovetailed into each other. The different heights of the stories resulted in different levels within individual flats whose rooms were located in both the old and the new buildings. The stairwell in the older building became superfluous and was transformed into living space. All in all, this was an intelligent and elegant solution.

This example of a peaceful coexistence between different architectural styles, of the acceptance of historical development, and of the preservation of a continuity between individual pieces of architecture and within urban design in general, was a harbinger of issues that would determine the discussion among architects in the 1980s. In 1971, however, when the small masterpiece on the Klopstockstrasse was created, the concept of postmodernism did not exist. Even if the modernist iconography was not a dogma for architects, the virtue of simplicity was unmistakably apparent in the best architecture of those years. This is true of two works by Josef Paul Kleihues, the block of flats on Vinetaplatz (1971–76) (fig. 12) and the main workshops for the Municipal Department of Refuse Collection (1970–74). It is also true of another building, whose originality and genius would unfortunately not be repeated by the architect. This was Ludwig Leo's building for the head offices of the Society of German Coast Guards (fig. 13) of 1969–71. Such simplicity is an early anticipation of high-tech so admired today, with the qualification that in this building, form is strictly the result of function and does not signal technology unto itself.

Around 1980

Despite the ignorance and craving for status that characterized the two mammoth projects of the 1970s—a residential complex built over the city freeway on Schlangenbader Strasse in the form of an apartment house fifteen stories high and a quarter of a mile long (Georg Heinrichs, 1976–81; fig. 14) and the ICC (Ralph Schüler and Ursulina Schüler-Witte, 1973–79; fig. 15)—a more sensitive perception of what was feasible and a respect for the traditional dimensions of the cityscape did slowly establish themselves. This was not solely

11

12

13

11. Planning Collective No. 1. Apartment house at Klopstockstrasse, Tiergarten.

12. Josef Paul Kleihues. Apartment block at Vinetaplatz, 1971–76. Landesbildstelle Berlin (Josef Paul Kleihues).

13. Ludwig Leo. School and Research Center, Society of German Coast Guards, 1973. Landesbildstelle Berlin.

14

15

16

14. *George Heinrichs. Residential Complex over freeway at Schlangenbader Strasse, Wilmersdorf (1976–1981), 1981. Landesbildstelle Berlin.*

15. *Ralf Schüler and Ursulina Schüler-Witte. Internationales Congress Centrum, Charlottenburg (1975–79), 1979. Landesbildstelle Berlin.*

16. *Rob Krier. Housing complex on Ritterstrasse, Kreuzberg. Ingo Wande.*

the fruit of more rational considerations and insights. It also owed much to general currents of thought resulting from the oil crisis and the recognition of the limitations of expansion.

With the construction of terraced houses on Ritterstrasse in Kreuzberg (one of the first IBA projects; figs. 16, 17), an attempt was made to build a large, connected architectonic form, in which the separate parts were designed by individual architects working within the constraints of a general consensus. The concept came from Rob Krier, and the architectural offices of Hielscher/Mügge, Group 67, and Planning Collective No. 1 were involved. Construction took place from 1979 to 1980. Despite the time-consuming voting process, there is a formal tension evident in this group of buildings. It can only be explained by the desire of each architect to distance himself formally from the neighboring facade, precisely because of the relatively few square feet with which each one had to work.

In the second and third phases of construction, which proceeded along the same organizational concepts (1981–83) and 1985–88), these formal flaws were avoided. The individuals receded behind a consensus. Tension was replaced by composure to the benefit of the overall design and its components.

Learning by Doing

Another attempt to deal with the relics of a Berlin that was gone and, in particular, to heal some of the wounds of reckless postwar traffic planning without denying the scars took place outside the context of the IBA. This was rarely the case in West Berlin during these years. The attempt was also expressed in a different language, a language characterized by neither a historicist nor mannered timidity but rather by a certain rigor.

Lewishamstrasse in Charlottenburg was created in a manner that is incomprehensible to us today (figs. 18, 19, 20) The street was simply cut through evolved block structures. It was lined by a number of leftover plots of land and lopped, open rear courtyards. The great merit of Jürgen Sawade's construction on this street lies in the fact that he closed the openings on a line parallel with the new street rather than with the old buildings. He thereby gave the street a new profile. Sawade did not attempt to undo what had been done by using remedies from nineteenth-century urban design. Instead, what had been ruined, either through the war or traffic planning, was not only accepted but transformed. It is this feature that is so unconventional about the architecture. The smooth fronts of the winter gardens are in keeping with the straightforward nature of the street and help to form a new face for it.

The husband and wife partnership of Inken and Hinrich Baller used very different methods but had the same goal with their apartment house on Lietzenburger Strasse. Here, too, in a neighborhood full of contradictions, the house—built on an infill site between two gable walls—was meant to be a mediatory influence without conforming or subordinating itself to the neighborhood. This historical street was widened after the war to ease the congestion on the Kurfürstendamm. Widening

17

18

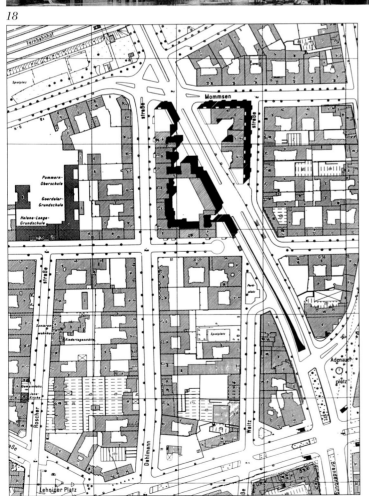

19

17. *Planning Collective no. 1.
Housing on corner of Ritterstrasse
and Alte Jakobstrasse, Kreuzberg.*
Uwe Rau.

18. *Jürgen Sawade. Apartment
houses, Lewishamstrasse,
Charlottenburg, 1980–81.* Siegfried
Büker.

19. *Site plan for the new
construction on Lewishamstrasse by
Jürgen Sawade, 1980–81.* Siegfried
Büker.

20. *Hans Kollhoff. Facade of the
new construction at Luisenplatz,
Charlottenburg, 1983–87.* Uwe
Rau.

it entailed the demolition of some of its old buildings and the loss of its harmonious appearance. To the left of one house was an old building from the turn of the century, to the right, an apartment house from the 1970s. There was a difference of more than eleven feet in the alignment of the two buildings. The new building, thirty-five feet wide, sought contact on both sides, moving back and forth in convulsive curves and organic concrete forms. Heavy traffic on the street led the architects to play excessively with reflecting planes and doubled-paned winter gardens. The result was a unique and idiosyncratic piece of architecture whose models—insofar as it even has any—can perhaps be found in the architectural fantasies of the Glass Chain, in particular those of Finsterlin. Common to these three examples—Ritterstrasse, Lewishamstrasse and Lietzenburger Strasse—is that they all deal in a conciliatory manner with the constructed past. They do so, however, in completely different ways, with totally contrasting architecture. And such contrast, in turn, is why they are typical of West Berlin. The pluralistic climate of this uprooted city, far removed from every convention, allowed for the development of such different architectural personalities as Scharoun and Fehling and Gogel, Eiermann and Baumgarten, Hämer and the Planning Collective No. 1, Kleihues, the postmodernists around Rob Krier, Sawade, and Baller. It would be hard to imagine starker contrasts. They, as well as many other architects of differing styles, played a role in the establishment of West Berlin's reputation for being open to the new and for paving the way into the provinces for this diversity through its programmatic building.

Today

There is no doubt that in the second half of the 1980s, the city's architecture was determined by the IBA. Its origins and aims are well known. The same can be said of its results, thanks to the national publicity elicited by this unique undertaking in the history of postwar architecture. The IBA also dedicated itself to the pluralism traditional to Berlin, even if it was a different pluralism from that which had placed its marks upon West Berlin during the 1960s and 1970s. Pluralism was now fostered by big names from outside the city, particularly from the international scene. In contrast, the problems that had to be solved were perculiar to Berlin. They were familiar problems; empty sites located between reminders of a prewar Berlin or beside the sins of the anti-city reconstruction after 1945 or on industrial and railway sites that had lost their function.

The fundamental contrasts among the individual participants in this great undertaking of the "critical reconstruction of the city" (Kleihues) is mirrored in its varying degrees of success. It was a new experience for many of the IBA's so-called guests to be confronted with an existing neighborhood or one that was just emerging. For Berlin, however, such a confrontation has been traditional, even if it has resulted in unique individual responses. One suspects that this lack of experience was why some of the IBA projects took refuge in architectural exaltation while the laborious struggle for functional groundplans—a struggle not visible from the outside—was lost.

The fireworks have gone out. Without a doubt they produced some beauties. The pluralism of styles celebrated triumphs. Individual themes can be perceived that could be the direction of contemporary architecture after the IBA. This direction will not be that of postmodernism, however, as manifested in Berlin in James Stirling's Science Center or Charles Moore's apartment complex at the Tegel Harbor. Far more likely, it will follow along the lines of the architecture of the 1920s and 1950s; it is young architects who are taking this path.

An example of this can be found in the manner in which Charlottenburg's Luisenplatz, neighbored by the palace and the Schinkel Pavilion, has been built up. In the tradition of many IBA competitions, the results of a feasibility study competition for the square (Andreas Brandt, Rudolph Böttcher, Yadegar Asisi) had to deal with two weighty problems: with the aura emanating from the palace and a building from the late nineteenth century that stood at odds with its environs in every sense of the word. The decision to let this thorn in the flesh of a harmonious realignment remain and to use it as the central point of a highly charged alignment network illustrates the transformation in the attitude toward historical structures. Less as a provocation of the old building but rather in reverence toward Knobelsdorff's palace wing (1740–45), on the other side of the street, the low, perhaps too low, block of buildings takes up the slightly corrected street line. Despite its conspicuous gateway, the architecture is consciously conservative, perhaps even timeless. It demands to be seen not only in reference to the palace and the Schinkel Pavilion, to which it forms a right angle, but also to its immediate neighbors.

And there it is: the virtuosic glass and brick wall by Hans Kollhoff and Arthur Ovaska which moves through the ensemble like a dervish (fig. 21). It forms the background, it cuts through the cube of the old building, creates a square, and contrasts with the somewhat stolid architecture of Brandt, Böttcher, and Asisi. It, too, is timeless but in a completely different sense. In this wall, elements of the 1920s, 1950s, and 1980s play with each other without creating any sort of disharmony. It relates to everything surrounding it, but nowhere does it curry favor. It lives from the grand gesture and from the clean detail. This wall gives Luisenplatz its own face. It coolly leaves the frivolity of postmodernism behind and shows the way ahead into the 1990s. In the best sense, it is worthy of Berlin.

Postscript

This essay was written before the fall of the Berlin Wall in November 1989. For this reason, major changes in the criteria for the architectonic development and urban design of the reunified city have not been taken into consideration.

In Search of Lost Research

Herbert Muschamp

Herbert Muschamp is architecture critic for the New York Times *and the author of* File Under Architecture *and* Man About Town: Frank Lloyd Wright in New York City. *He directs the graduate program in criticism at Parsons School of Design in New York City.*

"I'll be back one day," says Holly Golightly on the eve of her departure to marry a Brazilian diplomat in the movie version of Truman Capote's novel *Breakfast at Tiffany's*. "Me and my seven Brazilian brats. Because they must see this: I love New York."

I want to go back myself, back to that moment in New York circa 1960, when the film was made, back to Audrey Hepburn puffing on a cigarette as she surveys the city from the ledge of the Seagram Building Plaza. There they sit, side by side, these two refugees of the Weimar Republic: the Seagram Building, the triumphant bronze culmination of the vision Mies van der Rohe sketched out in charcoal in Berlin in the 1920s, and Holly Golightly, a shameless rip-off of Sally Bowles, the personification of free-spiritedness in Christopher Isherwood's *Goodbye to Berlin*. The two icons sit there in triumph; no longer symbols of a grungy bohemia or truculent avant-garde, they are now Hollywood stars. They are archetypes of New York at the moment when New York occupied the peak of prestige as the cultural capital of the world.

I've written before about this moment and the period leading up to it—the period that, in architecture, began with the Museum of Modern Art's 1932 exhibition, "The International Style." Most often, I've emphasized the negative side of the story: the draining away of European modernism's progressive ideological content, the reduction of its ideal of social responsibility to matters of form and style. But in going back to this moment now I want to trace the relief on the other side of the coin: to talk about the filling up of modern forms with an ideology of style. I want to recapture a moment when New York was not filled up with glass skyscrapers, when the architectural forms of modernism were multiplied not by construction companies but by movie companies. And I want to suggest how this content of style continued to serve a social mission, if in a form very different from that envisioned by CIAM, Team X, and other groups that continued to articulate a modern vision of the city well into this period.

Holly Golightly and the Seagram Building were figures in the dream of an aristocracy of style, a fantasy that in 1960 felt very real. This was not a new fantasy in the history of the world; the novelty lay in the absence or impotence of more traditional forms of aristocracy that have historically confined style's arbiters to the social fringes. The aristocracy of style was exclusive but not exclusionary. Peter Gay subtitled his study *Weimar Culture* "The Outsider as Insider," and that was true in New York to an even greater degree. Jews, women, and homosexual men—figures with severely circumscribed roles to play in earlier dispensations of cultural power—were the framers of this sensibility. In theory, at least, you did not have to be rich; you could live like Holly, out of a paper bag. You didn't have to be fancy; less was more. The doors of the world's richest city were declared open to anyone willing to ride the zeitgeist.

To be sure, a good deal of material wealth was involved in the creation of this moment, not only the financial empires concentrated in Manhattan but the whole material prosperity of the postwar United States. But the nature of wealth was un-

1. Mies van der Rohe. Drawing for a skyscraper, 1922. Museum of Modern Art, New York.

2

dergoing a remarkable transformation, a shift summed up by David Halberstam in his book about the media, *The Powers That Be*, when he describes "the American century" as one "whose early genius seemed to flower in production and whose later genius emerged, fittingly enough, in sales and promotion." New York at mid-century was the capital of the shift from production to consumption. And New York style, one might say, resided in the ability to articulate the juncture between these two systems—in knowing intuitively when to buy what and how to wear it against the backdrop of the surging consumer culture.

Perhaps the most conspicuous cultural episode in the history of this shift was Pop Art's displacement of Abstract Expressionist painting. Overnight, it seemed, a movement wedded to ideas of alienation, of opposition to social convention, had been upstaged by a new movement that celebrated convention and a change in the relationship of high art to mass culture. But the shift responsible for Pop Art's reception was not an overnight affair. By the 1950s, New York painters were already anxious about the encroachments of what they called masscult. What did it portend that Jackson Pollock, at work in his studio, was exposed through photographs to the readers of *Life* magazine? It portended, among other things, the erosion of a criterion: that artistic success could be measured, in part, by professional failure. And it portended the receptivity to an art movement that openly denied that criterion.

With architecture the problem was somewhat different. Modern architects had always seen their mission as one operating in the field of mass culture. The Museum of Modern Art's "Good Design" shows had been mounted to encourage public consumption of well-designed objects. Even so, though clearly founded for promotional purposes—to gain public acceptance of a particular vision of modern culture, MOMA was supposed to be above the crass values of the marketplace; part of the myth of museums is that they stand outside the normal course of contemporary events. At MOMA, we were supposed to focus on the intrinsic qualities of designed objects and overlook the systems designed to place these objects in circulation. But at what point would it become obvious that modern design, an aesthetic based on mechanical production, was now a matter of promotion?

Moreover, as Linda Nochlin observed, the canons of modern design "functioned to separate the 'tasteful' sheep from the 'philistine' goats." More than one script was provided for each object; there was the socialist narrative of mass redemption through reason and a capitalist script of status through privileged acquisition. At what point would it become clear that the acceptance of an aesthetic based on the ideal of mass culture depended on the taste of an elite? At what point would the art historical sense of the work style merge with the word's fashionable denotation?

In the late 1960s, I spent a year working at a place where an attempt was made to reconcile these two scripts: the New York branch of Design Research, a store that had been founded in the 1950s by Benjamin Thompson, an architect from Cambridge, Massachusetts. Describing the store in its 1967 edi-

3

2. *Mies van der Rohe with Philip Johnson. Seagram Building, 1958.* Ezra Stoller Associates.

3. *Installation of work by Frank Lloyd Wright, "Modern Architecture—International Exhibition," at the Museum of Modern Art, 1932.* Museum of Modern Art.

437

4. *Benjamin Thompson &*
Associates. Fulton Market Building,
South Street Seaport, 1983.
Steve Rosenthal.

tion, the *AIA Guide to New York City* came right to the point: "A modern architect's dream. Collected in one four-storied store are furniture, kitchen equipment, cutlery, dresses—in fact, everything that has been touched by the wand of good design. It could well be an exhibition for the Museum of Modern Art; but in this case the exhibits are for sale."

DR was literally "a modern architect's dream." Thompson was (and is) an architect of impeccable modern credentials. He was one of the young Americans who gathered around Walter Gropius when the Bauhaus founder emigrated to the United States to become chair of Harvard's Graduate School of Design. An associate of Gropius's at the Architects' Collaborative, Thompson later assumed that chair himself. His own architecture, even in recent years, has never strayed from the modern canon.

A few years ago, I ran into Thompson at the Design Conference in Aspen, one of the few places where unreconstructed modernists still set the tone. He didn't remember me, but I introduced myself and thanked him for one of the happiest years of my life. And it was. I loved working at Design Research. I worked in the store's display department; my job was to make sure that the exhibits looked good enough that they would sell. At the end of the year, I went off to architecture school, learned a lot about ideas and about the way architects talk to each other; but I never learned more about forms and about the ways we see them in context than I did that year at DR. I played with the classics as though they were toys: tables and chairs by Mies, Breuer, Aalto, Eames. I made sale signs with Le Corbusier's beautiful metal stencils. I ran around tacking panels of Marimekko fabric behind the new Italian designs. It made me proud to make these things sell—changing a light filter, moving a spot around, putting a bright dress at the front of a rack, going down to Little Italy to buy a particular kind of pasta to fill some glass jars.

Like other modernists, Thompson believed there was an affinity between the machine-made and anonymous handicraft; prominent among his wares were country chairs, Bennington pottery. For a while, the walls were hung with large pictures of Bernard Rudofsky's vernacular architecture, salvaged from the Museum of Modern Art's exhibition "Architecture Without Architects."

I loved to stay late on Friday nights to get the store ready for the Saturday crowds. I was often there until way past midnight; sometimes I would stop by on a Saturday afternoon, though it was my day off, just to see how sales were doing. It was a challenge to make the front window so beautiful that whatever was on display there—especially stock that hadn't moved for months—would sell out completely by the end of the day.

Thompson's dream came out of Gropius and the Bauhaus but did not merely copy it. In fact, in some ways, his vision attempted to remedy some of the problems modern architecture had brought in its wake. By the late 1950s, it was obvious even to many devoted admirers of modernism that the movement's impact on urban life was problematic. The Corbusian

438

conception of "towers in a park" had shattered the street and with it the order that made urban life comprehensible on a pedestrian scale. Jane Jacobs's 1960 book, *The Death and Life of Great American Cities*, brought wide public attention to this crisis.

One result, championed by Ada Louise Huxtable, architecture critic for the *New York Times*, was the movement toward architectural preservation. Another was the formation of the Urban Design Group, a city agency in the administration of Mayor John Lindsay, that sought to overhaul the standard solutions to urban renewal. Robert Venturi's comment that "Main Street is almost all right" reflected the reaction against the modern city.

Ben Thompson also had a vision of the city, but it addressed the issue of modern catastrophism from within the evolving canon of modern design. Thompson envisioned a modern city capable of renewing itself by translating the traditional concept of the agora in terms of modern design (the agora, not the factory, was his informing concept). He saw a city full of color, pattern, and shape, of attractive, active people leading attractive, modern lives. He took the fundamental, rational approach of Gropius and softened it with romantic edges. You could say that Thompson's idea was to accessorize the modern city; but actually there were more fundamental shifts going on. His inspiring social paradigm was not the factory but the agora. It was a capitalist's reinterpretation of a socialist's dream.

He promoted this vision quite aggressively. In the early days of DR, Thompson would come down regularly from Cambridge and present slide shows on the DR idea for the benefit of staff, customers, the press, and other guests. He would show the women in their Marimekko dresses and bright cotton hats, carrying big canvas bags with baguettes sticking out of them; dinner tables radiantly lit with masses of candles; public spaces adorned with his own line of butcherblock furniture (beautiful to look at, uncomfortable to sit in), or a domestic interior with his down-filled sofas (handsome to look at, heavenly to sit in). The words he spoke made it clear that this was not just a domestic but an urban vision; those women in their Marimekkos were angels of annunciation, dispatched from on high to carry the gospel of good design through the city's troubled streets.

My year at DR came at the very end of Thompson's dream. Thompson sold the business to a group of merchandizing experts who had ambitious plans for new stores, mail order, and cost accounting. We learned new words such as "unit control" and we acquired a new store manager who was always perspiring. Thompson had been promised creative control of the enterprise but had basically lost control; that's how things go in the agora. And in any case, the store had probably reached the end of its natural cycle. Marimekko dresses, which allegedly declared the wearer's independence from fashion, turned out to be as subject to fashion's laws as any mode of dress. And the same was probably true for the store's look. Different looks were coming in: sleek Italian, high-tech, country; postmodern, California organic; American southwest.

But it was hardly the end of Thompson's dream. Indeed, it was barely the beginning. Those who imagined he might fade away to the genteel clatter of TC-100 coffee cups had underestimated his stamina and the power of his urban vision. In the 1970s and 1980s, that vision emerged from the drawing boards—Thompson's drawing boards—to become the new paradigm for planning: the festival marketplace, a privately developed mix of shops, restaurants, and open spaces that organize consumption into a vast urban spectacle.

Not everyone loves these places. Ada Louise Huxtable, who appreciated South Street Seaport for its incorporation of older buildings into the commercial potpourri, wrote "it is a little hard to accept that at the end of the preservation rainbow is the shopping center. Even if it is called a Festival Marketplace." Perhaps it is harder still to contemplate that this consumer's paradise can trace its roots through Thompson to the Bauhaus and the "crystal cathedral" that in 1919 Gropius foresaw rising from the "hands of a million workers." How many of the young urban professionals who throng the outdoor areas of South Street Seaport during the early evening happy hour are aware of a connection between the place they're standing and an art school that was shut down for its radical social and artistic ideas?

It's with a shock that you recognize how nearly this picture was forecast by the modern framers. True, South Street Seaport is the handiwork of a million buyers, not workers; but what else would you expect to find at the end of an industrial economy? The architecture is not something you might feel drawn to consider great art; yet it is consistent with the Bauhaus aim to dissolve art into a quality of living. So what if that quality has taken the form of merchandise? This is a city that has bought itself back into being, to accommodate those for whom shopping is a form of self-invention more reliable that psychoanalysis, and your response to it may depend partly on whether you find capitalism today capable of forming or realizing anything but paltry dreams and partly on your willingness to allow the arrival at a destination to differ from your expectations. The modern utopia was widely and fairly criticized for being too removed from reality; and it may be no disgrace, for its visionaries or its builders, that it has turned out to look much like life.

1. Olaf Metzel. 13.4.1981, *1987.*
Collection of the artist (photograph
by Ulrich Gorlich).

Vicissitudes: The Art World in Postwar Berlin

Karl Ruhrberg

Karl Ruhrberg has published extensively on modern European art. His works include Der Schlussel sur Malerei von heute *(1965),* Twentieth-Century Art *(1987), and* Die zweite Moderne. *He was the founding director of the Kunsthalle in Düsseldorf, director of the Berlin Artist Program (DAAD), and most recently director of the Museum Ludwig in Cologne.*

The definition of Berlin is just as debatable as that of art. Berlin, or a stage set? Maybe . . . the Berliners . . . do not define art, even though they sometimes have to bear the consequences. Sometimes white. Sometimes black.
— *Marcel Broodthaers*

It must seem incredible to anyone who did not live through it—the war was over, German cities lay in ruins, there was nothing to eat, the situation was hopeless, but people wanted to hear music, see plays, look at pictures. Never have so many people realized in such a visceral way that humans do not live on bread alone; the issue of the social relevance of art, so hotly debated in later, more satiated periods, would have been incomprehensible at this time. Art had become a means of survival, it had a life-renewing effect,[1] it was a sign of hope in a new beginning. The hunger for pictures was not as innocuous as it is today; the cause was existential, not aesthetic. If art could not change the world, as experience had amply shown, then at least it could be a beacon of freedom, illuminating new paths, and, as Paul Klee defined art, picking out the outlines of potentially better worlds. That was the prevailing view in 1945, but euphoria did not last. The currency reform of 1948 and the ensuing economic miracle, which seemingly made everybody fat, happy, and sluggish of mind, put an end to idealistic illusions. Restoration triumphed, in everyday life as in political affairs. The West German bourgeoisie repressed the catastrophe, missing yet another chance to learn its lesson.

On the island of Berlin, in contrast, the clocks told a different time and there was no prosperity. The Soviet blockade at the end of the 1940s led to the development of a frontier-town mentality, diametrically opposed to the liberal cosmopolitanism of the prewar city. The consequences of this isolationist attitude are felt even today, despite the unification of the two unequal halves of Germany. For a long time this attitude was reflected in cultural life as well, even in the activities of the student movement and subculture, whose anti-imperialism at one point threatened to become anti-internationalism and whose regionalism often coarsened into xenophobia. This obstinate resistance to influences and ideas from outside meant that for some time, the Berlin art scene stewed in its own juices, attracting little more than local interest.

All of this, however, was still far in the future during the postwar years when German artists were attempting to re-establish their lost connection with international developments. Their belief in the healing powers of art—an aura of utopian hope that for one eyewitness[2] emanated from the paintings of the first hour—may have been naive, but it was also honest. So we today, with a postmodern cynicism born of the experience of a culture industry whose unscrupulousness has long surpassed Adorno's most rigorous diagnoses and has integrated art into show business would do better than to make fun of this attitude. Art in devastated Germany and Berlin was neither an economic factor nor a tourist attraction; it was the elixir of life. Not for everyone, admittedly, but certainly for many of the survivors. And when people gave coal for art, this was no pretty figure of speech, nor were the donors captains of industry or magnates investing in pictures for the sake of their image—it was a literal exchange involving Ruhrgebiet coal miners.[3]

441

This is all history, but our look at the revival of the art scene from the vantage point of the late 1980s is not just a sentimental journey into the past. What we can learn from it is that a painting is more than an investment that hangs on the wall. The sensory and intellectual essence of art and its appeal can be suppressed but never completely eradicated. Attempts to do so in both East and West have failed, and perhaps there is still reason to hope that the commercialization of art by an industry for which it is nothing but another product will be ultimately crowned by no greater success.

Berliners are known as hard-headed, skeptical people who are relatively unsusceptible to bathos and high-sounding phrases. Even during the worst years of the Nazi terror, niches of liberal resistance survived in the capital of the Reich, more so than in any other part of Germany. They were like patches of "calm in the eye of the hurricane," as the critic Heinz Ohff has written.[4] In the anonymity of the only German metropolis many persecuted artists found refuge; for a while even Joseph Goebbels, the Mephisophelean brain of the Nazi movement and secret admirer of such Expressionists as Emil Nolde and Barlach, hesitated to crack down on degenerate art in Berlin with the same fierceness as he did in the remainder of the Reich. Initially he was unwilling to countenance the closure of Berlin galleries that either openly or secretly opposed the official art policy.[5] Werner Doede's remark that in Berlin "the best minds always preferred to take the risk of opposition"[6] applied to a certain extent for the years 1933 to 1945. This stance found artistic expression in such works as the sarcastic and ironic depiction of a Nazi mass meeting entitled *Parade of the Zeroes*, a charcoal drawing of 1933–34 by Werner Heldt, who after 1945 was to capture the melancholy of a cityscape in ruins (*Berlin by the Sea*), or in the silent dignity of Karl Hofer's lost souls (*The Prisoners*, 1933; *Black Moonlight Night*, 1944).

In devastated Berlin, divided by the Allies into four initially open sectors, residents experienced more intensely than elsewhere the end of the war and the nightmare of the occupation, hoping for a chance to make a new start. The city soon began to play a leading role in the visual arts and in other fields. Rolling up their sleeves and digging in, and maintaining their brash self-confidence—as well as their chauvinism—even in such difficult situations as the blockade of 1948, Berliners overcame that other typical trait of theirs, skepticism. Euphoria echoed throughout the country, for all eyes were turned to events in postwar Berlin. The protagonists of the first chapter of postwar art were well known in Berlin and throughout Germany, but gradually, as artists from the Rhine and Ruhr areas began to set the pace, the Berlin scene at times seemed to propel itself into the backwater of developments.

Six weeks after the capitulation, the Berlin College of Art had already resumed its teaching activities under the direction of Karl Hofer. The name of this major painter, the classicist among German modernists, whose brittle, melancholy figuration bore a greater affinity to Hans von Marées and the constructive logic of Cézanne than to the Expressionists, in itself amounted to a program. Under Hofer's leadership, the so-called decadent artists were reinstated: Karl Schmidt-Rottluff, Max Pechstein, and Max Kaus, after years of ostracism,

began to set the tone. This was a natural development of an affinity for figurative, expressive art, which, along with realism, had dominated Berlin's art scene prior to the war. Ever since the artists of *Die Brücke* had moved from Dresden to Berlin—and even more recently with the New Fauves of recent years—there has been an underlying trend toward expressionism. The revolt of the original Fauves during the politically explosive Dada era in Europe remained episodic in Berlin. Despite the influence of such a major artist as Hannah Höch and the invention in Berlin of photomontage, not to mention the activities of the Fluxus movement between 1964 and 1976, Dada simply did not catch on.

Abstract artists, too, always had had a difficult time of it in Berlin. They were considered esoteric and withdrawn, despite the fact that they enjoyed the eloquent advocacy of no less a man than Will Grohmann, who with and even before Werner Haftmann was the doyen of art in Germany during the first postwar decades. An artist such as Theodor Werner, whose existential, coded images were symbols of metaphysical truths beyond mere metaphor and the visible world, was respected in Berlin but played a much more central role in the art world of Paris. That his name was not even mentioned in the comprehensive catalogue on the Berlin art scene published by the Museum of Modern Art in New York in 1987 is symptomatic.[7] A figure such as Wille Baumeister, who supplied the key arguments for the breakthrough of abstract art in Germany and, together with Gotthard Jedlicka, Alfred Weber, and others, vehemently defended it against conservative opponents grouped around Hans Sedlmayr at the 1950 "Darmstadt Talks"—as Grohmann would later defend it against Hofer—would have been barely conceivable in Berlin.

Other tendencies surfaced in Berlin, even during the years of renewal, when the scene was still open-minded and where, "as nowhere else, so much information was to be found in so limited a space."[8] An early and significant contribution to this was made by the French Cultural Department of the Allied Control Council. In 1946, it mounted an exhibition of modern French painting at the former Stadtschloss or City Palace (which four years later was demolished as a disgraceful monument to Prussian feudalism). The exhibition, which included works by Matisse, Picasso, Braque, and Chagall, but even more importantly, by Giorgio de Chirico, Max Ernst, and Salvador Dali, made artists and Berliners aware of all that had been going on around them during their twelve years of isolation. The Surrealists made the biggest impression, and with such painters as Mac Zimmerman, Heinz Trökes, and Hans Thiemann, Berlin became for a time the center of neosurrealism in postwar Germany.

Trökes was also the first artistic director of the Gerd Rosen Gallery on Kurfürstendamm, which opened its doors as early as August 1945. Its exhibitions included works by Werner Heldt, Alexander Camaro, Jeanne Mammen, Mac Zimmermann, and Juro Kubieck (who later was one of the first to report on Jackson Pollock's action painting, which was initially influenced by Surrealism), and the sculptors Karl Hartung, Bernhard Heiliger, and Hans Uhlmann (who even before the gallery opened had held the first art show in postwar Berlin).

2

3

2. *Karl Hofer.* Dance Macabre,
1946. Berlinische Galerie
(photograph by Udo Hesse).

3. *Heinz Trökes.* Moon Canon,
1946. Berlinische Galerie
(photograph by Udo Hesse).

4. Hans Uhlmann. Steel Sculpture,
1965. Rheinisches Bildarchiv,
Cologne.

Rosen attracted great interest in West Germany, as did the activities of the many reopened or newly established galleries that soon followed his courageous example in the 1940s—galleries such as Anja Bremer, Walter Schüler, and Rudolf Springer. Galerie Franz, which attempted to reunite the original Rosen group after one of its regular falling-outs, mounted an exhibition of the Zone 5 artists, whose name was an ironic allusion to the four zones of occupied Germany. The success of their project, however, could not prevent the gradual dispersal of what had been a loose association from the start.

The Zone 5 exhibition marked the end of the first phase of developments in the city's resuscitated art world. The gallery owners, of whom Rudolf Springer is still active, made an inestimable contribution, their commitment to art and artists having been a prime prerequisite of the profuse—sometimes overly profuse—cultural life of present-day Berlin. They deserve special respect for the fact that their work took place under the most adverse circumstances imaginable—in a heavily damaged city isolated from the rest of Germany and that, after the 1948 proclamation of a dogmatic Socialist realism in the East Berlin newspaper *Tägelicher Rundschau*, was ideologically divided in the cultural sphere as well, a city without hinterland, without an economic miracle, and hence without a group of established collectors.

After a number of more or less unsuccessful attempts, the Association of Friends of the National Gallery of 1929 was at last re-established in 1977–78, thanks to the efforts of the museum's director, Dieter Honisch. This was an unmistakable sign to hesitant collectors.[9] Under the imaginative leadership of its chairman, Peter Raue, the association was not only able to take up the tradition of its predecessor, but it also began a program of direct aid to artists in which members such as Hans-Hermann Stober did a great deal of good outside the National Gallery as well as within.

No one could have dreamed of this during the first dismal years after the war, whose mood has been wonderfully captured by Werner Heldt, an eccentric, suffering loner, in a series of Berlin paintings that began with *View from a Window with Dead Bird* of 1945. In his both stringently composed and lyrically evocative works—"abstract still-lifes," Werner Schmalenbach once called them[10]—the melancholy of the big city is translated into austerely unsentimental form and color. "There haven't been things like these . . . since Juan Gris," wrote Heldt's friend Werner Gilles,[11] indicating the frame of reference in which the Berlin artist's mature work rightly belongs. His importance, like that of his gifted compatriot, the constructivist sculptor Hans Uhlmann, has yet to be fully recognized.

In Werner Heldt's cityscapes, abstraction and concreteness exist in sensitive equilibrium. Completely out of balance, however, was the debate between representational and abstract art, which also took place in Berlin during these years. Postwar German abstract artists hoped to create a cosmopolitan language of color and form that would break down barriers, overcome mundane realities in favor of the spiritual in art, a kind of aesthetic Esperanto that would parallel those mathe-

444

matical formulas used by modern physicists to describe a reality not otherwise comprehended. For advocates of figurative art and of course for a large part of the public, this seemed to be little more than an escape into noncommitment and an expression of academic arrogance. The ugly vocabulary of the recent past, from "decadent" to "Jewish-infiltrated," reappeared, encouraged by such people as the composer Alois Melichar, who had every reason to hold his tongue. The saddest thing was that this brand of so-called healthy popular instinct found adherents among those who had so recently suffered under it—De Chirico, Oskar Kokoschka, and, in Berlin, Karl Hofer. Unfortunately, Hofer's understanding, and to some extent, legitimate skepticism of the craze for progress and of the partly naive and partly arrogant utopianism of his abstract colleagues turned into blind rage. This was among peers, all of whom had suffered as outcasts and had been persecuted during the Third Reich, and it took on a particularly bitter form in Berlin that would be repeated later in the political conflict of the 1960s and 1970s. Hofer, politically beyond reproach, did not hesitate to associate colleagues whose opinions on art differed from his with the very same Nazi ideology that had branded them, and himself, as decadent.

They found an eloquent defender in the person of Will Grohmann, a leading critic of the day and an instructor at Hofer's own College of Art. One of those "hacks," as the embittered Hofer was quoted as saying even as late as the 1978 catalogue of his exhibition in the Berlin Kunsthalle, Grohmann represented "a biased art criticism that made no attempt to understand his artistic oeuvre."[12] Grohmann's fulminant reply, in which he accused his opponent of "disaster-loving pessimism," was anything but balanced, nor even in every respect fair. This controversy was one of the most superfluous and absurd in the history of art. At its high point, the discussion came to a tragic, though only temporary, end with Hofer's death. As late as 1985, when figurative painting had long resumed its dominance in Berlin, Günter Grass, then president of the Akademie der Künste and himself a representationally oriented draughtsman and printmaker, found it necessary to reopen the old debate. Brushing the dust off outmoded arguments,[13] Grass associated abstract art of every variety, from geometric to gestural, with the restorative tendencies in the politics of the 1950s. Indeed, he understood this art as a confirmation of these tendencies. And this despite the fact that most of the artists he attacked were anything but artists of the establishment and had expressly refused to adapt to their newly rich society and its priorities. The oversimplifications of the prominent novelist, for whom ideological affiliation apparently determined the quality of art, were emphatically corrected by three other members of the academy—the artist Bernard Schultze, who was one of those attacked, and the art historians Werner Hofmann and Eberhard Roters.[14]

The attitude of Hofer and his successors, all the way to Grass, was assured of the support of the majority, including the politicians, in a city that has always had a realist–expressionistic orientation. Yet while the artistically interested younger generation of the 1950s tended to side with Grohmann—assisted by Hans Uhlmann, Alexander Camaro, and others—in the late 1960s and early 1970s, under the influence of the student

5. *Werner Heldt.* View from a Window with a Dead Bird, *1945.* Archiv für Kunst und Geschichte, Berlin.

445

6

7

6. *Wolfgang Petrick.* Beauty,
1974–75. Berlinische Galerie.

7. *Georg Baselitz.* The Great
Friends, *1965.* Museum Moderner
Kunst, Vienna, on loan from the
Ludwig Collection, Aachen.

revolt and its demand for a socially relevant, politically committed art, affiliations shifted 180 degrees.

The artistic echo of this turnabout was a critical style that came to be known as Berlin realism, whose protagonists included Petrick and Diehl, Vogelgesang and Sorge, Waller and Baehr. Its effectiveness, despite a few outstanding paintings that have managed to survive the changing fads and styles of the past decades, remained largely limited to the Berlin area. In contrast to doctrinaire socialist realism in the East, this West Berlin group assimilated a great range of stylistic means, integrating elements of Magic Realism, Surrealism, or Pop Art. The statement that if Picasso had been born later he would have painted like a Berlin realist,[15] was of course little more than a self-aggrandizing quip, particularly as most of the critical realists have since gone over to other styles.

Mention should be made in this context of the early painting of Georg Baselitz, who left East Germany for West Berlin in the late 1950s. In 1961, with his friend Eugen Schönebeck, he published the first *Pandämonium* manifesto, which was followed a year later by the second. Protesting the predominance of *l'informel* or action painting, which, in its most general sense, also describes the work of Baselitz's teacher Hann Trier, the two artists announced that the time had come for emotional realism. While Schönebeck—who was to give up painting entirely at thirty—attempted to find a synthesis between the original, not yet ideologically constricted principles of socialist realism and the gestural approach, Baselitz painted wild pictures in the style of an expressive, provocative realism with accusatory, obscene, and blasphemous elements. His works represented a protest, not only against the sterile academicism of routinely executed abstract works (as early as 1955 Werner Haftmann, arguing with more verve and less dogmatism that Hofer or Grass, had warned against the dangers of an abstract academy), but also against the bourgeois self-satisfaction and prudishness of West German society. This not surprisingly raised the ire of self-styled protectors of morals who once again felt it incumbent upon themselves to save the Western World from artists who, as the phrase went, befouled their own nest. In the end, however, Baselitz was not persecuted by the abstractionists but rather prosecuted by the district attorney. *The Naked Man* and *The Big Night Flushed* were confiscated from the Michael Werner-Benjamin Katz Gallery and only released two years later. It is sad that Baselitz, who with Markus Lüpertz and his far-less critical *Dithyrambs*, signaled the breakthrough of contemporary expressive art would later distance himself from his early powerful paintings.

The nonfigurative variety of expressive, gestural painting also had important adherents in Berlin. If the term "action painter" applies to any member of *art informel* in Germany, then it applies to Fred Thieler, a gruff East Prussian whose career was disrupted by political discrimination. For entire generations of students at the Berlin College of Art, Thieler provided the model of the devoted artist, teaching by example. If his sole theme was the dynamic process itself—with a deliberately reduced range of color sometimes augmented by roughly collaged surfaces—this was because his way of existing is to

446

paint. He works in a nonobjective, gestural style because, "you cannot live with ideologies." Even in Hann Trier's early *l'informel*-influenced phase, the other important teacher's canvases lacked the typical existentialist nihilism of the day; they were inventive, richly orchestrated in color and rhythm, and even frequently executed with both hands simultaneously. From his class emerged some of the best of the younger protagonists of contemporary realist and expressive art, of whom Baselitz, who succeeded Thieler at the college in 1983, is merely the most famous.

Gestural painting of concentrated expressiveness, whether figurative or abstract, had always played a key role in Berlin. The line runs from the generation following Thieler and Trier, whose most inspired and forceful member is Walter Stöhrer, all the way to the young Thieler student, ter Hell. What distinguishes Stöhrer from most of his gestural and spontaneous contemporaries is a rare combination of energy and precision, explosiveness and reflection, temperament and sensitivity to form. Color swaths are set in dynamic tension against graphic lines and citations from texts that inspire the artist. Painting becomes calligraphy. As Cézanne worked "parallel to nature," Stöhrer works parallel to literature. Calligraphy also plays a role in the vehement painting of ter Hell, who was initially influenced by Thieler, Rainer, Pollock, and others, but rather than echoing his readings it is a spontaneous, subjective expression of the younger generation's attitude to life: "It's me," "I want to live," "We want to love each other but don't know how."

A tendency to the emotionally charged is also evident in Berlin sculpture, most impressively expressed in the middle generation in the work of Rolf Szymanski. The human, in particular the female, figure is always the theme of his work. In the nearly baroque abundance of the swellings and hollows of Szymanski's pieces, joy and sorrow, vitality and destruction, history and the present moment coexist in close proximity. These contrasts lend Szymanski's sculptures a compelling intensity.

Ursula Sax works with contrasts in a different and very personal way. Her wooden sculptures, constructed of separate pieces, project freely into the surrounding space, combining the constructive with the expressive, stasis with kinesis, abstraction with figuration. Another Berlin sculptor of note is Rainer Kriester, whose works possess both classical calm and expressive force, heads and figures that stand as bronze or stone symbols of a precarious existence on the verge of the apocalypse.

The simultaneity of diametrical oppositions that resist chronological description and that are often forgotten in face of the fleeting triumphs of one style after another are perhaps nowhere so greatly in evidence as in Berlin. Stöhrer came to Berlin in 1959; in 1960, the actor Günter Meisner opened his Galerie Diogenes, devoted to the ZERO group and the circle around it; the year 1961–62 marked the publication of Baselitz's and Schönebeck's *Pandämonium*; in 1962 Markus Lüpertz arrived in Berlin and Christian Chruxin founded his gallery, Situations 60, for concrete and constructivist art. That

8

9

8. *Fred Thieler.* R-I-76-S, *1976.*
Berlinische Galerie.

9. *Ter Hell.* It's Me, *1980.*
Berlinische Galerie.

10
10. Wolf Symanski. Madonna of
Epheseus, *1967.* Galerie Brusberg,
Berlin.

11. Wolf Vostell. Miss America,
1968. Museum Ludwig, Cologne.

12. Walter Stöhrer. Large Black
Tuscany, *1980.* Sammlung der
Deutchen Bundesbank, Frankfurt
am Main (photograph by Philipp
Schönborn).

same year the Ford Foundation established the Berlin Artists' Program, which was transferred to the German Academic Exchange Service (DAAD) in 1965; Grossgörschen 35, established in 1964, became one of the city's most important self-help galleries and still serves Berlin artists as a public forum. The year 1964 also saw the opening of Michael Werner's and René Block's galleries, and the following year, Ludwig Gosewitz and Tomas Schmit moved to Berlin.

The stage was set for the fascinating play of contrasts that characterized the Berlin scene over the ensuing years: realism vied with neoexpressionism, abstraction with figuration, concrete art with happenings and Fluxus. The DAAD's Berlin Artists' Program played a major role in breaking through the isolation of the city's art scene and in providing it with international horizons.

The second postwar phase of artistic activity in Berlin began in the 1960s. Though it is still in process, the preferences have remained much the same as in the decades before. Critical realism, particularly in a form that has not been ideologically predetermined, and expressive art—especially in painting but also in sculpture—still finds a greater echo and larger audiences than other contemporary approaches. The 1960s, and above all the latter half of the decade, with the total disillusionment that followed the Kennedy assassination and the tensions arising from the political and moral disaster of Vietnam, were the heyday of the realists. Their vision of being able to change or indeed improve the world by taking an unmistakable political stance in their art in the end proved just as illusory as the early abstractionists' faith in progress and their belief that an internationally oriented art could break down all national barriers for good and reconcile every opposition in universal harmony.

While this sort of naivete could not appeal to a cynical younger generation, its members still had to do penance, at least in Berlin, for the naive credulity of their forbears. Those who remained true to abstraction, whether of the constructivist or monochrome variety, were forced to realize that their meditative imagery found little resonance beside the energy-charged gestural works by Thieler or Stöhrer. Paul Uwe Dreyer left Berlin for Stuttgart, Andreas Brandt for northern Germany; and Raimund Girke, a sensitive, intelligent artist with a richly differentiated palette, though a professor at the Berlin College of Art, for Cologne. Johannes Gecelli with his thoughtful parallel structures, Frank Badur with his precise and stringent color bands, and others working in a similar vein, have remained proud outsiders, more successful in venues outside the city in which they are based.

This isolation is not a recent phenomenon. Naum Gabo already felt it in the city that exerted a magnetic attraction on constructivists from East and West ever since the legendary exhibition of Russian art at Galerie van Diemen in 1922. Writing in his diary in 1931, the Russian sculptor in Berlin observed, "Without the opportunity to put my work in a living atmosphere it will die with me, it will never bear fruit."[16]

The history of happenings and Fluxus in Berlin took a not un-

similar course. René Block did his persistent and obstinate best to promote an art that was free in both the literal and the abstract sense. He lent his full support to Allan Kaprow and Wolf Vostell, the American and European founders of the happening, Ludwig Gosewitz, Tomas Schmit, articulate in both speech and image, and above all Joseph Beuys, the great guru. To the politically active students of the late 1960s and early 1970s, however, Beuys's social utopias seemed neither concrete nor radical enough, and his effort was insignificant in comparison to that in West Germany, Great Britain, the United States, or even Japan.

The strange thing is that the once-divided city with its irrational political, economic, and geographical situation—"Berlin (West): a surrealist cage; those inside are free," as György Ligeti once quipped[17]—should have exerted such a strong and continuing attraction on so many happening, performance, and Fluxus artists. It would be hard to name one who has not spent some time there, from Adi Koepcke to Dick Higgins, from Nam June Paik and Charlotte Moorman to John Cage, from Robert Filliou and George Brecht to George Maciunas, from Stanley Brown and James Lee Byars to Emmett Williams, who in the meantime has established a residence in Berlin.

Looking back from today's vantage point, as an increasingly widespread public interest in art threatens to be appropriated by increasingly ugly wheeling and dealing, one recalls with a certain sense of melancholy those evenings at René Block's gallery where people congregated to concern themselves intensively with works that did justice to Marcel Duchamp's fundamental tenet that art should be intelligent first and foremost. It is one of the more depressing episodes in recent Berlin art history that Block was at last compelled to abandon his gallery because the interest in his pioneering work was far less in Berlin than in the world at large. In this case, the worn phrase truly applies of the still-young man who has become a legend during his lifetime.

Not even Wolf Vostell, who came to Berlin from Cologne and was honored by large exhibitions, took part in a great number of happenings, and had major works accepted for the Berlinische Galerie, managed ultimately to feel at home in Berlin. At present he is based in Spain. Yet this artist who called himself an antidote to his former friend Beuys, with his egocentric and aggressive personality but above all with an expansive oeuvre that is critical of the times without being ideologically hidebound, is exactly the type of artist who would do Berlin good. Like many foreign artists who came to the city under the auspices of the Berlin Artists' Program—Emilio Vedova, George Rickey, Edward Kienholz, Eduardo Paolozzi, Laszlo Lakner, Marcel Broodthaers, Mario Merz, Armando, Bruce McLean—Vostell was fascinated by that "vibrato" of which Eberhard Roters speaks, by "that incessant motoric trembling often just noticeable under the surface of daily events that links Berlin's vitality through all its nerve fibers with occurrences throughout the world."[18]

The Berlin experience has shaped many artists and in many cases even changed their work. Yet the city has been guilty of

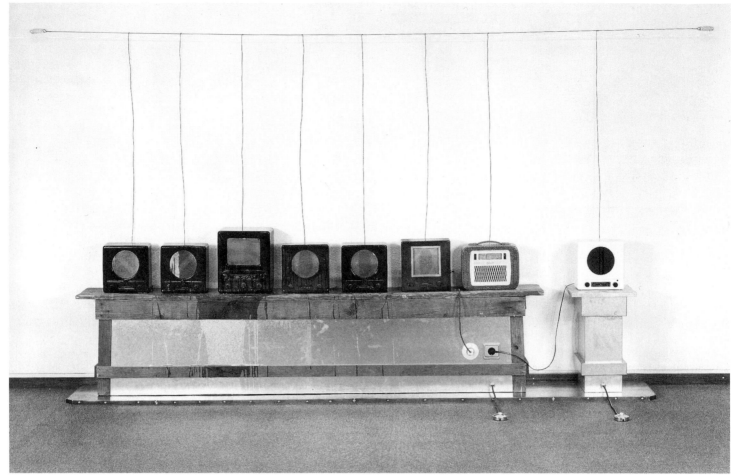

13

13. *Edward Kienholz.* Receivers of
the Volk—the Bench, *1976.*
Staatliche Museen, Preussischer
Kulturbesitz, Neue Nationalgalerie,
Berlin (photograph by Jorg P.
Anders).

14. *K. H. Hödicke.* Detour, *1984.*
Galerie Gmyrek, Düsseldorf.

14

not always repaying them in kind. While an artist such as Kienholz has become a Berlin institution over the years, Vedova's *Plurimi di Berlino* had to wait for the third Kassel *Documenta* to be seriously discussed, and Mario Merz's major, Berlin-related installation of 1974 attracted in the course of over four weeks a grand total of 592 visitors. Marcel Broodthaers, too, until his 1975 exhibition at the National Gallery, was a sort of hermit. Though Berlin has become a central theme for many artists, the city has not always deigned to take note of the fact.

On the face of it, the Berlin scene was dominated until far into the 1970s by its own version of politically committed realism. Yet there were rumblings beneath the agitated surface. Changes were under way that were to make Berlin, which since the early 1960s had always stood in the shadow of the Rhineland and its artists, from ZERO to Beuys, Richter to Polke, Graubner to Klapheck, into a center of contemporary art. That a re-evaluation of all values was under way was amply evident from the pathos of the *Pandämonium* texts he coauthored with his friend Schönebeck: "Negation is a brilliant gesture, not a source of responsibility." In conceptions like these, influenced by Nietzsche, the moralist was supplanted by the immoralist.

In the course of tone of the heated debates of those years, Markus Lüpertz replied to the bitter accusation that art was elitist and incomprehensible to the people by disarmingly stating: "I am the people who paint!"[19] Years before, in his *Dithyrambic Manifesto*, he had invoked the "grace of the twentieth century" and brashly proclaimed that it would be "made visible by the dithyramb I have invented."[20] Now, this was affirmative in the highest degree and diametrically opposed to the goals of artists who saw art as a weapon in the political struggle. The inevitable result was a schism with the critical realists, ending with the departure of Lüpertz, Hödicke, and Koberling from the Grossgörschen 35 artists' cooperative. Still, no one even suspected at the time that such conflicts held the seed of what Wieland Schmied has called the "most momentous change that has occurred in German art of the past forty years."[21]

This change was not only the result of the resigned acceptance of the political ineffectiveness of art that came at the end of the campus revolt; it also marked the demise of an avant-garde ideology that, paralleling a belief in scientific progress, had dominated twentieth-century art in Germany as elsewhere. While public interest still concentrated on the various current tendencies, from Pop to conceptual art, in Europe and the United States a shift from progressive to the postmodern art of the so-called trans-avant-garde was preparing. This paralleled a worldwide conservative movement in politics; also, Harald Szeemann announced at the Documenta V (1972) that art was turning inward and that Baselitz had renounced his own rebellious beginnings and from that point on painted for painting's sake alone. In Berlin, it was Karl-Horst Hödicke who, after exhaustive and thoughtful experimentation with all of the era's artistic means of expression, returned to painting and inadvertently became the role model for the New Fauves or Wild Painters.

This was the triumphal re-enthronement of painting, and indeed of sculpture as well, mediums that had long since been declared defunct by the protagonists of minimal and conceptual art, by happening and performance artists, by the Fluxus movement, and by all of their apologists. Serious doubts about the creative capacities of tradition artistic means were swept away. The sensory experience was rehabilitated after a long dry spell of an increasingly cerebral, purist art. It was an art in which Kandinsky's "great Abstract" and "Great Real"—the intellectual and sensual aspect of art no longer balanced each other. (An exceptional case was Eugen Schönebeck, whose doubts about this eventually led him to give up painting altogether at the age of thirty.)

Rebels tend to believe in the absolute truth of their principle and some artists, delighting in being able to break out the paint tubes, succumbed to the illusion that to become a major painter you only had to stop using your intellect. This was the source of the new superficiality, the discovery of the "dilettante as genius,"[22] which gave the public the pleasant feeling of at last being able to understand art. However, this reproach could not be directed at the pioneers of the new painting (among whom must include Max G. Kaminski, then in Berlin, now of Strasbourg). None of them made it easy on themselves; like Hödicke, they had to try many roads and take many detours. Bernd Koberling, to give only one example, passed through a phase of what he called special romanticism, imaginary landscapes painted on a canvas covered with synthetic material and conceptual imagery that radically questioned traditional form and content, before achieving the expansive, expressive approach that now characterizes his work, whose subject is still the utopian landscape, in which, as Koberling says, "beauty and revolt" precariously coexist.[23]

"Painting is on the upswing," wrote Marin Sorescu, a Rumanian guest of the Berlin Artists' Program in 1975. "I've been trying to hammer that into my typewriter after having looked around the galleries and museums and a lot of studios.[24] Two years after this was written, Berlin's most famous self-help gallery opened on Mortizplatz in Kreuzberg, with a performance by Salomé (alias Wolfgang Cilarz). Another three years later, from February to April 1980, the triumph of the "Neo-Fauves in Berlin"[25] was confirmed by an exhibition of *Heftige Malerei* (Vehement painting) including works by Rainer Fetting, Helmut Middendorf, Salomé, and Bernd Zimmer—all of whom, like Hödicke, had previously experimented with other contemporary approaches. The *Picture Change* had taken place, the *Hunger for Imagery* satisfied—thus the titles of a milestone show and book of the period—and expressive, spontaneous painting had replaced not only abstraction but realism in the public favor.

The turnabout did not come out of a clear blue sky. In 1979, two exhibitions had taken place concurrently in London on the theme of recent streams in Berlin art: *Berlin: A Critical View, Ugly Realism 20s–70s* at the Institute for Contemporary Art, and *13° E: Eleven Artists Working in Berlin* at the Whitechapel Gallery. In the former, an attempt was made to trace a line of development from Dix, Grosz, John Heartfield, and the realistic early Beckmann to the contemporary Berlin realists. But what the exhibition actually revealed were grave differences of style and content between the historical and current realists, as well an insecurity on the part of the politically programmed artists. The Whitechapel show had a much broader concept. With the painters Grützke, Hödicke, Koberling, and Lüpertz, the political conceptualist K. P. Brehmer, Dieter Hacker of the political agitation phase, with Wolf Vostell and Tomas Schmit, the exhibition pointed to yet unexploited potentials of creative work. That this group was still entirely undoctrinaire may be seen from the participation of Johannes Grützke, the initiator and so-called headmaster of the Schule der neuen Prächtigkeit (School of the New Splendor), founded in 1973, whose statutes proclaimed that "Splendor is born only of heightened sensibility."[26] Grützke's portraits and figure groups with their negation of easy aesthetic teachings and their tendency to the bizarre and trivial are testimonies of a strong expressive realism pushed into grotesque, endless variations of the artist's mirror image. "When I look at myself in the mirror," Grützke said, "I'm looking at the whole world. . . . It's always me, and I don't consider the world any better or worse than myself."[27]

Grützke has remained apart, having established no school in the traditional sense, nor indeed ever intending to. The astounding success of the four Moritzplatz Fauves, in contrast, has truly revolutionized the German art scene and contributed to the international breakthrough of the new German painting. In the wake of Baselitz, Lüpertz, and Koberling—who admittedly frown at being called mentors, let alone predecessors of the New Fauves—they managed something the critical realist had not, namely to clear the air of the odor of regionalism that had surrounded Berlin art. The most important contribution in this regard was surely made by Karl-Horst Hödicke. A critical involvement with Dada and neo-Dada, décollage and Pop, neorealism and the cinema provided the solid intellectual and artistic background for this outstanding draughtsman's decision to take up painting. Hödicke's artistic intelligence, love of experiment, and creative curiosity have assured him of influence far beyond the circle of his students and they have been major contributors to the vitality of today's German art scene. His painting, both topical and retrospective, reflecting on and reformulating history and myth, possesses an artistic and intellectual substance not always entirely matched by his pupils and imitators, whose work frequently seems threatened by the pressure to produce and succeed.

Now that the teleology of the avant-garde has finally broken down, it is permissible to make use of tradition and citations. The past is now available. Lüpertz for instance employs formal elements from the work of Werner Gilles, blowing them up to monumental proportions; a number of Hödicke's cityscapes reveal a definite influence on the past of Werner Heldt. And when Rainer Fetting gave a 1980 canvas the title *Return of the Giants* and entered the names Van Gogh and Gauguin for all to see, this itself represented a programmatic statement. Unlike their teacher, Hödicke, however, Fetting and his *confrères* Helmut Middendorf and Salomé let their private proclivities, their fears and obsessions flow into their imagery. These artist–individuals are at the same time representatives of a young generation, whose specific sense of life, which oscillates between a yearning for human communication, including that of the erotic variety, included a feeling of isolation and threat in the midst of a chaotic reality.

Bernd Zimmer, in contrast, concentrates on landscape and experiences of nature. An admirer of Mark Rothko and Barnett Newman, he has spoken of "the return of the object, but with the means of abstraction."[28] The best of Zimmer's canvases reveal a comparatively strong desire for composition and form. Unlike most of his colleagues, he is just the opposite of an asphalt cowboy, loving the open countryside because there one is not "permanently influenced by consumer goods and continually looking at window displays."

While the Moritzplatz artists and those with related approaches, such as the Swiss painter Luciano Castelli, who came to Berlin in 1978, focus on an immediate expression of their personal emotions, with Dieter Hacker, ex-constructivist and founder of 7. Produzentengalerie (7th Producers' Gallery), who contributed aggressively radical theses to the political discussion of art during the 1960s and 1970s, it is reflection on the reciprocal relationship between art and society that determines his work. The same holds for his return to traditional painting on canvas in 1976, which though it was tinged with a sad realization of the limited potential of art to bring about a change in consciousness, nevertheless triggered a second, astonishingly creative phase in his career.

A more concrete approach to political and social issues is found in the painting of Inga Barfuss and Thomas Wachweger, who live and work together in Berlin. Though the degree of abstraction of their abbreviated pictorial metaphors is higher than that of other young Berlin artists, the reference to reality of such canvases as *Development Aid* or *Defeated Hope* is much more direct and the aggressiveness of their attacks on social injustices more immediately apparent. A similar directness characterizes the self-consciously feminist paintings of Elvira Bach, who deals with her theme *When God Made Man, He Was Only Practicing* in unabashed raw colors and angular forms, and with direct reference to her own person. The comparatively unpolemical imagery of Hella Santarossa, in contrast, emerges from the graceful rhythms and movements of the dance. Barbara Heinisch, who attempted to bring the dynamics of color and of physical movement into direct relationship by letting nude models stride through the painting ground as she was working, has since left Berlin for the Rhineland. On the other hand, Eva-Maria Schön, creator of imaginatively meditative imagery and environments that conform to none of the current stylistic trends, has forsaken Düsseldorf for Berlin.

One excellent painter who stands beside the scene is Max Neumann, whose obsessively enigmatic figures, symbols and locales seem to transpose the world of E.T.A. Hoffmann into our own era. Another, more extreme example of how open Berlin has become despite its undiminished love of no-holds-barred criticism is Martin Rosz, an esoteric outsider who earned his living as a department-store employee, much too shy to court public notice. Yet noticed he was. His partly naive, partly sophisticated watercolors, frequently assembled to form an envi-

15

16

15. *Dieter Hacker.* The Day, *1985.*
Collection of the artist.

16. *Rainer Fetting.* Drummer and
Guitarist. *1949.* Berlinische
Galerie.

17

17. *Eva-Marie Schön.* Attempt to
Get Close to a Leaf, *1986.*
Collection of the artist.

18. *Max Neuman.* Untitled, *1984.*
Berlinische Galerie.

18

ronment, have as their subject the artist's own life, as he lives it both in the world and in his mind. And though the props have been derived from his everyday surroundings, Rosz's imagery, as in a modern novel, surpasses egocentricity to become a colorful myth for our day.

The number of Berlin's self-help galleries continued to increase into the 1980s. In 1978, Raimund Kummer, Hermann Pitz, and Fritz Rahmann opened their Büro Berlin with an exhibition called *Spaces*. The year 1979 saw the establishment of the 1/61 Gallery in Kreuzberg and Lützowstrasse Situations, followed in 1981 by the Quergalerie. Many of the artists involved have since won regional, national or even international acclaim, attesting not only to their self-confidence but to the high intellectual and aesthetic quality of their work in painting and sculpture. The Kreuzberg group, apart from ter Hell, included Reinhard Pods, who paints pictures about pictures; Gerd Rohling, who augments or confronts his socially committed vehement paintings with sculptural elements and found objects; Elke Lixfeld, who works in a serial approach and also carries out actions and performances; and the sculptors Frank Dornseif and Rainer Mang. The last two names indicate that in Berlin—as at the Düsseldorf Art Academy—sculpture has at long last emerged from the shadow of painting and found a place in the public eye, even though the so-called sculpture boulevard installed along Kurfürstendamm in 1987 can scarcely be called a successful *Gesamtkunstwerk*.

Originality and diversity are perhaps the most salient features of Berlin sculpture today. Much of it is characterized by the employment of unusual materials for unfamiliar ends. Frank Dornseif uses steel reinforcing rods to delineate figures in space, challenging viewers to flesh them out in their own imaginations. Rainer Mang works with cement and coal. Kummer, Pitz and Rahmen conduct a sort of big-city archaeology as a process of consciousness raising. They secure evidence not in the search for their own identity but rather with a sociocritical aim. On their *Spaces* show, Hermann Pitz commented: "Our idea was that we were going into a space where others had already been and left their traces. Nobody can say where art begins here and where life begins."[31] The same might be said of Raphael Rheinsberg's research into German history, as when he collects found objects at Anhalt Station to evoke the transient deceptive glory of the past and its destruction, when he arranges bricks from demolished Berlin buildings as memorial plaques to a bygone era, or when he exemplifies, with gleanings from the former Danish embassy on the Tiergarten, the most infamous period of German history in a chilling concentration of revealing details. This form of artistic criticism, in which past and present, life and art are reciprocally illuminated, has a greater long-term effect than ideologically more defined, topical agitation, which loses force as soon as the current situation changes.

One of the finest talents among young Berlin sculptors is Olaf Metzel, whose road-block assemblage, *13.4.1981*, an anti-monument to the battles between rebellious youth and militant police that took place on that date, was one of the most impressive and hence provocative works on the erstwhile sculpture boulevard. Although inspired by actual situations,

19. Martin Rosz. George Washington Hotel, New York, *1978.* Staatliche Museen, Preussischer Kulturbesitz, Neue Nationalgalerie, Berlin (photograph by Bob Leitner).

20. Gerd Rohling. Big Sleep, *1984.*
Berlinische Galerie.

Metzel's sculpture transcends the obvious to attain a historical dimension. This is true of the plaster busts of great men and women he belabors with sharp tools and "decorates" with outsized oak-leaves in order to raise awareness of "damaged" German intellectual history; it is also true of the relief of concrete and reinforcing rods entitled *Olympian Art*, which employs smashed symbols such as columns and Olympic rings, eagle, laurel wreath, and faces to evoke the perversion of classical ideals and the ruination of the Olympic idea.

By the 1980s, contemporary art in Berlin could no longer be accused of either provincialism or imitativeness, and in many cases it could even claim priority and true originality. Berlin painting and sculpture had once again become what they had not always been after the end of World War II: "one of the most sensitive indicators for the capturing and recording of the states of mind of a social organism at a certain place within a certain period of time."[32]

Notes

1. Lothar Klünner, "Zone 5," in *Weltstadtsinfonie, Sammlung Berlinische Galerie zu Gast in der Kunsthalle Emden* (Berlin, 1986).
2. Ibid.
3. "During that particularly harsh winter, members of the German theater in Hamburg . . . approached the works council of the King Ludwig 4/5 mine in Recklinghausen-Suderwich to `organize' coal so the show could go on in Hamburg theaters. . . . The singers and actors repaid them with a guest performance: *Art for Coal—Coal for Art*." This is how Thomas Grochowiak (*Kunstschätze in Recklinghausen* [Recklinghausen, 1972]) described the inception of the Ruhr Festivals sponsored since 1947 by the German Labor Union Association. Although they have since lost a great deal of their attractiveness, these festivals played an extremely significant part in the revival of cultural life in Germany after 1945, especially as their express aim was to bring the performing and visual arts to audiences that, initially at least, consisted primarily of working people.
4. Heinz Ohff, "Die Muse küsst den widerstrebenden Bären,: *Magazin KUNST* 3 (Mainz, 1976).
5. The Ferdinand Möller Gallery, for instance, showed until its closure in 1937 works by Feininger, Schlemmer, Heckel, and Nolde. Buchholz, to 1943, exhibited Beckmann, Barlach (prematurely terminated), Heldt, Hofer, Schmidt-Rottluff, and Blumethal; Galerie Nierendorf showed works by Rohlfs, Marc, and Scharl; and Galerie von der Heyde, as late as 1939, had paintings by Pechstein and Joachim Karsch, and in 1942, Karl Hofer. As late as 1943, the Prussian Academy of Arts presented an Otto Nagel exhibition.
6. Werner Doede, *Berlin, Kunst und Künstler seit 1870* (Recklinghausen, 1961).
7. Kynaston McShine, ed., *Berlinart, 1961-1987* (New York, 1987).
8. Wieland Schmied, "Typical and Unique: Art in Berlin 1945–1970," in McShine, ed., *Berlinart*.
9. *Verein der Freude der Nationalgalerie* (Berlin, 1978).
10. Werner Heldt, *Malerei und Zeichnungen*, (Düsseldorf, 1968).
11. Ibid.
12. *Karl Hofer 1898–1955* (Berlin, 1978).
13. Günter Grass, "Geschenkte Freiheit," speech to commemorate May 8, 1945, held on May 5, 1985.
14. Bernhard Schultze, "Gegen das Grass-Diktat," *Die Zeit*, May 31, 1985; Werner Hofmann, "Bekenntnis zählt—die pure Lust am Malen ist suspekt,: *art* 10 (October 1985); Eberhard Rogers, "Flucht in die Unverbindlichkeit? Zur Rede von Günter Grass," *Akademie der Künste, Anzieger* 4 (November 1985).
15. Jürgen Diehl, in a television broadcast on the death of Picasso, 1975.
16. Naum Gabo, diary entry for May 26, 1931, S.A. Nash and Jörn Merkert, eds, *Naum Gabo—Sechzig Jahre Konstruktivismus* (Munich, 1986).
17. Quoted in *10 Jahre Berliner Künstlerprogramm* (Berlin, 1975).
18. Eberhard Roters, "Kunst in Berlin von 1870 bis heute," in *Weltstadtsinfonie*.
19. In a discussion in the Akademie der Künste, 1973.
20. Markus Lüpertz, *Dithyrambisches Manifest* (Berlin, 1966).
21. Schmied, "Typical and Unique."
22. Walter Bachauer, in *Zeitgeist* (Berlin, 1982).
23. Quoted in "Berlin—Ein Pflaster für Künstler," *Art* 4 (April 1985).
24. Quoted in *10 Jahre Berliner Künstlerprogramm*.
25. Heinrich Klotz, *Die neuen Wilden in Berlin* (Stuttgart, 1984).
26. Manfred Bluth, Johannes Grützke, Matthias Koeppel, and Karlheinz Ziegler, eds., *Aufruf als Vorwort zu den Manifesten der Schule der neuen Prächtigkeit* (Berlin, 1973).
27. Quoted in Eckhart Gillen, "Comeback der Aussenwelt," in *Weltstadtsinfonie*.
28. Quoted in Klotz, *Die neuen Wilden in Berlin*.
29. Georg Jappe, "Die Republik der Einzelgänger," in *Strategy: get arts*, (Edinburgh, 1970).
30. Quoted in "Berlin—Ein Pflaster für Künstler."
31. Quoted in Michael Schwarz, "Kunst in Berlin seit 1977," in McShine, ed., *Berlinart*.
32. Roters, "Kunst in Berlin."

1. *Installation of the exhibition
"Fourteen Americans" at the
Museum of Modern Art, 1946.* The
Museum of Modern Art, New York.

The New York Art World Since 1945

Dore Ashton

Dore Ashton is professor of art history at the Cooper Union in New York City and the author of many publications on the arts, including Noguchi East and West *(1991),* Out of the Whirlwind *(1987),* Fragonard in the Universe of Painting *(1988),* A Fable of Modern Art *(1980), and* About Rothko *(1983). Ashton has curated exhibitions both in the United States and in Europe and edited* Picasso on Art *(1972) and* Twentieth Century Artists on Art *(1985).*

It is not a world, or if it is, it is part of the great world. If I had to think of a single word to qualify it, I would have to invent one as Henri Michaux did when he tried to sum up his experience with hallucinatory drugs. He converted an adjective into a noun: *extrêmement*. The art world in New York is a group of impingements. Its outlines are evasive and, like New York itself, almost impossible to contain in description. From the beginning, though, New York had two characteristics: it was founded with the sole aim of profit and attracted one of the most heterogenous populations in the world. A visitor in 1944 claimed he heard eighteen languages spoken.

This polyglot metropolis was and is culturally polyglot as well. The impingements I speak of are not only represented by institutions such as museums, or commercial nodes such as galleries, or broadcasting facilities such as newspapers and magazines. They are composed of groups and subgroups with exceptionally varied interests. One of those groups, of course, consists of artists, but paradoxically, they are not always part of the art world. This essay is about the art world, which means that the incalculable meaning of individual works of art or individual artists is regrettably left unmediated. Yet those meanings are impinged upon by the continuum that is the art world. Above all, by New York itself, which even Henry James could not quite get—speaking of the ambiguity element "matching in its mixture, with nothing else one had known elsewhere" and concluding, "I can only echo contentedly, with analysis for once quite agreeably baffled, 'Remarkable, unspeakable New York!'"[1]

"If the artist was in hell in 1946, now he is in business,"[2] wrote Allan Kaprow in 1964, a year when business was very good for New York's favored artists. His vision of the immediate postwar period, usually defined as the decade from 1945 to 1955, was informed by the work of Harold Rosenberg, whom he quotes at length from an article in 1952:

The refusal of Value did not take the form of condemnation or defiance to society, as it did after World War I. It was diffident. The lone artist did not want the world to be different, he wanted his canvas to be a world. . . . The American vanguard artist took to the white expanse of canvas as Melville's Ishmael took to the sea. . . . On the one hand, a desperate recognition of moral and intellectual exhaustion; on the other, the exhilaration of an adventure over depths in which he might find reflected the true image of his identity.

Rosenberg's summary of the "hell" of the artists he knew (most particularly Willem de Kooning, who was a sort of *chef d'école* of those who came to be called Abstract Expressionists) was a commentary on the moral order of things just after the war with which such artists as de Kooning and Robert Motherwell could concur. On the practical side, there was Clement Greenberg describing the physical discomforts of bohemia with its smallish lofts, decrepit stairways, cold water, and defined perimeters in downtown Manhattan, and seeing in the poverty a purity of intention that eventually would lead American artists to world acknowledgment, which is what happened. A younger but very influential critic (since he was editor of *ARTnews*), Thomas B. Hess was still equating hell with poverty and saw it as a sign of traditional American philistinism in 1950:

459

Rickety stairs and cold-water flats are not figures of speech; they exist, in the deepest Sartre sense, as do all the grey discomfort, bleakness and economic insecurity that go with them. Only nineteenth-century Paris has been as tough on its artists as our equally smug civilization.[3]

The American vanguard artists these commentators were examining were easy enough to identify in those days because they were relatively few. Even their physical haunts were well-known. They were mostly downtown, where artists had found small manufacturing lofts, and they patronized coffeehouses such as the San Remo on the corner of Bleecker and Macdougal streets, where later the Beat poets hung out; taverns such as the White Horse, at Hudson and Eleventh Street, where poets mingled with painters and where Dylan Thomas would make his sensational entry; and the Cedar Tavern at University Place between 10th and 11th streets that drew regulars such as de Kooning, Jackson Pollock, and Franz Kline. Then there was the Club at 35 East 8th Street, founded by an anarchic group of artists in 1949 who, as Irving Sandler has noted, kept sketchy records, had no sustained policy, and could rarely remember what had been voted or when.[4] "It must be stressed," he wrote, "that the Club never had a collective mission or promoted an esthetic program." Yet for many who wandered in and out, the Club had some conformation; it had some hierarchical stresses and the ambience of excitement was created by its more prominent members, who for one reason or another felt they were on the verge of important discovery. The fact is that by 1951, the Club was aware of itself as a repository for effective commentary on abstract expressionism and held at least four Friday evening symposia on the subject. By that time, the art world, or at least their art world, had reached out for general culture and included luminaries from other fields, among them speakers at Club gatherings such as Hannah Arendt, Paul Goodman, Joseph Campbell, Dylan Thomas, Edgard Varese, and John Cage. Their art world was also expanding to include important functionaries such as museum directors: Alfred H. Barr, Jr., of the Museum of Modern Art was very attentive to polyphonic talks at the Club, and James Johnson Sweeney of the Guggenheim paid his respects from time to time. The era of the collector as participant was yet to come.

I will not attempt to garner statistics to show that the economic situation in America after the war was entirely rosy. No need. America prospered during the war (although not her artists) and emerged, as everyone knows, a full-fledged consumer society, readying itself for the boom that commenced only days after the final days of the war. Close observers between 1945 and 1950 noted the quick growth of the luxury industry that naturally included art. But while they spoke of an art boom and pointed out that in 1940 New York had forty galleries and by 1946 had 150, they noticed a new type of collector—middle-class, under fifty and, for largely economic reasons, eager to buy works by living Americans, which cost less than their European counterparts. Left out until many years later were the denizens of downtown New York who comprised what would be called the New York School. The upwardly mobile (to use a phrase that was ushered in around that time) stayed comfortable on the middle road that, it is true,

would eventually take them to mecca, the Museum of Modern Art, but not quite yet.

So lucrative was the luxury industry, which subsumed the art industry, that in 1949, a popularizer, Russell Lynes, wrote a bestseller, *The Tastemakers,* in which he consistently capitalized "Art World." He pointed out that there had been a scarcity of consumer goods during the war but not of money. "But the postwar art boom cannot be explained as simply a mere matter of economic scarcity of supply and eagerness of demand. Its roots lie deeper than that in soil that had been carefully cultivated, fertilized, and watered for a long time by an eager band of tastemakers—museum officials, art critics, dealers, teachers and aesthetic messiahs. The group that now calls itself the Art World can compete as a pressure group with any commercial association of lobby in financial resources and public relations techniques."[5] Lynes described the American art world picturesquely as a "vast bureaucracy, hydra-headed and munificently financed." Moreover, he pointed out in a chapter called "Taste-Tax-Deductible" that corporations had gotten into the act and that "wealthy collectors in high income brackets are said to be financing dealers so that they can not only buy pictures cheaply but write off gallery losses on their income taxes"—a practice that still flourishes, if in far more complex ways.

This art world, however, was hardly the art world that harbored the future stars who, in the years immediately after the war, had not yet shared much of the hydra-headed monster's loot. A look at three artists destined (or doomed?) to become stars from the economic point is needed here.

Arshile Gorky, who had a strong position in the artists' milieu and was regarded by connoisseurs as a seminal figure in the Abstract Expressionist floriation, wrote to his sister in 1940: "The art business hasn't been so good this year, not a picture sold yet!" In 1941, concerned friends decided to donate his paintings to museums, but despite that, his student and biographer Ethel Schwabacher noted ruefully:

In the seven remaining years until Gorky's death in 1948 no further paintings were bought by museums or given to them. He did not receive any prizes or mention at the large national or international exhibitions. With few exceptions no important collectors acquired his work until after his death. He was not in demand as a lecturer, teacher, juror or committeeman.[6]

This, despite the considerable interest generated by his first important one-man exhibition at the Julien Levy Gallery in 1945 and his inclusion in "Fourteen Americans," an important exhibition at the Museum of Modern Art, in 1946.

His friend de Kooning, who had also enjoyed an underground reputation for years, fared hardly better. He had his first one-man exhibition at the Charles Egan Gallery in 1948, and it was greeted with enthusiasm by those in the art world who craved visual adventure but not by those with the need to possess. Hess noted that by the end of the 1940s "the situation of the American artist had not greatly changed. Sales were still so remote as to be almost unthinkable."[7] Two years after his

460

first exhibition (and he was no youngster: in 1950 he was forty-six years old) de Kooning had a one-man exhibition at the Venice Biennale and the year after, won first prize in the sixtieth annual exhibition of the Chicago Art Institute. In 1953, he had a *succès de scandale* with his Woman series but still, Hess wrote, "De Kooning's financial situation remained much the same—that is, terrible—even though 'Woman I' bought from the exhibition by the Museum of Modern Art soon became one of the most widely reproduced works of the 1950s."

Jackson Pollock had a far broader exposure to the general public than either Gorky or de Kooning and had engaged the interest of important functionaries of both museums and art publications early in his career. When Peggy Guggenheim gave him a contract and his first one-man show in 1943, she was able to interest the Museum of Modern Art, which later bought a painting. Pollock wrote to his brother Charles:

I am getting $150 a month from the gallery, which just about doesn't meet the bills. I will have to sell a lot of work thru the year to get it above $150. The Museum of Modern Art bought the painting reproduced in Harpers this week, which I hope will stimulate further sales.[8]

All the same, despite a middle-brow publication's attention, his next dealer, Betty Parsons, would write to Peggy Guggenheim in 1948 about "the terrible financial condition of the Pollocks." Within months, in one of the most popular weeklies in America, Pollock was important enough to be featured (*Life*, August 8, 1949) and belabored with an indignant, often insulting, text and lots of pictures. *Life* noted that Pollock was "virtually unknown in 1944. Now his paintings hang in five U.S. museums and forty private collections." Whether a bit of hyperbole was at work in the editorial office is hard to tell, but it is certainly true that the tide had turned for Pollock financially, bringing him to the position of a sought-after commodity.

Whatever financial success these so-called stars enjoyed was a result not only of their own efforts, which in all cases were confined primarily to the studio in those days, but to the concatenation of forces impinging on their fate. These included institutions that had also gained enormous prestige and, incidentally, money during the boom years, an art press that had finally managed to go beyond the boundaries of the knowing few and fashion, which took a big turn to the arts after the war.

These stars were, by 1950, largely identified with Abstract Expressionism, which was popularly identified only with the so-called wild men—the painters of large gestures such as de Kooning and Pollock. It would take a few more years for the New York School to be perceived as a movement that could not be characterized by mere stylistic traits. In his early, penetrating art criticism, Greenberg had seen a historical continuity that few others understood and that had more to do with the state of mind of the artist than with his competitive position on the world art scene (a side of Greenberg's criticism that lamentably appeared in the mid 1950s). Greenberg reviewed Pollock's 1943 show in the *Nation* (November 27, 1943), remarking that he was the first painter he knew of to have gotten

something positive from the muddiness of color that characterized much American painting. "It is equivalent, even if in a negative, helpless way, of that American chiaroscuro which dominated Melville, Hawthorne, Poe, and has been best translated into painting by Blakelock and Ryder." In his allusion to the brooding character of the only American tradition to which the modern painters could address themselves (as a few years later the young poets would), Greenberg focused on the abiding issues in American spiritual history: the struggle against materialism, philistinism, and spiritual isolation, all of which these earlier artists had confronted. Greenberg's literary antagonist—the other independent critic whose views were widely respected—Rosenberg, had also underscored the loneliness of the American artist and referred repeatedly to his cultural isolation and his frontiersman's state of mind. These two writers, and occasionally the scholar Meyer Schapiro, were not only attentive to contemporary issues in the arts but can be credited with writing the inner-circle history of the art world.

Such history probably has little to do with the art world, or even with a single highlighted movement known as Abstract Expressionism. Even artists whose work bore no resemblance to the visual styles that eventually got compressed into the sobriquet Abstract Expressionism shared many of their views on how to define art and how to locate meaning. In fact, the undercurrents were almost always running strong in the direction of ethics and morality and in this, the New York art world's artists shared with intellectuals all over the western world certain preoccupations.

It has become quite fashionable to analyze the artistic postwar decade in the United States only in sociopolitical terms, which is another way of saying that the handy facts, such as the economic boom and the concomitant Cold War mentality, are thrust upon the arts with resounding recriminations and left at that. The long list of Cold War degradations certainly had some impact on the state of mind of the artists, but their turning to individualistic positions must be seen as part of a worldwide inquiry to which they gravitated by instinct and experience. It would be more accurate to see in their attitudes the validity of the *idées forces* of their time. And those go back to the period between the world wars in which European artists had responded to the war partly by exploring the issues raised by Freud and Marx, and in many cases, by rejecting the standard logical historicism of the previous century. Aspects of the surrealist revolt against rationalism were to remain. They surfaced during the 1940s, particularly the late 1940s, when intellectuals but above all visual artists began to see the process of introjection as a legitimate ethical stance. Without discussing the individual attitudes of the many art world figures who openly discussed their situation, which they saw as difficult and sometimes desperate, it is possible to see that a prevailing concern was with fulfilling some kind of ethical imperative by means of their creative activity. That is why, when the echoes of the talk in Europe about existentialism sounded in New York, so many were engaged by its ideas, above all the ideas of ethical responsibility and individual acts. The resulting works of art, which as their authors occasionally remarked, had entailed risk, were not easily assimilated. The

461

truth is that despite the worldwide attention to the new American activities, particularly in painting, the Abstract Expressionists never effected the complete capitulation of the art world, as did later groupings.

Their role in intellectual history has yet to be defined, but I would have to allude to it, even in this quick survey, since in many ways it colored subsequent events. I think it is important to bear in mind that the formation of the artists in this movement was strongly affected by what they knew of the modern tradition, which included Baudelaire, Joyce, Rimbaud, Eliot, and Valéry among writers, and Picasso, Miró, Matisse, and Kandinsky among painters. (They did not know the Russian modernists other than Kandinsky.) All of these modernist forebears had touched upon the issues that would emerge after World War II in the writings of Camus, Sartre, and Merleau-Ponty, whose ideas quickly filtered into the New York studios after 1945. For Motherwell, Philip Guston, William Baziotes, Adolph Gottlieb, to mention a few, there was a natural flow of thoughts inspired by this tradition. Moreover, the impact of psychoanalysis—reflected in Joyce for instance—was received through works of art such as *Ulysses*. When a few artists discovered the works of Carl Jung, his theories, and particularly his idea of the collective unconscious merely coincided with insights they had already absorbed in their pilgrimages to the heart of the modern tradition. In their view, they upheld the highest principles evinced in the twentieth century by seeking authenticity and truth in the process of making works of art. In the view of so many recent critics, however, their preoccupation with their private spiritual lives and the significance of their choices were, on the contrary, an ethical failure in the face of the ravages of the terrible politics embarked upon by the United States known rather simply as the Cold War. The conformism of the postwar decade so often discussed was obvious enough, but as Harold Rosenberg once said, the painters alone were, and remained, anarchic enough to resist, unlike intellectuals in other disciplines.

Unquestionably, the postwar decade was blighted. The tone of official attitudes toward the arts may be gauged in its crudest manifestation in the 1949 statement of representative G. A. Dondero, who expostulated on the floor of Congress: "Art critics seem to enjoy complete freedom from directional supervision." While Dondero was a nuisance, other more insidious forces were at work, creating devastating inquisitions that left permanent deleterious effects on American culture, some noticed by prescient commentators (usually independents—which is to say, not wedded to an institution) such as C. Wright Mills. In *Gates of Eden*, a study of American culture in the 1960s, Morris Dickstein generously bestows the respect that Mills deserves and that had been unceremoniously withdrawn after he published a controversial essay about Cuba:

From early in his career Mills was no statistics man swimming in jargon but an almost novelistic observer of social change and the distribution of social power, the kind of observer who is also a citizen, who is committed, who makes judgments. He concluded "White Collar" (1951) with a troubled analysis of the political indifference of the men of the "new middle classes" (who are "not radical, not liberal, not conservative, not reactionary; they are inactionary; they are

out of it"). In the chapter on intellectuals, "Brains, Inc." he shows how more and more of the educated have become technicians and corporate hired hands, "unable to face politics except as news and entertainment," while "the remaining free intellectuals increasingly withdraw . . . they lack the will."[9]

The "inactionary" character of the postwar decade was a goad to more than a few intellectuals who produced "actionary" works with fervor, although most, as has so often been noted, settled into the good life that conformism promised. The year before Mills's book, David Riesman had published his study of the changing American character with the memorable title *The Lonely Crowd*, in which he discussed the middle class and attacked "political passivity and personal limpness." A few years later, the *enfant terrible* Norman Mailer declared in *The White Negro* that "a stench of fear has come out of every pore of American life, and we suffer from a collective failure of nerve."[10] He called the 1950s "years of conformity and depression" and raged against his own caste that had so handily found its mission in defending the American way. The middle-class art world certainly did not depart from the general tendency. It cheerfully adopted advanced art as a sign of cultivation; its members' status as cultural donors; and American omnipotence. But it is a grave error to charge the creators of advanced art with similar hypocrisy. Anarchistic in inclination (Barnett Newman enthusiastically wrote an introduction to Kropotkin's memoirs), they, by temperament and formation, resisted.

At least for a time they resisted. Many would soon be overwhelmed by the hydra-headed bureaucracy, which, by the mid-1950s, included vastly extended commercial systems of distribution of art; museums with eyes turned toward their turnstiles; corporations, and even the federal government, eager to use their products for various ends, some quite nefarious. In addition, the art world now encompassed a larger constituency. Artists thronged the downtown bastions, having been recently formed by the new art departments that had sprung up all over America in universities that had seen the value, finally, of the visual arts (which included the financial value, since art had become acceptable socially and the middle class was finally willing to subsidize its children's education as artists). Along with the new young artists arrived new young nonartistic intellectuals, armed with a high-class education and confidence in their academic credentials, who would begin to write art criticism in the flourishing art journals. From the mid- to the late 1950s, then, the ingredients of the New York art world visible changed, or rather, were augmented. Impinging forces, such as the dark reaction that had allowed some Americans to be jailed for their political convictions and others to be ruined by blacklists, did not diminish the exponential growth of the art industry, although they did prey upon the spirits of the artists.

In art world gatherings downtown there were signs of unease. At the Club in 1954, they worried through several panels under the title "Has the Situation Changed?"—which of course suggested that it had. Not long after, at parties, at the Cedar and the San Remo, and at openings uptown to which several older members of the downtown community had graduated, new and strident voices rose against almost everything including the art world itself. Among these lusty denouncers was Allen Ginsberg, who in many ways epitomized the dissent of the late 1950s and the paradox of instant fame for the dissenter, thanks to the relentless ingenuity of the communications industry. Pollock had been the first artist to be utilized by the powerful machinery of communications. (The fine art of publicity had made strides since the 1930s, when one of its founders, Edward L. Bernays, had gone so far as to consult the eminent psychoanalyst A. A. Brill, who, incidentally, cooperated.) When Ginsberg read *Howl* in 1955 in San Francisco, the news traveled fast, and when he turned up in New York a year later when the poem was published, the art world was there to welcome him—those uptown to welcome him as a court fool, those downtown to welcome him as an avatar of change from the silent early, to the obstreperous late, 1950s. He came proclaiming and singing—singing, like Whitman the undeniable father of them all, songs of himself and of nonconformity to the many selves who listened with relief to his great anger and despair. *Time* and the other household publications quickly saw the news value of the unwashed Beats and wrote regularly of their exploits, bringing Jack Kerouac, Ginsberg, Gregory Corso, and Edgar Rice Burroughs into the middle-class living room. But that in no way diminished their impact on the vanguard members of the art world. For a long time, similar voices, although in a more muted tone, had been tutoring the art world in unorthodox and unaccepting modes. Ginsberg's voice merged with an already steady chorus rising under the tutelage of such figures as John Cage, Marcel Duchamp, and Professor Suzuki, who was lecturing on Zen in the mid-1950s (and, in the background from Europe, as a kind of *basso continuo,* the activist voice of Sartre).

There are many ways to interpret the pronounced shift in values during the late 1950s that brought to the fore such artists as Robert Rauschenberg, Jasper Johns, and Claes Oldenburg, all of whom became notorious rebels in the artists' world and signal attractions in the art world. Rauschenberg is repeatedly quoted from his 1959 statement in a Museum of Modern Art catalogue: "Painting relates to both art and life. Neither can be made (I try to act in the gap between the two)." Although his use of old quilts, Coca-Cola bottles, strings, and real chairs affixed to his canvases had a certain shock value, it was a shock that, like the nineteenth-century's *frisson nouveau,* could be digested by an art public thoroughly conditioned to the consumer's game of novelty. From another point of view, Rauschenberg's rapid pace on the road to success can be seen as a fulfillment of earlier efforts to confront American life, particularly urban life, from a less lofty point of view than had prevailed among the previous generation. Surfeited with the ravages of doubt that had inspired so much vanguard art in the early 1950s, the new generation that rallied to Rauschenberg's banner sought hard evidence of daily existence—as hard to take, and unyielding, as detritus of New York's own streets. Rauschenberg's art was an urban art, but he was not urbane. This again is in an American tradition, perhaps best summarized by the rare and wonderful native essayist Guy Davenport:

Knowledge is a kind of ignorance, ignorance a kind of knowledge.

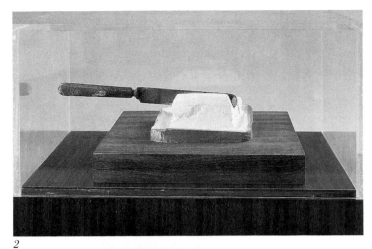

2

3

2. Claes Oldenburg. Cream Cheese with Knife, *1962. Leo Castelli Gallery, New York.*

3. Robert Rauschenberg. Sundog, *1962. Leo Castelli Gallery, New York.*

4. *Robert Rauschenberg.* Crocus, *1962.* Leo Castelli Gallery, New York.

This peculiarly American perception runs through our literature, welling up from our experience. . . . With forgivable innocence and forgivable arrogance, we mistook the knowledge of others for ignorance as often as we mistook our ignorance for knowledge. Learning has always therefore been a conversion for us. Our literature is one of persuasion and discovery, of vision.[11]

It is not difficult to extrapolate this insight to the visual arts and to understand the extraordinary appeal Rauschenberg's combine paintings had for Americans. The forebears, such as de Kooning, were also urban artists celebrating New York's diversity, but they worked in a context of the universal. The new artists, often harkening to John Cage's insistence on the empirical pleasures of each instant, could not accept the notion of no environment, which was said to be a principle in the paintings of de Kooning, Guston, and many others of their generation. Their recapture of visual innocence through the ingestion of the real in their own environment held broad and perhaps even profound implications for Americans seeking the conversion experience. On the other hand, they restored to Americans their interest in the practical documentary aspects of art, so that if a sculptor such as George Segal represented, as he did a few years later, a group of passengers on a bus, his realism was readily accepted as a vanguard manifestation, so penetrating is the American desire to find the real in its own locus.

Movement into the seething life of the New York City dweller appeared not only in the objects and paintings that could be seen in the singularly successful Castelli Gallery uptown where Rauschenberg and his friend Johns exhibited, but also in the cooperative galleries downtown run by artists. In the modest settings of artist's co-ops, for instance, Allan Kaprow first showed an environment (a deliberately tacky affair: a fragile structure made up of dirtied sheets of paper and tarred collaged scraps) and Claes Oldenburg first showed his chaotic, artfully artless ensembles of crude objects made from burlap, papier-mâché, and mud, simulating the aspect of the city. From these exhibitions emerged the theatrical phenomenon called happenings—wild and sometimes aggressive events combining mime, dance, film, scraps of dialogue, and artistic objects in motion. Happenings could be seen as ethical gestures; an attempt to kidnap the art from the art scene and to distance artists from the increasingly commercial atmosphere of the art world. But they, too, became occasions for bourgeois titillation. In no time, the storefront theaters of happeners were besieged by those who also attended Museum of Modern Art openings for their entertainment value.

If the earnestly rebellious creators of happenings inadvertently served the art world, they also opened an era and showed the way to the young. Marshall Berman generously credits such artists as Kaprow, Jim Dine, Robert Whitman, Oldenburg, and Segal with restoring modernism's century-old dialogue with the modern environment, adding:

The emerging New Left learned much from this dialogue, and eventually contributed much to it. So many of the great demonstrations and confrontations of the 1960s were remarkable works of kinetic and environmental art, in whose creation millions of people took

464

part. This has often been noticed, but it must also be noticed that the artists were their first—here, as elsewhere, unacknowledged legislators of the world.[12]

If these artists anticipated the radical cultural change ushered in by the 1960s, they themselves tended to remain ensconced in the art world, which by now had proved itself obdurately all-absorbent. Its ranks had swelled to include previously excluded groups (museums and their boards no longer scorned the presence of the newly rich or of such covertly maligned minorities as Jews) and even the world of fashion, also previously rejected, was now actively engaged. Calvin Tompkins in a curious note preparing the ground for his report of the Andy Warhol phenomenon observed:

During the late 1950s, the fashion crowd started to take an active interest in the New York art scene. . . . *Vogue* and *Harper's Bazaar* had duly noted the emergence of the New York School, had posed their mannequins against Abstract Expressionist, dripped-paint backdrops and informed their readers that "people are talking about" Jackson Pollock and Willem De Kooning, but there had been no real interaction between the worlds of art and fashion. Now, however, a new spirit was coming into vanguard art. Robert Rauschenberg and Jasper Johns had broken out of the Abstract Expressionist net Art was in. The fashion crowd, which knew Rauschenberg and Johns as display artists, realized with a slight start that people really were talking about Rauschenberg and Johns.[13]

They were not talking about certain other painters, however, who had also turned their attention to issues involving human destiny. (To give only two examples: the German-born painter Jan Müller had embarked on an impressive group of expressionist paintings in which hallowed romantic and Faustian themes were explored, and Lester Johnson moved away from abstraction, painting isolated figures in a twilight Manhattan, sustaining the existentialist note sounded first by the older abstract expressionists.) Although Meyer Schapiro was sensitive to the qualities of the minority artists, not many other critics could tear their eyes away from the extravagant, outer-directed artists about whom people were talking. In polyglot New York, it seemed that the art press could only talk one language at a time.

The 1960s. Although the packaging of decades offends my sense of complexity, there is no question about the reality of a block of time that encompassed so many eruptive events and engendered so much critical and often passionate commentary. The year 1960 ushered in worldwide agitation. There were student riots in Turkey, Japan, and South Korea; stirrings in England where the Aldermaston march initiated the still important struggle against nuclear weapons; and stirrings in America that heralded the Civil Rights movement and general protest against the sins of omission of the previous postwar years. The unforeseen popularity of a book published in 1960, *Growing Up Absurd* by the unconventional scholar Paul Goodman, can be taken as a legitimate sign of the times. Goodman touched the right nerve. An anarchist by temperament, an unaffiliated intellectual by profession, and a bohemian in his personal comportment, Goodman explained to America the crucial values that America had neglected to offer its progeny, and in so doing, found among the progeny a huge following.

5

6

5. *George Segal.* Bus Riders, *1962–64.* Hirshhorn Museum and Sculpture Garden, Smithsonian Institution, Washington, D. C. Gift of Joseph H. Hirshhorn.

6. *Jan Muller.* Walpurgisnacht Faust II, *1956.* Collection of Mr. and Mrs. Howard Wise.

7. *Lester Johnson.* Grey Head, *1964.* Zabriskie Gallery, New York.

8. *Group exhibition at the Green Gallery, 1961.*

7

8

The cultural radicalism that was the hallmark of the 1960s found its prophet in Goodman (abetted by Herbert Marcuse and Norman O. Brown, whose books in the 1960s were also fueling the protest movement).

There was plenty to be angry about. America's easily won hegemony in the postwar world, with its frightening military adventurism and scarcely concealed imperial designs, not to mention its domestic racism, was finally being challenged by many Americans themselves. Critiques abounded, not only in nondiscursive writings but in novels, poems, and visual works of art. Some of this critical outcrying bordered on wanton violence, as in Burroughs's works, both implosive and explosive, filled with unmitigated ire. In *The Wild Boys* (1969), Burroughs's drunk soldier exclaims: "When you want the job done come to the United States of America. And we can turn it on in any direction." Statisticians might tell Americans that the economy was just fine—the Gross National Product had doubled between 1955 and 1965—but many Americans were excluded from the prosperity. The young—including a growing number of intellectuals and artists—were not in a mood to be conned. Nor was John F. Kennedy's sloganeering very effective with the newly indignant, although it must be admitted that the art world found him quite to their taste.

Nothing short of tumultuous were the quick transitions in art world practices and preoccupations; cultural historians are still struggling to disentangle the period's cross-lines and contradictions. In 1962, for instance, Tomkins called Pop Art the *annus mirabilis*:

Nearly all the leading practitioners had their first uptown shows that year—Roy Lichtenstein at the Castelli (paintings of comic strips and household appliances), Jim Dine at the Martha Jackson (neckties and tools), Andy Warhol at the Stable (Campbell Soup cans, silk-screened Marilyn Monroes) and Jim Rosenquist (bill-board-sized auto parts) and Claes Oldenburg (giant "soft" hamburgers, ice-cream cones, etc.) at Richard Bellamy's Green Gallery.[14]

There were great differences in talent and even goals among the newly celebrated Pop artists, but one thing they all seemed to share was a disaffection with disaffection. By incorporating the products of corporations as though they were fitting subjects for art, they announced a willingness to accept what they sometimes called what is there. Far from being critical, they seemed acquiescent. Yet those who were represented in the brilliant 1961 exhibition of the Museum of Modern Art, curated by William Seitz, "The Art of Assemblage," sometimes made oblique references to the frauds in the land of plenty. Oldenburg exceptionally adopted the stance of a cryptocritic. All the same, he and all the others enjoyed instant fame perhaps because America saw itself in these works so much more clearly than it ever had in the works of the previous generation.

One of the disconcerting elements tunneling through the tangle of competing "isms" in the 1960s was the rise of the culture hero, which Marshall McLuhan in 1964 had tried to explain. Many artists agreed with him and demonstrated in their works that the medium had become the message. Still another prophet of the 1960s who is not too often mentioned in cultural reckonings but who was very much implanted in the period was Timothy Leary, whose hysterical message, "turn on–tune out" did turn on many artists, some of respectable talents, and others rank amateurs who, under the influence of LSD produced so-called psychedelic art. The new drug culture, alas destined to survive from the 1960s into our own period, had a certain cachet in the art world because after all, Andy Warhol was part of it. Drugs and sex were no longer the exclusive property of the lower urban classes. Warhol's allegiance to both did not scare off the upper-middle-class art fanciers or even powerful authorities such as Henry Geldzahler, the newly appointed curator of American art at the Metropolitan Museum. It hardly mattered that Warhol's work was basically dull, repetitive (even when that was supposed to be the point of it, it was boring), and lacking in ideas. What mattered was that a star was born whose personality (or deliberate lack of it) could be used in many ways by the culture industry. The stress on his person is of some interest since the personalities of those producing works for the art market would soon edge the works themselves off the page, as gallery announcements, reviews, and advertising began to focus more on the image of the artist rather than on the art. (Warren I. Susman in *Culture and History* traces the American shift from popular manuals on character to manuals of personality and notes that "The new interest in personality—both the unique qualities of an individual and the performing self that attracts others . . . extended to participants in high culture as well. . . . Every American wants to become a performing self." His conclusion is that the personality image suited a consumer society just as the character image had once suited a producer society.)[15]

In the more puritanical pursuits of artists, in movements such as minimalism, systemic art, primary structure, earth art, post-painterly abstraction, and cool art, personalities were not slighted in the tendency toward personality cultism. The lean, deadpan, repetitive structures of Donald Judd, for instance, were accompanied by Donald Judd himself as an advocate and critic. Artists more and more became involved in the propagation of their works, and several university-trained artists wrote some of the most searching and passionate essays of the decade.

In the face of rising social disorder in the mid-1960s, there was a strong tendency toward order and restraint in the works that were exhibited in institutions. A hot war, a cool art. Such symmetry was partly authentic, partly engineered by the art world's ever more efficient machine. After all, while the bland faces of post-painterly painting were neatly installed in the white-walled palaces, on the streets such unorthodox happenings as the giant puppets of the Bread and Puppet Theater were parading through the city, alerting citizens to the mayhem their taxes, and soon their sons, were committing far away in Vietnam. Mark di Suvero was organizing the Peace Tower, a giant messy affair in which hundreds of artists affixed their offerings in a public space. Ginsberg was rallying great crowds of dissenters intoning Eastern mantras, his echoing "oooooooom" finding grateful response in many of the troubled young aspirants to culture. Pandemonium was brewing, and a general malaise overtook America, which, among artists, sometimes

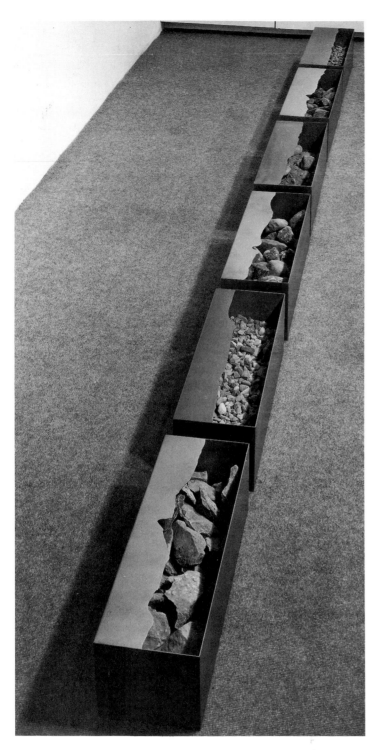

9. *Robert Smithson.* Six Stops on a
Section, *1968*. John Weber Gallery,
New York.

took the form of activities they hoped would be beyond the
pale, such as earthworks far from the Manhattan art world.
(But even earthwork artists were thwarted by the machine that
was right on hand to record their activities and market them in
the metropolis.) Both Robert Smithson and Robert Morris
fought back, taking possession of the columns of the art journals to offer thoughtful analyses of the deeply troubling aspects of their artistic lives.

Shortly before the paroxysms of the year 1968, which were
widely reported on television screens and frightened Americans who had not known that the flower children, the hippies,
the radicalized students, and a good many intellectuals could
really affect their lifestyle, as they were wont to call their existence, Smithson was working on an essay titled "The Sedimentation of the Mind."[16] Dark, brooding, full of Sartrean
nausea (although he would no doubt have been surprised to
hear it), Smithson's essay was rife with allusions to the uncontrollable forces weighing so heavily on sensitive spirits.
"One's mind and the earth are in a constant state of erosion,"
he said. "A bleached and fractured world surrounds the artist.
To organize this mess of corrosion into patterns, grids, and
subdivisions is an esthetic process that has scarcely been
touched." Like other artists aware of recent art history, Smithson understood that the romantic ideal of the pure artists, un-
contaminated by the mores of capitalist society, had been badly compromised, and he anxiously sought a way out:

As "technology" and "industry" began to become an ideology in the
New York Art World in the late 50s and early 60s, the private studio
notions of "craft" collapsed. . . . Deliverance from the confines of the
studio frees the artist to a degree from the snares of craft and the
bondage of creativity.

Acknowledging his heritage from the tense musing of Edgar
Allan Poe in such tales as the *Fall of the House of Usher* and
A. Gordon Pym, Smithson's diction is filled with the kinds of
words Poe marshaled to tell of the terrors lurking beneath our
consciousness. Smithson speaks of "primal ooze," "fissures,"
"faults," "corrosion," "the void," "time," and, of course,
"death." At the time, he was already contemplating ways to
give an image to his insights, and shortly after did, in fact,
supply such an image in the much-reproduced photograph of
his *Spiral Jetty* that, I believe, deeply touched an entire generation of serious young artists.[17] (It is perhaps relevant to
note that Foucault's archeological metaphor had not yet
reached American shores.)

A few months later, Morris published "Beyond Objects,"
which offered his view of the nature of perception and his reasons for his shift from hard to soft, from form to formless.[18] His
diction abounded with the geological words Smithson also favored, such as "stuff," "substance," "particles," "chunks,"
"slime." His reading of the contemporary artist's situation was
also comparable: "At the present time the culture is engaged
in the hostile and deadly act of immediate acceptance of all
new perceptual art moves, absorbing through institutionalized
recognition every art act." (Indeed, his own art acts were about
to be institutionalized at the Whitney Museum in a large retrospective in 1970.) Morris's interest in the nature of percep-

tion led him to a careful reading of a book that was one of the inner art world's discoveries in the late 1960s: Anton Ehrenzweig's *The Hidden Order of Art*.[19] The long gestation of the notion of the informal that had commenced almost forty years before found its way again into art world discourse, slightly diminishing the strong influence of positivist criticism deriving largely from Wittgenstein that had overtaken the art world during the 1960s. Ehrenzweig not only reopened the Freudian channel of interpretation but gave impetus to Morris and others in his challenge to the gestalt theory of perception. Morris makes clear the aspect of Ehrenzweig's work that interested him:

The art under discussion relates to a mode of vision which Ehrenzweig terms variously as scanning, syncretic or de-differentiated—a purposeful detachment from holistic readings in terms of gestalt-bound forms.

Like Carl Andre, Michael Heizer, and at times Eva Hesse, Morris felt an urgent need to dodge out of the quickly fashioned categories the art press, universities, and institutions were so eager to manufacture. If Judd and the minimalists talked about "holistic art," they would talk about whatever they could find that was not. The Spanish aesthetician Xavier Robert de Ventós later focused the argument more clearly:

Modern capitalism has become perversely ecumenical and humanist: nothing human is alien to it. No aspect of our most intimate lives fails to interest it and be an object of its planning. We are its object when it taylorizes our work and we are its object when it codifies our consumption. . . . The ubiquity and polyvalence of the new systems of control explain the fact that imaginative resistance to them also takes many forms. In a world of programmed behaviour, it is only natural to adopt irregular behaviors not yet colonized or integrated into the system: haphazard subsistence vs. planned "consumption" and the logic of "status"; camping or back packing vs. "tourism," a "laid-back" stance vs. "personalization"; the adoption of "perennial" philosophies vs. the commercial stimulation of trends or fashions' unisex and androgynous forms vs. commercially exalted secondary sex characteristics, etc. . . . An art understood as the symbolic rejection of a system of control that, since it no longer prohibits *anything* in particular but the *particular* itself, cannot be attacked by means of specific products—books or art works—which it will automatically assimilate and consume, but rather by means of the irregularity which may be introduced into everyday activities.[20]

The institutionalized art world, too, was craving such irregularity, and by the inexorable ironies so many commentators of mid-twentieth century culture have remarked, quickly regularized the irregular itself. Even Marcel Duchamp, who had always been the pride of the insiders in the art world, emerged in an exhibition in 1965 as a media star—irony of ironies! The art public (if there can be such a thing, since its definition is almost impossible) needed to fill its newly erected community centers, which is what the ubiquitous contemporary museum turned out to be. By the end of the 1960s, there were nearly two thousand museums and institutes of contemporary art in America, and their structures needed to be filled with objects with the regularity that an infant bird needs to be fed.

The climax of the 1960s was reached only in the 1970s with

10. Robert Smithson. Mirror Displacement, *Strumblehead, England, 1969.* John Weber Gallery, New York.

469

the conclusion of the war in Vietnam and the predictable economic recession soon after. Most of what was deposited in American culture during the 1960s, however, remained. Cultural commentators often try to characterize the 1970s as eclectic, lacking in spirit, gray, and finally, antimodernist. What really happened, according to Marshall Berman, was that "as the gigantic motors of economic growth and expansion stalled, and the traffic came close to a stop, modern societies abruptly lost their power to blow away the past."[21] That includes the immediate past, I think. The issues raised again and again by that part of the art world (mostly artists and a few forthright critics) that was galvanized by the Vietnam War remained active. When the Art Workers' Coalition called an Open Hearing in April 1969, the young art critic Gregory Battcock rose to denounce such public institutions as museums, reminding his excitable listeners that:

The trustees of the museums direct NBC and CBS, The New York Times, and the Associated Press, and that greatest travesty of modern times—the Lincoln Center. They own AT&T, Ford, General Motors and the great multibillion-dollar foundations, Columbia University, Alcoa, Minnesota Mining, United Fruit, and AMK, besides sitting on the board of each others' museums. The implications of these facts are enormous. Do you realize that it is those art-loving culturally committed trustees of the Metropolitan and Modern Museums who are waging the war in Vietnam?[22]

While much of what was said that night was equally hyperbolic, the fact remained that issues such as pressure from corporations to have a say in what museums exhibit (since museums were now becoming heavily dependent on corporate support); the degree to which museums were sensitive to minorities, especially blacks, Hispanics, and women; and their admission policies, were all alive during the 1970s and forced certain reorientations within the art world. Battcock's attack on Lincoln Center, however, was in one way unmerited. Among its more positive contributions was the New York Film Festival, to which its director, Richard Roud, brought numerous highly significant films, such as those of Godard, which would function very obviously in burgeoning seventies aesthetics.

One thing is certain: the art world had changed. Partronage had changed, artists had changed, and the nature of art business had changed. A veteran art dealer whose work in the 1950s and 1960s had been with young vanguard artists and poets and who modeled himself on the old ideal of the connoisseur-merchant, characterized one aspect of the change. Although John Bernard Myers, who became a private dealer in 1975, was certainly more of an Oscar Wilde, casting wicked and witty comments into an art world increasingly pleased with its image, he offered a revealing business sidelight in his memoirs:

The main difference in private dealing, I discovered, was the people involved. And what a lot of go-getters there turned out to be—all over town. The most nauseating group was the young married women with time on their hands who specialized in "Art for Offices"—sometimes whole suites of offices. . . . Some specialized in cheering up doctors' and dentists' waiting rooms or placing kinetic light-ups and movables opposite operating chairs. Other entrepreneurs engaged themselves in filling lobbies, courtyards, plazas and terraces of the new glass and steel edifices. . . . New business was pouring into foundries in Long Island, upper New York State, or New Jersey to "fabricate" jumbo-sized constructions by artists . . . who prepared mole-sized maquettes for elephantine productions. These celebrations could be found on the lawns of benign industrial plants, secure amidst the expensive landscape engineering, visible proof of business supporting art and improving the community.[23]

Myers was predictably averse to the grandiose activities of the newly activated nouveaux riches, yet the new constituencies for the imaginative activities that were called art with increasing liberality could not be so easily discounted.

In SoHo, where art galleries provided the main lure to suburbanites, who also shopped in the increasing number of chic boutiques in the midst of the artistic community, there were many possibilities. The fact is that the "go-getters" Myers so despised were forced to deal with the unaccustomed and to provide an audience to artists who remained serious and critical. The results were and are incalculable. Many artists, well aware of the snares in their situations, did not fall silent. The more they were patronized, the more they sought to elude the pitfalls—to elude, in fact, the domineering ambitions both of the empowered bourgeoisie and of the gatekeepers of success, the dealers. Increasingly they moved toward what Lucy Lippard called the "dematerialization of art." Or at least, the deaccessionability of permanent art. One of the key figures of the conceptualist art of the seventies was Carl Andre, whose portable antimonuments were not worth their weight in gold, if he could help it. Andre's voice and his persona (for his overalled, bearded image was as much a part of his legend as his bricks or styrofoam flagstones) ran out in quasi-Marxist tirades:

Instead of revolution emerging in the culture of history we have spectacle mired in the narcotizing ooze of publicity with no place to hide ourselves should we by chance come to some knowledge of our shame. As artists we have sold off inspiration to buy influence.[24]

Andre and many others whose installations of conceptual art, or art as idea, increased in the 1970s, tended to see the arts more and more as part of larger structures. In Andre's case, it was neo-Marxism. In the case of the art-language practitioners, it was structuralism, which later shaded into pure semiotics, and finally into deconstruction—points of view that tended to de-emphasize the ownable commercial value of works of art and in fact the notion of the unique work of art itself (and also the social responsibility of the artist in many cases). Undaunted, the art world joined the chorus, disconcerting the well-meaning artists who then had to look for other means of irregular behavior.

If the conceptualists tried to elude the toils of New York's ineffable mercantile instincts, there were others who used the old American saying, "if you can't beat them, join them" to try to subvert and convert. In the mid-1960s an endearing *exalté*, Billy Klüver, who was an engineer with Bell Labs, sought to "ellide" (not elude) his two loves, art and technology. Drawing on the interest of his friends among artists such as Jean Tinguely and Robert Rauschenberg, Klüver founded Experiments in Art and Technology, earnestly declaring in its charter in September 1966 that E.A.T. "initiates and carries out policies that expand the role of the artist in contemporary society and eliminate the separation of the individual from technological change."[25] Such an idealistic project inevitably came to grief, largely because corporations, on whom Klüver and company would have to depend, had no intention of handing over authority to artists. The debacles of the next few years provided disheartening evidence, as Max Kozloff pointed out:

They wanted the opportunity to create with the help of, but really to fall back on, exotic and costly technical systems, not realizing that the means of production—and hence control—would forever remain in the hands of the ruling classes who owned them.[26]

Yet such initial experiments with new sources of patronage certainly helped to fuel the battle against public indifference to the visual arts. From the so-called site-specific efforts of sculptors, who sought non-gallery or museum spaces to install temporary and sometimes deliberately ephemeral works, to the more solid enterprises of artists seeking public commissions through agencies such as the National Endowment for the Arts or various state and city agencies, a revived spirit of intervention in American culture was at work. It is true that federal agencies and well-endowed institutions exacted certain compromises, but increasingly, artists functioned as did the eminent courtesans of the eighteenth century (also great patrons of the arts) who had their *amants utiles* and their *amants honoraires*. Foundations, corporations, government agencies—were the useful lovers—museums and art magazines were necessary, if honorary. All were required for the patronage of the art, and each exacted a price. Kate Linker in an appropriately titled article "Public Sculpture: The Pursuit of the Pleasurable and Profitable Paradise" outlines the hazards of patronage and remarks on the mediocre results, asking "Does public art, then aspire to the condition of Muzak?"[27]

Certain kinds of public art, however, persist in challenging the governing powers and have grown rather than diminished in impact. Although Hans Haacke uses museums and art galleries as his primary platform, he addresses himself to a broad public that derives its information, and of course misinformation, from the collusion of corporations and the press, including the electronic press. His cultural critiques, which began years ago in more or less ecological terms, are now couched in a mocking way in the very language of corporate advertisers, such as when he attacks Mercedes Benz with its own image, while underlining the company's dealings with and even praising South Africa. Haacke's cunning adaptation of advertising techniques became more overtly political in the late seventies and eighties. In his 1988 work *The Freedom Fighters Were Here*, he contrasts the billboard mentality suggested by the movie marquee with a stark press photograph of the Nicaraguan tragedy. Haacke's gadfly technique generally focuses on the underside of the rock of the art world, exposing its verminous underpinnings, but the immediate horrors of America's Latin American transgressions required a direct and instantly affecting image. Even more specifically, public art was undertaken by Alfredo Jaar, a young architect from Chile who resides in New York and marshals his talents to cre-

11. Hans Haacke. The Freedom Fighters Were Here, *1988.* John Weber Gallery, New York.

12. *Alfredo Jaar. A Logo for America, 1987. Spectacolor sign, Times Square, New York, 40 seconds.*

ate multimedia works. When he created a Times Square billboard in colored light, *A Logo for Americans*, which flashed on the screen for thirty seconds every twelve minutes, more than one spectator remarked: "It makes you think." Jaar works, as he says, on two levels—galleries and museums, and public spaces—to communicate his message about the gap between Third World and the Western so-called developed world. Taking on North Americans in their own territory, he designed a map of the United States with the title *This Is Not America*, which instantly is transformed into a "U.S." with a message: "This Is Not America" is transformed into the word *America* that is modified with images of the two American hemispheres. Finally, the two are united as America. Since it is estimated that one-and-a-half million people pass through Times Square every day, Jaar's creation can be considered public art in an authentically broad sense. In view of the works of Haacke, Jaar, and dozens of others working with advertising techniques to deliver dissident messages, what is of significance is the willingness of the art world to assimilate even them and to consider them artists.

Defining art is one of the more perplexing problems of fin-de-siècle twentieth-century criticism. It is almost impossible to attempt to evaluate the role of criticism itself in the prolongation of the more serious concerns (or for that matter, the less serious concerns) that threaded through the art world after World War II. Looked at schematically (which inevitable falsifies), the corpus of art criticism reflects a restless and increasingly intellectualizing culture. The spokesmen for the first postwar vanguard were proud of their independent status and tended to belong to a category described by Victor Burgin, with some misprision, as "the empirical-intuitive Anglo-Saxon critical tradition."[28] The next generation, often well installed in academe, were inclined toward theory and in some cases had an absolute horror of intuitive response, preferring to buttress its convoluted arguments with those from Europe. In the very diction of the founding editorial of *October*, the savor of academe is strong, as is the commendable intention to wrest back criticism from the art journals that had become conspicuously acquiescent in vulgarizing so-called high art and oiling the wheels of the commercial behemoth. The high tone of the first issue of *October*, as well as its determinedly academic and exclusionary language, is caught in the editorial that mentions Eisenstein's *October* that "transformed the nature of an art paradigmatic for our century" and that "was, as we now know, propaedeutic for the realization of Eisenstein's two Utopian projects, *Capital* and *Ulysses*."[29] The references in that first issue were revealing: Walter Benjamin, Foucault, and several other newly discovered European intellectuals—reviving an old American reflex of a sadly colonial cast.

What is of interest, in view of the process of diffusion from the high-minded inner circles to the general public, is how quickly the preoccupations of the university-oriented new journals (for *October* is the ideal graduate student publication) were marketed to the art world. In 1979, *October* translated Derrida's essay "The Parergon" in which he instructed: "Deconstruction must neither reframe nor fantasize the pure and simple absence of the frame." In 1983, it published "Plato and the Simulacrum" by Gilles Deleuze, in which the author spec-

472

ifies that "The simulacrum is not a degraded copy, rather it contains a positive power which negates both original and copy, both model and reproduction." Aside from these luminaries and their often fanciful play with the notion of art, *October* also focused on Lacan (who, it should be noted, had already had an oblique influence on the far earlier generation of Abstract Expressionists who took his influence through their knowledge of the surrealist publications of the 1930s). Within months the diction of the so-called postmodern aestheticians was reflected in discussions of works of visual art that were dubbed deconstructionist or simulacrum art. Probably Victor Burgin, one of the most intelligent of the new conceptual artists, who eagerly rallied to new theories of art in their struggle to redefine its parameters, was mistaken to think that he and his co-workers were embattled:

Viewed in the overlapping illuminations of Marxism, semiotics, psycho-analysis and feminism, orthodox criticism was safe neither in its liberal humanism nor its phallocentrism; it was however, perfectly secure in its newspapers and magazines, its galleries and museums, its art schools and art history departments.[29]

On the contrary, he and the others had done their work perhaps too well. In the art centers springing up all over America (usually called museums but often more like the Kunsthalle in Europe), the communications industry works with lightning speed. If the *New York Times* covers one Sunday the new simulacrum art, the local go-getters all over the United States go and get it for the very next season. There is no cultural lag here. Moreover, the New York art world is no longer an entity of place. The volunteers in countless geographically dispersed art centers are as much a part of it as are artists from all over the world. (Consider only the astounding changes the new electronic possibilities have wrought on the institution of the art auction.) If there is a shift in taste, such as the quick switch from deadpan geometrism to deadpan expressionism in the stellar works of Frank Stella, the art world can catch up immediately. What they cannot catch up with are the tortoises in this classic race with invented time—those artists such as Jake Berthot or William Tucker, to mention only two—whose ideals do not coincide with current theories and whose activities as artists are still studio-bound and traditionally intuitive rather than a priori theoretical.

Since I am a believer in the Renaissance dictum "truth is the daughter of time," I cannot pretend to see the art world as it is today with perspecuity. Although it is now ostensibly illuminated with Klieg lights as opposed to the flickering lanterns of 1945, it is too complex an organism for topographical description. It is, as I suppose, a dependency of the great world and reflects what is probably a crucial upheaval in values of the world that can find definition probably only after the turn of the twenty-first century.

Notes

1. Henry James, *The American Scene* (Bloomington, Ind.: Indiana University Press, 1968), 208.
2. Alan Kaprow, "Should the Artist Be a Man of the World?" *ARTnews* 63 (October 1964): 34.

3. Thomas B. Hess, "Seeing the Young New Yorkers," *ARTnews* 49 (May 1950): 23.
4. Irving Sandler, "The Club," *Artforum* (September 1965): 27.
5. Russell Lynes, *The Tastemakers* (New York: Harper, 1949), 256 passim.
6. Ethel K. Schwabacher, *Arshile Gorky* (New York: Macmillan, 1957), 81.
7. Thomas B. Hess, *Willem de Kooning* (New York: The Museum of Modern Art, 1968), 72.
8. Francis V. O'Connor, *Jackson Pollock* (New York: The Museum of Modern Art, 1967), 33.
9. Morris Dickstein, *Gates of Eden: American Culture in the Sixties* (New York: Basic Books, 1977), 59.
10. Norman Mailer, *Advertisements for Myself* (New York: Simon and Schuster, 1982), 321.
11. Guy Davenport, *The Geography of the Imagination* (San Francisco: North Point Press, 1981), 202.
12. Marshall Berman, *All That's Solid Melts in Air* (New York: Simon and Schuster, 1982), 321.
13. Calvin Tompkins, *The Scene: Reports on Post-Modern Art* (New York: Viking, 1976), 43.
14. Ibid., 17.
15. Warren I. Susman, *Culture as History* (New York: Pantheon, 1985), 280.
16. Robert Smithson, "The Sedimentation of the Mind," *Artforum* 7 (September 1968).
17. The spiral jetty was subsidized by two art galleries that helped Smithson to pay for a twenty-year lease on ten acres of lakefront in Great Salt Lake, Utah. He moved some six thousand tons of earth to form the spiral in the lake, fully expecting rising tides to obscure and probably finally obliterate the image.
18. Robert Morris, "Beyond Objects," *Artforum* 8 (April 1969): 50.
19. Anton Ehrenzweig, *The Hidden Order of Art: A Study in the Psychology of Artistic Imagination* (Berkeley: University of California Press, 1957).
20. Xavier Robert de Ventós, *Heresies of Modern Art* (New York: Columbia University Press, 1980), 229.
21. Berman, *All That's Solid*, 332.
22. Quoted in Lucy Lippard, "The Art Workers Coalition," in Gregory Battcock, *Idea Art, A Critical Anthology* (New York: E. P. Dutton, 1973), 111.
23. John Bernard Myers, *Tracking the Marvelous* (New York: Random House, 1983), 268.
24. Carl Andre and Jeremy Gilbert-Rolfe, "Commodity and Contradiction or Contradiction as Commodity," *October* (Summer 1976):
25. Frontispiece for *Pavilion*, ed. Billy Klüver, Julie Martin, and Barbara Rose (New York: E. P. Dutton, 1972).
26. Max Kozloff, "The Multimillion Dollar Art Boondogle," *Artforum* 10 (October 1971): 72.
27. Kate Linker, "Public Sculpture: The Pursuit of the Pleasurable and Profitable Paradise," *Artforum* (March 1981): 61.
28. Victor Burgin, *The End of Art Theory* (Atlantic Highlands, N.J.: Humanities Press International, 1986), 161.
29. Ibid., 162.

1. Berlin's expressway network.
Landesbildstelle, Berlin.

Competition of the Fragments: Challenges for Tomorrow's Berlin

Michael Mönninger

Born in 1958 in Paderborn, Michael Mönninger studied philosophy, German literature, sociology, and music in Frankfurt. Since 1986 he has worked for the feuilleton of the Frankfurter Allgemeine Zeitung, *where he is primarily responsible for the topics of architecture, urban planning, monument preservation, and design. He received the Critic's Prize given by the Bundesarchitektenkammer in 1989. In 1990 he was in the United States on a grant from the Marshall Fund.*

It is West Germany's ruin that Berlin no longer exists.... What is now to be seen over there are provincial metropolises with local bigwigs, theater and radio conglomerates with competing cliques, academies in search of purposes that do not exist. What is missing is the awareness of a counterbalance. Berlin was such a counterbalance.... We are all supposed to be nice. And, after all, the nice people get the prizes. But what happens to those who want to do more than simply restore and carry on in the traditions of the oft-cited western world? What happens to those who want to continue to develop a still productive mind, even if it is sometimes overtaxed and aggressive, and imbue it with new colors through fresh ventures and incitements? One can watch the broad flanks of old Europe closing in front of them and hear them calling, "Stop, young man! No extremes! In the name of the western world, drown your sorrows in a glass of wine." Berlin would not have been a part of this and it will not be a part of it today.
—Gottfried Benn, Autobiography, *1961*

Even after the unification of the two German states, Gottfried Benn's polemic against the provincialism of the federal republic is as relevant today as it was when he wrote it. Before Berlin, which is itself currently undergoing a unification process, can again become Germany's capital and a European metropolis, the city must cope with challenges no Western metropolis has had to face. The propensity for what was pleasant and nice, a propensity that had become characteristic of both the West German and the West Berlin mentalities, has made the city extremely susceptible to feeble and petty-minded strategies for its redesign. Nobody yet knows how the pressing economic needs of this welfare state oasis, which was highly subsidized for forty years, will be met and how its new social and cultural conflicts will be mastered. Since the political unification, the question of Berlin's survival is even more urgent, for the city is not yet unified physically. If it were to take on once again the role envisaged by Benn, that of a counterbalance and a model for all of Germany, Berlin would need urbanists such as Rome once had with Pope Sixtus V, Paris with Georges Haussmann, Chicago with Daniel Burnham, and New York with Robert Moses.

In its center alone, Berlin's area and population have almost doubled overnight. The city is no longer held together by uniform ground plans and uninterrupted facades, as was characteristic of the nineteenth century. Berlin will provide an entire postwar generation of Germans—a generation whose sense of reality was formed in relatively small regional cities and was so sharply criticized by Gottfried Benn—with its first metropolitan experience. As a multicultural melting pot, Berlin is developing into a center of social conflict. Already many underprivileged areas of East Berlin are threatening to turn into slums; it will not only be immigrants from Eastern Europe who will settle in the concrete blocks in Marzahn, Hellersdorf, and Hohenschönhausen, but also residents of West Berlin who will be unable to afford to live any longer in the city's prospering areas.

The monocultural socialist state was responsible for using prefabricated parts to construct cratelike housing in which more than half a million people must live. The huge housing estate Marzahn, built between 1978 and 1988, has 61,600 dwellings; Hellersdorf, under construction since 1979, currently has 38,200 dwellings; and Hohenschönhausen (1980–

2. *View of the Cathedral,*
Karl Liebknecht Strasse.
Landesbildstelle, Berlin.

3. *Traffic jam on Frankfurter Allee,*
Berlin, January 1991. Ullstein
Bilderdienst.

2

3

89) has a total of 31,000. Altglienecke, the last project of this type planned by the German Democratic Republic government, was to have 17,000 dwellings. In comparison, the satellite towns in West Berlin seem almost idyllic. Gropiusstadt has 16,000 dwellings and the Märkisches Viertel has 17,000, and these are generally embedded in an intact infrastructure. When the huge housing estates in East Berlin were built, however, the only stipulation was that open areas be built up with such density that as many dwellings as possible would be created in record time. Basic supply facilities for the residents of these housing estates were usually forgotten by the planners. Before the war, many Berliners had already had a disparaging attitude toward the eastern areas of their city. This cultural topography of contempt for a more industrial, proletarian, and ethnic Berlin will be reinforced by the differences in the quality of its buildings and, eventually, by its poverty.

The prognoses for the city's growth are both impressive and frightening. In the next twenty years, its population is expected to increase by approximately 1.4 million inhabitants; 700,000 new positions will become available, and 1.8 million more cars will appear on its roads. At least 800,000 new dwellings and 86 million square feet of office space need to be built. An additional 242 million square feet are required for industrial and commercial purposes. Such growth is beyond the capacity of the city's center, and the green areas of the surrounding Land of Brandenburg are the first to be threatened with the prospect of becoming extensions of Berlin. The old Berlin star—strips of suburbs that radiate out into the countryside alongside the highways—will develop new arms and links, particularly toward the south, until the polyplike, rampant growth of this suburban carpet has covered an area twice the size of the Ruhr district.

The Planungsgruppe Potsdam, a provisional regional committee composed of Berlin senate and municipal authorities as well as residents representing Potsdam and Frankfurt an der Oder envisaged development along axes that would reach into Brandenburg and set the course for future spurts of growth. Between these axes there would be green strips pushing their way from outside into the center of the city. This design was based on Hermann Jansen's plan of 1910 that provided for a green ring and radical sections of greenery, thus focusing the committee's recommendations on star-shaped plan. At that time, however, one could not foresee the growth in automobile traffic. The plea for strips of suburbs only supported what was occurring anyway. The open land between the strips—Havelland marsh, Oranienburg heath, the Spree's flats, and the Nuthe valley—will be exposed to the constant pressure of expansion along the arterial roads until a shopping mall or a used-car dealer had gobbled up the last remaining meadow.

By itself, a conventional style of urban planning will be unable to master the dynamics of this development. This growth can only be steered with the new strategies of a building and planning policy that must have greater authority to implement its decisions and that must also develop Berlin in a manner prototypical for other Western European cities. There are many ways in which this could be done: an old Berlin tradition could be taken up and a nonpartisan *Stadtbaurat* (director of

city's Department of Urban Planning and Development) could be reinstated to mediate between investors and the city's needs; following the Dutch example, a so-called design team could be set up; or with the aid of data technology and computer simulation, planning could be undertaken that would allow for an ongoing process of decision making. The rush to place office buildings in the city's central area between Alexanderplatz and Kurfürstendamm recalls the major mistakes of postwar urban planning in Germany. From Atlanta to Frankfurt am Main, single-function business and commercial areas have led to the virtual depopulation of the inner city, separated living from working space, forced out the city's inhabitants, and created millions of commuters. In contrast, in Munich and Paris, skyscrapers and office complexes were only allowed to be built on the city's periphery, for instance in Arabella Park or La Défense, so that notwithstanding an astronomical rise in rents, it is still possible to live in the inner city.

Fortunately, similar plans have existed for some time in Berlin, and in some cases they are already in progress. The municipal administration has pinpointed nine prime areas for development that encircle the city and follow along the path cut by the interurban railway. As soon as it is completed in the east, this path is also foreseen as a *boulevard périphérique* for automobile traffic. These land reserves of the ring city consist of large, unused industrial sites, docks and railway yards, and traffic junctions. Seen clockwise from the west they include the traffic junction Westkreuz, and the planned construction over the Halensee ditch, the extension to the exhibition center and the construction of a teleport at the bus station ZOB beside the building housing the radio and television stations, Sender Freies Berlin; the area known as City-Westend between Charlottenburg and Siemensstadt; the western dock, from which shipping will be shifted toward the south, to the Teltow Canal and into a new eastern dock; the Wedding subway station, Schering industrial site, and Berlin-North train station; the area around the interurban railway station, Leninallee (which has already been earmarked for the Olympics); the traffic junction Ostkreuz at the Berlin-East railway station; the area along the Spree River between the city's center and Köpenick; Tempelhof Airport; the traffic junction Schöneberger Kreuz, where the existing cloverleaf is to be demolished.

Planners in Berlin have already developed a ring scenario based on the motto, "gentle on the inside, powerful on the edge." If the investment pressure exerted by single-function business and commercial centers were to be focused successfully, these satellite towns would relieve the strain upon the inner city and thereby be a far more formative influence upon the cityscape than the symbol-laden Potsdamer or Leipziger Platz. These two are currently at the center of a debate over the distribution of the building mass for the first and largest of many future investment projects. The project in question is Daimler Benz's Services Center, which is to measure over 700,000 square feet. At the moment, formal considerations are being used to produce little more than eyewash: Berlin's traditional eaves height of seventy-two feet will not be exceeded and the historical shape of the street building line will be respected. But if the center's function is endangered, this cannot be rectified by architecture.

The Berlin architect Hans Kollhoff has inveighed against the expected compensatory aesthetics of a supposedly human scale on Potsdamer and Leipziger Platz. He argues that instead of the flattened, broad, and bulky building style typical of Berlin, a great deal of space could be saved if Daimler Benz put up a slim tower the size of New York's Chrysler Building. It would contain the same amount of floor space; at the same time the surrounding area could still be used in a variety of ways. As long as Berlin does not alter its well-established hostility toward towers—a hostility already confronted by Mies van der Rohe—it will never achieve the metropolitan compression of a major industrial city.

But the privileged center will have few difficulties in finding investors of suitable concepts for its design. The real effectiveness of a planning policy for the entire city only becomes apparent in the bordering areas, where nobody would freely choose to invest large sums of money in buildings of high quality. At the most, the center can only serve as the measuring rod for the greater urban area. In its exemplary status or in its active competition with the bordering areas—its refusal to be bled dry—the center's architectonic and functional qualities can also exert a magnetic force upon these areas.

The ideal of a homogenous and centered city had been given up long ago by forward-looking architects. Instead, they envisage the city as a competition between fragments. The architect O. M. Ungers developed his concept of the city as archipelago for Berlin. He argues for a pluralistic, polycentric concept of clearly differentiated urban islands in the sea of the metropolis, in which each person can find a place of his or her choice. Referring to Tokyo, the architect Peter Wilson once used the metaphor of the holographic video disc for the city of the future. Each of its fragments still stores a part of the whole. Berlin already has a multiplicity of centers with completely different faces. One could not imagine a greater contrast than that which exists between the incunables of the 1950s, the relaxed design of the Hansaviertel beside the Tiergarten, and the severe order of Karl-Marx-Allee. It is only in the total elimination of a sense of space around Alexanderplatz—a landscape that brings Brasilia to mind—and in the wasteland of the *Kulturforum* that the two halves of the city have achieved similar configurations of modernity gone amiss.

East Berlin's center, between the former Foreign Ministry and the television tower, is a cemetery of deserted monuments. Whoever is not taken in by the economically unfeasible as well as culturally improper illusion of total demolition and reconstruction has to accept its existence as a kind of archaeological stratum that must be corrected and augmented by future urban design. A new type of planning gaining ever more attention from architects could be helpful here. It is directed toward transforming the planning sins of the 1960s. This type of concept has already been drawn up and partially realized for such buildings as the unimaginative Equitable Building in Manhattan and the former Shell Building in Frankfurt am Main as well as for dreary satellite towns in Amsterdam (Bijl-

mermeer) and Paris (Melun-Sénart).

Despite real estate speculation, a serious housing shortage, and a miserable economic state, there is a broad scope of possibilities for Berlin's future development. Half of the city's land is publicly owned. This is twice as much as in other West German communities. The municipal government therefore has considerable room to maneuver and cannot make excuses based on an ostensibly natural momentum or the tax exemption of private investors. From now on, every second mark will be gone from the city's budget because the subsidies from the federal government—in 1989, they still totalled thirteen billion marks—are coming to an end. It will then be absolutely vital that there be a municipal management team that comes up with more solid financing concepts than those of West German communities, which like to conceal their budget deficit before an election by selling off communal property quickly and cheaply.

In the future, urban planning in Berlin will have to be closely linked with its economic policy. The current orientation toward models such as Silicon Valley in California, the London Docklands, and other service industry centers could, however, be fatal for Berlin. It is still Germany's largest industrial center and therefore has a manufacturing potential that must be supported and developed. The impressive panorama of the industrial buildings near the river, especially at the upper Spree, only became apparent after the fall of the Wall. Such buildings can only be saved from their approaching collapse, however, by efforts reaching beyond the considerations of urban planning and involving economic and industrial strategies for revitalization.

Many city lovers have once again been smitten by the beauty of old European metropolises, above all that of Paris. Yet in the face of the revolutions in Eastern Europe, it is difficult to announce this to be the decade of democracy and human rights and at the same time for Berlin to argue in favor of planning methods that are relics of autocratic constitutions. A strict unity of urban planning and architecture is finally only possible in dictatorships where an order is imposed on large areas through the abuse of the rights of property and those of the individual.

If one complains about the virtual babel of different voices in the current discussion on the city, one should not overlook the fact that the appearance of our seemingly ugly environment has been shaped by a civic order that has successfully shaken off the binding power of political constraints. To some extent, our cities have run wild, but if one wants to find a way to a new democratic consensus of how they should be built, then there is no better model for such an attempt, no city that is architecturally richer and more open to the future than Berlin.

Until now Berlin has been something like the new Jerusalem for the Germans. Everybody prayed to it but nobody believed in it. Now that the city has returned to life overnight, Germany is faced with the greatest task of its postwar history: to create a city that can be an ecological, economic, social, and cultural model for a metropolis of the twenty-first century.

*4. Westhafen (western dock),
Berlin–Wedding, 1977.* Ullstein
Bilderdienst.

1

2

Competition of the Centers: A Cultural and Philosophical Comparison

Mathias Schreiber

Mathias Schreiber is editor of FAZ Zeitschrift, *the weekly color supplement of the newspaper* Frankfurter Allgemeine Zeitung *of which he was previously architecture critic and cultural editor. His publications include* Die unvorstellbare Kunst, Kunst zwischen Askese und Exhibitionismus, *and* Vierzig Jahre deutsche Moderne: deutsche Architetur nach 1945. *He has also published three collections of poetry.*

1. View from Rockefeller Center towards Central Park, 1977. Ullstein Bilderdienst, Berlin (K. Lehnartz).

2. Grosser Stern (Great Star) with the Victory Column in the Tiergarten. In the centre is the Brandenburg Gate and on its left, the Reichstag with the Platz der Republik. Landesbildstelle Berlin.

The center is powerful and empty. In geometry, the center of the circle is the point that is incapable of expansion, a nothingness around which everything else arranges itself. According to Henri Lefebvre, centrality originated "on the first occasion that things were collected." In his book *La Revolution urbaine*, he writes:

The center of the city fills to the point of saturation; it decomposes, it explodes. Sometimes it inverts its significance, organizes itself around a vacuum—the exception. In most cases, it is the precondition and cause of the concentration of everything in the world, nature, and the cosmos: agricultural products, industrial products, the products of man, objects and instruments, actions and situations, signs and symbols. Where does all this take place? Anywhere can become the focal point, the privileged place at which everything converges. Each urban space has this possibility and impossibility within it, its own negation. Thus, every urban space was, is, and will become concentric and poly-(multi-)centric. The form of urban space demands this concentration, this spreading moreover provokes it: crowds of people, groups of colossal buildings, evacuation, abrupt expulsion.

The power of the center is its ability to attract. Its attraction is also the source of its weakness, however, and overcrowding is often followed by exodus and flight. As a potential concentration of the world, the big city is truly monumental. With London in mind, Henry James defined the city as "the most complete compendium of the world." Seen in this light, the monumental architecture of the city center symbolizes the city's inherent monumentality—the concentric.

The statuesque nature of the city center's powerful buildings can be seen as an attempt to defy forces of concentration, dispersal, centrality, and evacuation, in other words halting them with the promise of orientation and visual permanence. Without really being able to guarantee centrality, the cathedral, the proud town hall, the bank skyscraper, the templelike opera house, the museum, all buildings of this nature struggle to stabilize the formation of the center. For the urban center is not a fact that exists once and for all; it is a process, a constant repetition of attraction and repulsion, position and negation, an eternal struggle for the position of the privileged place, an explosive mixture of antagonistic and compatible elements, a compendium of the world, which like every real lexicon, can very quickly lose its inner coherence and become provincial. Critics of the metropolis applaud and welcome this development as the new neighborhood culture.

A comparison of the fundamentally dissimilar cities of Berlin and New York with a view to this competition of the centers brings astonishing parallels to light. Both of these metropolises fulfill a function as centers located on the periphery. New York stands on the east coast of an enormous country where other competing islands of urban centrality are gradually emerging from Chicago to Los Angeles and Atlanta to Houston. For decades, Berlin was an island in the east; in the German Democratic Republic, the communist half of the divided country, it was an outpost of freedom in the middle of a dictatorship. This city effectively in exile rehearsed its role as the center of Germany, which it always represented—at least culturally. And it continued to do this after 1961 as a divided city with its historical center, the palace of the Hohenzollerns (of which now only a small part of the facade remains) and the so-called Museum Island, on the other side of the wall in the eastern half. Since the opening of the Berlin Wall, on November 9, 1989, East and West Berlin have been growing together again. However, even as the united capital city of a united Germany, Berlin remains a metropolis on the periphery. Right in the middle of the (former) German Democratic Republic, Germany's eastern and rather underdeveloped peripheral province, Berlin is much nearer to Poland than to Germany's western borders with the European Community.

New York is on the shore, just as for decades Berlin was at the wall—two truly eccentric centers. The center of Manhattan is empty. Central Park, albeit an imposing void, is surrounded by museums and company headquarters (fig. 1). In addition, it is the venue for numerous concerts, meetings, and other gatherings at which the inhabitants of the city can celebrate a frenzied awareness of their central significance. The Berliners emulate this with their rock concerts beside the former Reichstag Building near the Tiergarten. In both cases, the empty center functions as a location for concentrated, mass experiences, as a place for explosive and to say the least propaganda-like demonstrations of how the vacuum can be filled. The Berlin Tiergarten quarter with the Reichstag as its forecourt corresponds in a certain way to Central Park; since reunification, it is now directly beside the historical city center and can function in the way that Central Park does. A parallel can also be found in the way in which this area with its spacious park is bordered by the important cultural buildings that together make up the *Kulturforum* (culture forum). This corresponds to the institutions that surround Central Park (Museum of Modern Art, Metropolitan Museum of Art, Solomon R. Guggenheim Museum, Carnegie Hall, American Museum of Natural History; Rockefeller Center and the Chrysler Building can also be added to this list). At the Grosser Stern with its Victory Column and the powerful visual axis leading up to the Brandenburg Gate two spatial variants of urban monumentality are apparent: the avenue and the circular plaza with the memorial at the imaginary center of the circle (fig. 2). In what is now still known as West Berlin, this centrality motif in urban design is also repeated in the relationship between the Kurfürstendamm and the central building of the Emperor William Memorial Church.

Grosser Stern, Potsdamer Platz, Mehringplatz, Kottbusser Tor, Platz der Gedächtniskirche—large axes connect these competing and mostly circular, and, in each case, privileged places (fig. 3). The street network between these centers encloses the rectangular, sharp-cornered, and truncated blocks and seems altogether more natural and organic than Manhattan's rigid grid reminiscent of a Roman castrum; its strict right angles are only occasionally interrupted by slanted deviations such as Broadway. In Berlin, the baroque palace garden, such as that belonging to the Charlottenburg Palace, appears to be a continuation of the city street plan. Manhattan's organization, however, is determined by Anglo-Protestant sobriety and the pioneers' rough sense of order.

In both cities, the street plans provide the basic conditions

necessary for a volatile and lively competition for the role of the most privileged place within what is already a privileged place. In New York, centrality can be found in the fashionable business quarter between Fifth Avenue and Lexington Avenue on the east side of the island. As opposed to this, many of the city's inhabitants insist on the centrality of the western part of the island with colorful, tawdry Broadway, Columbia University, and Lincoln Center. And still others opt for Lower Manhattan with attractions as diverse as Greenwich Village, the powerful twin towers of the World Trade Center, and Chinatown (fig. 4). The center of the center wanders among these parts of the city. Similarly in West Berlin, the boroughs of Charlottenburg, Wilmersdorf, Schöneberg, and Kreuzberg (an area that has been greatly improved by the erection of numerous new buildings as apart of the International Building Exposition [IBA] in 1987) jealously watch the development of Tiergarten. This area, well aware that it borders the historical city center between the Museum Island and Unter den Linden has been rapidly catching up since the opening of the wall.

Roland Barthes said, in reference to Tokyo where the center is the Emperor's Palace, which is not used by the city's inhabitants, that the city center is a "kind of voided fire of what the community imagines as the center." Central Park and the Tiergarten quarter represent for Manhattan and Berlin what the Emperor's Palace represents for Tokyo. In the Tiergarten, where the Wall's empty death strip threatened for decades, trees are now being planted—greenery is intended to erase the memory of death. Barthe's void is a place where the city dweller's imagination liberates itself from the onus of continuous concentration by unharnessing itself and imagining the lost center of its own existence. The individual's dream of finding reconciliation with humanity is contained in the concept of the city as a place to come together. It is expressed in the notion of the city as a world, the metropolis. Without this longing for reconciliation, even the toughest realist would be unable to find the strength to cope with the nerve-racking day-to-day conflicts, triumphs and failures, and encounters.

The characteristic turmoil of this multi-layered phenomenon—the city—may be louder, faster, and more garish in New York, but it can, of course, also be found in Berlin. The city on the Spree compensates in political eccentricity and historical tension what it obviously lacks—compared with New York—in the dynamism of skyscrapers. What Adolf Behne wrote of Erich Mendelsohn's sweeping facade for the newspaper offices of the *Berliner Tagesblatt* applies basically to the whole of Berlin in the twenties and early thirties (fig. 5). This is not Potsdam or Neu-Ruppin, he wrote, "but city, modern city, concentrated, powerful life, confidence, affirmation, will and the pace of work." This is still the Berlin to which Alfred Döblin created a literary memorial in the novel *Berlin Alexanderplatz*. In this 1929 work, being alert is the primary virtue of the protagonist, the urban worker, whose name Franz Biberkopf (literally "beaver head") has connotations of that typically urban mix of animal directness and intellectual alertness. Using an abrupt filmlike cutting technique, Döblin creates a montage of scenes, perspectives, and photographs. The result is a collage made up of completely disparate impressions and languages that mirrors the modern pulsating city. The city appears as a

3. Potsdamer Platz with The Wall,
1986. Landesbildstelle Berlin.

*4. Skyline of Lower Manhattan with
Battery Park and the World Trade
Center, 1981.* Ullstein Bilderdienst,
Berlin (Financial Times).

monument made up of many voices where the coherent individual personality faces as great a threat as urban order. The formerly omnipotent narrator resigns and disappears into the stream of movements, confrontations, sounds, and images. Döblin's model for *Berlin Alexanderplatz* was John Dos Passos's New York novel *Manhattan Transfer* (1925). In a more radical way than Döblin, Dos Passos shows the city person as the puppet, subject to the will of the group. Siegfried Lenz described Dos Passos's image of Manhattan:

"In the artfully directed confusion of figures in 'Manhattan Transfer,' where as if by chance all paths cross, everything intersects, overlaps, and individual fates are reduced to mere episodes. The rebellion, the outbursts, the numerous repeated attempts to bring this bungled existence into line are doomed to fail and appear episodic in view of the stone giant's composed detachment. . . . Here, where winners go away empty-handed and nobody registers the lesson of history, where the day in question defines the aims and failure becomes a Woolworth experience—here, in this monstrous institution only one thing ultimately triumphs and that is movement. The movement of people and ferries, fire engines and ambulances—a numbing movement, which imposes itself as the ultimate meaning" (*Das Gesetz von Metropolis [The Law of Metropolis]*, 1979).

Life disintegrates into episodes, the novel becomes a collage, the individual—in the case of Dos Passos, the journalist, Herf—can only fail or flee. Seen and criticized in this way, the city becomes a paradigm for the modern age. In his book *Mechanization Takes Command*, Siegfried Giedion writes, "Our thinking and feeling in all their ramifications are fraught with the concept of movement." Forms of movement mold our daily behavior, how we feel, and our image of the universe. The city with its innumerable streams of traffic, canals, electricity cables and water pipes, elevators and motorways is one single moving machine (fig. 6). Moving television pictures bring urban life to the country with the result that it is no longer possible to halt the urbanization of even the most remote rural area. The fast city, the model for the Charter of Athens, is the metropolis as the absolute embodiment of the age of modern movement. In *Die Struktur der modernen Lyrik (The Structure of Modern Poetry*, 1956) Hugo Friedrich illustrates how modern poetry, for example, the work of Rimbaud, consists of "pure dynamisms" and visually abstract "dynamic directions." The fragments of reality are no longer "organized around a center." "Contrasting dynamics," "heat tracks of a feverish intensity," and "supramaterial conflictive relations"— are the concepts Friedrich employs to analyze modern poetry; but they can also be used to describe the structure of the modern city.

Public and private wealth is concentrated in the cities. According to Georg Simmel there is a profound, fundamental relationship between "the world of money and the supremacy of reason and intellectual life" *(Die Grosstädte und das Geistesleben [Cities and Intellectual Life]).* They share an unwavering objectivity in their approach to people and things, in that a formal justice is often coupled with ruthless "toughness." The origin of the much maligned toughness of city life, which, however, also provides opportunities for freedom and dropping out, can be found here. It can lead to the individual's breakdown just as easily as the furor of movement.

5. *Office building of the publishing house Rudolf Mosse. Built by Cremer and Wolffenstein, 1901–03. Remodelled and enlarged by Erich Mendelsohn, 1921–23.* Kunstbibliothek, Staatliche Museen Preussischer Kulturbesitz, Berlin.

6

The dream of the center of the city as a symbolic guarantee of personal and collective identity is also a protest against its toughness and neutrality, against the dissolution of life into fragments, episodes, and stages of movement without an integrating purpose. The empty, central, so to speak pathetic square, and the wide avenue (boulevard) that leads up to or away from it are a theatrical representation of this dream just as much as the monumental vertical projection. According to Rudolf Arnheim, this vertical projection indicates the direction of gravity and serves all other directions as an axis and a point of reference.

The archaic vertical is the sacred mountain. In Tartar mythology, an iron mountain is called the Center of the World. Athens is grouped around the Acropolis, Cologne around the cathedral. In Cologne, Münchengladbach, and Florence, the dramatic proximity of the city church and art museum marks the urban center although the vertical is still in the possession of the churches (fig. 7). Berlin and New York both lack such classical central forms. Similar to other churches in New York, St. Patrick's Cathedral (fig. 8) is a neo classical dwarf compared with the World Trade Center. This angular, elegant twin-towered building by the Japanese architect Monoru Yamasaki caricatures the towers of the Gothic cathedral with the pointed arches at its base. In Berlin, the old ruinous tower of the Emperor William Memorial Church and the new tower by Eiermann that stands beside it are always photographed from an effective worm's-eye view, as this creates the impression that the central motif is still intact. In reality, however, it is undermined by the nearby high-rise, the Europa-Center (fig. 9). On top of the flat roof of the building a striking trademark rotates, the Mercedes star, a symbol both of the matter-of-fact urban world and of the modern age of movement.

The monumental architecture with which New York celebrates its centrality in an almost vulgar manner is embodied in the powerful high-rise silhouette. It is as if this silhouette pulls the gridlike arrangement of streets into the vertical. The city dweller first becomes aware of the silhouette on leaving or approaching the city by ground, water, or air (fig. 10). In the center of the city, its profile remains at most a prescient image, a secret. The Berlin profile is incomparably more diffuse and varied. It still betrays traces—in the Western section—of the townscape that Hans Scharoun, in a complete failure to recognize its baroque and classical past, wanted to impose upon it. On the way from Kurfürstendamm to Kreuzberg, the Berlin pedestrian repeatedly encounters significant buildings or groups of buildings that provide a central and determining force for the surrounding space. However, the city as a whole remains indecisive, motley, coincidental and cannot be compared with the energy and concentrated power of New York. As a result of the critical reconstruction undertaken as part of the International Building Exposition, Kreuzberg has gained so much succinct force and ordered multiplicity, spatial centrality, and orientation that this district, formerly a virtual wasteland, is now replacing the area around the Emperor William Memorial Church and the zoo, West Berlin's center in the 1960s and 1970s. The centrality of the area around the zoo and the train station—a centrality that was painstakingly established after the war—was already threatened before the

7

6. *Times Square at night, 1969.*
Ullstein Bilderdienst, Berlin
(K. Lehnartz).

7. *St. Patrick's Cathedral surrounded by skyscrapers, 1969*
Ullstein Bilderdienst, Berlin
(K. Lehnartz).

8. *Kurfürstendamm with the*
Emperor William Church and the
Europa Centre, 1967.
Landesbildstelle Berlin.

opening of the Wall and the potential reestablishment of the old city center. A favored location, with its commercial elegance and concentration of business, this zone still represents one of Berlin's centers. Nevertheless, both in architectonic terms and as the focal point of a more sensual colorful style of urban life, Berlin's center had already shifted eastward to Kreuzberg before the opening of the Wall. This has resulted in a tense competition for the role of center—Kurfürstendamm can only hope to survive if it orientates itself toward an architecture that allows people to gather and meet.

Like the world, the universe lacks a center. For the Roman architect Vitruvius there was still a correlation between the universe, which rotated around its centerpoint, the world axis, and the built symmetry of sacred buildings, that is, temples on the one hand and the ideal proportions of the human body on the other. Vitruvius called this correlation consensus. In the eighteenth century, his French colleague the revolutionary architect Boullée described space as experienced by someone traveling in a balloon who drifts in boundlessness and is profoundly shaken "by the extraordinary drama of an immeasurable space." After Copernicus, the universe lost forever its ancient central axis and the earth its privileged location; from then on it has been viewed as boundless and immeasurable. The individual who moves suspended in this universe can experience but never understand it. Planetary sublimity becomes the central criterion of monumental architecture. Boullée was intoxicated by criteria such as "the simplest form" and "completely uninterrupted surface." The uninterrupted continuum of the glass and steel skin of a high-rise facade corresponds to this canon. Seen in this way, the American skyscraper shooting up to the sky is the ideal object for a point of view that desires planetary sublimity and simplicity (figs. 11, 12). And it is also logical that its beauty is apparent less to the old-fashioned pedestrian than to the observer moving by mechanical means such as the passenger in a balloon, airplane, or ocean liners, or to the car driver on a bridge.

The monumentality of Manhattan is abstract and based on a primarily surface and linear aesthetic. The line that projects from each corner of a high-rise into the sky marks the triumph of the boundless, the immeasurable space of space travel and astrophysics. The aerial and the linear repeatedly connect with each other to form a grid that imposes order to movement and makes it calculable. Provided that the modern metropolis has subjected itself to this correlation, it is a cold, clear abstraction that has flown in from the expanse of the universe. Within this abstraction, the supremacy of reason has built temples for itself, temples formerly built for the gods, those representatives of all that which could not be understood. The temples of abstraction are the administrative towers of companies, bureaucracies, and other institutions. The old temples, the churches, are insignificant beside them and as with the historical town centers of which only traces remain in Berlin and New York, they too take on the attributes of a museum (fig. 13). Due to the unusually high concentration of museums in Berlin (in both parts of the city), this deficit of centrality finds greater compensation here than in Manhattan.

It is often said that the museum is a particularly refined way

9

10

9. *View of Manhattan from the East River. On the left is the U.N. Building, on the right is the Chrysler Building.* Ullstein Bilderdienst, Berlin (J. Messerschmidt).

10. *Rockefeller Center, 1969.* Ullstein Bilderdienst, Berlin (K. Lehnartz).

of killing a city. The opposite is true. In his book *The City in History* (1963), Lewis Mumford said of the metropolis that it is "the best organ of memory man has yet created," and he identifies the museum as its "most typical institution." The "selected specimens and samples" presented in the museum make the world more accessible and conceivable. According to Mumford, the city invented the museum because "one of its own principal functions is to serve as a museum" (he is, of course, referring to the modern, public museum and not to royal collections of rare objects). The museum preserves testimonies of the distant and recent past, frequently in the form of burial objects or pictures of the dead. It is possible to see it as a secularized form of ancestral worship and as a cult of the dead. This cult enables the city's inhabitants to deepen their relationships with time. The museum, therefore, tends to slow down the hectic pace of the city. For this reason, it is sensible to design museum buildings as plaza and pedestrian complexes.

The avant-garde of the twenties wanted to abolish the museum and the academy and sought to reconcile art with the amnesiac technology of movement. In the culture of kinetic technology, time triumphs over space, and covering spaces ever more rapidly saves more and more time. In rebelling against this trend through the recollection of what has been and of the dead, the new museum culture aims for a spatial expression of the *Zeitgeist*, a deceleration of mere dynamics and a pictorial urbanization of the city. The city suddenly finds time again—time to present space as an image in front of which we try to visualize another era. It is possible to take a leisurely stroll through the new museums; with their squares, passageways, and stairways, they extend spatial invitations for such a stroll, even to those who do not purchase a ticket to enter the museum. The fact that, under the influence of these museum complexes, the consumer city is undergoing a step-by-step process of urbanization and cultivation is a clear external expression of the internal process to which we have referred.

In the vertical dimension of the centrality symbolism, Manhattan is triumphant. It can barely be compared to Berlin, this somewhat blurred and backward representation of the age of modern movement. To make up for this Berlin is catching up as a museum city. In the museum, the city center emerges as that which it always was—a gathering place. It gathers not only objects but also people; people who are willing to come together, to concentrate, and then passively affect the world around them. From this point of view, it is precisely as a traffic-free or dead zone that the inner-city museum complex actively contributes to urban vitality, to the city's attempts to fight against any threat to its centrality, and to remain a fascinating, empty center that poses a challenge to the imagination.

The genuinely European centrality ensemble is that of the cathedral or palace surrounded by the old town, the city as museum, and finally the museums themselves. As antiquated as it may seem, if this ensemble is understood as a museum-like compendium of time and of the world, then it is as least as elemental and as promising for the future as the American model, the abstract skyline city with its gridlike transport network and the central void (the park). The American metropolis, above all Manhattan, is a perfect image of the modern age. It elevates the scientific and financial abstraction to almost mythological status. It celebrates the metallic sheen of the objectivization and concretization of almost all of life's processes. It endows functional movement with an exuberant aesthetic quality—particularly in the evening light. This can be ideally illustrated by the mobile medium of film, for example in Martin Scorsese's *Taxi Driver*, where Manhattan by night provides a grandiose backdrop of turbulent, hectic lights. In the final analysis, the imaginary center of this metropolis is neither the park nor the square in the center nor any single skyscraper but rather the relationship existing between its linear and dynamic aesthetic and immeasurable space. It is only in this relationship that the excess of that which has been made hectically available finds a balance. The supremacy of reason is confronted with the immeasurable universe, with its mystery, and is thereby tempered and relativized. This has always been the center's task when faced with any kind of extreme.

The European city seeks its balance of movement and inwardness, rationality, and incomprehensibility more in a relationship to historical space than to the universe. Its tense center is formed by its quality as a museum and by modern movement. Its center, its dream of the reconciliation of the individual with the species, is more sensual, more visual, more melancholy, and probably more poetic than the American mold. In 1850, Richard Wagner outlined the idea of the *Gesamtkunstwerk*, in his work *Kunst der Zukunft (The Art of the Future)*: "The artistic person can only find complete satisfaction in the union of all art forms to a common work of art." Even if Wagner saw the standard for this unity of the arts in the theater, the idea can be transferred to urban features and architecture. The "union of all art forms" echoes Vitruvius's "consensus" of disparate elements and acts as the mediator between physical, architectonic, and cosmic order. The measure of the modern union of all arts, however, is to be seen in the correspondence between the act of knowing and what is known, between subject and object. At the center of this dynamic symmetry is a state of suspense: back and forth between spirit and object. The center as a standard for a new union of all art would therefore be the subject, which in view of the immeasurable whole of existence retracts his subjectivity, a subjectivity which tries to objectivize everything. The artistic unity that becomes visible and possible as a result of this process is not the rigid, static symmetry characterized by the portico of the Greek temple but the dynamic, fragile symmetry, the never-ending search for the central axis, the uncertain balance between the subjective, constant desire for knowledge and the experience of the paradoxical, infinite planetary and historical-existential expansions and contractions. Something of this resonates in Gottfried Benn's poem "A Word": "A word—a gleam, a soaring flight, a fire, a cast of flame, a shooting star—and darkness again, vast and monstrous in the empty space round world and me." These lines lend symbolic expression to the principal motifs of a modern aesthetic of the center: the planetary horizon that simultaneously liberates and restricts the isolated subject, the dynamism of uncertain movement through space and time, the balance of light and darkness, imagination and incomprehension, the center as void between the world and

490

11

*12. The Kulturforum in the
Tiergarten, Berlin, aerial view,
1989.* Landesluftbildarchiv, Berlin.

the subject. In the modern age, the static center of the ancient world disappears, it is transformed into a process of never-ending mediation between subject and world. This finds expression in modernist symmetry in the forms of asymmetrical elements and irritations. These are the apparently accidental fissures in the ordered schema, the barely perceptible shifts and imbalances in the dynamic equilibrium of forms and buildings.

Wagner's concept of the "union of all forms of art" corresponds to what I have called the museum-like quality of the city center and the role of the museum in the city center. When expanded to a Museum Island or to a *Kulturforum* as in Berlin (fig. 14), the museum represents the realistic and true *Gesamtkunstwerk* of our century. It encompasses all the artistic disciplines (music and literature, fine art, architecture, and arts and crafts) of almost all artistic ages. The greater the number of diverse works of art hanging or standing in individual museums, the greater is the desire of the individual work to achieve a sense of individuality and exclusivity. This contradictory process corresponds directly to the dialectic of the city concentrated in the center, subjects everyone and everything to its toughness, and thus provokes individualism in acts of dispersal and evacuation. The threatening collapse of the center forces the members to the periphery. This process is one which actually takes place in many cities, but for the present Berlin and Manhattan are protected against it—Manhattan because it is a real island, West Berlin because of the decades it has spent in isolation, and unified Berlin because of its insular progressiveness and attractiveness in the context of its underdeveloped surroundings.

It is precisely as an abstract, autonomous kinetic art that modern art, described by Hans Sedlmayer as having abandoned the center and therefore lost sight of man, is able to serve as a mediator. In the break in the context, in the provocation, in the protest, in the disruptive fire, and in the asymmetry arising from art's partial or complete rejection of the symmetry of representation, modern art confronts the omnipresent supremacy of reason and its limitations. Art has lost the central axis, even those artists who seek it have lost the fundamental order. It is precisely for this reason, however, that art has also gained the strength to resist the absolutism of reason. In the recent museum architecture, which is criticized by art historians for its tendency to absolutize the architectonic dimension, art and architecture, image and space are united. This is achieved through a confrontation with each element absolutizing its own individuality and as a result provoking the other to aspire to autonomy. As a *Gesamtkunstwerk* of spatial and visual art, the museum represents the union of the disparate. Its unity is to be seen in the active desire for autonomy on the part of its constituent elements. It is also in this respect that the museum is the true center of the modern city, for its inhabitants are linked by the fact that they simultaneously seek a collective urban identity and an individual identity. The dialectic of the city that Lefèbvre describes as the repeated play of concentration and evacuation, accumulation and dispersal is also the decisive dialectic of the museum. This constitutive tension among the works of art, which, as parts of a collection, clamor for individuality and autonomy, corresponds to the endurance test between autonomous architecture and art on display. It was in fact art that showed architecture how to strive for the much criticized autonomy.

Today museums and not churches are the places of worship where, through ritual, the city dweller becomes conscious of the privileged nature of the city and becomes a true inhabitant. New York, the abstract and kinetic metropolis, and Berlin, the historical and museumlike metropolis, are two extremely different, although sometimes very similar, urban versions of modernism. One is characterized by the supremacy of reason, the triumph of movement, relationship to the cosmos, and spatial abstraction, and the other by the concentricity of time and history that for decades was dramatically embodied in the Wall and the lavish museum collections. The absolute, perfect city that can only be imagined but never built would be Berlin-Manhattan—a unity of contradiction, the living reconciliation of time and space, history and abstraction, proximity to death and mechanism, intimacy, and the intoxication of speed. Berlin-Manhattan would be the ideal center between the extremes of Berlin and New York.

Observations

Burkhard Grashorn

Phillip Evans-Clark

New York and Berlin stand on either side of the mirror. They do not reflect one another for their respective positions are incommensurable, their destinies hyperbolic. Berlin is like a plane gliding in the night unaware of its position, oblivious to its destination, all lights shut off. There is something serene, awesome in its silent flight, something frightening also. New York is out of sight: two legs swathed in floral patterns of finely meshed black silk stockings; gold and silver pumps with high golden heels. The skirt? Also black, wavy, casting undulating shadows on the floor. The hands? Buried in taffeta. The face? Smiling, I suppose. The eyes? Big, surely. New York dances; tomorrow she'll die. "Skip the agony, toots."

Gustav Courbet's *The Origin of the World* had been lost for about a century when it finally turned up unexpectedly after the death of Jacques Lacan. Or so the story goes. Here it is: A close-up of a woman's naked trunk (you cannot discern her face), with open thighs (you cannot see her legs either), and her vagina six to eight inches from you face (depending). The question is, if culture (history) is that female sex, bursting in full daylight, how do New York and Berlin confront it?

In Fargier's video, *Le Trou de la vierge* (The Virgin's Hole), Sollers suggests that, within Western culture, a man glimpsing a woman's vaginal gape has no alternatives other than blindness or sublimation. The retinal encounter with the open sex instantly collapses for lack of words. The eye, rounding the curve of the vulva, glides gravityless (the friction of language is absent). The crash is imminent. The man, on the right, jerks his head away, blinded. The shockwave is so intense that it punctures two holes precisely in the orbit that had eyed the hole. An eye for an eye. Only the dotted white light on the afterflash remains. The myth folds. Language collapses. Bye, bye love. In Berlin, culture stumbles heedlessly.

The man on the left is seemingly better off. For one, he fights the vertigo. He remains planted in front of the picture.

Terrified by the sight of the folded cleft, he heads for more familiar features, the eyes, an entrance to the soul, so they say. (Bad luck, though, for Courbet's girl is headless.) He too cannot endure the glare of his reflected desire, but, unlike his neighbor, he projects his psyche onto one-eyed principles (archetypes, for example). The lady vanishes. The woman becomes Woman, Womanhood, Aphrodite, Isis, the Great Mother, the Great Mother Earth (thank God for the title). Her Holiness. The Holy hole. Holy but also fertile, that is, in transit toward a third being, hence a modest proposal. Language metastasizes and suffocates its object. In New York, culture acts as a sublimation for capital.

At this end of the Atlantic, history is lived through idolatry and bloated myths. What the New Yorker wants and requires is a socialized rite that tailors godheads after godheads (a market within the temple precinct is after all an old idea). Art has become the ultimate sacrificial lamb in the ritual of consumption. The artifact is born a reliquary. So devout is the New Yorker that he cannot stare at the naked body of history without rushing to the nearest church for necessary ablutions no matter how costly or painful: museums for donations, galleries for raw deals. A personal, mystical, solitary path away from the liturgies of the glamour industry and the tolling of the auction bell lies beyond the looking glass, worse yet, beyond desire.

Capital begets alienation, alienation begets fetishism, fetishism begets art, art begets desire, desire begets repression, repression begets the product, the product begets money, money begets the institution, the institution begets writing, writing begets history, and history embalms and immortalizes the entire process. And so the simulacrum goes. But behind the many effigies of God, there is nothing: not a single deity, savior, or prophet, not even a dog. Signs continuously gyrate like punctured balloons. Yet more dangerous is the saturated conscience that refuses the existence of the radical confusion of tongues (some people liken the whole thing to a Benetton ad). In New York, greed throttles the critical mind, and excessive vanity numbs the pain. New York can't see her future because she can't recognize her present: she does not know she needs redemption.

America had always looked upon herself as the child/pioneer. With this double identity, she could rally support for the truth of her ways. She dared the world with a perfect sense of patriotic infallibility. Yet her energy, good will, unflinching optimism, her strength and magic, are diminishing every day. Like Dorian Grey, she clings to her youth and so avoids confrontation with the mirror. Still, she ages. Military defeat, economic frailty, shifting morality roughed up her babyskin. Plagued from within, America is also haunted from within as she no longer symbolizes the New Eden. America is now an old child. And instead of throwing dice for an astounding Western world (Mallarme taught English), she now merely throws tantrums before a disillusioned audience.

The New York art world, which, at this point, mixes anything for an elusive rush, neatly personifies this type of tarnished youth. For beneath the hype, the speed, and the money, the stuff is going bad. Alternative practices groove with the airtight pretenses of the New York Academy, remaining alternative in name only. Concept art, by acting as the other pole, internalizes and reproduces the binary code characteristic of official thinking and hence is immediately sanctioned regardless of its content, message, or material. Worse, the redundancy of critical art enforces a schema of domination and violence similar to that within society. The current attempt to discredit painting reads more like corrupt evidence in a mock trail than an honest appraisal.

Barbara Kruger, a member of the conceptual tribe, sees no contradiction between her vitriolic epigrams against establishment and her constant presence in and around its many outposts. While insisting on the integrity of her approach, she welcomes official beatification. Strictly speaking, her art is a design. Couched in the glossy, finishing school aesthetics of Condé Nast, here the source for knowing what makes society tick, Kruger's works are no more handsome posters carping at the world. Their slick surfaces and sanctimoniousness distressingly hide their dogmatic content. Artists such as Kruger pretend to have the gift of second sight when at best they simply second-best the police.

Eric Fischl, a member of the painter's class, represents another form of closure. His dirty little world of soft porn morality does not so much reveal the obscenity of suburban living (if it did, no one would buy his works, which would amount to a modern form of crucifixion) as it glorifies a traditional take (realism) in a traditional medium (painting) for a traditional viewer (one who prefers figuration) in a traditional manner (an inflated version of academic easel painting). Fischl caters directly to taste and so revamps all the mystifying schemes (fetishistic technique, genre painting, sacredness of the image) that had given painting a bad name. What makes Fischl so lovable is that he manufactures cheap icons for small fortunes (this discrepancy alone tells all). Fischl and Kruger, in their different ways, seem terrified by change and so inhibit invention.

Traditionally, the child and the prophet are blessed with the gift of extended sight and inspired speech. Both figures are close to the artist because their position toward society is ambiguous: inside of the child, never sleeps. Insomnia, he simulates his concern for family when in fact his search for an identity is motivated by fear of the future. Jealous, cowardly, and noxious, he cauterizes his vices and masquerades his cure as an acceptable treatment. He does not encourage change because he has not seen it for years and so can no longer recognize it. New York supplants true change (progress) with hype and so kills insouciance. In this confusion, the artist suffers the most for he must trade in his best motivations— delight, amazement, purpose, and knowledge—for a pittance, a sale or a blurb in a magazine. Totally co-opted by society, he is forced to relinquish his gift of sight and his power of interpretation. In New York, the prophet died and was reborn as the trader. The imposter chokes the voice and fixes movement. In the end, this profound silence may signify that New York is impotent, a citadel without enemies.

If tradition in New York hallucinates, in Berlin, it is tabooed. After the war, Berlin had no view, but her own petrifying presence.

Instantly judged and convicted, Germany was given no time to assess the events of her recent past. Frazzled and sleepless, she faced persecution. So odious were her crimes that they required exemplary punishment. But neither the public confessions nor the weight of compensations conveyed the ultimate severity of the sentence. Far more destructive was the branding of Germany as evil. Not only did the world consider her satanic, but eventually so did she. No matter where Germany went, she was impregnated with the rancidity of sin. And while everybody recognizes and condemns the monstrosity of Nazism, few want to realize the enormity of its penalty: its mythical dimension.

Instead of fostering understanding through analysis, guilt paralyses the mind by fusing all evidence into one massive, infrangible boulder. Germany was left with no alternative than to transform the concrete reality of historical facts into an all-encompassing event. Ineffable and impenetrable, it dehydrated the German soil. As in the case of black holes where light once trapped cannot escape, any segment of German history once in contact with the event is irrecoverably lost. Unlocalized, the event threatens all aspects of German culture and then seals them off from history. Germany lives under a regime of pure terror, a terror that exceeds the nightmare of remembrance for it has no name.

"Now if you can you may tell how you saw me when I was undressed," hurls

497

Diana to a metamorphosing Acteon. Language collapses in the mythical event: the profanation of the godess's sex or the monstrosity of the Holocaust. And just as Diana's words induce irony and provocation, so Nazism appears as a derisive challenge. In the defiance of nomination, Nazism reveals its mythical dimension and hence its essence as play. As pure event, Nazism was impenetrable. As defial, it is pure irony. This double-take curses reason.

For a moment it looked as if a sophisticated rhetorical arsenal would do the job. Take Sibelberg's *Parsifal,* for example. By choosing Parsifal, Sibelberg sets a myth against another myth (an eye for an eye). Moreover, Parsifal is a recurrent figure in the Nazi fancy (hence its rhetorical potential for displacement through metaphor or synecdote). The story of Parsifal describes the loss of innocence and its aftermath, which also relates to the Nazi experience. Finally, Sibelberg uses the medium of film, his knowledge of theater, and the possibilities opened up by singing to avoid narrative complacency or worse, a reversed apology of Nazism. And yet, he fails. By throwing Nazism back onto the domain of innocence, Sibelberg exchanges one myth for another and so reinforces both. His Parsifal ends up covered with Nazi overtones. Nazism, through its genetic link to German romanticism (Wagner) and its mythology, appears as the legitimate progenitor of German culture. By using worn-out tropes, Sibelberg's *Parsifal* fails to address Nazism's irony and chokes on its own pomposity. Excess does not always lead to the palace of wisdom.

For Anselm Kiefer, on the other hand, Nazism is no longer a topic but the main motivation of his work. His first photographical work matched the irony of Nazism by turning the Nazi salute into a quick, personalized paper cutout. Even more radical are some of his later landscapes. In these works, the colors are hushed, the horizon line high, the light strong, the curvature of the image exquisite. There is no fear and no nostalgia in these vast fields of wintery muteness. The land is forlorn, yet not abandoned to death.

The solution to the Nazi riddle resided in the space of painting itself. By constructing personal mandalas and redefining Nazism within the terms of his desire, Kiefer breaks from the patterns of traditional connotations and resists their gravitational pull. A new event (the paintings themselves) rips the event apart. A tooth for a tooth. No game here, no tease, no excess. As Kiefer moves with the gorgon reflected on the surface of his canvas, he views it indirectly, and thus survives. At last, Nazism is consumed, its progressive, debilitating strangulation released. Unfortunately many works, and especially the most recent ones, do not follow suit.

Acteon sees Diana's sex; his pleasure is immeasurable and for it he must die. But death is incidental to the satisfaction of his desire. So too is the horror of Nazism incommensurable, but it carries no redemptive value. Germany irretrievably lost her innocence in the rectilinear grids of death camps. Nowhere is this loneliness more deeply felt than in front of Berlin's wall, the stigma of scarification. Berlin herself is trapped in the fold of the event and remains alive to tell the tale. The crucial difference between her condition and that of New York is that Berlin, though permanently disfigured, feels her pain, and hence can choose salvation. Art may contribute to creating the choice as it maps out alternative routes through the past and into the future.

"Other maps are such shapes, with
    their islands and capes!
But we've got our brave Captain to
    thank."
(So the crew would protest) "that he's
    bought us
the best—A perfect and absolute
    blank!"

The future is certainly not linked to either cities, nor to cities like them, but to one's position with regard to the city. Corporations, museums, and, in general, institutions are blank spots. They are autistic blank spots. Terminal stations. The future is not in or on the map, but sometimes around the borders, and it refuses to stand still. No longer primarily a social phenomenon, it is bound to existential choices—a question of scale. The future is literally utopic—without place. It can occur anywhere but not to anybody. It is the gift and the possibility of walking away. "There were too many blank spaces on the map. Therefore I had no obligation to force myself to fill them in. I was no guardian of the law."

This text was dedicated to Adrienne Baxter, Maria Nazor, and Luke Gray, who stubbornly continue to create and hope amidst ruined maps.

John Brademas

As president of New York University— the largest private university in the world, located in the heart of the most exciting city in the world— I have a good vantage point from which to dream about the future of New York.

Here's my scenario of a historic day in the life of the city in the year 2000. To mark the dawn of the twenty-first century, the president of the United States will visit the great metropolis of New York. Her itinerary follows:

10:00 to 11:00 A.M. Visits central Park to observe Helping Hands in action. The city's few remaining homeless tend parks instead of sleeping in them. After gardening, pruning, and planting, the helpers are provided shelter and meals in safe, clean facilities.

11:00 A.M. to noon. Joins Mayor John F. Kennedy, Jr. (an NYU Law School alumnus), for a walk down car-free Fifth Avenue. The area from Third to Eight avenues and 34th to 59th streets has for several years been off-limits to all vehicles.

12:30 P.M. At luncheon ceremonies at the United Nations, she welcomes other heads of state of U.N. member nations in hailing the tenth anniversary of the dissolution of apartheid in South Africa. In an internationally televised news conference, the president joins the democratically elected president of Libya to hear his explanation of Libya's pivotal role in crafting a binding Middle East peace accord.

2:30 to 3:30 P.M. Tours a midtown medical center's Resource Sharing center. The successful battles to conquer AIDS and tropical diseases such as malaria have sped sophisticated exchanges of information among major research institutions throughout the world.

3:30 to 4:30 P.M. Visits P.S. 7 to deliver a speech in which the president lauds the strides taken by the New York public-school system, largest in the United States, over the past decade to rebuild its physical plant, attract top-

flight teachers, and enhance the quality of instruction. The president praises the six percent dropout rate.

5:00 to 6:00 P.M. Hovercraft flight over recapture waterfronts of lower Manhattan and Brooklyn where plazas, promenades, and gardens have replaced crumbling docks and warehouses. Fishermen, swimmers, and boaters throng waterside parks.

6:00 to 7:00 P.M. Washington Square, where the president attends a special academic convocation and receives an honorary degree from New York University, the nation's foremost independent institution of higher learning, celebration its accomplishment in raising one billion dollars by the year 2000. NYU president announces that in the year just past, 1999–2000, so many more students applied than could be admitted that some had to settle for their second choice, Harvard.

7:00 to 8:00 P.M. Final stop: City Hall, where the president signs the new Federal Landmark Act, which grants generous tax credits for the restoration of old buildings and makes demolition of valuable, aging structures illegal without the approval of the Secretary of Preservation, her new Cabinet officer.

8:15 P.M. Departs New York from a splendidly refurbished Grand Central Station. Traveling via high-speed rail, the president arrives at Union Station, Washington, D.C., an hour later.

Rainer Fetting

Rainer Fetting. Southern Star
Passage, *1988.*

Rainer Fetting. Brush Pier
(A 350), *1987.* Raab Galerie,
Berlin.

Rainer Fetting. Evening on Devil
Lake, *1988.*

Rainer Fetting. Homeless Winter
(A 368), *1988.* Raab Galerie,
Berlin.

Rainer Hoynck

Berlin wants to go far
It probably needs to
Berlin wants to go too far
Does it need to?

Much of what is remarkable and
unique about New York results from
the cruel injustices that occur under
its skyscaping towers.

Berlin. Who is this? Definitely a
complex community which does not
speak with one voice and in which
controversial opinions prevail.

In many areas Berlin is still and once
more a city of innovation and
inspiration, of new ways of living, of a
contrary consciousness and of a
diversity of appropriations and needs.

Berlin will never, never be like New
York.

But Berlin can be compared to New
York. Here, too, processes are set in
motion that affect not only established
and influential areas of the city but
also other cities and countries. It too is
a place that moves.

What is necessary for Berlin is quality
rather than quantity as well as a sense
of proportion.

Saskia Sassen

Marketplace of Capital, Meeting ground of the Third World

The conditions are in place now. They will only get more acute.

New York can no longer be understood as one city. Some of New York is part of a transterritorial city that also encompasses London and Tokyo. This is an economic space for the management, control, and regulation of the global network of factories, offices, and financial markets that make up the world economy. In the late 1980s, this transterritorial space accounted for the eight-five percent of world capitalization, forty-two percent of all the assets of the twelve leading bank centers in the world, seventy-nine percent of the global investments in stock markets. The level of economic concentration accounted for by these three cities was higher than ever before.

And so are their built densities. The central business districts of these cities have reached the highest densities ever. Why has this happened in an era of global telecommunications capability that would allow for the geographical dispersal of economic activity? In New York City, a rather small area of Manhattan concentrates much of this activity. The Manhattan CBD, extending from 60th Street all the way down to the tip of the island, houses fifty-eight percent of the city's jobs in six hundred million square feet of non-residential floor space, one of the highest densities among major cities. Several new office towers have been added over the last few years.

Agglomeration persists and will continue to persist in the face of major telecommunication advances because globalization of economic activity has created new forms of centralization in order to manage and regulate this global network. It is precisely the spatial decentralization made possible by technological development that has created the new forms of centralization of top-level management, control, design, and servicing function.

The maintenance of centralized control and management over a a geographically dispersed array of plants, offices, and service outlets cannot be taken for granted or seen as an inevitable outcome of a world system. The possibility of such centralized control needs to be produced. Central for its development is the production of a vast range of highly specialized services and of top level management and control functions. It is not only a matter of the familiar issue of the power of large corporations, but also that of the work, the *practice* of global control: the specialized activities involved in producing and reproducing the organization and management of the global production system and the global labor force. The new forms of centralization entails a shift in the locus of control and management: in addition to the large corporation and the large commercial bank there is now also a marketplace with a multiplicity of advanced corporate service firms and financial institutions. Correspondingly, we see the increased importance of cities such as New York, London, and Tokyo, as *center* of finance and as *centers* for global servicing and management. The more globalized economic activity becomes, the higher this new form of agglomeration.

Because globalization of the economy keeps growing, we need more highly paid people to run the world economy and more transactions and more centralization and more tall buildings in as little space as possible in a limited number of strategic locations— New York is one of them. The fight for urban space becomes stronger, more acute, and more unsparing. The politics of this strategic trans-territorial space for global management contains no accountability to the people of a place. A politics of the margin. Immigrant communities, informal neighborhood economies, neighborhoods defending against gentrification, devastated areas where mostly women and children live, malnourished with high mortality rates and no future, the tent cities of the homeless. Retribalized spaces alongside the trans-territorial marketplace of the most advanced form of capital.

INDEX

A

Aalto, Alvar, 306
Abstract Expressionism, 437, 459–60, 461–62
Academy of Architecture (Berlin), 50, 57
Academy of Arts (Berlin), 182
Ackerman, Frederick L., 98, 245, 266, 268, 271
action painting, 446–47
Adams, Henry, 196
Adler, Felix, 173
Adler, Friedrich, 133
air shafts, 164–65, 175
Airship Hall, 55
Akazienhof, 87, 142
Aktion, Die (journal), 181, 190
Alexanderplatz, 52, 258
Allaire, James, 161
Allgemeine Elektricitäts- Gesellschaft (AEG), 15, 17, 24, 29, 47, 48, 50, 51, 139, 183
Alsenviertel (Königsplatz), 66
Altglienecke housing estate, 477
America: capitalism in, 23; garden city planning movement in, 93–107; German conceptions of, 281–85; leftism in, among artists, 361, 365; metropolises in, compared to Europeans, 490, 493; modernism in, 282, 360; post- World War II, 311; railroads, 18, 311; social reform and architecture in, 245–46; turn- of-the-century conditions, 94; World War I effect on American consciousness, 96–97
American Abstract Artists, 364–65
American Artists' Congress, 362
American Place, An, 358
American Radiator Building (Hood and Foulhoux), 334
Amerikanismus, 213, 218, 240
Ammann, Othmar Hermann, 45, 123, 125, 298–99, 302–9
Andrae, K. Paul, 252
Andre, Carl, 469, 470
Anhalt Station, 57
Anker, Alfons, 258
Anker stone construction, 157
Appalachian Trail, 97, 98
architects: vs. engineers, 49–50, 52, 55, 118–19, 237–38; as reformers, in garden city planning movement, 83–84; social conscience of, 427, 429
Architects' Association of Berlin, 134
Architects Collaborative, 404
architecture: as index of cultural climate, 232–34; new (*see* new architecture)
Arco, Graf von, 29
Arensberg, Walter, 204
Armory Show, 203
Arnhold, Eduard, 188
Arnim, Frederick William von, 61
Arnold, Bion J., 38
Arp, Hans, 347
art, human need for, 441–42
art criticism/critics, 472–73
Art Deco, 306, 334–36
Art Front (journal), 361
art informel, 446–47
Artists' Congress, 365
Artists' Union, 361–62
Art Nouveau, 187
"Art of Assemblage, The," Museum of Modern Art exhibition, 1961, 467
art patronage, 357, 358–59, 362, 364
Arts, The (journal), 358
Arts and Crafts Movement, 187, 234
Art Students League, 208

Art Workers' Coalition, 470
Asisi, Yadegar, 432
Association for Art (Berlin), 190
Association of Berlin Artists, 182
Association of Friends of the National Gallery of 1929, 444
Association of the XI, 186
Astoria Pool, 301
Athens Charter, 399
AT&T Building (Johnson), 335
autobahn, 309–10
Automobile Club of America, 124
automobiles, 102, 104, 123–25, 309–10, 311, 312
avant-garde, 190

B

Baader, Johannes, 344
Babij, Ivan, 343
Bach, Elvira, 452
backbuilding, 164
Badur, Frank, 449
Balla, Giacomo, 190
Ballard, William F. R., 275
Baller, Hinrich, 430, 432
Baller, Inken, 430, 432
Barclay-Vesey Building (McKenzie, Voorhees & Gmelin), 334
Barfuss, Inga, 452
Barr, Alfred H., Jr., 360, 460
Bartning, Otto, 253
Baselitz, Georg, 446–47; *Big Night Flushed, The*, 446; *Naked Man, The*, 446; observations, 376–77
Battery Park City, 276, 420
Bauer, Catherine, 245, 246, 268; *Modern Housing*, 268, 271
Bauhaus, 353–54, 399, 438
Baumeister, Wille, 442
Baumgarten, Paul, 425
Bauwelt (journal), 238
Bayonne Bridge, 43, 45
Baziotes, William, 462
Beach, Alfred Ely, 118
Beaux-Arts design, 38, 266, 271, 333, 334
Beckmann, Max, 192, 342, 351, 352; *Departure*, 352; *Hell*, 354–55; *The Night*, 352
Begas, Reinhold, 139, 188
Behne, Adolf, 238
Behrendt, Walter Curt, 151, 289, 324
Behrens, Peter, 24, 27, 48, 50, 51, 139–40, 244, 252, 253, 255, 256, 258, 260, 318, 323–24, 327
Bel Geddes, Norman, *Magic Motorways*, 311
Bell, Alexander Graham, 17
Bellamy, Edward, 94
Bellevue palace, 61
Bellows, George, 196, 198, 204
Belmont, August, 118
Belmont Lake, 301
Belt Parkway, 301–2
Berg, Max, 252
Bergson, Henri P., 202
Berlage, Henri P., 320, 322
Berlin: architectural styles, 30–31; art world in, 189–90, 192, 341–55, 441–57; compared to New York as center/city, 481–93; in early nineteenth century, 182–83; garden city movement, 139, 142; housing in, 22–27, 145–57, 241, 243–45, 256; industrial age in, 50–51, 130–31; inventors, 28–30; liberal bourgeoisie vs. conservative aristocracy, 182–83; peripheral location of, 481–82; post-unification, 475–78; post-World

War I, 240–41, 341–55; post-World War II, 395–408, 441–57; public transport systems, 143, 254–55; railroads, 51–55, 131, 136; railroad stations, 51–52; reconstruction of, 406–8; skyscraper debate in, 315–16; suburbs of, 139; as technological metropolis, 13–15, 30–31; Tiergarten, 58–69; turn-of-the-century conditions in, 84–85; urban planning in, 240–41, 249, 251, 255–56, 395–408, 475–78; waterways, 51; Weimar contrasted with, 353–54; Wilhelmine Period, 47–57, 134–39; World War II damage, 220, 395–96. *See also* East Berlin; West Berlin
Berlin: A Critical View, Ugly Realism 20s–70s exhibition (Institute for Contemporary Art, London), 451–52
Berlin Artists Program, 449
Berliner Elekricitäts-Werke, 15, 17
Berlinische Boden-Gesellschaft, 141
Berlin-Potsdam Railway, 51
Berlin realism, 446
Berlin Republic, 341–55
Berlin Secession, 187, 188–89
Berlin-Spandau Canal, 51, 136
Berlin Wall, 220
Berman, Marshall, *All That Is Solid Melts Into Air*, 312
Bernoulli, Hans, 86
Bernstein, Carl, 188
Best, George, 123
Bestelmeyer, German, 253, 260
Beuth, Peter, 50
Beuys, Joseph, 449
Biddle, George, 365
Bierbaum, Otto Julius, 187
Billing, Hermann, 253
Bing, Alexander, 98–101
biotechnic society, 231
Birkmire, William H., *Skeleton Construction in Building*, 332–33
Bismarck Monument, 139
Blackwood, Michael, personal recollections, 367–73
Blankenstein, Hermann, 133, 136
Blaue Reiter, 190, 346, 347
Bliss, Lizzie, 357, 360
Block, René, 449
Blum, Otto, 249, 251
BMT subway line, 119
boarding houses, Berlin, 155
Boarding-Palast, 155
Boccioni, Umberto, 190
Bode, Wilhelm von, 134
Boelsche, Wilhelm, 83, 184
Boller, Alfred P., 43
Bolotowsky, Ilya, 365
Bonatz, Karl, 396
Borsig company, 182
Böttcher, Rudolph, 432
Boullée, Etienne-Louis, 488
Bourke-White, Margaret, 362
Bowdin & Webster, 125
Boynton, Captain Billy, 211, 214
Brademas, John, observations, 499
Brahm, Otto, 183
Brandenburg Gate, 61, 130, 482
Brandt, Andreas, 432, 449
Braun, Ferdinand, 29
Brecht, Bertolt, *In the City Jungle*, 354
Breslau, 244
Breslau exhibition of 1929, 238
Breuer, Marcel, 260
bridges, New York, 20, 40–45, 119. *See also* specific bridges
Brighton Beach, 222
Brighton Beach Hotel, 213
Brix, Joseph, 249
Brody, Samuel, 276

505

Bronx River Parkway, 125, 298
Bronx-Whitestone Bridge, 45, 302
Broodthaers, Marcel, 451
Brook, Alexander, 359
Brooklyn and Jamaica Railroad, 35
Brooklyn-Battery Tunnel, 305
Brooklyn Bridge, 20, 40, 56, 121, 207
Brooklyn Bridge Southeast Urban Renewal Plan, 418
Brooklyn Rapid Transit (BRT), 119
Brown, Archibald Manning, 273
Brown, Capability, 72
Brown, Floyd De L., 338
Brown, Norman O., 467
Bruce, Edward, 362
Brücke, Die, 189–90, 346, 347, 442
Brunner, Arnold W., 117
Büchner, Georg, 89
Buck, Leffert L., 41, 121
Buckout, Isaac C., 36
Building Code of 1853 (Berlin), 146–47
building construction, rationalization of, 235, 237
building materials, Berlin, 133–34
building standards, 167–68, 169
Burckhardt, Jacob, 232, 233
Burgee, John, 414
Burgin, Victor, 472, 473
Burnham, Daniel H., 113, 318
Büro Berlin, 455
Burr, William H., 43
Burroughs, Bryson, 357
Burroughs, Edgar Rice, 463
Burroughs, William, The Wild Boys, 467
Bush Terminal Company waterfront complex, 34

C

Café Bauer, 17
Café des Westens, 181
cafes, Berlin, 61
Cafe Vaterland, 212, 220
Cage, John, 463, 464
Cahill, Holger, 364
Camera Notes (journal), 201
Camera Work (journal), 201, 206, 207
Camus, Albert, 462
capitalism, 23, 81, 84
carfloat terminals, 34, 35
Caro, Nikodem, 30
Carr, J. Gordon, 306
Carrá, Carlo, 190, 344
Carrère & Hastings, 41, 123
Carstenn, J. A. W., 139
Cassatt, Alexander, 38
Cassirer, Bruno, 188
Cassirer, Paul, 188
Cassirer Salon, 184, 188
Castelli, Luciano, 452
Castelli Gallery, 464
Cawdery, William, 214
CBS Building (Saarinen), 336, 414
Cedar Tavern, 460, 462
cellar dwellings, 160–61, 167
centralized housekeeping (Berlin), 155
Central Park, 70–79, 195, 482
Central Park Conservancy, 79
Central Park Zoo, 309
Chagall, Marc, 343
Chandler, Charles F., 169
Charity Organization Society (COS), 171, 174
Charlottenburg, 405–6
Charlottenburger Chausee, 61
Charlottenburg housing complex, 150
Charlottenburg Technische Hochschule, 29
Chase, Stuart, 97

Chase, Willam Merritt, 195, 196
Chelsea-Gansevoort piers, 33
Chicago School, 282
Children's Aid Society, 98
Cholera Epidemic of 1849, 160, 165
Chruxin, Christian, 447
Chrysler Building (van Alen), 335, 336, 338–39
Chrystie-Forsyth Houses, 271
churches, in West Berlin reconstruction, 424–25
Churchill, Henry S., 275
Circle, the (Berlin), 61
Citicorp Building (Stubbins), 335
cities: as collages/montages, 482, 485; as centers, 481; monumental and vertical architecture of, 487–88; public recreation and entertainment in, 211–22; as symbols, 231
Citizens' Association of New York, 167
Citizens' Committee on Lower Manhattan Redevelopment, 417
Città Nuova, 315
City and South London Railway, 38
City and Suburban Homes Company, 98, 174
City Housing Corporation (CHC), 99–107
City Planning Exhibition (Berlin), 86
city plazas (Hegemann and Peet), 289, 290
Civil Servants' Housing Association, 151
Clarke, Gilmore D., 125, 298, 301
classical modernity, 407
Club, The (New York), 460, 462
Coady, Robert, 206
Coleman, Glenn, 359
Collective Plan, 395–96
Columbus Circle, 414
Communist Party, U.S., 361, 365
community ideology, 84, 88–89
Competition for the Development of a Basic Plan for the Construction of Greater Berlin, 142–43, 249, 251
conceptualist art, 470
concrete, 24
Coney Island, 211–16, 220, 222
Congrés Internationaux d'Architecture Moderne (CIAM), 238
consensus architecture, 420
Consolidated Edison, 15, 17
Consolidation Act of 1882, 170
Constructivism, 343
consumption, vs. production, 437
Continental Corporation (Hanover), 140
Cooper, Alexander, 276
Cooper, Theodore, 43
Corbett, Harvey W., 301
Corbin, Austin, 38
Corso, Gregory, 463
Council of Hygiene and Public Health, 167
Country Club District (Missouri), 94
country house, English, 150
country house colonies, Berlin, 145
Courbet, Gustave, 185
courtyard gardens, Berlin, 141–42, 149
craft tradition, 141
Crane, Hart, 207
Cravan, Arthur, 206
Cremer and Wolffenstein, 134
critical reconstruction concept, Berlin, 406–8
Cross-Bronx Expressway, 312
Croton Aqueduct, 35, 43, 160
Croton Dam, 43
Cubism, 202, 233, 335, 342
Cubo-Expressionism, 342, 343
Cubo-Futurism, 342
culture heroes, 467

D

Dadaism, 189, 204, 206, 208, 320, 322, 343–48, 442
Dadasophs, 344
Daimler Benz, Services Center, 477–78
Davies, Arthur Bowen, 200, 203, 357
Davis, Lewis, 276
Davis, Stuart, 357, 359, 361, 362, 364, 365
De Chirico, Giorgio, 344, 345, 347, 445
deconstruction, 472–73
decoration, elimination of, 320, 322, 323
De Forest, Lee, 27
DeForest, Robert, 175
De Fries, Hans, 284, 285
Dehmel, Richard, 184
De Kooning, Willem, 459, 460–61
Delano & Aldrich, 125
Deleuze, Gilles, 472–73
demolition, vs. renovation, 427, 429
Department of Labor housing report of 1895 (The Housing of Working People), 172–73
Department of Survey and Inspection of Buildings (New York), 167
Derain, André, 345
Derrida, Jacques, 472
Design Research, 437–38, 439
Desky, Donald, 306
Deutsche Edison Gesellschaft für angewandte Electricität, 15, 17
Deutsche Gesellschaft zur Förderung des Wohnungsbaues Gemeinnützige Aktiengesellschaft (DE GE WO), 243, 244
Deutsche Werkbund, 150
Dewing, Thomas, 195
Dickstein, Morris, Gates of Eden, 462
Die weisse Stadt housing estate, 243
Dine, Jim, 464, 467
Dische, Irene, observations, 378–81
disease, housing and, 160
district controls (New York), 414–15
Dix, Otto, 342, 344, 345, 351; Big City Triptych, 354–55; Portrait of the Art Dealer Alfred Flechtheim, 354
Döblin, Alfred, 258; Berlin Alexanderplatz, 482, 485
Doesburg, Theo van, 234
Dolivo-Dobrowolsky, Michael, 29–30
Dondero, G. A., 462
Dornseif, Frank, 455
Dorotheenstadt, 61
Dos Passos, John, Manhattan Transfer, 485
Downing, Andrew Jackson, 72
Downtown Gallery, 358
Downtown Lower Manhattan Association, 417
draft riots, New York, 165–67
Draper, Earl, 94
Dreamland, 211–12, 216, 220
Dreier, Katherine, 359
Dreyer, Paul Uwe, 449
Duchamp, Marcel, 196, 204, 206, 207, 208, 359, 463, 469; Bride Stripped Bare by Her Bachelors, Even, 204, 206; Fountain, 207; Large Glass, The, 206; Nude Descending a Staircase, 206
dumbbell tenements, 168–70
Dundy, Elmer S., 214
Dunkel, Wilhelm, 287
Du Pont, Pierre S., 338
Durand-Ruel, Charles, 188
Durch (Berlin literary society), 181
Dutch architecture, 289
Düttmann, Werner, 404

E

Earle, Ellis P., 338
carthwork artists, 468
East Berlin: housing in, 401–2, 475, 477; socialist realism in, 396, 399
Eastman, Max, 200
East Village, gentrification of, 416
Ebe and Benda, 134
Eberstadt, Rudolf, 249
Ebert, Wils, 404
Eckartshausen, Karl von, 62
Eckstut, Stanton, 276
Edison, Thomas A., 15, 27, 28–29
Edison General Electric Company, 28
Edison Society, 183
Ehrenbaum, Hans, 190
Ehrenzweig, Anton, The Hidden Order of Art, 469
Eidlitz, Leopold, 117
Eiermann, Egon, 425
Einstein, Albert, 202, 233
Eisenstein, Sergei M., 89
electrification of railroads: Grand Central Station, 38; New York lines, 113, 116, 118; Pennsylvania Station, 40
electropolises, 14–20
elevated trains, New York, 19, 118
embellissement theory, 289, 291
Emerson, Peter Henry, 201
Emmerich, Paul, 151, 244, 253
Emperor William Memorial Church, 425, 487–88
Empire State Building, 336, 337–38, 339
End and Böckmann, 134
engineers, vs. architects, 49–50, 52, 55, 118–19, 237–38
English country houses, 150
English garden city planning movement, 83–84, 93–96, 266, 267–68
English garden tradition, 61, 72
English philanthropic housing, 267
Ensor, James, 192
Equitable Building (Graham, Anderson, Probst & White), 320, 323, 334
Equitable Life Assurance Company, 332
Erdmannsdorff, Friedrich Wilhelm von, 130
Erlach, Fischer von, 130
Ernst, Max, 344, 345
Eueders, Marie Elisabeth, 238
Europa-Center, 425, 487
European metropolises, compared to American, 490, 493
Evans-Clark, Phillip, observations, 496–98
existentialism, 461–62
Experiments in Art and Technology, 470–71
Exposition Universelle (Paris, 1889), 186
Expressionism, 189–90, 192, 335, 342, 343, 346, 347, 348–49, 351–52

F

Fagus Works (Benscheidt shoe last factory), 140
Fahrenkamp, Emil, 244, 260
Fair Lawn, N.J., 101
Falkenberg, 83, 86–91, 142
Falkenberg Festivals, 88–89
Fauvism, 342, 442
Federal Art Project, 362
Federal Theater Project, 364
Fehling, Hermann, 424
Ferdinand, Prince, 61
ferries, New York, 18, 33–34

Fetting, Rainer, 451; observations, 500–501; *Return of the Giants*, 452
Field, Hamilton Easter, 358
Fifth Avenue district, 414
Fintelmann, Ferdinand, 62
Fintelmann, Karl Frederick Simon, 62
Fire Island, 301
Fireland (Chausseestrasse), 51
Fischer, Samuel, 183
Five Points (New York), 161
Flagg, Ernest, 124, 173–74, 175, 266
Flatiron Building (Burnham), 318, 320
floor area ratios, 413–14
Fluxus movement, 442, 449
Force, Juliana, 358, 362
Ford, Henry, 23, 24, 102, 104, 220, 309
Forest Hills, 96
Form, Die (journal), 238
Förster, Paul, 83
Forster, William W., 291
Fort Washington Bridge, 45, 123
Fourier, Charles, 267
Frank, Adolf, 29, 30
Fränkel, Rudolf, 256
Frankfurt, 244
Frederick I, 59
Frederick II, 61; monument to, 130
Frederick William, Elector, 59
Frederick William I, 59
Frederick William II, 61, 130
Frederick William III, 62–64, 131
Frederick William IV, 134
Free Theater Association (Berlin), 183–84
Freie Strasse (journal), 347
Frey, Albert, 271, 273
Friedrich, Hugo, *The Structure of Modern Poetry*, 485
Friedrich Ebert-Siedlung large housing estate, 151
Friedrichshagen circle, 184, 187
Friedrichshain, 131
Friedrichstadt, 61
Friedrichstrasse, 52
Friedrich Wilhelm Strasse (Klingelhöferstrasse), 66
Friends of the South Street Seaport, 418
Fries, Heinrich de, 260
Fritsche, Johannes, observations, 227
Fuller Building. *See* Flatiron Building
Fulton, Robert, 34
Fulton Fish Market, 417, 418
functionalism, 399
Futurism, 202–3, 233, 315, 335, 342, 347

G

Gabo, Naum, 343, 449
Galerie Diogenes, 447
Galerie Franz, 444
Gallatin, A. E., 359–60
Gallery (Museum) of Living Art, 359–60
Gallery 291, 358
Garden Cities Association of America, 93, 94
garden city movement: Berlin, 139, 142; England, 83–84, 93–96, 266, 267–68; Germany, 81–91; New Jersey, 101–6; New York, 93–94, 96, 98–101, 106–7, 265–76; United States, 93–107
Garden City Zehlendorf, 151
gardens, English-style, 61, 72
Gardner, Isabella Stewart, 358
Gare d'Orsay, 19, 38
Gartenterrassenstadt, 141–42
Gay, Peter, *Weimar Culture*, 435

GE Building. *See* RCA Victor Building
Gecelli, Johannes, 449
Geddes, Patrick, 98
Geldzahler, Henry, 467
Gellert, Hugo, 361
Gemeinnützige Baugesellschaft Freie Scholle housing estate, 155, 157
Gemeinnützige Heimstätten Aktiengesellschaft (GEHAG), 157, 243, 244
Generalbesauungsplan (Berlin), 240–41
General Electric Company, 17, 28
gentrification, in New York, 415–17
Gentz, Heinrich, 130
Genzmer, Felix, 249
George Washington Bridge, 45, 123
Gerd Rosen Gallery, 442, 444
German Academic Exchange Service (DAAD), 449
German Expressionism, 346
German Garden City Association, 83, 85
German Opera House, 425
Germany: conceptions of America, 281–85; effects of Depression on, 245; garden city planning movement in, 81–91
Gessner, Albert, 142, 147, 149–50
Gibbs, Kenneth Gurney, *Business Architectural Imagery*, 333
Giedion, Sigfried, 232–34, 238, 411–12; *Mechanization Takes Command*, 485; *Space, Time, and Architecture*, 232–34, 240, 311
Gilbert, Cass, 45, 333
Gilbreth, Frank, 202
Gilly, David, 130
Gilly, Friedrich, 50
Gilpin, William, 72
Ginsberg, Allen, 463, 467
Ginsbern, Horace, 273
Girke, Raimund, 449
Glackens, William, 197, 198, 200
Gladden, Washington, 94
Gleisdreieck, rail junction at, 52
Godin, Jean Baptiste, 267
Goebbels, Joseph, 442
Goecke, Theodor, 85, 287
Goethe, Johann Wolfgang von, 62
Gogel, Daniel, 424
Goldhammer, Albert, 268
Goodhue, Bertram Grosvenor, 282
Goodman, Paul, *Growing Up Absurd*, 465–67
Gorky, Arshile, 460
Gosewitz, Ludwig, 449
Gotham Court, 161
Gottlieb, Adolph, 462
Gould, Elgin R. L., 98, 172
Graham, John, 364
Grand Central Depot, 36
Grand Central Parkway, 301–2
Grand Central Station, 19, 36–38, 113–14, 414
Grashorn, Burkhard, observations, 494–95
Grass, Günter, 445
Great Depression, 105–6, 245, 357, 360–61, 362, 364
Greater Berlin Nonprofit Building Cooperative, 86
Greater Berlin Settlement Association, 85
Greater New York Charter of 1897, 170
Greathead, James H., 19
Great Star (Grosser Stern), 59, 61, 482
Greenbelt towns (America), 231
Greenberg, Clement, 461
Greene, George S., Jr., 33, 34
greenhouses, 55
Green Houses (Gessner), 142, 147, 149
Green Party (Berlin), 184

Greenwich Village historic district, 415
Grenander, Alfred, 253, 254
gridiron layout, New York, 161–63, 265
Griscom, John H., 160
Grohmann, Will, 442, 445
Gropius, Walter, 22, 23, 24, 133, 134, 140, 234–35, 237, 238, 246, 353, 404, 438
Grossgörschen 35 artists' cooperative, 449, 451
Grosstadt, Hegemann's belief in, 292
Grosz, George, 320, 322, 342, 343, 344, 347, 348; *Eclipse of the Sun* and *Pillars of Society*, 354–55; *Republican Automatons*, 344
Group 67, 430
Gründerzeit, 183
Grützke, Johannes, 452
Guggenheim, Peggy, 461
Gurlitt, Fritz, art salon of, 188
Guston, Philip, 462
"Gutter Art" speech, of Wilhelm II, 188

H

Haacke, Hans, *The Freedom Fighters Were Here*, 471
Hacker, Dieter, 452
Haesler, Otto, 268
Haftmann, Werner, 442
Halbe, Max, 184
Halberstam, David, *The Powers That Be*, 437
Halpert, Edith, 358
Hamburg, 244
Hamburg Station, 47, 51–52, 57
Hämer, Hardt-Waltherr, 406, 427
Hansaviertel, 66–67, 399, 401, 425, 429
Hansson, Olaf, 184
happenings, 449, 464
Harden, Maximilian, 183
Harlem, gentrification of, 416
Harlem River bridges, 43, 45
Harlem River Houses, 273, 275
Harnisch, Otto, 147, 149
Hart, Heinrich, 81, 83, 184
Hart, Julius, 81, 89, 184
Haselhorst large housing estate, 151
Hassam, Childe, 195, 196
Hatfield, Robert G., 36
Hauptstadt Berlin competition, 396, 402
Hausmann, Raoul, 344, 345, 347
Haus Potsdam, 216, 218
Haus Vaterland, 211–13, 216–20
Havestadt & Contag, 249, 251
Haymarket Riot, 94
Heartfield, John, 343, 344, 345, 347
Heckel, Erich, 190, 192
Heckscher State Park, 299
Hefner-Alteneck, Friedrich, 29
Heftige Malerei (Vehement painting) exhibition, 451
Hegel, Georg Wilhelm Friedrich, 62
Hegemann, Werner, 146–47, 261, 285–93, 427; *American Architecture and Urban Planning*, 282; *American Vitruvius*, 290, 318
Heidelbergplan, 142
Heimann, Emanuel, 85
Heinisch, Barbara, 452
Heinrichs, Georg, 404, 429
Heins & LaFarge, 118
Heizer, Michael, 469
Hejduk, John, observations, 375

Heldt, Werner: *Parade of the Zeroes*, 442; *View from a Window with Dead Bird*, 444
Hellerau, 87
Hellersdorf housing estate, 475
Hell Gate Bridge, 43, 123, 299
Hempstead Lake, 301
Henri, Robert (Robert Henry Cozad), 196, 197–98, 200, 204
Henry Hudson Parkway, 301–2
Henselmann, Hermann, 399
Herder, Johann Gottfried, 62
Herpich building (Leipziger Strasse), 287–88
Herzfelde, Wieland, 343, 347
Hesse, Eva, 469
Heym, Georg, 192
Hielscher/Mügge, 430
High (Aqueduct) Bridge, 43
high-rise cities, mythology and monstrosity of, 315–27
Hilberseimer, Ludwig, 240, 255–56, 316; in Chicago Tribune Competition, 320, 322; *Grosstadtarchitektur*, 255; skyscraper design theory, 322–27
Hildebrand, Wilhelm, 43
Hille, Peter, 184
Hiller, Kurt, 192
Hillside Homes (Bronx), 268
Hine, Lewis, 198
Hirschfield, Christian Cay Lorenz, 62
historicity, in West Berlin, 423–32
historic preservation, in New York, 414–15
Hitchcock, Henry-Russell, 245, 268
Hither Hills, 301
Hitzig, Friedrich, 134
Hobrecht, James, 56–57, 131, 133, 249
Hobrecht Plan, 145, 147
Höch, Hannah, 344, 345, 442
Hoddis, Jakob van (Hans Davidsohn), 192
Hödicke, Karl-Horst, 451, 452
Hoeppener, Hugo (Fidus), 83
Hofer, Karl, 442, 445
Hoffmann, Franz, 253
Hoffmann, Ludwig, 134, 139, 152, 253, 254
Hofjäger, 61
Hofmann, Albert, 85
Hofmann, August Wilhelm von, 29
Hofmann, Hans, 364
Hofmann, Ludwig von, 186
Hofmann, Werner, 445
Hohenschönhausen housing estate, 475, 477
Hohenzollern Panorama, 55–56
Hohenzollerns, burial vault for, 134
Hohe Warte (journal), 83
Holleran, Leslie G., 125, 298
Holzbauer, Georg, 260
Hone, Philip, 159
Honisch, Dieter, 444
Höppener, Hugo (Fidus), 184
Hopper, Edward, 359
Hornbostel, Henry, 43
Hotel am Zoo, 425
housing: in Berlin, 22–27, 145–57, 241, 243–45, 256; in East Berlin, 475, 477; and new architecture, 238; in New York, 159–77, 245–46, 265–76, 312, 415–17
housing complexes, vs. housing estates, 157
Housing Study Guild, 271, 276
Howard, Ebenezer, 83, 93–96
Howe, George, 271
Hoynck, Rainer, observations, 502
Huckel, Samuel, Jr., 36
Hudson, Henry, 211

Hudson River, 18
Hudson River Railroad, 35
Huelsenbeck, Richard, 344, 347
Hufeisensiedlung, 23, 24, 243
Hufeland, Christoph Wilhelm, 62, 63
Huttenstrasse building (Behrens), 24
Hutton, William R., 43
Huxtable, Ada Louise, 439

I

Ihne, Ernst Eberhard von, 134
immigrants, in New York, 171–72, 197
Imperial German Embassy (Leningrad), 140
Impressionism, 188, 346
Independent Subway System (IND), 119
industrial age: architecture of, 47; in Berlin, 50–51, 130–31, 139–40; New York as symbol of, 231, 238
industrialization: and Americanization, 315; influence on new architecture, 238; uses of, in new architecture, 234–37
industrial revolution: in Berlin, 182; first, 13; second, 13–14, 27
Interbau competition, 399
Interborough Rapid Transit (IRT), 118–19
International Building Exposition (IBA) (Berlin), 390, 393, 406–7, 432
Internationales Congress Centrum (ICC), 429
International Exhibition of Modern Art (Armory Show), 203
internationalism, 212–13, 218, 222
International Style, 22, 24, 30, 282; Museum of Modern Art exhibition (1932), 435
Intimate Gallery, 358
inventors: Berlin, 28–30; New York, 27–29
Israel, Jozef, 185
Israel, Richard, 188
Italian architecture, 289

J

Jaar, Alfredo, 471–72; *A Logo for Americans*, 472; *This Is Not America*, 472
Jackman, Stephen E., 214
Jacob Riis Park, 301
Jacobs, Charles M., 19
Jacobs, Jane, 386; *Death and Life of Great American Cities*, 276, 439
Jakobowitz, Georg, 256
Jansen, Hermann, 142, 249; plan of 1910, 477
Jatzow, Paul, 141–42
Jawlensky, Alexey, 190
Jedlicka, Gotthard, 442
Jervis, John B., 35, 43
Jews, in Germany, 183
John Reed Club, 361–62
Johns, Jasper, 463
Johnson, Lester, 465
Johnson, Philip, 245, 246, 268, 414
Jones Beach, 298, 301, 310
Jordan, Wilhelm, 187
Journal of the American Institute of Architects (JAIA), 98
Joyce, James, *Ulysses*, 462
Judd, Donald, 467
Jung, Carl, 462
Jung, Franz, 347
Jungfern Bridge, 48
Justi, Ludwig, 188

K

Kahn, Albert, 306
Kaiser, Heinrich, 253
Kaiser-Friedrich-Museum (Bode Museum), 134
Kaisergalerie, 129
Kaiser Wilhelm National Memorial, 188
Kallmann & McKinnell, 386
Kampffmeyer, Bernhard, 81, 83, 89
Kampffmeyer, Hans, 84, 89
Kandinsky, Vassily, 190
Kant, Immanuel, 62
Kaprow, Allan, 449, 464
Kaufman, Louis G., 338
Kaulbach, W., 134
Kaus, Max, 442
Kayser and Von Groszheim, 134, 155
Keller & Reiner, 188
Kempinski firm, 216, 220
Kendall, Edward H., 43
Kent, Rockwell, 362
Kent, William, 72
Kerouac, Jack, 463
Kessler, Harry Graf, 183
Kienholz, Edward, 451
Kingsport, Tenn., 94
Kirchner, Ernst Ludwig, 188, 190, 192, 342, 347
Kleihues, Josef Paul, 390, 393, 429
Klein, Alexander, 253
Klüver, Billy, 470–71
Knickerbocker Village, 268
Knight, Richard Payne, 72
Knobelsdorff, Georg Wenzeslaus von, 61, 130
Knoblauch, Eduard, 134
Koberling, Bernd, 451
Koeber, G., 66
Koetter, Fred, 393
Kohn, Robert J., 98, 266, 268
Kohtz, Otto, 252–53
Kokoschka, Oskar, 190, 342, 347, 445
Kollhoff, Hans, 432, 478
Kollwitz, Käthe, 184
Königsplatz, 66, 69, 131
Kraffert, Hans, 253
Kreis, Wilhelm, 260
Kreuzberg, 487–88
Kreuzberg group, 455
Krier, Bob, 430
Kriester, Rainer, 447
Kroll's Restaurant (Berlin), 66, 69
Kronau, Leo, 216, 220
Kropotkin, Piotr, 83
Kuhn, Walt, 203
Kummer, Raimund, 455
Kuniyoshi, Yasuo, 359
Kurfürstendamm, 136, 145
Kyllmann and Heyden, 134

L

Lacan, Jacques, 473
Ladies' Mile historic district, 415
La Guardia, Fiorello, 309
laissez-faire, vs. social control, in New York, 159–60
Landauer, Gustav, 81, 184
land reform, and garden city planning movement, 84
landscape architecture, 61, 62, 72, 74
Landwehr Canal, 51, 64, 67, 131, 136
Lang, Fritz, 332
Langhans, Carl Gotthard, 61, 130
Lasker-Schüler, Else, 190
Lawson, Ernest, 200
Leary, Timothy, 467

Le Corbusier, 22, 24, 140, 238, 253, 271, 275–76, 291–92, 315, 332, 438–39
Leeuwen, Thomas van, 332
Léger, Fernand, 345
Leistikow, Walter, 184, 186, 187
L'Enfant, Charles, 385–86
Lenné, Peter Josef, 51, 57, 62–64, 66–67, 131, 133, 249
Le Nôtre, Andre, 72
Leo, Ludwig, 429
Lescaze, William, 271, 273, 306
Letchworth, 87, 94
Lever House, 413
Levittown, 104
Lewishamstrasse housing complex, 430, 432
Liberator (journal), 361
Lichtenstein, Roy, 467
Liebeg, Justus, 29
Liebermann, Max, 184, 185–86
Liebknecht, Kurt, 401
Liebnitz, Robert, 155
Lietzenburger Strasse housing complex, 430, 432
light, in New York tenements, 160–61, 163–64, 173–75
light wells, 149–50
Lilienthal, Gustav, 157
Lilienthal, Otto, 157
limited dividend housing, 98–99, 106, 265–66
Lincoln Center, 309
Lincoln Square Urban Renewal Area, 416
Lindengalerie, 129–30
Lindenthal, Gustav, 41, 43, 45, 121, 123, 299
Lissitzky, El, 343
Litchfield, Electus, 271, 275
Little Galleries of the Photo- Secession (Stieglitz and Steichen), 201
Lixfield, Elke, 455
Loewe, Ludwig, 139
Loewensohn, Erwin, 192
Loewy, Raymond, 306
Long Island Rail Road, 19, 35
Los Angeles, mass transit in, 311
Lower East Side, gentrification of, 416
Luckhardt, Hans, 244, 253, 258
Luckhardt, Wassili, 244, 253, 258
Luckman, Charles, 125
Luisenplatz, 432
Luisenstadt district, 406
Luisenstädtische Canal, 131
Luks, George, 197, 198, 200
Luna Park (New York), 211–12, 214, 216, 220
Lunapark (Berlin), 212, 216
Lüpertz, Markus, 447, 452; *Dithyrambic Manifesto*, 451; *Dithyrambs*, 446
Luther Bridge, 64
Lützowstrasse Situations, 455
Lux, Joseph August, 83
Lynes, Russell, *The Tastemakers*, 460
Lyon, Henriette, 83

M

Macbeth Galleries, 200
machine-aesthetic, 238
machines:and dadaism, 347; and new architecture, 234–37
Mächler, Martin, 254–55, 256; plan for Berlin, 251
Mackay, John Henry, 184
MacKaye, Benton, 97–98
Madison Square Garden (Luckman), 125

Madison Square Terminal, 34–35
Magic Realism, 343, 344, 345, 348, 446
Mailer, Norman, *The White Negro*, 462
Manet, Edouard, 185
Mang, Rainer, 455
Mangoldt, Karl von, 85
Manhattan Bridge, 20, 41, 121, 123
Mannesmann pipe plant (Düsseldorf), 140
Manship, Paul, 362
Marc, Franz, 190
March, Otto, 155
Märchenbrunnen fountain, 139
Marcuse, Herbert, 467
Marey, E. J., 202
Marholm, Laura, 184
Marin, John, 202–3
Mark Brandenburg, 139
Markgraffenstrasse, 17
Märkisches Museum, 139
Märkisches Viertel, 404–5, 425
Marschall Bridge, 48
Marsh, Reginald, 359, 362
Martin, Homer D., 196
Marzahn housing estate, 475
mass culture, 437–39
Masses, The (socialist journal), 200–201, 204, 207
mass production, for housing, 23–24
mass transit, 305, 311, 312
Matulka, Jan, 364
May, Ernst, 22, 23, 237, 240, 243, 268
Mayer, Albert, 271
Mayer, Hannes, 237
McAlpine, William J., 43
McGraw-Hill Company, 338
McKim, Mead & White, 19, 38, 113–14, 116, 323, 333
McLuhan, Marshall, 467
McMahon, Audrey, 364
Mebes, Paul, 142, 150–52, 244, 253
Mehring, Walter, 347
Meidner, Ludwig, 190, 192, 342
Meier-Graefe, Julius, 187
Meisner, Günter, 451
Mendelsohn, Erich, 253, 254, 255, 256, 260, 261, 287–88; *Amerika*, 282, 284, 318; *Amerika, Bilderbuch eines Architekten*, 240
Menzel, Adolf, 134, 136, 182
Merkel, Hermann W., 125
Merleau-Ponty, M., 462
Merz, Mario, 451
Messel, Alfred, 134, 139, 147, 152–55, 327, 425
Messer, Thomas, observations, 226
Metropolitan Board of Health, New York, 167
Metropolitan Museum of Art, 195, 357
metropolitan squares (Berlin), 258–61
Metzel, Olaf: *13.4.1981*, 455, 457; *Olympian Art*, 457
Meyer, Adolf, 140, 253
Meyers, Jerome, 198
Meyers Hof, 145
Michaelis Garten, 61
Michael Werner–Benjamin Katz Gallery, 446
Middendorf, Helmut, 451, 452
Mies van der Rohe, Ludwig, 24, 50, 140, 238, 253, 254, 258, 318, 322–27
Mietskaserne, 22, 133, 145–57
Mietvilla (rented villa), 155
Mills, C. Wright, 462
minimum-existence flat, 91
Mitchell-Lama Slum Prevention Law, 415–16
Moabit district (Berlin), 57, 59, 61

modernism, 181–92; in American architecture, 282; Hegemann's resistance to, 292–93; in New York art world, 357, 364–65; in New York housing, 268, 271, 276; popularity of, 360; vs. realists, 196, 201, 203, 208; social content of, 197
modernity, definition of, 407–8
Moest, Walter, 395
Möhring, Bruno, 52, 249, 252, 253
Moisieff, Leon, 123
Moldenschardt, Hans Heinrich, 405
Moltke Bridge, 64
Mommsen, Theodor, 182
Montauk Point, 301
Moore, Charles, 432
Morand, Paul, 327
Morgan, J. P., 17
Moritzplatz gallery, 451–52
Morris, Robert, 468–69
Moser, Karl, 271
Moses, Bella, 297
Moses, Emanuel, 297
Moses, Robert, 76, 79, 118, 222, 297–98, 299–312, 411
Moskowitz, Belle, 297
Motherwell, Robert, 459, 462
Mühsam, Erich, 89
Müller, Hans-Christian, 404
Müller, Jan, 465
Müller, Otto, 189
Mumford, Lewis, 97–98, 231, 268, 362, 365, 415; *Brown Decades, The*, 333; *City in History, The*, 490; *Sticks and Stones*, 282
Munch, Edvard, 186–87
Municipal Art Commission, 121, 123
Municipal Building (McKim, Mead & White), 323
Münter, Gabriele, 190
Murnau, Friedrich Wilhelm, *Sunrise*, 254
Museum Island, Berlin, 134
Museum of Modern Art, 360; "Art of Assemblage" exhibition (1961), 467; International Style exhibition (1932), 435; mass culture and, 437; 1936 Exhibition, 365; symposium on modern architecture (1948), 292–93
museums, as vital forces in cities, 488, 490, 493
Muthesius, Hermann, 141, 149, 155
Muybridge, Eadweard, 202

N

Nabokov, Vladimir, 343
Nalen, John, 94
Napoleonic Wars, 62, 131
National Association of Building Owners and Managers, 336–37
National Gallery (Berlin), 187–88
National Monument to Emperor Wilhelm I, 139
National Wildlife Federation, 97
naturalism, 181, 183
Nazi-Soviet Pact of August 1939, 365
neighborhood block housing, New York, 265–76
neighborhoods, 96, 265
neoclassicism, 131, 141
"Neo-Pathetic Cabaret" (Berlin poetry readings), 192
neosurrealism, in Berlin, 442
Neptune Fountain, 136
neue Frankfurt, Das (journal), 238
neue Gemeinschaft. See New Community
Neue Jugend (journal), 347
Neue Pathos, Das (journal), 190
Neuer See (New Lake), 64

Neue Sachlichkeit, 343–46, 348–53, 399
neues Bauen. See new architecture
Neuhaus, Friedrich, 51
Neumann, J. B., 358
Neumann, Max, 452
Neutra, Richard, 271, 282
New American Building exhibition, 281–82
new architecture, 232–38; in America, 282; in Berlin, 244–45; forms of, 238–40; in New York, 245–46, 268, 271; post-World War I, 237–38; and social reform, 241, 243–44; and urban and town planning, 240–41
New Art Circle, 358
New Club (Berlin), 192
New Community, 81, 83, 85
New Fauves, 442, 451, 452
New Gallery, Inc., 358
New Jersey: garden city movement in, 101–6; railroads, 35
New Masses (journal), 361
New National Gallery, Berlin, 50
New Objective Realism, 343
New People's Free Theater (Berlin), 184
News Building (Howells and Hood), 335, 338
New Secession, 189
New Society of Artists, 358
New York: ad hoc development of, 389–90, 411–15; architectural styles, 30–31; art world in, 195–208, 357–65, 459–73; bridges, 40–45, 119; compared to Berlin as center/city, 481–93; district controls in, 414–15; egalitarian design in, 386; garden city movement, 93–94, 96, 98–101, 106–7, 265–76; gridiron layout, 161–63; housing, 159–77, 245–46, 265–76, 312, 415–17; interwar years, 357–65; inventors in, 27–30; lower Manhattan restructuring, 417–21; midtown redevelopment project, 412–15; as mythological icon, 315–16, 318; new architecture in, 245–46; peripheral location of, 481–82; post-Civil War, 195–96; post-World War I, 106–7; post-World War II, 386, 389, 459–73; railroads, 34–40, 113, 116, 118; railroad stations, 36–40; real estate interests/greed in, 386, 389; skyscrapers of, effect on post-war European architecture, 315–16; subways, 19, 20, 118–19, 125; as symbol of modernity, 231, 238; as technological metropolis, 13–15, 30–31; transportation systems, 18–20, 34–40, 111–25; turn-of-the-century, 111, 113; urban planning in, 386, 389, 411–12, 414; waterfront, 33–34, 417–21
New York and Harlem Railroad, 34–35
New York and New Haven Railroad, 35
New York Aquarium, 222
New York Association for the Improvement of the Condition of the Poor, 98
New York Central Railroad, 35
New York City Department of Docks, 33
New York City Housing Authority, 245; 1934 competition, 271, 273
New York City Landmark Commission, 414–15
New York City Planning Commission, 245
New York Connecting Railroad, 43
New York Film Festival, 470
New York Hilton, 414

New York Pubic Library, 41
New York Sanitary Reform Society, 169
New York School, 460, 461
New York State Housing Law of 1926, 268
New York University, 359–60
New York Zoning Law of 1916, 334
Nichols, Othiel F., 41
Niederschönhausen housing complex, 150
Niemeyer, Oscar, 306
Nietzsche, Friedrich, 84
Nolde, Emil, 189
Nollendorf-Casino, 181
Nollendorfplatz, 55
Northern State Parkway, 299
Novembergruppe, 342–43

O

Ocean Parkway, 301
October (journal), 472–73
Odeum, 61
Oldenburg, Claes, 463, 464, 467
Old Law Tenements, 168, 176
Olmsted, Frederick Law, 71–76, 79, 116–17, 123–24, 195
Olympic Tower, 414
1/61 Gallery, 455
Onkel-Toms-Huette housing development, 24, 243
Oppenheimer, Franz, 83
ornament and decoration: Hilberseimer's elimination of, 320, 322, 323; prefabricated, in Berlin, 133–34
Orozco, José Clemente, 362
Otis Elevator Company, 28
Otto, Adolf, 83
Ovaska, Arthur, 432

P

Palmer & Hornbostel, 121, 123, 125
Palucca, Gret, 89
Pan (journal), 181, 187
Pan Am Building, 413, 414
Pandämonium manifesto, 446, 447
panoramas, 55
Paris, 13; art in, 185, 344–46
Park Avenue, 412–13
Park Belvedere, 416
Parker, Berry, 83–84, 87
parkway system (New York), 299–302, 411
Parsons, Betty, 461
Parsons, William Barclay, 20, 118
Pathetiker, Die, 190, 192
Paul Gerhard Church, 424
Paul Laurence Dunbar Apartments, 267
Peace Tower, 467
Pechstein, Max, 189, 442
Pennsylvania Hotel (McKim, Mead & White), 323
Pennsylvania Railroad, 19
Pennsylvania Station, 19, 35, 38, 40, 113, 114–16
Peoples Art Guild, 361
People's Free Theater (Berlin), 89, 184
Pergamon Museum, 134, 139
Perry, Lila Cabot, 196
Petersen, Richard, 249
Pevsner, Antoine, 343
Pfamfert, Franz, 190
philanthropic housing, New York, 176, 265–66
Philharmonic Hall (Berlin), 61, 425
Phipps Gardens, 268
photographers, in New York, 198

Picabia, Francis, 196, 204, 207; *Ici, c'est ici Stieglitz*, 204
Picasso, Pablo, 342, 345
piers, New York, 33–34
pittura metafisica, 344, 345, 347
Pitz, Hermann, 455
Planning Collective No. 1, 429, 430
Planungsgruppe Potsdam, 477
Platz der Republik, redesign of, 260–61
Plumber and Sanitary Engineer (magazine), 168–69
Pods, Reinhard, 455
Poelzig, Hans, 253, 254, 255, 260
Pollack, Jackson, 437, 461
Pop Art, 437, 446, 467
populist movement, New York, 171–72
Porsche, Ferdinand, 309
porte-cochère, 124, 173
Post-Expressionism, 348
Post-Impressionism, 357
Potsdamer Platz, 260
Potsdam Station, 260
poverty, in New York, 159–76
Prendergast, Maurice, 196, 200
Price, Thomas, 161
Price, Uvedale, 72
production, vs. consumption, 437
progressive reform movement, 198, 208
Prospect Park, 195
public art, 471–72
public health, 160
public recreation and entertainment, in cities, 211–22
public space/private space design, in skyscrapers, 333–34, 336
Public Works Administration (PWA), 268
Public Works of Art Project (PWAP), 362
Pullman Strike, 94
Pulvermühlengelände, 57
Puni, Iwan, 343; *Musician, The*, 343

Q

Qassowski, L., 133
Quebec Bridge, 20
Queens (New York), development of, 99–100
Queensboro Bridge, 20, 41, 43, 121, 123, 299
Queensbridge Houses, 273, 275–76
Quergalerie, 455
Quinn, John, 357, 358, 359

R

Raczynski Palace, 66
Radburn housing complex, 101–6, 268
Rading, Adolf, 256
Rahmann, Fritz, 455
railroad flats, 164
railroads: in America, 18, 311; in Berlin, 51–55, 131, 136; in New York, 18–20, 34–40, 113–18; urban, 17–20
railroad stations: Berlin, 51–52; New York, 36–40
Rappold, Otto, *Der Bau der Wolkenkratzer*, 252
Raschdorff, Julius, 136
Raskob, John J., 338
Rathenau, Emil, 15, 17, 139, 183
Rathenau, Walter, 183, 284
rationalization of construction, 235, 237
Rauch, Christian Daniel, 130
Raue, Peter, 444
Rauschenberg, Robert, 463–64

Ray, Man, 206, 359; *Rope Dancer Accompanies Herself with Her Shadow, The*, 206
Raymond, George W., 38
RCA Tower, 339
RCA Victor Building (GE Building) (Cross & Cross), 335, 339
Rea, Samuel, 38
realist artists, 196, 197, 198, 200, 201, 203, 208; space-time concerns of, 202–4, 233–34
recessed perimeter block housing projects, New York, 267–76
Reconstruction Finance Corporation (RFC), 268
Reconstruction Plan (Berlin), 396
Red Hook housing project, 273, 275–76
Reed, Charles, 38
Reed, John, 208
Reed & Stem, 38, 113–14
Refregier, Anton, 361
Regional Art Commission (Berlin), 187, 188
Regional Planning Association of America (RPAA), 97–101, 106–7, 245, 268
Reichsforschung-gesellschaft (Rfg), 238
Reichstag Building, Berlin, 260–61, 482
Reinhardt-Bühne, 89
Reis, Philipp, 17
renovation, vs. demolition, 427, 429
representational art, 444–46
Repton, Humphrey, 72
Reuter, Joseph, 253
Reynolds, William H., 216
Rheinsberg, Raphael, 455
Rhode, Gilbert, 306
Richards Kaffeegarten (Kempers Hof), 61
Riehmer (Hofgarten designer), 141
Riesler, Walter, 238
Riesman, David, *The Lonely Crowd*, 462
Riis, Jacob, 161, 171, 198
Ring group, 238, 254, 255
riots, in New York, 165–67
Ritter, Wilhelm, 298
Ritterstrasse housing complex, 430, 432
Rivera, Diego, 361
Riverbend Houses, 276
River Gardens, 271, 273
Riverside Drive, 116–18
Riverside Park, 116–18
roadways, New York, 123–25
Robert Fulton Memorial, 117
Robert Moses Massena Power Dam, 309
Robinson, Theodore, 196
Rockefeller, John D., 105
Rockefeller, Mrs. John D., 360
Rockefeller Center, 310, 338, 389, 411–12
Rockefeller family, New York properties, 386
Roebling, John Augustus, 40
Roebling, Washington, 40, 121
Roemerstadtsiedlung, 238
Roh, Franz, 348
Rohling, Gerd, 455
rookery dwellings, New York, 160–61
Roosevelt, Theodore, 171, 203–4
Rosenberg, Adolf, 186, 461
Rosenquist, James, 467
Rossi, Aldo, *L'Architettura della città*, 405
Rosz, Martin, 452, 455
Roters, Eberhard, 445
Roud, Richard, 470
Rouse Company, 420
Rousseau, Henri, 345

Rousseau, Jean-Jacques, monument to, 61
Rowe, Colin, 393
Royal Iron Foundry, 51, 131
Rudolf-Virchow-Hospital, 139
Russell, John, observations, 225
Russolo, Luigi, 190
Ruttmann, Walter, *Berlin, Symphonie einer Grosstadt*, 254

S

Sachs, Paul J., 360
St. Norbert's Church, 424
St. Pancras Station, 233
St. Patrick's Cathedral, 487
Salomé (Wolfgang Cilarz), 451, 452
Salon, Berlin, 182
Salon, Paris, 185
Salon of America, 358
Salzmann, Georg, 253
San Remo cafe, 460, 462
Santarossa, Hella, 452
Sargent, John Singer, 196
Sartre, Jean-Paul, 462, 463
Sassen, Saskia, observations, 503
Sawade, Jürgen, 430
Sax, Ursula, 447
Schad, Christian, 344, 345, 351
Schadow, Gottfried, 130
Schaefer, Heinrich, 244
Schamberg, Morton, 207; *God*, 207
Schapiro, Meyer, 361, 362, 365, 461
Scharoun, Hans, 24, 253, 254, 256, 395, 396, 402, 423
Scheffler, Karl, 316, 320; *Die Architektur der Grosstadt*, 261
Schermerhorn Row, 418
Schiller, Friedrich, 62
Schillerpark complex, 142
Schinkel, Karl Friedrich, 47, 48, 50, 55, 57, 131, 134, 323–24, 327
Schinkel Pavilion, 432
Schklovsky (artist), 343
Schlangenbader Strasse residential complex, 429
Schlemmer, Oskar, 353–54; *Paracelsus - The Legislator*, 354
Schlenther, Paul, 183
Schlichter, Rudolf, 344; *Roof Atelier*, 344
Schmidt-Rottluff, Karl, 188, 190, 192, 442
Schmieden, Heino, 133, 134
Schmit, Tomas, 449
Schmitthenner, Paul, 142, 260
Schmitz, Bruno, 155, 249, 251, 252
Schneider, Charles C., 43
Schön, Eva-Maria, 452
Schönebeck, Eugen, 451; *Pandämonium* manifesto, 446
Schöneberg Harbor, 51
Schöneberg housing complex, 150, 151
Schöneberg meadow, 67
Schrimpf, Georg, 346
Schule der neuen Prächtigkeit, 452
Schüler, Ralph, 429
Schüler-Witte, Ursulina, 429
Schultze, Bernard, 445
Schuyler, Montgomery, 116, 121
Schwarzes Ferkel, 181, 187
Schwarzkopff company, 182
Schwatlo, Carl, 134
Schwechten, Franz, 136, 216
Schwedler, J. W., 50, 55
Schwieger, Heinrich, 52
Schwitters, Kurt, 322, 347
Science Center (Berlin), 432
Scorsese, Martin, *Taxi Driver*, 490
Seagram Building, 413, 435

Sea Lion Park, 211, 214
Secession, 186
Sedan Panorama (Alexanderplatz Station), 55
Sedlmayr, Hans, 442, 493
See, Milton, 117
Segal, George, 464
segregated housing, and garden city movement, 104
self-contained cities (Howard). *See* garden city movement
Sello, Christian Ludwig Samuel, 61
Sert, Jose Luis, *Can Our Cities Survive*, 311
7 Produzentengalerie, 452
Severini, Gino, 190
sewage systems, Berlin, 56
Shinn, Everett, 197, 198, 200
Short, R. Thomas, 174
Shreve, Richmond, 273
Shultz and Simmons, *Offices in the Sky*, 336
Sickingenstrasse housing complex (Berlin-Wedding), 152, 155
Siedler, Eduard Jobst, 253, 256, 260
Siedler, Wolf Jobst, *The Assassinated City*, 405
Siedlungen (housing settlements), 22–23, 24, 244, 265
Siegesallee, 139
Siemens, George, 17
Siemens, Werner, 17–18, 28–29, 52
Siemens & Halske, 15, 17, 29, 52, 55, 183
Siemensstadt housing development, 24, 243
Simmel, Georg, 255; *Big Cities and Intellectual Life*, 255, 485
simulacrum art, 473
Sitte, Camillo, 84, 287, 324
Situations 60, 447
Sixties, The, 465–70
60 Wall Tower, 336
site-specific sculpture, 471
Skarbina, Franz, 186
Skoda, Claudia, observations, 224
skyscrapers: American, history of, 332–39; definition of, 331–32; economic impact of, 336–39; Germanization of, in Berlin, 251–54; as symbols, 315–16, 318, 320, 322–27
Slaby, Adolf, 29
Sloan, John, 196, 197, 198, 200, 204, 208
Smith, Alfred E., 98, 297
Smith, Henry Atterbury, 174
Smith, Stephen, 171
Smithson, Robert, *Spiral Jetty*, 468
Smokeless City housing estate (Steglitz), 151
Snook, John B., 36
SO-36 district (Berlin), 406
social classes: bourgeoisie vs. aristocracy, in Berlin, 182–83; intermixing of, in New York, 159–60
Social Democratic Party, 22, 84
socialism, 22, 200–201
socialist realism, 396, 399
social reform: and architecture in America, 245–46; garden city movement as means to, 84, 86, 94, 104; and new architecture, 241, 243–44
social unrest, in New York, 165–67, 361–65
Société Anonyme, 358, 359
Society of Friends and Young Artists (New York), 208
Society of Independent Artists, 206–7, 358
Soeder, August, 254

SoHo, 470
SoHo/Cast-Iron historic district, 415
Soil, The (journal), 206
Somervell, Brehon, 364
Sophie-Charlottenpark complex, 142
Sörgel, Herman, 327
Southern State Parkway, 298, 299
South Street Seaport, 418, 420, 439
Soyer, Raphael, 361
space design, effect on human psyche, 84
Spaces exhibition (Büro Berlin gallery), 455
space-time concerns, of modernist and realist artists, 202–4, 233–34
Speer, Albert, 251, 253, 261–62
Spengler, Oswald, 231
Sperry, Elmer, 27
Sperry Gyroscope Company, 27
Sprague, Frank Julian, 27, 28, 38
Sprague Electric Elevator Company, 28
Sprague Electric Railway and Motor Company, 28
Springer, Rudolf, 444
Springsteen, George, 268
Spuyten Duyvil and Port Morris Railroad, 36
Stadtbahn (S-Bahn), 52, 136
Stadthaus, Berlin, 139
Staff, Franz, 260
Stahl-Urach, Carl, 218
Stalinallee, 396, 399, 401
standardization, 235
Starin, John, 34
State Charities Aid Association, 98
State Park Plan for New York (Moses), 298
steel construction, 50
Steeplechase, 211–12, 214, 220
Steglitz housing complex, 150
Steichen, Edward, 201, 204, 207; *Flatiron Evening*, 320
Stein, Clarence, 98, 99–100, 266, 267, 268
Stein-Hardenberg reforms, 131
Steinway tunnel, New York, 20
Stella, Joseph, 196, 202, 207
Stern, Allen, 38
Stern, Henry J., 79
Stettenheim, Julius, 183
Stieglitz, Alfred, 196–97, 201–2, 203, 204, 206, 207, 358; *Flatiron, The*, 197; *Steerage, The*, 197
Stirling, James, 432
Stock Exchange, Berlin, 134
Stöhrer, Walter, 447
Stokes, I. N. Phelps, 175, 266
Stoughton, Charles, 125
Strack, Johann Heinrich, 134
Straumer, Heinrich, 253
stream-of-consciousness, 202
street courtyards, 149–50
Strindberg, August, 184, 187
Strong, Josiah, 94
Stüler, Friedrich August, 134
Sturm, Der (journal), 181, 190
Sturm Gallery, 190
Stuttgart, 244
Stuyvesant Town, 415
suburbs, Berlin, 139
subways, New York, 19, 20, 118–19, 125
Sullivan, Louis Henry, 281
Sullivan, Mrs. Cornelius J., 360
Sulzer, Johann Georg, 62
Sunken Meadow, 301
Sunnyside Gardens, 100–101, 105, 268
superblocks (garden cities), 102–4
Superdadaism, 344
Surrealism, 344, 442, 446

Susman, Warren I., *Culture and History*, 467
Suvero, Mark di, 467
Suzuki (Zen theorist), 463
Sweeney, James Johnson, 460
Synthetic Cubism, 343
Szymanski, Rolf, 447

T

TAC II plan, 404
Tappert, Georg, 189
Taronescher Kaffeegarten, 61
Tatlin, Vladimir, 331
Taut, Bruno, 22, 23, 24, 86–91, 142, 157, 240, 243, 253
Taut, Max, 237, 253; *Die neue Wohnung*, 235
Tautz, Paul Robert, 83
Taylor, Frederick W., 23, 202, 220
Taylorism, 235
Teague, Walter Dorwin, 306; *Design This Day*, 311
Tegel Harbor apartment complex, 432
Teichmanns Blumengarten, 61
Teltow, 69
Teltow Canal, 136
Tenement House Act of 1867, 167
Tenement House Act of 1879, 168, 169
Tenement House Act of 1901 (New Law), 175–76
Tenement House Committee: report of 1884, 170; report of 1894, 172
Tenement House Law, 161
tenement housing: New York, 161–76; origin of term, 163
Tent Place, 61, 69
ter Hell (Berlin artist), 447
Terminal City (Grand Central Station, New York), 114
terra-cotta facades, in Berlin, 133–34, 134
Tesla, Nikola, 27–28
Tessenow, Heinrich, 87, 256
Thieler, Fred, 446–47
13 E: Eleven Artists Working in Berlin exhibition (Whitechapel Gallery, London), 451–52
Thirty Years War, 59
Thomas, Andrew J., 266–67
Thomas Garden Apartments, 267
Thompson, Benjamin, 437–38, 439
Thompson, Frederic, 214
Throg's Neck Bridge, 45, 305
Tiergarten, 58–69, 131, 482
Times Square, restructuring of, 414
Times Square Center, 414
Titz, Eduard, 134
Todt, Fritz, 309–10
Tönnies, Ferdinand, 84
Toulouse-Lautrec, Henri, 187
Towle, Hubert Ladd, 124
town houses, Berlin, 147, 155
traffic: congestion, road building as cause of, 305; and redesign of metropolitan squares in Berlin, 258–61
trans-avant-garde art (postmodern), in Berlin, 451
Transportation and Building Museum, 52
transportation systems: Berlin, 254–55; New York, 18–20, 34–40, 111–25
Treasury Department Section of Painting and Sculpture, 362
Treasury Relief Art Project, 362
Tribeca, 420
Triborough Bridge, 45, 301, 302
Triborough Bridge Authority (TBA), 302
Trier, Hann, 446, 447

Trökes, Heinz, 442
Trump, Donald, 416
Trump Tower, 414
Tryon, Dwight W., 196
Tschudi, Hugo von, 184, 187–88
Tugwell, Rexford, 411
tunnels, railway, 19–20
Turmhaus (tower building), 316
Twachtman, John Henry, 196
Tweed administration (New York), 168
291 (journal), 204
type forms (Le Corbusier), 235

U

U-Bahn, 55, 136
Uhlmann, Hans, 444
Ulbricht, Walter, 396
Unemployed Artists' Group, 361
Ungers, O. M., 478
Unglaube, Felix, 260
uniform block frontage design, 324, 327
Unité, 425
United Nations, 412
United States. *See* America
Universal Pictures Building, 413
University Heights Bridge, 43, 45
University of Berlin, 29
Unter den Linden, 129–30; redesign of, 253, 288–89
Unwin, Raymond, 83–84, 87, 267–68
Upper East Side historic district, 415
Upper West Side, urban renewal of, 415–17
Urban Design Group, 439
urban planning and design: autocratic impulse in, 385; in Berlin, 56–57, 249, 251, 255–56, 395–408, 475–78; egalitarian city vision, 385–93; and garden city planning movement, 83–84, 86; in Germany, 47–48, 475–78; Hegemann's notions of, 285–93; and new architecture, 240–41; in New York, 386, 389, 411–21; post–World War I, 47–48; post–World War II, 386, 389, 395–408
urban street blocks, 265
Urbino, urban design of, 385

V

Valley Stream, 301
Vanderbilt, Cornelius, 35
Vanderbilt, William K., 114
van de Velde, Henry, 140–41
Van Eesteren, Cor, 253, 288–89
Vaux, Calvert, 71–76
Vedova, Emilio, *Plurimi di Berlino*, 451
Veiller, Lawrence, 174, 175
ventilation, in tenements, 160–61, 164–65, 173–75
Venturi, Robert, 386, 439
Venus Basin (Goldfish Pond), 61
Verists, 343, 344, 345, 348
Verrazano Narrows Bridge, 45, 125, 305
Vienna, 13
Vietnam War, 470
villa colonies, Berlin, 136
Village, The (journal), 94
Viollet-le-Duc, E. E., 123
Virchow, Rudolf, 182
Vitruvius, 488
Vogel, Hermann Wilhelm, 201
Volksgarten (Hirschfeld), 62
Von der Hude and Hennicke, 134
Vostell, Wolf, 449
Vroman, Guy, 125

W

Wachweger, Thomas, 452
Waesemann, F. A., 133
Wagner, Martin, 22–24, 240–41, 244, 246, 253, 254, 255, 258, 260
Wagner, Robert, 415–16
Wagner Housing Act of 1937, 245, 275
Walden, Herwarth, 190
Wallot, Paul, 136, 260
Ware, James, 168, 173–74
Warhol, Andy, 467
Warren, Whitney, 114
Warren and Wetmore, 38
Wart, John S. Van, 268
Washington, D. C., 385–86
Washington (Harlem) Bridge, 43
Washington Market (New York), 417, 420
Washington Square (New York), 267
waterfront development, New York, 33–34, 417–21. *See also* Battery Park City; South Street Seaport
waterways, Berlin, 51
Watson, Forbes, 358, 359
Weber, Alfred, 442
Weber, Max, 196, 202, 204, 207; *Chinese Restaurant*, 204; *New York*, 204; *Rush Hour*, 204
Weimar, 353–54
Weimar Republic, 23, 341–55
Weinberg, Robert C., 291
Weinert, Erich, 89
Weir, Julian Alden, 195
Weisbachgruppe housing complex, 152
Weissenhofsiedlung (Stuttgart), 238; exhibition of 1927, 238
Weisse Stadt (housing development), 24
Welfare City Exhibition, 324
Werefkin, Marianne von, 190
Werkbund, 234, 238
Werner, Anton von, 134, 136, 182, 185
Werner, Michael, 449
Werner, Theodor, 442
Wertheim Department Store (Leipziger Platz), 139, 152
West Berlin: image of a free society in urban design, 390, 393; post–World War II architecture of, 423–32
Western Railroad of Massachusetts, 34
West Side historic district, 415
West Side Improvement Project, 117–18
West Side Urban Renewal Area, 415–16
Wetmore, Charles D., 114
Whitaker, Charles, 98
White, Alfred T., 98
White, Stanford, 114, 119
White Horse Tavern, 460
Whitman, Robert, 464
Whitney, Gertrude Vanderbilt, 207–8, 358, 360
Whitney Museum of Art, 359, 360; 1935 Show, 364
Whitney Studio Club, 208, 358–59, 360
Whitney Studio Galleries, 360
Wiegand, Dr., country home of (Berlin-Dahlem), 140
Wiener Werkstätte, 335
Wildenbruch, Ernst von, 183
Wildwood, 301
Wilgus, William J., 38, 113
Wilhelmine Period (Berlin), 47–57, 134–39
Wille, Bruno, 184
William I, Emperor, 134
William II, Emperor, 188
Williams, William Carlos, 207
Williamsburg Bridge, 20, 41, 121

Williamsburg Houses (Brooklyn), 271
Wilmersdorf meadow, 67
Wingate, Charles F., 171
Winkler, E., 50
Wittig, Paul, 252
Wohnstadt Carl Legien, 243
Wolff, Eugen, 181
Wolff, Paul, 141
Wolff, Theodor, 183
Wölfflin, Heinrich, 232
Wood, Edith Elmer, 245
Wood, Silas, 161
Woolworth, Frank W., 333
Woolworth Building (Gilbert), 333–34, 338
Works Progress Administration (WPA), 362, 364
World Financial Center, 420
World's Fair (New York, 1939), 305–6
World Trade Center (Yamasaki), 337, 417, 487
World War I: effect on American art, 357–58; effect on American consciousness, 96–97, 204; effect on artists of Weimar Republic, 342; impact on housing in Berlin, 241; influence on American government planning, 266
World War II: damage to Berlin, 220; personal recollections of, 367–70. *See also* Berlin; New York
Worldwide Plaza, 414
Wright, Frank Lloyd, 234, 284
Wright, Henry, Sr., 100
Wright, Henry, 98, 245, 246, 266, 268
Wurster, Catherine Bauer, 97
Wyant, Alexander H., 196

Y

Yellow Houses (Gessner), 142, 147, 149

Z

Zech, Paul, 190
Zeckendorf, William, 412
Zehlendorf housing complex (Mebes), 150
Zehlendorf Plan, 395, 396
Zeilenbau housing layouts, 238, 271
ZERO group, 447
Zimmer, Bernd, 451, 452
Zone 5 exhibition, 444
Zorach, William, 365
Zum Hofjäger, 66
Zweckverband Gross-Berlin, 143